THE HISTORY OF MODERN SPAIN

THE HISTORY OF MODERN SPAIN

CHRONOLOGIES, THEMES, INDIVIDUALS

Edited by
Adrian Shubert and José Álvarez Junco

Bloomsbury Academic
An imprint of Bloomsbury Publishing Plc

B L O O M S B U R Y
LONDON · OXFORD · NEW YORK · NEW DELHI · SYDNEY

Bloomsbury Academic

An imprint of Bloomsbury Publishing Plc

50 Bedford Square	1385 Broadway
London	New York
WC1B 3DP	NY 10018
UK	USA

www.bloomsbury.com

**BLOOMSBURY and the Diana logo are trademarks
of Bloomsbury Publishing Plc**

First published 2018

British Library Cataloguing-in-Publication Data
Names: Shubert, Adrian, 1953- editor. | Álvarez Junco, José, 1942- editor.
Title: The history of modern Spain: chronologies, themes, individuals / edited by
Adrian Shubert and José Álvarez Junco.
Description: London: New York, NY: Bloomsbury Academic, 2017. | Includes
bibliographical references and index.
Identifiers: LCCN 2017042199 (print) | LCCN 2017042202 (ebook) | ISBN 9781472591999
(PDF eBook) | ISBN 9781472592002 (EPUB eBook) | ISBN 9781472591982
(hardback : alk. paper) | ISBN 9781472591975 (pbk.: alk.paper)
Subjects: LCSH: Spain–History–19th century. | Spain–History–20th century.
Classification: LCC DP203 (ebook) | LCC DP203 .H59 2017 (print) | DDC 946/.07–dc23
LC record available at https://lccn.loc.gov/2017042199

ISBN: HB: 978-1-4725-9198-2
PB: 978-1-4725-9197-5
ePDF: 978-1-4725-9199-9
eBook: 978-1-4725-9200-2

Library of Congress Cataloging-in-Publication Data
A catalog record for this book is available from the Library of Congress.

Cover design: danileighdesign.com
Cover image: (top) massimofusaro/Shutterstock;
(bottom) Indalecio Ojanguren/Diputación Foral de Gipuzkoa

Typeset by Deanta Global Publishing Services, Chennai, India
Printed and bound in Great Britain

To find out more about our authors and books visit www.bloomsbury.com.
Here you will find extracts, author interviews, details of forthcoming events
and the option to sign up for our newsletters.

To the memory of
Chris Schmidt-Nowara (1966-2015)
And Carolyn Boyd (1944-2015)

CONTENTS

Contents

LIST OF ILLUSTRATIONS

NOTES ON CONTRIBUTORS

Paloma Aguilar is Professor of Political Science at the Open University (UNED) in Madrid. She has also been Tinker Professor at the University of Wisconsin-Madison and Visiting Professor at Princeton University. She is the author of *Memory and Amnesia: The Role of the Spanish Civil War in the Transition to Democracy* (2001) and *Políticas de la Memoria y Memorias de la Política* (2008), and coauthor, with Leigh A. Payne, of *Revealing New Truths About Spain's Violent Past: Perpetrators Confessions and Victim Exhumations* (forthcoming). Her more recent contributions have been published in the following journals: *Journal of Spanish Cultural Studies, International Journal of Transitional Justice, Comparative Political Studies, and Politics & Society*.

Gregorio Álonso is Lecturer in Spanish History at the University of Leeds. He is the author of *La nación en capilla. Ciudadanía católica y cuestión religiosa en España, 1793–1874* and the coauthor and editor of *The politics and memory of democratic transition. The Spanish Model*, and *Londres y el liberalismo hispánico*. He is currently working on a monograph on the Atlantic dimensions of the Latin American independence processes.

José Álvarez Junco is professor emeritus in the Department of the History of Social Thought and Movements of the Universidad Complutense of Madrid. The author of a number of works on the political and intellectual history of modern Spain, his book *Mater Dolorosa: la idea de España en el siglo XIX,* won the Premio Nacional de Ensayo in 2002. In addition to being one of Spain's leading historians he is also a public intellectual whose articles appear regularly in *El País* and other major Spanish newspapers. Between 2004 and 2008 he was director of the Centro de Estudios Políticos y Constitucionales.

Edward Baker has written on literary and cultural themes ranging from Cervantes to modern and contemporary Madrid. Most recently he has collaborated with José Álvarez Junco, Gregorio de la Fuente, and the late Carolyn Boyd on *Las historias de España: Visiones del pasado y construcción de identidad,* vol. 12 of the *Historia de España* directed by Josep Fontana and Ramón Villares. At present he is writing a book, *Spanish/Literature, the Historicity of a Syntagma,* on the emergence and consolidation of a national literature in Spain from the last third of the eighteenth century to the Civil War.

Ángeles Barrio Alonso is Professor of Contemporary History at the University of Cantabria. She is the author of numerous books on unions and social movements including *Anarquismo y anarcosindicalismo en Asturias, 1890-1936* (1988); *El sueño de la democracia industrial. Sindicalismo y democracia en España, 1917-1923 (1996),* and *Por la razón y el derecho. Historia de la negociación colectiva en España. 1850-2012,* (2014).

Isabel Burdiel is Professor of Modern History at the University of Valencia. Her work focuses on the cultural and political history of nineteenth-century European liberalism. She has also been interested in the possibilities of biographical history and between 2008 and 2015 she directed the European Network on Theory and Practice of Biography: http://www.valencia.edu/retpb/. Her major publications include *La política de los notables*, (Valencia, 1987) and *Isabel II. Una biografía*, (2010), which won Spain's National History Prize in 2011.

Antonio Cazorla-Sánchez is Professor of History at Trent University, Canada. His work has focused on the social history of Franco's Spain. His latest books include *Las cartas a Franco de los españoles de a pié*. Barcelona: RBA, 2014; *Franco: The Biography of the Myth* (2013) and *Fear and Progress: Ordinary Lives in Franco's Spain (1936-1975)* (2009) both of which have been translated into Spanish.

Ángela Cenarro is Associate Professor of Modern and Contemporary History at the Universidad de Zaragoza. She is the author of a number of books on the Spanish Civil War and the Franco regime, including *El pasado oculto. Fascismo y violencia en Aragon (1936-1939)* (1992) *La sonrisa de Falange. Auxilio Social en la guerra civil y la posguerra* (2006) y *Los niños del Auxilio Social* (2009). She has recently coedited two collective volumes: *Pagar las culpas. La represión económica en Aragon, 1936-1945* (2014) and *Feminismos. Contribuciones desde la historia* (2014).

Jesus Cruz is Professor of Iberian History at the University of Delaware. His publications include *Gentlemen, Bourgeois, and Revolutionaries: Political Change and Cultural Persistence among the Spanish Dominant Groups, 1750–1850*, (2004), *Los notables de Madrid: las bases sociales de la revolución liberal Española* (2000), and *The Rise of Middle Class Culture in Nineteenth-Century Spain* (2011).

Rafael Cruz is Associate Professor in the Department of History of Political Thought and Social and Political Movements at the Universidad Complutense de Madrid. A specialist on the history of collective action and political violence, his most recent book is *Protestar en España, 1900-2013* (2015).

Julio de la Cueva Merino is Associate Professor of Contemporary History at the University of Castilla-La Mancha and a specialist on the history of Catholicism and laicism in modern Spain. In collaboration with Feliciano Montero he has edited *Izquierda obrera y religión en España, 1900-1939* (2012), *Laicismo y catolicismo. El conflicto político-religioso en la Segunda República* (2009), and *La secularización conflictiva: España, 1898-1931* (2007).

Gregorio de la Fuente Monge is Associate Professor of History at the Universidad Complutense de Madrid. He is author of *Los revolucionarios de 1868* (2000) and coauthor of *La Revolución Gloriosa* (2005), *El nacimiento del periodismo político* (2009), *Patriotas entre naciones* (2011), *Mujer y política en la España contemporánea* (2012), *Las historias de España* (2013) y *Líderes para el pueblo republicano* (2015), as well as editor of a special issue of the journal *Historia y Política* devoted to theatre and politics in nineteenth-century Spain.

Fernando del Rey Reguillo is Professor of the History of Political Thought and Social and Political Movements at the Universidad Complutense de Madrid. A specialist on the political history of twentieth-century Spain and Europe, his major publications include the monograph *Paisanos en lucha. Exclusión política y violencia en la Segunda República española* (2008) and the edited volume *Palabras como puños. La intransigencia política en la Segunda República española* (2011).

Scott Eastman is Associate Professor of Transnational History at Creighton University. He is author of *Preaching Spanish Nationalism Across the Hispanic Atlantic, 1759-1823* (2012) and coeditor of *The Rise of Constitutional Government in the Iberian Atlantic World: The Impact of the Cadiz Constitution of 1812* (2015). His research interests focus on the intersection of identity, colonialism, and culture across the nineteenth-century Hispanic Atlantic World.

Josefina Gómez Mendoza is Professor Emeritus of Geography at the Universidad Autónoma de Madrid (UAM). Her research has focused on the history of geographic and environmental ideas, forestry, sustainable cities, and landscapes. She is the author of a large number of books including *El pensamiento geográfico: de Humboldt a las tendencias radicales, Ciencia y política de los montes españoles, Atlas de los paisajes españoles, Urbanismo e ingeniería en las ciudades españolas del siglo* XIX. A past President of the UAM, she is a Full Member of the Spanish Royal Academies of History and Engineering, a member of the International Geographical Union Commission on History of Geography and elective member of Spanish Consejo de Estado.

Aitana Guia is Assistant Professor of History at California State University, Fullerton. Her areas of expertise are nationalism, migration, and minorities in postwar Europe. Her publications include *The Muslim Struggle for Civil Rights in Spain: Promoting Democracy through Migrant Engagement, 1985-2010* (2014) and *La llengua negociada: El manteniment del conflicte politic sobre la llengua* (2001). As a 2015/16 Max Weber Postdoctoral Fellow at the Robert Schuman Centre for Advanced Studies, European University Institute, Florence, Italy, Dr. Guia began her new research project on nativism in southern Europe.

Stephen Jacobson is an associate professor of history at the Universitat Pompeu Fabra (Barcelona) and the Director of the Institut d'Història Jaume Vicens Vives. He is the coeditor of *Endless Empire: Spain's Retreat, Europe's Eclipse, and America's Decline* (2012).

Geoffrey Jensen holds the John Biggs ´30 Cincinnati Chair in Military History at the Virginia Military Institute. The author of various books and articles on modern Spanish, military, and North African history, his most recent book is *Cultura militar española: modernistas, tradicionalistas y liberales* (2014).

Santos Juliá Professor Emeritus in the Department of Social History and the History of Political Thought at the National Open University (Universidad Nacional de Educación a Distancia) in Madrid. He has published widely on the social and political history of twentieth-century Spain, political violence, intellectuals, and historical theory. His book *Historias de las dos Españas* won the National History Prize in 2004. He also writes regularly on contemporary politics in *El País*. A full list of his publications is available at http://www.santosjulia.com/Santos_Julia/Santos_Julia.html.

Emilio La Parra is Professor of Modern History at the Universidad de Alicante. His research focuses on the political history of the late eighteenth and early nineteenth centuries. He is the author of, among others, *El primer liberalismo y la Iglesia. Las Cortes de Cadiz (1985), Manuel Godoy. La aventura del poder* (2002), *Los Cien Mil Hijos de San Luis. El ocaso del primer impulso liberal en España (2007)*. He has also served as director of the Biblioteca Virtual Miguel de Cervantes (http://www.cervantesvirtual.com/).

Mark Lawrence is a lecturer in the School of History at the University of Kent. He researches war, radicalism, and society in nineteenth-century Spain and the comparative history of civil war. He is author of *Spain's First Carlist War, 1833-40* (2014) and *The Spanish Civil Wars: a Comparative History of the First Carlist War and the Conflict of the 1930s* (2017).

Aurora G. Morcillo is a professor of History at Florida International University and the director of the Spanish and Mediterranean Studies Program in the Green School of International and Public Affairs at FIU. She has published four books to date: *True Catholic Womanhood. Gender Ideology in Franco's Spain*; *The Seduction of Modern Spain (2008)*, *The Female Body and the Francoist Body Politics; Memory and Cultural history of the Spanish Civil War* (2014), and *En cuerpo y alma. Ser Mujer en tiempos de Franco* (2015). She is currently working on a book to be called *Things Visible and Invisible: Women's Life Narratives in Franco's Spain*.

Javier Moreno-Luzón is Professor of Modern History at the Universidad Complutense de Madrid. He has also been guest researcher at the LSE, Harvard University, the EHESS of Paris, and UCSD. His work focuses on Spanish political history during the Restoration period (1875–1923). He has published several books and articles on political clientelism, liberalism, monarchy, and nationalism. His most recent book is *Modernizing the Nation: Spain during the Reign of Alfonso XIII, 1902-1931 (2012)*.

Rafael Núñez Florencio is a historian and philosopher with an extensive record as an author, critic, and popularizer. He has published more than 20 monographs, and hundreds of articles and reviews in cultural magazines as well as serving as director of a number of book series. His most recent books include *El peso del pesimismo. Del 98 al desencanto* (2010) y *¡Viva la muerte! Política y cultura de lo macabro* (2014).

Xosé Manoel Núñez Seixas is Professor of Modern European History at the University of Santiago de Compostela and Ludwig-Maximilians University Munich. His work focuses on comparative history of nationalist movements and national and regional identities, as well as on the study of overseas migration from Spain to Latin America and on modern war and war experiences in the twentieth century. Among his most recent books are *Camarada invierno. Experiencia y memoria de la División Azul, 1941-1945* (2016); (with J. Moreno-Luzón, ed.), *Metaphors of Spain. Representations of Spanish National Identity in the 20th century* (2017), and (with J. Moreno-Luzón), *Los colores de la patria. Símbolos nacionales en la España contemporánea* (2017).

Inbal Ofer is senior-lecturer in Modern European History at the Department of History, the Open University of Israel. She specializes in social history of twentieth-century Spain (gender and women's history, urban history and social movements). Among her publications are *Señoritas in Blue: The Making of a Female Political Elite in Franco's Spain*. Sussex Studies in Spanish History (2009) and *Claiming the City/Contesting the State: Squatting, Community Formation and Democratization in Spain (1955 – 1986)* (2017).

Diego Palacios Cerezales is a lecturer in European History at the University of Stirling. Diego has published widely on protest, policing, popular politics, and social movements in Spain and Portugal in the modern era. His books include *O poder caiu na rua. Crise de Estado e acções colectivas na revolução portuguesa, 1974-1975* (2003); *A culatazos. Protesta popular y orden público en el Portugal contemporáneo* (2011); *Estranhos corpos políticos. Protesto e mobilização no Portugal do século XIX* (2014). He is currently writing a transnational history of petitioning. More in https://stir.academia.edu/DiegoPalaciosCerezales

Leandro Prados de la Escosura is Professor of Economic History at Universidad Carlos III, Madrid. He is a Research Fellow at the Centre for Economic Policy Research (CEPR), a Research Associate at the Centre for Competitive Advantage in the Global Economy (CAGE), and a Corresponding Fellow of Spain's Royal Academy of History. He currently holds the Honorary Maddison Chair at the University of Groningen. He has contributed to the main journals in economic history and published and edited books on long-run growth and retardation in Spain, the economic consequences of Latin American independence, the costs and benefits of European imperialism, and British exceptionalism at the time of the Industrial Revolution. His latest book *Spanish Economic Growth, 1850-2015* will be published in 2017.

Pamela Radcliff is Professor in the Department of History at the University of California, San Diego. She is the author of several books and articles on popular mobilization, gender and women's politics and civil society in twentieth-century Spain. Her most recent books are *Making Democratic Citizens in Spain: Civil Society and the Popular Origins of the Transition, 1960-1978* (2011) and the *History of Modern Spain, 1808-2016* (2017).

Clara Ramírez-Barat is the Director of the Auschwitz Institute for Peace and Reconciliation (AIPR) Educational Policies Program. Before joining AIPR, she was a Senior Research Associate at the International Centre for Transitional Justice where her research focused on different aspects of transitional justice with a special interest on outreach, media, and the cultural sphere. She edited a book on the topic *Transitional Justice, Culture and Society: Beyond Outreach* (2014) and she is also the coauthor of forthcoming volume entitled *Transitional Justice and Education: Learning Peace* (2016).

Óscar Rodríguez Barreira holds a PhD from the Universidad de Almería, where he is a lecturer. In addition to a number of journal articles, he is the author of two books: *Migas con Miedo* (2008), *Miserias del Poder* (2013) and editor of one: *El Franquismo desde los Márgenes* (2013).

María Cruz Romeo Mateo is Professor of Modern and Contemporary History at the University of Valencia. Her research has focused on the political and social history of nineteenth-century Spain, and in particular Progressive liberalism and the participation of women in nineteenth-century society. She has coedited *La España liberal, 1833-1874*, (2014) with María Sierra and, with Salvador Calatayud and Jesús Millán *El Estado desde la sociedad. Espacios de poder en la España del siglo XIX* (2016).

Vicent Sanz is Professor of Modern History and member of the Instituto Interuniversitario de Desarrollo Social y Paz at the Universitat Jaume I in Castellón. His research focuses on the social history of work and social movements and on colonial policies in the nineteenth century. He is author of de *D'artesans a proletaris* (1995), and *Propiedad y desposesión campesina* (2000) and coeditor of *En el nombre del oficio* (2005), *A Social History of Spanish Labour* (2007) and *Tabaco e escravos nos impérios ibéricos* (2015) as well as of Berghahn Books' series Studies in Latin American and Spanish History. He created and directs the radio program *Hablemos de Historia*.

Adrian Shubert is University Professor of History at York University in Toronto. His major publications include *The Road to Revolution in Spain: The Coal Miners of Asturas, 1860-1934* (1987), *A Social History of Modern Spain* (1990), and *Death and Money in the Afternoon: a*

History of the Spanish Bullfight (2001). He is a Fellow of the Royal Society of Canada and a Comendador de la Orden del Mérito Civil. He is currently writing a biography of Baldomero Espartero.

María Sierra is Professor of Modern History at the University of Seville. She has conducted research programs concerning the history of liberalism in the nineteenth century (as shown in *Elegidos y elegibles). La representación parlamentaria en la cultura liberal* (2010), and has explored the notion of political culture in several studies, foremost, *Culturas políticas: teoría e historia,* (2010) and *Las culturas políticas contemporáneas en España y América Latina,* (2014). Her research interests include the study of gender and emotions within cultural explanation for political action. She is currently developing a research program on the history of the Roma.

Nigel Townson teaches history at the Complutense University of Madrid. Author of the award-winning *The Crisis of Democracy in Spain: Centrist Politics under the Second Republic, 1931-1936* (2000), he has also edited numerous works, including *Spain Transformed: The Late Franco Dictatorship, 1959-75* (2007), and *Spain is Different? A Comparative Look at the 19th and 20th centuries* (2015). He is currently writing the *Penguin History of Modern Spain, 1898–2016.*

Enric Ucelay-Da Cal was born in New York in 1948. His parents were both academics, dedicated to Spanish and Portuguese literature. His PhD dissertation on Catalan separatism at Columbia University was directed by the late Edward Malefakis. Ucelay-Da Cal was fortunate enough to spend his life teaching at universities in Barcelona; he is currently Senior Professor Emeritus in Contemporary History at the Universitat Pompeu Fabra. He is the author of several books, notably *La Catalunya populista: Imatge, cultura i política en l'etapa republicana, 1931– 1939* (1982), and *El imperialismo catalán: Prat de la Riba, Cambó, D'Ors y la conquista moral de España* (2003). Some 300 of his articles are available in pdf at enricucelaydacal.weebly.com.

Javier Zamora Bonilla is Professor of History of Political Thought and Social and Political Movements in the Faculty of Political Sciences and Sociology of the Complutense University of Madrid. He is chief executive of the Center for Ortega Studies in the José Ortega y Gasset – Gregorio Marañón Foundation and editor of the *Revista de Estudios Orteguianos.* He is the author of a biography of Ortega y Gasset (2002) and coordinator of the new critical edition of the Complete Works of the philosopher in 10 volumes (2004–2010).

CHRONOLOGY

1808	Popular insurrections against the Napoleonic invasion
1810	Start of independence movements in American colonies; convocation of the Cortes of Cadiz
1812	Cortes of Cadiz approves the liberal Constitution of 1812
1814	End of the war against Napoleon; Ferdinand VII returns to Spain and restores the Old Regime
1820	Rafael de Riego's *pronunciamiento* leads to restoration of the constitution; start of the Liberal Triennium
1823	French invasion restores Ferdinand VII as absolute monarch
1824	Battle of Ayacucho ends Spain's American empire except for Cuba and Puerto Rico
1833	Ferdinand VII dies; his widow María Cristina becomes regent; Carlist War begins; Javier de Burgos divides Spain into provinces
1834	Estatuto Real proclaimed
1836	Mendizábal's ecclesiastical disentailment law passed
1837	Constitution of 1837 proclaimed
1839	Embrace of Vergara ends Carlist War
1843	Isabel II ascends the throne
1844	Civil Guard created
1845	Constitution of 1845 proclaimed
1851	Concordat with the Holy See
1854	General O'Donnell's *pronunciamiento* opens the Progressive Biennium
1856	Madoz's civil disentailment law passed; O'Donnell's Liberal Union come to power
1856–62	O'Donnell's "prestige policies" lead to military intervention in Morocco, Indochina, Mexico, Santo Domingo, and Peru
1868	September revolution sends Isabel II into exile; Ten Years War in Cuba begins
1871	Amadeo I becomes king
1872	Start of new Carlist War
1873	Amadeo abdicates; First Republic proclaimed; Cantonalist revolt begins
1875	General Martínez Campos' coup ends the First Republic; Bourbons restored under Alfonso XII
1876	Constitution of 1876 proclaimed

1878	End of Ten Years War in Cuba
1886	Slavery in Cuba abolished
1879	Socialist Party (PSOE) founded
1888	General Workers' Union (UGT) created
1890	Universal male suffrage
1892	Bases of Manresa, first major document of Catalan nationalism; beginning of anarchist terrorism in Barcelona
1895	Last Cuban war begins; Basque Nationalist Party (PNV) created
1898	Spanish-American War; Spain loses Cuna, Puerto Rico and the Philippines to the United States
1899	Lliga Catalana created
1902	Alfonso XIII ascends the throne
1905	¡Cu Cut! Incident
1906	Law of Jurisdictions passed; Solidaridad Catalana created
1907	Solidadridad Obrera founded
1909	Tragic Week in Barcelona
1910	Anarchosyndicalist National Confederation of Labour (CNT) founded
1912	Spanish protectorate in Morocco established
1913	José Ortega y Gasset launches League for Political Education
1914	Spain declares neutrality in the First World War
1916	First national park established at Covadonga
1917	Juntas Militares de Defensa; Assembly of Parlamentarians; general strike single partral strike
1918	Start of "Bolshevik triennium" and *pistolerismo* in Barcelona
1921	Military defeat at Annual
1923	Primo de Rivera dictatorship begins
1930	Fall of Primo de Rivera
1931	Second Republic proclaimed; Women given the vote
1933	CEDA created
1934	Asturian revolution
1936	Popular Front wins elections; Military revolt starts Civil War
1937	Creation of Francoist single party, FET y de las JONS
1939	Civil War ends with Nationalist victory
1946	United Nations condemns Franco regime
1953	Franco government signs Bases Treaty with the United States and Concordat with the Vatican

Chronology

1955	Spain admitted into United Nations
1956	Major student protests
1959	Stabilization Plan
1962	Miners' strike in Asturias; opposition groups meet in Munich
1963	First Development Plan
1965	Student demonstrations; Leading intellectuals expelled from university posts
1968	Basque separatist organization ETA kills first victim
1969	Juan Carlos named Franco's successor as head of state
1973	ETA assassinates Prime Minister Luis Carrero Blanco
1975	Franco dies; Juan Carlos becomes king
1976	Widespread strikes; Law of Political Reform
1977	First democratic elections since 1936
1978	Constitution of 1978 approved in referendum
1979	Autonomy statutes for Catalonia and the Basque Provinces approved
1981	Attempted military coup; Spain joins NATO; divorce legalized
1982	PSOE wins majority in elections
1985	Spain joins the European Economic Community (EEC); abortion legalized
1986	Homosexuality decriminalized
1992	Spain hosts Olympic Games in Barcelona and World's Fair in Seville
1996	Popular Party comes to power
1997	Compulsory military service abolished
2000	Pedro Almodóvar wins first Academy Award
2001	Aznar government supports invasion of Iraq despite massive opposition
2004	Terrorist bombing of Madrid commuter train kills 191; PSOE returns to power
2005	Spain becomes third country in the world to legalize gay marriage
2007	Law of Historical Memory passed
2008	Beginning of economic crisis
2011	Popular Party wins majority in elections; start of Indignados movement; ETA declares end to its armed struggle
2014	Creation of Podemos party; independence referendum in Catalonia
2015	King Juan Carlos abdicates and is succeeded by his son, Felipe VI; national elections produce a hung parliament
2016	Second national elections lead to Popular Party minority government

CHAPTER 1
INTRODUCTION
José Álvarez Junco and Adrian Shubert

This book is the successor to *Spanish History since 1808*. That volume, which was conceived in the late 1990s and published in 2000, embodied a new revisionist interpretation which rejected long-prevailing ideas of Spanish exceptionalism and failure in favor of one which placed Spain securely in the European mainstream. That book was written at an optimistic moment, in the context of the democratic Spain that had emerged from the lengthy dictatorship of Francisco Franco, the still-recent celebrations of the 1992 Barcelona Olympics and Seville World's Fair, and the 1993 Maastricht Treaty and the upcoming introduction of the Euro. Today such optimism is difficult to appreciate, in Spain and elsewhere. In the case of the former, since 2008 the country has been suffering from the grave economic crisis which, at its height, produced unemployment of 25 percent—and 50 percent among young people; its political system is mired in paralysis and badly stained by corruption; the challenge posed by Catalan separatism looms larger than ever; and the post-Franco transition to democracy, once an object of pride, is now denounced by many as the origin of a despised "Regime of 1978." The European Union has its own serious problems: anemic economic growth, at best, an immigration crisis, the shocking rise of xenophobic political parties, "Brexit," and increasing skepticism about the European project itself. And all of this in the context of the ongoing "War on Terrorism" which began in 2001 and the election in November 2016 of a new US president who generates uncertainty and even fear.

In sum, today's Spain is not the Spain of 2000 because today's world is not that world. These realities cannot help but influence the tone of the book, but they do not diminish the underlying argument that since the end of the eighteenth century, Spain's history, although not identical to that of any other country, has been very much part of the European mainstream.

Consider, for example, our starting point, the conventional date for the beginning of Spain's modern history. In 1808, Spain was a pre-national, imperial monarchy, as were the other political units born in late medieval Europe. It was an amalgam of kingdoms and territories ruled by a single person, a vast and diverse political structure very different from a modern nation-state (however much nationalists emphasize continuity). After 1492, the European domains were joined by the American ones which, for centuries, would provide the crown massive resources, especially in the form of precious metals.

This political construction was underpinned by a powerful cultural identity born at the time of the Counter-Reformation, the expulsion of the Jews and Muslims and the unyielding ethnic cleansing enforced by purity of blood statutes by institutions like the Inquisition. Needless to say, this cultural identity was light years away from some of the basic characteristics of modernity, such as the plurality of belief, the freedom—or at least toleration—of religion, and the limitation of royal power by some sort of institution representing the people of the kingdom. But we would be mistaken in seeing in this a Spain that was substantially different from other contemporary kingdoms. And in many cases, Spain seemed more peaceful and, in a sense, tolerant than other regions: unlike France (which developed an arguably more absolutist monarchy than Spain) and the German lands, Spain avoided the devastating wars of religion of the sixteenth and seventeenth centuries; and if for the Dutch, Spain was the bitter enemy, for Irish and Scottish Catholics it was the hoped-for protector against England, the ruthless and detested oppressor.

But Spain was not just a kingdom; it was a composite monarchy which lacked a single administrative system, despite the best efforts of its rulers since Philip IV to impose one. In this it resembled the British monarchy, the Russia of the Romanovs and the empires of the Habsburgs and the Ottomans. It was less like France, although not radically so. There, Richelieu and Mazarin, chief ministers during the reigns of Louis XIV and Louis XV, had succeeded in imposing a relative administrative homogeneity. With the exception of the Inquisition and, in the eighteenth century, the army, the Spanish crown had been unable to establish institutions which functioned in all its dominions. And there was no place, like the British parliament, where the nobility could attempt to control the power of the monarch.

One significant difference between Spain and some other European monarchies, such as Britain and France, before 1808 was that there had not been a revolution which had radically and violently transformed the social and political structure or reinforced collective identities. But then the same could be said about most European polities at the time.

The Spanish Enlightenment and the Bourbon reforms of the second half of the eighteenth century saw Spain begin to make up some of the ground it had lost to its European rivals, but then revolution arrived with the traumatic Napoleonic invasion and the devastating war which followed. In addition to suffering enormous human and material losses, Spain saw the bulk of its empire in the Americas become independent. This was the last act of the Atlantic revolutions which began with the rebellion of the thirteen British colonies in North America in 1776 and their independence in 1783 and continued with the slave revolt in the French colony of Sainte Domingue in 1791 which produced the independent state of Haiti in 1804. From the Napoleonic Wars on, Spain would not only fail to maintain its position as a European great power; it would all but disappear as an international agent of any significance. And this represented a major difference from the two European monarchies which had been Spain's main competitors from the sixteenth through eighteenth centuries. France and Great Britain would build extensive new empires in the nineteenth century while Spain would not.

Having lost the bulk of its overseas territories, the Spanish monarchy found itself having to rebuild the state structure as the former imperial political, administrative, and fiscal structures had been rendered useless. One of the fundamental aspects of this transformation was reducing the power of the Catholic Church, seizing its lands, eliminating its fiscal system, and taking over key functions such as education, welfare, and controlling the official identity of its subjects through registries of births and deaths. Equally important was the need to rebuild a collective identity, this time not in monarchical, imperial, or religious terms but in modern, national ones. It was a process of massive scope: building the nation, secularizing society, reconstructing gender roles, rebuilding the legitimacy of the state while modernizing it, and inviting at least a part of the population to participate in political life in the name of national sovereignty.

All of this had to be done at a time when the Spanish state was weak and starved of financial resources. And in a country which had also lost most of its capacity for cultural innovation compared to the rest of Western Europe, in part because of its failing economy but also because of its very high levels of illiteracy, especially in the rural world which made up the bulk of Spanish society, there was not much in the way of modern ideological support it could summon. All of this meant that the strength of modern ideologies and identities, and especially national identity, was limited in the face of inherited traditions and identities, especially religious ones. There was certainly a national and liberal project advanced by modernizing urban elites, but it lacked sustained support from the political rulers. Throughout the entire nineteenth century, Spanish governments proved incapable of building networks of public schools and modern communications which would turn the country into a fully unified economic territory or, to use Benedict Anderson's famous concept, an imagined community. At a time when liberalism saw homogeneity as desirable and modern and when language was a major marker of identity, Spain continued to be the site of linguistic and cultural diversity, especially in comparison to France, the centralizing model all Spanish liberals aspired to. The result was a series of contradictions and problems, especially with the elites of the economically and culturally powerful city of Barcelona. These emerged most powerfully in the last quarter of the nineteenth century, and especially after the loss of the remaining colonies in 1898, but until then Spanish nationalism and Catalan cultural assertion coexisted comfortably.

Spain did have the benefit of borders which had been set after centuries of wars and treaties. This also meant that, after the war against Napoleon, Spain did not engage in military conflict with its neighbors and did not have to confront wars or other challenges which its fragile state might have been unable to withstand. It was largely for this reason that Spain remained strictly neutral in European conflicts, even when, for example during the Crimean War (1853–56), it was under strong external pressure to intervene. (By contrast, the small kingdom of Piedmont sent troops to fight alongside France and Great Britain as a way of winning allies who would support its aspirations in northern Italy.) On the other hand, Spain did not share the experience of the Ottoman or Habsburg empires, where foreign powers encouraged the centrifugal tendencies which would, in the end, see these ancient imperial monarchies fragment into a number of separate states. Spain was also able to keep its hold on its remaining colonies without serious problems, except for the Ten Years' War in Cuba (1868–78). And unlike Italy, Poland, or Germany, Spain did not experience a great wave of romantic nationalism. There were occasional nationalist outbursts, such as those provoked by the so-called War of Africa in 1859 to 1860—which was particularly strong in Catalonia—or the small naval incident with Germany in the Caroline Islands in 1885.

What really dominated nineteenth-century Spain was political instability. It started with a liberal revolution triggered by external causes. The occupation of the country by a foreign army, the absence of the entire royal family from the country, and the attempt to put a brother of the French emperor on the throne provoked a popular uprising which gave rise to a war of resistance which, with powerful British support, would last six years. This period also saw the summoning of a parliament, the Cortes of Cádiz, which legislated a liberal revolution, embodied above all in the "Political Constitution of the Spanish Monarchy," better known as the Constitution of 1812. The modernizing elites behind the work of the Cortes of Cádiz were weak and exclusively urban, and once the exceptional circumstances caused by the war were over, they had to confront the power of the monarchy and the conservative clergy in rural Spain. This was a struggle which lasted through most of the century, as the three Carlist Wars: 1833–40, 1846–49, and 1872–76, demonstrate. The first of these civil wars was at least as lethal as the Civil War of the twentieth century and, like it, became a major issue in the relations among the European great powers. These wars also contributed to one of the most distinctive features of Spain's political history: the ongoing prominence of military men like Baldomero Espartero, Ramón María Narváez, Leopoldo O'Donnell, and Juan Prim. They were behind most of the political changes of the years 1833–76. These changes were often engineered by military uprisings known as *pronunciamientos*, but rather than instituting military dictatorships their goal was to bring to power one of the major political parties of the period: the Progressive, the Moderate, or the Unionist. The result of all this was a dizzying instability which saw brief moments of advanced liberal government: 1810–14, 1820–23, 1837–43, 1854–56, and 1868–74, alternate with longer periods of restored absolute monarchy: 1814–20 and 1823–33, or more limited liberalism: 1834–37, 1844–54, and 1856–68. This situation was exceptional if we compare it with the British case but not if the comparator is France. The French Revolution (1789–1815) was followed by three more revolutions, in 1830, 1848, and 1870, foreign invasion, military defeat, and the loss of territory in the Franco-Prussian War (1870–71), as well as three changes from monarchy to republic.

Political life became more stable after 1875, although this half-century of peace was based on a rigged political system controlled by a narrow political elite which was supported by the Church and the military. Things were very similar in Italy and Portugal, which even had very similar words to describe them: *turnismo* in Spain, *rotativismo* in Portugal, and *transformismo* in Italy. There were differences of detail, but all three words describe a system in which power was shared by two main political parties which agreed to take turns in office without engaging in real electoral competition.

1898 was a key date. That year Spain was humiliated militarily by the United States and lost its remaining colonies in the Caribbean and the Pacific, most of which passed to American control. This triggered a traumatic period of self-criticism and multiple projects for "regeneration." (The word reflects the prevalent racial thinking of the time in a Europe concerned with "degeneration.") It was now clear that Spain was no longer a power nor even, again in the thinking of the time, a "superior race." There were similar developments in Portugal after the British Ultimatum of 1890 and in Italy following its defeat by the Ethiopians at Adowa in 1896. And even though it was not a colonial failure, France went through a couple of decades of self-criticism following the defeat at Sedan (1870) in the Franco-Prussian War. There were many different and contradictory reformist projects, which would, under the right circumstances, produce serious conflicts. Even though it remained neutral in the First World War, Spain was not immune to the fallout from the conflict, which produced a long series of dictatorships and civil wars which culminated in the Second World War. Starting in 1923, it endured the dictatorship of General Miguel Primo de Rivera (1923–30), another civil war (1936–39), and the dictatorship of General Francisco Franco (1939–75). By June 1940, only four democracies remained in Europe: Great Britain, Ireland, Sweden, and Switzerland. On the other hand, in 1945, unlike France, Italy, Germany, and others, Spain was not liberated from Fascism, thus creating a political and, in many senses, socioeconomic exception that, with Portugal, would last another three decades.

The lengthy Franco regime began with a period dominated by fascist forms with obvious similarities to Mussolini's Italy and Hitler's Germany. As time went on, this turned into a very particular kind of fascism, much closer to the Portuguese "New State" of Antonio Salazar or the mental world of France's Marshall Pétain, one based on a national-Catholic and military ideology. Due to its great longevity, the dictatorship went through a number of phases and, as a result, it is very difficult to apply the same label to it throughout.

Starting in the 1950s, and only after two decades of the regime's abject economic failure, the long-awaited economic takeoff and modernization finally got underway. Franco's death in November 1975 was followed relatively quickly by the creation of a parliamentary democracy. The Spanish Transition was part of what Samuel Huntingdon described as the "third wave of democratization" which hit Portugal and Greece at virtually the same time. The Transition has been the subject of much debate, but it is clear that it benefited from a welcoming European context, very different from the situation which confronted the Second Republic in the 1930s, and from the traumatic memory of the Civil War, a repeat of which virtually all Spaniards fervently wanted to avoid.

The democracy which is embodied in the Constitution of 1978 has been extremely stable, but it has also demonstrated a series of other characteristics, not all of them positive. These include control by two parties, the Socialist Partido Socialista Obrero Español and the conservative Partido Popular, both with rigid internal hierarchies; the absence of an effective division of powers which favors the executive at the expense of the legislature and the judiciary; and problems of financing political parties which have given rise to widespread corruption. Observers in France, Italy, Portugal, Greece, Belgium, and most Eastern European countries would find many similarities with their own realities. In the context of the severe economic crisis which began in 2008, this has led to strong criticism of the political system, the appearance of new political parties such as the Podemos (We Can) on the left and Ciudadanos (Citizens) on the center-right, and a major upheaval in the party system in Catalonia which has included the unprecedented rise of an overtly separatist movement. Interestingly, one thing these changes have not produced is a significant xenophobic, right-wing populist political party analogous to the Party for Freedom in the Netherlands, the Danish People's Party in Denmark, or France's Front National.

Historiography

The Franco regime affected the way history was written in Spain, as it affected so much else in Spanish life. Into the 1950s, historiography was very traditional, centering on chronological narratives of high politics. Economics, culture, and society very much took a back seat. The main subject was the Spanish nation and the approach was at once hagiographic and exculpatory: on the one hand historians sang about the glories of the Spanish past, on the other they explained away failures. Biography was mobilized as propaganda, to generate what Anna Caballé has called a "gallery of national heroes" who fit the regime's Catholic and nationalist ideology. Methodology was a straightforward positivist empiricism whose goal was to establish the facts. The regime also had its favored periods: the glorious imperial era that ran from Ferdinand and Isabella through the sixteenth century, which it saw as its inspiration. Later periods, marked by "decadence" and "decline" blamed on foreign influence, were ignored. The nineteenth century was the worst of all. As Franco said in a famous speech in 1951, it was a century that should be "erased from our history."

This situation began to change in the 1950s, in large part because of the influence of the French *Annales* school on some of the best historians of the time. The most significant was Jaume

Vicens Vives in Barcelona whose work on economic and social history, such as *Historia social y económica de España y América* (1957–59) and *Cataluña en el siglo XIX* (1961), influenced many younger historians there, in Madrid and Valencia. French influence even reached some historians who had been Francoists, such as José Antonio Maravall. There was another crucial factor in this shift: the connection between the writing of history and the emergence of a new culture of opposition to the regime. Concerned to explain the origins of the Civil War, they turned their attention to the nineteenth and twentieth centuries, explored economic and social conflicts, and revalued the liberalism of the nineteenth century that Franco so despised. The pioneer here was the University of Salamanca professor Miguel Artola, whose most influential books, *Los orígenes de la España contemporánea* and *Los afrancesados*, came out at the end of the 1950s.

The work of foreign historians of Spain, what Spaniards call *hispanistas*, became very influential starting in the 1960s. With access to sources, and to the freedom to write what they wanted, which were unavailable to Spaniards, they produced a more modern view of the country's modern history. The most important came from France: Ferdinand Braudel, Jean Sarrailh, Pierre Vilar, and Pierre Chaunu, and from the English-speaking world: Raymond Carr, Hugh Thomas, Gabriel Jackson, and Edward Malefakis. Three of these historians were especially influential. Thomas' book on the Civil War, originally published in 1961 and then in Spanish by the Paris-based opposition publisher Ruedo Ibérico, was truly groundbreaking. Vilar's influence came from his focus on Catalonia and his rigid Marxist approach with its emphasis on economics, so far removed from the idealism that permeated official histories. And from his position at St. Anthony's College, Oxford, Carr trained a group of young Spaniards: Juan Pablo Fusi, Joaquín Romero Maura, and José Varela Ortega, who became known as the "Oxford group."

Vilar's influence extended through one of his disciples, the Spanish exile Manuel Tuñón de Lara. Tuñón married his Marxism to the concerns of the *Annales* to produce a history which privileged economic forces and social struggles, but saw them connected to and influenced by politics and culture. His early books, such as *La España del Siglo XIX* (1961) and *La España del Siglo XX* (1966), were influential even though they were published in France. By the early 1970s, the regime's censorship had relaxed sufficiently to allow newer books such as *El Movimiento obrero en España* (1972) and *Metodología de la historia social de España* (1973) to be published inside the country. Perhaps even more important than his books was the series of annual Coloquia he organized in Pau starting in the early 1970s which were attended by large numbers of progressive young historians. The common denominator among them was an interest in the modern period, especially the Restoration, the Second Republic, and the Civil War, and within each period the priority they gave to the history of the labor movement. While all anti-Francoists, these young historians were also ideologically and politically diverse (within the left): socialists, communists, Trotskyists, or anarchists, and they wrote about the segment of the working class which coincided with their own political preferences. In all cases, the objective was to explore the past to delegitimize Francoism.

The labor history they wrote was traditional, focused on institutions such as unions and political parties, their leaders, ideologies, and the conflicts in which they engaged. It was, in short, political history with a new subject. On the other hand, their interest in the nineteenth and twentieth centuries distinguished them from their teachers who held university Chairs and who always privileged the early modern period.

The strong Marxist imprint on this generation's work meant that the central question was the "bourgeois revolution." History was driven by class struggle and passed through predetermined stages: feudalism, capitalism, and socialism. Bourgeois revolution moved a society from the first to the second, as had happened in France during the Revolution, and the "proletarian revolution" would carry it from the second to the third and final stage. The question historians of Spain debated was whether or not their country had experienced a bourgeois revolution. The consensus was that the revolution had been a "failure"; here the influence of Vilar was crucial. The Marxist approach also meant that the history of the urban working class was paramount and that the peasantry received much less attention, even though Spain was an overwhelmingly rural country into the twentieth century.

Things began to change in the 1970s and 1980s. The first social histories of the working class appeared—the journals *Estudios de Historia Social* and *Historia Social* appeared in 1980 and 1988, respectively—and the prominence of the working class as a historical subject began to diminish as historians explored other topics. Historians began to study the Franco regime and, reflecting international developments, women's history emerged at this time. The Barcelona-based Irish historian Mary Nash published her first articles in 1988.

By 2000, the historiography of the period dominated by Tuñón de Lara seemed very far away. There was no longer a dominant paradigm. Marxism had been displaced—again an international trend following the collapse of the Soviet Union—but nothing had taken its place. There were only multiple, partial visions. The idea that the Restoration was characterized by class domination exercised by an "oligarchy" or "power bloc" was replaced by the concept of clientelism, and one not peculiar to Spain, a form of mediation, between an urban political elite and a predominantly rural society. Social history was in the ascendant and cultural history was becoming important. The labor movement was no longer the center of attention; historians were interested in a variety of social movements such as feminism, environmentalism, pacifism, etc. If there was one topic that stood out for its prominence it was nationalism. This too was an international development but one which had special resonance as the hyper-centralized and Castilian-centric Spain of the Franco regime gave way to the decentralized "state of the autonomies." There was an enormous amount of writing about regional or peripheral nationals, much of it written in languages other than Spanish, mostly Catalan and Gallego.

What has happened in the last fifteen or twenty years? One striking feature of this historiography is the extreme imbalance in the interest historians have shown in the two centuries. In quantity, at least, the work devoted to the twentieth century towers over that devoted to the nineteenth. And interest in the twentieth century has been all but monopolized by the Second Republic, the Spanish Civil War, the Franco regime and, increasingly, the post-Franco Transition. The first thirty years of the century have received much less attention.

Despite this relative neglect, our understanding of the nineteenth century has changed significantly. The long-held view, well captured in the title of Jordi Nadal's 1975 classic *El fracaso de la revolución industrial en España, 1814-1913*, was that the century was essentially a write-off, an extended period in which Spain failed in every important way: economically, politically, socially, culturally, and diplomatically. Historians such as María Cruz Romeo, María Sierra, and Isabel Burdiel have shown that nineteenth-century Spanish liberalism was, in Burdiel's words, "a much more vital, richer and more diverse phenomenon than used to be thought." One historiographical development which has contributed much to this new vision has been the resurgence of biography. The manipulation to which the genre had been subjected during the Franco years had left it in ill repute, but it has been rescued and reinvigorated by new approaches, above all what has been called "biographical history." Isabel Burdiel, its outstanding Spanish practitioner, has defined this as "biographies driven by substantial historical questions . . . less a matter of who than how."

Our understanding of gender relations has become much more sophisticated as historians have looked beyond prescriptive literature and developed an understanding of political activity that is not limited to elections and legislatures—where the exclusion of women was unambiguous—they have seriously modified early ideas about the separation of the spheres and the banishment of women from public life. Rather than being predetermined, the roles of women were the focus of debates in which women participated and which were themselves a constitutive part of the liberal revolution. Gender was, in Mónica Burguera's words "an organizational category at the heart of [liberal and anti-liberal] political cultures . . . the extraordinarily powerful discourse around the complementarity of the sexes was unstable, contradictory, open and diverse." These debates did not simply pit liberals against their opponents. The two main branches of Spanish liberalism, Progressives and Moderates, differed fundamentally on the place of women in the new order. The domestic archetype known in Spain as the "angel of the hearth" was consolidated only in the second half of the nineteenth century.

Nationalism has continued to be a major topic but with some differences. Spanish, as opposed to peripheral, nationalism is now receiving serious attention. José Álvarez Junco's *Spanish Identity in the Age of Nations* (2016, Spanish edition 2001) and *Los colores de la patria: Símbolos nacionales en la España contemporánea* (2017) by Javier Moreno-Luzón and Xosé Manoel Núñez Seixas are but two examples. There have also been some interesting crossovers between work on Spanish and regional nationalisms. For example, Joan-Lluis Marfany has argued that men like Victor Balaguer and Bonaventura Carles Aribau, who were instrumental in launching the Catalan cultural revival known as La Renaixenca, were also important builders of Spanish nationalism. Historians have also begun to examine national identity through the lens of gender.

Another important feature of this rejuvenated vision of the nineteenth century has been the new place of empire, what we might call bringing the empire back in. Prompted by the centenary of the Disaster of 1898, historians such as Josep Fradera, Christopher Schmidt-Nowara and others have rethought the importance of the empire in Spain's nineteenth-century history. As Schmidt-Nowara put it in his contribution to perhaps the most important collection of essays on the subject, *Más se perdió en Cuba*, "in Cuba and the Pacific the empire was not the empty shell of the imperial grandeur of the past; rather it was a new imperial project on a scale without precedent in the long history of Spanish colonialism."

This new imperial history also formed part of broader new historiographical approaches, such as the rise of Atlantic and transnational history. Mexican historian Roberto Breña has described a distinctive Hispanic liberalism which emerged in Spain and informed the independence movements in its American colonies in the early nineteenth century, while Scott Eastman has explored one vector for its transatlantic transfer. And liberalism is increasingly being seen as a transnational phenomenon in Europe itself, in large part due to the experience of exiles. This was a common fate for Spanish liberals in the first half of the century, but at specific moments, such as during the Liberal Triennium, Spain was a promised land for liberals from elsewhere, particularly the Italian territories. The Constitution of Cádiz became a transnational document and the greatest symbol of international liberalism in the 1820s, inspiring revolutionaries in Portugal, Naples, Piedmont, and even Russia.

There have also been significant changes in the way the history of the twentieth century has been written. The debates over the Second Republic have become more polarized and heated, in part due to the popular success of nonacademic right-wing historians such as Pío Moa, in some cases with the stamp of approval of the well-known US Hispanist Stanley Payne. But there has also been a steady reappraisal of the regime, in part due to a number of important regional studies, such as those by José Manuel Macarro Vera and Fernando del Rey, and in part to major reassessments of politics at the national level, such as Nigel Townson's *The Crisis of Democracy in Spain: Centrist Politics under the Second Republic, 1931-36* (2000). A growing number of historians have criticized the long-standing politicization of the Republic's history, as well as highlighting what they see as its democratic deficit. This new approach to the period has been labeled as "revisionist" by defenders of the left orthodoxy, showing that the topic still generates great passion. The study of political violence during the Republic, while not a new topic, has become increasingly important and, as described by Eduardo González Calleja, has evolved from an emphasis on "the political to the social and cultural; from the base to the superstructure; from the calculus of individuals to collective action . . . from organized structures to opportunity structures and from ideologies to collective identities and political discourse and cultures."

The Civil War is increasingly being seen through the prism of total war. Michael Seidman and James Matthews have both produced innovative studies of how the war was waged, the former looking at the ways in which the Francoists their mobilized financial and economic resources, the latter exploring the use of conscription by both sides.

Francoist repression, both during the war and after, has attracted new attention. The first major study was Santos Juliá's *Víctimas de la Guerra civil* (1999) but the emergence of a grass-roots movement to exhume mass graves after 2000 provided a major impetus. The most high-profile work so far is Paul Preston's *The Spanish Holocaust: Inquisition and Extermination in Twentieth-Century Spain* (2012). The dominant metanarrative has been that from the outset of the war, the Francoist rebels had a plan to exterminate what they designated as the anti-Spain, what Francisco Espinosa has called "political genocide." In much of this work, the comparison with the Nazis is explicit. Sebastian Balfour has connected Francoist violence following the occupation of Republican territories during the war to the brutal tactics used during the Rif War in Morocco. This connection between violence employed in colonial conflicts and the increasing brutality of wars in Europe in the twentieth century has been an important recent trend in modern European history.

On the other side, ever since Albert Reig Tapia's influential 1984 book, *Ideología e historia*, the metanarrative about repression in the Republican zone has been that it was done by the masses, often criminals, in the context of the collapse of the state apparatus and without the involvement of Republican authorities. This narrative has been powerfully challenged by new research, above all that of Julius Ruiz, as shown most recently by his pioneering study of the massacre of Paracuellos in late 1936.

An intriguing new development, although outside the discipline of History strictly speaking, has been the application of archaeology to the study of the Civil War. Alfredo González Ruibal's *Volver a las trincheras* is the first book-length product of this approach.

The historiography of the Franco regime has also changed significantly. The previous dominance of political history, with its concern for categorizing the regime as fascist or not and its emphasis on studying its institutions and the resistance to them, has been reduced. Increasingly, historians of this period have turned their attention to social and cultural questions such as the experience of ordinary Spaniards and their attitudes toward the regime. The dichotomy consensus/resistance has been replaced by a more nuanced approach. As Antonio Cazorla-Sánchez, one of the leading historians of this period, has put it, historians "have become more skeptical about the myths of Spanish antifascism, less politically militant and have opened our eyes to the—at times contradictory—complexity of the histories of the people." There have also been two major, but very different biographies of Franco, one by Paul Preston, the other by Cazorla-Sánchez.

The past twenty years have also seen the insertion of an entirely new topic: historical memory, into the historiography of the Franco regime and post-Francoism. The field was launched by Paloma Aguilar's magnificent 1996 book *Memoria y olvido de la Guerra Civil Española*. Her conclusion, that the democracy created after the death of Francisco Franco was based on a "pact of forgetting" about the Civil War, became a hotly contested idea. And in an article written with Francisco Ferrándiz published in 2016 she herself qualified her original argument. The campaign to exhume mass graves and the 2007 Law of Historical Memory have given rise to much interesting work, often from other disciplines, for example Alison Menezes de Ribeiro's book, *Embodying Memory in Contemporary Spain* (2014), on memory discourse, Francisco Ferrándiz's exploration of the social impact of the exhumations, *El pasado bajo tierra: exhumaciones contemporáneas de la guerra civil* (2014), and Layla Renshaw's *Exhuming Loss: Memory, Materiality and Mass Graves of The Spanish Civil War* (2011).

Structure

To tell this story we have designed a volume which is more complex and ambitious than its predecessor. It is structured along three intersecting axes, a self-reinforcing structure which is further strengthened by generous cross-referencing within the text. The first section consists of seven chronologically defined chapters which provide the basic, largely political, narrative. The second section contains fifteen chapters which discuss individual themes across the entire period. The previous volume also had thematic chapters but these existed within the chronological periods which defined the book, for example "The Military and Politics" and "Church and State" for the period 1808–74, "Spain in the World" for the period 1875–1914, and chapters on competing nationalisms for that period and the period 1975–96. There were also some themes which did not receive chapters of their own, even on this limited basis. In some cases, as in "Gender" and "Migrations," this was a serious omission on our part. In others, such as "Environment," the available literature would not have sustained a distinct chapter. In at least one case, the "Politics of Memory and Transitional Justice," the theme itself became a significant one only after the book was published. Bolstering the thematic offers readers a second way of understanding the history of Spain beyond the political. It also reflects increased interest among historians in thematic approaches.

This kind of bipartite structure which combines chronology and themes is quite conventional. Adding a third section made up of a number of biographical sketches is not. There were various reasons behind our decision to do so. The first was pedagogical. It is our experience that undergraduate students, who are likely to constitute the bulk of the readers of this book, find having specific examples to illustrate general historical points extremely helpful. These biographies do that. Second, and related to this, both the chronological and thematic chapters are, of necessity, painted in broad strokes. Biographical sketches make it possible to include details, nuances, and complexities that the others cannot. They also add an engaging human dimension to the story. Third, the resurgence of biography which we mentioned above meant that there were a number of experienced and skillful authors we could invite to contribute and this, in part, shaped our selection of subjects. From among the vast army of possibilities we chose fourteen people, ten men and four women, from the worlds of politics and culture. (The number of these sketches was constrained by the overall length of the book.) Almost all will be new to English-speaking readers and many would be little more than names to university students and the general public in Spain. All of them, however, were important in their time and, more significantly for our purposes, serve to illustrate and bolster some of the more general points made in the rest of the book. This is not to say that they were the only important figures, or even the most important ones. Indeed discussions about this could prove a valuable classroom exercise and having students do their own biographical sketches an engaging assignment.

The contributors are also a diverse group. They are specialists in a number of different fields: political history, economic history, cultural history, social history, gender history, and military history, and they come from eight different countries: Canada, France, Germany, Israel, Italy, Spain, the United States, and the United Kingdom. They do not belong to a single historiographical school and, as a group, they bring a diversity of intellectual backgrounds, experiences, and outlooks. We believe that between them, the tripartite structure and the choice of authors have produced an unusually rich volume which offers a broad and nuanced vision of a complex and engaging national history which has always also been part of European and world history.

Further reading

Aguilar Fernández, Paloma, *Memory and Amnesia: The Role of the Spanish Civil War in the Transition to Democracy*, New York: Berghahn, 2002.

Aguilar, Paloma and Ferrándiz, Francisco, "Memory, media and spectacle: Interviú's portrayal of Civil War exhumations in the early years of Spanish democracy", *Journal of Spanish Cultural Studies*, 17, 1 (2016), pp. 1–25.

Anderson, Peter, *The Francoist Military Trials: Terror and Complicity, 1939-1945*, London: Routledge, 2010.

Andreu Miralles, Xavier (ed.), Click here to enter text.*Género y Nación en la España Contemporánea*, *Ayer*, 106, 2 (2017)

Balfour, Sebastian, *Deadly Embrace. Morocco and the Road to the Spanish Civil War*, Oxford: Oxford University Press, 2008.

Baumeister, Martin and Schüler-Springorum, Stefanie (eds.), "*If You Tolerate This.. "The Spanish Civil War in the Age of Total War*Click here to enter text., Chicago: University of Chicago Press, 2008.

Breña, Roberto, *El primer liberalismo espanol y los procesos de emancipacion de America, 1808-1824*, Mexico City: Colegio de México, 2006.

Breña, Roberto, "The Cádiz Liberal Revolution and Spanish American Independence", in Tutino, John (ed.), *New Countries. Capitalism, Revolutions, and Nations in the Americas, 1750-1850*, Durham: Duke University Press, 2016.

Burdiel, Isabel, "Historia política y biografía: más allá de las fronteras", *Ayer*, 93, 1 (2014), pp. 47–83.

Burdiel, Isabel, *Isabel II. Una biografía*, Madrid: Taurus, 2010.

Caballé, Anna, "La biografía en España: primera propuesta para la contrucción de un cánon", in I. Burdiel and R. Foster, eds, *La Historia Biográfica en Europa*, Zaragoza: Institución Fernando el Católico, 2015.

Cazorla-Sánchez, Antonio, *Franco: The Biography of the Myth*, London: Routledge, 2013.

Cazorla-Sánchez, Antonio, *Franco, Fear and Progress: Ordinary Lives in Franco's Spain (1936-1975)*. Oxford: Blackwell-Wiley, 2009.

Del Rey Reguillo, Fernando, *Paisanos en lucha. Exclusión política y violencia en la Segunda República Española,* Madrid: Biblioteca Nueva, 2008.

Eastman, Scott, *Preaching Spanish Nationalism Across the Hispanic Atlantic, 1759-1823*, Baton Rouge: LSU Press, 2012.

Fradera, Josep María, *La nación imperial (1750-1918). Derechos, representación y ciudadanía en los imperios de Gran Bretaña, Francia, España y Estados Unidos*, Barcelona: Edhasa, 2015.

Fradera, Josep María, *La nación imperial Colonias para después de un imperio*, Barcelona: Edicions Bellaterra, 2005.

González Calleja, Eduardo, "La historiografía sobre la violencia política en la Segunda República española: una reconsideración", *HISPANIA NOVA. Revista de Historia Contemporánea*, 11 (2013) http://hispanianova.rediris.es

González Calleja, Eduardo, *Cifras cruentaslas víctimas mortales de la violencia sociopolítica en la Segunda República española (1931-1936)*, Granada: Comares, 2015.

Graham, Helen, *The War and Its Shadow. Spain's Civil War in Europe's Long Twentieth Century*, Brighton: Sussex Academic Press, 2012.

Isabella, Maurizio, *Risorgimento in Exile: Italian Emigres and the Liberal International in the Post-Napoleonic Era*, Oxford: Oxford University Press, 2009.

Macarro Vera, José Manuel, *La Sevilla Republicana*, Madrid: Silex, 2003.

Marfany, Joan-Lluis, *Nacionalisme espanyol i catalanitat*, Barcelona: Edicions 62, 2016.

Matthews, James, *Reluctant Warriors. Republican Popular Army and Nationalist Army Conscripts in the Spanish Civil War 1936 – 1939*, Oxford: Oxford University Press, 2012.

Pan-Montojo, Juan (ed.), *Más se perdió en Cuba: España, 1898 y la crisis de fin de siglo*, Madrid: Alianza Editorial, 1898

Peyrou, Florencia, "The role of Spain and the Spanish in the creation of Europe's transnational democratic political culture, 1840–70", *Social History*, 40, 4 (2015), 497–517.

Preston, Paul, *Franco*, New York: HarperCollins, 1993.

Preston, Paul, The Spanish *Holocaust: Inquisition and Extermination in Twentieth-Century Spain*, New York: Norton, 2012.

Richards, Michael, *After the civil war: making memory and re-making Spain since 1936*, Cambridge: Cambridge University Press, 2013.

Ruiz, Julius, *'Paracuellos': The Elimination of the 'Fifth Column' in Republican Madrid During the Spanish Civil War*, Brighton: Sussex Academic Press, 2016.

Ruiz, Julius, *The 'Red Terror' and the Spanish Civil War. Revolutionary Violence in Madrid*, Cambridge: Cambridge University Press, 2014.

Schmidt-Nowara, Christopher, *Empire And Antislavery: Spain Cuba And Puerto Rico 1833-1874*, Pittsburgh: University of Pittsburgh Press, 1999.

Schmidt-Nowara, Christopher, *Slavery, Freedom, and Abolition in Latin America and the Atlantic World*, Albuquerque: University of New Mexico Press, 2011.

Seidman, Michael, *The Victorious Counterrevolution. The Nationalist Effort in the Spanish Civil War*, Madison: University of Wisconsin Press, 2011.

Simal, Juan Luis, "Letters from Spain. The 1820 Revolution and the Liberal International", in Isabella, Maurizio and Zanou, Konstantina (eds.), *Mediterranean Diasporas. Politics and Ideas in the Long Nineteenth Century*, London: Bloomsbury, 2016

SECTION ONE
CHRONOLOGIES

CHAPTER 2
THE CRISIS OF THE OLD REGIME: 1808–33
Gregorio Alonso

The arrival of the French Bourbon dynasty to the Castilian throne in 1700 with Philip V Anjou (1683–1746) provoked radical changes in the internal organization of the Hispanic Monarchy. The Iberian territories and the global overseas empire went through drastic modifications during the eighteenth century aimed at making its administration more rational and profitable. The schemes inspired by the so-called Enlightened despotism combined monarchical absolutism with modern ideas vaguely grounded on both French philosophy and British political economy. Gradual changes would make the old composite Catholic monarchy evolve toward an up-to-date Empire. These reforms included increasing degrees of centralization, the abolition of the Catalan *furs*, or Medieval charters, the militarization of the imperial administration, the introduction of new captaincies and viceroyalties in the American possessions, agrarian reform, and a more aggressive stance toward the Catholic Church labeled "regalism." Some positive effects of this new political approach could be felt under Charles III (1759–88) and Charles IV (1788–1808), although they also faced two extraordinary changes in the international stage.

The revolutions of 1776 in the United States and 1789 in France changed Western history permanently and had immediate consequences for all neighboring countries, including the Catholic monarchy of Spain. Between 1793 and 1795, French revolutionary troops occupied large sections of the north of the Iberian Peninsula. When the invasion ended, a combination of political realism and ambition led the Spanish government to sign collaboration agreements with the revolutionary French government that reached an end in 1805. The long-lived Hispanic monarchy had certainly faced major crises in previous times, but the depth, width, and nature of its fight against the new French empire under Napoleon Bonaparte made this one unique. With the fresh memory of the worst defeat ever experienced by the once invincible Spanish royal navy, inflicted by the British on the shores of Trafalgar (Cadiz), the Spanish authorities faced the largest and best trained armies that had ever crossed the Spanish border.

The 1808 political crisis showed some distinctive elements from the outset. First, never since the Middle Ages and the emergence of the Iberian Monarchies as leading actors in world politics had a Castilian monarch been made prisoner by invading forces. From April 1808 the Spanish royal family was taken hostage by Napoleon in the southern French city of Valençay (see Chapter 24). Secondly, this monarchical crisis also had the knock-on effect of generating an imperial power vacuum. Unlike the Portuguese monarch John VI, who fled along with his court to his Brazilian territories, the Spanish Bourbons decided to stay in Europe and agree to the terms of their abdication with Napoleon, who replaced Ferdinand with his older brother Joseph I. Finally, and even more of a novelty, never before then had it been the common people who led the rebellion against foreign invading armies once they crossed the borders in the autumn of 1807.

To these unprecedented changes needs to be added the fact that among the members of royal family there had been serious political discrepancies that predated the French invasion. Those different opinions, in fact, revolved around the actual position to be taken in the face of such an aggressive move, and the decision of Ferdinand VII, the son of king Charles IV, to forcefully remove his father from the throne and put an end to the ascendancy of the over-mighty prime minister Manuel Godoy (1767–1851). The latter had entertained a rather close relationship with the French representatives and diplomats of Napoleon in Madrid and held ambitious plans to become the regent of neighboring Portugal once the French had toppled the reigning dynasty. However, while Napoleon never meant to give Godoy access to the Portuguese throne, he badly needed his support to allow him to place his armies in the Iberian Peninsula and, once there, take both Iberian monarchies by storm. Well aware of Godoy's intentions, Ferdinand decided to intervene and, allied with the most conservative sectors of the court, launched a coup d'état against his own father on March 19 that year. Once Napoleon sensed that the window of political opportunity had been left open, he did not take long to send his men to take Spain's capital city. Once the French troops reached Madrid, the political fate of the Crown was sealed. Napoleon would take the entire royal family to France and replace the quarreling Bourbons with his older brother Joseph, who was acting as king in Naples at the time.

This rapid and confusing series of events triggered an unexpected popular reaction across Spain and Portugal that led to the outbreak of the Peninsular War that would last from 1808 to 1814. A mixture of xenophobia, exacerbated Christian bigotry, and localism fueled the feelings of large sections of the Spanish population for the following years and invested them with a strong will to resist any imperial decree affecting their lives and fortunes. The resulting unmitigated hatred against the invading forces materialized into a long and bitter campaign of attrition which would produce the devastation of the country as well as the loss of thousands of lives. The local people's reaction, their sustained war effort, and their ultimate victory over the invaders would in turn give raise to the heroic myth of the untameable Spanish people fighting "Napoleon's cursed war," a myth tainted with the dark colors of anti-French Romantic nationalism and Catholic fanaticism. These were the key local elements at play in the Spanish version of what David A. Bell has called the "first total war," one characterized by its levels of "sheer bloodshed and destruction."

The crisis immediately acquired Atlantic dimensions: the empty throne not only implied chaos in the metropolis but, even more importantly, triggered events which would bring to an end the already challenged control of the Castilian Crown over most of the American continent. The flames of the constitutional revolution that ignited in Madrid almost immediately had an effect in places as distant as Mexico City, Quito, Caracas, and Buenos Aires. It is only within the larger framework of the Atlantic revolutions that the 1808 effect and its reverberations can be properly understood. Not only did it mark the American collapse of the Iberian empires, it also signaled the beginning of the age of nations in the Hispanic world and a new stage of modernity.

The constitutional revolution that followed the breakdown of Bourbon absolutism started in New Granada, modern Colombia. The 1811 Constitution of Cundinamarca would be the first of a long series defining the geographical, juridical, and political limits of the newly independent republics across the Americas. The Latin American adoption of liberal rule as the favored strategy for declaring independence from the crippling Iberian grip on the continent needs to be framed within a dense network of family links, business interests, and trade needs. The independence process therefore begs for not linear accounts based on an alleged and shared hunger for liberty and requires historians to look into the dead ends of failed agreements that were explored until the very last minute, as shown by Roberto Breña for the largest and wealthiest of the new republics, Mexico, formerly New Spain. The influential Creole elites who led the process, as well as the royalist groups who opposed their plans, shared a sense of conservatism and a fear of race-based popular upheaval that found its origins in recently repressed instances of social revolution such as the rebellion of Tupac Amaru II in Peru (1780–82) and the successful slave revolt in the French colony of Saint Domingue that produced the republic of Haiti in 1804. On the other hand, despite the efforts of historians such as Marisa Laxo or Marcela Echeverri, most current versions of the end of the Spanish empire in continental America between 1811 and 1824 tend to ignore the substantial contributions to the achievement of national independence made by the descendants of Africans and people of mixed race.

The parliamentary and constitutional revolution that took place in the metropole also relied on popular leadership. The decreed replacement of the Bourbons by Joseph Bonaparte stirred outrage and led to popular mobilization against the invading troops and the new government. The opening event of this process can be located in Madrid on May 2 and 3, 1808, as famously portrayed by Goya's paintings. In political terms, the power vacuum left by the exiled kings was rapidly filled by revolutionary bodies of local patriots, known as *juntas*. These institutions arguably originated in sixteenth-century Aragonese *germanias* or Castilian *comunidades*, and claimed to replace the absent monarch and the represent national will, in a Rousseauian sense. The king's forced decision to leave the Peninsula had put an end to the preexisting social contract and popular allegiance to the reigning monarch. Liberated from their duty to submit to a foreign and illegitimate king, the *juntas* took power in order to preserve national integrity, protect national interests, and organize armed resistance against the Napoleonic armies.

Most historiographical writing on what would later be christened the Spanish War of Independence (1808–14) has emphasized the mixture of factors that led common Spaniards to rebel against Napoleon in the name of the fatherland. Nevertheless, their intentions and the connotations of the revolutionary process that it encompassed have far too easily been summarized borrowing the reactionary motto "¡Viva el Rey y la religion!" ("Long live the King and Religion!"). However, the meanings of patriotism in the springtime of 1808 were highly disputed and divisive. Those pejoratively known as the *afrancesados*, or Frenchified, also acted patriotically but instead of joining the *juntas* and the irregular armies (the *guerrillas*) that would soon populate the country, they chose to serve Joseph Bonaparte. These loyal subjects also thought of themselves as patriots and acted out of their legitimate political persuasion mixed with personal interests, as much as the Bourbon supporters did. In fact, a fair share of the nobility and influential echelons of the reforming high civil service embraced the Napoleonic cause and joined this group. The *afrancesados* stayed loyal to the absent monarchs, who had requested their vassals to comply with Joseph's rulings, and duly supported the newly established dynasty in order to guarantee peace and further reform the old structures of the Catholic monarchy. Among them there were highly powerful figures of all orders of life, including leading clergymen such as the *Inquisidor General*, or Chairman of the Holy Office of the Inquisition, Ramón José de Arce (1757–1844). Other ecclesiastical hierarchs, such as the Archbishop of Toledo, the head of the Catholic Church in Spain, Luis de Borbón (1777–1823), who sought refuge in Southern Spain, supported Liberal ideas.

The closest collaborators of Joseph I drafted and introduced the Constitution of Bayonne in July 1808. The document was a royal charter that decreed separation of powers, the abolition of feudal privileges and the tribunal of the Holy Inquisition, and divided the country into French-inspired departments. Spain thus became a part of a broader Napoleonic plan to create modernizing monarchies across Europe while putting them and their resources at the service of his personal empire. In fact, regardless of the legislative innovations based on revolutionary constitutionalism and codification, it would be Napoleon Bonaparte himself and his generals, not Joseph, who would take most political decisions.

In 1808, French troops took control of most of Spain and Portugal, and the local *juntas* joined forces to create a new Spanish government: the Supreme Central Junta. It was first convened in September 1808 in Aranjuez with thirty-five members and originally chaired by the Count of Floridablanca (1728–1808), the most able statesman of the reigns of Charles III and his son, and the brains behind most successful reforms in the previous decades. This Central Junta coordinated the war effort until January 1810, when it was replaced by the five-member Regency Council of Spain and the Indies which, in the absence of the king, would operate as the executive body and direct diplomatic efforts to guarantee British support. The latter objective was soon achieved, when on August 1, 1808 troops commanded by Field Marshall Sir Arthur Wellesley (1769–1852), better known as the Duke of Wellington, landed in Spain. The British intervention, resources, and support would prove to be of paramount importance for the combined Hispano-Portuguese struggle against the Napoleonic invasion. While war escalated and spread across the Peninsula, some leading figures of the Spanish political and military resistance successfully forced the Regents to call for a *Cortes* (parliament), which was opened on September 1810 in the city of San Fernando (Cadiz), which the presence of British naval vessels kept out of French control.

Despite the revolutionary nature of the rapidly developing political process, some recent works have highlighted the lines of historical continuity between the Old Regime and the Age of Liberalism. Gabriel Paquette, Antonio Calvo Maturana, and José María Portillo Valdés, among others, have convincingly argued that most relevant political actors of the political revolution that led to the formation of constituent Parliaments across the Atlantic and the reconfiguration of the main political institutions ruling the Metropole and the soon-to-be independent republics alike were already veterans of Spanish politics. Moreover, their worldviews and expectations, as well as some of the state-building projects they supported, had been shaped and widely discussed during the reigns of both Charles III and Charles IV. In particular, the strengthening of royal powers through regalist policies applied to the Catholic Church illustrated only one dimension of a more comprehensive plan for the expansion and diversification of royal jurisdiction. On the other hand, the French invasion also produced some crucial novelties. A case in point was the revolutionary Parliament that opened its doors in September 1810: the Cortes of Cadiz.

The Cortes of Cadiz (1810–14)

The deputies sitting at the *Cortes* included a significant number of clergymen, 97 out of 350, as well as lawyers, civil servants, local councilors, military officers, and noblemen. Despite this socially conservative cast, as their decisions show, a slight majority of them supported reformist ideas. Moreover, given the political revolution and the international and civil wars the country faced, the tasks and powers of the new Parliament could hardly be fully defined by the Regency. In principle, its main objective was to monitor and control the war effort and introduce the necessary reforms to guarantee the victory of the Spanish armies. From the first meetings on, however, it was clear that the deputies understood their mission in a more expansive fashion. In the absence of the king, the Cortes started its work by announcing its full loyalty to Ferdinand VII. By the same token, however, they also declared themselves as sovereign and promptly introduced some controversial measures such as freedom of the press. In their view, the country needed a well-informed public in order to have an enlightened debate on how to win the war and regenerate the old structures, corrupted by the ministerial despotism embodied by the widely hated premier, Godoy. The *Cortes* would thus aim to combine the efficiency of its policies with the defense and the expected benefits of freedom of ideas. These two measures were supported by the most forward-thinking deputies, the soon-to-be called *Liberales*, who were better organized and slightly more numerous than their opponents during the four years the *Cortes* met, between 1810 and 1814. This was the first time in history that the word "Liberal" was used to designate a political group, leaving behind its exclusively moral connotations. The same deputies would also be responsible for the introduction of the most radical reforms related to the right to vote, seigneurial rights, guilds, tax, and ecclesiastical reforms, and the abolition of the Inquisition, among others.

The bicentennial celebrations of the Cortes provided a golden opportunity for scholars to reflect critically on the purpose, the achievements, and the legacy of the first modern Parliament in Spanish history, as well as its shortcomings and pitfalls. Much has been written, for example, about the foreign influences—American, French, English, or otherwise—on the proposals and policies passed by the Cortes of Cadiz. However, the Spanish *Liberales* themselves denied any foreign influence and constantly proclaimed their loyalty to the ancient Castilian and Aragonese roots of their ideology and parliamentary proposals. However, revolutionary ideas permeated the deputies' collective psyche and, as recently put by Maria Cruz Romeo, it was the nation, as the emerging political subject, that was then the only locus where freedom was possible.

The Cortes' most important achievement was to create and proclaim the Constitution of March 1812, officially known as *The Political Constitution of the Spanish Monarchy*. And it was indeed in name of that nation, "consisting of all Spaniards of both Hemispheres" as Article 1 proclaimed, which the Parliament would, from its opening sessions, legislate a series of radical reforms. The idea that Spain was a single sovereign nation that comprised territories that stretched from the Philippines to Cuba can puzzle modern readers, but it also surprised some contemporaries, especially those in the high echelons of the colonial administration. Indeed, the transition from the Old Regime's imperial monarchy to the emerging imperial nation was anything but easy.

The declaration of national sovereignty, the unicameral nature of the legislative body, and the separation of powers, as well as the introduction of indirect universal manhood suffrage with some limitations based on race, education, and financial autonomy, ranked high among the most "democratic" measures introduced by the Constitution. On the other hand, some other decisions illustrated the corporatist and historicist underpinnings of their legislative activity. For instance, article 12, which declared that "the religion of the Spanish nation is, and ever shall be, the Catholic Apostolic Roman and only true faith; the State shall, by wise and just laws, protect it and prevent the exercise of any other," infamously sanctioned religious intolerance and perpetuated religious censorship of all publications. In so doing, the deputies established a long-lasting precedent that would be followed by all Parliaments until 1869. Yet the Cortes also prevented monks and friars, as members of religious orders, from becoming active members of Parliament due to the alleged incompatibility between their religious oaths and the constitutional one. Tellingly, incompatibility would also be referred to when it came to abolishing one of the most powerful and controversial institutions of the Old Regime, the Inquisition. According to its critics, the maintenance of this special court, half royal and half ecclesiastical, was entirely at odds with the spirit of change and reform that inspired the work of the Cortes. Revealingly, it would be a clergyman and former vice chancellor of the University of Salamanca, the theologian and professor of philosophy Diego Muñoz Torrero (1761–1829), who headed the parliamentary commission on constitutional matters, who would declare in January 1813 that "the Inquisition is incompatible with the Constitution" and the Cortes accordingly voted to abolish it.

Therefore, the first experiment with representative government with an absent king, the aforementioned search for compatibilities between the old and the new, and the imperial vocation of its scope and mandate, animated the 1812 Constitution. The first formulation of a Hispanic liberalism was also accompanied by a shared sense of loyalty with the allegedly healthiest and most respectable institutions inherited from the Old Regime. A constitutionally limited monarchy, a comparatively strong legislature, and ample enfranchisement of adult male citizens ranked high as its key features. Moreover, the aforementioned faithfulness to the conservation of intolerant Catholicism as the first duty of the king and the legislators alike would also be sanctioned by most Spanish and Latin American constitutions in the nineteenth century.

Life inside the Cortes was far from easy, however. The initial consensus around the need for coordinating the war effort and rejecting Ferdinand VII´s abdication quickly proved a rather narrow common ground. As soon as the first decrees were passed, symptoms of dissent and conflict between *Liberales* and conservatives started to emerge. The former advocated for more radical reforms inspired by the mixed influence of the British parliamentary tradition and some local adaptation of the French Revolutionary ideas. Cadiz, where the Parliament sat, was Spain's main trading port with the Americas and, for some decades, had been the Spanish haven for advanced-thinking writers, poets, and journalists. The ratio of printing houses, libraries, and cafés was rather high in Spanish terms and they constituted the ideal centers where Liberal principles could be produced, disseminated, and discussed. A commercial hub with a high number of foreign traders, diplomats, refugees, and businessmen was not the ideal setting for defending conservative ideals. Those who did often found themselves isolated both within and without the theatre, and later the church, where the Cortes held its sessions. A clear indication of this was the actual naming of the opposing groups. Whereas "Liberal" had a highly positive connotation in moral terms, the conservatives were labeled by local journalists as *Serviles* (Servile ones), highlighting their lower moral stance as well as their submissive attitude toward the traditional sources of authority. The use of Liberal as a political label, as Raymond Carr showed more than fifty years ago, was a truly global novelty that is one of Spain's major contributions to modern political lexicon.

The content of the 1812 Constitution demonstrated the balance of power within the Cortes and included a number of articles that can hardly be described as purely "modern" or "liberal" in full sense. The document aimed to set the general rules and principles under which the bi-hemispheric imperial nation would be run as well as to define the very nature of the internal and external limits, in legal as well as in geographical terms. In that sense, the role of the Catholic religion was critical. Its actual formulation also implied the sanctioning of the preexisting regalist interventionism in the internal organization of the Church. As a consequence, the Parliament would decree the reduction of the amount of the special ecclesiastical tax—the tithe—which Spanish farmers needed to pay. Moreover, the number of religious houses would also be reduced and their properties sold at auction as planned by the interim finance minister, José Canga Argüelles (1770–1843). This measure aimed to reduce the weight of *mortmain*, the inalienable ownership of real estate by noble or ecclesiastical corporations, and had some precedents in 1798, when some plots of land had already been alienated and sold. As then, in 1813 the new minister aimed to raise funds to reduce the national deficit and public debt and to finance the ongoing war effort against the retreating French troops. The Church, along with the Military Orders, the Crown, and the local councils would be the main targets of this policy (see Chapter 18).

The selling of ecclesiastical lands was the last nail in the coffin of the controversies raised by the place that the Catholic Church should play in the new regime. In fact, this issue was the most divisive between the *Serviles* and the *Liberales* at the Cortes. Along with the disentailment of the lands previously belonging to the suppressed religious houses, earlier that year the abolition of the Inquisition had been decreed. The reactionary sectors sitting in Parliament aired their discontent and wondered if the *Liberales* were willing to copy the revolutionary French de-Christianization policies. They failed to remember that whereas the French Assembly had introduced the Civil Constitution of the Clergy, by which ecclesiastics were forced to swear allegiance to civil laws and authorities, the Spanish Cortes had used its Constitution to make Catholicism the official and exclusive religion of the country. On the other hand, the civil authorities faced clear limitations in making modifications to the internal organization of the Church and accordingly denied Parliament legitimacy to regulate the activities of the Holy Office.

Despite its unrealistic ambition to become the supreme law of a vast empire, its internal contradictions and its short life, the Constitution of 1812 has widely been regarded as both the birth certificate of the Spanish nation and the soundest indicator of the arrival of political modernity to the Catholic monarchy. Yet the political life of the country would radically change with the return to the throne of the king, for whose right to rule many Spaniards, Portuguese, and British had given their lives. Ferdinand VII's arrival in 1814 would put an abrupt and bloody end to the first period of political experimentation with Liberalism as he would successfully reclaim his alleged right to enjoy "full sovereignty": absolutist monarchical rule.

1814–20: Back to the past?

As far as the notion of modernity is concerned, the clock started going backward in high politics early in 1814, right after the absent king crossed the Pyrenees and returned to Spain. On his return, King Ferdinand received a truly glorious and enthusiastic welcome from his loyal subjects. Since 1808 his royal persona had been through a process of official and popular idealization and sacralization, which reached its peak when Napoleon decided to release him. The Spanish representative of the Bourbon dynasty would shortly attempt to put that political capital to his own interested use and restore unrestricted, absolutist monarchical rule in Spain.

Across the Atlantic, however, the situation could not have been more different. Unimpressed by the meager representation granted to the American deputies at the *Cortes*, in growing areas of the empire the end of the Old Regime had become coterminous with the evaporation of Spanish dominance. The sacral figure of the King was now heavily criticized and identified with despotism too. Clear evidence of this development was the ceremonial shooting, burning, and destruction of royal portraits in New Granada. Events like these only prefigured the series of civil wars that would plague the colonies for the following decade and bring the end of Spanish rule.

Back in the peninsula, after the military coup led by General Elío and following the advice of the absolutist deputies of the Cortes who had launched the so-called Manifesto of the Persians, in May 1814, Ferdinand closed down the parliament and declared "the constitution and those decrees null and void, now and forever, as if those events never happened." Immediately after his return to power, a fierce campaign of repression led a group of Liberal deputies, journalists, and public figures either to prison or to exile. A number of them fled to France, England, and the Americas in search of safety, the first of a long series of political exiles that many nonconformist or dissident Spanish citizens would suffer in the years to come (see Chapter 19). The monarch was willing to restore the society of estates, along with all the privileges enjoyed by the nobility and the clergy, and supporters of absolutism cheered the reinstatement of the seigneurial rights, the guilds, and the tithe. Moreover, free speech and press freedom were duly abolished. These policies eventually met with some liberal resistance and in La Mancha region, for instance, there were street brawls when the commemorative Constitutional plaques that had previously been set in the main square of numerous towns and villages were destroyed.

The intended journey to the past was not achieved in its full expected depth, though. Monarchical restoration did not mean full ecclesiastical emancipation from civil control. For instance, the Inquisition was restored and replaced the Faith *Juntas* created by the Cortes. Their duties included press censorship, the spiritual welfare of the royal subjects, and control over their morals, including blasphemy and concubinage. In addition, the restored inquisitorial authorities would persecute liberals and *afrancesados* alike. Yet this revamped union of Throne and Altar was far from ideal, and the king carried on drawing heavily on forced donations by local parishes in order to refurbish the churches, chapels, and other buildings that had been destroyed during the war. It took little time for the bishops and the papal nuncio to denounce them, but to no avail. Due to the poor harvests, the situation became even worse in 1817. It was then that the finance minister Martín de Garay (1771–1822) imposed a "general contribution" on the religious orders that outraged the ecclesiastical hierarchy even further.

The international situation favored such monarchical excesses. The fall of Napoleon led most Western European monarchies to experience a short-lived period of revamped absolutism committed to wiping away all traces of the revolutionary legacy. The Habsburg chancellor, Prince Klemens von Metternich, coordinated diplomatic efforts to agree on the terms of the reestablishment of power of the fallen monarchical powers at the Congress of Vienna in autumn 1814. Moreover, in order to guarantee the success of the restored monarchies which had previously suffered under French rule, the first international peace-keeping organization ever founded was instituted with the revealing name of Holy Alliance. Despite its name, the Alliance was not a confessional organization and indeed included a variety of Christian rulers. Its primordial goal was not to defend any specific set of religious values but to safeguard the *status quo ante* 1789 on the Old Continent. Following the lead of Tsar Alexander I, the constituent members were Orthodox Russia, mostly Protestant Prussia, and Catholic Austria, which signed the foundational agreement in Paris on September 26, 1815. Its aims included returning powers and jurisdictions to the traditional ruling classes—the aristocracy and the clergy—in order to sustain the restored might of European monarchs. In so doing, they aimed to overcome the shock of the revolutionary period and set the ground for a lasting political regime that would keep the challenge of liberalism in check. The commotions of 1830 and 1848 which spread throughout Europe would later show the limits of their success.

Notwithstanding these coordinated efforts to repress revolutionary ideas, the flames of revolt burned brightly in the Latin American colonies. National bankruptcy and the demobilization of the armies in the Peninsula did not favor Ferdinand's desperate attempts to keep them. On another front, England lobbied the Spanish government to further its own interests by speeding up the process of Latin American independence and loosening Spanish grip on the Antilles. As a result, in September 1817 Ferdinand VII was forced to sign a treaty with England where he committed to abolishing the slave trade in his possessions north of the equator. The government and the King, under pressure from the Cuban elites who defended their vested interests in the flourishing cane sugar industry, never meant to comply with the treaty, much to the British authorities' dismay and despair (see Chapter 25).

The process of imperial collapse advanced rapidly under Creole military leadership. Generals like Francisco de Miranda (1750–1816), Simón Bolívar (1783–1830), José de San Martín (1778–1850), and Antonio José Sucre (1795–1830), along with civilians like Vicente Rocafuerte (1783–1847), spearheaded the liberation movements across South America. On July 9, 1816 the United Provinces of South America, comprising current-day Argentina, Bolivia, Paraguay, and Uruguay, declared independence from Spain. Santa Catarina and Río Grande del Sur in Brasil soon joined them. On August 7, 1819, Royalist forces were defeated in the battle of Boyacá and Gran Colombia was created, bringing together Venezuela, Colombia and Ecuador. Meanwhile in Mexico, the emancipatory impulse was temporarily blocked by the presence of 10,000 troops. In 1815, José María Morelos (1765–1815), who along with fellow Catholic priest Miguel Hidalgo y Castilla (1753–1811) had been the leader of the 1810 movement, was executed in Mexico City by the civilian authorities after having found guilty of treason by the Holy Inquisition. Similar results were achieved in the viceroyalty of Peru, where José de San Martín´s pro-independence efforts faced what became a stronghold of royalism between 1811 and 1821.

During the years between 1814 and 1820, political stability in the Peninsula was under threat and Liberal army and navy officers often menaced Ferdinand's rule. Most of these military men had been promoted during the Peninsular War and now feared being demoted and plotted to restore constitutional rule. The first of a long list of Liberal *pronuciamientos*, or coups d'état leading to popular revolt, took place in Pamplona in September 1814 under the leadership of the war hero General Francisco Espoz y Mina (1781–1836). Once the movement proved unsuccessful, and Espoz y Mina went into exile to France to save his life; some of his fellows were less lucky and were executed immediately. In May 1814, the conspiratorial plans of Field Marshal Juan Díaz Porlier (1775–1815) were discovered in Madrid and he was sentenced to spend four years at the inquisitorial dungeons at La Coruña. He would continue his conspiratorial activities there and launch a coup on the night of September 18, 1815. He proclaimed the 1812 Constitution and released a political manifesto, but some of the sergeants under his command betrayed him and Díaz Porlier was hung for treason in a public square on October 3, 1815. Similar failed attempts took place in Andalucia, Barcelona, Madrid, and Valencia in the following years, in an endless battle for the recovery of constitutional rule. The inability shown by neoabsolutism to gather support among large sectors of the armed forces, as well as the idealization of the potential of the 1812 Constitution, paved the way for these insurrections.

The combination of military insurrection and popular upheaval finally put an end to the first period of Ferdinand VII's absolutist rule in January 1820. The disgruntled and poorly armed military men due to embark for America to defend the Crown's authority over its colonies there headed a successful rebellion that ultimately managed to restore the Cadiz Constitution.

A second chance for the constitution of Cadiz: The Liberal Triennium (1820–23)

Andalucia would again be the region where the *Liberales* succeeded in advancing their cause and imposing constitutional rule upon the monarch. This time it all started in the town of Cabezas de San Juan (Seville). In January 1820, Colonels Rafael de Riego (1784–1823) and Antonio Quiroga (1784–1841) took the lead, arrested the commander of the expeditionary troops about to cross the Atlantic, and proclaimed the Constitution of 1812. In March, when the uprising was about to collapse, riots supporting it broke out in the northern province of Galicia. It was then that the rebels entered Madrid, joined forces with the crowds which surrounded the Royal Palace and imposed the Constitution on Ferdinand VII. Forced by the circumstances, he swore an oath on the Holy Bible to protect it and rule the country constitutionally.

In April 1820, a new government was put in place that soon became popularly known as the "Government of the Jailbirds" due to the fact that most of its members had served prison terms in the previous years. The occasion provided a second chance in power for the *Liberales*: men like Agustín de Argüelles, the leader of the parliamentary group at Cadiz, José Canga Argüelles (1776–1844), and Manuel García Herreros (1767–1836) became ministers. In power until March 9, 1821, this relatively moderate group reinstated indirect, universal manhood suffrage and the abolition of the Inquisition, and reintroduced freedom of the press. The new Liberal government also introduced the National Militia, a paramilitary corps formed by civilians devoted to protecting Constitutional rule and to educating the youth in Liberal values while being trained in the armed defense of the political regime.

Only eleven months later, the government faced a deep crisis that led to its demise. In his opening speech to the 1821 Cortes, King Ferdinand VII, never a convinced supporter of Liberalism, made some veiled criticisms of his own cabinet, alluding to its alleged lack of patriotism for not granting him the right to veto laws passed by parliament. This power struggle for determining the specific terms of shared sovereignty between the King and the Cortes, known as the Postscript Crisis, prefigured the deeper conflicts which would shake the highest level of Spanish governance during the Liberal Triennium.

The members of the new government were thus fully aware that the king craved far more powers than the Constitution had officially granted him. The institutional power given to Ferdinand VII, along with the disputed value ascribed to the restored 1812 Constitution, stirred debate among Liberal circles and started polarizing them. The most forward-thinking sectors, labeled *Exaltados* (Exalted Ones), developed new organizational strategies and built the Patriotic Societies as a combination of reading societies, debating clubs and secret organizations, laying the roots of modern political parties. The *Exaltados* also published a wide range of pamphlets along with some newspapers such as *El Relámpago, La Tercerola o El Zurriago,* where they defended their democratic, patriotic and sometimes anticlerical ideas, to indoctrinate the reading public. They supported popular sovereignty and the Cortes' veto on the King's decisions, as opposed to mere national sovereignty which implied unequal power sharing with the monarch; a unicameral legislature; and a significant reduction in the powers given to both the King and the Church. Among their leaders there were high-ranking military figures and war heroes such as Generals Quiroga, Riego, Espoz y Mina, and Evaristo San Miguel (1785–1862). On the other hand, the more conservative Liberal faction, the Moderates, defended the sharing of power with a strong monarchy, the creation of an aristocratic Senate, narrower access to suffrage, and a restricted role for the National Militia, as well as a closer understanding with the Catholic clergy in order to secure a strong relationship with the Church. They also rejected the need to reform the Constitution as requested by the most radical sectors of the *Exaltados.*

Even before the fall of the first Liberal government, General Rafael de Riego would be the victim of political reprisals for his open criticism of the Moderate government and his collaboration with Aragonese *Exaltados,* and on March 4, 1821, he was forced to resign as captain general of Aragon. His dismissal constituted the first step in an escalation of political tension between the two Liberal factions that in September would lead to the so-called battle of *Platerías,* named after the lane close to Plaza Mayor in Madrid, the scene of a popular mutiny against the government. Social turmoil and political conflict soon spread across the country and cities like Barcelona, Bilbao, Cadiz, La Coruña, and Seville followed suit, witnessing bloodless *Exaltado*-led upheavals. The *Exaltados* gathered momentum during the following months, and in July 1822 they formed a government headed by Evaristo San Miguel which pursued deeper reforms, mostly affecting the Catholic Church and its landed property. The new government launched a comprehensive reform of the religious orders. In September, parliament passed a law that ordered the reduction in the number of monks and friars as well as the sale of those lands owned by the religious houses due to be closed. The measure was heavily criticized by the Royalist and anti-Liberal press and enraged increasing sectors of the conservative public.

These occurrences rang alarm bells among anti-Constitutionalists who organized themselves to act on two complementary fronts: at the Royal Palace in the form of court conspiracies, and in the hills through reactionary *guerrillas.* In August 1822, a parallel government in defense of the unrestricted powers of the monarch was founded in the northern Catalonian town of Urgell. Led by the exiled Royalist Marqués de Mataflorida, the bishop of Tarragona and the Baron of Eroles, the Urgell Regency declared the King "unfree" under the Constitutional government and advocated the reestablishment of absolute rule and traditional privileges. On the international front, since January 1820 the emissaries of Ferdinand VII had regularly reported to their reactionary allies abroad. At a Congress held in Verona in October 1822, the governments of Austria, France, Prussia, and Russia invoked the counterrevolutionary doctrine they had set out at their Troppau meeting two years earlier to deal with liberal revolution in Naples authorized French military intervention to overthrow the Spanish government.

> States which have undergone a change of Government due to revolution, the results of which threaten other states, *ipso facto* cease to be members of the European Alliance, and remain excluded from it until their situation gives guarantees for legal order and stability. If, owing to such alternations, immediate danger threatens other states, the Powers bind themselves, by peaceful means, or if need be by arms, to bring back the guilty state into the bosom of the Great Alliance.

Along with these developments at the highest levels of European politics, liberalism was losing domestic support, as shown by increasingly overt hostility and armed resistance in rural areas. According to most sources, the lower clergy played a prominent role leading and recruiting support for the ultra-Royalist *guerrillas*. These informal units started their activities in Navarre and the Basque Country as early as the summer of 1820. They spread their influence to rural areas in other regions rather quickly and, apart from committing some thefts and other crimes, persecuted and assassinated *Liberales*. This "White Terror" also included kidnapping and demanding ransoms.

By July 1822, a failed attempt to topple the *Exaltado* government, organized by King Ferdinand and executed by his Royal Guard through a coup, took place. However, a good share of the population of Madrid joined forces with the National Militia and most of the Army to frustrate it. This failure to forcefully impose his will made Ferdinand VII revise his tactics; it also triggered his request for the armed intervention of foreign troops to finish off Liberalism in Spain. The King did so even at the high price of a risking another civil war that would, in the end, be particularly destructive in Catalonia and the Basque Country. The French army, known as the "100,000 sons of Saint Louis," crossed the Pyrenees into Spain on April 7, 1823. Only on August 31 did they successfully complete their campaign and restore Ferdinand VII to the throne with unrestricted powers.

Meanwhile, after more than a decade of constant political conflict and social turmoil, New Spain had declared its independence from the Hispanic Crown in September 1821 and created the Mexican Empire. General Agustín de Iturbide (1783–1824), a war hero in the struggle for national independence, led the political experiment of a newly established Catholic monarchy for less than three years before new insurrections in central America forced him to abdicate and imposed a federal republic. The viceroyalty of Peru, on the other hand, also witnessed further pro-independence battles that concluded in December 1824 at the Battle of Ayacucho, where the final defeat of the Royalist troops signaled the end of Ferdinand's dream of keeping continental America under his personal rule.

The Ominous Decade: A last attempt to restore absolutism (1823–33)

Unlike the period 1808–14, the French troops which marched into Spain in April 1823 found little opposition south of the Ebro River. Political quarrels, conspiratorial activities, ecclesiastical opposition, and lack of governmental stability, along with imperial failure, had taken their toll and left the *Exaltado* cabinet with few supporters. Moreover, once the news of the intervention reached Madrid, the government's decision to move itself and the Cortes to Seville to gain time and support proved to be unsuccessful. The invading troops and their supporters had gained some experience in Piedmont and Naples, where they had also intervened to overthrow the 1812 Constitution that had been previously adopted by Italian Liberal patriots.

For the next five years, around 45,000 French soldiers stayed in Spain to guarantee that absolutism would not be overthrown again. They made sure that the *Liberales* were kept at bay and that King Ferdinand's decisions were faithfully executed. This heavy international presence went hand in hand with the implementation of measures of political control over the population as well as the necessary economic reforms to reconstruct the material infrastructure of the country. However, French support proved of paramount importance in repressing ultra-Royalist forces too. In 1827, the so-called *Revolta dels Agraviats* (Revolt of the Aggrieved) set Catalonia aflame. Disgruntled farmers, lower clergy, and low-ranking military officers organized an insurrection against the government of the aging king in order to restore the Inquisition, abort the growing influence of the *afracensado* factions at the royal court in Madrid, and boycott planned tax reforms. The instant governmental reaction with the collaboration of most of the ecclesiastical hierarchy also accounted for the defeat of the insurrection that was rapidly spreading to the Basque Country, Valencia, and Andalucia. Nonetheless, the movement set a dangerous precedent that reemerged after 1833 under the banner of Carlism (see Chapter 3).

As far as the consolidation of absolutist rule is concerned, this time Ferdinand VII was better advised and his policies proved more effective than during his first restoration. A return to the Old Regime seemed unrealistic while the newly established Congress system provided some good examples of policy making without popular participation and established itself as a broader European trend. A National Police was created by royal decree on January 8, 1824. Police agents were expected to fulfill the traditional tasks assigned to similar corps such as keeping law and order; safeguarding civic peace; urban surveillance in collaboration with courts; or granting licenses for opening all sorts of establishments, business, and shops, among others. Interestingly enough, the royal decree also stated that the National Police would be a very useful tool for ascertaining the King's project of recovering his uncontested full sovereignty, and that it should therefore persecute the most vocal supporters of the previous regime, that is, "secret societies, formed by *comuneros*, freemasons, or *carbonari*, and any other dark sect that currently exits or will do so in the future." It was not only political repression that the new institution would carry out; it was also designed to guarantee and safeguard the satisfaction of the interests of the landed peasantry and the aristocracy who had supported the reestablishment of monarchical absolutism. Therefore, the Police was in charge of hounding all groups of agricultural wage laborers "who meet to raise the amount of their salaries." This decision to control the population and repress all political opponents following modern guidelines and using renewed institutional settings was at odds with the very nature and scope of absolutism in Spain. Moreover, the new police body shared jurisdiction and tasks with local militias that predated it, including the *migueletes* and the *miñones*, both based in the Basque Country. This phenomenon fully reflected, on the one hand, the resilience of the Old Regime's organizations in Spain and, on the other, the corporatist nature of its societal organization during this transitional period, which was based on collective, "natural" entities' such as families, parishes, guilds, councils, and privileged bodies, both ecclesiastical and lay.

As for the State and its institutional development, the second absolutist proved to be slightly more productive than the first. Between 1823 and 1832 new governmental offices were established and fresh legislation was implemented mostly due to the active involvement of the most conservative sectors of the reforming *afrancesados*. Unlike the *Liberales*, and probably due to French diplomatic pressure based on their military presence in Spain, those influential members of the elites with an *afrancesado* past were allowed to incorporate themselves into the new governments after 1823. On November 19 of that year, the King decided to appoint his first ever *Consejo de Ministros* (Cabinet Council), which was initially conceived as an advisory board to the monarch. It was to be chaired by the King himself and to hold meetings twice a week in which five secretaries would discuss and find ways to enforce the rulings dictated by the monarch. Víctor Damián Sáez (1776–1839), then the first secretary of the State and an anti-revolutionary priest, would chair it in case of the monarch's absence. On December 2, due to his excessive zeal persecuting Liberals and the condemnation of his activities by the members of the Holly Alliance, he was obliged to step down and was replaced by the Marquis of Casa Irujo (1763–1824). As compensation, he was appointed bishop of Tortosa in Catalonia.

In October 1824, the minister of justice Francisco Tadeo Calomarde (1773–1842), a representative of the most fervent opposition to Liberal ideas, implemented an education reform. The scheme fully reflected the minister's worldview and desire to divert Spanish university students from the allegedly mistaken pathways followed by similar establishments elsewhere in Europe. It thus reduced the curricular weight of modern sciences in all universities and reinforced the weight of the study of Law and Catholic theology. Calomarde would also be responsible for the opening of Seville's School of Bullfighting and closing down all universities in 1830.

But not all under absolutism was erratic repression and nonsensical folklore. While Ferdinand's health started to deteriorate, Luis López Ballesteros (1782–1853), finance minister from 1823 to 1832, took a keen interest in legislating on economic matters and designing tools for a better administration of the public treasury and the national economy. In 1828, a royal decree was passed creating a centralized accounting board, the *Tribunal Mayor de Cuentas*. The role of this new institution had already been designed in the Cadiz *Cortes* in order to rationalize and monitor the overall balance between income and expenses. Another initiative would be the creation of a new centralized bank of the realm, the Banco de San Fernando, that would replace the then existing Banco de San Carlos, whose debt it inherited. On top of setting interest rates and monitoring currency, the Banco was heavily funded by private investors, and around two-thirds of its stocks were in their hands. Its role would evolve after the death of Ferdinand VII with the outbreak of a new civil war and it would be in charge of balancing the public accounts and generating income to sustain the war effort against the Carlists. Moreover, this renewed zeal to monitor and control public expenditures accounted for the introduction of yet another innovative measure in 1828, the first annually released State's general budget.

This reformist impulse led to the late approval of the first Commercial Code in Spanish history introduced on May 30, 1829. The new Code aimed to replace the ancient *Libro del Consulado del Mar*, which had regulated maritime commercial transactions in Spain and the Mediterranean since 1320. Inspired by a combination of traditional sources, Napoleonic initiatives, and the guidance provided during the Liberal Triennium by the influential British philosopher Jeremy Bentham, it was devised to guarantee and further ascertain the Crown's jurisdiction on trade matters. The Code was not well received by the most conservative sectors of the Spanish society because of the two articles which ruled out religious orders and clergymen, who were protected by Canon Law, from legally acting as traders. In the same vein, the Stock Market opened its doors in Madrid on September 10, 1831. The institution allowed the government's officials to handle the bonds on the national debt at a point where international investment in Spain was growing. The Madrid Stock Exchange proved to be rather cautious in its beginnings and dealt with financial speculation with a firm hand. This trend was altered in the years after its creation when political instability and war affected its workings and the management of the State financial obligations under increasing pressure.

Finally, on November 9, 1832, when a civil war over royal succession was about to start, the Ministry of Development, *Ministerio de Fomento*, was founded in order "to secure the Throne upon a solid basis." Sharing some responsibilities with the Ministry of Finance and others with the National Police, the newly created institution was meant to control an extremely wide range of activities including all official statistics, the promotion of public wealth, welfare, public instruction, military conscription, economic and political management of local councils, and the general control of law and order. This ambitiously planned institution was intended to overcome previous mismanagement in some of these areas and embodied the dream of Royalist reformism. However, its establishment, consolidation, and functioning were severely boycotted by some members of the court, the Church and the Army, who saw it as a powerful threat to their privileges. On the other hand, the King's health as well as the questions raised by his changing last will and succession further threatened its successful introduction.

Although temporarily defeated and with its main leaders either in jail or exiled, since 1808 Liberalism had never stopped playing a role in Spaniards' hopes and political imagination. The exiled groups in France and England actively conspired to restore constitutional rule and organized a series of thwarted military insurrections countered by further executions and imprisonments. Supported by English Whig politicians and intellectuals, probably the best-known of such attempts was the expedition led by General José María de Torrijos y Uriarte (1791–1831). Departing from the British colony of Gibraltar, Torrijos and sixty comrades disembarked at the shores of Malaga province on December 2, 1831 to be detained by the absolutist authorities and shot nine days later. His tragic end led to his immediate conversion into a Liberal martyr and the arousal of renewed hopes for political change.

The last months of Ferdinand VII's life coincided with the increased agitation and military mobilization that initiated the First Carlist War. The warring sides represented the aspirations of María Cristina, the King's wife and mother of his three-year-old infant daughter Isabella (1830–1904) on the one hand, and his brother Carlos María Isidro (1788–1855) on the other. Far from being a family matter exclusively related the legitimate right to succeed the dying King, the country's future was at stake, with Liberals supporting the former and advocates of absolutism backing the latter. With the death of the monarch, a full-fledged civil war would erupt and devastate the country once again.

Further reading

The Political Constitution of the Spanish Monarchy, http://www.cervantesvirtual.com/obra-visor/the-political-constitution-of-the-spanish-monarchy-promulgated-in-cadiz-the-nineteenth-day-of-march--0/html/ffd04084-82b1-11df-acc7-002185ce6064_1.html

Álvarez Junco, José, *Spanish Identity in the Age of Nations*, Manchester: Manchester University Press, 2011.

Bell, David A., *The First Total War: Napoleon's Europe and the Birth of Modern Warfare*, London: Bloomsbury, 2007.

Centeno, Miguel A., and Agustín E. Ferraro (eds.), *State and Nation Making in Latin America and Spain. Republics of the Possible*, Cambridge: CUP, 2014.

Eastmann, Scott, and Sobrevilla, Natalia (eds.), *The Rise of Constitutional Government in the Iberian Atlantic. The Impact of the Cádiz Constitution of 1812*, Tuscaloosa: The Alabama University Press, 2015.

Fradera, Josep Maria, *La nación imperial (1750-1918). Derechos, representación y ciudadanía en los imperios de Gran Bretaña, Francia, España y Estados Unidos*, Edhasa: Barcelona, 2015 (2 vols.).

Fraser, Ronald, *Napoleon's Cursed War: Spanish Popular Resistance in the Peninsular War, 1808-1814*, London: Verso, 2008.

Paquette, Gabriel, *Enlightenment, Governance, and Reform in Spain and its Empire, 1759-1808*, Cambridge: CUP, 2009.

Portillo Valdés, José M, *Crisis Atlántica. Autonomía e independencia en la crisis de la monarquía hispana*, Madrid: Marcial Pons, 2006.

Shubert, Adrian, *A Social History of Modern Spain*, London: Routledge, 1990.

CHAPTER 3
THE TIME OF LIBERALISM: 1833–74
María Sierra

As was the case in much of Europe and the Americas, between 1830 and 1880, Spain experienced the definitive end to the Old Regime and the emergence of a new liberal political and economic order. Alongside the consolidation of legal changes and new institutions, social relations and dominant cultural references were transformed. The bourgeois order of a system of gender relations based on the idea of separate spheres exemplifies these changes (see Chapter 11). What happened in Spain greatly resembled developments in other Western nations with which it shared models and influences. These changes were sweeping and had major consequences. It is also the case, however, that some legacies of the past continued to play an important role. For example, the power of the old aristocracy did not disappear with the Old Regime. Similarly, and this is a more specifically Spanish development, the Catholic Church retained its influence, even though the disentailment of much of its property affected it greatly (see Chapter 18).

The construction of the liberal order: the design of the institutions and the economy of the new regime, its political practices and ideas about the public sphere, mostly took place during the reign of Isabel II (1833–68). The brief six-year period, known as the Sexenio Democrático, which followed her reign, saw an attempt to broaden the social base of liberal politics by going beyond the restrictive and elitist model of the previous period, but this would end in defeat at the hands of the most conservative form of liberalism, embodied in the Restoration of 1874.

The arrival of liberalism

The death of Ferdinand VII, the last absolute monarch, opened a crucial decade for the creation of the liberal order in Spain. Between October 1833 and July 1843, when first his widow, María Cristina de Borbón, and then General Baldomero Espartero acted as regents for the child-queen Isabel II who had been born in 1830, a number of crucial developments took place. The legal privileges of the Old Regime were abolished; the economy was transformed; political parties were created; and the world of culture was modernized. These were some of the novelties of that time of intense change. The writer Mariano José de Larra was right when he said that in those years Spaniards were "drinking their coffee after eating their soup" without bothering about the main course.

This sense of the acceleration of historical time should not hide the fact that until then the arrival of liberalism had involved a fair dose of reform and compromise with the Old Regime power structures. It was only their agreement to defend the throne of Ferdinand's daughter against the challenge from those ultraconservatives inclined to put his brother Carlos on the throne which made it possible for liberals to be incorporated into official political life. In the context of the dynastic struggle, liberals could accept the regent's offer to form a government even though she was not at all in sympathy with their goals and saw them as a means of ensuring her daughter would retain her throne. Of course, it was the most moderate liberals, led by Francisco Martínez de la Rosa, who she called to power. They brought in the Estatuto Real (Royal Statute), a quasi-constitution granted by the Crown which put the first timid limitations on royal power.

It is crucial to remember that the passage from absolutism to liberalism took place against the backdrop of the First Carlist War (1833–40), a lengthy and brutal civil war which shaped the process of political change. [In per capita terms, this war was more deadly than the much better known Spanish Civil War which took place one hundred years later (see Chapter 6).] Much of the aristocracy and the army backed Isabel II, but Carlos still had significant support. With its defense of the absolute authority of the King, the supremacy of the Church, and the permanence of the *fueros*, the valuable privileges enjoyed by certain regions of the country, Carlism, as it was called, had popular support in parts of Aragon, Catalonia, and Valencia, but above all in the Basque Provinces and Navarra.

Given that absolutism remained in place in many European states at this time, the possibility that it could be restored in Spain drove those who wanted to do away with the privileges of the Old Regime to act more decisively. The surprising military resilience of the Carlist forces, together with the excessive moderation of the first governments of the transition, provoked a series of movements in Spain's cities: juntas, citizen militias, newspapers, and other media demanded the formation of a more progressive liberal government. This mobilization brought Juan Álvarez Mendizábal to power in 1835 (see Chapter 26). After a brief return to more moderate government, a series of local uprisings and the military Mutiny of La Granja in the summer of 1836 forced María Cristina to name the Progressive José María Calatrava prime minister.

They brought with them a truly revolutionary program, one which fully justified Larra's quip. Between 1835 and 1837, they completed the dismantling of the Old Regime which had been started by the Cortes of Cadiz (see Chapter 2). They disentailed the lands of the Church, abolished seigneurial jurisdiction, and created a free market by bringing in a new legal concept of property. Mendizábal's ecclesiastical *desamortización* (disentailment), which nationalized much of the landed property of the Church and then sold it at auction as private property, was decisive (see Chapter 18). Among its social, economic, and political effects, it won the support of the new and old elites who bought the land. On the other hand, it earned the enmity of the Catholic Church and disappointed the peasants who were unable to benefit. The Constitution of 1837, with its division of powers and declaration of citizens' rights characteristic of liberal constitutionalism, inaugurated true representative government in Spain. The electoral law, which created a broad suffrage for the time extending beyond landowners to some tenants, was strongly influenced by British practice. In 1837, there were 257,000 voters; by 1844 the number had jumped to some 600,000.

María Cristina did her best to block the advance of this kind of liberalism, and she had the backing of the more conservative liberals who wanted to impose a more centralized and authoritarian model of the state (see Chapter 20). The conflict between Progressives and Moderates came to a head over the organization of municipal governments. The Progressives won in the short term: their campaign against the Law of Municipal Government in 1840 led to the resignation of the regent and her replacement by Baldomero Espartero, the most important Progressive military officer. He was overthrown three years later and the Moderates would return to power, and remain there for most of the rest of Isabel's reign.

The Moderates governed for a decade and during this time they shaped the country's institutional structure. Against the ideas of liberty and participation of the liberals who had fought against absolutism, they put the maintenance of order at the heart of their political model. For them, order was both a wall against anarchy and the very essence of modernity. In practice, it was the way of bringing cohesion to the diverse groups within the party: the aging survivors of the Cortes of Cadiz who had lost their revolutionary impulses, young romantics, a considerable number of recycled Carlists and absolutists, and authentic liberals.

The European context was on their side. The principle of order was widely touted as the foundation of "authentic" liberty and representative government as the best alternative to revolution. The combination of Parliament, monarchy, and elections with limited suffrage was seen as a happy medium, distant from both absolutism and democracy. The Moderates created a new constitution to embody these ideas, the Constitution of 1845. It would have a long life. It established the idea of sovereignty shared between the Crown and Parliament, with the former enjoying the power to appoint the government. It also created a senate whose members were appointed by the Crown, affirmed Catholicism as the official religion of the state and the only one which could be practiced in the country, and stopped regulating rights such as freedom of the press. At the same time, the electoral law of 1846 established a much more restrictive suffrage which deprived almost half a million people of a right they had enjoyed and left fewer than 100,000 people with the right to vote.

It is clear that for these conservative liberals, liberty and order went together easily. Indeed, the second was a precondition of the first and a generation of Moderate politicians which included men like José Pedro Pidal, Alejandro Mon, and Juan Bravo Murillo used their positions of power to create an efficient administration. In 1844 they created the Civil Guard, as a national police force charged with maintaining public order. In 1845 they reformed the Treasury, reorganizing taxes and improving the way they were collected. That same year they promulgated an Educational Plan, in 1848 a new Criminal Code and in 1852 laws on the civil service (see Chapter 20).

This concern among conservative liberals to endow the state with a strong, centralized administration which could effectively execute the orders of the government was nothing new and carried on from the enlightened reformism of the eighteenth century. In the 1830s, men such as Javier de Burgos had opted for a strong bureaucracy to serve the executive and the Moderates followed their lead in the 1840s. The starting point was the abolition of the historic regions and the division of the country into roughly equally sized provinces in 1833. Javier de Burgos was correct when he said that the administrative system the new state needed could not be built until the national territory was organized properly.

The minister of the interior, Pidal, was continuing this approach with his 1845 laws on local and provincial government. The appointment of mayors and the sharp reduction in the size of the electorate reduced the autonomy of municipal governments vis-à-vis Madrid. Likewise, administration of the provinces was put into the hands of the Jefe Político (Political Chief), later renamed the Civil Governor, who was appointed by the central government and given sweeping powers. All this ensured that Madrid enjoyed direct control of provincial and local administration. Finally, the electoral law of 1846 gave them oversight of elections, which became the basis of a dense network of politically useful clientelistic relations.

It is important to remember that this new state model was conceived for a country which still retained remnants of its once vast colonial empire and without which the history of the nineteenth century cannot be understood. The Constitution of 1812 had proclaimed a nation made up of "Spaniards of both hemispheres," but neither Progressives nor Moderates saw things the same way. As a result, the remaining colonies were left outside constitutional guarantees, made subject to "special laws," and put into the hands of Captains General who governed with greater or less degrees of authoritarianism (see Chapter 13). Only with the Revolution of 1868 would the inhabitants of these territories briefly enjoy the possibility of being represented in Parliament.

If the liberal model of the nation had no place for the overseas territories which, for the sake of administrative homogeneity, were reduced to neocolonial status, it did, paradoxically, find room for the survival of the *fueros* of the Basque Provinces. It is easy enough to understand why so many people who benefited from such important privileges as reduced taxation and exemption from military service resisted the imposition of legal equality. It is harder to understand why the Moderates, with their fetish for legal homogenization, allowed these ancient laws to exist within the modernizing national project they claimed to be pursuing. The fact is that the foral provinces lobbied intensely and Moderate governments, happy to find allies, allowed this exceptional circumstance to continue.

Political practices and informal spaces of power

As the examples of the overseas territories and foral provinces demonstrate, to understand the political life of Isabel's Spain it is not enough simply to look at the laws as they were written. It is also essential to examine the political interests which shaped their development. The nature of the liberal system is better appreciated by attending to the political practices which were established or consolidated during this period, practices which long survived the constitutional monarchical system which they underpinned. Many of these ways of understanding and practicing politics were shared by various parties during the Isabelline period and the Sexenio. The inclination to ensure the dominance of the executive over other branches of government and the suspicion of citizen participation were not the monopoly of the Moderates. That said, there can be no doubt that due to both their ideology and their long periods in power, the conservative parties, Moderates first and the Liberal Union next, were the principal practitioners of a series of political habits which distorted the parliamentary system from its very birth.

The most significant of these was the self-interested use that politicians made of the constitutional prerogatives of the Crown. The Moderates made use of the Queen, starting with the act of lowering the age at which she could rule in her own right which they did immediately after overthrowing the Espartero regency. They did so rashly, building and spreading a deplorable image of her with the goal of pressuring her politically. The reputation of queen as a capricious, fickle, and sexually voracious woman which was spread through the press and in caricatures, was promoted for the own benefit by politicians close to her for whom the idea of a weak ruler who had to be controlled for her own good and that of the country. The Moderate kidnapping of the Queen led in the medium term to a suicidal erosion of the legitimacy of the system itself. There can be no doubt that Isabel II, who had been raised in a profoundly aristocratic court culture suffered from the absence of a political education which would have helped her become the "other Queen Victoria," the Progressives talked about during the Espartero regency (see Chapter 27). In addition, she was controlled by the powerful personality of her mother and prone to favor confessors, friends, and lovers, all of which provided fodder for the construction of a negative image of the Crown. On the other hand, it is equally the case that her politicians played irresponsibly with the prestige of an institution which at this time was being built up in other countries.

The failure of the Moderates to endow the monarchy with the symbolic capital of new bases of legitimacy, whether as the arbiter of political life who stood above parties or as the mirror of the bourgeois morality of the period, is even more evident when put in a comparative perspective. While in Great Britain Queen Victoria sought to adapt herself to a model which combined the historic justification of the monarchy with the modern function of the symbol of social morality of her time, in Spain the media publicized the Queen's moral depravity. She was also at the focus of unofficial networks, known as camarillas, which sought to take advantage of her official powers. Many of the connections among business, politics, and social prestige which were established in this period came together precisely in this informal space of power.

If the Crown as an institution was not bolstered even though the constitution broadened its prerogatives, Parliament was also unable to assert its legitimate role as the legislative power. Under the Moderates it was the victim of systematic interference by the executive, which took away many of its powers. The undermining of the parliamentary system was as much the result of the frequent practice of governing by decree so as to avoid debate as it was of electoral manipulation and the corrupt construction of artificial majorities. Much of the legislation of the Moderate decade came into being with minimal input from Parliament, as the most important laws came fully formed from the cabinet without leaving any opportunity for real discussion. On the other hand, both the prevalent manipulation of election results and the common practice of selecting deputies from civil servants who owed their jobs and their salaries to the government which appointed them all but ensured that Parliament would obey the will of the executive. The negative image of the Cortes as a "tank of leeches"—an image painted on the walls of the Cortes building and referred to in an 1855 bill to bar deputies from holding civil service jobs—who lived off the public purse emerged from the early days of the system of representative government.

Governments were not all powerful, however, and frequently found themselves stymied by other authorities which did not appear in the constitution. The powerful role of the army in civilian politics is well known. There were, of course, the *pronunciamientos* and other potential uses of force as a mechanism for political change, something which no party which aspired to govern could ignore. But there was also the incredible political prestige enjoyed by military men in a country which had been brought into the modern age through warfare: the war against the French (1808–14) and the First Carlist War (1833–40). These included Espartero, a man from an extremely humble background who used the prestige he earned as the general who won the Carlist War for the liberals—he was popularly known as the Peacemaker of Spain—to become prime minister and even Regent. Without Espartero, one cannot understand the Progressive party, just as one cannot understand the Moderates without Ramón María Narváez, the Liberal Union without Leopold O'Donnell, or the evolution toward democracy at the end of Isabel's reign without Juan Prim (see Chapter 29). (The political prestige of military men in these years was not a uniquely Spanish phenomenon, as the careers of Jean-de-Dieu Soult in France, the

Duke of Wellington in Great Britain and Andrew Jackson and Zachary Taylor in the United States demonstrate). This is a very different phenomenon from that which would come later, when the army as a whole intervened in politics as the self-proclaimed savior of the fatherland (see Chapter 21).

In these years it was the Court which constituted the greatest threat to liberal governments. The fact that the Moderates manipulated her did not eliminate Isabel II's capacity as queen to interfere in the policies of her governments. And beyond the Queen herself, the entire Palace entourage: the rest of the royal family, the various cliques of courtesans, and the clearly absolutist culture they all shared, represented a problematic political front which liberals in power had to negotiate. The Queen mother and former regent, María Cristina, combined all the obstacles coming from within the system that confronted the authentically liberal section of the Moderate Party, the one which was most active in government between 1844 and 1854. The close personal relationship between María Cristina's second husband, Fernando Muñóz, a member of the royal guard who she had married in secret and who was later made a duke, and Donoso Cortés, the principal ideologue of the merging political right, and the astonishing wealth they both built through shady busy dealings had a lot to do with the popular demands that they be expelled from the country which were voiced once the Progressives finally displaced the Moderates from power following the Revolution of 1854.

The alternatives: From advanced liberalism to anti-liberalism

The Moderates governed Spain during the entire first decade of Isabel's rule, but they had to compete with a number of other political contenders: Progressives, Democrats, Carlists, Republicans, and Neo-Catholics. The most significant of these were the Progressives, or the "Party of Progress" as Salustiano Olózaga, their leading civilian figure, had proposed calling it. They were clearly liberal, less obsessed than the Moderates with the question of order and more open to change. While the Moderates were influenced by French doctrinaire liberalism, they were more oriented to British ideas. Both wanted a system which would balance the powers of Crown and Parliament, but the Progressives favored making Parliament the more powerful of the two. During the brief period of Isabel's reign in which they were in power, the so-called Progressive Biennium (Bienio Progresista) of 1854–1856, Parliament became a forum which could really affect the laws which were passed. Paradoxically, the much healthier parliamentary life of this period also undermined the executive capacity of the government as many laws, including the new constitution itself, were delayed for long periods by amendments coming from members of its own party as well as from the opposition groups. The conservative coup of July 1856 cut short a process which, in the long term, could have brought great benefits to Spain's parliamentary system.

The Progressives were also unable to bring into effect the new electoral law which was passed in 1856 and which would have greatly increased the number of voters. Even though neither they nor the Moderates supported full democratic suffrage even for men alone, there were significant differences between their respective electoral models. The Progressive law significantly lowered the economic requirements for the right to vote and further extended the electoral roll by giving to vote to members of a number of professions regardless of their economic situation. The greatest difference between the two lay in the area of local government: the Progressives supported local autonomy against the fierce centralism of the Moderates. Mayors were to be elected, not appointed by Madrid, and local elections had an even wider suffrage than did those for the national Parliament. This was a clear sign of their greater optimism about the participation of society in political life.

The Progressives saw their reform program as the engine for the transformation of Spanish society. Although their time in power was fleeting, the number of laws they passed designed to stimulate economic development is striking. Pascual Madoz's 1855 law continued and extended the disentailment of land by applying it to land owned by municipal governments. The laws on banks and credit societies increased the financial resources available for investment and the 1855 Railway Law launched the definitive takeoff of the country's rail network. On the other hand, the problems of the new economy and the greater freedom of expression permitted by the Progressives combined to produce protests against the horrible living conditions of the workers. Just before they were thrown from power, the Progressives introduced into Parliament a bill for Spain's first Labor Law.

The two main liberal parties also differed in how they understood civil liberties, especially freedom of expression and freedom of religion. The Moderates' Constitution of 1845 included an uncompromising assertion of Catholicism as the official religion of the state and the only religion which could be legally practiced in the country, and the Concordat of 1851 had given the Church important powers in the areas of education and public morality (see Chapter 18). In contrast, the Progressive's Constitution of 1856, which never actually came into effect, included an explicit statement of religious toleration which went beyond that in the Constitution of 1837. In addition, there were a number of legal measures which, in an attempt to separate religion from the state, authorized such things as civil burials. These would die with the Bienio and only be revived during the period known as the Six Democratic Years (Sexenio Democrático).

This ambition to secularize society was shared by the political families to the left of the Progressives. The Democratic party was created in 1849, bringing together the most advanced segments of Spanish liberalism with other groups such as utopian socialists like Fernando Garrido and republicans like Francisco Pi y Margall. The basis of the new party's program was universal male suffrage—giving the vote to women was inconceivable even for such advanced thinkers—as well as demands for other political and civil rights. Their critiques of inequality resonated in the those segments of Spanish society which suffered the punishing working conditions of the capitalist economy as well as the demands of the liberal state for military service and taxes which fell disproportionately on them (see Chapter 21). At a time when unions were illegal, the Democrats used the press and other methods to demand the right to free association for workers.

Democrats and Republicans paid more attention than the liberal parties to the politics of the street (this did not mean that they ignored electoral politics as they were present in both local governments and the national Parliament). Consistent with a social imaginary that made the people, first, and the working class, second the protagonist of history, these groups undertook initiatives designed to achieve greater political inclusion and the creation of citizenship. The press, literature, clubs, cafes, and *tertúlias* (get togethers) were the vehicles through which Democratic ideology was spread, both in the more favorable climate of the Espartero regency and the times of harsh censorship in the last years of Isabel's reign. Democrats and Republicans became used to the ups and downs of freedom of expression and were able to overcome the barriers to the spread of their ideas, undertaking an intense campaign of propaganda which won them a diverse social following which ranged from middle-class professionals like doctors and lawyers to members of the, for the most part urban, working class (see Chapter 17).

There were also political forces to the right of the Moderates, although at times some of these found their way into that party. Religion and the Church were central to the wide range of groups which composed this right wing. Carlism was undoubtedly the strongest. This ideology had its deepest roots in those parts of the country where special regional laws (*fueros*) continued to exist: Navarra and the Basque Country. Carlism had a mass base composed of small landowners and tenants and artisans with economic and moral ties to the old ways of life which were threatened by liberalism. For their part, Carlist leaders proved very adept at making use of the methods of the new liberal public sphere: newspapers, elections, and Parliament. The liberal regime thus had to endure the paradox of the presence in Parliament of a group of deputies who were avowedly opposed to liberalism and to parliamentary government. It is important to remember that the generous Embrace of Vergara between Espartero and the Carlist commander Rafael Maroto which had brought the First Carlist War to an end made possible the participation in political life of those who had fought against Isabel II and the liberals. Thus, to give but one example, the former Carlist officer Enrique O'Donnell would end up sitting in Parliament across from his brother, the great liberal politician, Leopoldo.

There was also a right wing within the Moderate Party. This included thinkers like Donoso Cortés, who talked about the need for a monarchy unconstrained by Parliament and the social authority of the Church and who questioned the legitimacy of the disentailment of Church land. Characterized above all by their determination to defend the interests and rights of the Church in Spanish life, they were known as the "Neo-Catholics." With the support of the Holy See, they used politics as a way to demand that religion have a central role in defining public morality and culture. They also enjoyed the support of the court and of the Queen herself, so it is little surprise that anticlericalism, with its demands the role of the Church and of Catholicism in public life, became one of the distinguishing features of all the most advanced political options (see Chapter 18).

Mobilization and third ways (1854–62)

The greater openness fostered by the Progressives during the Bienio permitted a marked increase in social mobilization. Some of this, such as the incipient protests by the working class, worried even the Progressives themselves. This fear of what was already be calling the "masses" prompted the creation of a liberal third way which sought to bring together the most liberal section of the Moderates and the most conservative section of the Progressives in what its leaders called a liberal union. In July 1856, this group led by General Leopoldo O'Donnell, launched a coup which dissolved Parliament and brought to an end the only Progressive government during the reign of Isabel II. From then until the Queen was deposed in September 1868, the Moderates and the new Liberal Union alternated in power while the regime became more and more closed in on itself.

The Moderates returned to power in 1856. Increasingly dominated by the Neo-Catholics, they used the supposed threat of social revolution to justify a series of laws intended to further strengthen the executive and increase the public presence of the Church. These included two bills passed in 1857: a Press law which established sweeping prior censorship and an Education Law which gave the Church a major role in public education. This increasingly authoritarian direction worried some of the more liberal elements in the party, some of whom had played major roles in building the state apparatus in the previous decade, who chose to join the Liberal Union. This was definitely a liberal party, although strongly marked by its rejection of the popular mobilization that the Progressives had permitted.

The party was officially born in 1858 when the Queen charged O'Donnell with forming a government. He made Posada Herrera Minister of the Interior with the mission of controlling the elections to ensure a Liberal Union victory. Under the slogan "conserve through progress," O'Donnell and his party formed the longest lasting government of the nineteenth century, from 1858 to 1862. Its priorities included promoting the maximum economic development compatible with the maintenance of social order. Posada Herrera and Antonio Cánovas del Castillo, another of the party's strongmen and one who would play a pivotal role in Spanish politics after 1874, embodied the party's ambition of balancing a prudent authoritarianism in the exercise of power with a certain amount of openness. Thus, the 1865 electoral law extended the suffrage beyond the tightly constricted limits allowed by the 1846 law, which was still in force.

Alongside this extension of the franchise, however, the government was increasingly manipulating elections. The Liberal Union even went so far as to openly defend the need to tutor voters through what it called "legitimate influences." The executive declared itself responsible for maintaining order during elections and block private interests which presumed to impose themselves on the general good. The system worked so well because Liberal Union ministers preferred to make arrangements with local elites over ramming things down their throats. This produced a way of connecting the central government with local powerholders which would have a long life (see Chapter 4).

Inventing Spain

Spain was born as a liberal state at the same time as it lost much of its empire, and its configuration as a modern nation took place in a century one of whose distinguishing features was the renewal of colonialism and the creation of new empires. The independence movements in Latin America deprived the Spanish Crown of extensive territories it had ruled for centuries, leaving it with Cuba, Puerto Rico, the Philippines, and little else (see chapters 13, 23). This process of territorial shrinkage, political and administrative reorganization, and economic adjustment had many consequences, relegating Spain to the second tier of European powers. At the same time, Spaniards developed discourses and images of their national identity which sought to explain the existence of Spain and the "nature" of Spaniards using historicist concepts similar to those used in other countries (see Chapter 15).

After the loss of its American colonies Spain assumed a secondary place on the international scene, and between 1830 and 1850 liberal elites fed a complex of cultural inferiority with respect to France and Great Britain. Spain was not isolated from the traffic in ideas and products but it had renounced an active role in international politics. The arrival of the Liberal Union broke this trend. Once in power, the party sought to raise Spain's international profile. The centerpiece was the bombastically named War of Africa (1859–60), which affirmed Spanish influence in Morocco, but it was followed by a series of less successful adventures in South America. The incorporation of Santo Domingo in 1861, in response to requests for annexation to prevent it from being swallowed up by Haiti, ended with Spain abandoning the island four years later. The "War of the Pacific," a series of conflicts with Perú, Ecuador, and Chile between 1860 and 1866, was a failed military operation that lacked any clear economic objectives. The intervention in Mexico, in the context of Napoleon III's efforts to make a Habsburg prince emperor, was also far from being a roaring success.

These colonial adventures were in part the result of lobbying by Caribbean business interests, but O'Donnell also saw them as a way of bolstering his own position by building a sense of national identity among Spaniards. Even here the results are questionable. It did work to place in the collective imaginary a number of myths and symbols of national identity. This was especially true of the War of Africa, which attracted a number of writers and artists who produced scenes' patriotic glory and created new national heroes, Prim foremost among them (see Chapter 29). On the other hand, there was no overall planning to the foreign policy of those years, something which was particularly clear in the case of Cuba, the jewel of Spain's remaining empire (see chapters 13, 25).

Parallel to this search for a place on the international scene, Spain's political and cultural elites took on the task of building and spreading a national collective imaginary. This work of creating myths and symbols took place in art, literature, and other media. All of them drew on history as the foundation for telling stories about the Spanish nation. Just as in other countries at this time of the creation of modern nation-states, intellectuals came up with images of the national past which were intended to be made into a valid collective identity for the present. The most liberal version of the Spanish past privileged the Middle Ages, which was reinvented as a time when, through its Cortes and municipal governments, Spain enjoyed political liberties. The rule of the Habsburgs, in contrast, was criticized for crushing the vitality of the Spanish people. So too was that symbol of religious intolerance the Inquisition which, they said, was responsible for Spain's material and cultural backwardness.

Using examples from the distant past as a way of justifying one's political program and disqualifying that of one's enemies in this way was part and parcel of the general phenomenon of the creation of national identities which took place in this period.

Nevertheless, even though the war against Napoleon had given rise to an early and intense burst of patriotic images and an initial identification of the ideas of people, fatherland, and nation which was publicized in catechisms, songs, newspapers, and plays, after 1833 the liberal version of the "essence" of Spain was not sufficiently strong to establish a consensus among elites and the general population over even a few basic references. Liberals were confronted with a belligerent anti-liberalism which had its own, contrasting patriotic identity. Reactionaries, traditionalists, and Neo-Catholics created a very different story of Spain's history, based on religion and the monarchy. In this version of the past, the era of the Habsburgs, with the epic colonization and evangelization of America, had been the zenith of Spain's glory while the arrival of the Bourbons and their imported reforms, which were alien to Spain's national traditions, had sapped the country's vitality. Liberalism had exacerbated a disease which could only be cured by returning the nation to its true essences. The "Glorious Revolution" of 1868 would intensify the fears of the most conservative sectors and reinforce this negative portrait of Spanish modernity.

The revolution of 1868

The rotation in power of the Moderates and the Liberal Union prevented any other party from coming to power in the last twelve years of Isabel's reign. Increasing repression led the Progressives to turn their backs on the regime and move toward the Democrats and Republicans. As the Moderate Party was curtailing the freedom of expression and forcing its opponents into exile, the idea that the only solution was to overthrow the Queen was gaining ground. This was even the case for some important groups within the Liberal Union since the abolition of constitutional legality and the closing of the Cortes affected them as well.

The Queen played an important role in the final phase of the decline of the regime. Ever more obsessed by her personal religious demons, she sought to shape the policy of the government on the contentious issue of the unification of Italy and its conflict with the Vatican. Favoring those groups most sympathetic to the interests of the Church, she wore down her ministers, irrespective of their ideological positions or their political capacity. The way in which she ungratefully did away with her most important protectors, Narváez for the Moderates and O'Donnell for the Liberal Union, demonstrates just how little she understood, or cared about, the basic logic of a constitutional and parliamentary system.

It is not the least bit surprising that the wave of protest that hit the last years of her reign would lead to a revolution which surprised no one. In 1865 university students who demonstrated in defense of Emilio Castelar, who the government had removed from his teaching position at the Universidad Central, were bloodily put down by the army and the Civil Guard on the so-called Night of Saint Daniel. In 1866, Juan Prim, the charismatic leader of the opposition led a failed attempt at a military coup. That same year there was a revolt by sergeants in the San Gil barracks in Madrid which was followed by extremely harsh punishments. As a committee of Progressives and Democrats and Republicans in exile was planning the revolution which would finally overthrow Isabel, the first barricades were appearing in the streets of the capital.

The "Glorious Revolution" as it was called sent Isabel II into exile and opened a promising period of change. "Long live national sovereignty!" and "Down with the Bourbons!," the cries which were most often heard at the time, nicely summarize the programs published by the revolutionary juntas which emerged in cities across the country. Demands for the vote for all men were accompanied by ones for the abolition of the hated sales tax on basic necessities, the *consumos*, and the *quintas*, the compulsory military service, as well as for freedom of expression, freedom of religion, the completion of the disentailments and other economic freedoms.

The revolution brought together a number of different movements into a temporary alliance against their common enemy, the Crown, and its allies, in anti-liberal circles and the Church which were opposed to any political opening. The elites of the Liberal Union had certainly become democrats from one day to the next, but in deciding to join the common front that the more advanced liberal groups had already created they agreed to leave the question of the nature of the new regime, and especially the central issue of whether it would be a monarchy or a republic, to the future Cortes. In this way, Unionists, Progressives, Democrats, and Republicans all brought their different political resources to a revolutionary outbreak which had the support of a military *pronunciamiento* as well as of the barricades and which created an atmosphere so heady that some participants would even shout "Down with what exists!" Not everyone wanted to go so far, especially those politicians who had held high office under

Isabel and who now sought merely to correct the reactionary course that the regime had taken. The diversity of objectives became clear almost as soon as the revolution had triumphed, but in the decisive first moments the powerful personality of Juan Prim asserted itself. He would manage to hold this heterogeneous coalition together until his assassination at the end of 1870.

Against the backdrop of an unprecedented freedom of expression, elections for a Constitutent Cortes, the first elections in Spain under direct, universal manhood suffrage, were held in January 1869. This Cortes was going to have to deal with two major matters: write a new constitution which would address the widespread demands for democratization and decide whether the new regime would be a monarchy or a republic. The latter question was decisive. After Isabel's overthrow, a part of the Democratic party had joined with former Unionists and Progressives in opting for the construction of what they called a "democratic monarchy." They drew on British and Italian models to demonstrate that democracy was compatible with monarchy which, they said, fit better with Spanish traditions. In their view, the problem with the former regime was not with its form as a monarchy but with the monarch herself and, even more, with the Bourbon dynasty which had brought the institution into discredit. The other, openly republican sector of the party, argued that only a republic was compatible with democracy, and it ended up creating new Federal Republican party.

The decision was made by a Cortes in which more than 200 deputies declared themselves monarchists and 85 republicans. There were also some 20 Carlists who had been elected in the traditional strongholds of the movement. Their participation in democratic elections was not an obstacle to a return to arms in 1872. Outnumbered and only recently organized into a party, the Republicans had to resign themselves to the monarchy, and many of its leaders chose to continue to work within parliament. However, some of its rank and file decided differently. The temptation to insurrection had already shown itself in the summer of 1869 when a wave of protest against the new monarchical constitution spread through the major cities and a number of smaller places in Andalucia and the Levante.

The Constitution of 1869 represented an important step in the deepening of liberalism. Along with universal male suffrage it set out in great detail, and for the first time, a broad series of rights including freedom of association, something the most organized sectors of the working class had been demanding for some time. The most controversial of these was, without doubt, freedom of religion, which was constitutionally guaranteed for the first time. The constitution did stop short, however, of the explicit separation of Church and State. Finally, the new constitution defined the regime as a democratic monarchy in which the powers of the Crown were much reduced and Parliament was the dominant partner.

The democratic monarchy (1870–73)

It was one thing to declare Spain a monarchy; it was something else again to find a monarch, especially after the Bourbons had been discarded. The search for a king from one of Europe's ruling families ran afoul of national rivalries and the new ruler, Amadeo of Savoy, a son of the King of the recently united Kingdom of Italy, was selected by the Cortes after a hiatus of almost two years. Prim was Amadeo's strongest supporter but he was murdered, in circumstances which remain murky to this day, just as the new king arrived in Spain. In fact, Amadeo's first official act in Madrid was to view his coffin.

The new democratic monarchy would have a short life, lasting from the end of 1870 to February 1873. For the first time in its history, Spain had a monarch who was genuinely willing to accept and support constitutional legality. His failure has been attributed to such factors as the supposed ungovernability of the Spaniards and his foreign origins (Amadeo was frequently mocked as "Macarroni I"). One thing is certain: the unyielding resistance to change of the most conservative sectors of Spanish society had a lot to do with it.

The reorganization of the Progressives and Demócratas gave rise to two new parties which dominated the political life of the new regime: the Constitutionalists led by Práxedes Mateo Sagasta and the Radicals led by Manuel Ruiz Zorrilla. The historiography of the period has been dominated by an image of divisiveness and factional conflicts, the continuation of the practices of clientelism and electoral corruption. However, while there was much of this, it is important to remember that there were elections, demonstrations were permitted and, in general, there was an unprecedented level of freedom. Many of these criticisms were made at the time by the most conservative and clerical political groups as a way of delegitimizing the new regime.

In spite of the difficulties, the governments of this period managed to pass important laws and achieve important reforms. These included legalizing civil marriage, passing laws on education, and disentailing mining properties. This last issue was important to the Democrats, who believed it would allow the industry to takeoff. Until this time, subsoil rights belonged to the Crown, which sold the rights to exploit the resources for limited periods of time. The nationalization of subsoil rights and their subsequent transfer to private businessmen encouraged foreign investment and helped turn Spain into the most important mining country in Europe.

On the other hand, giving greater freedom to private enterprise did not turn out to be a recipe for harmonious economic development. The regime had guaranteed the freedom of association, but Amadeo's governments found themselves having to deal with the increasing mobilization of the working class (see Chapter 17). The 1870 Public Order Law narrowed this right considerably. Even worse, in its fight against banditry and other types of crime resulting from severe social inequality, it was used by the Civil Guard as a license to kill people without trial. In 1871, with the events of the Paris Commune stoking fears of revolution among the political elites, the Cortes debated banning the International Workingmen's Association.

Relations with the Catholic Church were also conflictual even though the secularizing measures passed by government were quite moderate. Ecclesiastical reaction was particularly strong when it came to measures, such as civil marriage, the creation of a civil register of births and deaths, and a new law on burials, which asserted the power of the state in fundamental areas of daily life. They provoked fierce campaigns which, ironically, benefited from the new freedom of expression and association. This extreme reaction was also connected to the reactionary turn of the Holy See following the loss of the Papal States to the new Kingdom of Italy, a reaction which was embodied in Pius IX's Syllabus of Errors (1864) (see Chapter 18).

The Church was joined in its desire to bring down the new regime by important landowning and business interests, and especially those with connections to Spain's colonies (see Chapter 13). The campaign to end slavery in Cuba and Puerto Rico led to a bill on abolition introduced by the Ruiz Zorrilla government. In response, the landowners on the islands, supported by landowners in the metropolis, organized a pressure group which succeeded in preventing the law from being passed. This conflict was also related to the possibility of giving the colonies seats in the Cortes, but this too was defeated. Caribbean business interests along with financiers, investors, and agricultural interests in Spain all became increasingly hostile to Amadeo's democratic monarchy and gave their support to Cánovas del Castillo's new party, which sought to bring back the Bourbons in the person of Isabel's son Alfonso. In the end, the attempt by some artillery officers to pressure the King to change a senior appointment made by the government proved the final straw. On February 11, 1873 Amadeo abdicated.

The First Republic (1873–74)

Only hours after Amadeo announced his abdication, the Cortes, meeting as the National Assembly, voted to proclaim Spain a republic. Its life was fleeting, only eleven months, and full of challenges: disagreements among Republicans over what a republic should look like and, above all, the active resistance of the most conservative sectors of Spanish society. The death of the First Republic would bring to an end the attempt to make liberalism more authentic and more democratic which had started in September 1868.

The differences of opinion among Republicans were evident from the outset. Some advocated a French-style unitary republic while others wanted a more decentralized federal republic. Federalism had always been the stronger strain within Spanish republicanism, even before the creation of the Federal Republican party in 1869. As social mobilization increased, some Republican leaders came to favor a unitary state which would be better able to defend order, but Francisco Pi y Margall, the most important Republican politician, consistently defended federalism as the only political and administrative structure compatible with free will. After being elected president in June 1873, Pi tried to make his vision a reality and proposed writing a new, federal constitution.

Pi soon found himself facing popular demands for a quicker and fuller creation of the Federal Republic from below. This popular mobilization was the basis of what is known as the Cantonalist revolution. It was an extremely heterogeneous movement both in its ideology and is social composition. Revolutionary juntas were created and autonomous republics, or cantons, were proclaimed in a number of towns and cities. Their programs differed greatly. In some places, such as Valencia, the movement was led by men from the middle class whose program included respect for private property, while in others, such as Alcoy, Malaga, and Seville, the presence of working-class groups added an element of social revolution. And where the International Workingmen's Association was strong, the Cantonalist movement even had socialist or anarchist slogans. The Cantonalist revolt distracted the government from writing a new constitution and bringing in laws protecting workers and abolishing slavery. It also forced the government to rely on the army and the Civil Guard, which had political consequences. Pi y Margall resigned on July 18 and was replaced by another federalist, Nicolás Salmerón. He resigned after less than two months in office after refusing demands by generals to sign death sentences and was replaced by Emilio Castelar, an advocate of a centralized rather than a federal republic who was determined to restore order.

The Cantonalist revolt was only one of three armed struggles the First Republic was fighting. Only weeks after the Revolution of 1868 an independence movement had broken out in Cuba and a new Carlist revolt in northern Spain had started in 1872. These multiple conflicts made the Republic ever more dependent on the army at a time when military officers were becoming more politically conservative and less inclined to accept civilian authority. There was also an emerging ideology which saw the army as the savior of a fatherland threatened by "separatism" and social anarchy (see Chapter 21). On top of this, the Republic was isolated internationally. Only the United States and Switzerland, themselves both republics, had recognized it.

The army was not the only powerful institution with which the First Republic found itself in conflict. Its goal of putting the separation of Church and State into the constitution further angered an ecclesiastical hierarchy which had already been fighting the democratic monarchy. Catholic propagandists spread the image of the "good Spanish people," religious and traditionalist, who had been led astray by corrupt politicians. Together with the military's opposition to "separatism," these ideas made up the world view of right-wing Spaniards.

In this context, even Castelar's declarations that his top priority was to assert the authority of the government and restore order were insufficient to save the First Republic. When it started to look likely that Parliament would censure the president, and that this would allow the left to return to power, the army acted. On January 2, 1874, Manuel Pavía, one of the leading generals of the day, led some Civil Guards into the Congress and dissolved it. For the next few months General Francisco Serrano served as president of a military and authoritarian Unitary Republic in which there was no constitutional legality and which was justified by the need for a "robust power." Among its first measures was to restore good relations with the Church and to declare the International Workingmen's Association illegal.

Cánovas del Castillo, a highly experienced politician from Isabel's time, was able to take advantage of this situation to realize his project of restoring the Bourbon monarchy. He also enjoyed the support of colonial economic elites, whose money in large part financed the Bourbon's return to the throne in the person of Alfonso XII, the seventeen-year-old son of Isabel II. This marked the start of the "new-old" regime of the Restoration, a regime based on the agreement between political forces and the clientelistic organization of society.

Further reading

Álvarez Junco, José, *Mater Dolorosa. La idea de España en el siglo XIX*, Madrid: Taurus, 2001.

Andreu, Xavier, *El descubrimiento de España*, Madrid: Taurus, 2016.

Bahamonde, Ángel, and José Cayuela, *Hacer las Américas. Las elites coloniales españolas en el siglo XIX*, Madrid: Alianza, 1992.

Burdiel, Isabel, *Isabel II. Una biografía (1830-1904)*, Madrid: Taurus, 2011.

Burdiel, Isabel (Coord.), *España. La construcción nacional (1830-1868). T 2. América Latina en la Historia Contemporánea*, Madrid: Mapfre-Taurus, 2012.

Fradera, Josep, *Colonias para después de un imperio*, Barcelona: Bellaterra, 2005.

Fernández Sebastián, Javier, and Juan Francisco Fuentes (eds.), *Diccionario político y social del siglo XIX español*, Madrid: Alianza, 2002.

Pro, Juan Juiz, *Bravo Murillo. Política de orden en la España liberal*, Madrid: Síntesis, 2006.

Romeo Mateo, Maria Cruz, and Maria Sierra (eds.), *Historia de las culturas políticas contemporáneas en España y América Latina. T II: La España liberal*, Zaragoza-Madrid: Prensas Universitarias de Zaragoza-Marcial Pons, 2014.

Sierra, María, María Antonia Peña, and Rafael Zurita, *Elegidos y elegibles. La representación parlamentaria en la cultura del liberalismo*, Madrid: Marcial Pons, 2010.

CHAPTER 4
THE RESTORATION: 1874–1914

Javier Moreno-Luzón

Translated by Nick Rider

At the beginning of January 1875, seventeen-year-old King Alfonso XII arrived in Spain. He had spent a good part of his adolescence in exile, and his mother, the ex-Queen Isabel II, remained in Paris, from where she had abdicated in his favor in 1870. The young monarch landed in the port of Barcelona, where he was given a magnificent reception headed by the financial and business elites of Catalonia. In Cuba, Spain's principal colony and an important market for Catalan products, a war was underway against the independence movement. Shortly afterward Alfonso traveled on to Valencia, the city in which the military coup that had proclaimed him King on December 29, 1874 had been hatched. From there he went on to Madrid, the capital of his kingdom, where he proceeded across the city beneath triumphal arches and amid high expectations. The government was already headed by the politician who had led the movement in favor of the monarch's return, Antonio Cánovas del Castillo, raised to power by the pro-Alfonso (*alfonsino*) Generals. However, the King stayed in the city for only a few days, as he very quickly left for the north of the country to place himself at the head of the army that was fighting against the Carlists, supporters of a rival branch of the Bourbon dynasty. Thus began a new era in the political history of Spain: the Restoration.

In those first moments, the predominant mood was one of uncertainties. The new reign could have been just one more twist in the convulsive trajectory of Spain in the nineteenth century, full of military coups, civil wars, and constant changes in the political system, problems that had become further aggravated in the preceding years (see chapters 2, 3). Nevertheless, the Restoration brought something different. Spurred by the desires for peace and tranquility among a large part of public opinion, it managed to bring an end to two wars relatively successfully, laid the basis for a stable constitutional regime—the Constitution of 1876 was the most long-lived in modern Spanish history, since it would remain in force until 1923— and distanced the army from major political decisions. Some military leaders continued to play a prominent public role, and the army also gained greater autonomy by continuing to reserve for itself the task of maintaining public order. However, transfers of power were no longer carried out by force but through an agreed alternation in power between two major parties, Conservative and Liberal, which between them consolidated a new political system that was liberal in form, if not democratic. Until the political effects of the First World War began to be felt (especially from 1917 onward), this *turno pacífico* or peaceful alternation in power generally continued to function.

For decades, most historians judged the Restoration political system negatively. Many had inherited the contemporary critiques that decried the system at the end of the nineteenth and in the early years of the twentieth century. No one expressed this better than Joaquín Costa, an intellectual who summed up his opinion of the regime in 1901 in the phrase "*oligarquía y caciquismo,*" [oligarchy and cacique-ism (clientelism)]. For Costa, the Restoration was no more than a corrupt shell, exclusively at the service of the political elites and held up by local petty tyrants—the *caciques*—who helped these elites to falsify elections and keep Spaniards in submission. Other intellectuals subsequently added to this definition by referring, as the philosopher José Ortega y Gasset did in 1914, to the opposition between the "official" Spain and the "real" or living Spain, that is, to the disconnect between governments and their citizens (see Chapter 32). From these and other portrayals an image was built up of a system that was artificial and immobile, incapable of bringing forward reform and based upon a country that was sunk in backwardness, rural, and illiterate, and held apart from the international currents of progress. Spain lived, due to the faults of its rulers, on the margins of modernity, constituting an exceptional case in the Europe of its era. Later historians confirmed these impressions, and often added a class component, since, in the judgment of many, the politicians of that time served the interests of a power bloc made up of landowners and industrialists. In opposition to this dominant view, a few authors with a more classically liberal or conservative approach idealized the Restoration as an oasis of economic progress and political stability between two periods of turbulence, the *Sexenio* of 1868–74 and the phase that began in 1923 with the military dictatorship of Primo de Rivera.

Recent historical research into this period, which has progressed with special intensity since the 1990s, has altered these stereotypical and simplistic viewpoints. In-depth analysis of the political system has given us a more nuanced image of the forces of monarchism, which not only were not fossilized but also generated reformist projects. Even more so, our image of political life has become more complex, since mass parties and movements that had a growing presence both in the street and in the parliamentary arena have come into view. Politicians possessed autonomy from the most powerful economic interests and, although corruption was the norm in elections and many areas of public administration, the principal demands of organized groups played an influence in their decisions. In other words, one cannot speak of artificiality and a lack of connection between the political sphere and social realities, above all at a local level. All this took place in a society that, far from being sunk in paralysis, was developing and becoming urbanized—albeit in a slow, unequal, and unbalanced manner—a process that provoked conflicts which would have been unimaginable had Spain truly remained stagnant and immobile (see Chapter 17).

In addition, Spain was not isolated during this era of great transformations in Europe and America. On the one hand, it was affected by international trends, such as the globalization of trade and the colonial share-out between the great powers, which brought Spain's empire to an end in 1898, when the United States snatched away its last possessions in the Caribbean and the Pacific. On the other, Spanish political and social phenomena were similar to those experienced by other countries in the same period. Thus, the Restoration can be considered a regime comparable to others which, from Portugal to Italy and from Argentina to Mexico, similarly stabilized their respective political spheres after decades of violence. All of them, like the Restoration, arbitrated pacts between previously opposing elites, made systematic use of the falsification of elections, and relied on clientelist parties that encouraged corruption. Spain, like many other states in Europe and Latin America, enjoyed a constitutional regime that recognized basic rights and freedoms but also suffered serious deficiencies, one in which a transition to full democracy had scarcely begun. Nevertheless, the regime's difficulties arose out of the changes that were already underway, not the historic lethargy of Spanish politics and society.

The basic pillars of the political system

The proclamation of Alfonso XII at the end of 1874 represented much more than merely the return to the throne of the Bourbon dynasty, since it served to set in motion an ambitious political project conceived by Antonio Cánovas del Castillo. The last conservative statesman in a Europe of conservative statesmen (including Benjamin Disraeli in Britain and Otto von Bismarck in Germany), Cánovas was a veteran politician who in his youth had been active in the centrist sectors of liberalism. Of modest origins like other Spanish ministers, he was the son of a teacher who liked to present himself as an example of the social mobility that had been permitted by the liberal revolution in Spain, so different from the aristocratic tone that still dominated public life in Great Britain, Russia, Germany, and Austria-Hungary. He had also devoted himself to studying the history of the seventeenth-century era of Spanish decline, which gave him a nationalist vision of the past and a certain skepticism regarding Spain's true possibilities. In essence, his great project consisted of eliminating the factor that, in his view, had made political instability endemic in Spain: the exclusive pursuit of party interests. That is, the political monopoly customarily exercised by the party in power, which imposed its constitutional model on others and obliged the opposition to seek the aid of military commanders in order to gain power by means of coups d'état (see Chapter 21). What was needed therefore was to find a legal framework and mechanisms of political change that could be shared by the majority of the factions that up to that time had persecuted each other.

Initially, Cánovas imposed an authoritarian government, which enforced severe policies in the fields of public order and press censorship. However, he soon began to weave together the agreements and accords necessary to elect a new parliament and draw up a new Constitution, approved in 1876. Predominant within the new document were the conservative elements that had characterized the constitutional model of the Moderate Party, which had enjoyed hegemonic status during the reign of Isabel II and whose ideas had been expressed in the Constitution of 1845, although it also included some progressive features drawn from the Constitution of 1869. The fundamental principle that inspired the 1876 Constitution was the idea espoused by moderate liberals of cosovereignty or shared sovereignty between the parliament, the Cortes, and the King, in opposition to the progressive principle of national sovereignty, which gave primacy to the parliament. Behind the idea of cosovereignty one could see the belief in a Spanish "internal constitution" that was based on the centuries-long historic coexistence of the Crown with the traditional Cortes of the different territories. In practice, this meant giving an advantage to the King, who could freely appoint and dismiss ministers, and would equally be cohead of the legislative power, with the ability to dissolve parliament, as well as head of the armed forces and the controller of foreign policy. Meanwhile, governments needed to have the dual confidence of both the King and the Cortes, made up of two chambers: a Congress of Deputies elected by the citizens and a Senate which was partly elected and partly appointed by the King or drawn from the aristocracy, the Church, and the army. Cánovas considered monarchy, rather than one form of government that could be replaced by another, to be a permanent form of the state. The Restoration would not be a parliamentary monarchy of the kind that was taking shape in Great Britain or the Nordic countries, but a constitutional monarchy in which the monarch retained extensive powers, more limited than in the German Empire but similar to those of the Kings of Italy.

Alongside this preeminence of the Crown, the 1876 Constitution guaranteed basic rights and individual freedoms, such as those associated with private property, the rights of those arrested or detained and the freedoms of the press, assembly, and association. The area of religion was especially problematic in a country such as Spain, in which the powerful Catholic Church did not accept religious pluralism. The Constitution adopted an intermediate solution between the religious unity demanded by the right and the religious freedom defended by the left: Catholicism would be the official religion of the state but other forms of worship would be respected, so long as their observance was confined to the private domain. In reality, this Constitution stood out for its openness and flexibility, which enabled it to last much longer than its predecessors; it scarcely went into detail on many significant matters, and left them in the hands of a future legislative development in a way that allowed for a variety of different formulae. Suffrage is an excellent example: it permitted, without the need to revise the text of the Constitution itself, first a return to selective suffrage—restricted according to financial and professional criteria—and then subsequently the introduction of universal male suffrage.

Once the constitutional framework had been established, the political system was reinforced through the construction of two large parties that, inspired by the British example, would make it possible to integrate the majority of liberals into the new structure and then alternate in power. The first of them, the Conservative Party, was led by Cánovas himself, and rested on an accord between various tendencies of the Spanish right, from those of a centrist background such as the party leader to the more extreme sections of the old Moderate Party, who prompted a serious conflict at the outset of the Restoration by seeking to use the powers of the government to persecute progressive university professors. Added to these factions were the militant Catholics who, in accordance with the recommendations of Pope Leo XIII, were now willing to take part in the parliamentary system, in the same way that German Catholics were doing in the Centre Party or *Zentrum*, and many French Catholics in the *ralliement* that accepted the Third Republic. Only the Carlists, defeated in the civil war but still active, remained outside. In fact, the Catholic Church, still dubious of liberal structures but now protected by the State, recovered a good part of its old privileges under the Restoration, and experienced a period of splendor (see Chapter 17).

The Liberal Party, the second fundamental element in the system, took shape with greater difficulty. The decisive role was played by another veteran politician, Práxedes Mateo Sagasta, a clever and pragmatic engineer and a Freemason who had been tried as a conspirator in times of Isabel II and had headed governments during the six "revolutionary years" prior to 1874. Labeled the *viejo pastor*, the "old shepherd," because of his ability to hold together political flocks, Sagasta had the ability to bring together under his leadership a range of elements whose backgrounds were in the center and left wings of liberalism, but who all gradually agreed to accept the Constitution of 1876. This required that they accept shared sovereignty and the subsequent preeminence of the Crown, and therefore renounce the principle of national sovereignty, together with full freedom of religion and other progressive precepts. In exchange, they gained power on several occasions and were able to advance reforms that incorporated some democratic principles into the legal structure of the Restoration. To the left of the Liberal Party there remained republicans of various tendencies, some of whom continued to place their hopes unsuccessfully in a coup d'état, and the Socialists, who were still taking their first steps (see Chapter 30).

The Liberal Party carried out most of its reforms during what was known as Sagasta's "long parliament" between 1885 and 1890. It had previously passed a law on the press that ended the censorship imposed by Cánovas. From 1885 onward, however, the Liberals launched a range of reforming initiatives of major significance: the abolition of slavery in Cuba, an old desire of humanitarian groups; a law of associations that authorized workers' unions; trial by jury, so that citizens could take part in justice; and the Civil Code of 1889, which regulated family law and gave legal security to contracts and property rights, the equivalent of the Constitution in the private sphere. Although it followed the model of the *Code Napoléon* of 1805 in imposing uniformity across the country, the code also recognized some customary practices peculiar to different regions. The culmination of the Liberal program was the electoral law of 1890, which granted the right to vote to all males over 25 years old. Spain thus joined the European vanguard in extending political citizenship, which at that time consisted of only France, Switzerland, Germany, and Greece. Nevertheless, the Liberals were concerned not just with recognizing a right, but also with expanding the franchise. In contrast to the Conservatives' fear of socialism, the Spanish Liberals thought that this extension would not disrupt social order and would have scarcely any effect on the supremacy of the educated elites over the ignorant masses. The principal immediate effect of the measure was to attract into the ranks of the Liberal Party the more lukewarm republicans, who had called for such changes as conditions for their integration in the constitutional consensus.

Having been thus established during the first fifteen years of the Restoration, the two governmental parties took turns in power in accordance with the shared rules of the Constitution. The preeminence of the Crown made it the arbiter of this alternation, since it gave the monarch the ability to change governments without paying attention to parliamentary majorities. However, this royal prerogative was not employed in an arbitrary manner, but followed agreed-upon practices that also took shape during these years. It was used when there was a serious crisis, such as that caused by the early death of Alfonso XII in 1885, which led to the definitive consolidation of the system of alternation in power, or when the party in power split into opposing factions, and the opposition party seemed to be more united. The greater the internal unity in each party and the more widely their leaders were accepted within them, the less room for maneuver there was for royal intervention. When Alfonso died in 1885, his widow, the Austrian Archduchess Maria Christina of Habsburg-Lorraine, assumed the regency during the minority of her son Alfonso XIII, who was born shortly after the death of his father. Both the first Restoration king and his widow were attentive to their constitutional role and, though they were not passive, the system of alternation in power, backed by the strong leadership of Cánovas and Sagasta, operated well during their reigns.

Nevertheless, these mechanisms were only possible thanks to the massive level of electoral fraud that characterized Spanish political practice, and enabled all governments to win the elections they called. This had been happening in a systematic manner—with one exception—since 1834 so that the principal novelty brought by the Restoration was not electoral manipulation but the *turno pacífico* between the parties. That is to say, in the Spain that followed the introduction of liberalism, the habitual political processes functioned in a manner that was the reverse of the pattern indicated by modern representative thinking: governments did not emerge out of parliamentary majorities once elections had been held, but rather parliamentary majorities were fabricated from above by the governments previously appointed by the king, who granted them the right to call the election. To achieve this, these governments took advantage of the general lack of political mobilization among the electorate and the tools that were placed at their disposal by a highly centralized state (see Chapter 20). The Interior Ministry (*Gobernación*) gave the necessary orders to the civil governors of the provinces, whose functions corresponded to those of French prefects, although in Spain they were not themselves career civil servants. The governors in turn controlled the local mayors, who presided over municipal councils and, during elections, polling stations. Local institutions lacked autonomy of action, and the regions, despite Spain's cultural and geographical variety, did not even exist as separate administrations. This was a system of organization that, as had already been seen in the France of the Second Empire and would be seen again later in Portugal and Southern Italy, could readily be placed at the service of the executive power in order to elect a parliament.

Even so, the need to include the opposition demanded complex electoral negotiations. Prior to elections, the government had to agree with the other party in the *turno* and minority forces, for whom a few seats were reserved, on who the official candidates would be. At the end of these negotiations a kind of table or *cuadro* was drawn up to share out the seats, in which there was a box or *casilla* for each electoral district—hence the name of the system, *encasillado*—with a name written into each one for the probable successful candidate. This generally anticipated the results, although on some occasions several candidates from the same party competed among themselves, and there were also rebellious districts that defied the government. The Restoration system maintained an electoral map that favored the use of fraud, since it divided the country into small constituencies each of which elected a single member or deputy. Multimember constituencies existed only in certain cities, which tended to include an extensive rural surrounding area in order to drown out the urban vote. The addition of universal male suffrage did not change the panorama greatly, since governments continued to win all elections. Nevertheless, in the longer term the new voting practices did permit a notable increase in political mobilization in the cities, which led to defeats for governmental candidates in these urban centers, and, by comparison with the more traditional forms of electoral fraud, prompted an increase in more open corruption in the shape of the buying of votes.

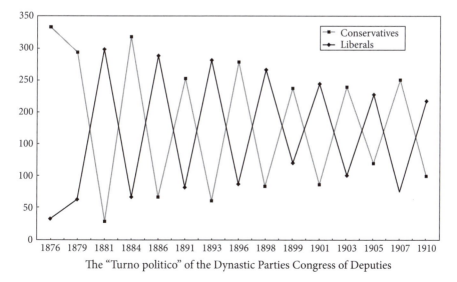

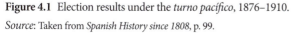

The "Turno politico" of the Dynastic Parties Congress of Deputies

Figure 4.1 Election results under the *turno pacífico*, 1876–1910.

Source: Taken from *Spanish History since 1808*, p. 99.

As in many other European countries, political parties in Spain were elitist or cadre parties made up of provincial notables who saw political life as a complement to their social position or a reward for their skill in administrative affairs. These were the so-called *caciques*, powerful local figures who took their exotic name from indigenous chieftains in the old Spanish Caribbean empire, who had acted as intermediaries between their communities and the colonial administration. As with their fellows in other parts of southern Europe—the Portuguese *influentes* or the *grandi elettori* in Italy—and in Latin America, but also in cities in the United States where immigrants turned for protection to local bosses, their preferred political weapons lay in the favors that they sought from their superiors and granted in turn to their clienteles. These could be individual—from obtaining a job to pursuing some matter through the public administration—or collective, such as a new road or a school. At election time, the *caciques* imposed limits on the negotiations of the *encasillado*, and facilitated the electoral fraud that was of most interest to higher authorities. In return, they saw their own local power reinforced. In fact, they were indispensable when it came to implementing many decisions of a state that was centralized, but weak. Beyond these clientelist networks, the parties also disposed of social clubs and newspapers that defended their interests. All these elements made up the framework of *caciquismo*, a phenomenon so solid that it survived beyond the Restoration regime.

At the top of these parties of notables were the parliamentarians, with a profile similar to that seen in other countries in the region. The aristocracy had only a reduced presence among them, although it was prominent in the Senate, with a predominance of recently created noble titles. In both chambers there was an abundance of the liberal professions and above all lawyers, the profession most closely associated with politics in Spain as it was in Italy, France, and Portugal. However, there were also frequently rural landowners and businessmen with interests in their home districts, especially those connected with the dynamic sectors of the economy, who had need of good contacts in the state. Some deputies had no connection at all with their constituencies, since they owed their election entirely to the government, but many others dedicated their time to taking care of petitions and requests from their followers at home around the ministries in Madrid. A growing number of them managed to establish a solid constituency base of their own, among whom the influence gained on the basis of favors won and granted gave them a certain freedom of action with respect to the government. Even though political demobilization was the dominant tone and electoral competition was scarce, this form of parliamentary representation articulated real interests, and was not at all artificial.

The Restoration parliament, in spite of its constitutional limitations and the lack of legitimacy it suffered due to its fraudulent origins, was the center of political life. It was there that the great debates took place and the reputations of its leading protagonists were at stake. As was the case virtually throughout Europe, one could not be a prominent politician in Spain if one was not a good orator. Parliament legislated, but it occupied itself above all in exercising a check on ministers through the means of parliamentary questions. The divisions inside the majority that supported the government were played out in the chambers, which consequently were the scene of many governmental crises. As was also habitual in European politics, the members were not divided into parliamentary groups subject to tight discipline, but rather each deputy or Senator enjoyed great freedom when it came to speaking or voting, which they did according to their own interests or those of their district. For example, the parliamentarians of areas that would be favored by particular economic policies often voted together, even when they belonged to rival parties. The norms of parliamentary behavior permitted obstructionism, although strong leaders such as Cánovas or Sagasta were generally able to prevent it. Spanish parliamentary life was distinguished from those of other European liberal regimes only by the enormous role played within it by electoral manipulation and *caciquismo*.

The agitated *Fin de Siècle*

The political stability of the Restoration existed alongside a modest but constant economic and demographic growth (see Chapter 9). The basic structures of the economy were modernized and the creation of a unified national market was completed; new industries emerged. However, Spain continued to be an agrarian country, one that was comparatively poor in the context of Western Europe, a country where in 1910 the primary sector—agriculture, stock-rearing, fishing—still generated 38 percent of Gross Value Added (GVA) in the economy, compared to 45.5 percent in 1870. For its part, the secondary sector—industry and mining—had risen from 16 to 26.8 percent of GVA. Real but gradual rate of development was not only inadequate to shorten the distances that separated Spain from the most advanced countries—Great Britain, France, or Germany—but allowed them to increase it, since the economies of these countries were growing more rapidly. Spain was less far behind Italy, but the only country it surpassed was small and stagnating Portugal. In addition, industrialization increased the inequalities between the Spanish regions, since those of the north and northeast, from Asturias to Catalonia, were developing far more than those of the south and west, such as Andalusia or Extremadura. Standing out among the economic innovations of this period was the incorporation of the Basque Country, principal location for the second industrial revolution in Spain, into the select band of European industrial regions. Up to this point it had only included one part of Spain, Catalonia. The Catalan textile sector continued to be significant, but the Basque iron and steel industry, spurred by the blast furnaces that made use of the iron ore of the province of Vizcaya and imported British coal as their source of energy, acquired extraordinary momentum. Between 1875 and 1901, the production of cast iron grew by a factor of eight. This industrial hub also gave rise to manufacturing plants producing machinery and shipping and the foundation of large private banks, which had been absent in Catalonia. Other advanced sectors, such as chemical and hydroelectrical industries, appeared from 1900 onward. Moreover, Spain was a major mining country—the first producer in the world of lead, and the second of copper—and benefited from the increase in demand across Europe. Not only did the greater part of its mineral production go for export, it was foreign capital that exploited the country's mineral deposits. Such was the case of the Río Tinto copper mines in Huelva (Andalucia), which could almost be considered a miniature British colony.

During the Restoration there was a notable increase in investment in transport and communications infrastructure. In contrast to other areas of Europe, Spain did not possess good navigable rivers, so it was dependent on other means of transportation. The construction of the railway network was almost completed in a little over half a century, so that between 1874 and 1907 it grew from 5,621 to 11,362 operational kilometers, while roadbuilding surpassed the railways in dynamism, the total network expanding from around 17,000 to 46,000 kilometers between 1874 and 1914. Seaports were similarly improved, and telegraph cables were laid. Overall, a national market was created without legal barriers or territorial privileges, articulated by means of a communications network that, following the French model, connected the center (Madrid) with every point around the periphery. This network was still deficient in many respects, but it reached the majority of the national territory and permitted regional economic specialization.

In the mid-1880s, the Spanish countryside began to feel the effects of the agrarian crisis that was spreading across a large part of Europe, prompted by the collapse in prices provoked by the arrival of cheap foodstuffs from the United States and Argentina, in what is known as the Long Depression. In Spain, this crisis first struck growers of cereals, which occupied the greater part of cultivable land, and olives. In Barcelona, for example, wheat from the American Midwest became much cheaper than wheat from Castile. The third element in the "Mediterranean triad" that dominated agriculture, wine, had in contrast undergone a brief golden era thanks to the phylloxera epidemic that ruined the vineyards of France, but this ended brusquely in the 1890s due to a French recovery and the arrival of the same plague in Spain. On the other hand, the Spanish primary sector also modernized, and some regions specialized in high-quality products for export, such as olive oil, Rioja wines, Andalusian sherry, or Valencian oranges. Other agriculturally based industries also appeared, such as those that produced flour, cork, canned fish or vegetables, and beer. Nevertheless, the equilibrium of rural society was still highly precarious and bad harvests caused hunger and food riots.

The malaise caused by the agrarian crisis at the end of the century prompted a wave of corporate organization, similar to those experienced in other European countries. Pressure groups were born such as the *Liga Agraria* (Agrarian League), which defended the interests of Castilian farmers. They combined with other organized interest groups, such as the Catalan textile manufacturers and the Basque iron and steel makers, around a common demand: an increase in tariffs to protect domestic producers from cheap imports. (Such tariffs had been introduced by other governments, from Germany to the United States.) These mobilizations succeeded in imposing protectionism as a permanent economic policy that from 1890 onward raised Spanish tariffs time and again to the point where, by the twentieth century, the Spanish market became one of the most closed in Europe. This was undoubtedly damaging to consumers, who were obliged to pay high prices, and was the foremost example of the influence of economic interests over political decisions during the Restoration. The different parties, even those such as the Liberal Party that had traditionally defended free trade, all accepted this kind of economic nationalism.

Spain's population, which was essentially rural, continued to be burdened by a high rate of mortality, which reached catastrophic levels among children. Moreover, in the final quarter of the nineteenth century, the country still suffered demographic crises such as a cholera epidemic that caused 120,000 deaths in 1885. It was only at the beginning of the new century, with a considerable delay by comparison with the more developed European societies, that Spanish society entered the path of the demographic transition, signified by a reduction in birth rates and a still greater fall in death rates. At the same time, there was an acceleration in the rural exodus to the cities, and a displacement of population from the interior toward the coast. During this period, Spain also joined the migratory pattern of Mediterranean Europe (shared with Italy and Greece). Emigration grew exponentially from 1904 to the outbreak of the First World War, which put a sudden break on the outflow: in that period, between 1.5 and 2 million Spaniards left the country. The record year for net migration was 1912, when almost 135,000 more people left Spain than entered the country (see chapters 11, 19).

Spain's cities, the scene of the innovations that changed the social and political panorama after 1890, also saw a great growth spurt. Around the turn of the century, Madrid and Barcelona each surpassed half a million inhabitants, and figured among the eighteen European cities with populations above that figure. Within them the middle classes associated with the professions, public administration, and trade expanded and began to organize themselves in defense of their collective interests. To a lesser extent, something similar occurred among the growing working class, in which the migrants arriving from the countryside swelled the numbers of the most wretched and insecure, packed together in *barrios* or districts that lacked the most elementary levels of health and hygiene. The situation of rural laborers and urban workers— what was known as the "social question"—had begun to concern the political elites, who in the face of the rise in labor organizations and workers' protests during these years began to take a few still-timid measures. In 1883 a Liberal government created the *Comisión de Reformas Sociales* (Commission for Social Reform), which collected information to serve as a basis for legislation, and would give rise twenty years later to the much more ambitious *Instituto de Reformas Sociales*. In 1900 the Conservatives passed Spain's first legislation on accidents at work and female and child labor.

At the same time, it was also during this period that the *ensanches* or "extensions" of many cities were built, new districts inspired by those of other European centers and seen since the mid-nineteenth century as a means of reducing the congestion in the historic centers of old cities. In the early 1900s even these old unhygienic cores were broken into with the marking out of great new avenues, such as the Gran Vía in Madrid or the Via Laietana in Barcelona. In 1888 the Catalan city had held the first Universal Exhibition organized in Spain, showing the world the power of the economic capital of the Iberian Peninsula. Its great emblem was a column with a statue of Christopher Columbus, erected at a time when the four-hundredth anniversary of the Discovery of America was approaching to symbolize the good commercial relationships between Catalonia and the American continent, which were especially vigorous in Spain's Caribbean colonies. A mass culture flourished in Spain's urban centers, nourished by the hundreds of newspapers published under the wing of freedom of the press, pamphlets and naturalistic novels, theatres, *zarzuelas*—Spanish operettas with regional or patriotic themes— and the modern form of the bullfight, which established the best *toreros* as popular heroes (see Chapter 11).

Meanwhile, official politics had followed its customary path through the 1890s, characterized by the *turno pacífico* and *caciquismo*, and disturbed only by circumstantial splits within the governmental parties, sometimes prompted by corruption scandals. In an era of heightened imperial competition, political attention was focused on the problems of the undersized Spanish empire (see Chapter 13). This was the case especially in 1895, when a new insurrection broke out in Cuba, followed a short time later by another in the Philippines. The first Cuban war had ended in 1878 with a peace agreement that gave the island parliamentary representation, but plans to concede it to an autonomous government would not be approved until 1897, and in the meantime the rise in commercial protectionism tightened the bonds restricting the colony's economy, reserving its market for Spanish products. These insurrections provoked patriotic demonstrations in Spain, and public opinion came together in an exaggeratedly patriotic *españolista* language, which became further exacerbated when the United States declared war on Spain in 1898.

This colonial war was unjust not only for the population of Cuba, subjected to a cruel regime, but also for the Spanish soldiers. Only the poor were obliged to fight, those who lacked the necessary resources to pay the financial charge that freed others from military service, which led to protests around the slogan "*¡O todos o ninguno!*" ("All or none!"). In addition, the greater part of the losses was due to tropical diseases and bad sanitary conditions not combat: 50,000 of the 221,000 soldiers that Spain sent to Cuba did not come back. The broader war of 1898 lasted only a few months—it took scarcely two battles of a few hours each for the Americans to finish with the Spanish navy—and demonstrated Spain's international isolation and irrelevance. The Liberal government of Sagasta, pressured by patriotic demonstrations and the threat of a coup from army officers who would not accept surrender without a fight, led the country to certain defeat. At a time when the great empires were expanding in Africa and Asia, Spain lost its last colonies. The sad spectacle of the repatriated troops, transported home in miserable conditions at the end of the war, provided the postscript to what from then on would simply be known as *el Desastre*, "the Disaster."

The humiliation of 1898 seemed to augur a new Sedan; that is, a political catastrophe on the scale of France's defeat by Prussia in 1870–71, the ramifications of which included the revolutionary outburst of the Commune and the replacement of the Second Empire by the Third Republic. However, none of this happened in Spain. There was not even a coup d'état, although General Camilo Polavieja (an expert on colonial matters) unsuccessfully offered to lead one with the support of Catholic sectors and the Catalan bourgeois damaged by the loss of the Cuban market, in a movement comparable to the wave of nationalism that had been headed by General Boulanger in France in the 1880s. Nor did the conspiracies concocted in Paris by Carlist or republican exiles get very far. There was no alternative to the constitutional monarchy of the Restoration, and the peaceful alternation of Conservatives and Liberals continued as it had done previously. Following the conclusion of a peace treaty, Sagasta was replaced in office by the Conservative who had inherited the leadership of his party after the assassination of Cánovas in 1897, Francisco Silvela.

Nevertheless, the *Desastre* brought with it a profound crisis of national identity, which added an agonizing sense of failure to the old awareness of Spain's backwardness compared to other European nations. In reality, this was one more case of the failure of the more vulnerable countries in the imperialist struggle, like the 1890 British ultimatum to Portugal to abandon its dream of a Portuguese African corridor between Angola and Mozambique, the grievous humiliation of Italy at Adowa in Ethiopia in 1896 or the French retreat before Great Britain at Fashoda in Sudan in 1899. A struggle that tended to be interpreted in line with the ideas of "social Darwinism"—the transposition of the biological theories of Darwin to social and political relations—as a conflict between vigorous or "living" nations and "dying" ones that were increasingly moribund, condemned to a slide into decadence. In Spain—as in other countries nearby—it became a cliché to speak of the superiority of the Anglo-Saxon nations or races over the Latin countries. Though there might be disagreement as to the reasons— biological, educational, religious—there was no doubting one particular fact: that Spain was a "dying nation."

The impact of the defeat coincided with the entry into the arena of public debate of a new actor: the intellectuals, men of letters who indicated the course for the country to follow, and who had an enormous impact in the expanding urban cultural market. In this regard the Disaster of 1898 was the equivalent of the Dreyfus affair, which was sending shockwaves through France during this same period, and which consecrated the figure of the modern intellectual. In Spain, prescriptions for overcoming the nation's state of prostration and backwardness proliferated in the so-called Disaster literature full of a heterogeneous mix of often contradictory and sometimes nonsensical solutions (see chapters 16, 32). The figures that best represented the mood of this time were a varied assortment of men who devoted themselves to diagnosing the ills of the fatherland, and proposing remedies for its regeneration. For this reason they are described as *regeneracionistas* (regenerationists). As did their contemporary Russia counterparts, the Spanish intelligentsia aspired to transform a backward country.

Some intellectuals also took part in the political mobilizations and agitation by business and economic organizations that burst into view immediately after the colonial defeat, and assembled a "regenerationist" reform program. Joaquín Costa, the most influential, directed the campaigns of the agricultural chambers, while fellow Aragonese businessman Basilio Paraíso did the same with the Chambers of Commerce. Their movement proposed measures such as the granting of votes to corporate bodies, reductions in taxes and, although it might seem contradictory, increased investment in public works. They were obsessed with hydraulic engineering projects, the aim of which would be to irrigate large areas of the arid regions of Spain and thus improve agricultural productivity (see Chapter 14). These were campaigns sustained by the middle classes in protest against the domination of the state and the economy by oligarchies, in a manner similar to those sustained by comparable groups in other countries such as the elements that made up French Radical Republicanism or American Progressivism. In 1901 some regenerationists formed a new but ultimately unsuccessful political party, the *Unión Nacional*.

This state of discontent also led to a rebellion against the fiscal policies of the Conservative government of Silvela, who had charged his finance minister with readjusting the state's accounts after the colonial wars, which had created an unsustainable debt. The increase in taxes provoked a closure of shops and a taxpayers' strike in Barcelona—the *tancament de caixes* in Catalan or "closure of the cash registers"—and other cities. The authorities suppressed these and other movements forcefully, and budget orthodoxy—what the Liberal politician and winner of the Nobel Prize for Literature José Echegaray called "the sacred fear of the deficit"—produced results, until a new colonial war beginning in 1909 in Morocco destabilized state finances once again. In effect, if the "Disaster" did not lead to a full-scale political catastrophe nor entail a grave economic crisis, it naturally affected sectors that had sold their products in the colonies. At the same time, it also led to the repatriation of large amounts of capital, which served to finance industries, banks, and insurance companies.

The most lasting aspect of the regenerationist ambience is to be found in certain arguments and forms of language that would leave a mark on the Spanish political agenda for decades. One was the insistence on particular policies, such as those on hydraulic engineering (see Chapter 14) and above all in education. In an atmosphere imbued with a preoccupation with education and pedagogy, the principal liberal educationalists linked to the *Institución Libre de Enseñanza* ("Free Institute of Education") founded in Madrid in 1876, drew up a program to improve education and connect Spain with advanced tendencies in all the academic disciplines. According to a popular expression at the time, the task at hand was to "Japan-ize" Spain, that is, to repeat the miracle that, by means of importing the most modern techniques and technology, had transformed Japan from an underdeveloped, feudal country into a world power. The Japanese military victory over Russia in 1905 made this model popular. Overall, regenerationism encouraged an increase in public spending on education and areas such as health, and consequently an increase in the number of public officials in these same fields, although the greater part of the state budget remained dedicated to paying off public debt and sustaining the armed forces.

The other great legacy of regenerationism was its acid critique of the political and parliamentary establishment mentioned earlier. The calls made by Costa, for example, for an "iron surgeon" (*cirujano de hierro*) who would close parliament by force and extirpate the cancer of *caciquismo* from national life were hugely influential. Spanish parliamentarism was represented in newspaper reports, press cartoons, and literature in highly derogatory terms: electoral fraud, generalized corruption, the abuse of power in the villages by *caciques*, time-wasting in parliamentary debates, and the lack of real ideological differences between the politicians of the main parties all made up an image that could only undermine the legitimacy of the constitutional regime. Consequently, calls were made not only for its reform, but also often for its destruction. The military dictatorships of the twentieth century, first of General Primo de Rivera and later Francisco Franco, both took advantage of these critiques and images to justify their actions.

Mass politics and monarchist reformism

In that turbulent turn of the century, the mobilization of the regenerationist middle classes combined with the emergence of new forms of political engagement which, as in other countries, left elitist and clientelist habits behind: socializing in party clubs and social centers, the large-circulation press, meetings and demonstrations, the celebration of holiday rituals, and the use of specific symbols. Political constellations were also created that extended through a range of associations of all kinds, including youth and labor groups and others created around leisure activities, such as choral societies and hiking clubs. Though they did not succeed in overturning the monarchist *turno*, these movements created strong political identities, and won local elections in cities. Moreover, regenerationism and the appearance of mass politics also had an influence on both governmental parties, driving them to put forward reformist proposals that they hoped would gain social support for the monarchy. Equally, however, during the first thirteen years of the twentieth century a series of serious political conflicts prompted further movements of mobilization on a massive scale, and led to clashes between the two monarchist forces that placed the whole Restoration system at risk.

The first of these conflicts arose in the field of nationalism and nationalisms. Spain was no exception in Europe, which was witnessing a proliferation of movements on the German model, which in opposition to the civic nationalism rooted in the French Revolution sought to find the national spirit—the *Volksgeist*—in language, religion, or race. These were years in which European and American states set out to "nationalize" their citizens through schools, the army, monuments, commemorations, and the dissemination of national symbols. Among Spanish conservative nationalists, a fusion had already been proclaimed between Catholicism and the national identity, but at this time the Castilian language also began to gain ground as a key element in nationality, in a process that confused Spain with Castile, its history and its landscapes. With some delay by comparison with other European states, the state began to take nationalistic initiatives in the educational field, the pace of which accelerated after the "Disaster," and in the commemoration of national glories like Miguel de Cervantes, the great national writer. Cities were filled with statues that extolled the links between local or regional identities, so very marked in Spain, and the national identity. Regenerationism, in effect, was nothing other than a particularly tormented form of Spanish nationalism. After 1898, paradoxically, closer links were established with Latin America, promoted by *hispanoamericanista* or "Hispano-American" associations that aspired to place the "mother country" at the head of a gigantic cultural community.

In a dialectical relationship with this growth of Spanish nationalism, various substate nationalist movements also developed, tendencies that were stronger in Spain than in countries where indigenous local cultures had not survived or the state had not suffered the loss of legitimacy caused by colonial defeat (see Chapter 10). The first political party was created in the Basque Country, although other types of nationalist organizations had been established earlier in Catalonia. Basque nationalism was as Catholic as the older Carlism of the region had been, and with a xenophobic attitude toward the thousands of Castilian migrants who had arrived in the Basque Country to work in industry. Catalan nationalism, preceded by a cultural renaissance that turned into a political movement through the experience of the campaigns that were launched in defense of Catalan civil law, were in favor of some form of decentralization or in support of local businesses. In contrast to Basque nationalism, which initially had scant electoral success, Catalanism succeeded in forming a party, the *Lliga Regionalista* (Regionalist League), that attracted a significant percentage of the electorate to vote for it and so defeated both Conservatives and Liberals. In addition, and in contrast with the stance of Basque pro-independence campaigners, the Catalanists of the *Lliga* also designed plans for the whole of Spain, the aim of which was to ensure that the particularities of Catalonia were recognized within a plurinational and decentralized state. This placed them at the center of Spanish parliamentary life from 1907 onward, as they negotiated their objectives with Conservative and Liberal governments. In 1914 the *Mancomunitat* or joint administration of the four Catalan provinces was created, the first regional administration in modern Spain (see Chapter 31).

The rise of substate nationalisms provoked the return of the army to politics. This was no longer a matter, as it had been in the previous century, of generals launching coups to seize power at the head of their respective parties, but of interference by the military as a specific corporate interest group. The regenerationist critiques of politicians, blamed for the colonial defeat, had gained currency in the officers' messes, and with them the idea that the army was the true guardian of national unity. In the absence of a modern police force, army officers were in charge of maintaining public order, and when serious conflicts occurred, local military commanders took over from the civil authorities and took command of events at regional and provincial levels, which made them indispensable to governments. They could also count on the support of King Alfonso XIII, whose reign started in 1902 when he turned sixteen. Strongly influenced by the nationalistic atmosphere that grew up around the "Disaster," the King considered himself a soldier committed to the regeneration of his country, and was prepared to intervene in political life (albeit initially without going beyond the bounds of the Constitution) more assiduously than his parents had done. Both the Crown and the armed forces initiated programs of "nationalizing" activities intended to raise national feeling, similar to others seen in other European monarchies, such as a rapid increase in the number of royal tours to different parts of the country and expanded public ceremonies in which new recruits to the army or navy swore loyalty to the flag. In 1906, a group of army officers violently attacked Catalanist newspaper offices, and with the support of the monarch, succeeded in ensuring that military courts would try insults or other offences against the armed forces in the press.

The second great conflict of the first years of the twentieth century was the confrontation between clericalism and anticlericalism (see Chapter 18). On the extreme right, the Carlists and integrist Catholics reorganized themselves and set up an extensive network of newspapers and *círculos* (social clubs) which achieved some success in elections in the Basque Country and Navarre. Moreover, even outside these religiously defined parties, Catholic civil society in general experienced an impressive level of growth in these years, driven, as in other parts of Europe, by a desire to "re-Christianize" society in the face of the modern advance of unbelief. A steady series of religious campaigns and pilgrimages succeeded each other, and giant churches, cathedrals, and monuments to the Sacred Heart of Jesus were built; in 1882, the construction of the Sagrada Família by architect Antoni Gaudí began in Barcelona. However, in contrast to the practice followed by the Church in Belgium and many other countries, the Spanish Catholic Church founded scarcely any workers' unions. Nor did a Catholic political party emerge: thanks to the monarchy and the influence the Church itself exerted in the Conservative Party, none was needed. The spearhead of the Church's expansion was in the schools controlled by religious orders, many of which had fled to Spain to escape the secularizing policies of the French Third Republic.

Faced with this pro-clerical expansionism, the left, aided by many intellectuals, made a banner of anticlericalism. It was equally prompted by a theoretical idea of secularizing the state and a desire to push back ecclesiastical influence over Spanish society, which in the view of some regenerationists had led to the decadence of Catholic nations compared to the rise of the Protestant countries. This cause gave new vigor to republicanism, which achieved some electoral victories when it managed to overcome its internal divisions, thanks to universal male suffrage. In cities such as Barcelona and Valencia mass republican movements arose, spurred on by populist arguments with a strongly anticlerical tone and the charismatic leadership of notable individuals such as journalist Alejandro Lerroux and novelist Vicente Blasco Ibáñez. These secularist and Spanish nationalist republicans clashed with the forces of clericalism, which included Basque and Catalan nationalists. Alongside these movements, a reformist republicanism also emerged among urban professionals, which had the support of the younger intellectuals headed by José Ortega y Gasset who called for a definitive "Europeanization" of Spain (see Chapter 32). These republicans demanded constitutional reform to restore freedom of religion, and were willing to accept the monarchy if, as in the United Kingdom or Belgium, it evolved into a true parliamentary monarchy and made itself compatible with democracy.

In the third place, the Spanish public arena was shaken by social and labor conflicts, which still included traditional food riots, but among which other forms of collective action such as strikes were increasingly widespread (see Chapter 17). Anarchist tendencies, opposed to any kind of political participation, were strong in Spain, rooted in regions where federalist republicanism had flourished previously, such as Catalonia and Andalusia. As throughout Europe, anarchists turned to terrorist attacks—what they called "propaganda by deed"—and assassinated prominent figures, including French president Sadi Carnot and King Umberto I of Italy. In Spain, anarchists attempted to kill King Alfonso XIII on his wedding day and assassinated two prime ministers, Cánovas del Castillo in 1897 and José Canalejas in 1912. However, following the model of French syndicalism, they also founded unions that employed the general strike as a revolutionary method in 1910–11. These unions formed the Confederación Nacional del Trabajo (National Confederation of Labour, CNT), the largest workers' organization in Spain. Marxist socialist organizations in line with the directives of the Second International began earlier but developed more slowly, and were divided between two branches, a political party, the *Partido Socialista Obrero Español* (Spanish Socialist Workers' Party or PSOE) and a union confederation, the *Unión General de Trabajadores* (General Workers' Union or UGT), both with a gradualist approach opposed to anarchist revolutionary adventures (see Chapter 30).

Carlists, nationalists, republicans, and Socialists all shared in the different aspects of mass politics of the period, since they all formed political communities "from the cradle to the grave" with multiple satellite organizations. If nationalists placed emphasis on traditional music or the national landscape, republicans and workers' movements insisted on the emancipatory virtues of education. All had their own particular symbols [the Basque nationalists invented their flag, the *Ikurriña*, with a design similar to the British one; Catalanists adopted an old folk song, *Els Segadors* (The Reapers), as their national anthem] as well as holidays (republicans celebrated February 11, anniversary of the First Republic of 1873; Socialists celebrated May 1 promoted by the International) and heroes (such as the martyrs of the Carlist tradition). In areas where these movements managed to take root, they displaced the governmental parties: in Barcelona not a single Conservative or Liberal deputy was elected after 1901. Their favorite field of operation was in the *ayuntamientos* or municipal councils, but they encountered greater difficulties in translating their influence to a national stage. In contrast to their German or Italian coreligionists who had built up substantial groups within their national parliaments by the turn of the century, the Spanish Socialists did not enter the Congress until 1910, and then only thanks to an electoral alliance with republicans that broke with the party's traditional rejection of any understanding with forces they considered bourgeois (see Chapter 30).

Regenerationist criticisms of political corruption and the lack of connection between the political system and Spanish society also affected the established official parties of the *turno*. Renewal came with the disappearance of their historic leaders Cánovas, murdered in 1897, and Sagasta, who died in 1903. The search for new leaders gave rise to confrontations between rival factions and a high degree of government instability up to 1907, which led to constant intervention by the young Alfonso XIII. The Liberal Party, given the difficulties it found in choosing leaders, effectively left their appointment in the hands of the King. Though it might seem contradictory, the Liberals, who knew their social base to be weak, encouraged this active role for the Crown, while the Conservatives preferred to confine the monarch to a symbolic role.

The Conservatives also took the initiative in renewal. Francisco Silvela, a subtle, gentlemanly figure who had denounced corruption in his party but retired early, formulated a program that was implemented by his successor Antonio Maura, a minister in Liberal governments prior to his change of party in 1902. Also a Catholic lawyer but with a much greater capacity for leadership, he was idolized by his followers. Maura proposed a "revolution from above" that would avoid a revolution from below by creating a bond between the monarchy and the Catholic upper and middle classes concerned with social order, similar to the alliance of support achieved by Bismarck in unified Germany. To set this in motion in 1907, he passed a new electoral law that introduced compulsory voting and removed polling stations from the control of local mayors, a measure that achieved only limited results, since clientelist culture did not recede in the rural world that still made up most of Spain. Maura also sought to reform local administration by dislodging the bases of *caciquismo*, but it was blocked by strong opposition from the left that distrusted the approaches Maura had made to Catalan regionalists and rejected the proposal for corporate voting. This was popular among regenerationists who believed that allowing economic associations, other organizations and individuals to vote would produce a more "authentic" representation of society. It would also favor Catholics, whose civil society organizations were the strongest in rural areas. His "long government" (1907 to 1909) was marked by a hardening of repression of anarchists and a certain stress on moral rigor seen, for example, in the prohibition of gambling. It also undertook nationalistic projects such as the construction of a new navy, which Spain had lacked ever since the "Disaster."

For its part, the Liberal Party found a new leader in José Canalejas. An ex-republican lawyer, Canalejas, was the Spanish representative of a new European liberalism in favor of more state intervention and equality of opportunity, exemplified by David Lloyd George in Britain and the Radicals in France. During his period in government between 1910 and 1912, Canalejas brought into reality the old demands of the left, such as obligatory military service—virtually ending the discriminatory system through which those with sufficient means had escaped it—and the abolition of indirect taxes on basic necessities. Similarly, he also sought to check the expansion of the religious orders that were coming into Spain from France, which led to a mobilization against him of the Church hierarchy and Catholic civil society, and extended labor legislation and the practice of state arbitration in strikes. The Liberals were attuned to the cultural concerns of the regenerationists, and so sponsored improvements in the working conditions of teachers, grants to study abroad, and the creation of scientific centers. Hence in 1907 they founded the *Junta para la Ampliación de Estudios e Investigaciones Científicas* (Council for the Extension of Studies and Scientific Research), which represented a huge step forward in the development of Spanish science and intellectual culture.

Conservatives and Liberals agreed on some matters such as foreign policy, since both wanted Spain to escape from the international isolation that had been evident in 1898. To do so they moved the country closer to the *Entente* that had been formed at the beginning of the new century by Britain and France, which implied taking charge of the colonization of northern Morocco, a key area in the international equilibrium in the western Mediterranean. However, this new colonial war became highly conflictive inside Spain, where it was associated with the business interests of the oligarchy. In July 1909, the embarkation of conscript troops destined for Morocco from Barcelona unleashed what became known as the *Semana Trágica* or "Tragic Week." In an atmosphere well fertilized by anticlerical movements, an anti-military riot evolved into generalized attacks on religious buildings and the burning of several churches and convents. The severe repression of these protests by the Maura government generated a Europe-wide campaign in defense of the libertarian educator Francesc Ferrer i Guàrdia, who was unjustly condemned and executed for his supposed responsibility for the disturbances, and undermined the agreements that had been reached between the two governmental parties. In a rare monarchist incursion into the field of mass campaigning, the Liberals had already joined republicans in demonstrations against Maura's right-wing policies, supported by the great progressive newspapers. However, they now demanded power, for which the Conservatives did not forgive them.

These bad relations between Liberals and Conservatives continued for years, and exploded after the assassination of Canalejas in 1912. The battle of the slogans of "¡*Maura No!*" and "¡*Maura Sí!*" illustrated the tensions created by the figure of the Conservative leader, who refused to alternate in power with the Liberal Party, and so broke a basic rule of the system. Both parties fragmented once again into yet more factions, which led to a further reinforcement of the powers of Alfonso XIII, who was seen by large sections of public opinion, including the republican reformists who aspired to replace the Liberals, as the savior of the nation. In contrast to the process that was taking place in the same period in the north and northwest of Europe, the Spanish monarchy did not evolve toward democracy, but toward a strengthening of royal power. Some characteristics of the Restoration remained: governments still won elections, and *caciquismo*, with its roots in the political demobilization of the countryside, permeated political and administrative life. However, the spread of regenerationist ideas and the explosion of mass politics had altered the panorama, intensified conflicts, and undermined the alternation in power between Conservatives and Liberals. Far from remaining stagnant and immobile, Spain, influenced by the transformations that were being experienced by other European societies, was entering a new period of uncertainty.

Further reading

Álvarez Junco, José, *The Emergence of Mass Politics in Spain. Populist Demagoguery* and *Republican Culture, 1890–1910*, Brighton: Sussex Academic Press, 2002.

Balfour, Sebastian, *The End of the Spanish Empire, 1898–1923*, Oxford: Clarendon Press, 1997.

Dardé, Carlos, "Fraud and the Passivity of the Electorate in Spain, 1875–1923," in E. Posada-Carbó (ed.), *Elections before Democracy*, London: ILAS/MacMillan, 1996, pp. 201–22.

González, M.J, "'Neither God nor Monster': Antonio Maura and the Failure of Conservative Reformism in Restoration Spain (1893–1923)," *European History Quarterly*, 32, 3 (2002), pp. 307–34.

Jacobson, Stephen, *Catalonia's Advocates: Lawyers, Society, and Politics in Barcelona, 1759–1900*, Chapel Hill: University of North Carolina Press, 2009.

Moreno-Luzón, Javier, "Political Clientelism, Elites, and *Caciquismo* in Restoration Spain (1875–1923)," *European History Quarterly*, 37, 3 (2007), pp. 417–41.

Moreno-Luzón, Javier, *Modernizing the Nation. Spain during the Reign of Alfonso XIII, 1902–1931*, Brighton: Sussex Academic Press, 2012.

Shubert, Adrian, *A Social History of Modern Spain*: London: Routledge, 1990.

Varela Ortega, José, "Aftermath of Splendid Disaster: Spanish Politics before and after the Spanish American War of 1898," *Journal of Contemporary History*, 15, 2 (1980), pp. 317–44.

CHAPTER 5
THE CONTESTED QUEST FOR MODERNIZATION: 1914–36
Nigel Townson

The period 1914–1936 was one of profound, tumultuous change in European history, to which Spain was no exception. Although a nonbelligerent during the First World War, it was deeply affected by the conflict in political, economic, and social terms. During the war and postwar period, the Spanish liberal regime, as in other European countries, was assailed by forces from the left and right. Nor was Spain made different by the collapse of the Restoration regime into military dictatorship in 1923. In reality, it mirrored the experience of many other European states, as nearly all of the republics that emerged in the wake of the world war succumbed to authoritarianism. The Spanish case proved exceptional insofar as the process proved reversible: the dictatorship eventually gave way to democracy, the republic of 1931 being the last to emerge in interwar Europe. Neither fascism nor communism constituted a major force in Spain until 1936, but their ideological impact and in particular their attack on liberalism strongly conditioned the interwar years.

Still, the fact that three very different political regimes were established in Spain over the course of just twenty-two years is incomprehensible without reference to the broader economic and social realities. Modernizing processes such as industrialization, urbanization, secularization, and the growth of the working and middle classes in the towns and cities during the 1910s and 1920s not only generated new political expectations, but also sharpened social tensions. The cultural and socioeconomic fragmentation fostered by modernization made the framing of a national political consensus more difficult than ever. The resulting struggle between competing visions of State and society revealed that Spain's quest for modernization, as in virtually all other parts of Europe, was a heavily contested, often violent process. Indeed, the outbreak of civil war in 1936 was merely an indication of the extent to which Spanish society had become irreconcilably polarized.

The war years (1914–18)

Up to the 1990s, the liberal Restoration regime (1875–1923) was generally characterized as a time of painstaking economic growth, social rigidity, and political immobility. The research of the past twenty-five years, however, has largely debunked this interpretation (see Chapter 4). The First World War did not herald a new economic era, but it did accelerate preexisting modernizing trends. Spain's neutrality during the conflict—a result of the country's peripheral international status and military irrelevance—permitted it to take advantage of soaring wartime demand while avoiding the ruinous costs of combat. Workers were sucked into the city from the countryside as industries such as iron and steel, shipbuilding, textiles, light metals, and especially mining all recorded extraordinary profits. Wartime demand also led to the foundation of Spain's first aeronautical manufacturer, *Hispano Aviación*. The surge in exports permitted Spain to post its first positive balance of trade in modern history, causing gold reserves at the Bank of Spain to rocket from under 350 million pesetas in 1914 to just over 2,000 million in 1917. The service sector grew even more rapidly than industry as reflected, for example, in the doubling in the number of bank branches between 1914 and 1920. Even Spain's agrarian economy, often portrayed as backward and stagnant, grew by 27 percent during the first three years of the war. Employers, desperate not to interrupt production, granted substantial wage raises, between 20 and 50 percent in the case of Catalan workers. Overall, the Spanish economy grew substantially during the war.

Yet this is not the whole story. The growth in employment was offset to an important degree by a drastic fall in emigration and the return of many workers from abroad. The economic upswing was also extremely uneven. Asturias, the Basque Country, and Catalonia may have benefited hugely from the war, but other regions did not. Many sectors of the economy may have boomed, but others, such as the fruit export business, fared badly. In fact, both imports and exports were adversely affected by railway disruption and the crippling shortage of shipping: imports plummeted in both volume and value between 1914 and 1918, while exports dropped in volume by a third. The massive rise in the value of exports was due to inflation, but this simultaneously hit living standards hard as it consistently outstripped wages. The price of basic foodstuffs, for example, climbed by 67 percent during the war years: bread riots became commonplace in towns and cities from 1915 onward. Mounting social desperation was reflected in a sharp rise in muggings and robberies, while in Madrid alone there were 28,000 beggars during the winter of 1917–18, according to the newspaper *El Sol*. The urban situation was made worse still by overcrowded and squalid housing. To alleviate the widespread misery, local authorities handed out bread and even money to hungry mobs. The national authorities did little. The Liberal Cabinet of 1915–17 failed to control prices effectively or to prevent the export of food, raw materials, and manufactured goods that were considered vital to domestic living standards. The prime minister, the Count of Romanones, promised aggrieved union representatives to take action, but did next to nothing. The government did try to raise a tax on war profits and money for public works, which would have lessened the distress, but both initiatives failed. The mass misery and deprivation prompted the socialist and anarcho-syndicalist movements—traditional rivals—to hold a general strike in December 1916, the first in Spanish history. Despite the strike's success, the government, in the words of one union boss, stuck with its policy of "suicidal inhibition."

Opposition to the Restoration regime was not just the result of the socioeconomic crisis. Public opinion in Spain was deeply divided over the war in Europe. While the military, the Catholic Church, and conservatives in general were *germanófilos*, or supporters of the German cause, republicans, socialists, and regionalists were *aliádofilos*. Criticism by the latter of the Restoration system was muted by the support of the Liberal Count of Romanones for the Allied cause and by the conviction that the king too was sympathetic to it. As it became apparent that neither the Liberal nor the Conservative governments were willing to make a diplomatic gesture in support of the Allies and that the king was more of a *germanófilo* than an *aliádofilo*, progressive opinion went on the offensive, spurred on not only by the fall of the 300-year-old Romanov dynasty during the Russian Revolution in March 1917, but also by the sudden closure of the Cortes in February 1917 and the suspension of all constitutional guarantees the following month.

Still, the catalyst for the "crisis of 1917" was not the anti-Restoration opposition but, ironically, a pillar of the conservative establishment: the army (see Chapter 21). In late 1916 and early 1917, *Juntas de Defensa* (Defence Councils), a type of unofficial trade union, had sprung up in barracks throughout Spain to defend the interests of the officer corps. Their chief grievance concerned the system of promotions, above all the favors increasingly dispensed by the king, which tended to benefit either those on active service in the Moroccan Protectorate, Spain's last major colony, or those with links to the court. The regenerationist rhetoric of the protesting officers, with their manifesto call for "renovation", along with their brazen defiance of king and Cabinet, convinced the political opposition that the *Juntas* might become an ally in its struggle against the Restoration system. Sympathy for the *Juntas* was arguably underpinned by the hope that they might, as in the nineteenth century, topple the government by means of a *pronunciamiento* (a military uprising in favor of a political party or movement). But this misread the motivation of the *Juntas*. The overriding objective of the upstart officers was their own corporate self-interest: the reform of the promotions, not the political, system. This was, in Gerald Meaker's words, a "revolt of the bureaucrats." Once the Conservative government of Eduardo Dato met the officers' main demand on June 1917, there was little likelihood of them joining forces with the republicans, socialists, and regionalists, all of whom they viewed in any case as subversive.

Despite the disarming of the *Juntas*, the opposition still decided to hold an "Assembly of Parliamentarians" on July 19. The Assembly called on the government to hold clean elections to a constituent Cortes, which would then decide the fate of the Restoration. But this was a muddled venture from the outset. For the Lliga Regionalista de Catalunya, the driving force behind the meeting, the Assembly formed part of an ambitious strategy that was designed to displace the landed and financial elites in Madrid in favor of the modernizing industrial and commercial classes. The Lliga also aimed to establish a federal State in Spain that would give Catalonia far greater autonomy. It was no coincidence that the Assembly was held in Barcelona, or that forty-six of the sixty-eight politicians present were from Catalonia. Still, the roadmap drawn up by the Lliga leader, Francesc Cambó, was decidedly conservative (see Chapter 31). It was unlikely to be seconded by the Lliga's republican, socialist and Reformist allies, especially since the lynchpin of Cambó's plan was the Conservative leader Antonio Maura. For good measure, Cambó called on the *Juntas* to back a "profound renovation" of the nation rather than limit themselves to a "sterile act of indiscipline." However, the plan failed because neither Maura nor his followers attended the Assembly. In any case, it is difficult to see how the Lliga's progressive allies could have cooperated with Maura as they regarded him as a dangerous reactionary.

Against the background of a deteriorating socioeconomic situation, the insubordination of the *Juntas*, the Assembly of Parliamentarians, and the increasingly revolutionary climate in Europe, both the socialist trade union movement, the *Unión General de Trabajadores* (General Union of Workers, or UGT), and the anarcho-syndicalist *Confederación Nacional del Trabajo* (National Confederation of Labour, or CNT), believed that the time had come for a "revolution" in Spain. Yet the socialists' revolutionary plan was distinctly limited. They regarded the establishment of a "bourgeois" republic as the next step in the march toward socialism. The Assembly, they believed, would advance that plan. For the socialists, the "revolution" was to consist of a peaceful general strike in support of a bourgeois republic. CNT syndicalists also viewed the creation of a republic as a necessary step on the road to liberation, but for the hardline anarchists within the CNT, the strike was an opportunity to launch a violent social revolution that would sweep aside the monarchy. They were convinced that a few days of street fighting would bring about the triumph of liberation socialism. Thus the "revolutionary" strike was undermined from the very beginning by its contradictory aims.

As it happened, the general strike badly misfired from the start. A railway stoppage, cleverly provoked by the government, led the UGT and CNT to bring the "revolution" forward to 5 August, even though preparations were incomplete. The strike was ferociously repressed by the government; eighty workers lost their lives and many hundreds were injured. It failed not only because of its calamitous organization, conflicting goals, and the severe repression, but also because it received little extra-union support. The *Juntas* actually played a prominent role in the repression, the republicans mostly rejected the strike as premature and the Lliga was simply terrified by it. Moreover, in October 1917 Cambó abandoned the Assembly once the king invited him to help form a government (see Chapter 31). The Assembly then split, the left blaming the Lliga leader for his "betrayal." The conflicting aims of the *Juntas*, the Assembly of Parliamentarians, and the trade unions during the "crisis of 1917", together with the lack of a coordinated strategy, rendered the opposition to the Restoration ineffective, above all once it became clear that the *Juntas* were not interested in changing the system, but their own corporate interests.

The failure of the Restoration opposition in 1917 was all the more painful because the very political edifice that they were attempting to demolish was itself in a woeful state. The *turno pacífico*, or prearranged rotation in power of the dynastic parties, had folded in 1913 as a result of the disputes between and within them. Between 1914 and 1917 the Count of Romanones and Eduardo Dato managed to keep a much-diminished version of the *turno* afloat, but the events of 1917 not only finished off the *turno* completely, but also fractured both parties irremediably. The Liberals and Conservatives governed thereafter not as parties, but either through a single faction or by cobbling together different factions. The exception was Maura's "national" government of 1918, which lasted seven months. This fracturing of the monarchist landscape brought instability and poor government: the average Cabinet between 1914 and 1923 lasted a mere five months, the *Cortes* were closed for lengthy periods, and no complete budget was passed by parliament between 1914 and 1920. In the meantime, the monarchists proved incapable of reforming the political status quo in such a way as to provide the constitutional monarchy with greater stability and legitimacy.

The crisis of dynastic politics was due only in part to ideological divergences. First, it was difficult to establish an undisputed leader in loosely assembled parties of notables that were bereft of the norms and procedures that generally characterized mass parties. Second, the fragmentation of these parties was heightened by the fact that they were bound together to a considerable extent by personal ties based on the exchange of resources, otherwise known as "clientelism": a politician or "patron" would obtain a public post or contract for a "client", and in exchange the "client" would provide the "patron" with their political support, most importantly at election time (see Chapter 4).

The dynastic parties were therefore divided into personal factions which, in turn, were subdivided into a mosaic of clientelistic networks. The very rootedness of these networks meant that parliamentary support for a leader depended to an important extent on his ability to meet the demands of the different *clientela*; that is to say, it was conditional on his access to the resources of the central administration. For example, numerous Liberals abandoned

Romanones for García Prieto in 1917 not as a result of an ideological dispute, but because the latter was more likely to return to power than the former. The sheer strength of the networks not only made it extremely difficult to establish an uncontested party leader, but also to undertake sweeping political reform. Still, the centrality of clientelism to party politics is far from exclusive to the Restoration system, despite what is often thought. It has remained an indelible feature of Spanish politics ever since, characterizing—to varying degrees—the Primo de Rivera dictatorship, the Second Republic, the Franco dictatorship, and democratic Spain. Needless to say, clientelism is not peculiar to modern Spain, as similar practices have proliferated throughouts Southern Europe and to differing extents in the rest of Europe.

Postwar years (1918–23)

The postwar period brought no respite for the beleaguered Restoration political order. The organized working class, especially the anarcho-syndicalist movement, was to present a major challenge to the system (See Chapter 17). This was first manifested in the peasant insurgency that engulfed the southern regions of Andalusia, Extremadura, and the Levante between 1918 and 1920. Both anarcho-syndicalist and socialist peasants took to rioting, crop burning, the invasion of estates, assaults on the homes of landowners, clashes with the Civil Guard, and the proclamation of "Bolshevik-style" republics in towns and *pueblos*. These uprisings were not a product of the postwar economic slump—landless laborers, for one, were much better off in 1918 than in 1914—but of rising expectations. "Russia has been the beacon flare", observed the American writer, John Dos Passos, on visiting the region. As in Germany, Italy, and Hungary, the Russian Revolution was of epic inspiration to workers in Spain. That said, the Russian Revolution only meant one thing for Spain's southern peasantry: the seizure of the land that they worked. As one manifesto put it, "It is no longer a time for requests or demands. It is the time to 'seize' . . . 'Peasants, let us follow our Russian brothers and quickly begin the era of social justice that we desire so much." Not until the Maura government of 1919 sent 20,000 troops to the south under General Emilio Barrera was the so-called Bolshevik Triennium finally extinguished.

By this stage, an even greater working-class insurgency was unfolding in the northeast of Spain. In January 1919 the CNT, then at its peak, launched a strike in Barcelona against the Ebro Power & Irrigation Company, popularly known as *La Canadiense* because its head office was in Toronto. This company was critical to the life of the city as it supplied energy to both the homes and the factories. The ostensible origin of the stoppage lay in a handful of dismissals, but its raison d'etre was to secure full and unequivocal recognition for the CNT. The anarcho-syndicalists wanted to guarantee the future of their movement in the conviction that it would eventually establish itself as one of the leading forces not only in Catalonia, but in all of Spain. During the 44-day stoppage Barcelona was plunged into darkness, making it seem like "the end of the world" according to one union leader. Meanwhile the CNT's textile, gas, water, and remaining electrical members came out in solidarity, and the socialists trade unions threatened to do the same. An alarmed government brokered a deal on March 17 that recognized all of the workers' main demands: the eight-hour day, a general wage rise, the release of nearly all those under arrest, and no reprisals against strikers. This was an extraordinary, unparalleled victory for the CNT. However, the intransigence of its extremists, who believed that the revolution was at hand, along with that of the hardline employers and military authorities, both of whom were determined to crush the CNT, wrecked the deal. The government's conciliatory approach, which was based on the pragmatic premise that the employers and syndicalists had to establish a means of coexistence, had been derailed by the extremists on both sides.

The conflict soon became a vicious circle: the revolutionaries, inspired by the Russian Revolution and the Bolshevik Triennium, waged war on industry bosses, the police, and dissenting workers, while employers enforced the lockout, fired union activists, and hired their own thugs to combat the violence of the CNT. The situation was further exacerbated by the resurrection of the *Somatén*, a civilian paramilitary group of up to 8,000 members, and by the army's heavy-handed approach, which included the use of machine guns, cannon, and the cavalry. The captain general not only backed this strategy, but made matters even worse by hiring hitmen to assassinate anarchists and their republican lawyers. As if this was not enough, the CNT also came under assault from the Carlist-backed *Sindicato Libre* (Free Union), which claimed 150,000 members in 1922. The anarchists alone were responsible for around 350 dead and wounded between 1917 and 1923. High-profile victims of the gangster-style warfare included the CNT leader Salvador Seguí, the Archbishop of Zaragoza, and the Conservative Prime Minister Eduardo Dato in 1921. The governments of these years veered disconcertingly between reconciliation and repression, but the struggle was ultimately settled by the ferocious General Severiano Martínez Anido who, as Civil Governor, waged a dirty war against the workers that included the infamous *"ley de fugas"* (Law on Fleeing), or shooting of prisoners on the pretense that they were trying to escape. By 1923, the ruthless repression, together with the postwar economic crisis, had crippled the CNT, losing it two-thirds of its members.

During the revolutionary conflict in Barcelona the army had achieved an astonishing degree of autonomy. It had been instrumental in rupturing the Romanones-sponsored settlement of March 1919 and then toppling the government the following month. In maintaining public order it acted as a State-within-the-State, pursuing its own punitive agenda often despite the views of the civilian authorities. The origin of this newfound assertiveness lay in the triumph of the *Juntas* in 1917. Since then, the *Juntas* had become a major protagonist of national politics, intimidating ministers, overturning governments—such as that of Eduardo Dato in 1917 or that of Joaquín Sánchez de la Toca in 1919—and installing the reactionary Juan de la Cierva as Minister of War in 1918. They effectively vetoed the formation of a Liberal Cabinet between 1919 and 1921 on the grounds that the Liberals were too weak in the face of the revolutionary threat. The political influence of the *Juntas* was nonetheless limited by their divergences with the *africanistas*, those serving in Morocco, who bitterly resented the privileges extracted by the mainland officers from the politicians, especially promotion by seniority rather than by merit. A reassertion of civilian power by the governments of 1922–23, however, led the army to close ranks: while the suppression of the *Juntas* alienated the peninsular soldiers, the *africanistas* were infuriated by the decision to place the Protectorate in Morocco under civilian command.

Military and civilian relations were to reach their nadir as a result of the shambolic retreat of the Spanish army at Annual in July 1921, during which 10,000 soldiers were killed at the hands of Rif tribesmen. This devastating reverse resonated all the more strongly within Spain, as it echoed not only Italy's humiliation at Adowa in Ethiopia from 1896, but also the "Disaster" of 1898. As if this were not bad enough, the army was now subjected to a campaign, spearheaded by the press and parliament, demanding "responsibilities" for the calamity. The campaign became a clamor once General Picasso completed his investigation into the debacle. The report painted a sorry picture of the Spanish army in Morocco, highlighting not only the army's strategic blunders, but also its many other shortcomings, including its endemic venality. The lengthy parliamentary debate over Picasso's findings made relations between the civilian and military authorities even more inflammatory than ever.

The ongoing confrontation between the politicians and the soldiers was heavily conditioned by the army's resolute conviction, fostered during the nineteenth century, that it—as opposed to parliament or the parties—embodied the national will. This belief had been disarmed during the early part of the Restoration by the determination of the regime's architect, Antonio Cánovas del Castillo, to keep the armed forces out of politics, which he duly achieved by appeasing them with control of the Ministry of War and the colonies. Humiliated by the "Disaster," the military had occasionally intervened in politics after 1898, most notably in 1905–6 in order to settle accounts with its critics. During the First World War, the army, convulsed by the twin threats of separatism and revolution, came to regard itself once more as the savior of the *patria*, a conviction that was bolstered by the revival of Spanish nationalism. Powerfully shaped by the nationalist fervor that gripped Europe during the First World War, as well as by the rise of Catalan regionalism and the working-class insurgency at home, the resurgence in Spanish nationalism was distinguished by a counterrevolutionary zeal and ardent religiosity. The liberal nationalism which had held sway before the war was now swept aside by a more combative and conservative genre, for which the nation was unequivocally identified with Catholicism, the monarchy, the empire, and the army. Some conservative intellectuals drew on contemporary forms of nationalism, such as filofascism, but many others looked to the past, rethinking the National Catholicism which had first been formulated during the late nineteenth century by the philosopher Marcelino Menéndez Pelayo and which would later triumph under Franco. This bellicose imagining of the nation may not have crystallized in a single movement or party, but it was sanctified by the State. In 1918, to take a leading example, 12 October was declared a national holiday, the *Fiesta de la Raza* (Holiday of the Race). Officially, this commemorated the day that Columbus set foot in the Americas, but it also happened to be the day, known as *el Pilar* (the Pillar), that Saint James received a vision from the Virgin Mary as she sat atop a pillar. In other words, 12 October was at once a secular *and* a Catholic commemoration, a means of fusing the nation's identity with Catholicism. This upsurge in Catholic nationalism climaxed with the dedication of Spain to the Sacred Heart of Jesus on May 30, 1919 by none other than the king himself (see Chapter18). Dressed for the occasion in military attire and attended by the entire Cabinet, which was gathered around an altar adorned with the national flag, Alfonso XIII consecrated Spain to the Sacred Heart of Jesus. The symbolism was unequivocal: the defining features of the Spanish nation were its Catholicism, monarchy, armed forces, and, by extension, its empire.

The febrile nationalist climate explains the army's political protagonism only in part. This was due, above all, to the complicity of the king. As head of state, Alfonso XIII was the key political player in Restoration Spain: he could appoint and dismiss ministers at will, as well as convoke and dissolve parliament as he saw fit. He was, in short, the arbiter of Spanish politics. He was also the commander-in-chief, enjoying extensive powers of patronage within the armed forces, something which he had exploited from the very beginning of his reign in order to create a military following that was personally loyal to him. Indeed, the Ministers of

War acted for many years as the personal agents of the monarch by accepting uncritically his constant "recommendations." During the First World War, Alfonso's undisguised sympathy for the army took a new turn. It was he who freed *Junta* leaders in 1917 without even consulting the prime minister; it was he who permitted the army to topple Cabinet after Cabinet; it was he who let the army repress the workers in Barcelona with impunity; and it was he who allowed the *Juntas* to install the hardline Juan de la Cierva as Minister of War. Traumatized by "the sinister effects of the Russian Revolution", noted a British diplomat, and increasingly disenchanted by civilian politics, he aided and abetted the ever greater involvement of the army in politics.

The king's embrace of a militantly Catholic and counterrevolutionary nationalism reflected his belief that the protection of his dynasty lay not in liberal parliamentarianism, but in an authoritarian regime. The postwar crisis of liberalism in Europe and the fall of the Romanovs and other dynasties, such as those in Germany and Austria-Hungary, increasingly convinced the king that the people's will ultimately resided in *his* person and that the Constitution had become a tiresome and unnecessary shackle upon his freedom of action. The final straw was the parliamentary debate over Annual, during which the socialist spokesman, Indalecio Prieto, accused the king of bearing responsibility for the military catastrophe. During the summer of 1923, Alfonso XIII spoke of the need for a "transitory dictatorship" and contemplated setting up a *Junta de Defensa Nacional* (National Defence Council) under his direction to replace the government. Antonio Maura advised him that the monarchy's future would be best served if the king himself were not to lead an authoritarian regime, but to leave this to the army. When General Miguel Primo de Rivera declared his coup d'état on September 13, 1923, six of the eight captain generals awaited the response of the monarch rather than immediately support him. The king responded by appointing Primo as his prime minister and then by dissolving the Cortes.

There has been much debate ever since as to whether the coup cut short a democratic reconfiguration of the political system—Raymond Carr's "strangling of a new birth"—or whether, on the contrary, it was already defunct. It can perhaps be argued that neither was strictly true. On the one hand, the reformist aspirations of García Prieto's government of 1922–23 had already encountered serious opposition, as shown by the clash with the Church over freedom of conscience and with the army over Morocco, and were unlikely to radically renew the system. On the other hand, it is clear that dynastic politicians of both hues were actively seeking a solution to the long-standing crisis of the system, as shown by the passing of a number of notable reforms, including the introduction of the first eight-hour working day in the world. What is undeniable is that Alfonso XIII could have done much more to defend and advance civilian power at the expense of the military, rather than the other way around. Had he done so, the constitutional regime of 1876 would have stood a far better chance of survival. It is also undeniable that by ratifying the *coup d'état* of Primo de Rivera, the King had taken the considerable risk of linking the future of his dynasty to that of a politically naïve and temperamentally unpredictable General. Not that the Spanish response to the crisis of liberalism following the First World War was at all unusual. On the contrary, there was to be a very long list of European countries, including Hungary in 1919, Italy in 1922, Portugal, Poland, and Lithuania in 1926, Yugoslavia in 1928, and Germany in 1933 that were, like Spain, to turn their backs on parliamentary liberalism in favor of right-wing authoritarianism.

The Primo de Rivera dictatorship (1923–30)

Arguably the least researched period of modern Spain, the dictatorship of Primo de Rivera has been the subject of only four general studies, three of which were published more than twenty-five years ago. This sparse coverage pales in comparison with the myriad accounts of the Restoration, the Second Republic, and the Franco dictatorship. The Primo de Rivera regime is often treated as an awkward, somewhat irrelevant *interregnum*, divorced from the Restoration before it and the Republic that came after it. Yet this is a mistake. The dictatorship was inextricably linked to both periods. On the one hand, the Primo years marked the triumph of the authoritarian currents that had been on the rise during the 1910s and early 1920s. On the other hand, the trajectory of the Republic is inexplicable without taking into account the extent to which right-wing authoritarianism was strengthened under Primo. In addition, the dictatorship is important in its own right: it broke with the constitutional regime of 1876 and heavily conditioned the future of the Bourbon monarchy. And it was at once a paradigm and an object lesson for the regime that replaced the Republic: the Franco dictatorship.

The Primo de Rivera dictatorship first dealt with the forces that had in large measure brought it about: Catalan separatism and revolutionary anarchism. The CNT was banned, its leaders arrested, and its activists hounded. By 1924, anarcho-syndicalist violence had dwindled into insignificance. Meanwhile, the Catalan flag was prohibited, the *Mancomunidad* dissolved, and usage of the Catalan language increasingly curbed. But Primo de Rivera did not limit the repression to Catalanism and anarchism alone. He also crushed the incipient Communist Party, and he was equally determined to eliminate parliamentary liberalism, dismissing "the old politics" as "the falsest and cruellest legal tyranny known to History." The two dynastic parties were banned, the Cortes closed, all constitutional rights suspended, and a system of strict censorship was introduced. Government was now embodied in a Military Directorate, with military men initially occupying all the civil governorships.

The visit of Primo de Rivera and the king to Mussolini's Italy in November 1923 indicated that fascism might become the template for the nascent regime, not least because Alfonso XIII boasted that the General was "my Mussolini", while Primo himself found much to admire in the Italian dictatorship. Certainly there seemed to be "borrowings" from fascism: the *Organización Corporativa Nacional* (National Corporative Organization, or OCN) that appeared to pursue the fascist dream of superseding the struggle between capital and labor; a much more active economic role for the State, including the establishment of State monopolies such as Telefónica, CAMPSA, and Iberia; and the creation of an official party, the *Unión Patriótica* (Patriotic Union, or UP). Still, the similarities with Italy were limited: the workers that participated in the National Corporative Organization were not fascists but mainly from the Socialist UGT, while the right to strike was retained; State intervention in the economy and State-led monopolies did not distinguish fascism alone; and the *Unión Patriótica* was not made up of fascists, but authoritarian Catholics and *Mauristas*. Nor did the *Unión Patriótica* possess a fascist ideology, as indicated by the fact that its motto, "Patria, Religion, Monarchy", was a reworking of the Carlist one. The UP concerned itself with patriotic parades and masses, while acting as a recruitment agency for the public sector. Despite the dictator's diatribes against *caciquismo*, the UP represented a new form of clientelism.

The Primo de Rivera dictatorship signaled above all the triumph of the authoritarian tendencies that had originated in the aftermath of 1898 and had grown vertiginously during the First World War. The ideology of the dictatorship was counterrevolutionary and nationalist, rejecting parliamentary liberalism while embracing Catholicism, the monarchy, the army, and the empire. At the same time, the new regime drew powerfully on the post-1898 rhetoric of regeneration. Primo portrayed himself, in the words of the regenerationist thinker Joaquín Costa, as an "iron surgeon" who would forge a "new Spain." One of the pillars of Costa's modernizing vision was the nationalization of the masses. The dictatorship made the most serious effort thus far to inculcate the Spanish masses with a national identity. National symbols were emblazoned on public buildings, the only flag permitted was the Spanish one, and civil servants had to work in Spanish alone. In the regime's discourse, the *patria*—rather than the monarchy or Catholicism—was the key identifying element; that is to say, sovereignty was considered to reside above all in the nation, which in Primo's thinking had the State as its "permanent representative organ." It was no coincidence that the single party was called the *Unión Patriótica*, as opposed to *Unión Monárquica* or *Católica*, or that an official newspaper was titled *La Nación*. Heritage sites were now dubbed "national" monuments and the 6,000 schools that were built under Primo were "national" centers of learning where the pupils were drilled in the "national" language and versed in their "national" glories. In everyday life, nationalist imagery proliferated as never before, such as on stamps, banknotes, sweet papers, almanacs, and so on. The exalted *españolismo* of the dictatorship was reflected in the high-profile celebration of the *Fiesta de la Raza* each year and in the two international Exhibitions held in Spain in 1929, both of which were naturally organized around a *Plaza de España*. In contrast to the old liberal vision, this new nationalism was not self-pitying and angst-ridden, but assertive, populist, triumphalist.

The dictatorship was genuinely popular during its early years. This was partly because its ideas resonated with a substantial swathe of conservative opinion, though its support was not limited to the right. The UGT not only participated in the National Corporative Organization, the lynchpin of which was the *comités paritarios* (arbitration committees) which negotiated working conditions and settled disputes, but also took part in local government, the provincial administration and national economic councils. The President of the UGT, Francisco Largo Caballero, even joined the Council of State in 1925. But why did the socialists collaborate with the military dictator, especially one that repressed another union, the CNT? The UGT worked alongside the dictator precisely because he removed its archrival, thereby providing the UGT with an unprecedented opportunity. Indeed, by 1928 the socialist trade union had acquired a record 235,000 members and established itself in areas such as rural Andalusia and Castilla-La Mancha that had hitherto been controlled by the CNT. The socialists also benefited from the suppression of the Communist Party. In reality, the UGT leadership was not so much liberal or democratic in outlook as corporatist. From the perspective of Largo Caballero, the chance for the UGT to embed itself within the interstices of a corporatist State—albeit a right-wing one—was too good to be missed.

Support for the dictatorship was also due to its achievement in solving the Moroccan question. In September 1925 the Spanish army, in tandem with the French, defeated the Rif tribes at Alhucemas. A few months later, their leader, the infamous Abd el-Krim, was captured. By July 1927 the war was over. The pacification of Morocco generated such an upsurge in support for the regime that the dictator, despite having promised to rule for just ninety days, was encouraged to undertake the institutionalization of the regime, starting with the replacement of the Military Directorate by a Civilian Directorate in late 1925.

Even more important in terms of the regime's popularity was the boom of the 1920s (See Chapter 9). During the dictatorship the economy grew at the redoubtable rate of 5.5 percent *per annum*, a product not just of the favorable international context, but also of the State's interventionist policies. This marked a new departure in Spanish economic policy-making, reflecting its regenerationist commitment. An essential element of Costa's vision was the implementation of a massive program of state-funded public works, especially the construction of roads, reservoirs, and schools. Thus the extraordinary budget of 1926 was designed to improve the country's road network as well as the exploitation of the country's water resources, thereby extending electrification and the amount of land under irrigation. The Hydraulic Confederations' Board, which introduced irrigation systems to 180,000 hectares of land in Costa's home region, Aragon, was a notable result of this policy. A total of 9,455 kilometers of road were also built, including the first *nacional* or trunk roads. The boom of the 1920s brought about far-reaching social and economic change. By boosting the industrial and service sectors it led to a huge expansion in the urban working and middle classes. In fact, by 1930 less than half the workforce was located on the land for the very first time in Spanish history. In other words, Spain had shifted, under Primo, from an agrarian to an industrial and service economy. The accelerated modernization of Spanish society was evident in a multitude of ways: in economic terms, by the ever greater presence of new technologies such as cars and telephones; in cultural terms, by the rise of professional sport as a branch of the modern leisure industry, especially the launching of the Football League in 1928; in artistic terms, by the Iberian Artists' Exhibition of 1925 and the emergence of the "Generation of 1927"; and in gender terms, the reform of local government led to the appointment of the first female councilors and mayors. From this perspective, the dictator had indeed overseen the emergence of a "new Spain": an urban, modern, and increasingly educated and secular one.

The fact that Primo's *putsch* of 1923 had failed to provoke mass protests or a general strike had been indicative not only of the incapacity of the monarchists to mobilize the populace in defense of the Restoration system, but also of the disarray and demoralization of the anti-Restoration forces: the CNT was exhausted, the republicans were at a low ebb, and the socialists were still rebuilding after the failure of 1917. The first attempt to overthrow the dictatorship was undertaken not by the republicans or organized working class, but the monarchists. The coup of 1923 had returned Spain to the nineteenth century insofar as it had legitimized the use of violence in order to achieve regime change. In 1926, a group of Liberals linked up with disaffected elements in the army in an effort to dislodge the dictator by means of a *pronunciamiento*, but the conspiracy was foiled. In 1929, a wider-ranging conspiracy, centered on the exiled Conservative leader José Sánchez Guerra and including republicans and anarcho-syndicalists, was also thwarted.

By this stage, the dictatorship was nonetheless in serious trouble. Ironically, Primo had managed to alienate a bulwark of the army. The promotion by merit and outright favoritism that came to characterize the dictatorship after 1926 disenchanted the artillery corps above all, which had abided by a system of promotion by seniority since 1891. The protestations of the Corps eventually led Primo to disband it, which notably strengthened the military opposition to the regime. The employers' associations, initially among Primo's most fulsome supporters, had also become hostile to the dictatorship because they bitterly resented State intervention in the economy, especially the *comités paritarios* and the attempt to introduce an income tax. A further source of protest was the students, outraged by the recognition of two private Catholic universities (which ended the State monopoly on higher education), by the persecution of liberal academics, and by the closure of the Central University in Madrid. Virtually all progressive intellectuals, such as the philosopher José Ortega y Gasset (see Chapter 32) or the celebrity doctor and humanist Gregorio Marañón, had also become disenchanted by the dictatorship, in addition to liberal institutions such as Madrid's prestigious *Ateneo* (Atheneum). Still, the most important reason for the dictatorship's catastrophic loss of support was the currency crisis. In 1928 the peseta began to drop in value as a result of the State's mountainous debt, the deficit in the balance of payments, and the withdrawal of foreign investment. Unable to halt the plummeting of the peseta, the Minister for the Economy, José Calvo Sotelo, resigned on January 20, 1930. By now, a number of generals were so disillusioned by the regime that they had gone over to the republican cause, while more conservative ones were urging Alfonso XIII to revive the Restoration order. The situation was made more unstable still by the dictatorship's manifest failure to develop its own institutions, the king and the dictator both rejecting a draft constitution in 1929. Overwhelmed by the economic crisis and the ever-expanding opposition, Primo de Rivera decided to consult the captain generals, but not one of them supported him. So he, too, resigned on January 28, 1930.

The fall of the Primo de Rivera dictatorship, like that of the Restoration before it, was due in large measure to its inability to respond effectively to the interests of the rapidly expanding urban working and middle classes. During the first third of the twentieth century, Spain underwent massive change as millions of peasants abandoned the land, the towns and cities doubled their populations, and literacy, secularization, and associational life all advanced considerably. By the end of the 1920s, the modernizing ideals and political aspirations harbored by the "new Spain" had simply superseded the purview of a Catholic authoritarian such as Primo de Rivera.

The demise of the dictatorship did not make the fall of the monarchy inevitable, despite the damage done to the Bourbon brand by its symbiotic relationship with the military regime. Nonetheless, both Alfonso XIII and the Restoration politicians demonstrated during the course of 1930 and early 1931 that they were still too remote from the realities of modern, urban Spain to provide a solution to the ongoing political crisis. They were too wedded to the politics of factionalism, dynastic infighting, and clientelism to undertake fundamental political reform. They also badly miscalculated the national mood by taking over a year to organize a new round of elections. By contrast, the republicans and socialists were much more in tune with the expectations of a modernizing society and were hailed as the saviors of the nation, as opposed to the discredited forces of the *ancien régime*. This explains why the republican-socialist coalition was able to turn the nationwide municipal elections of April 12, 1931 into a plebiscite on the future of the monarchy. The victory of the dynastic parties in the countryside did little more than confirm the durability of their clientelistic networks. On the other hand, the triumph of the republicans and socialists in the cities, where the vote was relatively free, provided a much more accurate idea of the state of public opinion. Indeed, Alfonso XIII found himself completely alone: neither the Cabinet nor the army nor even the Civil Guard would stand by him. On the day he went into exile, April 14, 1931, the Second Republic was proclaimed, Spain's third regime in less than a decade.

The Second Republic: (1931–36)

Work on the Second Republic has been blighted from the outset by historians of both the left and the right viewing it as a political battlefield in which they have to defend their respective "sides." Even today, there are a good many historians who skew their accounts by passionately upholding the cause that most closely approximates their own political prejudices. Thankfully, there have always been historians who have striven to understand the Republic in all its complexity, and not just as a Manichean morality tale in which left confronts right.

The great promise of the Second Republic was that, in contrast to the Restoration or the Dictatorship, it would construct a political order that did justice to the transformation of Spanish society over the previous three decades. Modernization, democratization, and secularization were the keynotes of the "revolution." As Minister of War Manuel Azaña put it, "for us the Republic is . . . an instrument of construction, for remaking the State and Spanish society from their foundations to the very top." During the first nine months, the republicans and socialists went a long way toward achieving their aims. The provisional government of April–June 1931 decreed a whole raft of reforms: the republicanization and streamlining of the armed forces; the commitment to "sow Spain with schools," in the words of the Minister of Public Instruction; and the reinvention of the *comités paritarios* in the form of the *jurados mixtos* (arbitration boards) which, unlike the former, would be extended to rural workers; and the Municipal Boundaries and Obligatory Cultivation decrees, both of which were designed to improve the lot of rural workers. The Constitution of December 1931 signaled a seismic shift in Spanish history. Following decades of struggle in defense of women's rights and in particular the courageous performance of Clara Campoamor during the constitutional debates (being opposed not only by many male deputies, but also by the only two other female representatives in the Cortes, the republican Victoria Kent and the socialist Margarita Nelken), women finally obtained the vote and were able to cast their ballots in a national election for the first time in 1933. This was shortly after women in Britain got it (1928), but long before those in supposedly more "advanced" nations such as France (1944), Italy (1946), and Switzerland (1970). The Constitution also separated Church from State, removed the Church from the educational arena, recognized freedom of conscience, and no longer made full citizenship dependent upon being a Catholic. Other long-denied rights were also granted, such as civil marriage, divorce, and civil burial. Numerous articles in the Constitution contained extensive lists of reforms, thereby committing future governments to their realization. Article 45, for example, obliged the State to regulate "coverage for illness, accidents, unemployment, old age, invalidity and death; the employment of women and children and especially maternity leave; the working day and the minimum and family wage; annual paid holidays; the conditions of employment of Spanish workers abroad": in short, the prospect of a fully-fledged social security system.

These wide-ranging reforms were all the more remarkable as they were undertaken in the midst of the Great Depression. Spain may not have been as deeply affected by the Crash of 1929 as most other European countries due to its high tariff walls, but sectors such as mining, building, metallurgy, and certain agricultural exports were badly hit, while rising unemployment was exacerbated by endemic structural underemployment. The example set by the new regime was also remarkable because most of the republics established during the interwar period—of which the Spanish one was the last—had already collapsed. At a time when more and more of Europe was succumbing to a tide of right-wing authoritarianism, the

Second Republic stood out not merely as a new democracy, but also as one that was prepared to tackle the challenges of modernization through far-reaching reform.

But the Republic was afflicted by serious fault lines from the outset. Within the republican-socialist coalition that triumphed in the general election of June 1931 (winning more than 400 of the 473 seats), there were two visions of the Republic: for the left republicans and socialists, the Republic was meaningless without substantial reforms (which in practice meant *their* reforms), but for the moderate republicans, the principal objective was to establish the regime as a parliamentary democracy. While not opposing reform, the moderates held that change should be calibrated according to its support: only in this way, they argued, would the new regime be consolidated. The first fissure produced by these conflicting visions occurred in October 1931 when the two Catholic ministers, Premier Niceto Alcalá-Zamora and Interior Minister Miguel Maura, resigned over article 26 on the grounds that it constituted a frontal attack on the Catholic Church. The second split took place two months later when the Radical Party, by far the biggest of the republican parties and the chief representative of the industrial and commercial classes, departed the Cabinet as a result of its divergences with the Socialist Party. By this stage, the government, although still enjoying a parliamentary majority, had effectively been reduced in social terms to a minority: the socialist working class and the most progressive elements of the urban middle classes, while against it stood at least half the working class and most of the urban and rural middle classes. The uncompromising and sectarian outlook of the political left had rapidly reduced its support. Further fissures lay within the left itself, as became clear over the next two years as the left-republican-socialist governments under Manuel Azaña struggled to advance their reformist agenda.

Within the republican camp there were fault lines that ran even deeper than the party divisions. The first major problem was fiscal policy. Despite the Great Depression, the damaging debt passed on by the dictatorship and the low taxes that prevailed in Spain, the governments of the Republic never introduced an effective income tax and never accepted deficit spending. As a result, their policy-making promises often outran their ability to deliver. Thus the left-wing governments of 1931–33 were unable to fulfill their pledge to "sow Spain with schools" because of a lack of funds. Equally, the Agrarian Reform Act of 1932 was only partly implemented because the resources to execute this complex and demanding piece of legislation were not available. The Radicals' pledge to establish a Ministry of Health once in power was similarly ditched for fiscal reasons. As a result, the rhetoric of the republicans and socialists was repeatedly undone by reality. This created widespread disillusionment, which in turn undermined the credibility and legitimacy of the Republic.

An even more momentous problem, though, was the patrimonial attitude of the left toward the Republic. For the forces of the left, the Republic was *their* regime: just as the right had governed Spain for the last fifty years, so the left could now expect to rule Spain for the foreseeable future. This attitude had devastating consequences. First, the left did not view the Constitution as a framework of national consensus and integration. On the contrary, they consciously pursued a left-wing agenda that alienated many sectors of society. The most salient example was article 26. The article's separation of Church and State was expected (and accepted) by the ecclesiastical hierarchy, but its exclusion of the Church from all educational and business activities deprived the Church of both its public *and* private sources of income. It was no surprise that Catholics, who comprised half the political community, rejected the 1931 Constitution. Far from consolidating the Republic through a process of compromise and transaction, the constitutional proceedings made the regime's future inherently uncertain by excluding the Catholics. Obliging conservatives to place constitutional reform at the center of their agenda was hardly a recipe for stability. Second, the patrimonial attitude of the left led it to grossly underestimate the right. In the 1931 general election, the right-wing forces, disorientated and disorganized, failed to muster more than 30 deputies, which tended to confirm the left's preconceived idea that the Republic was not of the right. However, in early 1933, a Church-sponsored party, the Confederación Española de Derechas Autónomas (Spanish Confederation of Autonomous Rightists, or CEDA), was founded with an alleged 700,000 members—more than any party in Spain. In April 1933, the CEDA nearly defeated the ruling coalition in the municipal elections. And in the 1933 general election the CEDA won 115 seats—more than any other party. The left's self-serving identification of the Republic with its own cause had clearly been a monumental miscalculation.

The left-wing politics of exclusion did not affect the forces of the right alone. All of the socialist-inspired labor legislation was designed—as it was under the Primo de Rivera Dictatorship—to strengthen the UGT at the expense of the CNT. Anarcho-syndicalist strikes and protests were also suppressed with a severity that was not applied to socialist ones. This approach debilitated the syndicalists within the CNT, while playing into the hands of the anarchist extremists. The syndicalists managed to dominate the National Congress of June 1931, but increasingly lost out thereafter to the radicals, as shown by the rise in strikes and the uprisings of January and December 1933. The breach between the Republic and the CNT lost the regime the potential support of a large part of the organized working class while greatly radicalizing the social and political climate. This not only hardened attitudes on the right, but also weakened the socialists' commitment to the Republic by dragging them to the left in an effort to compete with the CNT.

Still, sectarianism was not the sole province of the political left. Ideologically, the CNT rejected the political parties, the Cortes, the electoral system, and the State. While the syndicalists were prepared in practice to work within the system, the anarchists were not. Like the Communists, who were relatively insignificant, their goal was the overthrow of the "bourgeois" Republic. The main force on the right, the CEDA, adopted the Vatican's "accidentalist" formula of judging a regime by its content, not its form. In doctrinal terms, the CEDA was corporatist and authoritarian rather than democratic and liberal, but, in contrast to the explicitly anti-republican forces of the right, the CEDA was "accidentalist" or *posibilist*—disposed, in theory, to work within the regime. This was not an opportunistic ploy, but formed part of a wider Catholic strategy, endorsed by the Church, of collaboration with the Republic. However, the stance of the CEDA remained ambivalent and threatening. Farther to the right, the Alfonsists, the Carlists, the *Bloque Nuevo* (New Block), and the Falangists were viscerally anti-republican and, like the CNT and the PCE, had a vested interest in exacerbating political and social tension in order to undermine the Republic.

The two years of center-right dominance following the general election of November 1933 have been stigmatized as the *Bienio negro* or "Black Biennium" on account of the supposedly reactionary and regressive governments of this period, which are unfavorably contrasted with the progressive administrations of the *Bienio reformista* or "Reformist Biennium." Central to this thesis is the claim that the right "won" the 1933 election before demolishing most of the first biennium's legislation during the first nine months of 1934. This is a myth. In the 1933 election, the left returned around 100 deputies, the center 177, the non-republican right 152, and the anti-republican right 44. The outcome was a hung parliament. A centrist government under the Radicals was then formed with the parliamentary support of the CEDA. The non-republican right did not enter the government until October 1934 and the right did not achieve a majority in the Cabinet until May 1935, while it never secured the premiership. Still, the moderate republicans have been criticized ever since for "betraying" the Republic by acting as the "puppets" of the CEDA. The *raison d'être* of the centrists' coalition with the CEDA was that the Republic could not be consolidated in opposition to the Catholic community and that it was incumbent upon them to at least try to integrate the posibilist right, thereby driving a wedge between the non-republican and anti-republican right.

Up to October 1934, the two Radical-led governments did not act as marionettes of the non-republican right but, on the contrary, battled to defend a politics of transaction. This was highlighted by the three major conflicts of the summer of 1934: the peasants' strike and the disputes with the Catalan regional government and the Basque local authorities. In each case, the government strove to secure a constructive compromise, but it was repeatedly undermined by the dogmatism and opportunism of the left and the hectoring exigencies of the right. Nor did the governments destroy the reforms of 1931–33 *en masse*. The only major piece of legislation that was overturned was the Municipal Boundaries Act, which was unpopular with all but the socialists. Otherwise, the Radicals struggled to uphold the labor legislation, as shown by their loss of support among the industrial and commercial classes, the mainstay of their social base.

In October 1934 the entry of three members of the CEDA into the Cabinet sparked a socialist revolutionary strike, a full-scale uprising in Asturias, and the declaration of a Catalan State within "the Spanish Federal Republic" by the Catalan regional government. The strike and the Catalan revolt were soon queled, but the Asturian revolutionaries held out against the army for two weeks. Many historians justify the socialist rebellion—as did contemporary socialists—as a doomed if heroic attempt to defend the Republic against "fascism." In reality, the socialists broke with the left republicans in September 1933 and then with the Republic itself in November 1933 because they had lost power. Rather than join forces with the left republicans as a parliamentary counterweight to the center-right, the socialists decided to jettison the regime altogether and take the revolutionary highroad.

October 1934 was the turning point of the Second Republic insofar as the uprisings and subsequent repression polarized politics to an unprecedented extent. It would remain the quintessential point of reference until the outbreak of civil war in July 1936. October 1934 was a disaster for the left, now marginalized and repressed, as well as for the center, as its declared *leitmotiv* of "a Republic for all Spaniards" had been heavily discredited. The victors were the forces of the right, above all the triumphant CEDA. For the latter, October 1934 furnished a magnificent opportunity to advance its plan for power at the expense not only of the left, but also the center. Over the following year, national politics would be dominated by the fight between the center and the CEDA over the scale of the repression and the extent of the counterrevolution. In Cabinet, Radical defiance of the CEDA's vindictive desire to carry out all the death sentences passed down by the military courts led to numerous crises. The fact that only two of the sentences were approved by the governments of 1934–35 showed the determination of the centrists to avoid greater polarization. On the other hand, the Radicals did far too little to curb or defuse the repression in other areas: the prolonged states of exception, the vicious military clampdown in Asturias, the trials that dragged on into 1936, and the indiscriminate persecution of leftists nationwide. In the villages of Castilla-La Mancha, to take one example, there was "an unbreathable atmosphere within the local communities." The Radicals also violated their own centrist credentials by taking advantage of the left's prostration to replace local councils in towns and *pueblos* throughout the country with their own handpicked appointees. All of this only served to poison the political climate still further.

At least the Radicals blocked the CEDA's counterrevolutionary program at almost every turn, including its putative reforms of the trade unions, the press and the electoral system. They also dragged their feet over the CEDA's proposed overhaul of the Constitution. The one major legislative victory of the right was the repeal of the Agrarian Reform Act. By mid-1935, cooperation between the two parties was, in the words of the CEDA leader, "practically nil." The patent lack of harmony within the ruling coalition was graphically revealed by the Straperlo scandal, which engulfed the Radicals in late 1935. Instead of defending its ally, the CEDA exploited the situation in order to advance its own ambitions. The CEDA stratagem, however, backfired as President Alcalá-Zamora preferred to call a general election rather than let the authoritarian CEDA boss, José María Gil Robles, become prime minister.

The general election of February 1936 between the left-wing Popular Front and the right-wing Counter-Revolutionary Coalition was bitterly contested. The narrow victory of the Popular Front returned the left to power, but the workers' organizations refused to join the Cabinet, so a weak left-republican government was formed. Power shifted from the Cortes to the streets and squares during the spring and summer of 1936 as the trade unions came to overshadow both the parties and the government. Worker mobilization secured the mass release of imprisoned revolutionaries, the readmission by employers of blacklisted laborers, and the imposition of new and better contracts. Meanwhile, rural workers in the south and west seized and settled land on their own account rather than wait for the resurrection of the Agrarian Reform Act. The government rubber-stamped the workers' gains by hurriedly passing retrospective legislation. Among the workers there was a strong presentiment of revolution, but not a single organization was prepared to take the initiative. On the right, the legalism of the CEDA was increasingly displaced by the "catastrophist" solution of the far right: the street violence of the Falange and the incendiary rhetoric of figures such as José Calvo Sotelo was designed to justify a military revolt against the Republic. Recent research reveals that around 400 political assassinations took place between January and July 1936, an astonishing figure, even if compared to troubled states elsewhere in contemporary Europe. The murder of Calvo Sotelo on July 13 was the catalyst for the military uprising that had been in preparation since the general election. By this stage, Spanish society had become deeply divided, which is why the failed coup rapidly degenerated into civil war. Ultimately, the Second Republic, like the Restoration and the Dictatorship before it, had proven unequal to the formidable challenges thrown up by a society in the throes of headlong modernization.

Further reading

Álvarez Junco, José, *Dioses útiles: Naciones y nacionalismos*, Barcelona: Galaxia Gutenberg, 2016.
Álvarez Tardío, Manuel and del Rey Reguillo, Fernando (eds.), *The Spanish Second Republic Revisited: From Democratic Hopes to Civil War (1931-1936)*, Brighton: Sussex Academic press, 2012.
Ben Ami, Shlomo, *Fascism from Above*, Oxford: Oxford University Press, 1985.
Boyd, Carolyn P., *Praetorian Politics in Liberal Spain*, Chapel Hill: The University of North Carolina Press, 1979.

Gómez-Navarro, José Luis, *El régimen de Primo de Rivera: reyes, dictaduras y dictadores*, Madrid: Cátedra, 1991.

González Calleja, Eduardo, *La España de Primo de Rivera: la modernización autoritaria 1923-1930*, Madrid: Alianza, 2005.

Meaker, Gerald H., *The Revolutionary Left in Spain, 1914-1923*. Stanford: Stanford University Press, 1974.

del Moral Vargas, Marta, *Acción colectiva femenina en Madrid (1909-1931)*, Santiago de Compostela: Universidade de Santiago de Compostela, 2012.

Moreno-Luzón, Javier, *Modernizing the Nation: Spain during the Reign of Alfonso XIII, 1902-1931*, Brighton: Sussex Academic press, 2012.

Preston, Paul, *The Coming of the Spanish Civil War: Reform, Reaction and Revolution in the Second Republic*, Second edition, London: Methuen, 1994.

Quiroga, Alejandro, *Making Spamiards. Primo de Rivera and the Nationalization of the Masses*, London. Palgrave McMillan, 2007.

del Rey Reguillo, Fernando, *Paisanos en lucha: Exclusión política y violencia en la Segunda República española*, Madrid: Biblioteca Nueva, 2008.

del Rey Reguillo, Fernando, *Propietarios y patronos: La política de las organizaciones económicas en la España de la Restauración (1914-1923)*, Madrid: Ministerio de Trabajo y Seguridad Social, 1992.

Townson, Nigel (ed.), *Is Spain Different? A Comparative Look at the 19th and 20th Centuries*, Brighton: Sussex Academic Press, 2015.

Townson, Nigel, *The Crisis of Democracy in Spain: Centrist Politics under the Second Republic, 1931-1936*, Brighton: Sussex Academic Press, 2000.

CHAPTER 6
THE SPANISH CIVIL WAR, 1936–39
Angela Cenarro

The military revolt

On the afternoon of July 17, 1936, the garrisons of Melilla, Tetuan, and Ceuta in Spanish Morocco rose in revolt against the Second Republic. The revolt spread to the mainland the next day, when a number of officers across the armed forces chose to support it. The conspirators, led by General Emilio Mola, were not expecting that their uprising would lead to a long war; they anticipated that it would quickly bring the appointment of a military directory which would replace the civilian government, as had happened in September 1923. However, some features of their preparations revealed characteristics that were different from the previous interventions of the army in Spain's political life. One was the use of violence to put down the resistance they anticipated. This explains why Mola said in his orders: "Keep in mind that our action has to be extremely violent to defeat the enemy, which is strong and well organized, as quickly as possible."

A second new feature was the existence of a parallel civilian conspiracy, whose goal was to guarantee that the military had the materiel and human resources to succeed. Thus members of the monarchist parties, the editor of the newspaper *ABC*, and the journalist Luis Bolín rented a plane in London to fly General Francisco Franco from the Canary Islands to Tetuan, where he was to take command of the Army of Africa. Likewise, there were negotiations between the two most significant political organizations of the anti-Republican right: the Falange Española y de las JONS and the Carlist Comunión Tradicionalista, both of which had paramilitary organizations which could be incorporated into the rebel forces. Following the instructions of its leader, José Antonio Primo de Rivera, who had been in a republican prison since June, the Falange quickly offered unconditional support. Agreement with the Carlists was more difficult as some of their leaders demanded the creation of a corporatist monarchy, but Mola was eventually able to count on the more than 8,000 men of their armed militia, the *requetés*.

The rebels did not have a defined political program, and it took almost a year for the nature of the regime they would create to become clear. The only thing that was clear was their desire to do away with the government that had been formed following the elections of February 1936. Control of the situation lay with the military: the most significant figures became members of the Junta Defensa Nacional in Burgos. Under the symbolic leadership of General Miguel Cabanellas, it was created on July 24 "to assume all the powers of the State and be the legitimate representative of the country to foreign powers." Four days later, they declared martial law in all the territory under their control.

The uprising did not turn out as they had expected. It failed in the major cities of Madrid, Barcelona, Bilbao, Valencia, and Malaga. These were the most industrialized parts of the country, with a strong, well-organized labor movement. The regions where the rebellion was successful were the agricultural regions of central and northern Spain, which were characterized by small- and medium-sized properties and deeply rooted Catholic beliefs. Nevertheless, this black-and-white vision of a progressive Spain confronting a reactionary one, which would feed the myth of the "two Spains," is not sufficient for understanding the reasons for the success or failure of the coup. The role of the police, the Civil Guard and the Assault Guard, was crucial: where they sided with the military rebels or stood aside, as in Galicia, Aragon, and much of Andalucia, the rebels were able to take control of such important cities as La Coruña, Zaragoza, and Seville. On the other hand, the revolt was often defeated where a section of the army and the security forces stood against it.

This alliance—or its absence—was crucial. This was the case in Barcelona, where the Assault Guard and the police of the Catalan regional government fought alongside the *Confederación Nacional del Trabajo* (CNT), the *Partido Obrero de Unificación Marxista* (POUM), and *Partido Socialista Unificado de Cataluña* (PSUC) in many parts of the city. In Madrid, where the majority of the officers and men of the security forces remained loyal to the government, General Fanjul was forced to hole up in the Montaña barracks with 2,000 troops and some 500 Falangists where they were unable to resist the joint attack by Civil Guard and armed militias on July 20.

The most significant response to the coup came from trade unions and workers' parties that declared general strikes and gathered outside government buildings to demand the distribution of weapons. The attitude of the government was based on a different logic, that of maintaining public order at the same time as it tried to get the rebel officers to stand down. The prime minister, the moderate Republican Santiago Casares Quiroga, refused to distribute weapons to the workers' parties and unions, but feeling overwhelmed by the situation, he resigned on the afternoon of July 18. He was succeeded by José Giral and a cabinet composed solely of Republicans. Giral took some crucial decisions, especially agreeing to give weapons to the workers' organizations. He also requested arms from the government of France and decided to use the massive gold reserves of the Bank of Spain to finance these purchases.

By the end of July, the front line divided Spain into two zones defined by radically different political and social projects. In a few weeks, the Republic had ceased to be a democratic regime confronting (as did other contemporary European democracies) problems in consolidating itself, and had become immersed in a total war. It was facing a sector of the Spanish officer corps, the Morocco-based Army of Africa, and thousands of volunteers ready to follow their orders, as well as, from the end of July, the two fascist powers, Germany and Italy.

It was not, however, that the officer corps was not monolithically in support of the rebellion and its goal of doing away with the Republic. Only four of the eighteen Divisional Generals who controlled the most important units (Cabanellas, Queipo de Llano, Goded, and Franco), only fourteen of fifty-six brigadiers, and approximately half of 15,000 officers joined the rebellion. The so-called *Alzamiento Nacional* (National Rising) actually split the army. This made the contribution of the Army of Africa, and especially the Foreign Legion and the indigenous *Regulares*, 1,600 officers and 40,000 soldiers with actual combat experience, particularly important to the rebel cause.

Historians and other commentators have asked how it was possible for Spain to be the scene of such a barbaric and bloody civil war. Long-standing cultural constructions of the peculiarity of the Spaniards (such as the supposedly violent and passionate nature that led them to solve differences by violence, and prevented them from functioning in a liberal-democratic system) have been abandoned. But the debate over the causes of the war remains alive. There has been much talk of the "failure" of the Republic, the result of the errors of the principal republican leaders, but the Civil War was the result of a number of factors. It was the product of tensions that had been building up for decades, tensions which were only sharpened by the Republic's attempts to resolve them by parliamentary means in a context of increasing social mobilization and the limited democratic culture of the most important political organizations.

Spanish society was marked by a number of what Ronald Fraser called "points of rupture," conflicts caused by unresolved structural problems: unequal land ownership, the immense power of the Catholic Church which was challenged by the secularizing policies of the Republicans and the left, and regional nationalisms, especially in Catalonia, which hardline defenders of the unity of the fatherland never understood. In 1930, republicans and socialists had signed an agreement to overthrow the monarchy, which they saw as the only way to do away with these historic problems. With the proclamation of the Second Republic in April 1931, their reformist project ran into enormous difficulties. The disagreements among the leaders of the parties that should have been the foundation of the new regime, Alcalá Zamora, Azaña, Prieto, and Largo Caballero among others, deprived the Republic of the stable coalition it required to consolidate itself, and deprived it of support from the middle and working classes. The insurrectional tactics of the CNT in 1932 and 1933 and the radicalization of the *Partido Socialista Obrero Español* (PSOE), which would reach its peak in October 1934, spread ways of speaking and acting that left little room on the left for democratic values. For its part, the right debated between the strategy of accidentalism promoted by CEDA leader Gil Robles and that of maximalism (doing away with the Republic by force), advocated by monarchists and fascists, but they all shared the goal of ending the redistribution of power embodied by the Republic. The collapse of Alejandro Lerroux's Radicals meant the end of any possible center party.

These fissures and weaknesses ended up creating irreconcilable divisions because the rebel officers, by breaking the rules of the political game, imposed force of arms into a situation where, until then, peaceful negotiation had been possible. As Julián Casanova has put it, if the Republic had to deal with the challenge of the left and the harassment of the right, both of which repudiated the system of representative government, the "death blow" came "from within, from the heart of its means of self-defense, the military." It is impossible to predict what the future of the Republic might have been, but without this attempted coup, the crisis of the 1930s, which followed a similar path to that of other European countries, would not have led to a civil war.

Spain at war: Between reaction and revolution

The failure of the rebels' plan to take power across Spain at once had unforeseen consequences. Most significantly, it disrupted the state's mechanisms of coercion, that is the military and police institutions, which deprived the Republican government of the resources required for centralized control of the resistance. As a result, the authority of the government evaporated and the power vacuum was filled by the workers' parties and the unions, especially the UGT and CNT, which led the resistance to the rebels. In the first days, their leaders and militants distributed arms, attacked the rebellious garrisons, and took part in street battles to defeat the coup's supporters. Organized into committees and militias, they took charge of transportation and supplies and even managed, as in the case of those who left Catalonia and the Levante, to take back control of some areas, or as the Barcelona daily *La Vanguardia* put it "to march on the traitors in Zaragoza."

These workers' committees and militias, the embodiment of the people in arms, were the display of a revolutionary process that, in the circumstances, was the inevitable response to the attempted coup. Far from being the creation of a preconceived plan, they emerged as a result of the power vacuum that the uprising had created. Their goals did not include seizing political power as the Bolsheviks had done in Russia, but rather to destroy the existing political and social hierarchies. Their targets were property, the state, religion, and anyone who opposed them. The first task was to destroy and purify so that a new order, a nebulous "egalitarian paradise," could be created. Extrajudicial killings carried out through the rituals of *paseos* and *sacas* (looting and confiscation of property) were daily occurrences everywhere the revolt failed, but they took place with greatest virulence in rural areas far from the front and the major cities. In Madrid, political parties and trade unions created some 200 *checas* or prisons, while in Barcelona, ground zero of the urban revolution, there were some 700 patrols under anarchist control.

As José Luis Ledesma has demonstrated, this brutal explosion of violence that claimed some 55,000 victims, most of them in the summer of 1936, was the result of a number of interconnected logics. The first was the reaction to the coup, which explains the sudden and explosive character of the "red terror" in July and August. A little later came a dynamic of reprisals and revenge, so that many massacres came immediately after rebel bombings of cities or episodes of repression in the territory they controlled. For example, the mass executions in the Badajoz bullring on August 15 and the bombing of the Argüelles district of Madrid triggered the *sacas* at the Modelo prison on August 22–23, where some thirty people, including a number of important right-wing leaders, were killed. Violence was also a way of demonstrating control over a territory, and in small communities, of settling disputes over land or religion. This is why repressive rituals had social support, such as the "popular trials" which took place during the day, where assembled residents delivered the verdict, or the militias' use of blacklists compiled by local people to help them make arrests.

The victims were those who represented economic, social, cultural, and political power. They were local bosses (*caciques*), landowners, sometimes even smallholders, Catholics from all levels of society, local fascists and rightists, and even members of the lower class who had ties of affection or dependence to the elites. The representatives of the Catholic Church were eliminated with particular fury, as the death toll makes clear: 6,549 male clergy and 283 nuns. Sometimes the men were humiliated or tortured before being killed. This was a brutal response to the Church's historic ties with the powerful, one that demonstrated that this violence also had a cultural and symbolic side intended to uproot this alliance by force (see Chapter 18). The collectivization of the means of production and the distribution of power were other characteristics of the revolution. The former was the result of the desire to build a new social order, starting with a more equitable distribution of wealth, as well as of ensuring that production would be directed to supporting the war effort. The proper running of firms was a priority; there was no single blueprint which was applied everywhere, and as a result there were various ways in which companies were expropriated and union control imposed. In rural areas, the unions collectivized the land so that it could be worked by groups of peasants, the community as a whole, or by commercially oriented cooperatives. Once the revolutionary fervor of the first few weeks had passed, the UGT and CNT became more open to the "individualist" option of allowing smallholders to continue to work their own land outside the collective so long as they did not use hired labor.

Finally, the bewildering array of powers, or counter-powers, initially embodied in the revolutionary committees, was proof that power was being exercised in a more dispersed way at the local, provincial, or regional level. On the other hand, there was neither the will nor the capacity to construct a new, centralized, nationwide revolutionary order. For a number of months, the Barcelona Anti-Fascist Militias Committee, whose powers were taken over on September 26 by the Generalitat headed by Lluís Companys, coexisted with a huge number of local and neighborhood committees, some provincial or regional committees (such as those in Valencia and Asturias), and defense committees (*juntas de defensa*) such as those in Madrid and Vizcaya. The autonomous Basque government soon replaced this last one, with José Antonio Aguirre of the PNV as president. The closest the revolution came to creating an autonomous government was the Regional Defence Council in eastern Aragon, headed by Joaquín Ascaso of the CNT. These organisms, which were always run by the political parties of the Popular Front and the unions, served to exercise control on the parts of the country that remained loyal to the Republic, organize the economy, and maintain public order. They institutionalized the exercise of violence through their "popular tribunals" which significantly reduced the kind of repression that had marked the first weeks of the war, although they did not eliminate it entirely.

On the other side of the front, the war facilitated the wave of behind-the-lines repression that left a trail of blood. The exact number of victims is still unknown, but local studies carried out by historians point to a minimum of 140,000 between the war and the postwar period. As in the Republican zone, *paseos* and *sacas* and the absence of any legal protections were the order of the day in rebel territory during the first weeks. Starting in October, when the rebel failure to capture Madrid first made the prospect of a long war likely, trials carried out by military courts became common. By then, the initial explosion of violence in the summer of 1936 had claimed almost 80 percent of those who would be killed during the entire war. This mass slaughter involved many people beyond the soldiers who gave the orders: Falangists, Carlists, and local rightists all too happy for the opportunity to settle accounts with Popular Front politicians, civil governors, mayors and town councilors, labor leaders, and the rank and file. The victims included workers and peasants but also doctors, teachers, professors, and intellectuals such as Federico García Lorca, probably the most famous victim of all. Many women were also victims. In addition to being killed or imprisoned, they were often subject to punishments which attacked their bodies and their female dignity. There were rapes in both rearguards but only the rebels humiliated women by shaving their heads and forcing them to drink castor oil.

The logic of war, the elimination of the enemy, mixed with desires for vengeance in which the old conflicts over class or religion overlapped with deep hatred between residents of small rural communities which were given free reign once the military opened the door to violence. Moreover, as the war went on and the rebels took control of more territory formerly controlled by the Republic, the excesses that characterized the summer of 1936 were repeated. The idea of purifying the social body of the nation, which was an essential step toward creating the kind of undivided national community that was the goal of modern counterrevolution, appeared in many of the Francoists' proclamations and appeals for the citizens of the New Spain to collaborate in "the serene justice of the Caudillo." The seizure of property of people "hostile to the National Movement" and the purge of civil servants were processes set out in new laws, which called for local authorities and ordinary citizens to take part: by denouncing people or giving evidence, they held the power of life and death over their enemies.

At the same time as they were carrying out this process of exclusion by force of arms, the rebels were laying the foundations for their new political order, "New Spain" as they called it. These were two parallel processes. Immediately after the uprising began, thousands of men enthusiastically signed up as "volunteers of July 18." There were 35,000 of them at the start of the war, double that number by October, and between 90,000 and 100,000 during the rest of the conflict. Enrolled in militias which, unlike those in the Republican zone, were under the control of the central authorities, they constituted the human foundation on which to build the new state which would also find room for economic elites, the conservative middle class, smallholding peasants, and Catholics.

The rebels were initially without a leader, but in October Francisco Franco proclaimed himself *Generalísimo* of the armed forces and "head of the government of the Spanish state" in a decree of the Junta de Defensa Nacional, which gave him all-inclusive powers. Then, in April 1937, he issued the Decree for Unification, which merged the Falange with the Carlist Comunión Tradicionalista into a new organization, Falange Española y Tradicionalista de las Juntas de Ofensiva Nacional-Sindicalista (FET-JONS) of which he was the leader. All other political organizations were abolished. This new party, which would be the only legal one in Spain until 1977, became the bureaucracy that sustained the regime from the beginning until the end (see Chapter 7).

The Catholic Church also had a major role in the building of this new state. Angered by the secularizing legislation of the Republic, it saw the opportunity to retake the ground it had lost. It gave the uprising, as well as the actions of its leaders—repression included—its blessing, proclaiming the war to be a "crusade" against the enemies of Spain, who were also the enemies of religion. Bishop Pla y Deniel of Salamanca, author of the September 1936 pastoral letter *The Two Cities*, and Cardinal Gomá, the primate of Spain, who promoted, at Franco's request, the *Joint letter of the Spanish bishops to the bishops of the whole world concerning the war in Spain*, of July 1, 1937, led this renewed fusion of the sword and the cross which came to be known as National Catholicism and which enjoyed the support of almost the entire Church hierarchy and clergy (see Chapter 18). The regime also drew on the feelings of lay Catholics who had been mobilized against the Republic and whose religious fervor was heightened further by anticlerical actions in the Republican zone, such as the symbolic execution of the statue of the Sacred Heart of Jesus on the Cerro de los Angeles just outside Madrid, the burning of churches and religious images and the slaughter of clergy. The failed attempt by the Republican air force to bomb the cathedral of El Pilar in Zaragoza on August 3, 1936 provoked processions and other religious displays across rebel-held territory. Both the demonstrations of religious belief (such as field masses, pilgrimages, and the displays of crucifixes, flags, and scapularies) and the way in which apologists for the rebellion designated the conflict as a "holy war" led to the Civil War being considered a "war of religion." The support of the Church was absolutely essential in gaining the rebels international recognition and the support of its citizens. At the same time, the Church did well out of the bargain. As Frances Lannon has said, the Franco regime "protected it, covered it in privileges and silenced those who opposed it."

The Frontlines: The division of Spain and the internationalization of the conflict

At the end of July, Spain was divided into two irreconcilable zones by a frontline which moved over the course of the almost three years of war. During that first summer and inspired by the methods used by the Spanish army in the colonial wars in Morocco, Franco led his Moroccan troops on a slow advance through Andalucia and Extremadura, which allowed him to carry out a brutal "war of annihilation" against the "enemies of Spain." The four months which his troops took to reach the gates of Madrid also created the conditions for Franco to assert his personal power over the other members of the Junta de Defensa Nacional. In fact, the delay in launching the attack on the capital changed the course of the war. Thanks to the creation of its new Popular Army and the support provided by the International Brigades, the Republican government was able to put up an effective defense. With Franco's troops only a few kilometers away, the government moved to Valencia on November 7 and left the capital in the hands of a Defence Committee headed by General José Miaja.

The people of Madrid adopted the slogan "they shall not pass," unveiled by Communist leader Dolores Ibárruri (see Chapter 34), and turned it into a symbol of antifascist resistance. Madrid became the first major European city to suffer systematic aerial bombardment. This began at the end of August and became more intense during the fall and winter of 1936. Various measures were taken to protect the civilian population, such as organizing refuges, but these were inadequate in the face of modern military techniques. By April 1937, the bombing had claimed some 1,500 lives. The battle for Madrid also saw one of the greatest massacres which took place in the Republican rearguard. In a situation defined by a power vacuum in the capital and the presence of Franco's army nearby, the public order arm of the Junta de Defensa, with the collaboration of the security forces and the connivance of some members of the Republican government, murdered 2,500 prisoners, half of them military men, in the towns of Paracuellos and Torrejón de Ardoz in a number of *sacas* during the month of November.

By then, a number of things about the Civil War had become very clear. One is that although the causes of the war were completely endogenous, that is, due to internal conditions and domestic tensions, it very quickly became an international conflict. Another, closely related to the first, is that the Spanish Civil War was an early example of modern warfare, with devastating effects on the civilian population of aerial bombardment and large-scale population movements, some spontaneous others forced, driven by fear of reprisals.

The arrival at the end of July of 20 Junker transport planes and their crews sent by Nazi Germany allowed Franco to airlift his Moroccan troops to the mainland (naval vessels loyal to the Republic prevented the troops from crossing any other way). Mussolini also sent 12 Savoia bombers. By the end of the war, the two fascist powers would provide Franco with 1,600 planes, 200 canons, 1,000 combat vehicles and massive amounts of bombs, machines guns, and other weapons. In addition, there were 80,000 Italian soldiers, most of them in the Volunteer Corps (*Corpo Truppe Volontarie*; CTV) and 19,000 German soldiers in the Condor Legion. The two dictators were moved by ideological concerns (such as anticommunism) as well as geostrategic ones (preventing a possible alliance between Spain, France, and the Soviet Union, which would be a problem for Hitler and an obstacle to Italian expansion in the western Mediterranean). It was also a symptom that the battle that was being fought in Spain was the same one which was dividing Europeans and which would lead to war in September 1939.

The Republic, however, did not receive the support it needed from the Western democracies, especially France and Great Britain. At a meeting held in London on September 9, 1936 (a meeting to which Spain was not invited), representatives of 28 European nations signed the Non-Intervention Agreement (NIA) in which the promised not export or reexport war materiel to either side. Proponents of the agreement emphasized the importance of containing the conflict within Spain and preventing it from becoming internationalized, but in practice the NIA deprived the Republic of the military resources it needed to prosecute the war. The initiative for the agreement came from the French Popular Front government of Léon Blum, who was influenced by the controversial nature of the Spanish situation among French public opinion as well as by the British government's policy of appeasement, the refusal to risk a war with Germany by antagonizing Hitler.

As a result, the only European ally on whom the Republic could count for support was the Soviet Union. How to respond to the Spanish conflict was not an easy decision for Stalin. Since September 1935 he had been advocating the strategy of popular fronts against fascism and he was far from eager to get involved in an armed conflict, but after analyzing the situation for a few weeks, Soviet military aid began to reach the Republic in October. This assistance (700 planes, 400 combat vehicles, and 2,000 pilots, advisors and secret police (People's Commissariat for Internal Affairs; NKVD) agents) was very important, but it was far less than that received by the Republic's enemies. In addition, the Comintern, although itself divided over the position it should take toward the Spanish conflict, undertook the formation of the International Brigades: 35,000 volunteers from 53 countries, a diverse set of backgrounds and various political affiliations who were recruited through local Communist Parties (the largest number, around 10,000, came from France). There were 5,000 from Germany and Austria, 2,500 from the United Kingdom, 2,800 from the United States, and 1,600 from Canada. Almost a quarter of the total were Jewish, many of them exiles from Nazi Germany. Based in Albacete, the IBs, who were often used as shock troops, played a significant role in the defense of Madrid and in a number of other battles, and were the most powerful demonstration of international antifascist support for the embattled Republic.

A series of battles during 1937 put the unequal capabilities of the two armies on display. Around Madrid, the battles of the Jarama and Guadalajara (February to March) did not bring any significant changes to the territory held by the two sides. On the other hand, the fall of Malaga in February and Bilbao in June were major losses for the Republic. The collapse of the northern front was especially serious, as it meant the loss of mines and heavy industry essential for the war effort.

These battles also had serious effects on the civilian population. On February 7, with Francoist and Italian forces only a few kilometers from the city, thousands of citizens of Malaga, terrified by reports of earlier atrocities, fled toward Almería along the coastal highway that connected the two cities. By foot or in cars, entire families with children and grandparents undertook a journey that lasted days while being subjected to aerial bombing and shelling from naval vessels offshore. Between 3,000 and 5,000 people died from illness, suicide, or repression.

The Republican victory at Guadalajara brought the offensive against Madrid to an end, and Franco turned his attention to the north (the Basque Provinces and Asturias) which were isolated from the rest of the Republican zone. This campaign demonstrated the rebel superiority in the air. Both the Italians and the Condor Legion used the most modern planes and introduced a new tactic, attacking the population behind the lines to intimidate and demoralize civilians. On March 31, Italian bombers attacked Durango killing 250 people. On April 26, Guernica was leveled almost completely by the Condor Legion, which in a premeditated experiment in new techniques, dropped bombs and incendiary devices, and then machine-gunned the terrified people who tried to flee. The attack lasted three hours and claimed 300 victims, 5 percent of the town's population. This horrific event was immortalized soon after by Pablo Picasso in his painting, *Guernica*. Aerial bombing continued until the end of the war, especially in Catalonia and Levante, with 11,000 victims, the vast majority in the Republican zone.

On December 22, 1937, the Republicans launched an offensive that encircled Teruel and occupied it after weeks of house-to-house fighting inside the city itself. The only provincial capital the Republic managed to retake during the war, this small victory had special significance and generated renewed morale among Republican troops. The battle of Teruel was fought in horrible winter weather and the civilian population was evacuated to Valencia. However, a few weeks later in February 1938, the Francoist army retook the city. Franco ordered his troops (who were already in Aragon) to undertake an offensive that led to the complete occupation of the region (as well as part of the province of Lérida) by April. The Levante campaign came later that spring. These defeats, pessimism, and the belief that the war was lost spread through Republican ranks.

During the first two years of the war, the Francoist forces had demonstrated their superior ability to supply the armies at the front as well as the rearguard. Enjoying a numerical advantage thanks to the presence of Moroccan, Italian, and German troops as well as greater amounts of aid in the form of weapons and other war materiel, Franco had opted for a war of attrition. The Francoists also made much more effective use of their resources. There were many new organizations, campaigns (such as the Ficha Azul voluntary donation and the Día del Plato Único, in which restaurants served only a single dish but charged for a full meal), or civilian committees which, controlled by the emerging government, the Falange, or local elites, raised large amounts of money that helped provide a number of subsidies to soldiers and working families. The rebels recruited 1,260,000 men between the ages of 18 and 32, while the Republicans had to draft 1,700,000 between 17 and 44, and the older men were usually less effective soldiers. Toward the end, during the battle of the Ebro, the Republic sent 17 year-olds, the famous "baby bottle draft," into combat. Lack of pay and problems in feeding the troops sapped morale as well as prompting desertions, which were much more numerous than in the Francoist army.

Military defeats and especially the loss of Malaga had an impact on politics, increasing the divisions in the cabinet. The Socialist leader Francisco Largo Caballero replaced Giral as prime minister at the start of September 1936 at the head of a cabinet which included Republicans, Communists, and anarchists as well as members of his own party. His government's main goal was to rebuild the Republican state that had collapsed in July by creating a regular army, nationalizing war industries, and attempting to assert its authority across the entire Republican zone. For months, however, it faced the autonomous activities of local committees and regional governments as well as some resistance to militarization. For their part, the Communists, who had enjoyed a considerable increase in numbers during the fall, criticized what they saw as Largo Caballero's only limited ability to restore discipline and assert state authority. They were also opposed to the presence of the unions (especially the CNT) in the cabinet. The coalition began to split apart.

The most dramatic demonstration of these tensions came with the "May Days" of 1937 in Barcelona so graphically described by George Orwell in his book *Homage to Catalonia*. The situation in the Catalan capital became increasingly complicated due to shortages of basic necessities and the arrival of large numbers of refugees from other parts of the country. Armed groups also remained beyond the control of the regional government (the Generalitat), which was now run by republicans and socialists. On May 3, the minister of security ordered his forces to take control of the telephone building that had been occupied by the CNT. With help from the POUM, they fought back. The struggle lasted for four days and left 400 dead. It also brought the defeat of the CNT, which lost its political and military power, and the banning of the POUM and the persecution of its members.

This bloody episode was not caused only by rivalries between political and union organizations; it was the radical expression of the differing projects that coexisted in the Republican zone and the "antifascist resistance." On the one hand, there were the revolutionary conquests which had made room for the militias and the committees; on the other, there were the demands for the rebuilding of the Republican political and social order, respect for private property and an end to the autonomy of the militias and armed groups outside the army. If reestablishing state authority had been the government's goal since the beginning of the war, the "May Days" represented an acceleration of this process, not a turning point, as many have claimed.

This episode produced a government crisis that led to the fall of Largo Caballero and his replacement by Juan Negrín, another Socialist, at the head of a coalition of Republicans, Socialists and Communists. President Azaña considered Negrín to be the best person to undertake the dual task of prosecuting the war and undertaking diplomatic negotiations in Europe. On May 1, 1938, Negrín issued his famous "Thirteen Points," a declaration of his government's goals: the independence and territorial integrity of Spain, national sovereignty, the rights of citizens, respect for private property, and freedom of conscience and religion. It also proposed a general political amnesty after the war. These proposals were consistent with Negrín's strategy, summarized in the slogan "to resist is to win," which aimed at ending Non-Intervention. This policy meant prolonging the suffering of the civilian population, but Negrín thought it was essential to keep fighting until war broke out in Europe as well as having the possibility of negotiating a dignified surrender that would spare Spaniards from reprisals. However, the Munich Pact of September 1938 (in which France and Great Britain accepted Hitler's occupation of part of Czechoslovakia) meant that any possibility of the democratic powers providing support to the Republic were over.

Rearguards

The Spanish Civil War was a "total war," a type of war characteristic of the twentieth century in which the separation between the front lines and the rearguard no longer existed. In such wars, the rearguard has to be organized to serve military goals, which means that groups such as women, children, and men not serving in the army are drawn into the logics imposed by armed conflict. The Francoist and Republican governments both sought to exert control over industry, supplies, and transportation, as well as to meet the material needs of soldiers and civilians in the form of hospitals, canteens, and the rationing of basic necessities. Propaganda and maintaining the morale of the civilian population were also crucial, especially for the Republic, which had to deal with much more intensive aerial bombardments, fears of espionage and ever greater shortages of food and other goods. Faced with the collapse of the state and the international isolation of Non-Intervention, it faced much greater challenges than did the Francoists in organizing the war effort and attending to the needs of the population.

The experiences of the two rearguards were very different. As the Francoists conquered territory controlled by the Republic, civilians were evacuated or displaced. According to a report by the League of Nations, 7,000 people had flooded into Madrid by the end of 1936. Two more years of war brought the people of the capital shortages of bread, coal, and electricity, and rationing put limits on food consumption. During February 1939, hundreds died of starvation. More than 300,000 refugees from the north, the center, and from Malaga reached Barcelona and the surrounding towns in 1937, and early in the year they constituted 10 percent of the total population. The result was a shortage of basic foodstuffs and other necessities, which was exacerbated by geographic obstacles that made transportation and supply more difficult. Inflation quickly took off despite requisitioning by local committees and price controls. The policies of economic liberalism applied by the Generalitat midway through 1937 only furthered the spiral of price increases, speculation, and black markets that even rationing could not control.

Dealing with the needs created by a conflict of this type was an important challenge for the two governments, who quickly created new institutions to organize evacuations and tend to the displaced, such as the Republic's National Committee for Refugees (Comité Nacional de Refugiados), created in October 1936, and Refugee Aid and War Relief (Auxilio de Refugiados, Beneficencia de Guerra) created by the Francoists, among others. Assistance also came from abroad, from organizations devoted to alleviating the horrible conditions of the civilian population. International Red Aid (Socorro Rojo Internacional), the Quakers, the National Joint Committee for Spanish Relief in the United Kingdom and the Swiss Committee to Aid Spanish Children (Comité Suizo de Ayuda a los Niños de España), all worked with the Republic. The Francoists did not enjoy this sort of organized international solidarity, although they could count on Catholic organizations like the Bishops Committee for the Relief of the Spanish Distress and General Relief Fund for the Distressed Women and Children of Spain.

The war affected children especially strongly. They were at the center of policies designed to protect civilians as well as the recipients of heavily ideological messages about the meaning of the war. The Republic designed a network of children's colonies (colonias infantiles) where children removed from near the front or cities subject to aerial bombing could live a relatively normal life and begin to recover physically and psychologically. By November 1937 some 8,600 children were housed in 160 such colonies in Catalonia, Valencia, Aragon, Cuenca, and Albacete. Many others (some 33,000 according to Alicia Alted) left Spain altogether. The largest number, around 20,000 from northern Spain, went to France; in early 1939 they were joined by 68,000 who crossed the border from Catalonia with their families. Thousands more were welcomed for temporary stays in Belgium, the Soviet Union, and the United Kingdom, which received 4,000 Basque children who were evacuated during the Francoists' northern campaign in the spring of 1937. Mexico also welcomed Republican child refugees. At the end of the war, Francoist authorities or the Church organizations charged with receiving the children often made repatriation difficult. A significant number of children remained in their new country until they were adults, or never returned to Spain at all.

Aiming to realize their goal of creating a Spain which was "One, Great, and Free" with a plentiful and healthy population, Francoists focused on projects designed to preserve children's health, starting with the care of pregnant women. They also built daycares, camps, and children's homes as well as institutions to take care of pregnant women. The Falange's Social Help (Auxilio Social) was born with this purpose (underpinned by a eugenic outlook), but during the war it took on wider responsibilities (see Chapter 37). Education in the rebel zone drew on Catholic and hierarchical ideas. In fact, baptizing children in the Republican zone was a priority. On both sides of the lines, the smallest children were profoundly affected by the experiences adults imposed on them. But as Verónica Sierra's research has shown, they were also able to process and communicate them through the drawings they did in the colonies or the thousands of letters they sent from the Soviet Union, but which never reached their families.

As in the other total wars of the twentieth century, the work done by women in the rearguard was crucial to sustaining the war effort. The mass mobilizations undertaken by political organizations on both sides allowed thousands of women to enter the public sphere for the first time. On the Republican side, in July 1936 women even joined the militias to fight at the front, but they were an exception. The image of young women dressed in blue workmen's overalls and carrying a rifle, which appeared frequently in the propaganda posters in the early days, represented a radical break with the dominant model of gender roles, and quickly became a symbol of the revolution and the struggle against fascism. The experience was short lived. Women soon put down their weapons to contribute to the struggle from behind the lines. Although there was no formal prohibition against women serving in the Popular Army being created by the Largo Caballero government, the expectation was that they would not. The slogan "Men at the front, women at work" was not just an official one; it was echoed by the two main women's organizations, the Agrupación de Mujeres Antifascistas, which attracted middle- and working-class women, and the anarcho-feminist Free Women (Mujeres Libres).

The war did not shatter the dominant system of gender roles, but it did reshape it (see Chapter 11). And it did so on both sides of the lines. Women gained access to experiences that had been denied them, although always in the rearguard. The work they undertook, which was almost always unpaid, was considered an extension of their natural female and maternal characteristics, so that they came to have a prevalent role in questions of health and social welfare.

In the Republican zone, women replaced men in some collectivized factories and farms. In September 1936, the Agrupación de Mujeres Antifascistas was charged by the Republican government with organizing the Women's Aid Commission (Comisión de Auxilio Femenino) that was to produce consumer goods and supply the front lines. Its discourse combined the defense of full citizenship for women in the face of the fascist threat with female activism and the maternal model. As Mary Nash has argued, the militia woman was quickly replaced as the main symbol in the Republican rearguard by the ideal of the "combative mother" who remained in the private sphere while she resisted and generously gave her sons to the antifascist struggle. For their part, the anarchists advocated a more radical model in which the emancipation of women through their active participation in the resistance as well as through education and work was a priority for the Republic. In the end, the demands of war overpowered feminist demands.

Women in the Francoist zone undertook similar activities, but the meaning attached to them was very different. All women worked within the framework of social welfare or taking care of the needs of the troops. In October 1936, Mercedes Sanz Bachiller founded the Auxilio Social, based on the model of Nazi Germany's *Winterhilfe*. Her organization created a network of soup kitchens and canteens for poor civilians and refugees. Frentes y Hospitales (Fronts and Hospitals), another branch of FET-JONS, ran laundries, sewed uniforms, and sent blankets and other goods to the troops, while Pilar Primo de Rivera's Sección Femenina mobilized young women to serve as nurses after receiving quick basic training. Regardless of which organization they worked in, all women had to be members of the SF; as a result, by the end of the war, the SF had 600,000 members. While Falangist women's organizations reproduced the hierarchy and control typical of fascist-type organizations, they also created spaces for political engagement and personal self-realization for their young members (see chapters 11, 37).

During the three-year siege of Madrid, the 6,000 members of the Hermandad del Auxilio Azul (Blue Aid Brotherhood), the largest of the organizations that existed in the capital, made a significant contribution to the Francoist "Fifth Column" there. They supported people being persecuted by providing medical services, attending to prisoners' families, or obtaining ration cards. In addition to Falangist ideas of self-denial and sacrifice, these women had wartime experiences that opened the doors to reformulating gender roles, doors which would be slammed shut again after the "victory" in 1939.

Both sides used the experiences of the civilian population as material for a nationalist mobilizing discourse. Republicans appealed to the "people in arms" against the Moroccan, German, and Italian invaders and made use of symbols deeply rooted in Spain's history, above all the War of Independence of 1808–1814. This nationalist discourse saturated Republican propaganda, giving the Republic at war a new legitimacy, reinforcing its capacity to mobilize the population and unifying the war effort around some commonly shared and emotionally powerful principles, which also served to distract from its internal political tensions and contradictions. It was also part of a war culture that painted the enemy as an "other," a mercenary, a foreigner, or a traitor to the fatherland.

This appeal to patriotism was something both sides had in common, and both made use of similar icons, symbols, and slogans. The *Virgen del Pilar*, invoked by both sides but with different meanings, was one example: for the rebels, she was the emblem of "Hispanidad" and the "Race" (her saint day, 12 October, celebrated as Columbus Day in the United States, is supposedly when Columbus arrived in America, thus the connection with the empire), while for the Republic she was identified with the Spanish people. That said, the Francoists sought to claim a monopoly on the idea of the Spanish nation (there was a reason for calling themselves the Nationalists) and established a link with the heroes of the medieval Reconquest and the imperial glories of the Golden Age, while Republicans put greater emphasis on myths of resistance against foreign invaders like the Romans, Carthaginians, or the French.

The end of the war

The rebels reached the Mediterranean in the summer of 1938. The territory under Republican control was seriously reduced in size and cut in two. From then on the story of the Republic was a struggle for existence, behind the lines as well as at the front.

The battle of the Ebro (July to November 1938) was an offensive designed by General Vicente Rojo to relieve the threat to Valencia by reuniting the two parts of the Republican zone that had been separated by the Francoist advance: Catalonia and the area around Madrid. It was the last chance for the Popular Army to take the initiative but this longest and largest battle of the war turned out to be a defeat that was costly in both men and materiel. After the autumn, the assistance coming from the Soviet Union was reduced, which made it even more difficult to meet the basic needs of soldiers and civilians. For those who had provided the moral support for the Republic in the midst of aerial bombing and shortages, the situation became unbearable. Women took part in the black market or stood in lengthy lines to get their hands on rationed items. As things worsened in late 1938 and early 1939, the Republic collapsed from within. No longer able to provide its citizens with a life of dignity, its legitimacy eroded rapidly.

The Francoists occupied Catalonia at the end of January 1939. In February, an exodus of half a million refugees, civilians, and soldiers alike crossed the Pyrenees into France. President Manuel Azaña and a number of cabinet ministers did likewise. France and Great Britain officially recognized the Franco regime while the war was still going on. At the end, only Negrín wanted to continue the fight, in the hopes of avoiding reprisals against Republican supporters. The final blow came from an internal coup, what Paul Preston has called an "unnecessary tragedy." Colonel Segismundo Casado, commander of the Army of the Centre, supported by Socialists like Julián Besteiro, anarchists like Cipriano Mera, and others opposed to Negrín's "fight to the end" strategy, formed a National Defence Council (Consejo Nacional de Defensa) in Madrid to negotiate an unconditional surrender with Franco. This civil war within the Republic led to the worst possible defeat. It left 2,000 people (mostly Communists) dead, and destroyed plans to evacuate thousands of Republicans. Franco entered Madrid with almost no resistance, and his army's advance was followed by a brutal repression unleashed against left-wing militants and the civilian population.

The defeat of the Republic was a turning point in Spanish history. It was the tragic end to the attempt to modernize the country politically, socially, and culturally, an attempt at widespread reform that had run into immense difficulties and powerful enemies from the outset. The military rebels and their supporters, the great protagonists of the "victory" of 1939, ushered in a new era defined by terror, poverty, and the division of society into "winners" and "losers." Some 50,000 people were executed after the war had ended. The "New State" also created repressive laws (such as the Law of Political Responsibilities of February 1939, which had 300,000 cases by the end of 1941, and the Law of Repression of Masonry and Communism of 1940). There would be no place for reconciliation (see Chapter 7). Catholics, Falangists, and local elites monopolized political institutions, and they filled public spaces with their praise of the Caudillo and ceremonies honoring those who had died "for God and for Spain." From this perspective, the Civil War cleared the way for a long military dictatorship, one similar to other fascist and authoritarian regimes in Europe, but one that would end only with Franco's death in November 1975 and would have immense human, social, and cultural costs for Spanish society.

Further reading

Baumeister, Martin, and Stefanie Schüler-Springorum (eds.), 'If You Tolerate This.' The Spanish Civil War in the Age of Total Wars, Frankfurt-New York: Campus, 2008.
Casanova, Julián, A Short History of the Spanish Civil War, London: I. B. Tauris & Co. Ltd, 2012.
Graham, Helen, The Spanish Republic at War, 1936-1939, Cambridge: Cambridge University Press, 2002.

Graham, Helen, *The Spanish Civil War. A Very Short Introduction*, Oxford: Oxford University Press, 2005.

Ledesma, José Luis, "Una retaguardia al rojo. Las violencias en la zona republicana," en Francisco Espinosa (ed.), *Violencia roja y azul. España, 1936-1950*, Barcelona: Crítica, 2010, pp. 147–247

Moradiellos, Enrique, *El reñidero de Europa: las dimensiones internacionales de la Guerra Civil española*, Barcelona: Península, 2001.

Nash, Mary, *Defying male civilization. Women in the Spanish Civil War*, Denver: Arden Press, 1995.

Núñez Seixas, Xosé Manuel, *¡Fuera el invasor! Nacionalismos y movilización bélica en la Guerra Civil española (1936-1939)*, Madrid: Marcial Pons, 2006.

Preston, Paul, *The Spanish Civil War: Reaction, Revolution and Revenge (updated 80th anniversary Edition)*, Glasgow: William Collins, 2016.

Sierra Blas, Verónica, *Palabras huérfanas. Los niños y la Guerra Civil*, Madrid: Taurus, 2009.

CHAPTER 7
THE FRANCO DICTATORSHIP, 1939–75

Óscar Rodríguez Barreira

The end of the Civil War left the dictatorship that had been created during the conflict in control of the entire country. Although it called itself the "New State" and offered some modern responses basically associated with fascism to the crises of capitalism and democracy that had marked the 1930s, in a number of important respects the regime was essentially a return to the past. It represented a victory of the traditional elites and power holders over the political challenges presented by republicanism, the working class, regional nationalisms, and other emancipatory and democratizing movements, such as feminism. Armed force allowed these elites to maintain their power for forty years, as well as to bring Spain into the postwar capitalist bloc in a particularly unequal and reactionary way. This would be the beginning of the end for the Franco regime, but it would come at the price of suffering for many Spaniards.

This discussion of the dictatorship comes in five parts. The first deals with one of the regime's cornerstones: its use of violence and repression. It also examines ways it attempted to legitimize them and the legal and administrative tools it created to carry them out. As important as they were, however, the police and other security services could always rely on the loyal collaboration of a significant part of Spanish society. The regime destroyed the public sphere, but it also created a fearful society which policed itself and retreated into purely private life. The destruction of the public sphere enhanced the arbitrary use of power by the dictator and the political families that supported it. The second section analyzes the use Franco made of his unlimited power as well as describing the three pillars on which it was based: the Army, the Church, and the Falange. All were deeply mired in corruption and clientelism and drew on two of the most reactionary and anti-liberal ideologies of the twentieth century: national syndicalism and national Catholicism. Over the forty years he was in power, Franco drew on people from these three pillars and gave greater or lesser influence to these ideologies, all in the name of his overriding goal: keeping himself in power in the face of changing national and international contexts. The result was a series of processes of fascistization and defascistization, some merely superficial, others more profound.

The next two sections explore the effectiveness of these policies and their impact on Spanish society. The first deals with the regime's attempt to make Spain a closed and self-sufficient economy, a policy known as autarky. This produced hunger and misery, which affected many Spaniards but did so in ways that were shaped by politics, geography, and gender. Combined with repression, this led to most of the protest and resistance during the first twenty years after the end of the war taking the form of what has been called the "weapons of the weak." The second looks at another factor that militated against more direct expressions of protest: migration and the economic growth of the 1960s. Spain's "economic miracle" can only be understood as part of the golden age of western capitalism and as the product of the exploitation of many ordinary Spaniards. Unlike what happened in Europe's democracies, the Franco regime did not promote a social contract that provided social peace and a share in the benefits of growth.

Instead, growth was based on state coercion of working Spaniards. Together with generational change and the emergence of new political cultures and forms of protest, this led to a cycle of protest between 1973 and 1977. This protest did not bring down the regime, but it prevented the regime from surviving the death of the dictator in November 1975.

The final topic is an exploration of the debate over the nature of Francoism, a debate that was long dominated by the question of whether or not the regime was fascist. Since the mid-1990s, a dominant interpretation that characterizes the regime as "parafascist" or "fascistized" has emerged. This approach takes into account both the regime's longevity and its malleability, characteristics which require dividing its life into different periods or phases based on economic, social, and political features which remained constant as well as those which changed over time.

Winners and losers

The Civil War and its violence were both the midwife and stepmother of Francoism. Thus, the enormous and brutal bloodshed that the war produced politicized and mobilized the supporters of Francoism, who signed a blood pact with the dictator. It also traumatized and paralyzed the rest of Spanish society for which the idea of a new civil conflict was an unbearable thought, and who chose to accept, or at least resign themselves to, the cruel division between the winners and losers imposed at the end of the conflict (see Chapter 6).

The repression carried out by the Franco regime was legitimized by a simple but brutal distortion: assigning the guilt for starting the Civil War to those who had defended the legal order. On February 15, 1939, rebels declared that the government of the Republic had been illegal and all opposition to the military uprising constituted a crime of military rebellion. Anyone who had not supported it, or who was opposed to it, was considered a Marxist rebel. This was a political offence that was retroactively applied to October 1934. This operation was based on the state of war that the rebel National Defence Council had proclaimed on July 28, 1936 and which remained in effect until April 7, 1948. The Franco government also established a series of laws that further deepened the division between the winners and the losers. This legislation included the Law of Political Responsibilities (February 9, 1939), the Law of Purification of Officials (February 10, 1939), the Law for the Creation of Penal Colonies (November 8, 1939), the Law Against Freemasonry and Communism (March 1, 1940), the Law for the Internal Security of the State (March 29, 1941), and the Law of Public Order (September 30, 1959).

This legislation was designed to justify the social exclusion of the vanquished as well as to punish, humiliate, and, if necessary, eliminate any dissent or opposition to the dictatorship. The varying rhythms and intensity of violence make it possible to distinguish five different phases of repression (see Figure 7.1). The first stage was marked by an indiscriminate and extensive violence that developed during the Civil War. The second, of great intensity and cruelty, exponentially increased the prison population and intensely applied the summary proceedings (1939–41). The third phase covered the two years between 1941 and 1943, which saw a smaller number of people on death row and in prison population thanks to the application of the first measures to reduce sentences, pardons, and probation. This was succeeded by the five years between 1944 and 1949, when the dictatorship experienced moments of weakness due to the defeat of the Axis powers in the Second World War and the struggle of the guerrilla (1947–49).

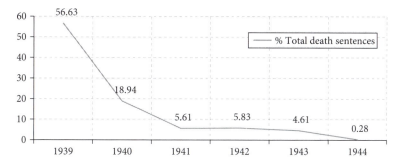

Figure 7.1 The evolution of death sentences, province of Madrid, 1939–44.

Source: Julius Ruiz; Franco's Justice . . .

The fifth and final phase began in 1950, at which time the violence, despite appearing lethal at certain moments, was reduced due to the international context and Spain's strengthening relations with the United States.

A third of the victims of Francoism, some 50,000 people, were executed after the end of the Civil War. These data show the cruelty of the dictatorship, especially when compared with the victims of Italian Fascism or with the justice leveled at collaborators in postwar Western Europe (9,000 victims in France, 15,000 in Italy, 265 in Belgium, and 100 in the Netherlands). Francoist repression also had clear class and political profiles. The majority of those executed were workers and day laborers, military men loyal to the Republican government and political party activists linked to the republicans and the left, including lawyers, journalists, and teachers. It is more difficult to quantify the number of prisoners during the postwar years. According to official data, in 1939, 270,719 prisoners lived in the overcrowded Franco prisons. This figure dropped to 233,373 in 1940 and to 124,423 in 1942. However, the actual number of prisoners was far higher. The situation reached the point that one of the reasons the dictatorship began to implement measures to reduce the prison population was its confessed incapacity to maintain the basic conditions of hygiene and sanitation. Typhus, tuberculosis, and starvation were widespread throughout the prison population.

The day-to-day experience of repression was arbitrary, suffocating, and complex. In addition to the important labor of the political police of the single party (the National Delegation of Information and Investigation), the dictatorship had a number of other police forces: the Civil Guard, the Catalan Militia (*Somatén*), the Municipal Police, the Naval Police, not to mention large numbers of local collaborators. The punitive intention of the Franco regime was so vast that ordinary people were able to use it to advance their own interests and settle personal accounts. Such instrumental use of repression was similar to that which took place in other dictatorships; it also highlights the moral misery in which ordinary Spaniards lived, as well as the construction of hierarchical power networks through the use of informing and denunciations. Small-scale power struggles, quarrels, and social conflicts, some of which went back many years, got settled in this legal context. For women, the everyday use and abuse of repression was more obvious, humiliating, and public. The traditional gender order meant that they were less likely to be executed or even sent to prison, but in contrast, those who had been involved in politics were publicly accused of a lack of morality, had their heads shaved, forced to swallow purgatives, and displayed in the busy streets and avenues.

The most obvious consequence of this level of suffocation and control was the destruction of the public sphere and the flight of ordinary people into private life. As we shall see later, the reconstruction of public spaces of dissent would be delayed for fifteen years and led by a new generation of Spaniards that had no direct experience of the Civil War. Changes in the international context presented the regime with a new challenge that it met by creating a new tool, the Public Order Tribunal (TOP) in 1963. This led to a decreased application of military justice in sociopolitical conflicts. However, it did not mean that such conflicts disappeared or that the regime demonstrated a more benevolent attitude toward dissent. Of the approximately 53,500 people who were tried by the TOP by the time it was abolished in January 1977, 75 percent were convicted.

Power and political changes

Francisco Franco's dictatorship was built on the experience and outcome of the Civil War. Franco used the three years of the conflict to concentrate and accumulate all the authorities and powers of the New State while at the same time constructing the mythical story of the victorious Leader chosen by the grace of God (see chapters 6, 35). The creation of the Falange Española Tradicionalista y de las Juntas de Ofensiva Nacional Sindicalista (FET-JONS) through the merger of all political groups in the Nationalist zone was a major step in the process of transforming the small fascist party into a large organization which he would use as a dependable, bureaucratized mechanism. This would become one of the three pillars on which Franco based his absolute power; the other two were the Army and the Church. The counterrevolutionary coalition contained different interests and sensitivities, among which Franco played the role of arbiter, one whose price was total loyalty. This system turned the political power under the dictatorship into a dense network of clientele and patronage, a network that always ended with same person: the dictator.

Apart from these three pillars, the various ideologies in the Nationalist coalition and the networks of clientelism and patronage tightly connected to political and economic corruption, politics during the dictatorship was subject to the ups and downs of two major political cultures: one stemming from fascism, the other from national Catholicism. During his forty-year dictatorship, Franco utilized the differences and divisions among his supporters to perpetuate his power by giving greater prominence to one or another depending on national and international circumstances. Thus, the Second World War and the initial success of the fascist powers were key in the process of the fascistization that was promoted by Ramón Serrano Súñer, a key figure in the Franco regime. This fascistization, however, was more cosmetic than substantive. The process of fascistization fundamentally affected the areas that dealt with propaganda, control, recruiting, and social mobilization. These took a visible, legal form with the approval of the Work Charter or the Press Law (1938) or conversion, during 1940, of Falangist organizations like the Youth Front (FFJJ), the Women's Section (SF) (see Chapter 37), and the Spanish Trade Union Organization (OSE) into state institutions that monopolized policies regarding youth, women, and workers, respectively.

If international politics was the key to fascistization, then domestic politics and economic distress were what led to defascistization. The military and economic weakness of a country destroyed by civil war was key to Hitler refusing Franco's terms to enter the Second World War. In addition, the Falangists' own excesses generated enough discomfort in the Church and in the Army that in May 1941 they slammed the brakes on the fascistization politics of Serrano Súñer, and did so further during the summer of 1942. The attack by a group of Falangists in the Basilica of Begoña (Bilbao) against some carlist military officers, along with the changing course of the war, facilitated the start of policies of defascistization and the gradual rise of a new strongman: the ultra-Catholic admiral Luis Carrero Blanco.

Defascistization did not suggest, as some have claimed, the elimination of the single party. In any case, the dictator found the mostly docile and faithful version of the FET-JONS a very useful counterweight against the international pressures and the offensives launched by monarchist generals from 1943 to 1947 to restore the Bourbon monarchy in the person of Don Juan, the son of King Alfonso XIII. Franco's new strategy was to make a strong turn to the national-Catholic positions, and starting in 1943, the regime's public discourse accentuated its Catholic, Spanish, and anti-communist character. This new line was then embodied in a new cabinet, which Franco appointed in July 1945 including personalities from Catholic Action. The post of Secretary General of the Movement was left vacant until 1948. In terms of foreign policy, the new government moved closer to the Vatican and the United States. Internally, it approved laws like the 1945 Charter of the Spaniards, a putative bill of rights, which was applauded in the sermon of cardinal Pla and Daniel for its Christian orientation, or the March 1947 Law of Succession to the Head of State, that defined the regime as a Catholic, social, and representative state.

The official start of the Cold War in 1948 reaffirmed the strategy of the dictatorship, which at the beginning of the 1950s saw a new government with Carrero Blanco in an important position. The main policy directions of this government included the gradual abandonment of economic autarky, military agreements with the United States—even if Spain was left out of the Marshall Plan—and the signing of a Concordat with the Vatican. Domestically, it adopted more open—or at least tolerant—education and university polices. This later led to a new conflict that provoked riots between Falangists and protesting students in February 1956. The resolution to this conflict, which included a government crisis, did not mean the end of friction between these two political cultures. Instead, this entered a new phase when the Falange tried to take back political influence through three new bills: the Law on the Principles of National Movement, the Organic Law of the National Movement, and the Law of Regulation of the Government. This offensive was another Falangist failure and a success for Carrero Blanco's national-Catholic policies. These enjoyed even greater prominence when a new cabinet appointed in 1957 included technocratic ministers from Opus Dei and the reduced role of the Falange.

During the 1960s, the rivalry between political cultures persisted despite the supposed end to their infighting. Both Falangists and Catholics renewed their membership and political strategies, but it would be the latter who, now under the banner of Opus Dei technocrats, would succeed in realizing the goal of political institutionalization and economic development without political liberalization. Their project sought a technocratic administration with the central role played by a corporatist—not democratic—Parliament crowned by the naming of a successor to Franco. The development of this political project was marked with milestones like the enactment of the Law on the Legal Regime of the State Administration (1957), the Law of Administrative Procedure (1958), the Law on Fundamental Principles on the National Movement (1958), and the Organic State Law (1966). The climax came in the summer of 1969 when Franco proposed the appointment of Juan Carlos, grandson of Alfonso XIII, as his successor at the head of the Monarchy of the National Movement that maintained the institutions and principles of the regime. This successful program of political institutionalization by the technocrats was overshadowed only by the MATESA scandal, a case of corruption involving the diversion of public funds that involved two ministers and various officials linked to Opus Dei. Paradoxically, this governmental crisis did not produce a move back toward Falange; instead, the government appointed in October 1969 was clearly Catholic and technocratic, and made clear the fracture among the Francoist elites and the end of the political game that the dictator had refereed so well. It also meant the exhaustion of the two conflicting political projects: the fascist one had failed while the national-Catholic had been too successful. The other died from success.

This brand new structure soon collapsed for two reasons: the social change that the regime's economic policies had produced and the new international context, specifically the beginnings of European economic integration, of which the regime and its economic elites wanted to be a part. This final phase of the regime was soon turned into a deathwatch by the assassination of Admiral Luis Carrero Blanco, the man who had overseen the institutionalization of the regime, by the Basque separatist organization ETA in December 1973 and the collapse of the Portuguese and Greek dictatorships in April and July 1974, respectively. This crisis completed the fragmentation of the Francoist political class and opened a window of opportunity for opposition movements, a window that opened even wider when the dictator died on November 20, 1975.

Misery, Domination, Autarky

Postwar Spanish society can be defined with two adjectives and one common desire. In 1939, a hungry and traumatized people desired nothing more than to recover some kind of peace and normalcy. However, Francoism never intended that all the Spaniards would overcome the trauma of conflict and live without fear. On the contrary, Franco used the memory of the Civil War constantly, convincing Spanish society that they did not know how to live in peace. He took over their collective pain and distorted history to help him stay in power.

At least during the 1940s, the dictatorship was unable to resolve the problem of hunger. Even worse, its economic policies only exacerbated economic misery, resulting in a famine between 1939 and 1941 that was harsher than the better-known German occupation of the Netherlands during the winter of 1944–45. The big difference in the Spanish case, one it shared with the USSR in the 1930s, is that the famine was not provoked by a foreign military occupation, but by the economic policy of its own autocratic government (see Chapter 9). This policy was based on the three fundamental pillars of self-sufficiency, authority, and state intervention. In the Francoist philosophy, Spain was a rich country that did not need imports for its development. Once the borders had been closed, the only thing Spain needed to flourish was discipline and order from its economic actors. This was a massive mistake. The growth of the black market and the plummeting economic data were unstoppable. Rebuilding an economy that was as tied to the rest of the world as Spain's was would require the development of an economic policy that guaranteed the importation of raw materials, energy products, and capital goods. Instead,

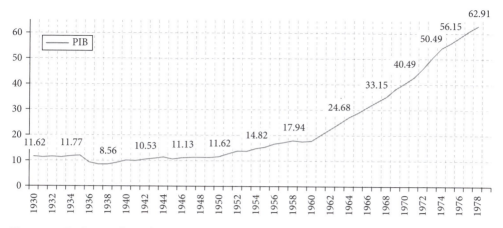

Figure 7.2 Evolution of Spain's GDP, 1930–79 (1995 = 100).
Source: A. Carreras & X. Tafunell, Estadísticas históricas . . .

autarky curtailed any chance of recovery. While Spain needed between ten and fifteen years for its main economic indicators to return to pre-Civil War levels (see Figure 7.2), Germany, Finland, France, and Holland needed only three years to recover to their pre-Second World War GDP levels; Greece and Belgium needed only four; and Italy only five despite having experienced substantial destruction during the Second World War.

The impact of the policy of autarky had an overwhelming effect on macroeconomics and on the daily lives of the population. During the 1940s, Spaniards' real wages were around half of 1935 levels, and per capita income did not match the 1935 level until 1953. Official food supplies became reliable only in 1943, and even then it was very scarce. While Spaniards recognized that there had been horrible hunger during the Civil War, the memory of the 1940s was seared into their minds, and for many, the postwar period was even worse: there was "nothing at all." The memory acquires an element of truth when one compares Spain's rationing with what was implemented in wartime Europe. In Germany, France, Holland, Norway, and Belgium, ration levels generally ranged between 1,200 and 2,000 calories per day. Even in Germany, postwar rationing never fell below 1,100 calories. In Spain, on the other hand, the official rations for 1941 fell 66 percent below minimum levels for proteins and carbohydrates, and the Rockefeller Foundation calculated that a modest Spanish family was getting the equivalent of only a third or a fourth of the nutrition it needed. This estimate is consistent with the grotesque figures for official food supplies that historians have calculated for the provinces of Jaén and Almería, and explains how 200,000 Spaniards died of starvation-related causes in the postwar years.

Not all Spaniards suffered these conditions equally. Those who had depended on the 150,000 people executed by the regime suffered most, but the number increases exponentially if we consider everyone who was a victim of the regime's broad repressive repertoire. It was precisely during those years of hunger that thousands of men and women were crammed into hundreds of prisons and concentration camps. There they died of starvation and from endemic diseases while their spouses and children on the outside fought malnourishment and struggled to help them. The difficult situation of prisoners' wives and children was compounded by the Law of Political Responsibilities, which, just like the military repression, mainly affected the 1939 poor. Thousands of families had their property and belongings confiscated by these courts just when they most needed them. In addition, many were victims of purges and found themselves fined or even dismissed from their jobs. While economic policy plunged the entire country into misery, the division between the winners and losers turned the survival of the latter into an illusion.

In this way, the regime placed a large part of the population outside the law. A minority went into the hills to fight in the guerrilla, but reaction of the vast majority was resignation or political passivity. When it came to the question of daily economic survival, however, Spaniards reacted differently, turning breaking the law into something that was both common and considered acceptable. They concealed crops, stole food from the fields, in train stations and in ports, and constructed an active black market. This last was a multifaceted phenomenon that resulted in some people connected with the regime taking advantage of their contacts and position of impunity to great personal fortunes. Alongside the black market there was the "gray" market, a form of compensatory justice of the weak against the wrongs committed by the powerful or the State. As well as using it for economic purposes, ordinary Spaniards turned the gray market into a form of hidden protest or boycott of Francoist economic policies.

The *guerrilla* was something very different, a product of the end of the Civil War and the regime's policies of exclusion that led some of the vanquished to "head for the hills." This was the origin of the first *guerrilla* groups, some of which did not have any particular political ideology, although most of them eventually ended up under the hegemony of the Spanish Communist Party (PCE). The struggle of the guerrillas was clearly an unequal fight. Although it initially had the support from a large sector of the peasantry, by 1947–48 it became a suicidal fight that ended in utter defeat. Between 1943 and 1952, around 2,500 *guerrillas* were killed, and a similar number ended up in Francoist prisons. In addition, approximately 22,000 "contacts" were also arrested. Thus, despite the harsh conditions of life and work, the vast majority of the population avoided direct confrontation with the regime, opting instead for a hidden resistance that was carried out anonymously. This hidden resistance included boycotts, sit-down strikes, jokes, rumors, and mass absences from Falangist rallies. The choice of these forms of resistance was closely linked to the excessive costs of harsh repression and the need to protect and safeguard their own families. Spaniards had learned that direct confrontation was not effective and that, despite being humiliating and not always effective, it was often better to cause the authorities moral dilemmas by using Catholic language and appearing to show them respect and gratitude in the hope that the regime would react positively.

Given all this, it is not surprising that in the early 1950s there were voices from within the regime itself that acknowledged the failures of autarky. These were prudent critiques that produced timid changes in economic policy in the direction of greater liberalization and less state intervention (the most significant measure was the elimination of rationing books). These changes were helped by credits given by American banks following the 1953 treaty that permitted the United States to establish military bases in Spain. However, these credits paled in comparison to the assistance provided under the European Recovery Program (Marshall Plan). While France received $2.4 billion, Germany and Italy $1.29 billion, Austria $977.7 million, Greece $515.1 million, and even neighboring Portugal $50.5 million, Spain was excluded and got nothing at all.

Meanwhile, in Spain, the imbalance between prices and salaries persisted, and earning a livelihood in the countryside became even more complicated. During the 1950s, the purchasing power of the average European citizen doubled, ushering in the consumer society.

Not in Spain, however: the inflation that lasted until the 1960s delayed the construction of a mass consumer market. The arrival of consumerism also required the migration of people from the countryside to the city. If this movement had already occurred in areas of large estates in the 1940s and 1950s, in the 1960s it reached regions with very small landholdings (see Chapter 19). A similar phenomenon occurred throughout Europe, but in Spain it came much later and had less impact (see Figure 7.3). For example, more than 46,000 inhabitants migrated from Zamora province during the 1950s, a loss of population greater than that produced between 1920 and 1950. This dynamic would intensify during the 1960s contributing to the decline of the traditional peasantry all over Spain. If in the 1950s most migrants were landless peasants, now an increasing number of small farmers joined them. These migrants ended mostly in the country's big cities, although close to a million of them went to work in economically booming Europe.

Development, emigration, protest

The 1950s marked the beginning of the unequal golden age of the global economy. It was a period of splendor that was primarily shaped by and benefited the Western economies. The years from 1950 to 1973 witnessed an explosive growth in the economy. Global manufacturing production quadrupled during the 1950s, while international trade of manufactured goods increased tenfold. While Spain remained mired in Francoist autarky, with its interventionism and protectionism, the neighboring economies grew at a rate of 5 percent due to widespread abandonment of protectionist policies and the increase in public spending. The mere removal of barriers to international trade was a huge advance in overcoming economic stagnation; it also allowed the start of a gradual process of integration among the European economies. Even before the 1957 Treaty of Rome—which created the European Economic Community (CEE)—Germany, Italy, France, Belgium, and the Netherlands benefited from international trade among themselves. The second key element explaining European growth was the increase in labor productivity, a reality linked to industrialization and the growth of the service sector. This development was made possible by policies in a number of countries that invested in the strategic sectors and encouraged social pacts between employers and workers, which created virtuous circles of growth based on higher government spending, the implementation of a progressive income tax, the creation of welfare states and moderate increases in salaries.

In contrast, the Spanish "economic miracle" of the 1960s was less the successful outcome of good government policy than the result of a correction of previous policies which freed the Spanish economy from the shackles preventing it from benefiting from the economic expansion of the postwar world. The 1959 Stabilization Plan allowed for an influx of foreign capital into Spain: $40 million in 1960, $322 million in 1965, and $697 million in 1970, which contributed to the country's industrialization. The results were immediate. Between 1960 and 1974, the economy grew at a rate of 7 percent and productivity increased at an average of 5.9 percent. This increase in productivity was based mainly in the industrial sector, which grew at a rate of 10 percent annually. However, this unprecedented growth did not have the same effects as in the rest of Europe. The regime did not encourage a social pact between capital and labor and ongoing repression made any redistribution of wealth through progressive taxation or welfare policies less urgent. The result was a modern, urban, and industrialized country with extreme levels of inequality.

The difference between the highest and lowest incomes grew between 1964 and 1967, and began to decline only after 1970. On top of long-standing class divisions, this unequal growth meant that in 1974 the top half of the population possessed 79 percent of the national income.

Class was only one kind of inequality: there were also marked inequalities among Spain's regions. The meager Plans for Development in the 1960s reduced investments in infrastructure so that industries were concentrated in regions where they already existed, although new industrial centers emerged in Madrid, Zaragoza, and Pamplona. The result was that in 1968, half of Spain's industrial workers were concentrated in Madrid, Catalonia, and the Basque Country. Extremadura, Galicia, and Andalusia represented the other side of the coin. In 1975 their per capita GDP was only 47.1, 59.5, and 62 percent, of the European average, respectively.

The boom was possible only through the sacrifice and exploitation of ordinary people. Economic growth did transform Spain into a mass consumer society, but access to it was so unequal that, unlike the rest of Europe, throughout the 1970s Spanish families remained units of production with relatively low levels of consumption. While the majority of young Europeans spent their time studying, or, if they worked, saving their salary or spending it on entertainment, most young Spaniards still worked and gave a part of their salary to their families in order to help defray collective costs. These personal efforts and the family strategies enabled them to acquire access goods such as electrical appliances (washing machines, refrigerators); motorcycles or cars, such as the iconic SEAT 600; or holidays on the Mediterranean coast (see Figure 7.3).

Newly opened borders allowed people, as well as goods and money, to pass. Two kinds of population movements, migration and tourism, were important factors that drove economic growth. The sun, the beach, and favorable currency exchange rates encouraged millions of French, Britons, Germans, and Scandinavians—themselves beneficiaries of the progressive policies Spaniards lacked—to choose Spain as a vacation spot. The growth in tourism was exceptional. Spain received one million tourists in 1954; two million in 1957; four million in 1960; and 19 million in 1969. These travelers not only left their money, which contributed to tourism revenue that exceeded $297million in 1960, but also prompted social and cultural

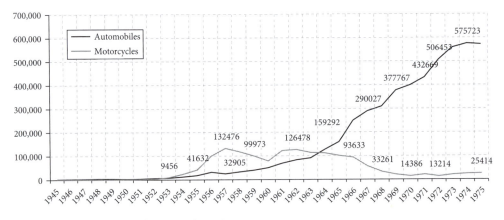

Figure 7.3 Automobiles and motorcycles in Spain, 1945–75.

Source: A. Carreras & X. Tafunell, Estadísticas históricas . . .

changes undesired by the dictator. Foreign tourists not only consumed and gave employment to hotel and restaurant workers; they also lived among the Spanish and publically exhibited the benefits of freedom. European workers, for example, enjoyed paid vacations and good salaries that permitted them to travel. They also behaved in ways the most recalcitrant sectors of the regime feared. In their view, short skirts and bikinis were morally corrupt. Just as in the Greek and Portuguese dictatorships, the most traditional sectors viewed the customs of foreigners as forms of Americanization and immorality that could end up shaking the pillars of authority, religion, and tradition that underlay their regimes.

In spite of this, the regime sought to use economic growth, new economic values, and leisure to generate political passivity and consent. It was a relatively successful strategy as conformity reigned among the majority of Spaniards. However, a general lethargy coexisted with a growing and active minority, especially in the universities, factories, in neighborhood and community associations, and in groups connected to regional nationalisms which helped open windows of political opportunity which later turned into cycles of protest (see Figure 7.4). Events between 1973 and 1977 made the continuation of a dictatorship without Franco seem unimaginable. However, for Spaniards, the main political value was the maintenance of peace, or avoiding another civil war. This meant that protest was generally peaceful, but also that once Franco died, the silent and passive majority would support, indeed consider inevitable, the democratization of the country. If the pro-Franco military established the lines that could be crossed, the collective action of the conscious minority marked what could be maintained. This new situation, along with the growing desire of the economic and political elites to join the CEE, allowed for the difficult road toward Spanish democracy.

The immediate strategy for opening those windows was to take advantage of the cracks in new Francoist legislation. These laws did not liberalize the dictatorship but they did turn a very restrictive regime into one where spaces of social protest could be found. Key among these laws were the Collective Agreement Act (1958), which permitted labor negotiations; the Law on Political Rights and the Professional Employment of Women (1961); the Law of Conciliation and Arbitration of Labour Disputes (1962), and the reformed Civil Code of 1965, which regulated labor conflicts. The Associations Act (1964) facilitated the creation of neighborhood associations, while the Press and Publications Act (1966) ended prior

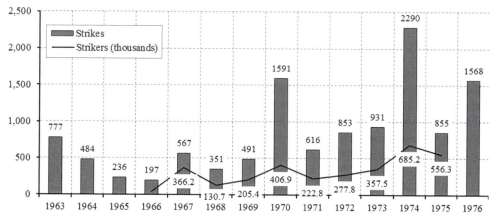

Figure 7.4 Number of strikes and strikers, 1963–77.

Source: A. Carreras & X. Tafunell, Estadísticas históricas . . .

censorship. Furthermore, the Organic Statute of the National Movement (1968), and reforms to the civil code in 1970, 1972, and 1975, reduced the brazen legal discrimination against women (see Chapter 11).

Active minorities utilized this new legislation to create open spaces that were safe for dissent: union halls, parishes, and university classrooms. The immediate strategy was to promote participation in collective action that avoided openly political objectives and focused instead on wages, better working conditions, improvements in the quality of education and the construction of new public services like water, sewers, and parks for neighborhoods. These claims were framed in a growing struggle for the right to self-organization. A new covert democratic political culture was brewing that, in a quiet way, manifested the hopes of popular sovereignty as a source of power and legitimacy: the right to demand rights. The activist minority utilized a diverse repertoire of political actions that included strikes, occupations, sit-ins, marches, boycotts, hunger strikes, petitions, lighting rallies, and demonstrations.

Strikes were frequent after 1967, while the assassination of Carrero Blanco at the end of 1973 marked the beginning of an extensive and radicalized cycle of protest. Students and workers, who were a part of the traditional political minority, joined hands with the residents of neighborhoods, housewives, feminists, the peasantry, and activists fighting for cultural freedoms. Complaints and protests became increasingly varied, but if there was one demand that all these groups shared in common, it was amnesty for political prisoners. This demand implicitly included the demand for the free exercise of the rights of citizenship: freedom of expression, freedom of assembly, and the right to strike.

The peaceful and restrained nature of these protests also affected opposition organizations. Since the 1950s, the Communist Party (PCE) had advocated a policy of national reconciliation, adopting the strategy of peaceful national strikes and alliances with other political forces as the way to achieve change. A corollary to this strategy was a policy of approximation to (and an infiltration of) worker, student, and intellectual circles. During this time, the PCE experienced a series of schisms and tumults. One was the expulsion of party leaders Fernando Claudín and Jorge Semprún in the mid-1960s; both had become highly critical of the PCE's official line that maintained that the Franco regime and Spain's capitalist system were on the verge of collapse. Another crisis was the creation of two competing forces: the Communist Movement (MC) and the PCE (Internacional). In spite of those setbacks, the PCE was able to evolve and make itself into the point of reference for the political opposition, embracing the de facto reformist theory of "Eurocommunism." For its part, the Socialist party (PSOE) was much less significant. It was badly divided between the leadership in exile and a growing group of younger people within Spain who enjoyed the support of French Socialists and German Social Democrats. These younger Spanish Socialists were also influenced by the ideas and political strategies of those parties: democracy was a core element of socialism, and Marxism was simply one other tool for analyzing society. The key goal was to win elections, and this meant gaining the support of the middle class. This group, led by Felipe González and Alfonso Guerra, won a major victory at the 1974 party congress in Suresnes (France).

Another key organization in the opposition to Francoism was the Workers' Commissions (CCOO). The CCOO chose to work in the open rather than clandestinely, and did so by running candidates for elected positions in the official union organization (OSE). A downside to this strategy was that it left its militants vulnerable. In February 1967, the

Supreme Court banned CCOO on the grounds that it was merely the union arm of the Communist Party, a decision that was followed by two years of severe repression. There were other opposition unions, the Socialist UGT, the anarcho-syndicalist CNT, and the social Catholic Unión Sindical Obrera (USO), but they were smaller and had less impact than the Workers' Commissions.

The exceptions that prove the rule about the peaceful nature of political opposition were the regional nationalist movements, particularly the Basque terrorist organization *Euskadi ta Askatasuna* (Basque Land and Liberty, or ETA) (see Chapter 10). This organization had its roots in the Catholic Universidad de Deusto and the youth wing of the Basque Nationalist party (PNV) in the late 1950s and early 1960s. For ETA, the situation of the Basque Country was analogous to colonies such as Algeria and Vietnam, which were fighting for their independence. This meant that the Basque situation was different from that in the rest of Spain and justified the use of armed struggle. ETA ideology contained a strong dose of revolutionary socialism, and in 1967 it defined itself as a socialist movement for Basque national liberation. In June 1968, ETA claimed its first victim, a Civil Guard named Pardines, the beginning of a long and bloody history which would include the assassination of Carrero Blanco in 1973 and which would claim 829 victims before the organization declared its armed struggle over in 2011.

Definitions, chronologies

The construction of the academic literature about the Franco dictatorship centered on the debate among sociologists, political scientists, and historians about the nature of *franquismo* and how it could be defined. This controversy was also connected to the international debate about the political and social support for fascism and, therefore, intended not only to describe the main features of Francoism, but also to compare it to the different types of dictatorships (conservative, military, fascist, totalitarian, authoritarian, and developmentalist) that ruled in Europe after the end of the First World War. The debate was heated and produced numerous competing definitions and typologies, although these could be divided into two large groups. The first group concerned itself with the specific characteristics of Francoism and described its ideological foundations, political forms, and social support. The second emphasized the European historical context that had given birth to the Franco dictatorship and its "historical mission." It also examined the levels of repression during the economic, political, and cultural crisis of the liberal system.

The definitions chosen by the first group (conservatism, authoritarianism, developmentalism, and clientelism) were essentially descriptive and emphasized the regime's longevity, adaptability, and the central roles of the Church and Army. It gave particular importance to Spain's perceived economic and cultural backwardness in the years between the two world wars, which it saw as an obstacle to the emergence of real fascism or totalitarianism. In contrast, the second group was more materialist and interested in finding the roots of the regime, although it too used many different descriptors: modern despotism, Bonapartism, cleric-fascism, or fascism. These expressions described the construction of a reactionary coalition that, despite the complex balance of forces that existed within it, had adopted political solutions similar to those in Germany or Italy: the creation of a single party with organizations for youth, women, and workers; corporatist and autarkic economic policies; anti-parliamentarianism; repression and the destruction of the labor movement. This was a series of policies intended to produce one overriding goal: stabilizing capitalism and ensuring the continuing domination of the financial, industrial, and landowning elites.

Despite their differences, these two approaches did agree on some things. For example, those who defined Francoism as an authoritarian regime accepted that there was a fascist, or at least fascist-like, period between 1936 and 1945. On the other hand, those who defended the fascist character of Francoism admitted its peculiarities, such as the limited political clout of the single party and its inability to turn itself into an instrument of mobilization of the masses. Thus, in the mid-1990s a third option started gaining support, one that defined Francoism as "para-fascist" or a "fascistized" dictatorship. Roger Griffin defines these as dictatorships composed of counterrevolutionary coalitions similar to fascism, but in which the fascist component is subordinated to state power, which is generally held by traditional elites. At certain moments these regimes adopt a fascist appearance: one party, cult of the leader, ultranationalist, etc., and even selectively co-opt fascist political leaders. Once they become part of a pragmatic regime prepared to adapt itself to changing contexts and circumstances, these fascist politicians themselves adapt. This approach is useful for describing a number of regimes in addition to Franco's: Vichy France, the Metaxas dictatorship in Greece, Engelbert Dollfuss's Austria, or Portugal under Salazar. However, the very longevity and adaptability of the two Iberian dictatorships and their political leaderships demands that they be seen not only as regimes which became fascistized, but also as regimes that threw off their fascist trappings.

Policies, adaptations, and historical contingencies all require the construction of a chronology or periodization of the nearly forty years of the Franco dictatorship. But establishing periods or phases is itself controversial. These phases often depend on the historiographical focus of each author or the political, social, and economic aspects that they consider crucial. However, most researchers have agreed to establish at least two major periods, with 1959 as a major breaking point. This was the year in which autarky was abandoned for a more liberal and open economic policy embodied in the Stabilization Plan (additionally, Spain had joined the International Monetary Fund, or IMF, in 1958 and would become a member of the Organization for Economic Co-operation and Development, or OECD, in 1961). These measures opened the Spanish economy to free-market capitalism (and the international markets), which resulted in an accelerated economic growth that fundamentally transformed Spanish society.

Defining these two major periods is not the end of the question of periodization. Taking national and international politics as points of reference, there are generally deemed to have been five periods in the life of the regime, three before 1959 and two after. "First" Francoism is divided into the years of the Civil War (1936–1939) in which the regime was configured; a second "fascist" or national-syndicalist phase during the Second World War, and a third national-catholic phase between 1945 and 1959. "Second" Francoism is also generally divided into two phases: the first featuring an authoritarian economic development marked by the rise of the Opus Dei (1959–69) and the second and final stage, "late Francoism," or the final crisis of the regime (1969–75).

If, however, we take economic and social development as a point of reference, there is a general consensus on dividing the life of the regime into three major periods. The first, defined by economic autarky, comprised the years from 1939 to 1952 and was characterized by an economic recession that reached unprecedented levels of famine between 1939 and 1942.

Autarky generated food shortages well into the second half of the 1940s, isolated the Spanish economy from the global markets, and was accompanied by interventionist policies that tried to regulate production and trade and invested significant public funds in industrialization. These policies produced an unmitigated economic disaster that the regime tried to alleviate in the second stage (1952–59). In those years, it abandoned some measures like rationing, but did not dismantle the interventionist and protectionist system. These timid measures did produce economic growth of four percent annually that by 1953 had returned per capita income to pre-Civil War levels. However, the imbalances of the system at a macroeconomic level were such that at the end of the 1950s, Spain was experiencing rampant inflation, structural unemployment, and an immense budget deficit. This situation, and the threat of default on its foreign debt, resulted in the adoption of the Stabilization Plan in June 1959. The Plan would result in a third stage of development, the "economic miracle" between 1960 and 1973–74. The economy grew around 7 percent per year and there was a radical social transformation from a rural society based on agriculture to an urban society based on the service and industrial sectors. This brief "golden age" of Spanish capitalism was brought to an end by the 1973 oil crisis. This demonstrated that the greatest virtue of the economic policies of the 1960s was that it did not hinder Spain from benefiting from Europe's economic boom. On the other hand, the effects of the oil crisis also resulted in a social and economic crisis during the Transition, which increased the social mobilization that politicians tried to alleviate through the Moncloa Pacts of 1977.

In an optimistic poem, "The ephemeral tomorrow," Antonio Machado wrote that "the vain yesterday will produce a tomorrow which is empty, and thus fleeting." Less lyrically, but with greater realism, Enzo Traverso claimed that during the present, the past, and the future engage in a dialogue when they both constantly create and reinvent themselves. In this way, times of crisis are perfect for revisiting our interpretations of the past. The crisis which started in 2008 shook Europe to its roots, making visible conflicts within Europe as well as the existence of a profound North-South divide.

Looking at the "vain yesterday" of the Spanish dictatorship—as well as those in Portugal, Italy and Greece—can help us understand not only the dominant political culture in these countries, but also their problems in integrating into the patterns of the countries of northern and central Europe. The Spanish experience, along with the Greek, appears to support the thesis that the overthrow of a regime dominated by mechanisms of extraction will bring a new elite which will exploit the same set of extractive mechanisms, or renovated ones. Real democratization can come only from below and over a long period of time if old vicious circles are to be turned into new, virtuous ones. Moreover, the histories of civil war and dictatorship in southern Europe kept them out of the post-Second World War social contract, and in the case of Spain, delayed its participation in the golden age of western capitalism by a decade, a delay which mortgaged the future of its lower classes, a mortgage they continue to pay.

Further reading

Carreras, Albert, and Xavier Tafunell, *Estadísticas históricas de España, siglos XIX y XX*, Bilbao: BBVA, 2005.
Cazorla, Antonio, *Franco. The Biography of the Myth*, New York: Routledge, 2014.

Cazorla, Antonio, *Fear and Progress: Ordinary Lives in Franco's Spain, 1939-1975*, Oxford: Blackwell, 2009.

Cruz, Rafael, *Protestar en España 1900-2013*, Madrid: Alianza, 2015.

Griffin, Roger, *The Nature of Fascism*, London: Routledge, 1993.

Judt, Tony, *Postwar: A History of Europe since 1945*, New York: Penguin, 2005.

Preston, Paul, *Franco. A Biography*, London: Harper Collins, 1993.

Ruiz, Julius, *Franco's Justice: Repression in Madrid after the Spanish Civil War*, Oxford: Clarendon Press, 2005.

Saz, Ismael, *España contra España. Los nacionalismos franquistas*, Madrid: Marcial Pons, 2003.

Saz, Ismael, "Fascism, Fascistization and Developmentalism in Franco's Dictatorship," *Social History*, 29, 3 (2004), pp. 342–57.

Townson, Nigel (ed.), *Spain Transformed: The Late Franco Dictatorship, 1959-1975*, Houndmills: Palgrave, 2007.

CHAPTER 8
FROM DEMOCRATIC TRANSITION TO CONSOLIDATION AND *CRISPACIÓN*: 1970s–PRESENT
Pamela B. Radcliff

After forty years of dictatorship, in the 1970s Spain began a political transition to what would become the longest and most stable period of democratic government in its history. In the afterglow of what was universally considered to be a successful transition to (and consolidation of) democracy, the only major debates in the first couple of decades revolved around which factors contributed most to Spain's achievement. The question was important, not only in comparing the dramatically different outcomes of Spain's first and second twentieth-century democratic transitions, but in the hopes of creating a blueprint that other countries could follow in the subsequent succession of transitions from authoritarian rule. In global terms, Spain continues to be celebrated as one of the few fully consolidated democracies of the so-called third wave transitions, which began with southern Europe in the mid-1970s and culminated in Eastern Europe in the early 1990s. Not surprisingly, however, within Spain the consensus and satisfaction that marked the early years of democratic rule have been supplanted by a more combative political culture, in which disagreements about the past, present, and future direction of the country have raised questions about both the "model" transition and the quality of the democratic polity that resulted from it. These questions have been exacerbated since 2008 and the "great recession," which has brought confidence in the functioning of Spain's democracy to an all-time low. At the same time, there remains a fundamental broad consensus about the basic framework of democratic government that did not exist in the 1930s. It may in fact be the sense of security about Spain's democratic stability that has provided an invisible perimeter for the politics of *crispación* (tension or conflict) among the current generation of "grandchildren" of the transition.

The transition to democracy

The initial celebratory view of the "model" transition was framed in both domestic and global terms. Domestically, the relatively peaceful and consensual transition from dictatorship to democracy contrasted dramatically with the turbulent and polarizing democratic experiment of the 1930s, which had ended in civil war. Globally, Spain negotiated an essentially uncharted path, laying the groundwork for what would become a new model for other authoritarian regimes transitioning to democracy. When Franco died in November 1975, there was no prefabricated blueprint, meaning the outcome was neither defined nor predestined. Thus, there was not yet either an international democracy project or a developed scholarly discourse to lend either logistical or theoretical guidance or support. It is true that the neighboring Portuguese dictatorship had recently been overturned in the Carnation Revolution of April 1974, but Spanish elites did not want to imitate either the military intervention or the tumultuous revolutionary process in which Portugal was still embroiled at the end of 1975. Later the two Iberian countries would be held up as vanguard success stories in what came to be called the "third wave" of democratic transitions, but in the moment it was clear only that some sort of transition was underway. The exact periodization of Spain's transition and consolidation is still debated, but the Constitution of 1978 marked the end of the formal institutional transition to a democratic regime, and most historians agree that consolidation was secure by 1982, or at the latest, 1986.

Although for a long time there was broad scholarly and popular consensus regarding the success of Spain's "model" transition, not everyone has agreed about its essential ingredients. Since the early 1980s, Spain's transition has been marshaled as evidence of the importance of a range of factors, from economic and social modernization, to global support, elite decisions, and civil society mobilization. Each of these factors is highlighted by a competing interpretive "school" that makes claims about the key ingredient to success. After decades of debate, the most convincing synthesis is that the Spanish transition emerged out of a favorable confluence of all these ingredients, although the exact ordering of each factor is still debatable. While the Spanish transition continues to be an object of study for comparative social scientists seeking to unlock the universal secrets of success, it is also increasingly a subject for historians, who are situating the process in the long-term trajectory of Spanish political evolution.

Origins of the transition

From this contextual historical perspective, Spain had more resources than the majority of the "developing" nations of the "third wave" with which it was often grouped. In social and economic terms, by the 1970s Spain had completed its long transition from an agrarian and rural to a largely industrial and urban society (see chapters 7, 9). While there is no automatic relationship between development and democracy, some threshold level of economic development and distribution of wealth seems to be necessary to create the infrastructure of communication, education, and welfare that sustains the fundamental bonds between a community of democratic citizens. Rising standards of living do not automatically create the basis for democratic consensus, but huge extremes of poverty and wealth are difficult to negotiate within a democratic system.

Equally important in creating a more favorable environment for democratic transition than in the 1930s was Spain's geographic location in Western Europe. Thus, the fact that Spain's transition occurred in a confidently democratic Europe clearly structured the choices that could be made when the opportunity to create a new regime opened up. In contrast, in the Europe of the 1930s, democracy was only one, and not even the strongest, game in town. Furthermore, the increasing commercial, economic, and cultural ties established between a liberalizing southern Europe and its democratic northern neighbors brought this way of life into public view in a way that had not been true during the early more insular decades of the dictatorship. Within Spain, the aspirational myth of joining an advanced "Europe" dated back to at least the late nineteenth century, surviving as a persistent counter-narrative to the Franco regime's embrace of the motto that "Spain is different" (see Chapter 15). During the transition, "Europeanization" and "democratization" became almost fused as interchangeable values.

In addition to more favorable economic, social, and international conditions, Spain had significant usable political capital, despite the forty years of authoritarian rule. The country had a long, if unstable, history of constitutional government dating from the early 1800s, and a parallel trajectory of popular political mobilization, even though the latter was never fully incorporated into a functional democratic system. An active public sphere had continued to grow and develop until the forcible demobilization after 1939, but it already begun to recover in the 1960s, when semilegal trade unions, student movements, dissident church groups, Catalan and Basque cultural organizations and neighborhood associations emerged, sometimes directly opposing the regime but often simply organizing for discrete changes in their everyday lives.

Both types of grassroots organization had an erosive impact on the legitimacy of the dictatorship. Oppositional movements disrupted the Franco regime's narrative of "25 years of peace" (proclaimed in 1965) and its strategy of bolstering legitimacy through economic growth (see Chapter 7). More diffusely, interest group associations opened an autonomous, or semiautonomous space inside a dictatorship that enhanced pluralism and often forced the authoritarian state into opening a dialogue. Through engaging in this dialogue, civil society organizations learned how to articulate collective interests and make demands, as well as developing the skills and habits of self-government. This expanding civil society mobilization was not powerful or coherent enough to overthrow the dictatorship or even to dictate the terms of the transition. But the "push from below" helped convince some regime elites of the need for reforms and strengthened the hand of democratic opposition forces once the formal transition period opened.

The eventual willingness of a group of Francoist elites to open a dialogue with the democratic opposition was a key element of the Spanish model, which combined "top down" negotiations with the push "from below." Beyond the general favorable conditions of a threshold level of economic development and a friendly European neighborhood, Spain's transition was made by human actions and decisions, both collective and individual. Competing schools of thought have emphasized the primacy of one or the other, but in reality, both were essential parts of a dynamic decision-making process.

At the same time, it is important to emphasize that before Franco's death no moves toward any sort of democratic political transition had been prepared or initiated from above. The *continuistas* or the "bunker" maintained control, rejecting even limited proposals for greater openness and representation, while Franco proclaimed that everything had been effectively "tied down" to secure the survival of the dictatorship after his death. But even if the reformer faction had taken the reins, they had no plan for regime transition, as was evident in the cosmetic changes proposed by the first government installed after Franco's death. It was not until Franco's designated successor, King Juan Carlos, initiated the formation of a new government in July 1976 with the appointment of Prime Minister Adolfo Suarez, that a more open-ended process was set in motion.

The institutional transition: July 1976 to December 1978

The institutional political transition occurred between July 1976 and December 1978, when a new democratic Constitution was handily approved by the voters. In the immediate aftermath, admiring observers emphasized the speed, the relative peacefulness, and the spirit of compromise and consensus that produced a settlement acceptable to most major players as well as the majority of the population. In the midst of the process, however, there was both uncertainty and conflict, not only about how to transition to democracy, but about what kind of democracy it would be.

One axis of this uncertain process was the interaction between elite negotiations and an increasingly massive popular mobilization of citizen and labor groups. Not surprisingly, the agendas and goals of all these players differed dramatically, as did their competing visions of the contours of a future democratic government. Some envisioned a liberal representative monarchy while others imagined a more participatory socialist democratic republic, and still others, especially in the Basque Country and Catalonia, hoped for a radically decentralized federal system or even independence, in the case of ETA. Thus, the transition began not only without a clear blueprint regarding the process of moving from an authoritarian to a democratic regime, but without consensus about the meaning of democracy itself.

The dynamic relationship between the "push from below" and elite actions was evident from the moment of the King's appointment of Suarez, which was made in the context of a burgeoning wave of popular mobilization as well as the unification of the democratic opposition in the Democratic Coordination or *Platajunta*, in March, and the first mass demonstration of 75,000 people in Barcelona in February. In addition to mobilizing in defense of a range of specific issues, the popular opposition was coalescing around demands for political rights, amnesty, and a complete institutional rupture to a democratic republic. Because all of these demands and actions were still illegal, and the repressive apparatus of the Francoist regime remained in place, protesters were arrested, beaten, and even shot, as in a police raid in Vitoria in March, in which five striking workers were killed. Faced with the Francoist "bunker" on the one hand, and the democratic opposition which denied his legitimacy on the other, King Juan Carlos gambled on a young man who had held posts in the Franco regime but had no investment in holding on to the past.

Over the next crucial six months, Adolfo Suarez proved to be an astute politician who launched a transition process and convinced most of the key players to participate. He began by promising to lead Spain to a "modern democracy," institute political pluralism and hold a free election within a year's time. He first approached the key players of the dictatorship, presenting his plan for political reform to the military leadership, the *Movimiento* and finally, in November, to the *Cortes*, which voted overwhelmingly to endorse his plan, even though it would lead to the dissolution of that body. There is probably no single reason that explains the acquiescence of many of the Francoist elites to the dismantling of the dictatorship. The perhaps grudging agreement of the military not to interfere at this point was due in part to their institutional duty to serve Franco's successor, Juan Carlos, in part to the pressure exerted by reformist defense minister Gutierrez Mellado, and in part a result of Franco's longer term efforts to separate military and political authority in order to secure his personal dominance. In terms of the political elites in the *Cortes*, some may have believed they could still be elected in a democratic system while others might have feared that failure to accept a negotiated transition would lead to a more radical rupture (the Portuguese scenario). Indeed, all of these internal negotiations were taking place in a context of still-intensifying popular mobilization, including, in September, 100,000 people marching in Madrid in the name of "bread, work and liberty" and another million publicly celebrating Catalonia's national holiday, the Diada, with calls for amnesty, freedom, and autonomy, and, in November, a general strike with at least one million workers demanding freedom, amnesty, and wage increases.

In any case, once Suarez had secured the legal authorization from the existing regime institutions, he held a referendum on December 15, in which 94 percent of voters, representing a solid 77 percent turnout, responded in the affirmative to his plan of negotiated transition. The meaning of that "yes" vote is difficult to interpret, and once again there were probably varying motivations among the general population. In strategic terms, the resounding "yes" vote further weakened the remaining bunker, but it also undermined the opposition's demand for rupture, since the *Platajunta*'s call to abstain from voting was ignored by most Spaniards. The opposition and later critics of the transition argued that the referendum was held in a climate of fear, with the government insinuating that a "no" vote might unleash a revolution, a military coup or a return to civil war. Public opinion polls taken at the end of the dictatorship indicate that the majority of the population valued peace and economic prosperity over "democracy" or "freedom," which is hardly surprising after four decades of Francoist insistence that these latter values would lead only to disorder and chaos. Some have disparaged this mentality as "sociological Francoism," while others see a healthy rejection of extremist politics and an attraction to moderate or centrist views on the part of a population weary of ideological struggles and ready for reconciliation. The preference for centrist positions defined significant turning points in the transition process, most notably the June 1977 parliamentary elections, in which Spaniards voted overwhelmingly for center-left and -right parties.

Whether fear or moderation weighed more heavily in the popular vote in December, it helped convince the main parties of the democratic opposition that a complete rupture was no longer viable. At the same time, Suarez' plan to incorporate and negotiate with opposition groups, as long as they agreed to certain ground rules (most notably the monarchist form of the state), provided further inducement to accept a compromise position of "negotiated rupture." Thus, the major statewide opposition parties, the Socialists (PSOE) and the Communists (PCE), as well as the center/right Catalanist party, Democratic Convergence of Catalonia (CDC) led by Jordi Pujol, all agreed to participate with the government in a process to establish a constitutional monarchy. In return, Suarez legalized political parties (February 1977), trade unions (March), and, most dramatically, the PCE (April). The PCE under Santiago Carrillo had already considerably moderated its rhetoric since the 1930s, having adopted a discourse of democracy and national reconciliation since the 1960s, but its legalization was a huge symbolic gesture that could be viewed as the key turning point in Suarez' credibility with the opposition.

The next step in the negotiated rupture was the June 1977 parliamentary election, for which almost 79 percent of the eligible voters turned out. In the run-up to the elections, 78 political parties were legalized, including Adolfo Suarez' new party, the Union of the Democratic Centre (UCD). With a panoply of choices from extreme left to extreme right, the results narrowed the field to what some political scientists have called an "imperfect bi-party system." That is, two-thirds of the votes (and over 80 percent of the seats in the weighted electoral system) went to two parties, the center-right UCD (34 percent) and the center-left PSOE (29 percent), with another 18 percent divided evenly between the conservative Alianza Popular (AP) (8.8 percent) and the left-wing PCE (9.3 percent). The exception, which also further complicated the bi-party model, was the regional vote. Thus, at the statewide level, 2.8 percent was received by the Catalan Nationalists and 1.7 percent by the Basque PNV. Within Catalonia, however, 16 percent voted for the centrist Catalan coalition led by Pujol and another 19 percent for the Catalan Communist party (PSUC), followed by the PSOE, with the UCD in fourth place.

The largest statewide party, the UCD, was actually a coalition of more than a dozen small groups whose ideologies ranged from Christian democratic to social democratic and liberal. Its victory reflected both Suarez' popularity and his visibility as well as his access to state-controlled media, but it also represented a familiar demographic bloc of rural and middle-class voters. Most of the PSOE's votes came from another familiar bloc of urban and industrial middle and working classes. The most activist working class and student left voted for the PCE/PSUC (as well as for other small revolutionary parties), but party leaders and supporters were shocked at the poor electoral showing of the party (outside of Catalonia) that had stood at the forefront of opposition to the Franco regime. On the other side of the spectrum, the AP of Francoist minister Manuel Fraga represented direct continuity with the Franco regime, with more than a dozen ex-ministers on its slate. Significantly, the older leadership of both the AP and the PCE based their legitimacy in the past, while both the UCD and the PSOE showcased young leaders with modernizing, vague platforms of progressive but orderly change.

The June 1977 elections marked an important turning point in the transition dynamic, when the major parties that emerged victorious from the elections began to hash out the institutional contours of a new regime in the constituent congress. For the next year, during which the text of a new Constitution was written, revised, and debated in the Parliament, the reins of the transition process were taken over by the small group of major party leaders, who eventually reached the much-vaunted consensus that permitted some ex-Francoists, Christian Democrats, Liberals, Socialists, Communists, and Catalan Nationalists (but not Basques) to sign on to a single document. In contrast to 1931, in which a majority center/left coalition had won an absolute majority in the face of disorganization on the right, this constituent assembly was evenly divided between left and right, so consensus required overcoming significant divisions. This feat was accomplished by narrowing considerably the options on the table as well as the room for popular participation. In fact, some of the thorniest issues were resolved at a famous dinner when representatives of the major political groups agreed to a series of compromises that allowed negotiations to move forward.

This process of elite transaction and consensus continues to be both praised and criticized. Defenders argue that it was the only way to produce a constitution acceptable across the political spectrum, one that would create the unconditional loyalty to the democratic system of all major groups that was never achieved in the 1930s. For critics, the process of back room negotiations between a handful of individuals reduced the transparency and participatory nature of creating a new democracy. Grassroots citizen groups like the Neighborhood Associations (AAVV), small left-wing parties like Red Flag (BR), the Revolutionary Organization of Workers (ORT), and the Marxist-Leninist Communist party (PCE-ml), feminist organizations and local union branches continued to demonstrate and argue for what we might call a more communitarian form of direct democracy in which citizens would participate directly in decision-making, especially at the local level. Many also hoped to wrest control away from the economic and political elites who had dominated the social order and repressed any acknowledgment of the Civil War losers for forty years. Those who maintain this critical view today argue that the elite-pacted transition set in motion an overly statist and neoliberal democratic regime that has been resistant to civic participation. Opinion continues to be divided as to whether the elite pacts were cornerstones of the successful transition, betrayals of popular democracy, or perhaps both at the same time. In any case, they illustrate the trade-offs that were made in defining both the process of transition and the contours of the new democracy.

At the time, there was no question that the main political leaders viewed consensus as the essential path to a functioning democracy. On a symbolic level, consensus epitomized the opposite of civil war and the hope for national reconciliation. The majority of the young political class aspired to transcend the polarization of the past, and many seem to have accepted what had become a widely shared view of the Civil War as a collective tragedy with guilt on both sides. More practically, the UCD had formed a minority government that required collaboration with other parties in order to move forward. The combination of the practical necessity and the shared commitment to avoiding another civil war at all cost created a climate in which the willingness to reach agreement across Civil War battle lines became as much of an end goal as a means.

In this spirit, even before work was begun on the constitution, the new government embarked on a series of pacts that prepared the ground for broad spectrum negotiations, including the Amnesty Law (see Chapter 22), the Moncloa Pacts, and the provisional reinstatement of the Catalan and Basque autonomous governments. In each case, the agreement required compromise across previously unbridgeable political terrain. The Moncloa Pacts (October 25) proposed bringing the representatives of capital and labor together in a social and economic agreement. Specifically, the pacts called for freezing wages and other austerity measures in order to bring down inflation and the foreign deficit, with a promise of broader structural changes in the future to bolster worker security and benefits. The reinstatement of the Generalitat (29 September) legitimized Catalan nationalists' claims to autonomy by inviting the exiled president of the Generalitat in the 1930s, Josep Tarradellas, to return to his post. In turn, Tarradellas agreed to recognize the unity of the Spanish state and to wait for the reinstatement of the Catalan statute as part of a new Constitutional order. The reinstatement of the Basque General Council (December) did not have the same success in incorporating the Basque nationalists into the negotiated transition.

The centerpiece of the pacted transition was the lengthy 160-article Constitution, which emerged after 18 months of laborious negotiations. The first draft was drawn up by the Constitutional Commission of the *Cortes*, with representation of the UCD (3), PSOE (1), PCE-PSUC (1), AP (1) and the Catalan and Basque nationalists (1). The draft text was debated in the Commission in May 1978, and in the Congress and Senate during the summer, culminating in a vote on October 31 in both chambers with only a half dozen "no" votes in each chamber and another fourteen abstentions in the Congress. All groups supported the final draft except some AP members and all the Basque nationalists, who withdrew early from the negotiations and abstained in the final vote because their demand for a preconstitutional recognition of Basque sovereignty was denied. Reaching broad consensus was a delicate process that threatened to be derailed at various points, but was finally secured by the famous back room deals, which produced a combination of compromises and vague wording that bridged the various positions.

Both compromises and ambiguity are evident in the Constitution's treatment of such historically contentious issues as religion, the territorial organization of the state, individual and social rights and economic organization. Since the monarchist form of the state had been part of the "ground rules" of the negotiated transition, it removed one of the key historical divisions in Spanish politics from the field of contention. Agreeing on the place of religion and the Church in the Constitution required a combination of compromise and ambiguity. Thus, the Constitution clearly rejected any state religion and guaranteed freedom of religious practice, while recognizing the special place of the Catholic Church in Spanish society and opening the door to public financing of religious education. More ambiguously, it neither constitutionalized rights like divorce or abortion, which were key demands of feminist groups and the left-wing parties, nor closed the door to implementing them in future legislation. On economic and social organization, the Constitution clearly reached for inclusive language, recognizing private property and the free market as well as a "mixed" economy with a public sector and economic planning. Mostly yielding to the demands of the left parties, the document spelled out an extensive list of political, civil, and social rights. These rights were framed within a state that was defined as both democratic and social and guided by the principles of liberty, equality, pluralism, and even the right to participation.

One important group targeted in this inclusive language was women. In all but one clause, the Constitution followed a gender equality framework that promised women equality before the law and forbade discrimination on the basis of gender or other categories in Article 14, while Articles 32 and 35 spelled out a series of rights that apply to both sexes, including the right to property and privacy, the right to work and to judicial appeal, and other rights previously denied women. The one major exception was Article 57, which directly contradicted Article 14 with its assertion of male privilege in the royal line. Aside from this one contradiction, there was ambiguity as well in the confident assertion of equality with little concrete language or discussion about how it would be implemented.

Perhaps the most contentious issue involved the territorial organization of the state, which pitted peripheral nationalists against unitary Spanish nationalists. In this case, Article 2 recognized, for the first time in a single paragraph, the indissoluble unity of the Spanish nation and the right to self-government of the nationalities and regions that constitute it. Adopting the term nation to describe both Spain and its constituent parts was an unprecedented symbol of conciliation, but also an example of an "apocryphal compromise" in which contradictory demands were acknowledged without explaining how they would be simultaneously respected. In any case, the crucial details of how autonomous governments would be established, whether the "historical" nationalities of Catalonia, the Basque Country and Galicia should have special privileges, and what the distribution of powers would be, were all left for future discussion. The ambiguity and imprecision of some of these formulations left many uncertainties, but in the moment, the symbolic achievement of nearly universal consensus was presented as evidence of Spain having left its fratricidal past behind.

The one major exception to this culture of consensus was the Basque Country, which followed its own transition path, characterized by high levels of violence and conflict, and ending in low levels of support for the Constitution as well as strong semi- or non-loyal political movements. Some analysts have defined the Basque problem as a case apart, a virtual failed transition, one that tarnished, while not derailing, the larger consolidation of Spanish democracy (see chapters 7, 10).

The democratic era: 1978–present

From transition to consolidation, 1978–82

The approval of a Constitution marked the beginning of a new phase, when the young democracy began the road to consolidation, defined as the unquestioned legitimacy of the democratic system among all major political actors and a majority of the population. Consolidation was no more preordained than was Transition, but it occurred relatively quickly. Most observers point to the 1982 general election as the key turning point, because it fulfilled the basic requirement of a peaceful shift of power from one governing party (UCD) to another (PSOE). Although these elections symbolized the formal consolidation of the democracy, there were other moments of what we might call reconsolidation that confirmed the initial trajectory, most notably the 1996 parliamentary elections, when the PSOE lost after fourteen years in power. In this period of initial consolidation that lasted barely more than three years, there were significant challenges and threats that extended the uncertainty of Spain's democratic future. In this period, the government had to turn the "apocryphal compromise" of regional autonomy into reality (see Chapter 10), devise a strategy to combat terrorism, hold municipal elections that would lead to the democratization of local governments, survive an attempted military coup in February 1981 and finally, reconfigure the party system after the collapse of the governing UCD in the 1982 elections.

An important aspect of consolidation that had not been resolved in the constituent phase was the democratization of local governments, many of which still had their Francoist-appointed mayors and city councils. Municipal elections were held in 1979, but it was not until 1985 that the central government produced a statute regulating the institutions and powers of local governments. During the transition, one of the key claims of the citizen movement, comprising mostly neighborhood and other locally based organizations, was that these citizen groups participate directly in decision-making at a local level and not simply through voting for representatives. These hopes were dashed after the 1979 local elections, as the major parties took charge of the new city councils.

And yet, local government became an alternative site of democratization that could transform citizens' everyday relationship with their community in important ways. Especially in urban centers, many social movement activists joined the new local administrations, either as elected officials or bureaucrats, working to implement some of the demands of the neighborhood associations to build schools, create recreation facilities and parks, and otherwise democratize access to the city. Significantly, the majority of cities elected left-wing Socialist and Communist majorities, who often created coalition governments with ambitious egalitarian social agendas that contrasted with the moderate tone and rhetoric of national politics. In fact, the notion of municipal government as a source of opposition and democratic empowerment vis-à-vis the central government has remained a recurrent feature of Spanish democracy up to the present.

As regional and local governments were defining their relationship with the central government, leadership at the national level began to dissolve after the 1979 parliamentary election, which had closely reproduced the results of 1977. Despite Suarez' many achievements and his popularity at the end of the transition, his party proved too heterogeneous to chart a coherent path through a fragile period. Thus, for example, debate over the laws authorizing public financing of religious schools (March 1980) and permitting divorce (1981) each divided the Christian and secular democratic wings of the party, as did disagreements among liberals and social democrats as to how to deal with the ongoing economic problems. Suarez himself finally resigned as prime minister at the end of January 1981, the beginning of the end of a party that had relied almost solely on his presence to hold it together. An indication of how unconsolidated the democracy seemed at that point was the suggestion of PSOE leaders that they might need to set up a government of "national concentration" led by an army officer.

The combination of the government crisis and the unwavering terrorism provided the spark for an attempted military coup on February 23, 1981, although dissatisfaction and even plotting had begun as early as 1977. One of the consequences of the negotiated transition was the continuity of Francoist personnel, particularly in the armed forces, in which more than two-thirds of the brigadier generals had fought in the Civil War, but also in the police and judicial systems (see Chapter 21). By all accounts, it was the King's actions that diffused the crisis and prevented the military uprising from spreading to garrisons around the country. As Franco's designated successor, his was the only authority that many of the military leaders acknowledged. As a result, when he called the other military leaders and ordered them not to join the coup, most felt obliged to follow his orders. After hours of public uncertainty, the King appeared on television to announce that he had taken all measures to maintain constitutional order. The King's path from Francoist successor to defender of democracy has made him one of the heroes of the transition, but his evolution also occurred within a larger context in which democratization of the monarchy had become the best route to preserve it. Confirming this context, on February 25, hundreds of thousands of Spaniards brought their support for democracy and the Constitution into the streets in the largest yet of citizen demonstrations. Ironically, the attempted coup had the ultimate effect of helping to consolidate democracy, including the legitimacy of its monarchist head of state. While many Spaniards had accepted the monarchist form of government as a necessary price of the consensus, the King's behavior during the coup convinced most that the monarch was an asset to democratic consolidation, rather than an obstacle, as in the past.

In the wake of the failed coup, the parliamentary election of October 1982 was viewed by many at the time as an important moment of democratic affirmation and consolidation, as reflected by the 80 percent voter turnout. Perhaps most remarkable was that the election marked a seismic shift in voting behavior at the same time that it boosted confidence in the stability of the democratic system. The election brought a dramatic absolute victory for the PSOE. The UCD vote collapsed, while the AP, fortified by a coalition with Christian democrats who defected from the UCD, jumped into second place. The PCE continued its decline, while the CiU and the PNV confirmed their hegemonic status in Catalonia and the Basque Country.

The PSOE victory was more than a default outcome of UCD disintegration. Since 1979, the PSOE leadership under Felipe González had pushed through changes in its platform and its image, most notably the abandonment of Marxism. New PSOE voters included a big chunk of former PCE voters but also about a third of former UCD voters, plus about two million first-time voters, many of them young people. In a sign of how much had changed, up to a third of practicing Catholics voted for the Socialists. With the ideological and demographic shift of both leadership and constituency, the PSOE had completed its transformation to a cross class party of the center-left with a platform of democratic consolidation and modernization.

After the uncertainty of the transition and early years of consolidation, the next important turning point was the 1996 election. The intervening phase of the democratic regime was defined by the stability of one-party hegemony, with PSOE absolute majorities into the early 1990s. Only then was the conservative opposition leadership able to convince enough voters that it could be trusted to take the reins of government. Until then, it was still tainted by its links with Francoism, symbolized by founder Manuel Fraga. The makeover began in 1989 when the leadership baton was passed to a young conservative, José María Aznar, and the name was changed to the Popular Party (PP). After 1996, when the PP formed its first government, the party system finally stabilized around the "imperfect bi-party" alternation between two main statewide parties that covered a broad range of positions and captured about two-thirds of the votes, with the remaining votes split between the left-wing IU and the regional parties. While democratic institutions were fully legitimated before this, the 1996 election confirmed the principle and practice of peaceful rotation as a normal, and, for many observers, a necessary element of democratic consolidation.

Democratic government under PSOE leadership: 1982–96

The era of PSOE-led governments, lasting from 1982 to 1996, with the last three years in a coalition with CiU, constituted the most productive era of democratic institutionalization in Spain's modern history. Whatever the final balance on the achievements and mistakes of the Socialists in power, the stability and longevity of a strong majority government able to map out plans for the medium and long term was mostly beneficial for the fledgling democracy. The PSOE oversaw the implementation of the system of autonomous governments, created the blueprint for local government, subordinated the military to civilian rule, brought the welfare state closer to European, levels and negotiated Spain's entry into European institutions and onto the global stage, a process that culminated in 1992 with the Olympics in Barcelona and the World Exposition in Seville. Over and above specific policies, the PSOE presided over a process of gradual normalization of democratic government. At the same time, it disappointed many of its original supporters, was unable to end terrorism or recurring unemployment and was increasingly beset by a series of corruption scandals that revealed a deeply clientelistic culture and a patrimonial attitude toward public resources. Finally, while its centralized, hierarchical structure produced coherent government programs, it was also generally impervious to popular pressure from civil society. However, when voters finally penalized the PSOE with defeat at the polls in 1996, it paradoxically further confirmed the normalization of democratic practice.

In the wake of the recent failed military coup, one of the first projects of the PSOE was to remove the threat of military intervention from democratic politics. The largely successful military reform reduced the number of senior officers, but more importantly, it restructured the chain of command under the civilian leadership of the prime minister and the defense minister. Integrated into the Western European defense system and deployed on humanitarian missions, the Spanish army lost its capacity for autonomous political action and, more gradually, its association with repressive public order.

An even more dramatic transformation occurred with the implementation of the state of autonomous communities, which turned Spain from one of the most centralized states into one of the most decentralized, mostly carried out under Socialist leadership. Within a year, the government had negotiated the approval of statutes for all the remaining autonomous communities, and affirmed that both fast and slow track governments would end up with the same powers and resources (symmetrical federalism). The eventual level of devolution was dramatic, including authority over urban planning, education, health care, police, environment, and finances. Devolution also increased heterogeneity, from Catalanization of the education system in Catalonia to varying levels of social benefits as the percentage of state expenditure controlled by the autonomous governments rose from 8 percent in 1983 to 25 percent in 1992. While it remained more difficult to integrate the Basque Country into the self-government framework, the 1988 Ajuria-Enea Pact between all the political parties in that region except HB marked a hopeful turning point, when the PNV affirmed its democratic nationalism against the unapologetic terrorism of ETA. While points of disagreement existed between the central and autonomous governments over powers and finances, during this period all major parties outside the Basque Country seem to have accepted the devolution process as a legitimate framework of territorial organization.

Internationally, the Socialists pursued further integration into Europe, the Cold War "West," and more broadly, the world, after decades of isolation and marginalization. First, the PSOE completed the arduous negotiations granting Spain, along with Greece and Portugal, entry into the EEC, which went into effect in January 1986. More contested was the PSOE's *volte face* on membership in the NATO military alliance, which shifted from a promise to leave the organization in 1982 to the insistence in 1986 that it would be irresponsible to do so. The government held a referendum on the issue in March 1986, which resulted in a close victory for the PSOE that further confirmed its hegemony but also its shift toward the center. A majority seemed to accept González' argument that Europe, the West, democracy and modernization were all part of a package that would finally complete the migration of Spain from the margins to the European core. For many on the left, however, the NATO campaign marked the culmination of a long process of disillusionment with a party that had retained little of its "socialist" origins.

Within the European core, the PSOE was not alone among Social Democratic parties in moving ever farther away from their working-class roots and the promise of a softer capitalism, but the betrayal of its base was particularly poignant in the Spanish case. The Spanish Socialist party only came to power (along with the French) when the heyday of social democracy was over. Since the oil crisis of 1973 and the increasing pressure of global competition, the postwar welfare states that had paid for generous social benefits with booming economic growth were in crisis. In Spain, the PSOE was faced with this crisis in a young democracy whose welfare state was still in its infancy. In this context in which workers had been waiting for decades for a government to represent their interests, the neoliberal economic policies of the PSOE felt like a stab in the back. With the goal of making the Spanish economy more competitive, the government cut spending in the face of inflation, privatized public companies, and eased the way for the closure of uncompetitive heavy industry like mining, steel, and textiles, accompanied by the loss of tens of thousands of jobs. With unemployment reaching 22 percent in 1985, there were not enough new jobs in the service sector to replace the old ones. The labor unions, both the Socialist UGT and the Communist CCOO, took an increasingly combative stance toward the government in trying to resist these policies. But the left opposition was not strong enough to pose a governing alternative, especially at a moment when international communism was on the point of collapse and stronger labor movements had been broken by neoliberal governments in the United States and the United Kingdom.

At the same time as it pursued neoliberal economic "adjustment" policies, the PSOE had a social democratic face as well. Thus, the government invested heavily in infrastructure, constructing a national highway system and building high-speed trains, and expanded basic welfare state services, including health and pensions, which had been well below the European norm. They increased spending on schools, but instead of trying to create a single public school system and close religious schools, which had been the controversial program of the Second Republic, the PSOE chose a conciliatory path, which not only recognized a double network of public and private schools but granted a significant subvention for private Catholic schools. While there was a certain tension between neoliberalism and state spending in the PSOE's economic policies, the economic recovery that began after 1985, aided in part by EEC markets and subsidies, lowered unemployment somewhat (to 16 percent), and helped maintain an uneasy balance until recession hit again after 1992.

By the early 1990s, economic recession was one of several issues that came together to undermine the PSOE's long hegemony. The recession with its spike in unemployment revealed that the Socialists had not resolved the structural problems of the Spanish economy. The ongoing unsuccessful anti-terrorist struggle was another issue, as 300 more victims fell to ETA attacks during the Socialist era. More important, however, was the public scandal exposed in a series of media and judicial investigations that accused and eventually tried government officials for supporting a "dirty war" against ETA during the 1980s, which included torture, abduction, and the assassination of about two dozen people. Concurrent with the investigations, a series of corruption cases involving government officials began to paint a picture of a governing party that acted with indifference to the rule of law and in violation of the public trust. While none of the scandals were linked personally to Felipe González, even the sins of omission were glaring in a party that was as tightly centralized and hierarchical as the PSOE.

In that context, the 1996 election can be viewed as at least a partial victory for Spanish democracy. The defeat of the PSOE in a solid turnout demonstrated that the electorate was willing to hold the party accountable, and that the media and the judiciary were capable of acting as "watch dogs" to monitor government activities. Further, at a time of disgust and frustration with the ruling party, the percentage of Spaniards who believed that democracy was the preferred system of government never faltered, increasing from 70 percent in 1980 to 76 percent in 1995. Equally important, enough of the electorate felt confident that they could penalize the PSOE without endangering the democracy by either abstaining or voting for the opposition PP. While the new era of competitive elections and viable opposition parties led to a resurgence of more confrontational politics, one could argue that the flip side of *crispación* was a functioning pluralist system that was more sustainable in the long run than the single-party hegemony of the 1980s. At the same time, the long PSOE hegemony also contributed to democratic consolidation, providing the stability to implement a sustained program of institutionalization at the local, regional, state, and European levels that, in most cases, established a solid foundation for the Spanish democratic state, if perhaps less so for a flourishing democratic society. Without denying the various critiques of the PSOE era, or minimizing the imperfections of the practice of democracy in Spain, it may be that these are issues shared by other consolidated European democracies, not unique products of Spanish difference.

From consolidation to Crispación: PP and PSOE alternation from 1996 to 2011

From 1996 to 2011, the stability of single-party rule was replaced by the high drama of competitive elections and shifting majorities between the two major statewide parties, as well as growing tensions between statewide and region-based parties, with polarizing rhetoric aimed at solidifying each party's base. The PP governed for 8 years, from 1996 to 2004 (in coalition with CiU from 1996 to 2000), before it was voted out of power as a result of its handling of the biggest terrorist action in Spain's history, the bombing of the Madrid train station on March 11, 2004 by Islamic militants. The PSOE, having renovated its leadership after the crisis of confidence of the 1990s, also won two consecutive terms, from 2004 to 2011, after which it was voted out for its handling of the economic crisis that began in 2009. While the Transition formulation of consensus politics had been abandoned long ago, the lack of a viable opposition party during the 1980s kept political debates muted. The culture began to shift in 1993, during the last (minority) PSOE government. It was in fact when the PSOE feared it was on the brink of losing during the 1993 election campaign that the party broke what had been an implicit agreement not to instrumentalize the past, by linking the PP to Francoism. Since then, Spanish democracy has had to adapt to this style of high stakes polarized politics, in which almost everything turns into a partisan battle.

So what does this culture of *crispación* mean for Spanish democracy? Few would celebrate partisan polarization as a symbol of democratic health, and yet not everyone agrees whether it is a sign of disease or simply post-consolidation normalization. Was the willingness to take the gloves off a sign that the ring itself was viewed as secure, with the added luxury of a long period of economic growth from 1994 to 2008? Or did *crispación* reflect the resurgence of an unresolved polarized past that had festered untreated since the Transition and limited the quality of Spanish democracy? Not surprisingly, there is evidence for both viewpoints.

Thus, one could argue that the political fireworks disguised an underlying consensus between the main parties on various issues, which provided a secure base from which to launch attacks. Both parties shared the desire to raise Spain's profile on the world stage and leave behind its semi-peripheral status in the first world. They also shared a hybrid approach to economic and social policy, balancing neoliberalism and welfare state protection, in an unstable equilibrium that relied on the long growth cycle for sustainability. Likewise, they agreed on the general parameters of anti-terrorism policy, which included police action, collaboration with the French government, and the illegalization of HB, ETA's political arm. Conversely, both accepted the constitutional framework of autonomous governments and continued the process of devolution, while neither statewide party accepted the most radical demands of the pro-independence nationalist parties, or fully embraced their concept of multiple sovereign nations. Obviously, there were differences of style and degree on these issues, but not major ruptures. Furthermore, the fact that the traditional left, reconstituted in the IU since 1986, continued to lose votes after 1996 suggests that most Spaniards did not see a viable alternative outside this centrist framework, except in Catalonia and the Basque Country.

In contrast to the underlying framework, each party stoked the flames of contention around a series of symbolic issues related to Spain's broader sense of identity, which did seem to resonate with broader rifts among the populace. For example, after several decades in which Spanish nationalism was the discredited province of far right-wing groups like Fuerza Nueva, after 1996 the PP embraced an unapologetic Spanish nationalism that appealed to a sector of the population. This nationalism was reflected in gestures like the installation of the largest (Spanish) flag in the world in Madrid's Plaza de Colon (October 12, 2001), or in the party's proposal (1997) that the unitary character of Spain's historical trajectory be a guiding principle of the school curriculum. Externally, the PP asserted its national independence from Europe, supporting the United States in the 2003 Iraq War, against the wishes of the major European countries. When the PSOE returned to office in 2004, the government withdrew Spanish troops from Iraq and turned back toward a more pro-European orientation, while rescinding the PP's educational guidelines. Religious identity has also become repoliticized, even though only about 20 percent of the population call themselves practicing Catholics who think the government should take the views of the Church into consideration. One of the most contentious religious and political issues was same-sex marriage, whose legalization by the PSOE in 2005 was challenged by the PP in the Supreme Court, which ruled in favor of the law in 2012. The PSOE's left-wing cultural program included a landmark 2007 law mandating "effective equality" between women and men, including parity in government and private business and electoral lists.

Perhaps the most potent symbolic battleground has been the past, which, from the mid-1990s, was increasingly mobilized by both sides in the so-called memory wars in defense of competing visions of Spain (see Chapter 22). The current debate in Spain has revealed precisely the lack of consensus, not only about memory politics during the Transition, but about the longer trajectory of twentieth-century Spanish history leading up to that moment. Taking shape in both popular and academic historical scholarship are conflicting master narratives (including various intermediary positions) that assign distinct political meanings to the Transition and what it produced. For conservatives, the "pacted" Transition was the result of a gradual process of democratization that began during the Restoration liberal regime (1875–1923), was derailed by the radical and intolerant Second Republic (1931–36), and facilitated once again by the stability and economic growth provided by the Franco regime in its later phases, after it had left its violent past behind. The contrasting left-wing narrative argues that the only source of Spain's democratic tradition lies not in the elitist and corrupt Restoration regime, but in the popular democratic Second Republic, which was brutally crushed by a fascist dictatorship that derailed the country's political modernization for forty years and contributed nothing to the democratic Transition.

The reconsideration of the terms of the transition also informed the growing *crispación* in the relations between Madrid and the historical nationalities, especially in Catalonia and the Basque Country. With some qualifications, the polarization situated both statewide parties, which sought to remain inside the Constitutional settlement, against the nationalist parties, which asserted the sovereign right to self-determination. The turning point came in 1998, with the Declaration of Barcelona, in which parties representing the three historical nationalities declared that the framework of autonomous communities laid out in the Constitution had not gone far enough to recognize the multinational reality of nations within a nation. In the same year, the PNV concluded the Pact of Estella with HB, which won the 1998 regional elections on the platform of the right of the sovereign Basque people to decide their future vis-à-vis the Spanish (and French) state, a platform that was consolidated in the Plan Ibarretxe, approved by the Basque Parliament in 2004 and rejected even for debate by the PP and PSOE in the Spanish Parliament in 2005.

In 2003 in Catalonia, after twenty-three years the CiU lost control of the Generalitat to a new Catalan nationalist coalition, led by the pro-independence Esquerra (ERC) and the Socialist Party of Catalonia (PSC), which drew up a plan to revise the Catalan autonomy statute. Although the PSOE supported the general concept, the version it pushed through the Congress in 2006 fell short of what the Catalan parties had initially proposed. The PP went further, stoking anti-Catalan sentiment and challenging the constitutionality of the new statute. See chapter 10 The 2010 ruling by the Constitutional Court rejecting some of the articles of the Statute was the final blow to a negotiated solution. The failure of statute reform undermined the credibility of the PSC/ERC coalition, which lost again to the CiU in 2010, but it also dramatically increased independence sentiment in Catalonia.

Beyond party politics, how has the culture of *crispación* affected the quality of democratic participation at the grass-roots level? Since the 1980s, there has been an ongoing critique of what some have called a "low intensity" democracy, marked by low levels of membership in political parties and NGOs, and weak civil society mobilization. On the other hand, there is evidence that the population is less passive and disengaged than these statistics suggest. First, it is notable that turnout in elections has remained consistently solid since the late 1970s, between 70 and 80 percent of eligible voters, with more coming out in highly competitive elections. Thus, while *crispación* may have increased the population's cynicism about politics, it hasn't soured the investment in the electoral system. Further, from the outset, the population has had the capacity to mobilize massively at certain critical moments, such as during the Transition and after the February 1981 coup. In 1997 there were huge demonstrations against ETA killings after the assassination of a city councilman, and in 2004, 35 percent of Spaniards participated in demonstrations, mostly in opposition to the government's participation in the Iraq War. Although mobilization fell again after the withdrawal of Spanish troops, since then there has also been a trend of greater interest in politics, which has been rising in an inverse relationship to the declining sense of satisfaction with how Spanish democratic government is functioning. What seems clear is that Spaniards will continue to debate the deeper quality of their democratic polity and level of civic engagement.

How can we summarize the state of Spanish democracy in the period between 1996 and 2011? On the one hand, the democracy showed every sign of continued consolidation at an institutional level, rising to the challenge in an era of growing polarization. Where polarization in the 1930s led to large sectors of the population pursuing their goals outside the legal framework when their party lost an election, in this recent period *crispación* did not convert any of the major statewide parties to "semi-loyalty." At the same time, the nationalist parties in Catalonia and the Basque Country, supported by growing portions of their populations, have become increasingly semi-loyal to the framework of a Spanish democratic state. However, even if both of these nations eventually seceded, the Spanish democratic state would still survive, albeit with different territorial boundaries. For the rest of the country, in 2011 it was still unclear how much the politics of *crispación* reflected deep cleavages that bode ill for Spain's future democracy as opposed to normal divisions that were mobilized to define opposing political camps.

2011-present: Crisis and uncertainty

The last few years have been the most tumultuous for the Spanish democracy since the early years of consolidation, beset by economic crisis from 2008 and political crisis from 2011. The "Great Recession" hit Spain particularly hard in two vulnerable areas: high levels of unemployment (peaking at 26 percent in 2013) and inequality. Partly a result of these economic woes, the political crisis also included the territorial challenge and declining faith in the major parties. The crisis exacerbated existing schisms, destabilized what had been common points of reference, but at the same time showcased Spaniards' capacity for grassroots mobilization in a crisis.

Confidence in both major political parties is at its lowest point, with barely over half the population voting for one of the two parties in the 2015 and 2016 general elections, down from two-thirds in 2011. Outside the electoral arena, there has been a surge in popular mobilization. Between 2011 and 2012, the number of public demonstrations or meetings rose from 18,000 to 45,000, taking shape in the so-called 15-M *indignado* movement, a predecessor of Occupy Wall Street, that was launched in May 2011 in the name of the 99 percent against the 1 percent. Anger at both parties is also linked to the perception that corruption is an endemic problem that crosses political lines, now framed as evidence that all political elites represent the interests of the haves against the have-nots.

Grassroots mobilization also fueled the formation of two upstart reform parties, the left-wing Podemos ("We can") and center right Ciudadanos ("Citizens"), which together won over a third of the votes in the December 2015 (24 percent and 14 percent) and June 2016 general elections (21 percent and 13 percent). The June election was called because the fractured December vote had produced neither a majority nor a governing coalition. While some had predicted that the PSOE might be finished, its support held steady at 22 percent, while the PP recovered slightly from 29 percent to 33 percent. Even though Podemos formed a coalition with IU for the June election, predictions that it would absorb the PSOE's voters did not pan out. It was only at the end of October that a new government, again from the Popular Party, was formed.

The crisis was also the spark for a rapid deterioration in the ongoing tensions between the central government and Catalonia, as financial meltdown heightened the debate over whether the Catalan economy was contributing too much or its fair share to the rest of Spain. The Catalan government campaigned to turn the regional elections of September 2015 into a referendum on independence, and a pro-independence coalition won just under 50 percent but a majority of seats, further increasing uncertainty about the future. Although the Basque situation has improved dramatically with ETA's definitive cessation of armed activity in October 2011, the Spanish government has still not responded to ETA's request for negotiation over its prisoners, and nonviolent independence parties have surged in recent regional elections, so the larger issue of the future relationship between the Basque Country, Catalonia, and Spain is, to say the least, unresolved.

Perhaps even more disquieting has been the uncertainty around what had been stable compass coordinates: Europe and the King. The King, once the stabilizing figure above warring politicians, squandered all his political capital in various misadventures, from a corruption case within the royal family to an ill-advised elephant hunting safari in Africa, leading to his abrupt abdication in favor of his son, Felipe, in June 2014, and a revival of interest in republicanism. And finally, the European strategy which promised to bring Spain from the periphery to the core has reversed itself, with Spain grouped among the southern European poor relations who are indebted to Northern European "haves," while the class divide itself has weakened faith in Europe across the continent.

While it is difficult to predict where all of these trends will lead, it appears that most Spaniards still envision the path forward within the framework of democratic government, although not necessarily within a single nation-state or even a monarchy. Whether the two main parties restabilize or are replaced by multiparty coalitions, the upstart parties have been operating within the democratic system, seeking election in local governments, a traditional site for popular empowerment and participation. And throughout the crisis, Spaniards continue to demonstrate engagement on both levels, filling the streets in protest demonstrations and going to the polls in healthy turnouts. In contrast to the mass mobilization of the 1930s, which could never be fully integrated into the democratic system, thus far the current wave of mobilization and the introduction of new parties seems to be aimed at reviving the democracy, not torpedoing it. In any case, whatever direction the current political and economic crisis takes, it is too uncertain of a moment from which to evaluate the entire course of the Spanish transition and democracy.

Spain's transition to and consolidation of a democratic regime has been viewed through multiple and competing lenses since the late 1970s, some aimed at celebrating Spain's achievement and others at pointing out the deficits of both processes. For the first couple of decades, the dominant narrative focused on what had worked, contrasted with what had not worked in Spain's first democratic experiment of the 1930s. From this perspective, after forty years of dictatorship, Spain carried out a relatively peaceful and consensual transition to a democratic government, which was consolidated within a few years and remained unchallenged in its basic parameters. This is the Spanish model that continues to be celebrated in comparative democratization and consolidation scholarship, as the star pupil of the "third wave" of transitions. The more critical view that has taken shape in recent years focuses on the tradeoffs that were made to achieve this smooth process, including the suppression of popular participation and the decision not to confront the demons of the Francoist past, all of which has resulted in a "low intensity" democracy. Between the extremes of a model case and a disaster, most scholars today would probably agree that the period is a balance of light and shadow, whose complexity defies a simple categorical judgment. The complexity of Spanish democracy is reflected in the ongoing dynamic between grassroots mobilization and elite politics, which have shaped its evolution from the outset, especially at particular moments of crisis. It is also reflected in the dynamic relationship between local, regional, and state level politics, all of which constitute channels of democratic decision-making and negotiation beyond what the Madrid government mandates. Spanish democracy at the start of the twenty-first century is the untidy sum of all these moving parts, making it, like every democracy in the world today, an ongoing work in progress.

Further reading

Alonso, Gregorio, and Diego Muro (eds.), *The Politics and Memory of Democratic Transition: the Spanish Model*, New York: Routledge, 2011.

Balfour, Sebastian (ed.), *The Politics of Contemporary Spain*, London: Routledge, 2005.

Cousins, Christine, Monica Threlfall, and Celia Valiente (eds.), *Gendering Spanish Democracy*, London: Routledge, 2005.

Dowling, Andrew, *Catalonia since the Spanish Civil War: Reconstructing the Nation*, Eastborne, UK: Sussex, 2013.

Gunther, Richard, Jose Ramon Montero, and Joan Botella, *Democracy in Modern Spain*, New Haven, CT: Yale, 2004.

Jerez-Farran, Carlos, and Samuel Amago (eds.), *Unearthing Franco's Legacy: Mass Graves and the Recovery of Historical Memory in Spain*, Notre Dame: University of Notre Dame Press, 2010.

Radcliff, Pamela, *Making Democratic Citizens in Spain: Civil Society and the Popular Origins of the Transition*, Basingstoke, UK: Palgrave Macmillan, 2011.

Tusell, Javier, *Spain: From Dictatorship to Democracy*, Oxford: Blackwell, 2007.

SECTION TWO
THEMES

CHAPTER 9
THE ECONOMY
Leandro Prados de la Escosura

How much economic progress has Spain achieved and what has been its impact on living standards since the end of the Peninsular War? In an attempt to answer these questions, this chapter assesses long-run economic growth and income distribution. Section I describes trends in output and investigates their determinants. Section II focuses on how the fruits of economic progress were distributed over time. The final section places Spain's performance in an international perspective.

Long-run economic growth

Between 1815 and 2015, the three alternative ways in which Gross Domestic Product (GDP) can be defined (the total amount of goods and services produced; the total expenditure on consumption and investment; and the total income accruing to workers and proprietors of capital and natural resources) multiplied 69 times, which implies an average cumulative rate of growth of 2.1 percent per year. As the increase did not take place at a steady pace, five main phases may be established: 1815–50, 1850–1950 (with a shift to a lower level during the Civil War, 1936–39), 1950–74, 1974–2007, and 2007–15. In the phase of fastest growth,

Figure 9.1 Real GDP and GDP per capita, 1815–2015 (2010 = 100) (Semi-logarithmic scale).

the so-called Golden Age (1950–74), GDP grew four and a half times faster than during the previous hundred years (almost 7 times faster than the early nineteenth century), and twice as fast as 1974–2007. The Great Recession, which started in 2008, represented a fall in real GDP of 8 percent between 2007 and 2013, and in 2015 the GDP level for 2007 had not been recovered.

Changes in the composition of GDP by type of expenditure are revealing of the transformation experienced by the Spanish economy over the last two centuries. The share of total consumption remained stable at a high level up to the late 1880s, followed by a decline that reached beyond the First World War. It recovered in the early 1920s, helped by the rise in government consumption, stabilizing up to mid-1930s. The Civil War (1936–39) and the Second World War (despite the fact that Spain was a nonbelligerent country) account for the contraction in private consumption and the sudden and dramatic increase in government consumption shares in GDP. The share of total consumption only fell below 85 percent of GDP after 1953, in which a sustained decline that reached a trough by the mid-2000s began. Such a contraction in the share of total consumption conceals an intense decline in private consumption paralleled by a sustained rise in government consumption that resulted from the expansion of the welfare state and the transformation of a highly centralized state into a *de facto* federal state. Investment oscillated around 5 percent of GDP in the second half of the nineteenth century, except for the railway construction boom of the late 1850s and early 1860s, when it doubled. From the turn of the century a long-term rise brought the relative size of investment to above 30 percent of GDP in 2006. Phases of investment acceleration are associated with those of faster growth in aggregate economic activity, namely the late-1850s to mid-1860s, the 1920s, mid-1950s to early 1970s, and since Spain's accession to the European Union (1985) to 2007.

Nonetheless, the long-run increase in investment was punctuated by reversals during the world wars and the Spanish Civil War, the transition to democracy (1975–85), and the Great Recession (2008–13). Since investment can be defined as a deferred consumption—it implies sacrificing present consumption in order to obtaining higher future consumption— the question of why Spaniards invested so little for such a long time emerges as a topic of further research. Was it due to uncertainty, to government policies, or to the lack of investment opportunities?

The integration of Spain into international markets also increased, but it did not follow a steady pattern. Three main phases can be distinguished. The first saw a gradual rise in openness (that is, exports plus imports as a share of GDP) since the nineteenth century stabilized in the early twentieth century at a high plateau. The second, from the early 1920s to mid-century, saw a sharp decline. Finally, starting in the 1950s, a cautious but gradual exposure to international competition took place, facilitated by the reforms associated with the 1959 Stabilization and Liberalization Plan, and accelerating after the end of Franco's regime. It is worth stressing the correspondence between investment and imports trends, which suggests that economic growth was stimulated by international trade.

The changes in the composition of GDP by economic activity also reflect the deep transformation associated with modern economic growth (Figure 9.2). Agriculture's share underwent a sustained contraction over time, which intensified during the late 1880s and early 1890s, the 1920s, and 1950–1980. There was a temporary reversal due to the autarkic policies of the 1940s. The evolution of industry followed an inverse U shape, expanding its relative size up to the late 1920s and resuming its relative increase after the 1930s and 1940s backlash, to stabilize at a high plateau, and then dropping sharply after the mid-1980s. By 2010,

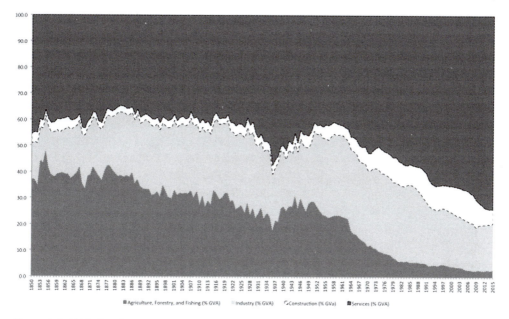

Figure 9.2 GDP: Supply composition, 1850–2015 (%) (current prices).

the relative size of industry had shrunk to practically one-half of its peak in the early 1960s. The construction industry remained stable below 5 percent of GDP until the mid-twentieth century, although there were more expansionary phases in the late 1850s to early 1860s, 1920s and 1950s. Starting in the early 1860s, it exhibited a sustained increase that peaked around 2005, more than doubling its relative size. The end of the construction bubble during the Great Recession implied a return to the levels of the mid-1960s. Services made a high and stable contribution to GDP, fluctuating around 40 percent, between the mid-nineteenth and mid-twentieth centuries, except for the 1930s–40s parenthesis of depression, civil war, and autarky, and then expanded from less than one-half to three-fourths of GDP between the early 1960s and 2015.

Comparing the composition of GDP by sector of the economy to that of labor may be illuminating (see Figure 9.3). Agriculture's share (measured in hours worked) exhibits a long-run decline from above three-fifths to less than 5 percent by the early twenty-first century. Again, it was not a smooth line. It fell more gradually up to 1950, intensifying in the 1920s and early 1930s, reversed during the Civil War (1936–39) and its autarkic aftermath, and then accelerated its contraction over 1950–90, when it shrank from half the labor force to one-tenth. Agriculture provided the largest contribution to employment until 1964, when it still represented one-third of total hours worked. The evolution of the relative size of services presents a mirror image of agriculture's, taking over as the largest industry from 1965 onward and reaching three-fourths of total hours worked by 2015. Industry's steady expansion, save for the Civil War reversal, overcame agriculture's share by 1973 and peaked by the late 1970s, when it reached one-fourth of employment, to initiate a gradual contraction that has cut its relative size by almost half by 2015. Construction, in turn, more than trebled its initial share by 2007, sharply contracting as the sector's bubble ended during the Great Recession.

As already observed in GDP composition, an initial phase of structural change—in which the agricultural sector contracted and that of industry expanded, only broken by the postwar

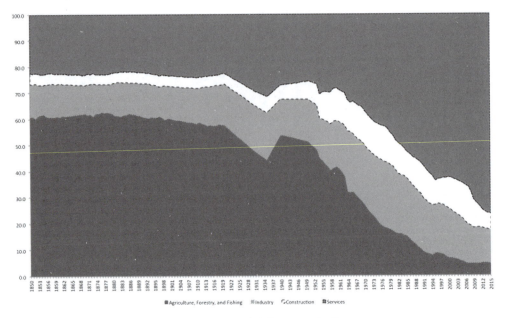

Figure 9.3 Employment composition, 1850–2015 (%) (hours worked).

falling behind—gave way to a second phase since 1980, in which the relative decline also involved the industrial sector, while employment in services accelerated its escalation. Thus, although it is true that sheltered and uncompetitive industries collapsed due to liberalization and opening up following the end of the Franco regime and the accession to the European Union, the shift into services is part of the general pattern associated with higher income levels in advanced countries.

What did these changes mean for Spaniards? To what extent did a larger amount of goods and services affect individuals' living conditions? GDP can be divided into GDP per capita and population. Since population trebled, real GDP per capita experienced an 18-fold increase between 1815 and 2015, growing at a cumulative annual rate of 1.4 percent. The implication is that output per person drove total GDP expansion (Figure 9.1). Such an improvement, though, took place at an uneven pace. After growing at a moderate 0.4 percent per year between the end of the Napoleonic Wars and the mid-nineteenth century, per capita GDP growth rose to 0.7 percent per year between 1850 and 1950, doubling its initial level in one hundred years. During the next quarter of a century, the so-called Golden Age, its pace accelerated more than 7-fold (at an annual rate of 5.3 percent), so that by 1974, per capita income was 3.6 times higher than in 1950. Although the economy decelerated from 1974 to 2007, and annual growth per capita slowed down to 2.5 percent, per capita GDP in 2007 was more than double its level in 1974. The Great Recession (2008–13) shrank per capita income by 11 percent, but by 2015, its level was still 83 percent higher than at the time of Spain's EU accession (1985).

What steered such a remarkable rise? GDP per capita depends on the amount of work per person and the level of productivity of this effort. GDP per capita and labor productivity (measured as GDP per hour worked) evolved side by side over 1850–2015 (Figure 9.5). Although the number of hours worked per person shrank—from about 1,000 hours per person

Figure 9.4 Real GDP per capita and per hour worked, 1850–2015 (2010 = 100) (Semi-logarithmic scale).

per year to fewer than 700—labor productivity grew at a faster pace: it increased 23-fold against 16-fold for GDP per capita. The main reason for the decline in hours worked per person was the reduction in hours worked per fully occupied worker, which fell from 2,800 hours per year in the mid-nineteenth century to fewer than 1,900 in the early twenty-first century. Thus, it can be claimed that long-term gains in output per capita were entirely attributable to productivity gains, with phases of accelerating GDP per capita, such as the 1920s or the Golden Age (1950–74), matching those of faster labor productivity growth. A breakdown of the gains in labor productivity into the contributions made by the productivity increase within each economic sector and by the shift of labor from less productive to more productive sectors (that is, structural change) indicates that structural change accounts for over a third of the aggregate labor productivity growth since 1850.

But what underlies the ability to produce more per hour worked? Is it a more abundant use of capital broadly defined (that is, encompassing physical and human capital) or a more efficient use of the available capital? Physical capital is understood to be the flow of productive services provided by an asset that is employed in production. Capital assets are produced goods that are not consumed but used for production (dwellings, infrastructure, machinery, transport material). Human capital is understood as the flow of productive services provided by the knowledge, skills, competencies, and attributes embodied in individuals, including schooling and skills acquired through work experience.

We can heuristically break down labor productivity trends into the contribution of human and physical capital and that of efficiency gains, also called total factor productivity growth. In Spain, labor productivity growth over the long run was accounted for, in similar proportions, by broad capital accumulation (physical and, to a lesser extent, human capital) and efficiency gains. Furthermore, main spurts in broad capital accumulation and in efficiency gains tended to coincide, as can be observed during the years of the railway construction (1850s–80), electrification (the 1920s and 1950s), and the adoption of new vintage technology in the Golden Age (1950–74) (Figure 9.5).

Nonetheless, a closer look reveals a clear divide before and after 1950. Between 1850 and 1950 (with the exception of the 1920s), capital deepening (namely, an increase in capital per hour worked) was the leading force, contributing two-thirds of labor productivity growth, while in the 1920s and between 1950 and 1985, efficiency gains were the hegemonic force, contributing two-thirds of labor productivity growth in the Golden Age (1950–74) and one-half in the 1920s and during the democratic transition (1975–85). Furthermore, the acceleration of labor productivity growth in the 1920s and the Golden Age was almost exclusively attributable to efficiency gains. From 1986 onward, broad capital accumulation became the main driver of labor productivity growth again, while efficiency gains stagnated and even declined.

Thus, while in the 1920s and between 1950 and 1985 efficiency gains largely explained the labor productivity increase that accounted for the improvement in GDP per capita, during 1986–2007 the increase in GDP per capita was dependent in roughly similar proportions on the number of hours worked per person (that resulted from employment creation) and on labor productivity (which in turn derived from a more intense use of capital). Hence, a more extensive (rather than intensive) kind of growth characterized the post-1986 period that corresponded with that of Spain's full membership of the European Union.

How do we account for such a reversal in the source of labor productivity growth from efficiency gains to capital accumulation? It can be hypothesized that as economic growth took place, Spain got closer to the technological frontier, making further gains in efficiency more difficult. Moreover, structural change, namely the shift of resources (i.e., labor) from lower labor productivity sectors to those of higher productivity (i.e., from agriculture into manufacturing), was a permanent change that had largely taken place by the time of Spain's

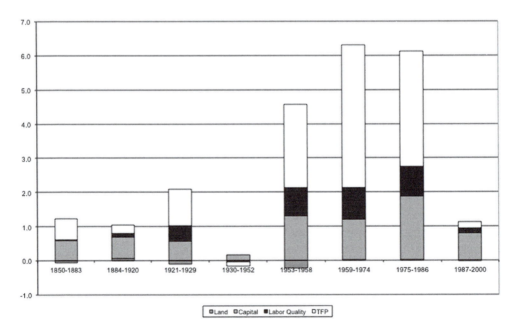

Figure 9.5 Labor productivity growth and its sources, 1850–2000 (annual cumulative rates %).
Sources: Prados de la Escosura and Rosés (2010).

accession to the European Union. Thus, Spain would have exhausted its catch-up potential and efficiency gains slowed down adjusting to the growth in total factor productivity in the most advanced countries. However, a summary inspection of the evidence suggests that this has not been the case, as Spain stayed at the bottom of the growth in total factor productivity among the OECD countries between the mid-1990s and the eve of the Great Recession (2007). Thus, an alternative explanation is required. Comparative evidence indicates that firms' expenditure on research and development are lower in Spain than in most OECD countries. The same is true for cases of investment in intangible (intellectual property) and human capital. The context is further aggravated by a low degree of competition of products and factor markets. Furthermore, the reallocation of resources toward services and construction has taken place in a context of lower investment and innovation that led to declining efficiency.

After the overview presented so far, a closer look at the different phases of Spanish economic performance in which growth rates deviate from the long-run trend, as a result of economic policies, access to international markets, and technological change, can be illuminating.

1815–50

During the nineteenth century, Spain underwent a complex transition from a colonial empire under absolutism to a modern nation with a liberal system of property rights (see chapter 3). The liberal regime reforms included a redefinition of rights that implied that all citizens became equal before the law. The liberalization of commodity and factor (that is, capital and labor) markets suppressed guilds, the Mesta and *mayorazgo*, and brought with it the disentailment of landed property, introduced a Commercial Code and new legislation and regulation on mortgages, patents, banking, and the stock exchange. Moreover, liberalism represented parliamentary control of public revenues and expenditure. In short, serious obstacles to reform emerged, with civil wars and military takeovers as major setbacks that deferred the completion of the transition to the last quarter of the nineteenth century (see Chapters 3, 4, 20).

The loss of the mainland colonies in the Americas, a result of the Napoleonic Wars, had negative effects in the short run on capital formation: government revenues, trade, and manufacturing industry; but the overall impact on GDP was much lower than previously assumed in qualitative assessments, and concentrated in particular regions. Moreover, the more competitive and flexible sectors of the economy eventually adapted to new circumstances, particularly commercial agriculture, and oriented supply toward the growing markets in northwest Europe. Furthermore, if a direct link could be established between Latin American independence and the fall of the *Ancien Régime* in Spain, the loss of the colonies would have contributed significantly to the modernization of Spain.

Thus, the early nineteenth century represented a turning point leading to sustained progress evidenced by population increase, agricultural productivity growth, urbanization, and international trade expansion, which acted as a stimulus to economic modernization, introducing a more efficient allocation of resources.

1850–83

The growth of output per capita between 1850 and 1883 nearly doubled the average for the period of 1850–1950. Institutional reforms that brought greater economic freedom lay beneath such significant growth (see Chapter 3). Opening up to international trade and foreign capital made it possible to break the close connection between investment and savings and contributed to the economic growth. It can be argued that economic success was partly the result of a "reconstruction effect" after the civil wars, political instability, and the social unrest of the early nineteenth century. Nonetheless, despite the persistence of political instability (which included the 1854 liberal uprising and the 1868 Glorious Revolution) a robust economic performance took place during this period. This suggests that an improved definition and enforcement of property rights, as well as openness to goods and ideas, contributed to offset political instability.

1883–1920

Growth slowed down during most of the *Restauración* (1875–1923). Restrictions on both domestic and external competition help explain sluggish growth during 1883–1920 despite the *Restauración*'s institutional stability, that should have provided a favorable environment for investment and growth. Increasing tariff protection, together with exclusion from the prevailing international monetary system, the gold standard, may have represented a major obstacle to Spain's integration in the international economy. Although economic links between the metropolis and the colony were already weak, Cuba's War of Independence caused substantial macroeconomic instability, which together with a sudden stop in international investment, reduced capital inflows sharply leading to the depreciation of the Peseta and in turn increased migration costs, reducing the outward flow of labor. Cuban independence had little direct economic impact on Spain's economy, but a large indirect one as it intensified protectionist and isolationist tendencies. The First World War hardly brought any economic progress and GDP per capita shrank, a result that challenges the conventional view of the war stimulus for growth through import substitution.

1920s

The 1920s represented the period of most intense growth prior to 1950. The hypothesis that Government intervention, through trade protectionism, regulation, and investment in infrastructure, was a driver of growth has been widely accepted. The emphasis on tariff protectionism, however, neglects the fact that Spain opened up to international capital during the 1920s, allowing the purchase of capital goods and raw materials and thus contributing to growth.

1929–50

The period from 1929 to 1950 (which includes the Great Depression, the Civil War, and the postwar autarchic policies) can be defined by economic stagnation and shrinking GDP per capita (see Chapter 7). The Depression, measured by the contraction in real GDP per capita, extended in Spain, as in the United States until 1933, with a 12 percent fall (against 31 percent in the United States). With GDP per capita falling at –3.1 percent annually, the Depression was milder than in the United States but similar in intensity to Western Europe's average, challenging the view of a weaker impact due to Spain's relative international isolation and backwardness. The Civil War (1936–39) prevented Spain from joining the post-Depression recovery and resulted in a severe contraction of economic activity (nearly a one-third drop in real per capita income) but did not reach the magnitude of the impact of the Second World War on the main belligerent countries of continental Western Europe. The weak post–Civil War recovery meant that it took fifteen years (until 1954) to return to the prewar GDP per capita peak level (1929), compared to the six years that it took on average to return to the pre–Second World War peak in Western Europe.

In the search for explanations of Spain's idiosyncratic behavior, the hypothesis that the larger loss of human capital vis-à-vis physical capital contributed to the delayed reconstruction can be put forward, as the destruction of physical capital during the Civil War was about the Western European average during the Second World War, but the exile after the Civil War and, possibly to a larger extent, the internal exile resulting from the new regime's political repression, meant a significant depletion of Spain's limited human capital.

1950–74

The change in trend that began after 1950 ushered in an exceptional phase of rapid growth lasting until 1974. During the 1950s, increasing confidence in the viability of Franco's dictatorship after the US-Spain military and technological cooperation agreements (1953), together with the regime's moderate economic reforms, favored investment and innovation, which contributed to accelerated economic growth. The institutional reform initiated with the 1959 Stabilization and Liberalization Plan, a response to the exhaustion of the inward-looking development strategy, set policies that favored the allocation of resources along a comparative advantage and allowed sustained and faster growth during the 1960s and early 1970s. However, without the moderate reforms of the 1950s and the growth they provoked, it seems unlikely that the Stabilization Plan would have succeeded. Thus, the new available evidence blurs the view of a neat discontinuity between autarchic (1939–59) and moderately free market (1959–75) periods.

The post-1975 era

The oil shocks of the 1970s happened at the time of Spain's transition from a dictatorship to a democracy (see Chapter 8). During the transition decade, per capita GDP growth fell to one fourth of that achieved over 1959–74. Was the slowdown exogenous, simply a result of the international crisis? Did it derive from the Francoist legacy of an economy sheltered from international competition? Was it caused by the policies of the new democratic authorities? Accession to the European Union (1985) heralded another long phase of per capita GDP growth that came to a sudden halt with the Great Recession (2008–13). What explains Spain's comparatively deeper contraction and weaker recovery? Answering these questions provides a research agenda for historians.

It is worth pointing out that the post-1975 era introduced a pattern according to which phases of acceleration in labor productivity correspond to those of sluggish progress in GDP per person, and vice versa. Thus, periods of sluggish (1975–85) or negative (2008–13) per capita GDP growth were paralleled by vigorous or recovering productivity growth. However, during the "transition" decade, labor productivity offset the sharp contraction in hours worked (resulting from unemployment) thus preventing a decline in GDP per capita. In the Great Recession (2008–13), however, the timid improvement in output per hour worked was not enough to offset the contraction in employment and, hence, output per person fell sharply, in a similar fashion to the contraction experienced during the Great Depression (1929–33). Conversely, the years between Spain's accession to the European Union (1985) and the eve of the Great Recession (2007), particularly after 1992, exhibited a combination of substantial per capita GDP gains and slowing labor productivity. Thus, during the three decades after Spain joined the EU, more than half the doubling in GDP was due to the increase in hours worked per person.

The opposite trends in GDP per capita and per hour worked since the mid-1970s can be attributed to the fact that the Spanish economy has been unable to combine employment creation and productivity growth, with the implication that sectors that expanded and created new jobs (mostly in construction and services) did not succeed in attracting investment and technological innovation.

Income distribution

How were the fruits of growth distributed? Did economic growth percolate through to reach the lower income groups? Was there a growth-inequality trade-off, so higher living standards resulting in economic growth compensated for higher inequality?

Trends in aggregate inequality measured by the Gini coefficient are provided in Figure 9.6. (The Gini coefficient measures the extent to which the distribution of income (or consumption expenditure) among individuals or households within an economy deviates from a perfectly equal distribution. A Gini of 0 represents perfect equality, while an index of 1 (100) implies perfect inequality). The evolution of inequality presents the shape of a wide inverted W with

Figure 9.6 Income inequality, 1850–2015: Gini coefficient.

peaks in 1918 and 1953. Different phases can be observed in the evolution of inequality. A long-term rise is noticeable between the mid-nineteenth century and the First World War, reaching a peak in 1918. Then, a sustained reduction in inequality took place during the 1920s and early 1930s stabilizing in the years of the Civil War (1936–39) and the Second World War. The decline in inequality was sharply reversed during the late 1940s and early 1950s, with a peak in 1953 similar to the one reached in 1918. A dramatic fall in inequality took place in the late 1950s and early 1960s. Thereafter, inequality stabilized up to the present at comparatively low levels, fluctuating within a narrow 30–35 Gini range.

How can these inequality trends be interpreted? In the early phase of globalization (from the early nineteenth century to the First World War), the fall in inequality during phases of opening up to international competition (the late 1850s and early 1860s, the late 1880s and early 1890s) and the rise in inequality (from the late 1890s to the end of the First World War) coinciding with a return to strict protectionism, could be predicted with Stolper-Samuelson's theoretical framework, which posits that protectionist policies favor the scarce factors of production (in this case, land and capital) while penalizing the abundant one (labor). At the turn of the nineteenth century, this tendency would have been reinforced by the fact that tariff protection did not push out workers as in other protectionist European countries (i.e., Italy and Sweden). The depreciation of the *peseta* in the 1890s and early 1900s made the decision to migrate more difficult as the cost of passage increased dramatically. This explanation fails, however, to explain the rise in inequality between the mid-1860s and early 1880s that could be attributed to a rise in capital and land returns relative to wages associated to the railroad construction and to the exploitation of mining resources after its liberalization, and not least to the agricultural export boom.

The reduction in inequality during in the 1920s and early 1930s, a period of globalization backlash, would demand a different explanation, as other forces conditioned the evolution of inequality. Accelerated growth, capital deepening, and structural change all helped reduce total inequality in the 1920s. Wage inequality rose with rural-urban migration and urbanization, given that urban wages were higher and with a larger variance than rural wages, but the gap between returns to property and labor declined. Institutional reforms that included new social legislation, especially the reduction in the number of working hours per day, and the increasing voice of trade unions, contributed to a rise in wages relative to property incomes.

The fall in inequality during the early 1930s (years of increasing restrictions to commodity and factor mobility) is, again, at odds with the Stolper-Samuelson model. Forces pushing for redistribution were in place in Spain. On the whole, a reduction in the gap between returns to property and labor more than offset the rise in wage inequality. The Great Depression possibly had a negative impact on the concentration of income at the top of the distribution, that is, returns accruing to proprietors. Wages (in nominal and real terms) rose in a context of trade unions' increasing bargaining power and labor unrest. During the Second Republic, new legislation that tended to increase labor costs, threats to land ownership, and workers' attempts to factory control created insecurity among proprietors, leading to a severe investment collapse and provoking political polarization in Spanish society (see Chapter 5).

The fact that the Civil War broke out after a decade and a half of declining inequality and the economic growth of the 1920s (that led to the alleviation of absolute poverty) demands explanatory hypotheses. Did the Civil War have economic roots? Unfulfilled expectations to share increases in wealth by those at the bottom of the distribution during the Second Republic may contribute to explaining the social unrest that preceded the Civil War. Furthermore, the shrinking gap between returns to property and to labor in a context of social unrest, including threats to property during the early 1930s, provides a potential explanation for the support lent by a significant sector of the Spanish society to the military coup d'état that triggered the Civil War.

How can the rise of inequality during the autarchic years be interpreted? Wage compression took place as a result of the re-ruralization of Spanish economy (the share of agriculture increased in both output and employment) and the ban on trade unions. A parallel decline in the concentration of income at the top during the 1940s took place simultaneously. Thus, while inequality was falling within both labor and capital returns, polarization between property and labor caused a rise of total inequality. International isolation resulting from autarchic policies intensified these trends, with inequality rising as scarce factors, land, and capital were favored at the expense of the abundant and more evenly distributed factor, labor.

A dramatic decline in inequality started in the late 1950s and reached into the early 1960s, that is, prior to the phase of liberalization and opening up that followed the 1959 reforms. The spurt of economic growth in the 1950s brought improvements in living standards, urbanization, and an increase in the labor share within the national income. Furthermore, populist policies by Franco's Minister of Labor, led to a substantial pay rise across the board in 1956. A careful investigation of the process of inequality reduction is warranted.

Openness favored labor as the abundant factor and thus contributed to reducing inequality while stimulating growth and structural change that, in turn, played a significant role in keeping inequality at moderate levels.

The rise in savings, helped by the financial development that accompanied economic growth, facilitated access to housing ownership which, in turn, helped reduce the concentration of property incomes. The diffusion of education likely played a role in the decline of inequality by reducing the concentration of human capital. Moreover, the decrease in regional disparities, conditioned by technological catch-up, the generalization of basic education, and convergence in employment composition, also impinged on income distribution. Furthermore, the increase in social expenditure in the late age of Francoism (1960–75) must have had an effect on reducing inequality.

As income distribution became more egalitarian and growth accelerated from the late 1950s onward, absolute poverty (that is, those living on 2 dollars a day, as measured today by the World Bank) was practically suppressed by the mid-1960s. Perhaps the successful transition to democracy in the last quarter of the twentieth century had its roots there.

Increasing political participation after democracy was reinstated in 1977 led to a progressive fiscal reform and to substantial increases in public expenditure on social transfers (unemployment, pensions), education, and health that had a strong redistributive impact. However, phases of declining and rising inequality have alternated since the restoration of democracy, resulting in levels of inequality that have remained within a 30–35 Gini range.

Thus, it can be argued that the social transfers and progressive taxation brought by the welfare state allowed the maintenance of inequality levels within the 30–35 Gini range, while the "market" Gini (that is, the measure of inequality before social transfers) increased. In fact, evidence for the twenty-first century shows that, in the absence of social transfers, income inequality reached similar levels to those of the early 1950s. A similar finding is obtained for OECD countries. Why Spain, along other OECD societies, has become so unequal before progressive taxation and social transfers demands careful investigation.

Spain in comparative perspective

Spain's long-term GDP per capita growth followed a similar path to that of the Western European nations, although its level remained systematically lower (Figure 9.8). Moreover, the improvement in Spain's GDP per capita did not fit a steady pattern, a feature it shares with Italy and Germany, but that is at odds with the steady progress experienced by the United Kingdom, the United States, and to a lesser extent, France. These findings lend support to the view that the roots of most of today's difference in GDP per person between Spain and other advanced countries should be searched for in the early modern era. However, a closer look reveals that long-run growth before 1950 was clearly lower in Spain than in the advanced countries. Sluggish growth over 1883–1913 and not taking advantage of its neutrality during the First World War partly account for this. Furthermore, the progress achieved in the 1920s was outweighed by Spain's short-lived recovery from the Depression that was brought to a halt by Civil War (1936–39), and a long-lasting and weak postwar reconstruction.

Thus, Spain fell behind between 1815 and 1950 (Figure 9.8). The nineteenth century and the early twentieth century witnessed sustained per capita GDP growth while paradoxically the gap with industrialized countries widened over 1883–1913. The gap deepened further during the first half of the twentieth century.

The opposite was the case from 1950 to 2007. The Golden Age (1950–74) and especially the period after 1960 stands out as a phase of outstanding performance and catching up to the advanced nations (a feature shared by countries in the European periphery: Greece, Portugal, and Ireland). Slow but steady growth after the slowdown in the transition to democracy years allowed Spain to keep catching up until 2007. The Great Recession reversed the trend,

Figure 9.7 Comparative real GDP per capita, 1815–2015 (1990 Geary-Khamis Dollars) (semi-logarithmic scale).

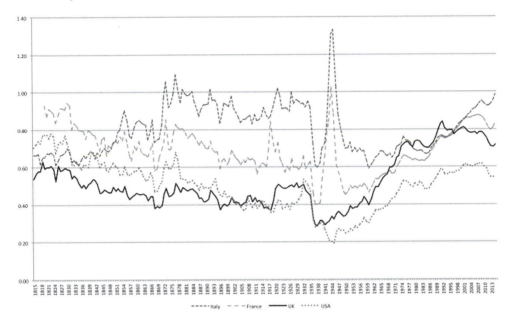

Figure 9.8 Spain's relative real GDP per capita, 1815–2015 (1990 Geary-Khamis Dollars) (Spain as a percentage of each country's level).

although it remains too soon to establish whether this is a temporary episode or the beginning of another phase of falling behind.

On the whole, Spain's relative position to Western countries has evolved along a wide-U shape, deteriorating to 1950 (except for the 1870s and 1920s) and recovering thereafter (except for the episodes of the transition to democracy and the Great Recession). Thus, at the beginning of the twenty-first century Spanish real GDP per capita represented a similar proportion of United States and Germany's income to the one in mid-nineteenth century, although it had significantly improved with respect to the UK and kept a similar position to that of the 1870s with regard to France.

In terms of income distribution, during the last century and a half, Spain matched the evolution of OECD countries, except for the autarchic period that followed the Civil War in which Spain's inequality was far above the European average.

Over the last two centuries, income per person has improved remarkably, driven by increases in labor productivity which derived from a more intense and efficient use of physical and human capital per worker. Up to 1950 and from 1986 (when Spain became part of the European Union) factor accumulation dominated long-run growth, while efficiency gains led productivity growth in the 1920s and during the period 1953–86. The reallocation of resources from lower productivity sectors (i.e., agriculture) toward sectors with higher productivity contributed significantly to the acceleration of productivity growth. Exposure to international competition represented a decisive element behind growth performance, with sluggish growth and retardation associated to closeness and accelerated growth and catching up to openness.

From a Western European perspective, Spain underperformed up to 1950. Thereafter, Spain's economy caught up with advanced countries until 2007, with the years 1960–74 standing out for their outstanding performance and the transition to democracy (1975–85) as the exception.

Income distribution did not follow a linear process. After an upswing in inequality up to the First World War, a declining trend initiated in the interwar years, and although reversed in the post–Civil War autarchy, resumed strongly in the late 1950s and early 1960s, stabilizing at a relatively low level in the last half-century. Higher levels of income per capita were matched by lower inequality, suggesting that Spaniards' material well-being improved substantially during the modern era.

Further reading

Calvo González, Oscar, "American Military Interests and Economic Confidence in Spain under the Franco Dictatorship," *Journal of Economic History*, 67, 3, (2007), pp. 740–67.

Fraile Balbín, P., and A. Escribano, "The Spanish 1898 Disaster: The Drift Toward, National-Protectionism," in P. K. O'Brien and L. Prados de la Escosura (eds.), *The Costs and Benefits of European Imperialism from the Conquest of Ceuta, 1415, to the Treaty of Lusaka, 1974, Revista de Historia Económica* 16 (1998), pp. 265–90.

Martin Aceña, Pablo, "Spain during the Classical Gold Standard Years, 1880-1914," in M. D. Bordo and F. Capie (eds.), *Monetary Regimes in Transition*, Cambridge: Cambridge University Press, 1993, pp. 135–72.

Martínez-Galarraga, Julio, Joan R. Rosés, and Daniel A. Tirado, "The Long-Term Patterns of Regional Income Inequality in Spain (1860-2000)," *Regional Studies*, 49, 4 (2015), pp. 502–17.

Nadal, J., "The Failure of the Industrial Revolution in Spain, 1830-1914," in C. M. Cipolla (ed.), *The Fontana Economic History of Europe*, 4, 2 (1973), pp. 532–626.

Prados de la Escosura, Leandro, *Spanish Economic Growth, 1850-2015*, London: Palgrave Macmillan, 2017.

Prados de la Escosura, Leandro, "Inequality, Poverty, and the Kuznets Curve in Spain, 1850-2000," *European Review of Economic History*, 12, 3 (2008), pp. 287–324.

Prados de la Escosura, Leandro, Joan R. Rosés, and Isabel Sanz-Villarroya, "Economic Reforms and Growth in Franco's Spain," *Revista de Historia Económica-Journal of Iberian and Latin American Economic History*, 30, 1 (2012), pp. 45–89.

Sánchez-Albornoz, Nicholas (ed.), *The Economic Modernization of Spain, 1830-1930*, New York: New York University Press, 1987.

Simpson, James, *Spanish Agriculture: The Long Siesta, 1765-1965*, Cambridge: Cambridge University Press, 1995.

Sánchez Alonso, Blanca, "European Emigration in the Late Nineteenth Century: the Paradoxical Case of Spain," *Economic History Review*, 53 (2000), pp. 309–30.

Tortella, Gabriel, *The Development of Modern Spain. An Economic History of the Nineteenth and Twentieth Centuries*, Cambridge, MA: Harvard University Press, 2000.

CHAPTER 10
NATION AND NATIONALISM
Xosé M. Núñez Seixas

Since the beginning of the twentieth century, Spain has been an example of a pluriethnic state, where several ethnonationalist movements compete with state nationalism. Together with Canada, Belgium, and the UK, it also constitutes a case of an advanced capitalist society where ethnoterritorial competition remains one of the main factors affecting its political evolution. The unsolved national question makes Spain sometimes appear as an example of nation-state which failed to become a fully homogenized political community during the critical period 1850–1945. Nevertheless, it would be misleading to conceive Spain in terms of a multinational state similar to Eastern European examples, where different ethnic and linguistic communities coexist without sharing social space. On the contrary, mixed marriages, linguistic assimilation, multiple identities, and hybridization have been a constant feature of Spanish history, and intergroup conflict has been almost nonexistent. The country's European borders have not undergone alterations since the eighteenth century, nor have the electoral results of ethnonationalist parties in some territories (Catalonia, the Basque Country, Galicia, and, to a more limited extent, the Canary Islands and other regions) made them fully hegemonic. In other words, Spain may be considered an unfulfilled nation-state, but it is also an imperfect multinational state, since the alternative national identities have not yet managed to impose their social hegemony within their territories.

The liberal revolution and the emergence of the nation

The Spanish political community in the Hapsburg period (sixteenth and seventeenth centuries) was a composite monarchy, integrated by a diversity of territorial, juridical, and social bodies with diverse duties and rights. Its main principles of legitimacy were dynastic loyalty and Catholic faith. The Bourbon dynasty reduced the extent of territorial privileges, yet some of them (like the Basque and Navarrese *fueros*) persisted. Likewise, the concentration of power in the monarchy and the spreading of the principle that the political body situated under the authority of the sovereign had to be as homogeneous as possible regarding laws and customs was crucial to set the basis of a modern protonationalism, which just lacked the idea of the nation as a source of sovereignty.

As elsewhere in Europe, at the beginning there was Napoleon. The Peninsular War (1808–14), later renamed the War of Independence, against the Napoleonic invaders marked the beginning of modern Spanish nationalism and national identity. However, during the conflict and its aftermath a high degree of semantic ambiguity persisted in the public sphere regarding the different meanings of the concept of nation and homeland (*patria*). Its overwhelmingly local character also characterized wartime nationalist mobilization, and most symbols of anti-French resistance had just a local dimension. Yet, the first Spanish liberals, who gathered at the first Cadiz parliament (*Cortes*) in 1810–12, crafted a modern concept of the Spanish nation, regarded as the sovereign body of citizens placed under a common law (see Chapter 2). This liberal concept also incorporated an organic-historicist bias: Spain was considered to be a community shaped by history and culture, and the examples of anti-despotic resistance in the medieval and early modern past, like the revolt of the Castilian *Comuneros* in the sixteenth century, as well as the medieval city parliaments of the Crown of Castile, were regarded as the forerunners of an authentically Spanish liberalism. The preliminary discourse of the Cadiz Constitution (1812) affirmed that sovereignty resided "essentially in the nation" which assembled "all Spaniards from both hemispheres," and the different territories of the Empire were listed. However, the reluctance of metropolitan deputies to give equal representation to the overseas territories heralded the process of desegregation of the overseas empire, which took place in different stages between 1810 and 1826. Only the islands of Cuba and Puerto Rico, as well as the Philippines, remained attached to Spain (see chapters 2, 13).

The prevailing concept of the Spanish nation in traditionalist and (from 1833) Carlist thought adapted Hapsburg protonationalism to the new elements provided by cultural romanticism. According to them, Spain possessed a national spirit (*Volksgeist*), which was reinforced by the adaptation of the positive side of external stereotypes about Spaniards, stereotypes that had been outlined by foreign travelers and writers since the seventeenth century: a mixture of honor, bravery, and mysticism. The unity of the Spanish monarchy was compatible with respect for regional diversity, since national identity was mostly the outcome of Catholic faith and dynastic loyalty.

The impact of the loss of most American colonies between 1810 and 1824 was low: most Spaniards regarded them as territories of the king and not part of the new nation, which was to be built within its European borders. Exiled liberals and intellectuals were aware of the increasing necessity of nationalizing the new polity through the spreading of a narrative on the virtues of the Spanish character and the glorious periods of the national past, which emphasized myths of resistance against the Roman conquerors; struggles of medieval kings and knights against the Muslims; the conquest of America; and the resistance against Napoleon, as well as the establishment of some myths and symbols and the definition of a literary canon. A new national history of Spain played a prominent role in this program, beginning with the *Historia general de España* by Modesto Lafuente (1850–67). So too did the diffusion of historic themes in painting, the creation of museums and libraries, the establishment of an iconography of the nation by the press, and the increasing diffusion of symbols such as the red and yellow flag.

The period inaugurated by the reign of Isabella II in 1833 was marked by the construction of a new liberal state, which embodied the nation (see Chapter 20). However, several historians have underlined the relative weakness of the social diffusion of an articulated feeling of national belonging in the Spanish population, and have attributed this to several factors: (a) the persistence of territorial imbalances in the level of economic modernization, particularly concentrated in some regions of the periphery, which caused economic and political elites not to coincide and social communication to advance slowly (most Spaniards maintained a local worldview); (b) the territorialization of inner political splits: the confrontation between absolutists and Carlists on the one hand and liberals on the other hand, with the subsequent division of liberals between moderate (centralists) and revolutionary liberals (supporters of decentralization) overlapped with the idealization of the *fueros* and local liberties by democrats and republicans. Thus, an implicit association between decentralization and deepening of democracy emerged, paralleled by the defense of the territorial *Fueros* by the Carlists; (c) the limited efficiency of nation-building policies carried out by the state. Here the focus on a poorly financed system of national education, which was placed under the tutelage of the Catholic Church and was unable to spread a common culture or patriotic values, as well as the persistence of a socially discriminatory military service unable to incarnate the notion of the nation in arms and the difficulties met by the diffusion of some national symbols. The state carried out the task of propagating the new myths, erecting monuments, and promoting civic rites and ceremonies inadequately. However, other symbols rooted in popular culture, from bullfighting to some musical genres, also played an informal role in mass nationalization.

The territorial restructuring of the state into forty-nine provinces after 1833 slowly eroded social attachment to the old regions, which persisted throughout the nineteenth century as a frame of reference for both revolutionary liberals and supporters of the *ancien régime* alike. Local law codes and mores, particularly in the sphere of Civil Law, lasted until the end of the century and even beyond. Regional and local identities also developed, though they were mostly seen as complementary dimensions of Spanish identity. And many cities, Bilbao and Seville for example, themselves became places of memory and identity building. This highlighted the existence of overlapping processes of territorial identity building in modern Spain.

Last but not least, after the Peninsular War there was the lack of a foreign "other." Despite occasional rhetoric about the reintegration of Gibraltar, Spain did not really aim at annexing border regions. The country came late to the colonial race of the last third of the nineteenth century, and gained just small territories in Africa. The splendid little wars fostered by the *Unión Liberal* government in 1859–62, such as the "War of Africa" (1859–60); the expeditions to Mexico (1861–62), and Cochinchina (1857–63); the annexation of Saint Domingue (1861–65) and the Pacific War (1863–66) were short and involved a limited number of soldiers, although the African campaign of 1859–60 gained the enthusiastic adherence of Catholics and Republicans alike, who endorsed patriotic mobilization. (It was also highly popular in Catalonia.) At the same time, the last Caribbean colonies (Cuba and Puerto Rico) were accommodated within the national imaginary as an "overseas Spain," not just simple colonies but two more territories of the Spanish polity, even though they always remained outside the legal regime of the metropolis. After 1858, Cuban separatists were regarded as backward slaves who wanted to amputate a member of the national body and impose racial anarchy. The Spanish-American War of 1898 favored an outburst of patriotic rhetoric. Yet, after the defeat, Spanish nationalism turned increasingly toward the defense of national integrity against its internal enemies, especially in Catalonia. The Moroccan wars between 1907 and 1927 did not contribute to the creation of a new national unity against a foreign other.

Was nineteenth-century Spain an example of weak nation building and failure of state building, which preceded the emergence of peripheral nationalisms in the following century? Spanish historiography is far from reaching a consensus on this point. Certainly, some nation-building policies were weak in comparison with some other European nation-states. Yet, the diffusion of national symbols, such as the flag, was greater than supposed by twentieth-century historiography. Moreover, many subnational claims have to be interpreted as region-building processes that, in the end, related to a multifaceted construction of Spanish identity based on its regional and local diversity, a pattern that is also found elsewhere. Compared with other European polities, the Spanish case was not so exceptional. Moreover, civil society was able, through informal means, to generate its own mechanisms of national identification, which related to the local, the regional, and the national sphere in concentric ways. The subsequent difficulties of Spanish nation building to impose its hegemony on some regions of the periphery related to the difficult transit from an imperial polity to a national, postimperial one.

Moderate liberals were mostly in favor of state centralism. Yet, the victory over the Carlists in 1839 did not bring about the end of the *Fueros*, and some of their laws persisted in a new form. Thus, a lasting situation of territorial exceptionality that even persisted through the end of the Third Carlist War in 1876 was created. Spanish conservative thinkers, in fact, never entirely agreed with the maintenance of the provinces, which they saw as an alien, French invention, and maintained a certain nostalgia of the preliberal concept of composite monarchy, now reframed as a "federative monarchy."

For radical liberalism, nostalgia for the medieval assemblies and provincial liberties was a way to resuscitate an authentically Spanish democratic tradition. The short period of the Democratic Sexennium (1868–74) was marked by permanent political instability (see Chapter 3). This became especially evident during the First Republic (1873), which was marked by some local revolts that aimed at the proclamation of a federal republic. From that moment on, federalism became associated with political turmoil. However, it was also incorporated into the political vocabulary of the Spanish left as the preferred state structure. At the same time, Spanish federalism was internally heterogeneous, and its projects oscillated between (a) a federation based on the free association of municipalities and provinces up to the nation; and (b) the conversion of the "ancient kingdoms" and territories—including Portugal—defined by language and history into the units which should shape the federation, a trend represented by Francesc Pi i Margall. On the other hand, many Republicans, such as Emilio Castelar, believed that the new nation should be built on a common cultural basis crafted by a strong central state.

The workers' movement that emerged in the last quarter of the nineteenth century also took up these interpretations. Socialists, anarchists, and communists oscillated between two extremes: federalism as a magic recipe to radically democratize the state (an option particularly embraced by the Catalan workers' movement) and a fierce centralism, sometimes counterbalanced by municipal autonomy, which held that only a strong central state could carry out the task of transforming society. However, the political dialogue between federal republicanism and some peripheral movements also favored the emergence of hybrid political cultures. Two additional elements were the influence of the philosophy of Karl Krause, which enhanced the role of territorial entities as parts of an organic concept of society, and the influence of *fin-de-siècle regeneracionismo*, whose rather vague proposals could also be interpreted as a claim to regenerate the nation starting from the empowerment of municipalities and regions, which would reform the nation from below (see Chapter 4).

Origins and development of substate nationalisms

During the last quarter of the nineteenth century, a number of new political actors emerged in the Iberian periphery, particularly in Catalonia, the Basque Country, and Galicia, but also in Valencia. Most had their origins in regionalized evolutions of progressive liberalism, federal republicanism, and local Carlism or Basque *fuerismo*. They created associations and groupings that first embraced regionalist creeds, and later, once they had shifted to define their territories as *nations* and not as regions or ancient nationalities, became substate nationalisms, that is, social and cultural movements which aimed at achieving self-determination in the long term for their territories, and some form of self-government in the short and midterm. This process led to the articulation of regionalist movements between 1868 and 1875 in Catalonia, Galicia, and the Valencia region, flanked by a literary revival of vernacular languages (known as the *Renaixença* in Catalonia and *Rexurdimento* in Galicia) and the development of regional history writing, which aimed to reinforce the role of the regions and "ancient nationalities" within the mainstream of Spanish national history. Symbols and traditions, from dances to flags, were codified and transformed into alternative national icons. This steadily led to the development of a new national discourse that made those nationalities the subject of sovereignty. The turning point was noticeable in Catalonia at the end of the 1880s (Enric Prat de la Riba), as well as in Galicia (Manuel Murguía) and later on in the Basque Country (Sabino Arana). Although there was no teleological line leading from regionalism to substate nationalism, all new nationalists jumped from one stage to another.

These movements reframed the discourse of territorial identity in nationalist terms, and therefore laid the basis for alternative nation-building projects that challenged the Spanish one. The 1898 disaster and the subsequent legitimacy crisis of the idea of the Spanish nation also contributed to the increasing success of alternative national projects in the periphery, which gained the adherence of relevant sectors of the population they targeted. This happened particularly in the case of Catalanism, mostly represented until 1923 by the Lliga Regionalista, a Catholic and Moderate Party that also aimed to modernize the Spanish political system (see Chapter 31).

In the Basque case, the frustration of broad sectors of Viscayan society in face of rapid industrialization after 1880 and the consequent mass influx of immigrants from other parts of Spain combined with the radicalization of a part of the supporters of the ancient *Fueros*. The peculiar personality of Sabino Arana, founder of the Basque Nationalist Party (PNV) in 1895, decisively impregnated the ideological profile of the emerging nationalist movement. Arana crafted a new ideology based on racism, anti-Spanish sentiment, Catholicism and radical pro-independence positions. In Arana's view, the Basque nation was based on race and history. While after Arana's early death in 1903 the PNV would adopt an increasing political pragmatism that permitted it to endorse autonomy as a short-term goal, these essential traits persisted into the 1930s and well beyond.

From the start of the twentieth century until 1936, substate nationalist movements experienced a steady growth of social and political influence. In the Catalan case this became evident after 1901; in the case of Basque nationalism after 1905–06, and in the Galician case, although to a lesser extent, after 1916–18. In the 1907 elections, the electoral coalition Catalan Solidarity, which brought together Catalanists, Republicans, and other parties, won the overwhelming majority of the Catalan seats in the Spanish Parliament. However, the movement diversified internally and new Republican, left-wing and radical Catalanist groupings emerged. Yet, all of them shared some basic tenets: the relevant role ascribed to the Catalan language and history in their idea of the Catalan nation, and the will to intervene in Spanish politics to reform the state. On the eve of the First World War, Catalanism had shaped a broadly interclass social movement. After 1906, Basque nationalism underwent similar dynamics of social and political growth, spreading from Vizcaya to the other provinces and obtaining its first great electoral success in 1918.

Concepts of Spain during the first third of the twentieth century

Throughout the period 1900–1936, both traditionalist and liberal-progressive currents of Spanish nationalism experienced a noteworthy continuity. Both trends shared a pessimistic view of recent Spanish history as an imperial decadence marked by backwardness and isolation. Yet, both their interpretation of the national past and their proposals for the future diverged. Catholic-traditionalist nationalism was influenced by the historicist interpretation of Antonio Cánovas del Castillo and, in particular, by the work of historian, literary critic, and philologist Marcelino Menéndez Pelayo, who crafted an interpretation of Spanish national history deeply marked by Catholicism and royalism. In his view, Spain was an outcome of a diversity of kingdoms and traditions, united by the monarchy and the Catholic faith. As he put it in his most famous formulation: "Spain, evangelizer of half the world. Spain, hammer of heretics, light of Trent, sword of the Pope, birthplace of Saint Ignatius. That is our greatness and our glory. We have no other." This view was further developed by thinkers and political leaders such as Ramiro de Maeztu, the Carlists Juan Vázquez de Mella and Víctor Pradera, and the heterogeneous group behind *Acción Española* during the 1930s, alongside several currents of the anti-Republican right during that period. They also paid more attention to the ethnic foundations of Spanish identity, history, and national spirit. This trend was to lay the foundations of national-Catholicism, which became the hegemonic creed during the Franco regime (see Chapter 7).

On the other hand, until the 1930s, Republicans, liberals, and the "bourgeois" left embraced liberal-democratic Spanish nationalism. They mostly accepted the interpretation of national history advanced by nineteenth-century liberals, but also acknowledged the influence of philosophers such as José Ortega y Gasset (*España invertebrada*, 1920), who emphasized the role of Castile in Spanish unity and the necessity of building a new "project," a community of destiny under the aegis of Castile (see Chapter 32). They also stressed the necessity of building the nation through the education of its citizens, who were to become aware of their rights and duties: active citizenship was an urgent prerequisite for constructing a modern nation. For them, the people were the reservoir of the historical essence of the Spanish nation, and the only thing needed to reawaken its innate qualities was education. The necessity of coming to terms with Catalan republicans and progressive Catalanists, who were indispensable to building a Spanish republic, forced Spanish republicans to nuance their centralist views and display flexibility regarding the territorial structure of Spain (see Chapter 5). Moreover, Ortega y Gasset's influence was multidirectional: in fact, the minority fascist groups that emerged in the 1930s, particularly the Falange of José Antonio Primo de Rivera, adhered to the idea of Spain as a "mission," based on a shared goal and not exclusively on blood, soil, or language.

The task of Spanish cultural nationalism since the first decade of the twentieth century was of particular relevance. This was promoted by institutions such as the Institución Libre de Enseñanza and the Centro de Estudios Históricos, and drew on the theories crafted by intellectuals and writers who after the 1898 crisis "reinvented" the idea of Spain, rediscovered the Castilian history and tradition, and emphasized the role of the Castilian language as a national marker for Spain. This also meant a rediscovery of Latin America. A new project of "cultural expansion" toward the Spanish-speaking American republics took shape. Developed after the first decade of the twentieth century by intellectuals as ideologically different as Rafael Altamira and Ramiro de Maeztu, this Hispanoamericanism searched for the roots of the

Spanish grandeur in the reconstruction of its cultural and economic links toward its former American empire.

There was also a concept of Spain as a multinational or multiethnic polity that emanated from substate nationalisms. Leaving aside some pro-independence factions, three main projects coexisted. One was multinational federalism, which advocated Spain transforming itself into a plurinational federation (in the form of either a Republic or of a Monarchy), composed of four organic nations defined by ethnocultural criteria: Galicia (with or without Portugal); Catalonia (with or without Valencia and the Balearic islands); the Basque Country (with Navarre) and Castile. A second was the idea of a bilateral agreement between an individual nation and "Spain," that is the rest of the Spanish polity. This claim was particularly present in the Basque case—updating the "foral pact" between the monarchy and the Basque territories. The third was the short- and medium-term acceptance of decentralization from above, where access to administrative and political autonomy was granted, in theory, to all Spanish regions, but where the precedence and "differential quality" of the authentic stateless nations was preserved. This latter option prevailed both in the period 1914–23 and during the Second Republic, and became the most realistic way for substate nationalists to achieve some of their political objectives, either through a fusion of provincial governments (*Mancomunidades*), or under the form of a regional autonomy, as the Republican Constitution of 1931 established. However, substate nationalists always regarded autonomy for all Spanish regions with reluctance, since they considered asymmetry of treatment as recognition by the Spanish state of the peculiarities of Catalonia, the Basque Country, and Galicia.

From renationalization from above to the Republican decentralization

The dictatorship established by the coup d'état of General Primo de Rivera strove toward an authoritarian renationalization of Spain (see Chapter 5). After some vague promises of healthy decentralization, the military government forbade the official usage of regional languages and the public exhibition of regional flags, as well as the teaching of culture, history, and language of Catalonia in the schools. Likewise, the dictatorship attempted to incarnate a new Spanish nationalism through its cultural policies, the mobilization and militarization of youth, and the reinforcement of ceremonies and nationalist contents in the curricula taught at primary schools. However, this endeavor of renationalizing Spain completely failed, and social support for substate nationalisms did not substantially diminish. While some of their activists opted for cultural activities within Spain, others fostered political opposition against the dictatorship abroad. Radical catalanists, led by Francesc Macià, were especially active in conspiring with Republicans, anarchists, and even Italian antifascists. The prestige he acquired and the links he forged with Spanish republicans facilitated the consolidation of Macià's role in Catalan politics after the end of the dictatorship.

After the fall of Primo de Rivera, substate nationalists reemerged and adopted different strategies in the face of foreseeable political change. Conservative Catalanists failed in their attempt to broaden the support to the moribund monarchy through the creation of a Spanish center party. In a parallel way, Catalanist and Spanish republicans cooperated closely and signed the Pact of San Sebastián (August 1930), which granted the former the achievement of Catalan autonomy within the future Spanish republic. In 1930–31, a new political hegemony was built in Catalonia thanks to the political synthesis between social-reformist and federal republicanism on the one hand, and left-wing and radical Catalan nationalism on the other hand. In March 1931, they merged to create a new party, *Esquerra Republicana de Catalunya* (ERC). Basque nationalists played the card of strategic pragmatism and, after an initial period of collaboration with Basque-Navarrese Carlists based on their common Catholicism, shifted politically toward collaboration with republicans and socialists. This opened the path for the PNV toward becoming a modern Christian-democratic party. In Galicia, nationalists proved unable to reunite and create a common political platform. Some nationalists merged with local republicans to set up in 1929 an autonomist organization, which played an important role in the subsequent years.

From its inception, the nascent Republic adopted a decentralized structure. This was a consequence not only of the commitments of San Sebastián, but also of the political weight of Catalan nationalist republicans. On April 14, 1931, the Republic was proclaimed in Madrid and other towns, while in Barcelona, Francesc Macià called into being the "Catalan Republic" within a still nonexistent Federal Spanish Republic. This move forced the Republican provisional government to negotiate a solution: the creation of a provisional regional government in Barcelona, which adopted the name of *Generalitat* of Catalonia, seen as a restoration of the self-governing institutions abolished by the Bourbons in 1714. The parliamentary elections of June 1931 clearly displayed that peripheral nationalisms enjoyed remarkable social support: while ERC obtained a majority of Catalan seats, the PNV achieved more than a quarter of the Basque votes, and Galician nationalists obtained noticeable results, although they ran on different tickets.

The new Republican Constitution defined Spain as an "integral State," a sole political nation that also encompassed regions provided with statutes of autonomy. Only those territories where a majority of votes opted for it were, after a complex procedure, given the right to have access to home rule. The Catalan statute was passed by referendum in 1932; the Basque one in November 1933; and the Galician one in June 1936. However, only in the Catalan case was decentralization effective before the outbreak of the Civil War.

Catalan nationalists consolidated their social support during the Republican years and also saw their political protagonism reinforced. The ERC's hegemonic role was based on its embracing a polyvalent creed, which blended the tradition of catalanism, federal republicanism, and social reform; charismatic leadership exerted first by Macià and then by Lluís Companys; and the passive support of many anarch-osyndicalist workers. Despite claiming self-determination for Catalonia in the long term, the ERC accepted the framework of Republican home rule and governed the *Generalitat* pragmatically. Conservative Catalanism experienced a shift to the right, placing the defense of Catholic religion as its main priority. Both parties were flanked by diverse minority Catalanist organizations that covered a wide political spectrum, from Christian democrats to Communists, who aimed at reconciling Catalan self-determination with a Spanish revolution.

Galician nationalists founded a unified party in December 1931 (the *Partido Galeguista*, PG), which adopted a progressive-republican orientation and was in favor of self-determination for Galicia within a multinational state, yet focused in the short term on achieving an autonomy statute. The party broadened its social basis and was on the way to becoming a mass organization when the Civil War broke out. Some other regionalist groupings emerged in Andalusia, Valencia, and Aragon, all of them rooted in variegated traditions of local republicanism.

The electoral victory of the right in the parliamentary polls of November 1933 froze the process of regional devolution. It also caused center/periphery tensions to increase and to overlap with political polarization between the right and the left, as Companys' failed proclamation of the Catalan Republic within the Federal Spanish Republic in October 1934 made evident. From the end of that year, most factions of substate nationalisms linked their political fate to that of the Spanish republican left, which was still open to accepting claims for home rule. Both left-wing and progressive Catalanists and Galician nationalists, as well as some factions of Basque nationalism, joined the Popular Front, while the *Lliga* entered a coalition with the rest of the right-wing parties. Only the PNV stood on its own.

Civil War and Francoism

The Spanish Civil War meant the clash of Spanish and peripheral nationalisms on the one hand, and the confrontation between different variants of Spanish nationalism on the other (see Chapter 6). Both Republicans and rebels appealed to similar slogans and historical myths to endorse their cause, refusing to label the conflict as a civil war, and presenting it instead as a war of national liberation against a new invader: either Soviet communism for the Francoists or international Fascism for the Republicans. Communist and socialist propaganda referred to the heroes of May 2, 1808 as forerunners of present militiamen fighting the Fascists, while General Franco defined the uprising as "our new War of Independence." The left insisted on the idea that the Spanish people (the popular classes) were the authentic representatives of the nation's virtues, threatened by a clique of landowners, capitalists, bishops, and military who had betrayed their homeland and accepted foreign dominance.

The outbreak of the Civil War presented substate nationalists with a difficult choice. Catalan Catholic nationalists gave priority to the defense of religion and social order, as did some Galician and Basque nationalists, but most factions, including the Catholic PNV, aligned themselves with the defense of the Republic. They expected that the Spain that would emerge after a Republican victory would evolve toward a multinational federation. In Catalonia, the ERC in theory kept the regional government in its hands. However, anarcho-syndicalist and revolutionary militias exerted real power, and after 1937 the government of the Republic attempted to erode the "excessive" autonomy that Catalonia had enjoyed thanks to the wartime circumstances. In January 1939, when the Francoist army conquered Catalonia, many Catalan nationalists felt that the Spanish "Republican" invasion had been followed by a new Spanish invasion of a different political color.

Until 1975, Spanish nationalism was practically monopolized by Catholic-traditionalist discourse, with some additional Fascist touches. Francoism consecrated the hegemony of a traditionalist version of Spanish identity, which centered its nationalist discourse on the essentialist affirmation of a Catholic Spain, basically identified with Castile. It argued that Spanish history had produced a *Volksgeist* whose best contemporary expression was the myth of *Hispanidad*. Educational policy, the militarization of youth, military conscription, and public ceremonies were among the fields where this renationalizing program was expanded and promoted. However, Francoist nationalism failed to uproot the hidden peripheral national identities in some regions. The Franco regime moved to impose a single state language, and the Catholic Church always prevented the Fascist factions from taking control of the education system. Moreover, state repression was perceived in some areas, particularly in Catalonia and the Basque Country, as a kind of "Spanish occupation." Thus, the dictatorship contributed to reinforcing the social cohesion of the Catalan and Basque nationalist communities, whose durability was assured by their relationships based on family and private networks. On the contrary, in Galicia, the Civil War interrupted a dynamic of social expansion of the nationalist movement.

State repression and the survival of the peripheral nationalist legacy, along with the partial failure of Spanish "authoritarian nation-building," permitted substate nationalisms to remain alive—although silent—during the 1940s and 1950s. After 1960 their main characteristics changed, however. This corresponded with the deep transformations experienced by Spanish society: modernization, industrialization, and several new waves of internal migration toward the Basque Country and Catalonia (see Chapter 19). There were also important ideological mutations within substate nationalist movements. In the Catalan case, a new doctrine emerged, influenced by social Catholicism and Christian personalist thought under the patronage of broad sectors of the Catalan Church, which favored anti-Francoist mobilization by Catholic and left-wing groups with the support of a large portion of Catalan civil society. At the beginning of the 1960s, the influence of Marxist-Leninist ideology on the younger generation of nationalist activists, along with the popularity of "internal colonialism" doctrines in Europe, contributed to the emergence of new nationalist parties that marked an ideological rift with their predecessors. The depth of this break was much larger in the Basque Country and Galicia than in Catalonia. In 1959, Basque Land and Freedom (*Euskadi Ta Askatasuna*, or ETA) was founded, and from the mid-1960s evolved to embrace violence and terrorist tactics. Some currents in the Canary Islands' left wing also interpreted the peripheral situation of the archipelago in colonial terms.

The monopolization of Spanish nationalist discourse by Francoism and the antidemocratic right had significant consequences for the whole spectrum of Spanish nationalism, particularly when it was forced to present a democratically legitimized face in the last years of Francoism and during the democratic transition. At that time, any form of Spanish nationalism was automatically identified with the defense of the old tenets advocated by Francoism. As a result, the Spanish left-wing opposition was forced toward adopting federalist and even pro-multinational stances. But the combination of peripheral nationalism and socialism within a federal project for Spain reached a stable level only in the case of left-wing Catalanist parties. As a consequence, the 1960s and 1970s were a period of uncertainty concerning how to articulate a future democracy territorially. The Spanish Communist Party (PCE) followed a strategy of theoretically demanding the recognition of the right to self-determination for the Basque Country, Catalonia, and Galicia, and at its 1974 and 1976 conventions, the Socialist Party (PSOE) also affirmed the right to self-determination for "Iberian nationalities" while expressing its preference for a federal State.

The territorial question in the Spanish transition and democratic consolidation

After General Franco's death in November 1975, the unsolved national question in Spain emerged as one of the factors that would most influence the process of democratic transition (see Chapter 8). Some of the majority parties and currents within peripheral nationalist movements played an important role in that process, and in several cases—particularly the Catalans—they displayed a high level of political pragmatism, giving the reestablishment of democracy priority over their own goals of self-determination. The reestablishment of democracy brought about an ambitious attempt to achieve a consociational solution to the problem of the territorial articulation of the state and the satisfaction of peripheral nationalist demands.

During the early 1970s, the pressure exerted by the democratic opposition had increased greatly in certain regions. This was particularly noticeable in Catalonia, where in 1971 a multiparty plural platform (the Assembly of Catalonia) was set up in order to advocate a common program, which included political amnesty, democratic freedoms, and the reestablishment of the home rule statute of 1932. In the Basque Country, the first half of the 1970s was marked by the virulence of ETA's terrorist activity and by the strong repression carried out by Francoist police, which, after the Burgos trial of 1970 and the killing of Admiral Carrero Blanco in 1973, made ETA appear as the incarnation of the Basque fatherland's fight against the dictatorship. This seriously damaged the legitimacy of the Spanish state in the Basque Country and paved the way for the difficulties in integrating Basque nationalism into Spanish democracy after 1975. ETA's terrorism did not cease until 2011, leaving behind more than 900 victims. The anti-Francoist opposition in other regions, such as Valencia, Aragon, and the Balearic Islands, also advanced demands for autonomy, although their impact was much weaker. The timid offers of administrative decentralization that emanated in 1976 from the post-Francoist government were soon overwhelmed by pressure from the left wing and peripheral nationalist organizations.

The social influence that peripheral nationalisms enjoyed was clearly felt in the results of the first democratic parliamentary elections held in June 1977: Catalan nationalists reaped 26.9 percent of the vote in their region, while Basque nationalism reached 39.3 percent. The polls also demonstrated the persistence, although greatly weakened through political fragmentation, of Galician nationalism (6.7 percent), as well as the emergence of a new, leftist Andalusian regionalism and a recently formed Canary Islands' nationalism. It became clear that under conditions of full political democracy, the peripheral nationalist movements enjoyed a marked consolidation.

Moderate Catalan nationalism incorporated new ideological ingredients, such as Christian Democracy and even social democracy. The main nationalist party, Democratic Convergence of Catalonia (CDC), was founded in 1974 by the charismatic Jordi Pujol. Two years later it merged with the Christian-democrat Democratic Union of Catalonia (UDC) to form the highly successful electoral coalition Convergence and Union (*Convergència i Unió*, or CiU), which won all regional elections between 1980 and 2012. Until the second decade of the twenty-first century, this current within Catalan nationalism was characterized by strong pragmatism, aiming at the largest possible degree of self-government within the framework of the Spanish state and the European Union. For this reason, CiU advocated full development of regional devolution to Catalonia. According to Catalan nationalists, political autonomy had to be constantly "deepened," although they never specified the final point. The model defended by CiU leaders for thirty years was a kind of bilateral relationship between Catalonia and the rest of Spain. But the party also came to terms in Madrid both with Spanish socialists and conservatives. On the other hand, separatist options were almost marginal in electoral terms between 1977 and 1992. After 1992, the Catalan independence movement received a new impulse from the old ERC, which fell under the control of a separatist leadership.

In the Basque Country, peripheral nationalists gained social and electoral hegemony after 1977. Nevertheless, the support for Basque nationalist parties is internally very fragmented. Nationalist electoral results vary strongly in each of the Basque Provinces, and even within individual provinces there are strong variations between rural and urban working-class areas and Spanish-speaking versus Basque-speaking areas. Urban and Spanish-speaking districts tend to be less nationalist, a trend that became more accentuated during the 1990s.

Basque nationalism was divided into two main camps. On the one hand, there was the PNV, whose main emphasis now was on the "historical rights" (the ancient *Fueros*) and the Basque language as basis for the existence of a distinctive nation. The PNV upheld a broad social reformism in accord with its interclass appeal, but it also demonstrated permanent tension between a far-reaching pro-independence discourse and constant political pragmatism. Although the party has never given up the possibility of achieving self-determination for the Basque Country, it was also in favor of exploiting the autonomy statute in place since 1980.

The second group within Basque nationalism, the so-called patriotic left, constituted a broad social movement linked to ETA. This trend advocated a set of slogans: self-determination and total independence for Euskadi, socialism and "reunification" of all Basque territories in Spain and France. This program has insured that the "patriotic left" remains in frontal opposition to Spanish democracy. Attempts at building nationalist alternatives that could shape a sort of "third road" met little success.

In contrast, Galician nationalism maintained a much lower profile, and never surpassed 26 percent of the vote in any election. The reasons for this weakness lie in the extreme fragmentation of the political spectrum of Galician nationalism; the radicalization of nationalist demands in the transition period which were not supported by the Galician electorate during the 1970s and 1980s; and the great difficulties of consolidating any moderate right-wing nationalist organization, especially due to the regionalist turn taken by the right-wing Popular Party (PP) after 1980. Thus, the political expression of Galician nationalism has been overwhelmingly monopolized by the left, mainly by the Marxist-Leninists, with a populist strategy, represented since 1982 by the Galician Nationalist Bloc (BNG) on the one hand, and the reformist socialist and democratic left on the other. The latter current was subsumed into the former at the beginning of the 1990s, allowing the BNG to achieve significant results throughout the 1990s and the first decade of the twenty-first century.

Peripheral nationalist movements have also extended their influence to other spheres of civil society, such as culture and labor relations. In Catalonia, Euskadi, and Galicia they have contributed decisively to enhancing the status of the non-Castilian languages. In the field of labor relations, the peripheral nationalisms (particularly in the Basque Country and Galicia) also maintain a strong degree of influence through their own trade unions.

Apart from these three main "historical" nationalisms, the existence of newly emergent peripheral nationalisms in other regions of the country deserves mention. Nevertheless, the political influence of this group of minority nationalist movements remains quite limited, and their ideological position is sometimes a mixture of regionalist proposals and imitation of Catalan dynamics. Three main groups can be identified. The first is composed of more or less openly pan-Catalanist nationalist parties in the Catalan-speaking Balearic Islands and Valencia, where political nationalism has so far been much less successful. The second group is composed of those minority movements that seek to promote a newly fashioned national identity based on declining local languages such as Asturian and Aragonese. A third group consists of nationalist movements which are not based on any claim of linguistic difference, but whose electoral success has been greater thanks to their ideological ambivalence, which makes them closer to the "autonomic regionalisms" which will be mentioned below. Two movements are particularly noteworthy: Andalusia and the Canary Islands, whose electoral results since the mid-1990s were notable, although decreasing.

The state of the autonomous communities: A satisfactory solution?

The political solution to the national question that was achieved by the Constitution of 1978 combined the conception of Spain as a single political nation with the existence of autonomy statutes granted to all regions. Part VIII creates the so-called State of the Autonomous Communities. The new state was initially conceived as a decentralized structure, composed of seventeen "autonomous communities" which reframed the existing provinces, and which were neither uniform nor equal in size, population, or economic weight. Thus, Madrid became a uniprovincial community, as did the new regions of Cantabria, La Rioja, and Murcia. In contrast, Andalusia brought together the eight provinces of Almeria, Cadiz, Cordoba, Granada, Huelva, Jaen, Malaga, and Seville. Between 1979 and 1983, each of the new regions elaborated its own home rule statute.

From the outset, the autonomous communities were divided into two groups. The first was composed of the so-called historical nationalities: Catalonia, the Basque Country, and Galicia, those regions that had approved a home rule statute by referendum prior to the Civil War. The other group consisted of the remaining fourteen regions. In reality, the extension of a decentralized state structure to the entire Spanish territory was the result of a political agreement among the various political actors that intervened in the shaping of the Constitution, as a part of the pacted elite settlement that brought Spanish democracy into being (see Chapter 8). Basque and Catalan nationalists pressed for achieving self-government within the framework of a multinational state. This claim was unacceptable to the right-wing parties, the Union of the Democratic Centre (UCD) and especially with the Popular Alliance (AP), which tolerated nothing but mild administrative decentralization. In theory, the left advocated a federal solution. Nevertheless, UCD was eager to achieve a compromise with moderate Catalan nationalists and adopted a more flexible position.

In the end, the right to achieve autonomy was extended to all the regions, while at the same time different routes toward levels of home rule were established, the fastest and highest being accorded to the three "historical nationalities." Sovereignty was held by the Spanish state, which in turn transferred broad powers to the autonomous communities and strengthened them with legislative and executive powers in many areas (i.e., agriculture and fishing activities, transport, culture and education, public health, tourism, commerce). At the same time, the central state maintained legislative preeminence in other areas, as well as the monopoly on taxation (with the exception of the exemption enjoyed by the Basque Provinces and Navarre, the "Economic Agreements" dating back to 1878).

One of the key characteristics of the 1978 Constitution is its ambiguity concerning certain crucial concepts. On the one hand, it affirmed that Spain is the sole existing nation, and hence the sole collective entity enjoying full sovereignty; but on the other, it also recognized the existence of "nationalities" and regions, while the difference between a nationality and a nation was not clearly established. Article 2 of the Introductory Section of the Constitution reads that it is based "on the indivisible unity of the Spanish Nation, common and indivisible Fatherland of all the Spaniards. It acknowledges and guarantees the right to autonomy of the nationalities and regions which form it and the solidarity among them." The Constitution also set out two different paths for achieving autonomy. One was the "fast track" defined by Article 151 reserved for the "nationalities" (Catalonia, the Basque Country, and Galicia), which were later joined by Andalucia. The other was the Article 143, which defined a "slow track" for the rest of regions.

The State of the Autonomous Communities was conceived as a negotiated solution. The pragmatism of the central state leadership also helped to achieve that formula of coexistence. Nevertheless, a majority of the Basque nationalists did not accept the 1978 Constitution: the "patriotic left" rejected autonomy outright, while the PNV did not take part in the framing of the Constitution, and did not accept it because it failed to recognize the Basque "historical rights" (a new label of the *Fueros*) in a fashion which affirmed Basque sovereignty. A majority of Basque voters (55.5 percent) abstained in the Constitutional referendum held in December 1978. Catalan nationalists, on the contrary, called for an affirmative vote on the Constitution, which was approved by the overwhelming majority of the Catalan electorate.

On the other hand, not all parties that participated in the elaboration of the Constitution were convinced of the long-term survival of the autonomic system. Strong criticisms were directed at Part VIII of the Constitution by AP leader Manuel Fraga, and were sustained by the party in the following years. For example, it opposed the term "historical nationalities." Federalism as a final goal endured among some currents of the left, especially among the ranks of Catalan socialists and (post)-Communists.

The institutional framework of the State of the Autonomous Communities contained several ambiguities. The system did not establish any detailed delimitation of spheres of competence among the central government, regional governments, and municipalities. The financing system was left aside, and no efficient mechanism was established to ensure equalization transfers between richer and poorer regions. Finally, there was no provision for a parliamentary forum that would allow coparticipation in the government's tasks by the regions, nor was any mechanism for the participation of the autonomous communities in the formulation of Spain's European policy after 1986. These deficits made the evolution of the system heavily dependent on short-term political negotiations between the central government and the nationalist and regionalist parties.

Moreover, the establishment of new administrations provided regional elites with new opportunities for political activities and careers. This dynamic also led to a proliferation of regionalisms in many of the newly created autonomous communities. Some of these parties, like the Aragonese Regionalist Party (PAR) or the Navarrese People's Union (UPN), advocated the defense of "regional identity" and the final goal of achieving an autonomy statute by imitating the tactics developed by the peripheral nationalists, but they never claimed self-determination. Moreover, new regionalisms were a perfect tool for providing local elites with renewed democratic legitimacy, or simply an ideal umbrella to give refuge to a variety of political actors. It was no coincidence that the real reinforcement and proliferation of new autonomic regionalisms took place after the spectacular collapse of UCD in the 1982 parliamentary elections. Many regional sections and leaders of UCD in Aragon, the Canary

Islands, and Valencia joined new regionalist organizations, which stood at the subsequent regional elections and obtained significant results.

The increasing dynamic of regional identity affirmation promoted by autonomous administrations helps explain the constant necessity for regional elites to justify their own power position by demanding equal treatment with the "historical nationalities." Regionalist parties such as the PAR and Canary Coalition saw themselves having to increase their pressure by rhetorically upholding the aim of transforming their regions into "nationalities." Not even the major nationwide parties (PSOE and Popular Party) have been able to escape the pressure exerted by their regional branches, which find themselves demanding full devolution to the "slow track" autonomous communities.

Spanish nationalism at the end of the twentieth century

The new territorial framework drawn up by the 1978 Constitution forced Spanish nationalism to redefine, or at least to revise, itself. The two main tendencies of Spanish nationalism since 1975 corresponded to the democratic right and the left, and Spanish nationalism of Catholic-traditionalist origin became politically marginal. The whole of Spanish nationalism since the end of Francoism may be characterized by two constant features: the search for a new identity and democratic legitimacy; and, at the same time, confrontation with the peripheral nationalisms.

Right-wing Spanish nationalism clearly suffers from legitimacy problems inherited from Francoism, and is strongly marked by its permanent opposition to peripheral nationalist claims. Since the second half of the 1980s, political messages coming from the Right have been quite contradictory however. On the one hand, the political praxis of the PP in Galicia and the Balearic Islands was characterized by the promotion of a sense of regional "autonomic" identity and fostering of "self-identification." This was counterbalanced, however, by the same party's policies in the Basque Country and Catalonia, where confrontation with the peripheral nationalists and exploitation of the language conflict was a frequent strategy.

Nevertheless, it has to be noted that right-wing democratic nationalism has made some attempts to undertake a task of ideological reformulation symbolized by the "recovery" of the historical legacy of Republican reformism from the 1920s and 1930s. According to José María Aznar, the conservative prime minister between 1996 and 2004, Spain was a historical reality forged in the fifteenth century and unified by the agency of the Monarchy and the existence of a common project for the future. This historical tradition sustains the legitimacy of the Spanish nation, which is defined as a single nation, albeit a multicultural one. Nevertheless, the democratic right has fully accepted the autonomic model established by the 1978 Constitution. At the same time, Spanish conservatives advocate the greatest possible degree of homogenization of competencies for all regions.

Since the mid-1980s, the left has increasingly recovered a form of Spanish nationalist discourse which can be traced back to the traditions of regenerationism and liberal republicanism, and which incorporated the appeal to "modernity" and the full integration into the European common project symbolized by the EU. This discourse aimed at combining belief in the existence of a Spanish political nation with the recognition of different cultural nations. According to this, the variegated character of cultural nations and a single political nation represented by loyalty to the 1978 Constitution makes it possible to refer to Spain as a "nation of nations." As a parallel element, Jürgen Habermas' concept of "patriotism of the Constitution" enjoyed much popularity on the Spanish left. Yet, this discourse was not totally free from the inherited idea of Spain as an old nation built upon the existence of a common culture and a common history since the late Middle Ages. In fact, others remained loyal to the Jacobin legacy and upheld the need for a strong central state that would serve as instrument for social reform. The sporadic proposals of the Spanish left for federalization of the State model could not elude the existing gap between those who, on the one hand, advocated an "asymmetric federalism" which should take into account "national" differences; and those who on the other hand support "symmetric" federalism.

Nations of multiple identities

At the end of the twentieth century, there is a complex balance between Spanish state nationalism and the stateless nationalisms, and it could be even said, as Juan J. Linz pointed out, that Spain constitutes a paradoxical example of the failure of both state and minority nationalisms. Neither Spanish nationalism nor Catalan, Basque, or Galician nationalism has been able to impose itself as the hegemonic doctrine and exclusive identity in the territories they aim at. During the 1980s, the electoral trend seemed to be toward an increase in social support for minority nationalist parties, but during the 1990s the tendency had ended, except in Galicia.

Spain not only constitutes a paradoxical example of the failure of opposing nationalisms that "block" each other, but also gives us a clear picture of the limits of nation-building policies carried out by both state and regional governments within democratic contexts. "Classical" instruments of nation building are being constantly questioned by the more pragmatic approach demonstrated by the citizens submerged within a global society. On the one hand, the democratic state has not been successful either in convincing all the citizens of the periphery of the new legitimacy of the Spanish nation. On the other, in spite of the resources and power competencies at their disposal, the Basque and Catalan regional governments have also proven less efficient than expected in promoting the exclusive new *national loyalties*.

The autonomy system has shown itself flexible enough to provide an adequate framework for resolving the territorial tensions of Spanish democracy. Nevertheless, it is far from being entirely consolidated. Peripheral nationalists continued to demand a further reform of the territorial structure of the state, which would recognize its multinational character. However, until the first decade of the twentieth century, survey data suggested that in the short term, open secession did not have overwhelmingly majority support, either in Catalonia or in the Basque Country. On the other hand, the consolidation and social acceptance of the State of the Autonomous Communities, either in its present shape or in a more "federalized" version, enjoyed the support of a majority of the population in all Autonomous Communities.

Since 1975, collective identities in Spain have been multiple and heterogeneous. While certain traditional vehicles of Spanish cohesion, and especially anything that refers to *national* symbolism, is weaker than in other countries, sociological studies and several opinion surveys have demonstrated that even in the Basque Country and Catalonia, a peculiar form of "dual patriotism" predominates: the shifting coexistence in the same person of identification with the peripheral nationality along with a feeling of solidarity or identification with Spain as a whole. In this sense, opinion surveys demonstrate how those who feel Basque/Catalan etc., *and*

Spanish to a greater or lesser degree constitute the majority of the population in the periphery. Dual identity, with a stronger emphasis on the Spanish pole, also predominated in Valencia, Andalusia, and Aragon. Even in those territories where minority nationalisms have a strong foothold, dual patriotism persisted among a majority of the citizens.

The overall picture is, thus, quite complex. One can state that a permanent "historical balance" between Spanish and peripheral nationalisms has been achieved. Dual patriotism is the predominant identity (to a greater or lesser degree) in Catalonia, the Basque Country, the Canary Islands, and Galicia, but this does not mean that it is uniform and unchangeable. A collapse of the democratic system, a hypothetical situation of sudden loss of legitimacy by State institutions, or a far-reaching social and economic crisis might have unpredictable consequences on national allegiances and nationalist tensions. This was, to a great extent, the new scenario created by the impact of the economic crisis on Spain since 2008, whose impact has been particularly evident in Catalonia. Here, long-term factors (the results of the nation-building policy carried out by the Pujol governments since 1980s) and short-term phenomena (the growing political frustration caused by the failure of the reform of the autonomy statute since 2004, which should recognize the distinctive quality of Catalonia within the State of the Autonomous Communities) were accompanied by the reframing of the pro-independence discourse by the main actors of Catalan nationalism. In the wake of the devastating effects of the economic crisis, they gave priority to civic values over cultural issues and the achievement of an independent state within the EU as an instrument to improve the welfare of all Catalan citizens. This objective would be achieved through the peaceful mass mobilization of Catalan civil society. Although the supporters of full independence in Catalonia did not surpass the threshold of 48 percent of the voters in the 2015 regional elections, it is uncertain how this territorial issue will evolve in the near future.

Further reading

Álvarez Junco, José, *Spanish Identity in the Age of Nations*, Manchester: Manchester University Press, 2011.

Balfour, Sebastian, and Alejandro Quiroga, *The Reinvention of Spain: Nation and Identity Since Democracy*, Oxford: Oxford University Press, 2007.

Corcuera Atienza, Javier, *Origins, Ideology, and Organization of Basque Nationalism, 1876-1903*, Reno: University of Nevada Press, 2006.

Eastman, Scott, *Preaching Spanish Nationalism Across the Hispanic Atlantic: 1759-1823*, Baton Rouge: Lousiana State University Press, 2011.

Goode, Joshua, *Impurity of Blood: Defining Race in Spain, 1870–1930*, Baton Rouge: Louisiana State University Press, 2007.

Holguín, Sandie, *Creating Spaniards: Culture and National Identity in Republican Spain*, Madison, WI: The University of Wisconsin Press, 2002.

Mar-Molinero, Clare, and Angel Smith (eds.), *Nationalism and the Nation in the Iberian Peninsula: Competing and Conflicting Identities*, Oxford/Washington DC: Berg, 1996.

Mees, Ludger, *Nationalism, Violence, and Democracy: The Basque Clash of Identities*, Basingstoke: Palgrave Macmillan, 2003.

Moreno-Luzón, Javier, and Xosé M. Núñez Seixas (eds.), *Metaphors of Spain. Representations of Spanish National Identity in the 20th century*, Oxford, NY: Berghahn, 2017.

Quiroga, Alejandro, *Making Spaniards: Primo de Rivera and the Nationalization of the Masses, 1923-30*, Basingstoke: Palgrave Macmillan, 2007.

Smith, Angel, *The Origins of Catalan Nationalism: 1770–1898*, Basingstoke: Palgrave Macmillan, 2014.

CHAPTER 11
GENDER
Aurora G. Morcillo

This chapter will examine the gendered historical narrative of contemporary Spain in the nineteenth and twentieth centuries. It will focus on the way the values of the Enlightenment have led to a visible and an invisible side of history. The main argument running through the chapter will be to consider the intellectual debates and cultural symbols in the construction of Spain and its modern identity, which was gendered from its inception. Spain's quest for modernization is inseparable from the quest for gender equality. Mary Nash points to the significant impact of Catholic values in the construction of gender roles in Spanish social and political relations. The tension between traditional Catholic values and secularization are also central to understanding the war of the sexes throughout the modern period. Therefore, I will focus on national symbols and on how education and visual and material culture became the battleground where the forces of religious tradition and continuity engaged the forces of change and secularization. The invention of the modern Spanish nation is populated with gendered metaphors that constructed individual and national selves.

The enlightenment background

Enlightened thinkers looked to secular education to redeem the country from backwardness and religious superstition and to bring it closer to the rest of Europe. Identified by some as the "Spanish Voltaire," Benedictine friar Father Benito Jerónimo Feijóo y Montenegro (1676–1764) was one of the first (and most important) figures of the Spanish Enlightenment. His *Teatro Crítico Universal,* written between 1726 and 1740, was an eight-volume work in line with the encyclopedic style of the times divided into *Discursos* (treatises) that examined a range of themes from politics, philosophy, and history, to literature and theology. In the first volume Treatise XVI, *Defensa de las mujeres* (*In Women's Defense*) Feijóo inserted the "woman question" into the scientific discussion of his time, highlighting how some of the many authors who defended women's inferiority were, in fact, not only disrespectful but also immoral and less than virtuous in their own behavior. "Scathing against women," he asserts, "many times, if not always, goes hand in hand with a disorderly [Sexual] inclination towards them."

Little has been published in English about the participation of Spanish women in the Enlightenment debate. This is not exclusive of the Spanish case. Women thinkers like Josefa Amar y Borbón (1749–1833) had raised their voices in defense of education echoing the sentiment of Father Feijóo. She became a strong defender of women's talent and contribution to the common good through education in her treatise *Discurso sobre la educación física y moral de las mujeres* (1790). This work laid the groundwork of enlightened feminism in the same fashion as Mary Wollstonecraft's *The Vindication of the Rights of Women* (1792) for the

Anglo-Saxon world, or French revolutionary Olympe de Gauges' *"Declaration of the Rights of Woman"* (1791). Daughter of one of the court physicians, Amar y Borbón received an excellent education and spoke Greek and Latin as well as Italian, French, and German. She was a champion of Enlightenment values for the rights of women and their pursuit of happiness.

Josefa Amar y Borbón is not the only free thinker hidden from the visible side of history; several Spanish women forgotten in the historical record ascribed themselves to the women's rights cause and belonged to an enlightened minority. For example, the writer, translator, and poet Margarita Hickey Pellizoni (Barcelona, 1753–93); poet and dramatist María Rosa Gálvez de Cabrera (Malaga, 1768–1806); and mathematician María Andrea Casamayor y de Coma (1700–80).

The liberal revolution

The first half of the nineteenth century is particularly important when examining gender dynamics, since it is when the foundations of the modern nation-state and the liberal revolution were established. The gender question was central to the process of nation building. Traditional historiography, however, has chronicled a few of the lives and contributions of some "ordinary" women, making them exceptional examples, like those who participated in the War for Independence (1808–14), characterizing their participation either as victims or as "virile" heroines. No doubt their stories are part of the narrative of the nation (to use Homi Bhabha's terminology) in the modern era, but they somehow are the exceptions to the rule while the general human experience is always collapsed on the male one, regarded as universal.

Feminist historiography of the Napoleonic invasion and Spanish War for Independence has moved away from the heroic depiction of mythologized historical figures like Manuela Malasaña or Agustina de Aragon, putting emphasis on how Agustina for example was a "mujer del pueblo," (ordinary woman) immortalized in one of Goya's "Los desastres de la Guerra," in charge of supplying provisions to those defending the siege of Portillo in Zaragoza. This portrayal served a dual purpose: on the one hand she became an anomaly, since a woman's place in liberal bourgeois discourse is to be a domestic "Angel of the Home," and on the other hand serves as a shaming mechanism against the enshrined masculine by the same liberal ideology of separate spheres (public/private = male/female). In this bipolar scenario, each gender plays a predetermined social role where bravery is the realm of manliness in opposition to helpless femininity.

Recent scholarship has shown how patriotic participation on the part of Spanish women in the Napoleonic war went beyond that bipolar representation. They engaged in the intellectual debates through *tertulias* (in the same manner as the Salons in France). Some of the most important of these political and intellectual gatherings were organized by women on both sides of the ideological spectrum, either liberal or anti-liberal, defending their patriotic convictions. These conservative women included Frasquita Larrea (1775–1838), who was influenced by the German Romantics and Mary Wollstonecraft, and created one of the most important *tertulias* in Cadiz. Larrea was the wife of Nicolás Böhl de Faber (1770–1836) (theorist of a reactionary romanticism), and mother of Cecilia Böhl de Faber (1796–1877) who would become a well-known writer under the pseudonym Fernán Caballero.

On the opposite ideological side and linked to progressive liberal circles was Margarita Pérez de Morla (1790–?). She studied in England where she met Lord Byron. Perez de Morla led the liberal *tertulia* in Cadiz in opposition to the one Larrea hosted. Women partook in the patriotic debates emerging in the midst of the Napoleonic invasion through their writing in newspapers and through their propagandist action, although they were not allowed in the Cortes of Cadiz Assembly debates or even to be part of the public in attendance.

During the Romantic period of the first three decades of the nineteenth century (see Chapter 15), women expressed their views on their social role through newspaper articles and women's journals such as *La Ilustración*. These include *Album de Damas* (1845) by the Cuban Gertrudis Gómez de Avellaneda (1814–73), a renowned writer and progressive thinker who lived most of her life in Spain and addressed major public issues. In 1842 she published *Two Women*, a novel in which she defended divorce; in 1845 she published the antislavery novel *Sab* that predated *Uncle Tom's Cabin* by American writer Harriet Beecher Stowe. Her third novel *Espatolino* was a condemnation of the terrible situation of the prison system at the time. The *Liceo* in Madrid offered a public forum to a number of women including Gómez de Avellaneda and Carolina Coronado (1820–1911), leader of the so-called *hermandad lírica* with minor poets and writers like Robustiana Armiño (1820–90) and Amalia Fenollosa (1825–69). Their works highlighted the ambivalent meaning of the new liberal femininity vis-à-vis domesticity and individual liberty. New scholarship began to explore some of the debates concerning the essential access to citizenship for women at the time.

A wealth of political and intellectual debates brings the discussion of gender relations and modernity to the fore. In the constituent assemblies of 1812 and later in 1837 and 1845, there was no discussion on women's access to citizenship. According to Mónica Burguera, these constitutional debates are but the "tip of the iceberg" of a very rich participation of women in the liberal discussions outside the institutional realm per se. The traditional approach to the participation of women in the modernizing process of the liberal revolutions emphasized the separate spheres (public/private) doctrine, assigning the public the male nature while the private remained the space of women. It is important, as Burguera notes, to distinguish between the symbolic public realm and the public spaces both men and women actually inhabited at the time. In the period between 1812 and the mid-1850s, an associative movement among women born from the Enlightenment debates emerged as part of the public arena. This movement had philanthropic and charity inclinations in general but it also helped channel their political participation. This female association movement presented two models: first, a conservative elitist associative tendency based on the belief of the moral superiority and charitable role of women in the public realm, represented by the Junta de Damas de la Sociedad Matritense.

The second associative movement developed around the progressive social circles led by Juana María de la Vega Countess de Espoz y Mina (1805–72), symbol of the exiled liberal defenders of the progressive liberal constitutionalism (see Chapter 27). The Countess received the institutional support of the Instituto Español which, after 1841, was closely associated with Espartero's progressivism, and she directed its bulletin. The women belonging to this group were educated, of middle-upper social standing, rational yet pious, openly political but faithful wives and committed to social betterment. One of the most significant free-thinkers of this movement and foremothers of Spanish feminism was Concepción Arenal (1820–93). Arenal dedicated her work *La beneficiencia, la filantropía y la caridad* (1860) to the Countess Espoz y Mina. One of nineteenth-century Spain's most important feminist and abolitionist voices,

Arenal attended law school at the University of Madrid dressed in men's clothes as higher education was forbidden to women until the 1880s. She was appointed inspector of prisons and of correctional establishments for women between 1863 and 1868. Some of her works include *La mujer del porvenir* (1869), *Oda a la esclavitud* (1866), and *La educación de la mujer* (1880).

The associative philanthropy project fit well with the progressive principles of the time, which advocated for a political transformation emerging from an open and participatory civil society. As Burguera reminds us, there was a contradictory legacy forged first within liberal progressivism and later elaborated by democratic republicanism. Progressivism first incorporated the principles of social reform during the Regency of Baldomero Espartero. The "social question" was indeed a "social revolution" that aspired to engage all classes and both sexes and that brought to the fore debates on "the woman question," which will be discussed below. The contradictory legacy, between the free individual and the gender-specific roles attached to men and women, in which men were in charge and women were subaltern, remained latent in the different political factions that gave birth to the revolutionary democratic movement of 1868 and endured within the Spanish left and its articulation of different feminist outlooks.

Educating women in the art of homemaking remained central to gender discourse well into the twentieth century. The predominant discourse on piety and subordination fanned by the Catholic parameters remained at the center of the debate on the "woman question" in the second half of the nineteenth century. The outstanding example was prolific writer María del Pilar Sinués de Marco (1835–93), who explained in her best-selling manual *El Angel del hogar* (1859) "neither beauty nor wealth or noble birth can, by themselves, make any woman happy. We find many women with these advantages who weep tortured by a pain without a name, by an endless despair. Happiness for women resides in the home, among their family: there, she is queen and almighty; there moreover, she is the providence."

The Restoration

During the nineteenth century reform of the educational system centered was an important topic of debate. These public discussions served as an ideological battlefield, in which the forces of secularization engaged the forces of tradition. Spain's secular movement gained momentum with the introduction of the ideas of Karl Christian Fredrick Krause (1781–1832), an obscure German philosopher, and with the founding of the *Institución Libre de Enseñanza* in 1876. Krausists rejected faith as the guiding norm for human knowledge and hence refused the involvement of the church in the learning process. In contrast, traditionalists (or neo-Catholics) embodied the antithesis of Krausism. The Krausist drive to educate women began after the revolution of 1868 with a series of "Sunday Lectures" about the education of Spanish women. Women's education was intended to enhance female natural qualities such as purity, piety, domesticity, and subordination. The new liberal government of the Spanish First Republic promoted what is known as "republican motherhood" to produce well-educated mothers to strengthen its republicanism.

The discussion of what came to be called the "woman question" took place in the 1870s in the context of the educational debate raised by American Protestant educational missions, which established the International Institute in Madrid and the Free Institution of Learning (FIL). These institutions and the secular ideals they embodied had to confront Spanish Catholic conservatism as they advocated coeducation and the instruction of women. The Association for Women's Education (Asociación para la Enseñanza de la Mujer) was founded on October 1, 1870. This institution gave Spanish women access to higher education within different schools: School of Governesses (Escuela de Institutrices); School of Commerce (Escuela de Comercio); and the School of Postal and Telegraph Services (Escuela de Correos y Telégrafos). The Association was created with private funds. Unfortunately, only upper- and middle-class women benefited from these educational options, which offered better quality than the official alternative offered at the Normal Schools (Escuelas Normales de Maestras).

Toward the end of the nineteenth century, other social forces entered the educational debate: an active proletariat and especially anarchist and regional movements (particularly in Catalonia). Within the context of broader social and political debates, discussions on education at the turn of the century revolved around two important issues: the propriety of coeducation and the right of access to higher education and professional training for women. Lacking an organized women's movement in the manner of the United States and Great Britain, the Spanish debate on the "woman question" in the 1880s remained limited to the elite circles of the FIL and the writings of a few educated women such as Concepción Arenal (1820–93) and Emilia Pardo Bazán (1852–1921) (see Chapter 28). The combined efforts of the Protestant missionaries, the Krausists, the FIL, and a few extraordinary women led to official reforms such as a revision in 1877 of the 1857 Public Education Law, which was the basis of the public school system until 1970, and recommended the creation of Normal Schools in each province to improve the education of Spanish girls.

Early education for girls was not a priority, and very few women had access to a college education by the end of the nineteenth century. The few who studied were only able to receive a certificate of attendance, not a formal diploma, and the first degree was awarded to a Spanish woman only in 1888. The next year, Martina Castells Ballespí became the first woman to gain a doctoral degree in medicine and surgery. She died as a result of a difficult pregnancy, and anti-feminists exploited this to sustain their conviction that education was pernicious for women whose main goal, according to social convention, should have been maternity. Opposition to the right of women to be educated had strong supporters in the Hispano-Portuguese pedagogical conference of 1892 celebrated in Madrid. Their arguments made biological determinism the unquestionable reason to exclude women from the classroom. Dr. Fernando Calatraveño pointed out in his speech how only a small elite could escape women's "natural destiny," mediocrity:

Women will never be anything but mediocre . . . their nervous system controls their organism, their periodic ailments, pregnancy and breastfeeding, their organs: ovaries, uterus and breasts imprint a different function with the male sex . . . their brain is one hundred grams lighter than the men's, a detail of capital importance.

Arguments like this prevented the extension of suffrage rights to women until 1931, even though universal male suffrage was granted in 1890.

In the creation of a series of legal codes during the last third of the nineteenth century (the Penal Code of 1870, the Commerce Code of 1885, and above all the Civil Code of 1889), women were treated as legal minors always requiring a male guardian. They could not work or enter into any commercial transaction without their father or husband's permission. Adultery was penalized with four years' imprisonment in the case of women and only small fines for the husband, and men were only punished if they brought their mistress to live in the family's home. All this legislation solidified the separate spheres doctrine and consolidated a rigid gender inequality.

There was no reason to fear the crumbling of the gender status quo. At the turn of the twentieth century, the illiteracy rate was alarming. In 1900, 63.8 percent of the population was illiterate; 55.8 percent of those were men versus 71.5 percent women.

The labor movement did not offer better options for Spanish working women. In the cultural milieu that perpetuated a double moral standard, women were regarded as lesser working people who were paid accordingly lower wages than their male counterparts. Rather than supporting a united working-class cause, the separate spheres doctrine turned male workers against women because they regarded them as a threat to what the patriarchal culture expected of men: to be the sole breadwinners.

The royal decree of October 26, 1901 extended the curriculum for the girls' schools, and the law of June 23, 1909 made primary education compulsory until age twelve. By 1930, the illiteracy rate among women had dropped to 47.5 percent, whereas male illiteracy was 36.9 percent. 52.6 percent of Spanish girls attended primary schools versus 54.3 percent of boys, and there were 37,642 women students at the secondary level or in professional training. The university, however, was less populated by Spanish women, with a total of only 1,724 female college students.

Mass feminism had not yet taken root in Spain; rather, there was an elitist women's movement that developed further during the 1920s and 1930s with the growth of the labor movement and the discussion of the "social question." A few Spanish intellectuals opened a debate on the relation of the sexes that tried to explain male/female differences in light of the times, "scientific" discoveries, and the nascent eugenics fad. New psychological and sociological arguments revitalized the already stale notion of biological determinism. The ideas of Freud, Simmel, and Nietzsche influenced Spanish thinkers like Gregorio Marañón and José Ortega y Gasset to argue that men and women were different not only physically but psychologically as well. Marañón, a liberal-minded physician, defended the equality of men and women in political rights; the access of women to public office; and the availability of contraception and divorce; but at the same time he continued to worship motherhood. "Women," he wrote, "must be first of all and in spite of everything else mothers. . . . Marriage was not created for the pleasure of the couple but for the purpose of reproduction." Spanish intellectuals agreed with the Freudian idea that women's character was basically passive and self-effacing. They elaborated the dyad of motherhood/obedience as the only possible fulfilling option for the female.

This reductionist essentialism that sought to rationalize conventional misogyny led José Ortega y Gasset (see Chapter 32) to write: "If the male is the rational individual; the female is the irrational person. A woman offers a man the magical opportunity to deal with another being with not reason." His ideas about female identity and morphology, cloaked with a pseudo-scientific veneer, were prevalent for half a century. With *Estudios sobre el amor*, he embraced Western philosophical tradition on womanhood. For Ortega, "woman was first of all for man a prey—a body that can be seized." For Ortega y Gasset, women's right to vote or to gain an academic degree was not the way to help them influence history:

There is no other force in human condition stronger than the biological force that women possess which is to attract men with accuracy and efficiency. Nature has made this the most powerful means of selection and a sublime force to modify and perfect the species.

According to Ortega y Gasset, while men's worth was the product of their actions, women's worth was based on their inner essence, their "being." It was precisely their female essence and not their actions that attracted men. Hence, the female role in history resides, according to Ortega y Gasset, in their passive existence, and therefore he placed them outside of history. "Everything women do," declared Ortega, "they do it without doing it, simply by being there: glowing."

The Second Republic and the Civil War

The Second Republic brought a radically new approach to gender issues (see Chapter 5). The Constitution of 1931 declared the secular nature of the state and repudiated the Catholic Church's role in political matters. The Republican Constitution also granted Spanish women the right to vote and fostered progressive legislation on family and educational issues. But these changes were controversial even among progressive women. Clara Campoamor, a member of the Radical Party, was a chief defender of women's suffrage, but socialists Victoria Kent and Margarita Nelken opposed it, fearing that masses of Catholic women would vote for the right. A law passed on September 9, 1931 protected working mothers between the ages of sixteen and fifty. The state recognized the validity of civil marriage and the equality of legitimate and illegitimate children; and, in March 1932, it legalized divorce. Republican educational policy sought to eradicate illiteracy for both sexes, and women's access to and opportunities in higher education greatly improved during the Republican years. The presence of women in colleges grew slowly and although small, this growth was indicative of the official interest in education. Such progress would abruptly come to an end with the outbreak of the Civil War in 1936 and the victory of conservative Catholic forces by 1939. During these three years of conflict, the Republican school system began to be dismantled on the nationalist side, and the Francoist educational apparatus started to take shape.

The impact of the Civil War on women was complex. For the first time, a woman headed a ministry on the Republican side: Anarchist Federica Montseny was appointed Minister of Health in September 1936, and in her role, she helped legalize abortion. Women also organized female branches of the communist and anarchist movements, but both political organizations disagreed about the best possible strategy to win the war, and this strongly impacted any improvement in women's rights. In the context of the civil war, women's demands for emancipation became a secondary issue.

The most important Communist female organization was the Anti-fascist Women's Association (Agrupación de Mujeres Antifascistas), created in 1933. Their activities included raising funds and collecting clothing for the soldiers, creating kindergartens and shelters, and filling the jobs men had left behind when they went to the front. Communist propaganda, voiced by party members like Dolores Ibárruri, fostered traditional female nurturing qualities and duties as mothers and caretakers whose place was on the home front (see Chapter 34). Among anarchists, the most important female organization was Free Women (Mujeres Libres). Founded in 1936 by Lucia Sánchez Saornil and Mercedes Comaposada, this organization disappeared with the end of the war in 1939. Free Women acknowledged the double struggle of working-class women as both workers and women. For these libertarian women, education provided the key to emancipation. To this end, they developed a set of programs with two separate but related goals: *capacitación* (the "preparation" of women for revolutionary engagement) and *captación* (their active incorporation into the libertarian movement).

At the Libertarian Institutes (Institutos Libertarios), anarchist women sought to overcome illiteracy, but their classes also included a new understanding of what it meant to be a woman. They explained that a woman had to take her own initiative and seek her independence. Literacy courses were supplemented with classes in mechanical skills, childcare, and nursing and medical assistance. All of these were useful later in the war effort as women substituted men in the workplace and served as nurses in hospitals at the front or in their hometowns. Free Women also showed deep concern for birth control education and what they called self-conscious motherhood. "What we wanted," said Mercedes Comaposada, "at the least, were self-conscious mothers. People should be able to choose whether and when and how to have children and to know how to raise them . . . and they shouldn't have to be one's own children, there is need to take care of other people's children, of orphan and the like."

Some women, known as *Milicianas*, actually took up guns and fought, but they were few in number. They were also controversial, being denounced as, among other things whores and manly. Their active participation in the frontlines led to the exaltation of a few martyrs for the Republican cause, such as Lina Odena, a nineteen-year-old *miliciana* who was killed at the front in Granada. Women were pulled out of the frontlines by early 1937 by order of Largo Caballero, then Minister of War. Like their counterparts on the rebel side, women were to cover the rearguard duties, and to encourage them on their motherly destiny during wartime, Dolores Ibárruri, the Communist leader would address them in passionate speeches.

Founded in 1934, the Sección Femenina de FET y de las JONS (the Falangist Female Section of Falange) organized women on the nationalist side (see Chapter 37). By September 1936, Falange Española had 320,000 members, of which 80,000 were women. During the Civil War, the Female Section grew even more significant. The organization's objective was to create a female population subservient to the regime's needs.

During the conflict, the Female Section's social and cultural functions were crucial for the new state's indoctrination of the Spanish people. The duties performed by Falangist women during the war consisted mainly in assisting the wounded and children and creating sewing workshops, as well as a new service called Laundresses of the Front (Lavaderos del frente), organized groups of women who followed the soldiers to the front to wash and mend their clothes. In October 1936, the nationalist government created "Winter Aid" (Auxilio de Invierno), a replica of the German *Winterhilfe,* to manage all welfare services. Two months later, the National Committee of Winter Aid (Delegación Nacional de Auxilio de Invierno) was established under the direct supervision of the Female Section. Eventually, Winter Aid was renamed Social Aid (Auxilio Social), the most important welfare apparatus of the Francoist regime. The war situation demanded a well-organized war relief apparatus, so by the decree of October 7, 1937, Spanish women were expected to fulfill the so-called Social Service (Servicio Social), a mandatory six-month community/front service rendered to the state.

The Female Section thus secured for itself a portion of power, since its long-term task was to direct the state's social services. By using a discourse of abnegation and sacrifice in line with that of the Catholic Church, the state found its social services covered free of charge. Decree 378 of November 28, 1937 officially regulated the Social Service as a national duty for all Spanish women between seventeen and thirty-five years of age to reconstruct the fatherland; only married or disabled women could be exempted. For the rest, it was mandatory to show a document, issued by the Female Section, certifying completion of the service in order to obtain any professional diploma, to practice a career, or to hold public office.

The 1937 decree represented the first step toward the nationalization of Spanish women. At the same time, the official discourse contained inherent contradictions. On the one hand, women were expected to participate in the public sphere through the Social Service, and they were encouraged to join the Female Section of the Falange. On the other, their work was defined explicitly as secondary to the masculine task of the state; they were to be mothers and wives preserving the sanctity of the home. With the end of war, the new state-institutionalized Female Section of the Falange was the only female organization entrusted with the task of creating the Francoist new woman, whose Christian virtues came to be essential to the reconstruction of Spain.

Even those areas of Spanish life that would be modernized rested upon the restoration of old Catholic traditions. These would be the parameters regulating social relations that were articulated around the dichotomization of politics (Francoist/anti-Francoist) and gender roles. Gender ideology itself became crucial in defining the state, its territory, and authority. Spiritual/Catholic values, authority, and discipline were to govern an important institution: the family. Social and gender relations blended in the family, and women (as mothers) represented an essential element in the reconstruction of the fatherland. The preamble to the Spanish Charter defined the new state as the guardian of Catholic doctrine, and Article 6 declared state protection for practice of the Catholic religion, tolerating no other public religious expressions. Article 22 declared the state's recognition and protection of the family as a natural institution and pillar of society, with rights and obligations superior to human law. The same article also proclaimed state support for large families and decreed that marriage was to be indissoluble. Such an arrangement of social relations by the state implicitly followed Catholic Church doctrine.

The Franco regime

During the dictatorship of Francisco Franco, the Female Section of Falange became the mediator between the state and Spanish women. The participation of Spanish women in the reconstruction of the fatherland was thus defined within the discourse of abnegation, one of the Catholic feminine virtues. Spanish women were expected to help those in need, easing their pain and bringing happiness into their lives. The Decree of 1941 proclaimed that Spanish women were obligated to fulfill the Social Service. To qualify for all public jobs in Spanish society, women had to prove that they had rendered their services to the fatherland. Articles 3 and 4 prescribed fines of 50–5,000 pesetas to those employers who hired women without a Social Service certificate. The Decree of February 9, 1944 made service indispensable in obtaining a passport or belonging to any cultural association, but gave special dispensation to nuns and to daughters or wives of men of the nationalist side killed during the war, another example of how the regime favored its supporters and their relatives (see Chapter 7). The same year, by the Decree of 21 November, all women enrolled at a university also had to present a Social Service certificate.

Social Service was intended, above all, to instill domestic values in Spanish women, whose future was to become mothers and wives. In addition to imposing national service on Spanish women, the new state, in its zeal to protect the family, created the Board for the Protection of Women (Patronato de Protección de la Mujer) in 1942. Furthermore, sexually related crimes such as abortion and any kind of contraceptive propaganda (Law of December 24, 1941), as well as cohabitation without marriage, and women's adultery (Law of May 11, 1942), were severely penalized. Likewise, wartime casualties made it crucial to repopulate the country, thus good mothering became a national imperative. Franco's demographic goal was to create a population of forty million. Maternal and infant care received special attention from the Ministry of Health, which by the Law of July 12, 1941 reorganized the appropriate institutions. "The application of this law," reads Article 2, "reaches pregnant and nursing women, and those who take care of either their own children or the children of others; as well as the child from birth until he is fifteen years old." The law established a web of health centers in both cities and rural areas to assist mothers and children. The centers were under the supervision of the Ministry of the Interior and the General Commissary of Health with the joint assistance of the Female Section, Social Help, syndical organizations, and the Secretary of Welfare.

Article 15 established a National School of Infant Care "to prepare competent personnel of both sexes." Each child under fifteen years of age was issued a health book to record his or her clinical history: vaccinations, illnesses, pathological incidences, etc. At the Institutes and Services of Infant Care, a division called the *lactario* obtained and kept the mother's milk. To complement this law, the Ministry of the Interior issued the order of December 20, 1941 to educate nursing women in good mothering. It prescribed that during the first five days of each month, infant care centers were to provide free classes and lectures that mothers were required to attend (Article 3). After four lectures on infant care, health, and hygiene matters, the final session concentrated on the state's demographic policy and needs, addressing topics such as: "What Spain provides for mother and child," "Protection for the working mother," and "the danger of working for good mothering." Its motto was "the caudillo wants forty million Spaniards."

To help them perform well as mothers and to deliver healthy citizens to the new state, the government prevented Spanish women from entering the labor force. As early as 1938, the Francoist labor system and social order was defined in the *Fuero del Trabajo* (Labor Charter). By the order of March 9, 1939, the government made it mandatory to educate workers in the *Fuero's* principles. The Spanish labor charter followed the Italian *Carta di Lavoro* (1927), echoing the Catholic social doctrine prescribed in Pius XI's encyclical *Quadragesimo anno* (1931) which rejected the class struggle and proposed fraternal cooperation between workers and employers using a corporate structure ruled by religion. Women, according to the encyclical, needed protection from the "crime" of having to work.

Thus, working-class women were considered by the Catholic Church to be, first of all, mothers bound to fulfill the only purpose of Christian marriage: reproduction. The Labor Charter prohibited female and children's labor at night, regulated home labor, and forbade married women from working in factories and workshops. In this context, women's national duty remained confined to the home, and to this end, the regime issued a series of legislation regulating and protecting women's labor opportunities. The order of December 27, 1938 proposed an increase in male workers' salaries so that they could provide for their families as breadwinners and keep their wives at home (Article 3). In addition, the order prohibited married women's employment when their husbands' incomes were sufficient (Article 4).

Under the Francoist policy of autarky, women's national duty remained confined to the home. The Decree of March 31, 1944 regulated piecework at home in which an entire family worked for entrepreneurs in a putting-out system (Article 116). All married women needed their husbands' permission to practice any "trade or industry" (Article 132); even if they were separated, the husband's consent was mandatory and his signature required in his wife's contract (Article 133). The key issue in women's access to the labor market was moral protection. Married women could work only under the supervision of their husbands, doing piecework at home. To work in a factory, they needed to obtain his consent, which had its own bureaucratic form.

As the regime was welcomed into the Western orbit with the help of the United States in the 1950s, women's bodies continued to be the site of contention. As in the early modern period, piety, circumspection, order, and hygiene composed the essence of the Catholic female ideal in the 1950s and 1960s. The last two decades of Franco's regime gave birth to contested discourses on women's bodies and their social role in a growing economy in need of skilled labor. In order to confront the changing social reality, the state reformed the civil code in 1958. This reform was intended to amend the legal status of women, ruled since 1938 by the Civil Code of 1889. With the sponsorship of the Women's Section of Falange, the regime implemented further reforms that led to the Law of Political and Professional Rights for Women passed in July 1961. Sponsored by the Female Section of Falange, the spirit of Christian domesticity dominated the law. But at the same time, in an attempt to catch up with the modernization brought by American dollars, this legislation opened access for women to certain professions such as magistrate, or a career in the Foreign Service.

The "Spanish model of modernization" and the modern woman contained in it is crucial in the transitional period from autarky to consumerism of the 1950s and 1960s, in which gender relations evolved to adjust to foreign models of modernity, namely Americanization as it appeared in cinema and magazines. Some of the most important transformations in the social and cultural values of the 1960s and early 1970s were generated by the avalanche of tourists that visited Spain; the millions of Spaniards who moved from rural areas to the cities and the hundreds of thousands of emigrants who left Spain to work in France, Germany, and Switzerland, bringing with them a new way of understanding gender relations (see Chapter 19).

The consumerist economy that Spain gradually adopted in the 1950s and 1960s opened the way to the new modern Western woman, a sexualized consumer who left behind the official ideal of "True Catholic Womanhood." At the end of Franco's rule, Spain had done much to ready itself for integration back into Europe. The 1950s and 1960s represented an in-between moment in which cultural inscriptions of femininity—what Catholic womanhood had meant until then—suffered a transformation that could be traced in women's bodies. Women's bodies therefore were not only physical organisms, but rather the loci of historical meaning.

Transition and democratic Spain

When Franco fell ill in mid-October 1975, most of his ex-followers and servants aligned themselves in post-Francoist factions. As Franco's health and body deteriorated rapidly, the medical bulletins turned into the regime's vital signs. On November 4, the morning press releases from Madrid revealed Franco's worsening condition: "The symptoms of congestive cardiac arrest are mild and the ventricular extra-systoles have disappeared. It continues the blackened hemorrhagic defecation. Hydropsy has increased and a collateral abdominal circulation has developed. A mycosis in the mouth was rapidly controlled. Nonetheless, the pulse was normal and the blood pressure too." Statements like this using seemingly aseptic medical terms revealed the grave state of political affairs. Franco's body's breakdown was also the breakdown of Francoism.

There is in the scholarship an explicit connection between political transition and images of women's bodies in the common metaphor of *destape* (uncovering or revealing) in which the symbolic landscape of the naked bodies of women signified a political opening: the aged body of the dictator, connected to tubes, deteriorating in the hospital just as his regime was in the last days of November 1975 sustained artificially. Further studies may benefit from exploring the ways in which the counter-images of seductive womanhood that appeared in the popular culture from the 1960s to the end of the dictatorship undermined the regime's gender discourse and prepared the way for the transition of the 1970s.

In 2001, writer Francisco Umbral remembered the transition to democracy in an article for the twenty-fifth anniversary of *Interviú*, the iconic magazine of the period entitled "Los cuerpos y los siglos" ("The Bodies and the Centuries"). He remembered Marisol and other actresses who had posed nude in front of the camera with a nostalgic tone:

> Then it materialized in front of us mortals the forgotten Pepa Flores, with her Marisol outfit, in her naked Marisol, and her golden bangs rescued us from our multiple jobs; and those breasts a bit excessive gave us back our faith in summers, and those little girl hands made us the boyfriends of all the adolescent girls of the decade, and those bratty nymph glutei where the word was made flesh and reigned among us. And those clear eyes, intense, sad, of the color of a green moon when we had never seen a green moon. [Those eyes] paralyzed the national life, paralyzed democracy in a crosswalk, and we believed again in general strikes, in free love unions, in socialism, in mayors dying in bulk, and in a Model Transition which only Pablo Castellano disliked, while the rest of us found our place under the little girl's double suns.

Democracy was on display, naked, like a woman. During and after the transition, nudity was presented in the debates as a gendered issue: on the one hand, the mainstream press and the intellectuals that identified themselves as "*Progres*" (Progressives) regarded the new wave of eroticism as women's acts of rebellion against the prudish Francoist past; but on the other hand, it showed how the control and misogynist political discourse was a prerogative of heterosexual men, particularly self-proclaimed free-thinkers. Feminists at the time protested the commodification and sexist discussion of women's sexuality as a metaphor for liberty. For example, in 1976, the feminist journal *Vindicación Feminista* would protest in its pages remarks by Juan Luis Cebrián, editor of the prestigious newspaper *El País*, in *Interviú*:

> I remember with horror those films with a girl of golden braids and high-pitched voice; films, in truth, I did not watch in their entirety but only the trailers; then when the girl grew up the situation changed and I moved to her team due to mere aesthetic sensitivity.

I want to say that I do not like how Marisol sings, I think she is a mediocre actress, even when Bardem directs her, and certainly there is between her and me no rational or intellectual identification. However, *Marisol has been one of the few object-women that we have been able to display at the European level. Here [in Spain] object-women always are fat and short and they wait for their husbands at home to go to the neighborhood's movie theater. Marisol, at least, is a valuable object.*

These voices were drowned out, denounced as uptight or hysterical.

Again, women's sexuality was regarded as a measurement of Europeanization and a prerogative of men's sexual liberation. The erotic-political language was not new or even original as it was part of a misogynist genealogy. However, it made clear to some political factions at the time and to scholars today how gender equality remained a second priority in the quest for freedom. Far from being a trivial or frivolous examination of the Transition, the symbolic representation of the female body (whether as *Mater Dolorsa, Hispania, Niña Bonita* or *Naked Marisol*) exposed the subliminal contempt and conventional misogyny of the Enlightenment principles Equality, Liberty, and Fraternity still present in the twenty-first century in Spain and other Western democracies. While the mass media is saturated with crude pseudo-pornographic imagery, the policing of citizens' bodies (women and men) remains at the center of Western democratic legislations on issues that range from reproductive rights, abortion, gay marriage, and, more recently, how Muslim women dress.

The 1960s and 1970s experienced a growth of women's organizations and a feminist movement as a consequence of two major transformations: The Second Vatican Council called by Pope John XXIII meant a liberalization of social Catholicism, and the generation gap became visible in the Catholic Action student and workers organizations' commitment to the poor and the older establishment. The National-Catholic consensus showed signs of crisis. Young women participated in the religious grassroots movements that were part of the student resistance against the dictatorship and also joined the workers unions. The second transformation came with the Decree of 1964, which allowed the establishment of associations: homemakers associations had been already established in the 1963 under the Women's Section's patronage, allowing housewives to gain some political skills as they also joined the neighborhood associations that eventually would be under the control of the clandestine workers' unions.

After publishing several books on the female condition, in 1960 Maria Laffitte, countess of Campo Alange founded the Seminario de Estudios Sociologicos sobre la Mujer (SESM, Women's Sociological Studies Seminar) with a group of university friends who aspired to establish a feminist agenda. Founding members were: Lili Alvarez, Concepción Borreguero, Elena Catena, Mary Salas, Pura Salas, and Consuelo de la Gandara. This group remained active until 1986, when Maria Campo Alange and Consuelo Gandara died.

Particularly important in the 1960s was the Democratic Movement of Women (Movimiento Democratico de Mujeres MDM). Born in 1965 with a feminist agenda and to fight against political repression, the group brought together women from the PCE (Communist Party) and the PSOE (Socialist), some women from social Catholic organizations as well as independents. They supported the dual political militancy of their members to their parties and to the feminist movement as well as interclass organization, as they understood it was essential to undo all hierarchies both political and patriarchal. During their first period of clandestine activism, the groups met in members' homes, bars, churches, and occasionally in schools. In 1967, they published a petition signed by 1,518 people entitled "For Spanish Women's Rights." This document demanded social promotion for women; nurseries for working mothers; equal pay; access to birth control; reform of the civil code; and the legalization of abortion and divorce. In 1975, declared by the United Nations International Women's Year, the movement adopted a new name: Democratic Women's Movement/Women's Liberation Movement. The group elaborated its own law proposals for the legalization of abortion and divorce. More pressing, however, was the legalization of feminist organizations. This legalization became a reality in 1978.

The 1970s represent the most active and important period of feminist activity. Several reforms were introduced that led to the legalization of contraception in 1978. An article published on January 22, 1977 in *El País* reported that there were 400,000 abortions per year in Spain, but it would take another decade to see the legalization of abortion on July 5, 1985. Divorce and changes to adultery laws were other important demands of the feminist associations that emerged around neighborhood and housewives associations and in parallel to the major left-wing parties. Divorce was legalized on July 20, 1981. In the twenty-first century, domestic violence was the focus of the government. José Luis Rodríguez Zapatero's Socialist government approved the Law of December 28, 2004 against gender violence. It also legalized gay marriage in July 2005, making Spain the third country in the world to do so.

The strategy of many women who were members of the PSOE or the PCE during the Transition was to work within parties to achieve equality. Today, there are many more women in political life, thanks to the introduction of the so-called zipper lists (one woman, one man arrangement for the left-wing parties). Following the June 2016 elections, 48 percent of Unidos Podemos and 42 percent of the PSOE deputies were women. Leadership, however, remains a male-centered arena, even in the new movement Podemos. No national party has ever had a female leader, and women like Socialist Susana Díaz, president of the autonomous government of Andalucia, or Soraya de Santamaría of the Popular Party, who is vice-president of the national government, remain very much the exceptions. This is a clear symptom of how misogyny is present in the entire ideological spectrum inherited from the Enlightenment. The moves toward gender equality have not been easy or swift. Spain is leading Europe in matters of gender equality at least *de jure* while there is a death toll of 80–100 women on average killed by their domestic partners each year.

In the aftermath of the Constitution of 1978, gender relations were increasingly at the center of democratic debates. As it did for the forefathers who drafted the 1812 Constitution known as "La Pepa," in 1978 democracy was incarnated symbolically in another Pepa—Pepa Flores. In the twenty-first century, there was strong a Spanish feminist mentality active at the academic level, albeit not so visible on the streets. Today, many women walk alongside (feminist) men and stake claim to the streets of a country with a rich history of gender equality strife. The challenge in the early twenty-first century is to continue fighting for inclusive equality. Democracy is the arena where we can better achieve gender parity. However, the reactionary forces of tradition hold the power to inhibit the progressive accomplishments of the last century. There is no dictator to blame now, only our political responsibilities as citizens.

Further reading

Álvarez Junco, José, *Spanish Identity in the Age of Nations*, Manchester: Manchester University Press, 2013.

Aresti, Nerea, *Masculinidades en tela de juicio. Hombres y género en el primer tercio del siglo XX*, Madrid: cátedra, 2010.

Burguera, Mónica, *Las damas del liberalismo respetable. Los imaginarios sociales del feminismo liberal en España (1834-1850)*, Madrid: Cátedra, 2012.

Cazorla Sánchez, Antonio, *Fear and Progress: Ordinary Lives in Franco's Spain, 1939-1975*, Chichester: Wiley-Blackwell, 2011.

Cenarro, Angela, *La sonrisa de Falange*, Madrid: Crítica, 2005.

Cruz, Jesús, *The Rise of Middle-Class Culture in Nineteenth-Century Spain*, Louisiana: University Press, 2012.

Cruz Romeo, María, and María Sierra (eds.), *Historia de las culturas políticas en España y América Latina. La España liberal 1833-1874*, vol. II, Zaragoza: Marcial Pons-Prensas Universidad de Zaragoza, 2014.

Fuentes, Juan Francisco, and Pilar, Garí, *Amazonas de la libertad. Mujeres liberales contra Fernando VII*, Madrid: Marcial Pons, 2015.

Labanyi, Jo, *Constructing Identity in Twentieth-Century Spain: Theoretical Debates and Cultural Practice*, Oxford: Oxford University Press, 2002.

Labanyi, Jo, and Helen Graham (eds.), *Spanish Cultural Studies: An Introduction: The Struggle for Modernity (Science Publications)*, Oxford: Oxford University Press, 1996.

Morcillo, Aurora G., *True Catholic Womanhood: Gender Ideology in Franco's Spain*, De Kalb: Northern Illinois University Press, 2000.

Morcillo, Aurora G., *The Seduction of Modern Spain. The Female Body and the Francoist Body Politic*, Lewisburg: Bucknell University Press, 2010.

Morcillo, Aurora G. (ed.), *Memory and Cultural History of the Spanish Civil War and Fracoism: Realms of Oblivion*, Laiden and The Netherlands: Brill, 2014.

Nash, Mary, *Defying Male Civilization*, Arden Press, 1995.

Radcliff, Pamela, and Enders Victoria, *Constructing Spanish Womanhood*, Albany: SUNY Press, 1998.

Shubert, Adrian, *A Social History of Modern Spain*: London: Routledge, 1990.

Smith, Theresa Ann, *The Emerging Female Citizen: Gender and Enlightenment in Spain*, Berkeley: University of California Press, 2006.

CHAPTER 12
WAYS OF LIFE: CITIES, TOWNS, AND VILLAGES
Jesus Cruz

Between the years 1808 and 2008, Spaniards experienced the most profound transformation in their ways of life ever seen in the history of the country. This transformation was not exclusive to Spain, as it was the consequence of the process of industrialization and democratization in the West and other parts of the world that began in the second half of the eighteenth century. In this long stretch of time, the country changed from being a predominantly agrarian society with profound social divisions and limited mobility, to a modern urban middle-class democracy and consumer society.

The historical dynamics of this transformation have been object of controversy and revision among historians. Up until the 1990s, the prevailing point of view maintained that until the mid-twentieth century, Spain remained socially backward, with a predominantly rural population dominated by traditional ways of life, and lacking a significant middle class. Consequently, Spain lagged behind the rest of Europe, and its lack of socioeconomic progress was the reason for the political instability and social turmoil that characterized Spanish history until the Spanish Civil War. According to this approach, social modernization did not occur until the 1960s and was a consequence of the successful economic policies under General Franco's rule. The idea of a frustrated long nineteenth century, marked by political instability and economic and social failure, has been convincingly challenged by a number of studies which describe a long period of slow but steady transformation in all aspects of Spanish life, beginning in 1808 and accelerating in the years around the First World War. In other words, the roots of present-day middle-class consumer ways of life can be found in the nineteenth century.

Beginning in the 1980s, terms such as "way of life" and "everyday life" have been broadly used by social and cultural historians as an alternative to the pervading approaches of the 1970s, inspired by modernization theory as well as Marxism. Followers of the Marxist or modernization methods studied societies from the perspective of class structure, and conceived social class as an aggregate of people sharing economic and political positions. The study of class formation was addressed by means of quantifying methods and the formulation of patterns of collective behavior. This understanding of societal dynamics tended to establish rigid associations between class and political, cultural and economic choices such as nobility and feudalism, bourgeoisie and liberalism, or working classes and socialism.

In the last two decades, the influence of cultural anthropology and sociology has brought a "cultural turn" to the study of the history of societies that questions the exclusive value of group quantification and classification. Cultural historians do not necessarily reject the notion of class, but instead use the lens of individual experience to understand the complexities of the social process. Under this approach, class identity results from the accumulation of individual cultural practices including value systems, beliefs, norms of conduct, symbolic meanings, and even forms of political organization and economic activity. Consequently, to understand social dynamics, cultural historians take into account personal interests, opinions, behaviors, and behavioral orientations. Culture forms categories, or patterns, in which ideas and values are tidily ordered. These patterns constitute cultural systems or lifestyles. Seen this way, a way of life is a cluster of conventional models of thought and behavior that is transmitted from one generation to the next by way of a learning process, never through genetic inheritance. Thus culture is malleable and should not be considered outside of its economic and social context. The number of ways of life in any given society can be as broad as the diversity of its individuals, however some ways of life appeal to larger segments of individuals, eventually becoming hegemonic. These will be the focus of this chapter. We will start with an exposition of the general demographic trends to frame the two main spaces of social life: the urban (cities and towns) and the rural (villages).

Population

At the end of the eighteenth century, Spain had about eleven million inhabitants, three million more than in 1700. During the nineteenth century, the country added another seven million inhabitants. Another thirty million were added during the twentieth century, creating the current figure of forty-seven million inhabitants. These numbers show that Spain's historical demographic cycle followed the pattern of other southern European countries such as Italy and Portugal, characterized by a mild demographic takeoff starting around 1750, slower growth than Britain and Germany during the nineteenth century, and a considerable demographic expansion during the twentieth century.

All Western countries experienced a transitional period between the Old Regime demographic cycle (characterized by its weak growth) and the modern one distinguished by spectacular population rise. In Spain, that transition happened during the nineteenth century. Until the 1830s, population growth was slow due to the persistence of distinctive trends pertaining to the traditional demographic cycle: a weak rate of natural increase caused by high mortality rates. Despite timid advances in medicine, nutrition, and hygiene, episodes of catastrophic mortality caused by epidemics, war, and famine continued to slow population growth. After the 1830s, a small but sustained reduction in mortality rates produced a slow rise in demographics. Population growth became possible due to rising birth rates and a mild reduction in infant mortality rates. Nonetheless, mortality rates remained high until the 1900s, below the rates found in Russia and some areas of Eastern Europe, but higher than the Italian rates. Epidemics killed 800,000 people. The cholera outbreaks of 1834 and 1855 were especially lethal. Through the 1850s, the estimated rate of annual growth was 0.44 percent, a mean of about 132,000 new inhabitants per year. This marked a significant demographic jump, though still far from the 14.5 percent rates of England during the same period.

The rate of population growth in Spain remained below Western European standards until the mid-1920s. One main factor contributed to this comparative slowness: sustained high mortality. During the 1870s, many Northern European countries implemented national plans to improve public health, which resulted in dramatic outcomes in the fight against infectious diseases and the consequent reduction of mortality. It took longer for the Spanish state to implement similar policies. It was not until the approval of the *Reglamento de Sanidad Provincial* in 1925 and other improvements in public health policies in 1926 and 1927 that

Spain's mortality rates reached the levels required to allow fast growth. In 1900, the death rate in Spain was 26/000, still considerably higher than the average of 20/000 in France, Germany, and Britain. By 1930, the Spanish mortality rate had fallen ten points to sixteen per thousand. A significant portion of this reduction occurred in infant mortality, which was reduced from a rate of 32.6 percent in 1910 to 28 percent in 1930. Between 1900 and 1930, the country added five million births, reaching a population of 23.6 million. These changes marked the end of the long demographic transition that Spain initiated during the last third of the eighteenth century.

The nineteenth-century demographic transition was caused by a change in the socioeconomic structures of the country and particularly mass migration from the countryside to the cities (see Chapter 19). The process of urbanization started to reach European levels in the years around the First World War, although this was interrupted by the Spanish Civil War and its immediate aftermath. By 1950, the Spanish population was growing at a faster rate than the rest of Western Europe. The number of inhabitants rose from 28 million in 1950 to 38 million in 1985. These Spaniards were also taller, lived mainly in cities, worked in the service sector, and enjoyed Western European living standards. At the same time, starting in the 1970s, Spain entered the cycle of demographic decline characteristic of developed societies caused by the fall of fertility.

In sum, the history of Spain's modern demographics shows that the country followed a European path characterized by a slow but sustained improvement with a definitive incorporation to modern patterns around 1910. Similar patterns are found when looking at the evolution of Spaniards' ways of life.

Nineteenth-century urban ways of life: The rise of middle-class culture

For most of the nineteenth century, Spain remained mainly a rural country with an urban network that grew at a much slower pace than in northern and central Europe. Spanish cities grew at a faster rate than rural zones, but by 1900 only 21 per cent of Spaniards lived in towns larger than 20,000 far from the 39 percent of France and 75 percent of Great Britain. It is also true that demographic growth in general occurred in urban centers and comprised in part the expansion of the middle classes. In Spain as in the rest of Europe, the middle classes (also known as the bourgeoisie) became the social group that imposed the way of life dominant in present-day Western societies. In doing so, they did not sweep away the ways of life of the nobility prevalent in the early modern age. Instead, some aristocratic practices were admired, embraced, adapted, and incorporated into the new bourgeois way of life.

That the nineteenth-century bourgeoisie, despite being no more than a 30 percent of the social body, were the creators of Spain's contemporary ways of life can be evidenced in many aspects of daily experience. They introduced values such as a respect for intimacy, a taste for comfort, and a commitment to sports as a means of improving health and beauty or to make a profit. They popularized summer vacations as something entertaining, invigorating, and even profitable, and promoted travel as an educational and recreational experience. They valued entertainment as a means of personal enjoyment and enrichment, as well as an avenue for social relations. In sum, the nineteenth-century bourgeois promoted a hedonistic culture that ultimately freed luxury from moral censure as long as it benefited wide sectors of society. According to their value system, to furnish a home with elegance, to dress following the dictates of fashion magazines, or to adopt certain habits imported from societies considered more advanced was not only pleasurable but necessary for social progress. While they did not dispute the existence of class distinctions, they adhered to the utilitarian principle according to which social progress meant bringing the benefits of their way of life to the greatest possible number of individuals.

Bourgeois cultural practices were promoted in four main ways: the elaboration and dissemination of new rules of conduct aimed at establishing a dominant code of behavior; the promotion of consumer culture as a means of facilitating economic growth and bringing about collective happiness; the establishment of a material culture with distinctive symbolic components that provided class identity; and the promotion of new forms of sociability, high culture, and leisure to express their ideals of urban civility.

To understand the rules of conduct that the new bourgeois code of behavior aspired to we can look at the contents of the numerous courtesy and etiquette books that began to be published after 1820. This kind of *urbanidad* (urbanity) literature embodies what it meant to be a bourgeois in Spanish society. The social ideals introduced by these manuals, ones that would be reproduced throughout the nineteenth century, were *el hombre fino* and *la mujer fina* (the refined man and woman). The refined man was the equivalent of the English dandy (*dandi*), a term these books introduced into the Spanish vocabulary. The main difference between the bourgeois social archetype and pre-nineteenth century ones was that, at least in theory, refinement was not exclusive to the nobility. Any member of society, by embracing the required norms of conduct, could become a refined person. Refined men and women constituted an exclusive polite society known as *sociedad de buen tono*. This social space was more open than the aristocratic courtesan circles of the *ancien régime*, but was still highly exclusive.

One of the main attributes of the refined person was elegance. Men and women both followed fashion with discretion, becoming modern consumers who visited shops, read fashion magazines, and cared about the cleanliness of their clothes and body. Fashion was central to expressions of modernity, and there were many commodities that conduct manuals recommended consuming. For instance, some emphasized the health benefits of tobacco smoking and portrayed it as a distinguished and beneficial habit practiced by men and even women after elegant dinners, theatre soirees, and other genteel social gatherings. The manuals suggested the consumption of other imported items like tea and coffee, and provided suggestions for decorating one's home and entertaining guests.

The most frequent form of the bourgeois ritual was the social visit. The social life of nineteenth-century well-to-do Spanish families consisted of a continuous coming and going from one's home to the homes of members of the same social circle. The *día del santo* (Name Day, known also as *visitas del día*) was the most frequent among the social rituals of religious meaning celebrated by families and close friends. The polite always performed courtesy visits to relatives or friends to celebrate the *día del santo* and birthdays. Parlor life was characteristic of bourgeois nineteenth-century society, but other forms of social gatherings were meaningful as well, ranging from dinners and banquets for special occasions to evening parties, balls, and receptions. To have guests at one's table or to be invited to the table of someone within one's social circle was a symbol of social success. As it became one of the practices most characteristic of bourgeois society, norms for behavior at the table also assumed importance as part of the new way of life, and were set out in the manuals.

Bourgeois civility emphasized the home as a transitional space between the public sphere and the private sphere. Although the home was considered a sacred and inviolable domain, it was not a space limited to the family. For that reason, its decoration, aesthetic appeal, and comfort were fundamental to the new bourgeois ways of life and the construction of bourgeois identity. The nineteenth-century middle classes were the major promoters of the culture of domesticity and the principle of "home sweet home." The family home was conceived as a sanctuary for the refined man and above all for the refined woman, who was depicted as the "angel del hogar" (angel of the home), taking care of all things related to domestic life. There were even books and magazines on this topic directed specifically to middle-class women (see chapters 11, 26, and 27).

The process that transformed the domestic spaces of dominant groups and brought about the modern home began in Spain during the mid-eighteenth century. In that transition we find the development of the essential components of present-day middle-class life: domesticity, privacy, hygiene, and comfort. In Spain, the culture of domesticity originated and evolved in much the same way as it did in the rest of Europe, although it took hold more slowly given the particularities of Spanish social and economic development; its transformation into a hegemonic practice did not happen until the second half of the nineteenth century, much later than in England and France.

The making of the middle-class home was a central manifestation of the expansion of consumer culture. The home constituted a major component of the new bourgeois material culture aiming to create a distinctive symbolic language of class identity, but there were many others. During the nineteenth century, the most transcendental was fashion and clothing. Recent studies on the history of modern consumer culture focus mainly on the clothing industry to discuss the existence or nonexistence of a "consumer revolution" stirred by the middling ranks in some parts of Europe beginning in the early modern period. Scholarship in Spain shows that in some cities and regions beginning in the last third of the eighteenth century, the consumption of textiles experienced a moderate ascent. Consumer expansion occurred mainly between the upper and middle classes; in Spain the first signs of mass consumerism were not evident until the 1920s. But despite these limitations and differences, Spain experienced sufficient transformation to claim a berth within the group of Western societies that gave birth to modern consumer society. The *hombre fino* and the *mujer fina* were the new consumer subjects in need of acquiring an array of new symbolic objects (clothes being one of them) to perform in the diverse spaces for social interaction of the bourgeois public sphere.

The birth of a Spanish fashion press around 1820 and its consolidation in the second half of the nineteenth century constitutes the most significant manifestation of this historical development. The fashion magazine formed part of the new public sphere and was a major vehicle for the diffusion of bourgeois culture. From an ideological perspective, major segments of the nineteenth-century fashion press espoused and divulged the conservative values, principles, and worldviews of Victorian culture. Despite their conservative and gender-based content, these publishing initiatives were unequivocal carriers of modernity because they created the fashion system as it exists today: an industry with wide economic and cultural ramifications.

Again with some delay in comparison to northern Europe, the first Spanish fashion publication with financial continuity, *Correo de las Damas*, did not appear in Madrid until 1833, sixty-five years later than its counterpart in France. Nevertheless, the social functions, technological aspects, and overall historical significance of this aspect of nineteenth-century modernization in Spain were comparable to that in the rest of Europe. The surge in fashion publishing after 1833 occurred at a moment of political liberalization that was beneficial for the press in general (see Chapter 3). By the end of the century, there were four well-established fashion periodicals that lasted into the twentieth century (*La Moda Elegante, La Última Moda, El Salón de la Moda,* and *El Eco de la Moda*). All had a clientele that extended beyond Spain and Portugal to Spanish America. Cadiz and Madrid boasted the early magazines, while by the end of the century Barcelona shared the bulk of fashion publishing with Madrid. This shift is consonant with the emergence of Catalonia as the most industrialized region with a strong middle class. Barcelona became the main commercial city in nineteenth-century Spain. The first Spanish modern department store, *Almacenes El Siglo*, opened its doors in that city in 1885, later than the opening of department stores in Britain or France, but before Italy, Denmark, Austria, and Russia.

The consumption of fashion by middle-class men and women was linked to their need to perform in the diversity of spaces for social interaction in the new bourgeois public sphere, an unequivocal sign of a country's incorporation into modernity. During the nineteenth century, the Spanish middle classes created a multiplicity of these spaces; while some were unequivocally Spanish, most were similar to those established elsewhere in the Western world. For the most part these were spaces for the enjoyment of decorous, productive, and cultivated entertainment, what some thinkers of the Enlightenment called the "pleasures of the imagination."

The theatre became the most important of these pleasures of the imagination. Next to bullfighting, theatre was the most popular spectacle in nineteenth-century Spain. Among the more than one thousand plays written over the course of the century, many focused on themes of bourgeois culture: emotional dilemmas, social aspirations, political debates, and economic assumptions of an emerging middle-class identity. Above all, the theatre was an essential site of social interaction for the middle-class public, one of the primary places for the construction of *sociedad de buen tono*. The gentrification of the playhouse occurred during the eighteenth century. In major cities, the traditional socially mixed *corrales de comedias* were replaced by *teatros de comedia* with new repertoires and higher prices that were less affordable for the lower ranks of society. In the nineteenth century, theatre provided ready access to refined and influential society, and attending a play became a symbol of social distinction. A writer for *La Luneta*, a well-known theatre magazine of the mid-nineteenth century, lamented that a large portion of theatre audiences attended merely to gossip and chat. At the beginning of the century, Madrid had only two main theatre houses. By 1900, both Madrid and Barcelona had a dozen main theatre houses and two large opera houses. There were also a similar number of secondary playhouses affordable to popular audiences that started to proliferate during the 1860s. These venues, known as *café-teatro* or *teatro por horas* (theatre by hours) covered a variety of spectacles such as plays, circuses, *zarzuelas* (operetta), and vaudeville.

After the theatre, the public space par excellence where polite society gathered was the opera house. Unlike the theatre, opera had always been an exclusive form of entertainment. Yet, by the end of the nineteenth century, the bourgeoisie controlled its patronage, and opera was one of the public spaces that best represented the nexus between old and new elites. Both Madrid and Barcelona built opera houses, but opera was also performed in theatres and other spaces in the main as well as secondary Spanish cities. In Madrid, the building of the Teatro Real was backed by court, aristocratic, and bourgeois circles that wanted the city to become the symbolic capital of the new liberal state. In Barcelona, the impetus to build the Teatro del Liceo came from a bourgeois organization, the Liceo Filarmónico de Isabel II, and demonstrated the ascent of the bourgeoisie, who wanted to enhance Barcelona's national and international stature.

Liceos were a sort of civil association integrated by independent members with the goal of promoting the arts: music, drawing, poetry reading, plays, etc. This kind of group was usually patronized by young wealthy individuals who gathered under the teaching of consecrated artists to learn or to enjoy performances. *Liceos* were not gender specific; both men and women could participate in this form of artistic gathering. The first known *liceo* was established in Madrid in 1837 at the initiative of the artist José Gutierrez de la Vega, who held a weekly Salon in his study. The Liceo Artístico Literario of Madrid counted on the attendance of prestigious writers and artists of the city's Romantic clique, such as the writer José Zorrilla, the painter Antonio María Esquivel, and many others. Barcelona's Liceo Filarmónico performed similar functions, although it evolved into the solid institution that was able to open the first opera house in Spain in 1847. What was peculiar about *liceos* in comparison to other circles of bourgeois civic sociability already studied was the active involvement of women. The participation of young as well as older ladies was even incentivized with reductions in the admission fee and in many cases the offer of free admission.

Other nineteenth-century public spaces that facilitated the rise of middle-class sociability in Spain were casinos, athenaeums, museums, and pleasure gardens. Spanish casinos were not exclusively for gambling: they were a combination of an English club and an Italian public café: a private organization based on selective membership and funded by maintenance fees that served an essentially recreational function centered on board games, drinking, and male sociability. The first casinos opened in the 1830s, and within thirty years there were 575, operating in all Spanish provinces except for Soria. By 1895, there were more than 2,000 active casinos, making them the most frequented place for upper- and middle-class male sociability.

Athenaeums promoted cultural, scientific, and political debate as well as scholarship, with the ultimate goal of contributing to the moral and intellectual formation of citizens. In a country where academic institutions remained attached to and controlled by tradition, the athenaeums represented alternative platforms for freedom. The first athenaeum opened in Madrid in 1835 and became a model to export to other parts of Spain. By the beginning of the Spanish Civil War, there were about 500 athenaeums in different parts of Spain, some with very specific ideological profiles mainly in the spectrum of the political left. Besides promoting intellectual debate, athenaeums also sponsored scientific laboratories, art exhibits, and university extension courses. A small number of athenaeums have survived to the present day, thanks to their libraries, which were at the center of athenaeum life; Madrid is the best example.

Museums also helped articulate polite bourgeois society, largely through exhibitions that portrayed the historical underpinnings of national identity. Before they became spaces for education and entertainment of the masses in the first third of the twentieth century, museums were sites used mainly by the middle classes to display civility and modernity. In the nineteenth century, the major Spanish museums were located in Madrid. The earliest was the National Museum of Natural Sciences, which opened to the public in 1815. However, the largest and most important was the Prado Museum—called *Museo Real de Pintura y Escultura*—opened on November 19, 1819. The Prado was comprised of paintings and sculptures from the royal collections, and soon became an institution with an international reputation. It was Spain's main museum and the only one in the country comparable to the major museums of Europe. By the beginning of the twentieth century, Madrid had three emblematic cultural sites—the Prado, the Archaeological, and the Natural Science museums—symbols of progress made toward the recreation of a city that would represent Spanish national civilization and modernity.

The pleasure garden was a variety of public space that proliferated in all western cities beginning in mid-eighteenth century and that disappeared in the early 1900s. Known in Spain as *jardines de recreo*, these were extensive and privately owned entertainment complexes within the city or in its suburbs. They were generally seasonal, opening their gates in late spring and closing them in early autumn. Access to these parks required the payment of an entrance fee. Pleasure gardens reflected the democratic spirit of the nineteenth-century liberal bourgeoisie but, at the same time, its restrictive limits. Openness was controlled to ensure selectivity and order by offering high-priced activity programs such as operas, classical music concerts, and balls that required strict etiquette for admission. The first modern pleasure garden in Spain, the Jardín de Tívoli, a small park across from the main entrance of the Prado Museum with a theatre and a coffee house, opened in Madrid in 1821, a few months after the installation of Spain's first fully constitutional regime. New gardens were opened in Madrid and Barcelona during the 1830s and 1840s, modeled after gardens in London and Paris, but always of smaller dimensions. It was not until 1853 that the first Spanish gardens that could fully compete in size and quality with those in the rest of Europe were inaugurated in Barcelona. The gardens, called Campos Elíseos, featured elaborate landscapes with rows of trees, flowerbeds, parterres, statues, and fountains. They contained a theatre, an artificial river, and attractive new rides, the most exciting being Spain's first roller coaster. The Campos Elíseos were also the site of a variety of musical initiatives, the main one being the choral music movement led by the Catalan composer and civic activist Anselm Clavé (Campos Elíseos opened in Madrid in 1864, sponsored by a Catalan entrepreneur). The last pleasure garden of Madrid was called the Jardines del Buen Retiro. The novelist Pío Baroja, who frequented the gardens in his youth, described summer nights in the Buen Retiro as "the meeting place for politicians, aristocrats, bankers, and other members of Madrid's elegant society." El Buen Retiro was closed in 1904 to build Madrid's Palacio de Comunicaciones (Post Office Palace). By 1900, most pleasure gardens had disappeared from western cities, swallowed up by urban expansion.

In addition to its practice of cultivated leisure, nineteenth-century middle-class ways of life had a hedonistic and hygienic side. Some forms of bourgeois leisure activity, such as traveling to new places, combined intellectual enrichment with sensuality. Others, such as summer vacationing, pursued the relaxation of the spirit and the pleasure of the senses. The bourgeois obsession with health and hygiene was manifest in this social group's engagement in the practice of sports for the care of the body. In Spain, bourgeois tourism and vacationing started in the 1820s and found its moment of maturity in the last third of the nineteenth century during the Restoration (1874–1923) (see Chapter 4). Starting in the 1830s, writers and journalists reported the exodus from the major cities that occurred every summer. Most well-to-do groups escaped from Madrid and Barcelona during the hottest weeks of the summer to vacation in nearby countryside areas where prominent families acquired summer villas. Owning a villa was nonetheless the privilege of the few; most Spanish nineteenth-century vacationers rented rural houses, single rooms, or, most likely, found their lodging in spa resorts. In Europe and Spain, mid-nineteenth-century spas functioned as what some historians have called "parlours of Europe": chosen centers of sociability frequented by polite society during the summer season. By the last third of the nineteenth century, Spain had a selective number of spas with grand hotels, mainly located in the Pyrenees, Catalonia, Cantabria, and the Basque Country, that could compete with the most famous hotels established in other parts of northern and central Europe.

Spain's contribution to the history of vacationing and tourism in Europe can be best observed in seaside resorts such as San Sebastian and Santander. Spanish seaside resorts began appearing in the 1820s and were well established by the 1840s. The expansion of the railroad after 1850 made travel more accessible to the new middle classes. International travelers shared their experiences with the distinguished summer vacationers in the Cantabrian beaches, the diverse clientele of the spas, and the most modest tenants of rooms in rural houses near the big cities: all were pioneers of the modern practice of touristic traveling and vacationing.

The final contribution of the nineteenth-century middle classes to the making of modern ways of life was the practice and commercialization of sports. As in other parts of Europe, the practice of modern sports in Spain originated with the army at the beginning of the century. By 1913, there were about 360 societies dedicated to the promotion of sports in Spain. The majority of these associations were football (soccer) clubs, though all sports of the time were represented and groups were spread all over the Spanish map. There were clubs in all provincial capitals and in many secondary cities; Barcelona had the greatest numbers followed by Madrid and Valencia. Membership in these sports associations was mainly drawn from the middle and upper classes but some sports, such as soccer, reached the popular groups, symbolizing a new era in the history of the ways of life of many Spaniards.

Urban and rural subaltern groups

In cities and towns, the popular groups constituted the largest part of the population and their ways of life were diverse. The upper ranks (owners of small shops, butchers, specialized artisans, etc.) were a minority that shared middle-class living existences. The larger portion (composed of workers in crafts, industry, and domestic service) did not enjoy most of the benefits of modernization.

Until the First World War, the ways of life of most urban workers were not that different from their counterparts under the *ancien régime*. The abolition of the guilds in the nineteenth century destroyed traditional paternalistic relations between masters and apprentices and the life of many among the latter did not benefit from this measure. Many among these apprentices, shopkeepers, and assistants lived more as domestic servants than independent workers. Until the last decade of the century, industrial workers were still a small group, concentrated in a few regions: Catalonia, Basque Country, Asturias, and Madrid. Their ways of life were characterized by deprivation and hardship due to their low acquisitive power and tough working conditions. Working hours were long, an average of twelve hours a day at the beginning of the century, with little time for leisure, family or social life. Political and trade union pressure made a reduction of one or two daily work hours possible by the end of the century, but only in a few occupations.

This being said, some new forms of popular sociability and renovated forms of popular entertainment did emerge during the nineteenth century. The street, the patio, and the public market were the most common urban spaces where members of the lower ranks socialized. Evening gatherings (*las veladas*) were for chatting, singing, or drinking from spring to fall on the patios of working-class buildings, and have been represented in operettas and literary texts. The lack of space and comfort in lower-class apartments invited the outdoor celebration of most common family rituals: baptisms, birthdays, and weddings. Because modest houses lacked running water, refrigeration, and gas, women had to take frequent trips to the public fountains and markets, thus engaging in an intense community life. The tavern and the workshop were the most typical spaces for male sociability. The French socialist Flora Tristan (1803–44) described the tavern as "the temple of the worker," the only place where he could enjoy the pleasures of leisure. Taverns were for chatting, drinking cheap wine, playing games, engaging in fights, discussing politics, and planning revolutions. While taverns were opened in all parts of the city, in some cities the tendency was to move them from the downtowns to the emerging working-class neighborhoods in the suburbs. The number of taverns grew with the expansion of the city. Between 1852 and 1871, the population of Malaga, for example, grew by 20 percent; the increase in the number of registered taverns, from 155 to 248, was much greater.

The most frequent form of male socialization happened in the urban workshop. Spanish workshops tended to be of small dimensions and scarcely mechanized. The pace of work was slow, with lots of small breaks for smoking, chatting with visitors, gossiping with neighbors, or discussing politics with everyone.

The main forms of leisure of the Spanish urban popular groups before the arrival of the movie theatre were the bullfights, the dance halls, and the seasonal urban fairs. Modern bullfighting as a consumer spectacle affordable to the laboring classes, especially the artisans, emerged during the eighteenth century. By 1900, major cities and towns had built bullrings that were commercially quite profitable. Bullfighting was the earliest form of commercialized mass leisure in Spain. Bullfighters became popular icons comparable to present-day sport stars. From spring to fall, Mondays at five in the afternoon was the designated day and time for the *corrida*, as the church opposed their celebration on Sundays. Modernizers opposed this tradition, concerned by its negative impact on labor productivity. Bullfighting became more structured after the first national bylaws dictated in 1853, a trend that continued until the transformation of the strictly regulated spectacle bullfighting of the present day. After bullfighting, the most affordable forms of popular leisure were the numerous urban fairs (*verbenas*) organized to celebrate a patron saint or other religious holidays. People could attend the *verbena* to enjoy free outdoor dancing, and spend a few coins on refreshments or on the variety of available low-cost attractions. Also affordable for the popular youth were a number of dance halls that opened on Sundays and holidays from early afternoon to early evening. Some became legendary, as was the case of the Baile del Elíseo in Madrid, depicted in the Spanish operetta (*zarzuela*) La Gran Vía and in other literary texts.

Some new forms of popular sociability emerged during the nineteenth century. Mutual aid societies were a transitional hybrid between the old church and guild brotherhood and the modern trade union. The first *Sociedad de Socorros Mutuos* was authorized in 1839. By the end of the century, there were more than 700 active mutual aid societies, making them the major form of association in the country. The purpose of this kind of society was to provide help to members in case of sickness, unemployment, or death. By law, members were not allowed to engage in politics or activities that could be considered political. However, with the passage of time, many mutual aid associations surpassed these limits and carried out practices that created new cultures of popular sociability. Some went beyond the supply of traditional forms of mutual help by offering evening classes, cultural activities or small libraries. Most associations developed democratic practices such as the direct election of officers or the adoption of functioning norms and policies in open membership meetings. The same can be said of the rest of the other major forms of association: cultural circles of artisans, choral societies, and popular lyceums and athenaeums. These were popular versions of their bourgeois counterparts, and all had a main common mission: to provide education to those who could not afford school or college. Some of these organizations, like *El Fomento de las Artes* in Madrid, became platforms for the intelligentsia of the democratic, republican, and socialist opposition that emerged after the 1840s (see Chapter 17).

The ways of life of the inhabitants of the nineteenth-century Spanish village, especially those belonging to the lower ranks, have not been sufficiently researched. A substantial number of studies exist on the economic and social outcomes of the changes in property structure carried out by the successive laws of disentailment (see Chapter 3). Recent studies of the history of consumption in some Castilian agrarian towns and villages show a rise in the demand of clothes and linen since the end of the eighteenth century pulled out by the middling ranks. Something similar happened with the commercialization of the sewing machine, a technology linked to the expansion of the middle classes. A significant portion of the sales of Singer machines in the early stages of the expansion of the company in Spain went to the Andalusian countryside. The middle and upper segments of agrarian Spain may have been participants in the rise of middle-class ways of life already discussed.

In the end, the large majority of inhabitants of nineteenth-century villages and agrarian towns, the largest segment of Spanish population, remained economically poor and culturally traditional. There were substantial regional differences due to environmental, historical, and cultural reasons. But for all (small farmers cultivating unproductive property in northern Spain, or wage-earning landless peasants in the south), living conditions were rough, characterized by deprivation, hard work, and a lack of opportunities. In fact, this was the way of life of the majority of people in a country with predominantly agrarian economic and social structures and a deep gap between urban and rural living conditions.

The twentieth century: The making of a modern middle-class democratic and consumer society

It was around the years of the First World War that Spain started to accelerate the definitive completion of the process toward becoming a modern middle-class democratic and consumer society. The country needed to add the cycle of massive migration from the countryside to the cities, and to consolidate a large, better-educated middle class, with the acquisitive power to massively access the markets of consumer durables and real estate. However, the process would be slow, tortuous, and uneven. Slow because it took seventy-five years to be fully accomplished.

Tortuous because in its early stages it did not produce sufficient results, and was unable to neutralize the threat of a social revolution when the first Spanish democracy was established in 1931. And uneven because it was temporarily interrupted by the Spanish Civil War, and was not fully accomplished until after the death of the Franco dictatorship in 1975.

The first major episode of massive migration from the countryside to the cities started around the years of the Great War (see Chapter 19). During the 1860s, the municipal authorities of the major Spanish cities, along with the central government, developed plans for urban expansion, such as the Plan Cerdá for Barcelona (1859) and the Plan Castro for Madrid (1860). What drove Cerdá and Castro and other planners in secondary cities was the building of new neighborhoods for the rising bourgeoisie. In the 1920s, however, the main concern of urban planners, municipal authorities, and doctors was how to create adequate living spaces for the mass of immigrants that were moving to the cities.

Urban infrastructure may not have improved as much as growth demanded, but significant progress was made. Electricity began replacing gas in the 1880s, and by the 1930s it had reached most of the Spanish territory. In 1919, the first subway line was inaugurated in Madrid, and by that time most of the city's public transportation was already mechanized. Cesspools were a thing of the past and most houses in the major cities and towns had running water and sewage systems. New theatres, casinos, museums, athenaeums, parks, and other similar public spaces were opened, as well as public services such as hospitals and schools. The first telephone company and the first radio stations were inaugurated and soon expanded their services to different parts of the country. Along with this material progress came the broadening of existing forms of sociability. For the first time, Spanish masses had access to transportation, communication, leisure, and political activism.

The economic crisis of the 1930s and the Spanish Civil War put the process of economic and social modernization on hold. The material progress of the 1920s was insufficient; it did not reach the broader portion of society. A substantial segment of the growing urban working classes lived in neighborhoods where urban infrastructure was still deficient. Working-class apartments were small, were poorly ventilated, and had only one toilet shared by all neighbors. Many lacked running water. The living conditions of smallholding farmers in the interior and day laborers (*jornaleros*) in the south remained at or below the level of subsistence. The Second Republic, the first fully democratic regime in Spain, made colossal efforts to improve the living conditions of Spaniards, with very limited success because of adverse economic conditions. Nonetheless, the Civil War was not exclusively the consequence of this failure; in other words, it did not occur because Spain was socially backward. As in many parts of Europe, Spanish society became trapped in the maze of political extremism in an international context of weak democratic leadership, rising totalitarian ideologies, and diplomatic instability.

The definitive transformation of Spain into a middle-class consumer society took place during the 1960s under the Franco dictatorship (see Chapter 7). However, here we must separate the material progress generated by economic growth from the cultural progress toward the building of an open democratic society. The former came about after the implementation of the Stabilization Plan of 1959 that allowed a long period of industrial expansion and economic growth. The latter did not fully unfold until the death of Franco and the restoration of democracy after 1975 (see Chapter 8).

The most immediate social consequence of economic improvement triggered by the Stabilization Plan of 1959 was the expansion of the middle classes. A study in 1957 estimated that 38.8 percent of Spaniards were middle class, with significant regional variation (60 percent in the Basque Country, and 23 percent in Galicia). By 1963, the middle class was 47 percent of the Spanish population and the upper class was 5 percent. For the first time in the history of the country, the poor were not the majority. By 1975, the largest social group in Spain, 56 percent of the total population, was middle-class.

The way of life of this new social majority followed the course set by the nineteenth-century bourgeoisie, with modifications generated by technological development and cultural change. Its main characteristic was an unprecedented expansion of consumer habits to attain the level that social scientists call "consumerism." The phenomenon was not exclusive to Spain: it was a Western European trend that historians have described as the "Americanization of Europe." The average Spanish middle-class family aspired to own an apartment for the creation of their home sweet home. In Spain, the 1960s marked the beginning of a period of expansion in the real estate market that, with ups and downs, lasted until the crisis of 2008. Spanish homes were soon filled with a variety of new material objects. Coal stoves were replaced by gas and electric ones, ice boxes by electric refrigerators, and, after 1956, radio faced increasing competition from television. More families could afford a moped or a small car. First, many Spaniards drove the Italian Vespa with sidecar; later, the small Spanish-made SEAT 600 that could transport families to Sunday picnics in the countryside near the cities, or to the vacation resorts on the Mediterranean and Atlantic beaches. Some even escaped beyond the Pyrenees to experience the joys of democratic Europe. Two new department store chains, El Corte Inglés (1940) and Galerias Preciados (1943), opened branches in most Spanish cities. The American-style supermarket (nonexistent in the 1940s) became part of the urban landscape of cities, towns, and even villages. By the 1970s, soccer overtook bullfighting as the most popular form of entertainment; the Spanish *Liga* became the most profitable form of commercial leisure, and the soccer player became a new popular icon.

Material welfare inevitably brings cultural change. The generation born in the 1950s grew up watching American shows such as *Ironside* or *Columbo*, observing as American police officers read detainees their Miranda Rights. Viewers were thrilled; there was no such thing as Miranda Rights in Spain! Summer vacationers in Mediterranean beach resorts, especially young men, enjoyed the liberal habits of European tourists. A weekend in Torremolinos or Benidorm could be the most exciting life experience for sexually repressed young Spanish men. During the 1960s, British and American pop music was screened on Spanish television and on a variety of newly created radio programs captivating Spanish youth. The Catholic Church and the most conservative segments of Spanish society portrayed boys who let their hair grow as effeminate and girls wearing miniskirts as morally loose, but the average Spanish family started to allow their sons to wear psychedelic shirts and their daughters' colorful stockings and unconventional wigs. The fashion boutiques, a new kind of small shop usually owned by young female entrepreneurs, proliferated in the streets of middle-class neighborhoods, first in Madrid and Barcelona and soon in provincial cities and towns. *Boutiques*, as they were called in Spanish, supplied fashionable clothing at affordable prices to the rising crowd of young and middle-aged consumers. The traditional Spanish *taberna* (an establishment that served only wine and liquors) and the popular Spanish bar needed to compete with modern and clean cafeterias that included in their menus sodas, pancakes, sandwiches, ice cream, and pastries, and often had names such as "California" or "Nebraska" to emphasize their modernity. In the 1970s, two new kinds of drinking establishments were opened in cities, towns, and even villages: the "English-style pub" and the *bar de copas* (cocktail bar). Unlike the traditional pub, the Spanish version started as a cocktail bar where young Spaniards met, mainly at night, to socialize. Some pubs of the mid- and late 1970s in Barcelona and Madrid became emblematic public spaces where members of the anti-Franco intelligentsia gathered.

While Spaniards had reached European material standards, they were still culturally deprived. Franco allowed the Beatles to perform at the Madrid Bullring of Las Ventas on July 1965 with a discrete display of police to control possible rioting. However, the Rolling Stones did not play in Spain until the end of the dictatorship in 1976, and a number of Spanish songwriters were classified as subversive by Franco censorship and their songs were forbidden. In 1972, groups of Spaniards organized bus excursions to Perpignan in Southern France to watch Bernardo Bertolucci's film *Last Tango in Paris*, banned in Spain by Franco's censorship. In 1975, a municipal police officer in the provincial city of Cáceres gave a bookseller a fine because he was displaying the poster of "a naked woman" in his storefront; it was a poster of the eighteenth-century painting of the *Maja Desnuda* by Francisco de Goya. The officer justified his action, arguing that it was a case of public scandal because he saw youngsters and kids paying unusual attention to the window display of the bookstore. The dictatorship suppressed cultural practices and forms of sociability characteristic of modern democratic middle-class consumer societies such as political rallies, public festivals, and street demonstrations. Social activities that Spaniards were able to exercise in the 1930s and before were not restored until the death of Franco and the restoration of democracy.

The years immediately after the death of the dictator on November 20, 1975 were of both political and social transition toward an open and free society. In its material components, Spain was already a middle-class consumer society; culturally, it was a society breaking the barriers imposed by the dictatorship. The drastic gender divisions imposed after the Spanish Civil War started to naturally collapse in the 1960s, when many women entered the labor force and became professionals (see Chapter 11). The sexual revolution of that decade captivated Spanish youth while Franco's censors banned indecent movies because they had sex scenes or nudity. Rock, fashion, environmentalism, and democratic values were embedded in the lives of many Spaniards despite the barriers imposed by Franco's regime.

After the death of the dictator, the country finally completed the modernizing process interrupted by the Civil War in 1936 by recovering old democratic and civic traditions and creating new ones. Along with the first fully democratic election of June 1977, Spaniards strengthened the civic society created in the late years of the dictatorship through a variety of platforms such as neighborhood associations, grassroots cultural clubs, and spontaneous initiatives that promoted freedom of speech and creativity. A manifestation of that civic, cultural, and artistic energy was the rise in the 1980s of the youth countercultural movement known as *La Movida* (the Going On). The vanguard of the movement emerged in Madrid and was known as *La Movida Madrileña* (The Madrid Scene). *Movidas* could be understood as Spanish versions of the radical European and American punk subcultures. They had expressions in a variety of cultural fields including music, photography, painting, design, graffiti, comics, and film, and were a demonstration of the desire of Spanish youth to break with the cultural taboos imposed by the Franco regime. The filmmaker Pedro Almodóvar, the best known of these artists, became a global cultural figure.

During the 1990s and up to the crisis of 2008, the ways of life of Spaniards evolved to meet European standards, although Spanish society still remained closely attached to some of its habits and traditions. The Spanish economy benefited from its integration into the European Union in 1987, and especially from the implementation of the European Monetary Union in 2002. The Euro brought to Spain years of economic growth with an expansion of the middle classes and a rise of consumerism. In the last two decades, Spaniards have evolved into one of the most secularized peoples in Europe, having the lowest rates of church attendance, being among the societies with the highest number of non-married couples and approving what is considered one of the most liberal laws regarding gay marriage in the world. At the same time, with some slight regional differences, Spaniards keep the most peculiar daily schedules in Europe, lunching around 3:00 p.m. and dining around 10:00 p.m. They share with other southern Europeans a strong commitment to family and community life. While the nuclear family prevails, familial loyalties, solidarities, and dependencies are still valued over individuality and privacy. Even regarding consumer habits, particularities are noticeable. During the years of economic prosperity, Spaniards favored investment in real estate instead of education or culture. In 2008, Spaniards had the largest number of vacation homes among Europeans, a phenomenon that led to the creation of the worst real estate bubble in Europe.

In sum, in the decades between 1975 and 2008, democratic politics, progressive values, and economic improvement transformed Spanish society into one of the freest and most inclusive in the world. At the same time, the economic crisis made evident some of the shortcomings of the Spanish way of life and, in particular, what is distinctive of Spain in the context of the contemporary democratic middle-class consumer societies of Europe.

Further reading

Cruz, Jesus, *The Rise of Middle-class Culture in Nineteenth-century Spain*, Baton Rouge: Louisiana State University Press, 2011.

Díaz Barrado, Mario Pedro, *La España democrática (1975-2000) Cultura y vida cotidiana*, Madrid: Editorial Síntesis, 2006.

Gracia García, Jordi, and Miguel Angel Ruiz Carnicer, *La España de Franco (1939-1975)*, Madrid: Editorial Síntesis, 2001.

Juliá Díaz, Santos, *Hoy no es ayer: ensayos sobre historia de Espan a en el siglo XX*, Barcelona: RB, 2010.

Morcillo, Aurora G., *The Seduction of Modern Spain: the Female Body and the Francoist Body Politic*, Lewisburg: Bucknell University Press, 2010.

Radcliff, Pamela, *Making Democratic Citizens in Spain: Civil Society and the Popular Origins of the Transition, 1960-78*, Basingstoke: Palgrave Macmillan, 2011.

Rueda Hernanz, Germán, *España 1790-1900: sociedad y condiciones económicas*, Madrid: Ediciones Istmo, 2006.

Serrano García, Rafael, *El fin del Antiguo Re gimen (1808-1868)*, Madrid: Editorial Síntesis, 2001.

Shubert, Adrian, *A Social History of Modern Spain*: London: Routledge, 1990.

Shubert, Adrian, *Death and Money in the Afternoon: A History of the Spanish Bullfight*, New York: Oxford University Press, 1999.

Stapell, Hamilton, *Remaking Madrid: Culture, Politics, and Identity after Franco*, New York: Palgrave Macmillan, 2010.

Zozaya, Maria, *Identidades en juego. Formas de representación social del poder de la elite en un espacio de sociabilidad masculino, 1836-1936*, Madrid: Siglo XXI, 2016.

CHAPTER 13
EMPIRE AND COLONIES
Stephen Jacobson

The "Spanish Empire" usually conjures up images of the early modern period when Habsburg Spain (the first world power in history) inaugurated an era of Western global hegemony in which a clutch of small European states colonized vast non-European lands. The monarchy colonized much of the Americas and part of the Philippines by employing classical models of administration and tribute collection with their roots in the Roman and Holy Roman Empires and the Spanish Reconquest. Settlers and missionaries spread disease and the gospel, decimating native populations and converting the survivors and their descendants to Christianity. The crown extracted fantastic quantities of silver from the mines of Potosí (in today's Bolivia) and Zacatecas (in today's Mexico), and used them to finance a powerful fiscal-military state, which defended Catholicism against Germanic Protestants on the European continent and Islamic Turks in the Mediterranean. Merchants shipped the first African slaves across the Atlantic. The Manila Galleon set sale every year from Acapulco to the Philippines, where it exchanged silver for Chinese fineries, opening up the Celestial Empire to American trade. The crown instituted the first "pigmentocracy" in which skin color and lineage determined privilege and opportunity, planting the European weed of racism across the ocean.

Spain forfeited its status as a great power with the loss of its last European possessions in the Seven Years' War (1756–63) and the independence of its continental American colonies (1808–24). Yet, Spain remained an imperial power. In the mid-nineteenth century, it boasted the third most populous overseas empire in the world next to Britain and the Netherlands. The rich island of Cuba, the "pearl of the Antilles," was one of the most coveted possessions of the globe, producing one-third of the world's cane sugar by 1855 and 40 percent by 1860. The island's tobacco sector occupied much less cultivable land than sugar but yielded high profits, and, in some isolated years, may have rivaled sugar in export value. Puerto Rico became a crowded colony with large coffee and sugar sectors. The Philippines offered privileged commercial access to China, and came to harvest valuable exports in hemp, sugar, tobacco, and coffee. The other Pacific territories included the Mariana and Caroline archipelagos. Initially, these were forgotten places reserved for valiant missionaries and enterprising military governors, some of whom amassed small fortunes. By the latter decade of the nineteenth century, imperial rivals (particularly newcomers such as Germany, Japan, and the United States) eyed these islands as potential bases for coaling and laying submarine telegraph cable to vie for the control of strategic shipping lanes dominated by Britain.

Most of the empire disappeared following defeat to the United States in the Spanish-American War of 1898. Puerto Rico, the Philippines, and Guam became American colonies, while Cuba became nominally independent. In 1899, Spain sold its remaining islands in the Micronesia to Germany. After this date, Spain's chief imperial ambitions lay in Morocco. The Treaty of Fez (1912) established a Spanish protectorate in the mountainous Rif region of the northern coast to which the sparsely populated province of Tarfaya in the southwestern coast was added. Together, the "northern" and the "southern" zones encompassed about one-fifth of the Sultanate, the remainder of which was under French administration. The prosperous city of Tetuan, occupied almost a year after the signing of the Treaty, became the capital. In 1939, the Spanish Sahara (today Western Sahara) was incorporated into the Protectorate. Considered the "hinterland" of the Canary Islands by some rather imaginative geographers, Spanish troops had taken control of this vast expanse of land in the 1880s. In 1934, Spain occupied the last Moroccan territory, the coastal enclave of Ifni, to the north of the southern zone of the protectorate.

The other colonial possession in Africa was Spanish Guinea (today Equatorial Guinea), a group of islands in the Bight of Biafra in the Gulf of Guinea and a mainland enclave along the Muni River. The island of Fernando Po (today Bioko) was the most developed part of the colony and the focus of Spanish colonialism. Spain first established its authority over the islands after Britain abandoned its antislaving base on Fernando Po in 1832 due to high death rates from malaria and other tropical diseases, even for sub-Saharan Africa. Although Britain relinquished its claims, the Spanish governor continued to be British until 1858, Fernando Po remained a coaling station for British and North American ships for decades, and British commerce dominated. Pidgin

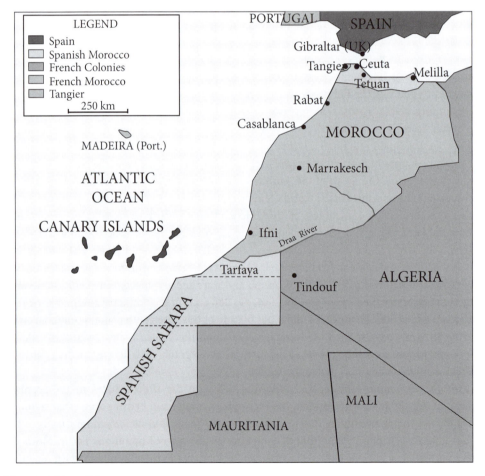

Map 13.1 Map of Morocco.

English served as the *lingua franca* well into the twentieth century. Spain began the colonization of Fernando Po in the 1880s after attempts to settle a few Valencian families and some 15,000 repatriated Afro-Cubans in the 1850s and 1860s failed due to inhospitable conditions. In 1885, the Society of Africanists and Colonialists sent exploratory expeditions to the Muni River estuary, and in 1900, France and Spain came to an agreement on the mainland borders of Spanish Guinea. The use of quinine as a prophylactic against malaria made European colonization possible in all of Africa. In the twentieth century, Spanish Guinea became Hispanicized.

Spain's overseas possessions remained a vast collage of peoples. Immigrant Spaniards and creoles of Cuba, Puerto Rico, and the Philippines were at the top of the hierarchy. In the middle, but often intermixed with the elite, were Spanish speakers distinguished from native populations. These included Spanish and Chinese *mestizos* in the Philippines. The latter were known as *Sangley*, an enterprising merchant class. The *Fernandinos* of Fernando Po spoke English, possessed English surnames, and practiced Protestantism before the Spanish began their civilizing mission in the 1880s. Many were descendants of recaptured Igbo slaves from Southern Nigeria who the British had repatriated to the island in the 1820s and 1830s. They mixed with immigrants from Sierra Leone and other migrants, captives, and runaways. Initially involved in the palm oil trade, many Fernandinos became planters once cocoa began to replace palm oil as the island's chief export toward the end of the nineteenth century. In the late nineteenth and early twentieth century, black creoles dominated the cash-crop export economy of the colony.

The Spanish governed various native groups, most of whom were unknown to peninsular Spaniards. North Africans included the various Jibala and Sahrawi tribes of the Rif region and the Western Sahara. In the Gulf of Guinea, the Spanish ruled various Bantu peoples on the islands, the coast, and the interior. In Puerto Rico and Cuba, the aboriginal natives had died off with colonization in the sixteenth century, but many rural creoles had deep roots. In Puerto Rico and Cuba, the *jíbaro* and the *guajiro* were romanticized terms used for proud hill dwellers who maintained their dignity while living in miserable conditions, faced with the degrading and predatory forces of an empire keen on converting them into hired hands. Slaves, free blacks, and mulattos were also born on the islands. Few had individual or family memories of Africa and did not claim any other *patria* as their own.

The Philippines was Spain's most extensive and the most populated overseas territory. In 1903, the United States census reported that some seven million of its people were "civilized," while another 650,000 souls belonged to the "wild tribes." All in all, the population was more than six times that of Puerto Rico and four times that of Cuba. Census takers estimated that 10 percent spoke Spanish, a figure that might have been too low. Until the arrival of Spanish missionaries in the sixteenth century, the region lacked any unifying religious, linguistic, or political tradition. Various Malay peoples, separated by mountains and waters, spoke multiple languages and held a variety of belief systems. On the most populous island of Luzon, numerous ethnolinguistic groups (Tagalog, Kapampangan, Pangasinan, Iloco, Cagayan, Bikolano, and Igorot) inhabited various regions, and many were divided into smaller tribes that spoke dialects that were not mutually intelligible. Various peoples lived on the central archipelago, known as the Visayan Islands. The southernmost island of Mindanao also exhibited great geographic, ethnographic, and religious diversity. The north belonged to the Visayan world, while the southwest was the home of the Magindanao, the dominant ethnic group of the southern Islamic peoples.

The Philippines Islands and Regions

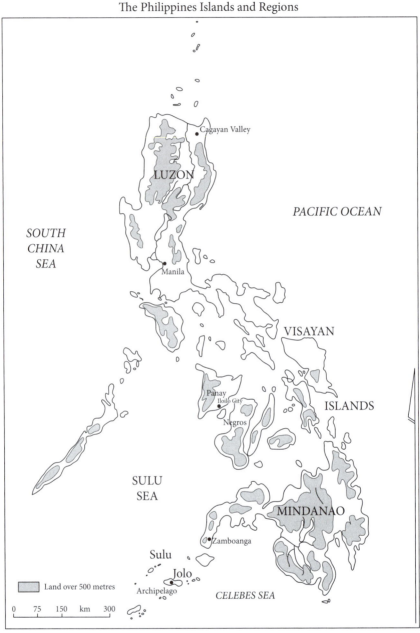

Map 13.2 Map of the Philippines.

The Philippines differed from the Caribbean possessions because large swaths of territory remained independent of Spanish authority for much of the nineteenth century. Until permanent military garrisons became established in the middle decades of the century, it was impossible to pacify the most conflictive zones, and even at century's end, many of the "wild tribes" had not been assimilated into colonial culture. In Luzon, the most resistant group were the Igorot on the Gran Cordillera Central, the central mountain range. This group of diverse peoples had staunchly resisted military and ecclesiastic incursions for centuries, and the fiercest tribes threatened contiguous zones. The Spanish began to make progress in the Cordillera in 1846 after a provincial military governor named Mariano Azcáriz carried out a scorched-earth campaign, vowing to take three native heads for every Spanish one. In the Philippines Exhibition of 1887 that was held in Retiro Park in Madrid, two human zoos showcased the grand ethnic diversity of this vast but little-known possession. In the first, the Igorot (also referred to as *salvajes*) were exhibited half-naked in their native g-strings. In the second zoo and in the craft and industry pavilions, the more civilized *indios* of the other "races" represented the Hispanized, Christianized, tribute-paying, and trouser-wearing colonial subjects.

Even more threatening to the Pax Española were the so-called *Moros del Sur*, Islamic slave raiders from the sultanates of Magindanao and the Sulu Islands. By the late eighteenth century, they arrived with forty to fifty gunships with up to 3,000 men touting heavy artillery. Guided by assimilated former slaves familiar with the terrain, they wrought havoc upon lowland towns. From 1775 to 1848, some 2,000 to 3,000 captives per year arrived in Jolo in the Sulu Islands, then the principal emporium of the slave trade. At the high watermark of the trade in 1848, the Sulu Sultanate harbored 10,000 "fishers of men" with a deadly fleet of 200 ships. In February of that year, the captain general of the Philippines, Narciso Clavería, who had previously supervised the campaign against the Igorot, attacked the Balanginga islands, the center of operations for Sulu slave raiders. He had at his disposition three steam gunboats, ordered from Britain specifically for the campaign. Troops razed to the ground forts, towns, villages, crops, and trees, and converted the islands into a wasteland. In the ensuing years, the Spanish transferred much of the Balanginga populace (as well as other groups in the Philippines) to the frontier region of the Cagayan Valley in northeast Luzon, where more hands were needed for tobacco farming. Although sporadic marauding continued for another three decades, steamship patrols kept the waters reasonably safe. By the late 1840s, commerce could be conducted smoothly throughout the Philippines.

During the third quarter of the nineteenth century, Spanish military objectives turned south to the Islamic sultanates, which had long resisted colonization. Historically, Spain's presence in the Islamic south was limited to a large garrison, trading center, and prison settlement on the western coast of Mindanao near the Sulu Islands in Zamboanga. There, the inhabitants profited from steady traffic from whalers and a brisk regional commerce in Chinese luxury products, opium, and local foodstuffs: rice, edible birds' nests (considered a delicacy in China), shark fins, wax, and other tropical foods. In 1849, the Spanish conquered Davao and established a port in the southeast. Two years later, they founded a naval base at Pollock Harbor at the mouth of the Pulangi River with the goal of penetrating the Cotabato Basin, the heartland of the Magindanao. In 1861, military operations commenced. Still, it took another twenty-five years to secure the upper river valley, and various parts of the island revolted in late 1890. The captain general of the Philippines, Valeriano Weyler, suppressed the uprising by employing counterinsurgency tactics that he would later perfect in Cuba and which enhanced his reputation as the "Butcher." He and his engineers "reconcentrated" civilians into fortified towns and constructed extended lines of wire, trenches, gun emplacements, and makeshift forts to prevent guerilla bands from melting into the villages.

The Sulu Islands constituted a rich, centralized maritime state that had thrived since the late eighteenth century due to fine relations with the British East India Company and its country traders. The "Reign of Jolo," as the Spaniards called it, boasted a thriving trade in Asian goods and flesh, including slaves from the Philippines and other islands in the Malayan world; silks, satins, brassware, and porcelains from China; pearls, mother of pearl, and tropical foods from the Sulu Islands and Mindanao; and arms and opium from Britain and its colonies. Chinese, British, Dutch, and German merchants from Borneo, India, Singapore, and southern China frequented the islands. In 1851, the Spanish invaded Jolo and forced the Sultan to sign a treaty, which recognized the sovereignty of Queen Isabel II and granted Spain exclusive trading rights. The Sultanate, however, ignored its terms, enjoying British protection for an additional two decades. In 1871, Spanish ships blockaded Jolo, and in 1875, the captain general of the Philippines José Malcampo put a definitive end to the "autonomy" of the Sulu Islands. Nine thousand soldiers aided by twenty-two steam gunboats carried out a vicious campaign. They razed towns to the ground and established Spanish military authority on Jolo.

In many respects, the Philippines were a typical Southeast Asian colony of the liberal era. Pacification was accompanied by the establishment of free trade, which was followed in turn by the transformation of the natural environment and the large-scale production of cash crops for export. Spanish liberals opened Manila to international shipping in 1835, and in 1855, a Progressive government added three more regional ports: Iloilo City, Zamboanga, and Sual. Monoculture replaced subsistence agriculture to such an extent that the Philippines changed from a rice exporter to a net importer. As occurred elsewhere, the arrival of cheap textiles from Britain was the most pernicious consequence of free trade, destroying thriving cottage industries. The history of Iloilo City (the second most populous city in the colony and the center of the sugar boom) speaks volumes of the transformative effects of liberal empire. In the space of a few decades, it became transformed from a port that exported textiles from the island of Panay to one that imported textiles and exported sugar from the nearby island of Negros. In a similar manner, immigrant pioneers turned western Negros from a practically uninhabited jungle into a bastion of sugar production. To be sure, the destruction of native textiles industries in Panay and in northwestern Mindanao caused massive social dislocation. Some families suffered poverty, others migrated to new frontiers, and others converted into hired or tenant labor. Not all natives, though, were victims. Many entrepreneurs took advantage of new opportunities and entered the planter and commercial classes.

The Tobacco Monopoly was the most glaring exception to the free trade ethos. It was the chief source of revenue for the colonial government, bankrolling the Moro Wars and the pacification of Luzon. In 1817, the Spanish government abolished the monopoly in Cuba and opened up of all of its ports to free trade. However, it maintained the monopoly in the Philippines where consumers were more plentiful. In the Philippines, the colonial government also raised revenue by direct taxes and by monopolies on recreational consumables and activities, such as palm wine, betel nut (a narcotic), and cockfighting. The Tobacco Monopoly was a colonial bureaucracy unto itself: a behemoth of administrators, intermediaries, customs police, warehouses, collection points, and retail outlets (*estancos*). It sold cigars, cigarettes, and snuff to an addicted populace who believed in their medicinal qualities. It was big business, and some was reserved for export. In 1880, the Spanish abolished the monopoly, by then riddled with corruption and considered a vestige of mercantilism. In its place, the privately owned Philippine Tobacco Company (Tabacalera) absorbed much of the infrastructure.

The presence of mercantilist practices in the liberal age was by no means exceptional in the colonial world. What made the Philippines a peculiar colony was that foreigners were responsible for much of the physical transformation and the commercial success of the colony. The Spanish were involved in the production of traditional crops primarily for internal consumption, such as rice, tobacco, vegetables, and fruit, but they had less of a role in new cash crops and in international commerce. As one Spaniard lamented in 1879, "the Philippines is an Anglo-Chinese colony under a Spanish flag." Large British and American merchant houses dealt primarily in textile imports and hemp and sugar exports. These enterprises, in turn, pumped in the credit that kept the supply chains flowing. Most middlemen were Chinese or *Sangley*, and the few Spaniards engaged in the procurement of export goods tended to work for foreign firms. The inability of the Spanish to take advantage of commercial opportunities was evident in the Sulu Islands where the Chinese replaced the Tausug as the merchant class in the wake of Spanish conquest. Until Spain issued a protectionist tariff in 1891 allowing for Catalan textiles to compete favorably, most imports came from Britain. In 1885, one Spanish journalist complained that Spain's Transatlantic Steamship Company sent only one expedition per month to the Philippines while England sent eight, and that passage from Liverpool to Manila cost half that from Barcelona.

The governance of the Philippines shared similarities and differences with the Caribbean colonies. On one hand, it resembled that of Cuba and Puerto Rico insofar as the captain general, the provincial governors, and their aides and administrators were army officers who wielded dictatorial powers. They were not subject to even a symbolic version of a colonial assembly, which, if one had existed, could have given creole, *mestizo*, and native elite some input into governance. In 1861, Spain created the Overseas Ministry, but it was poorly staffed and exercised minimal oversight over the military central commands. One Spanish constitution after another promised that "special laws" would govern the overseas territories, but such special laws were never written. The result was a legal vacuum that had the effect of investing authorities with discretionary (if not arbitrary) authority. Colonial subjects could not invoke constitutional rights, although they could win and lose criminal, civil, and mercantile cases in courts of ordinary justice under Spanish codes of law. On the other hand, the governance of the Philippines differed from the Caribbean colonies due to the large role played by the religious orders, which essentially doubled as a colonial civil service. Spanish military officials and bureaucrats were poorly trained, and most regarded a Pacific posting as an occupational hazard. Few saw the advantages of acquiring local knowledge given that they were ordinarily rotated out after a few years. In contrast, Augustinians, Recollects, Dominicans, and Franciscans spent extended periods of time in the colony, learned the local languages, and acted as effective intermediaries.

These four religious orders were the primary agents of colonization and Hispanicization. They ran the parishes, helped compile the censuses for tax collection purposes, participated in local tribunals, and organized primary, secondary, and university education. They recruited, collaborated with, and reported on the performance of the *gobernadorcillos*, the local governors (or *caciques*) who served as the native representatives in the pyramidal system of colonial rule. The religious orders operated their own *haciendas* and were also in the business of moneylending, their clients ranging from humble peasants to large commercial houses. They exported some of their profits to Spain, where they went to charitable projects and other "good works," although some found their way to London, where they invested in government bonds.

These four religious orders also continued to supply missionaries throughout the nineteenth century to convert pagan peoples in highland areas of the Philippines and the Mariana Islands.

In areas of recent conquest, the Spanish offered opportunity to other orders, eager to make their presence felt in the colonial world. In the strategic and dangerous Islamic south, the Spanish sent in the Jesuits, who were permitted to return to the Philippines after being expelled from all Spanish territories in 1767. Their success rate was modest among Islamic peoples, and they frequently suffered violence and disease. In 1858, the Jesuits were dispatched to Fernando Po, although, like the early colonists, they could not endure the pestiferous conditions. When the Spanish dedicated more resources to the colony in the 1880s, the Claretians, sponsored by the Transatlantic Steamship Company, were the chief vectors of Hispanicization. Following the Congress of Berlin (1884–85), Spain began its occupation of the Caroline Islands. In 1886, a steamship arrived from Manila to the island of Yap. On board were a provincial governor, a group of Spanish military officials, Filipino troops, convicts, and Capuchin friars.

Many European and American observers claimed that the conspicuous role of the Spanish friars was proof positive that Spain was not fit to govern modern colonies. In Spain, democratic and anticlerical intellectuals also saw the orders as a relic from the past and an impediment to modernization in the Philippines, Micronesia, and Fernando Po. The poor reputation of the religious orders, the persistence of slavery in the Caribbean, the arbitrariness of military governance, and the lack of any long-term plans for self-government in the colonies hampered the emergence of a persuasive civilizing ideology in Spain. In 1870, the democratic overseas minister, Segismundo Moret (author of the first law phasing out slavery in the Caribbean in 1868), attempted to remedy this situation. He proposed an ambitious but ultimately unsuccessful plan to replace the religious orders with lay teachers in the Philippines and to convert the Dominican University of Saint Thomas in Manila into a secular institution. As a powerful politician for the Liberal Party in the 1880s, Moret backed associations born in the wake of the Congress of Berlin, such as the Ibero-American Union and the Society of Africanists and Colonialists. They published periodicals, organized scientific expeditions, and sponsored conferences. They equated Spanish imperialism in Africa, and informal authority in Latin America, with material well-being, spiritual and racial harmony, improved infrastructure, the exploitation of natural resources, the facilitation of commerce, and the triumph of science and technology.

The idea that Spain was a modern nation equipped to carry out a civilizing mission gained purchase among educated classes and lent legitimacy to colonial enterprises in Morocco and Spanish Guinea. In the twentieth century, cultural and diplomatic initiatives sought to depict Spain as the chief representative of authentic Hispanic values and European culture and science on both sides of the Atlantic. During the period of Spanish rule in the Philippines, however, evangelizing ideologies prevailed over civilizing ones. Complicating matters, the Philippine church was wracked with intense internal conflicts between Filipino clergy, who saw themselves as the defenders of native rights, and Spanish friars, depicted as reactionary agents of colonial oppression. In 1872, Filipino officers mutinied in Cavite (on the southern shores of Manila Bay), the first political act of rebellion. After repressing the mutiny and executing its instigators, the Spanish also murdered three native priests who had been outspoken critics of colonial authority but were unconnected to the mutiny. Thereafter, westernized Filipino *ilustrados* denounced the abuses of the military and the clergy as the chief ills of Spanish imperialism, and advocated the disentailment of the friar estates. Conflicts within the church, and between the church and the *ilustrados*, were the most visible sources of tension leading to the Philippine Revolution of 1896.

In contrast to the Philippines, Spanish elites considered Cuba and Puerto Rico "overseas provinces" rather than "colonies." Various politicians made this distinction during the Democratic Sexennium (1868–74) when Cuba and Puerto Rico were requested to send deputies to the Spanish *Cortes*, an invitation not extended to the Philippines. However, such a distinction was lost on many Caribbean subjects who saw themselves as victims of an imperial power that exercised arbitrary governance, maintained slavery, denied them citizenship, and exploited them economically. In Puerto Rico, the first act of rebellion took place in September 1868 in the coffee-producing region of Lares. The military suppressed it quickly, but the *Grito de Lares* echoed in the eastern Cuban province of Manzanillo where *Grito de Yara* set into motion a major war. In both Caribbean islands, small-time planters protested against the extortionist practices of Spanish export firms, high taxes by the colonial government, and in the case of Cuba, colonial policies that favored the larger plantations owners in the more affluent sugar-producing regions in the west. By promising abolition upon independence, these planters forged an alliance among slaves, free blacks, and poor creoles. In eastern Cuba, the rebellion mushroomed into the Ten Year's War (1868–78), a conflict in which the Spanish sent some 180,000 troops across the ocean, the largest colonial conflict in Spanish history. Half of them died.

In Morocco, the baldly extractive objectives of metropolitan business interests also led to unrest. The first native revolt against the policy of "peaceful penetration" in the twentieth century took place outside Melilla in 1908, where Spanish iron-ore mines caused major social disruption. Spain mobilized some 42,000 troops in July 1909 to put down an uprising. It is revealing that unlike the colonial campaigns of the nineteenth century, ordinary Spaniards showed little enthusiasm for African imperialism. The call-up of troops provoked a massive revolt in Barcelona, known as Tragic Week (see chapter 17). Although appeals to a civilizing mission helped generate support among the elite, most Spaniards were fed up with imperial adventurism regardless of whether it was justified by anti-Moorish crusading discourse or by a more "modern" civilizing ideology. New working-class parties saw the empire in Morocco for what it was: a sliver of territory that served the ambitions of army officers, mining interests, and a government overeager to maintain a seat at the table in world affairs, even one of a minor power.

An empire in decline? Spain in the Caribbean

To many, Spain had long been an empire in decline, because those regions colored yellow on the world map (red being reserved for Britain) were hardly visible after the "disaster" of 1898. This thesis was at the heart of Lord Salisbury's famous "dying nations" speech, delivered at the Royal Albert Hall in May 1898 in which he equated the possession of colonies with the survival of the fittest. In Spain, the jingoist journalist Gonzalo de Reparaz echoed Salisbury in an influential article, "The Spanish Empire: What There Was and *What Remains*," published in August 1898 in the magazine of the influential newspaper *ABC*. Reparaz, the chief propagandist for the Society for Africanists and Colonialists, sought to reverse the trend of degeneration and to lend momentum to a new imperial drive in Morocco so that Spain would once again join the ranks of the healthy and virile. Intentions aside, the idea that Spain was an empire that had been declining for centuries became one of the mantras of the Black Legend, repeated throughout the twentieth century.

For those who lived in Spain's colonies, however, the reality was quite different. In the nineteenth century, few would have recognized the characterization of an empire in decline. It never would have occurred to many Filipinos who had been brought under Spanish authority by way of steam gunboats, Remington repeating rifles, permanent garrisons, and fortified trench lines. Nor would it have occurred to creoles in Cuba and Puerto Rico who witnessed the arrival of waves of immigrants, merchants, army and navy officers, colonial governors, judges, tax collectors, engineers, skilled and unskilled workers, slaves, and indentured servants. Newcomers sometimes replaced creole elites. Locals felt preyed upon by metropolitan and foreign commercial and banking interests, who drew on lines of credit extending from London, New York, Paris, and Barcelona, and sent profits to Europe. However, many local elite did business and intermarried with immigrant pioneers and colonial authorities. Together, they implemented novel ways to make profits, move the frontier, exploit labor, clear tropical forests, plant export crops, build railroads, and penetrate sparsely populated regions existing on subsistence agriculture. Ultimately, Spain and other "dying nations" were unable to compete in Lord Salisbury's Social Darwinist contest to paint the globe red. However, until the United States defeated Spain in 1898 and expelled Spain from the Caribbean and the Pacific, the tentacles of the empire grew increasingly strong with each and every year.

Cuba was the nucleus of the imperial system for political and human reasons, in addition to fiscal and economic ones. The allegiance of its creole community to the mother country during the Latin American wars of independence earned it the title the "Ever-Faithful Isle." During the nineteenth century, it received the lion's share of Spanish immigration: from 1860 to 1880, some ten to fifteen thousand Spaniards settled there each year. Puerto Rico, in contrast, received a higher percentage of its immigrants from the French Caribbean, France, and Venezuela. By the 1880s, net immigration of Spaniards to Puerto Rico per year was often under one thousand. Increasing numbers of Spanish emigrants settled in the Philippines, especially after the pacification of the islands in the 1850s and the opening of the Suez Canal in 1869, which reduced costs considerably and travel time from four to two weeks. In 1845, only 4,000 Peninsular Spaniards lived in the colony, but by 1894, the census reported more than 75,000 Spaniards. Still, the metropolitan presence was diluted by the fact that most Spaniards were concentrated in Manila, and that most migrants to the Philippines were Chinese.

Immigration patterns to Cuba changed in the 1870s and 1880s due to the gradual abolition of slavery and indentured service. Following the Ten Years' War, the Spanish freed the slaves in eastern Cuba, and many freed men and women migrated to the cities where they competed with Spaniards and creoles for jobs in tobacco factories and in skilled-labor professions. As free blacks migrated to the cities, many Spanish migrants headed to Argentina and Uruguay. By the 1880s, these countries became the primary destination of Spanish immigrants and attracted much skilled labor. In Cuba, many unskilled Spanish migrants arrived in rural areas, some of it temporary "swallow immigration" from the Canary Islands and Galicia. Organized by specialist companies, these workers arrived for the harvest and then returned to Spain.

Immigration to Cuba was also promoted for political reasons. In the 1840s, the percentage of the slave population was at its zenith. Voices cried out to "whiten" the island and abolish slavery or risk slave revolt and race war. In the end, neither Puerto Rico nor Cuba became "plantation societies" as did British Jamaica or French Martinique. Immigration, in addition to low population growth among slaves, ensured that whites outnumbered blacks and mulattos. Among immigrants, Catalans from Barcelona and the coast occupied a conspicuous role in commerce. In Puerto Rico, the Catalan presence was resented to such an extent that as early as 1810, the town government of San Juan requested that Catalans be sent home, since "rarely do they build factories, establish *haciendas*, or do anything but export the capital that they have saved." It is probable that by "Catalans" the Puerto Ricans also meant Mallorcans, who, along with Catalans and Corsicans, came to dominate credit and commerce in the coffee trade.

The largest industrial sector of the Spanish economy, Catalan textiles, was also interconnected with Cuba. Industrialists were dependent on Cuban and Puerto Rican sugar to access North American cotton. Ships followed triangular or quadrangular trade routes, leaving Barcelona and other Catalan ports with wines, liqueurs, and finished goods. They stopped in the Caribbean where they would exchange their cargo for sugar to be delivered to New Orleans, Mobile, or Charlestown where they swapped sugar for cotton to be brought back to Barcelona to feed the city's looms. Another permutation on this cotton route was one in which ships first headed to Buenos Aires to pick up beef jerky (*tasajo*), which would then be delivered to the Caribbean or the United States where it was used to feed slaves. Madrid and Castile also benefited from the riches of the Antilles. In 1860, Cuba remitted more than 5 million pesos annually (4 million USD) to metropolitan coffers. Castilian wheat farmers also exported flour to the Caribbean colonies. As such, the Antilles were more complementary to the peninsular economy and the treasury than the Philippines, whose exports chiefly went to Britain, the British colonies, the United States, and China. There were no triangular routes that converted Philippine hemp and sugar into strategic imports coming to Iberia. Morocco was similar to the Philippines. Foreign capital participated in Spanish mining corporations, and most iron exports went to Britain, Germany, France, and the Low Countries.

The most visible representatives of the empire in the metropole were the *indianos*, immigrants to Cuba and Puerto Rico who returned to Spain, bringing back capital, which they invested in industry, banking and real estate, while maintaining active business interests in the colonies. In Spain, the strong economic linkages between Catalonia and the Caribbean colonies converted Barcelona into as much as an *indiano* as a Catalan capital. Not all *indiano* families in Barcelona were Catalans. The most powerful *indiano* of his day was Claudio López y López, who left the province of Santander and became rich in Cuba as a merchant and slaver (*negrero*). After arriving in Barcelona in the 1850s, he founded the Transatlantic Steamship Company, Hispano-Colonial Bank, and the Philippine Tobacco Company. He proudly displayed his title, the Marquis de Comillas.

Like Claudio López, many *indianos* grew up poor and were eager to display their wealth by constructing sumptuous palaces and making lavish donations to church, state, and town. Until 1898, nobody living along the Catalan and Cantabrian coasts or the Balearic Islands would have ever recognized the label of Spain as an "empire in decline." To take one example among many, during the 1880s the López family contracted a distinguished coterie of modernist architects and sculptors from Barcelona, including Antoni Gaudí, to transform the sleepy Cantabrian fishing village of Comillas into a fashionable seaside resort. At the International Exhibition of 1888 held in Barcelona, Antonio López contracted Gaudí to design the pavilion for the Transatlantic Steamship Company in the form of a Moorish palace. Many *indianos* hired modernist architects to construct their capacious homes, family chapels, and summer residences. Steeped in imperial symbolism, the Moorish palace was a preferred motif. One of the most opulent mansions in Barcelona was modeled after the Alhambra of Granada.

Constructed on the Vía Laitana, it was the home of José Taltavull, an *indiano* plantation owner originally from Menorca.

It is probable that powerful men in the empire, though not formally represented in the Spanish Cortes, influenced decision-making in Spain to a greater extent than those in states with more extensive overseas possessions. The Cuban plantocracy could throw its weight around in Madrid through metropolitan economic associations representative of international commercial interests and through their close contacts with *indianos* who acted as intermediaries. Some Spanish heads of government were particularly sensitive to colonial matters. In the rest of Europe, it is a challenge to name a prime minister or president who had previously served as a colonial governor. In nineteenth-century Spain, at least four heads of government, all military men, served as captains general in the colonies: Leopoldo O'Donnell (Cuba), Juan Prim (Puerto Rico) (see chapter 29), Francisco Serrano (Cuba), and Camilo Polavieja (Philippines). To be sure, the maintenance of authoritarian military governance in the empire reinforced the praetorian inclinations of the officer corps when it returned home. This was made clear in July 1936 when Francisco Franco, former commander of the foreign legion in Morocco, contacted Italian diplomats in Tangier to arrange the airlift of the Army of Africa to the Iberian Peninsula. By so doing, he turned a military coup into the Spanish Civil War.

The Empire's workers: Slave, indentured, coerced, and free labor

The centrality of Cuban sugar to the economy and treasury put Spanish politicians in an uncomfortable position with respect to slavery. If they had their druthers, most liberals probably would have preferred to enforce the two treaties abolishing the slave trade that Spain signed with Great Britain in 1814 and 1835. If this had occurred, slavery would have disappeared in a matter of decades. By the outbreak of Civil War in the United States in 1861, even most Cuban planters recognized the need to promote a transition from slave and indentured to free labor. In 1868, the Spanish *Cortes* passed the Moret Law, also colloquially known as the "Law of the Free Wombs." Approved a year following the definitive prohibition of the slave trade, it declared all children of slave parents free and emancipated all slaves over the age of sixty. By 1868, however, many viewed the law as too gradualist, a compromise offered to those who sought to prolong a dying institution. The Spanish government definitively abolished all forms of slavery in Puerto Rico in 1873 and in Cuba in 1886, only two years before it was abolished in Brazil.

For much of the nineteenth century, however, the economic system in Cuba, and, by extension, the balance sheets of the Spanish treasury and the health of the Spanish economy, depended on sugar, and sugar depended on slavery (see chapter 25). Domestic economic associations pressured Madrid to preserve and prolong slavery for as long as possible, while working-class organizations turned a deaf ear to abolitionists who struggled to make their voice heard. Plantation owners claimed to have few alternatives, given that Cuba did not have a large creole or native population that could be converted into a labor force as existed in the Philippines or the more densely populated Puerto Rico. White creoles and free blacks preferred to claim land on the eastern frontier to toiling away on sugar plantations. Cuba had vast tracts of virgin soil, covered by forest, perfect for sugar planting but less than ideal for recruiting wage earners or finding tenants. The province of Matanzas grew to become the center of sugar production in Cuba and the world. It was transformed from a region dedicated to timber, cattle ranching, tobacco, and coffee to a sugar monoculture. In the late eighteenth century, the province was populated by a mere 7,000 people, 2,000 of whom were slaves. By 1862, it was the global leader in sugar production with a population of 194,000 people, 90,000 of whom were slaves.

From the late eighteenth century to the definitive suppression of the slave trade in 1867, Cuba imported some 800,000 slaves, more than the total number of slaves shipped to all of Spanish America previously. Only Brazilians generated more demand, purchasing some two million captives in the nineteenth century. The ferocity of Britain's steamship patrols in Africa and the Caribbean made the trade a risky though potentially lucrative affair. More Spanish ships were brought to the International Tribunal of Sierra Leone than those of any other country. Frustrated with the difficult tasks of trying to intercept slave ships in order to catch slavers red-handed, the British navy also bombed Spanish and Brazilian slave "factories" located on the west coast of Africa. The treaties and the abolition of slavery in Latin America and the other European Caribbean colonies phased out most of the inter-American trade, which had been intense in the early decades of the nineteenth century. By the middle decades of the century, most new slaves arrived in Cuba and Puerto Rico after suffering transatlantic crossings from Spanish factories. Planters preferred to replenish slave populations with African *bozales* purchased from Spanish factors, called *mongos*. American-born slaves with more sophisticated ideas about manumission and slave revolt were considered risky.

On the eve of the end of the slave trade in 1867, Cuba had a slave population of 370,000, and Puerto Rico around 40,000. The difference between the high number of slave imports and the low number of slaves was chiefly due to demographic factors: an unequal ratio of males to females, low birth rates due to malnutrition and low life expectancy and high death rates. Although not all slaves worked in rural settings, the plantations were killing fields for those sent there. Manumission was another reason that the slave population grew slowly. Peninsular judges were not always as friendly to slave owners as were the captains general. Together with ambitious and creative slave litigants and their lawyers, they molded the continental law to carve out a jurisprudential tradition with novel manumission devices. In Cuba and Puerto Rico, manumission was more common than in the United States, though less common than in Brazil. The influence of free blacks in Cuban society prevented the creation of a Jim Crow society in the wake of abolition as occurred in the United States following the Civil War.

It was one of the typical paradoxes (or, more accurately, hypocrisies) of empire that Spain permitted the continuity of slavery in the Caribbean while prohibiting it elsewhere. Slavery was illegal in the Philippines, where thousands of Queen Isabel's subjects were hauled away to the Sulu Islands where their knowledge of Spanish (and ability to communicate with Europeans) made them prize assets to the commercial state. The Spanish also made slavery illegal in Fernando Po and freed slaves there in 1859. The chief reason for this measure was, in the most cynical of fashions, to use the Guinean islands as a base for moving captives to the Caribbean. The theory was that Fernando Po's reputation as a place of contracted (as opposed to slave) labor would enable the Spanish to transport captives from the west coast of Africa to the islands where they would be regrouped and sent to Cuba. The French were employing this strategy to avoid British patrols, using the West African island of St. Louis and Gorée as fronts for shipping Senegalese captives to Reunion. This was precisely the scheme of Julián Zulueta, the chief representative of the Cuban plantocracy who originally came from the Basque Country. From 1858 to 1862, he and some other investors founded the company Expedition for Africa, which transported Africans in ships carrying US flags from the Dahomey coast to Cuba by first making stops in Tenerife or Annabon, the second largest of the Spanish islands in the Bight of Biafra. In the end, the Spanish never converted their possessions in the Gulf of Guinea into conduits to move captives to Cuba, even though this was their sole interest in the island and the mainland.

Spanish slave traders, like their counterparts elsewhere, were a varied lot. Some were true Conradian personages who basked in a life devoid of legal and moral codes. This was the case of Pedro Blanco, a native of Malaga, who operated on the Gallina Coast in Sierra Leone from 1821 to 1845. There, he married the daughter of an African ruler, lived in a mansion, had multiple wives and a harem and was rumored to carry on an incestuous relationship with his sister. A few years before the British bombarded his principal factories in 1842, he moved to Havana where he ran into troubles with the Cuban elite and Spanish justice because of his reputation as a tavern brawler and a rapist, and his scandalous sexual affairs with his nephews and various men of color. Others, however, carried on their affairs with more discretion. In 1864, the British Consul considered Cadiz the European center of the slave trade, and its slavers among the most elegant men in Spain. In Cadiz, the Consul debated slavery with Antonio Vinent, a merchant from Menorca who defended the heinous institution and continued slaving even after the British had destroyed his factory in Corisco in 1840. By the 1870s, the former ship captain turned senator and marquise hosted opulent balls in his palace in Madrid. It was there that the capital's elite held a solemn ceremony for Alfonso XII upon his arrival to assume the Spanish throne of the Restoration Monarchy in 1875.

The Cuban sugar industry was so voracious that slave labor alone was insufficient. It was increasingly dependent on indentured migrants, known throughout the world as "coolies." The chief source of coolie labor for Cuba and Peru was China, where British firms in Amoy (today Xiamen), Hong Kong, and Shantou organized the recruitment of Chinese laborers in the 1840s. Between 1847 and 1873, more than 120,000 Chinese contract laborers arrived in Cuba. Normally bound by eight-year contracts to Cuban plantations, they were housed and treated the same as slaves, and quite often renewed (or were coerced into renewing) the terms of their indenture. The long coolie voyages often had higher death rates than African slave ships. Mutinies were frequent, given that many boarded against their will after having been tricked into signing up or sold by their families to pay debts. In theory, the dearth of female coolies prevented the emergence of a distinct Chinese ethnicity in Cuba. The Spanish government, however, made some efforts to force coolie traders to ship females. In 1847, an advertisement in the *Diario de Havana,* read: "For sale: A Chinese girl with two daughters, one of 12–13 years and the other 5–6, useful for whatever you may desire."

The coolie trade underwent a major shift after the British began to clamp down on traffic to Cuba in 1858 and the Mexican government prohibited the recruitment of Mayan *yucateros* as indentured servants in 1861. In search of alternatives, traffickers used Portuguese Macao and Philippine ports as gates of departure. To be sure, after 1858, many of the "Chinese" coolies were Filipino *Sangley* and natives of other East Asian ports including Saigon. In 1858, the Spanish and French undertook the invasion of Vietnam, and in 1861, the two countries, together with Britain, also invaded Mexico. One of the incentives of the O'Donnell government to participate in these adventures was to develop an alternative source of contract labor for

Cuba. Such considerations also weighed heavily when Spain decided to annex the Dominican Republic in 1861 (see chapter 23). In 1873, Spain signed a treaty with China, which definitively ended the trade in indentured servants.

Coerced or semi-forced labor also existed in other territories of the empire. Puerto Rico did not suffer such acute labor shortages, but it was difficult to convince the landless to work for pittance wages especially if they managed to eke out subsistence livings by other means. In order to oblige the reluctant, the colonial government in 1849 required all landless laborers (*jornaleros*) to seek employment actively on landed estates or suffer prison sentences (another form of forced labor). The law required them to carry notebooks (*libretos*) in which their employers recorded their work and evaluated their performance. On the other side of the Atlantic, the island of Fernando Po was also a magnet for coerced labor given that the native Bubi population proved not only resistant to enslavement but also reluctant to work as wage laborers or tenant farmers. Fernando Po planters contracted thousands from Cameroon and the Windward Coast of Liberia in the nineteenth and early twentieth centuries to work on cocoa plantations. By 1930, Europeans had replaced black creoles as the elite, and owned the majority of the island's land. Spanish plantations came to produce practically the entire cocoa and coffee export crop. In 1943, amid the Second World War, Britain and Spain came to an agreement to regularize the supply of Nigerian workers to Fernando Po, and in 1960, Franco renewed the agreement with the Republic of Nigeria. Many souls remained there until 1973, when the Nigerian government brought home 60,000 citizens from Equatorial Guinea.

In the Pacific, planters also employed coercive mechanisms or worse. In Micronesia, stories abounded of inhabitants of small islands being kidnapped and put to work as wage laborers on larger islands. In the Philippines, the large *haciendas* of the religious orders around Manila were notorious for maintaining tenant farmers in a state of perpetual indebtedness. In order to meet tributary obligations and pay their "debts," peasants had to accept orders on what to plant and how to use the land, and had to follow strict work regimes or suffer physical punishment. Debt peonage was also present in sugar and food production, although it was not present everywhere. The Tobacco Monopoly had the effect of coercing labor even though tobacco farming was not too demanding. By the 1860s, however, the Monopoly fell behind on payments, and tobacco production itself came to resemble what was, for all intent and purpose, forced labor.

Decolonization

It would be an easy task to compile a list of the "weaknesses" of the Spanish empire, and then convert these weaknesses into the reasons that Spain lost much of its second empire half a century before other European countries. Such a list, which is by no means exhaustive, would include the following: the lack of a convincing or well-defined civilizing mission; the absence of a well-trained colonial service in the Filipino languages or in Arabic; the dictatorial powers of the captain general and the lack of representative political bodies; the tensions created by the religious orders in the Philippines; the inability of the metropolitan market to absorb colonial exports; and the rapacious and usurious practices of metropolitan commercial interests that preyed upon creole and native farmers. These factors led colonial elite and middle classes to participate in associations with few allegiances to the metropole that increasingly favored independence. However, it is not true that such reasons were alone sufficient to explain why Spain differed from other European countries. After all, Great Britain did not exhibit many of these weaknesses, and yet it also encountered similar problems. It almost lost its rich colony of South Africa to creole rebels in the Boer War (1899–1902) just after Spain lost the Cuban War (1895–98). Furthermore, the last country to decolonize in Europe was Portugal, a second-tier empire with similar limitations. It would be wrong to equate the timing of decolonization with the strength or weakness of the metropole.

Geopolitical rivalries were the principal reason that Spain lost most of its colonies in 1898. In concrete terms, the United States replaced Spain as an imperial power in the Pacific and the Caribbean. The victory of the United States in the Spanish-American War triggered an "imperial transition" that became manifest in other parts of the globe in the ensuing decades. By the early twentieth century, American corporations, politicians, a jingoist press, and an enthusiastic populace aimed to convert the Caribbean into an "American lake." Americans viewed the Philippines as a bridge to gain greater access to China and to join Britain, France, Holland, and Japan as imperial powers in Asia. After the Second World War, the United States continued its expansionist ambitions when it expelled the Netherlands from Indonesia in 1949 by threatening to cut off Marshall Aid. Under this lens, the loss of the Spanish colonies in 1898 was the first phase in the exercise of ascendant American formal and informal power that reached its apex during the Cold War.

It is likely that if the United States had not intervened in Philippines and Cuba, Spain would not have lost these wars, at least not at that time. In the Philippines, many islands were unaffected by the Revolution of 1896, which came to halt with the Peace of Biak-na-Bato in 1897 and the death and exile of key leaders of the *Katipunan*, the chief rebel group. In the Caribbean, the Spanish army suppressed isolated Puerto Rican rebellions; and the Cuban War was a civil war in which much of the west favored the mother country. Spain was arguably winning a brutal war of attrition in Cuba when the United States entered the fray. In the ensuing Spanish-American War of 1898, the decisive moments were the battles of Manila Bay and Santiago, in which a superior United States Navy decimated Spain's Pacific and Atlantic fleets. It is crucial to recognize the role that Filipinos and Cubans played in their own independence, but it is unclear whether they would have prevailed without American intervention. One potential outcome was increased autonomy for the colonies. The pivotal influence of foreign powers in determining the victors of a war of independence was not exceptional. After all, the British lost thirteen of its colonies in North America in 1783 primarily because of French (and Spanish) support for the rebels.

Another reason why the loss of Spanish colonies resembles an early case of decolonization is that like the Boer War, the Philippine and Cuban Wars were "dirty wars." Spain sent more than 200,000 troops into Cuba, more than any European power had sent to any colonial war beforehand (although the British soon sent more to South Africa). Spanish troops constructed reinforced trench and barbed wire lines to isolate rebels and prevent them from dissolving into civilian populations. Rebel troops, in turn, waged a "total war," avoiding the battlefield and provoking great suffering among civilians. Their most effective strategy was to burn the cane fields to deprive the colonial government of sugar exports and hence food imports. Starving peasants poured into the cities, where the Spanish army rounded them up into concentration camps and some 170,000 Cubans (some ten percent of the island's population) perished. In the Philippines, General Polavieja employed many of the same tactics as his counterpart in Cuba,

General Weyler, although the scale of the human devastation never reached such genocidal proportions. One of the last actions of the Philippine War speaks volumes about its conduct, and foreshadowed Cold War conflicts in Vietnam, Indonesia, and Malaysia. In the historically conflictive Cordillera Central, the Spanish commander Eduardo Xandaró attacked the Igorot town of Sagada in July 1898 in search of *Katipunan* rebels hiding among the civilian population. He returned to his garrison with eighty-four heads.

The outcome of the Rif War (1921–27) also hinged on foreign intervention, although in the case of Morocco, the international scenario favored Spanish interests. European powers were eager to defeat Africa's first native-led war of independence in order to prevent a domino effect in the Islamic world. It was also a dirty war in which Spain became the first nation to employ chemical weapons against a civilian population. Ultimately, French intervention was determinative. In October 1925, the key battle at Al-Hoceima Bay featured the first amphibious tank landing in history. It took the form of a Blitzkreig attack reminiscent of the last offensives of the First World War and the first in the Second World War. The joint Hispano-French land campaign featured 90,000 men descending upon a Rif Army of 20,000. Only in 1927, after the last signs of resistance had been suppressed, did a significant number of Spanish migrants settle in the Protectorate.

The decisive role of foreign intervention in determining the outcomes of wars of independence in Cuba, the Philippines, and Morocco evidenced a broader phenomenon. In many instances, Spanish territorial claims depended on the permission, acquiescence, or agreements between greater powers. In the Philippines, for example, Britain permitted the annexation of the Sulu Islands in the 1870s, once the Foreign Office became worried that Germans were encroaching in the area. Spain attended the Congress of Berlin (1884–85), where European powers divided up Africa, as an observer rather than a participant. During the proceedings, Britain again supported Spanish claims to disputed territories (the Caroline Islands, the Western Sahara, the Muni River estuary) in order to counteract French and German ambitions in the zones. The geopolitical interests of Great Britain were also responsible for the promotion of Spanish ambitions in northern Morocco, given that London was not eager to have the French opposite them at the Strait of Gibraltar.

International pressures were also manifest during the process of postwar decolonization. In 1955, Spain gained admission to the United Nations. However, it was not a member of NATO, and it could never negotiate from a position of strength. In every respect, the decolonization of Morocco followed the French lead. The French-Moroccan agreement of March 1956 was followed by a Spanish-Moroccan agreement in May. The Kingdom of Morocco included the French protectorate and the Spanish northern zone. The cities of Ceuta and Melilla had never been integrated into the Protectorate, so they remained part of Spain. In November 1975, following the signing of another agreement in which Spain ceded the Western Sahara to Morocco, King Hassan announced that Ceuta and Melilla could remain Spanish as long as Gibraltar remained British. Today, calls to annex Gibraltar receive little echo in international circles given the existence of these Spanish cities in North Africa.

The 1956 agreement, however, did not include the enclave of Ifni and the Western Sahara. Although these territories had less symbolic value to the Franco regime than the Rif, the resolution of their future was more complicated. The city of Sid Ifni was like Ceuta and Melilla insofar as Europeans outnumbered natives. In October 1957, Moroccan troops invaded Ifni, sparking Spain's last colonial war. Moroccan objectives, however, were not limited to Ifni.

Rather, they included the entire Western Sahara and ultimately the territory to the south that later became Mauritania, then under French authority. For their part, the Sahrawi people wished to negotiate the formation of a separate state and strove to avoid being absorbed into a "Greater Morocco." With the aid of the French, the Spanish defeated Moroccan armies in 1958. Upon negotiating a peace, Ifni and the Western Sahara remained Spanish, although Morocco incorporated the sparsely populated southern zone of the Protectorate, the province of Tarfaya. In 1969, under mounting international pressure, Spain ceded Ifni to Morocco. The Franco regime maintained its authority in the Western Sahara to shield the Sahrawi people from Moroccan aggression, while also protecting Spanish mining concerns in phosphates.

The decolonization of Equatorial Guinea occurred in 1968. Many thought this would be any easy process since only 9,000 Europeans lived in the colony, the majority on Fernando Po. All the same, negotiations leading up to decolonization were complicated. The wealth of the colony meant that much was at stake. Equatorial Guinea had high levels of literacy, the highest per capita exports on the continent, and high per capita government spending. Another problem was that urban creoles and the minority Bubi and Ngowé ethnicities feared a government of the majority Fang. The presence of a dictatorship in the metropolis also complicated things. Spanish diplomats negotiated the writing of the constitution and the holding of a referendum and general elections behind closed doors in an attempt to shield information from Spaniards who were denied the same rights as the Guineans. In 1969, the fiery independence leader Francisco Macías won democratic elections, and he turned the republic into a brutal dictatorship. In 1979, dictator Teodoro Obiang (educated at the military academy of Zaragoza) led a coup d'état. At the present time, Equatorial Guinea is the richest country in Africa on a per capita basis due to its petroleum reserves, although it has one of the worst records on human rights and corruption. Spanish remains the official language.

Spain ceased to be an empire upon becoming a democracy. Six days before the death of Franco, on November 14, 1975, Spain signed the Tripartite Accords with Morocco and Mauritania. In return for lucrative fishing and phosphate concessions, Spain transferred the "administration" of the Western Sahara to the two African signatories on the understanding that they recognize the Sahrawi people's right to national self-determination. At the time, it was common knowledge that neither country had the intention of holding a referendum on independence. Spain had little room for maneuver given that Morocco had taken advantage of Franco's illness by invading the region two weeks *before* the signing of the Accords. One week before, the famous "Green March" took place. Some 350,000 Moroccan civilians carrying Korans and Green Flags (representative of *jihad*) poured into the Western Sahara. The United Nations also favored rapid decolonization, characteristically unconcerned with minority rights. Spain's abandonment led to the Western Sahara War (1975–91) between Morocco and the SADR (Sahrawi Arab Democratic Republic) and its Polisario liberation army. In addition to Moroccan objectives, Polisario guerillas also carried out attacks against Spanish mining interests and kidnapped Spanish fishing boats as bargaining chips.

Today, the United Nations Council on Human Rights estimates that more than 90,000 Sahrawian refugees live in camps in western Algeria and an additional 20,000 live in northern Mauritania. In 1976, the socialist leader Felipe González visited the camps in Tindouf Algeria, and, a year later, the PSOE and other leftist parties in Spain called for the repudiation of the Tripartite Accords. However, once in power, the PSOE disremembered these promises. The Constitution of 1978 did not include national self-determination for Basques and Catalans, so Spanish politicians were reluctant to recognize such a right for a minority in Morocco (or anywhere else for that matter). Moreover, the PSOE signed a number of agreements forging closer economic links with Morocco and tabling disputes over Ceuta and Melilla. If the brutal and corrupt dictatorship of Teodoro Obiang in Equatorial Guinea is a colonial legacy of Francoism, then the plight of the Sahrawian Refugees is one of the many stains on Spain's transition to democracy. In this respect, the Spanish experience of decolonization was much the same as imperialism. The historical record, though checkered, was altogether unexceptional.

Further reading

Balfour, Sebastian, *Deadly Embrace: Morocco and the Road to the Spanish Civil War*, Oxford: Oxford University Press, 2002.

Balfour, Sebastian, *The End of the Spanish Empire, 1898-1923*, Oxford: Clarendon Press, 1997.

Bergard, Laird W., *Cuban Rural Society in the Nineteenth Century: The Social and Economic History of Monoculture in Matanzas*, Princeton: Princeton University Press, 1990.

Casanovas, Joan, *Bread, or Bullets! Urban Labor and Spanish Colonialism in Cuba, 1850-1898*, Pittsburg: Pittsburg University Press, 1998.

Delgado, Josep M., "Eclipse and Collapse of the Spanish Empire, 1650-1898" in Alfred McCoy, Josep M. Fradera, and Stephen Jacobson (eds.), *Endless Empire: Spain's Retreat, Europe's Eclipse, and America's Decline*, Madison: University of Wisconsin Press, 2012, pp. 43–54.

Fradera, Josep M., and Christopher Schmidt-Nowara, *Slavery and Anti-Slavery in Spain's Atlantic Empire*, Oxford: Berghahn Books, 2013.

Garcia Balañà, Albert, "The Empire is No Longer a Social Unit: Declining Imperial Expectations and Transatlantic Crises in Metropolitan Spain, 1858-1909" in Alfred McCoy, Josep M. Fradera, and Stephen Jacobson (eds.), *Endless Empire: Spain's Retreat, Europe's Eclipse, and America's Decline*, Madison: University of Wisconsin Press, 2012, pp. 92–106.

de Jesus, Ed. C., *The Tobacco Monopoly in the Philippines: Bureaucratic Enterprise and Social Change, 1766-1880*, Manila: Ateneo de Manila University Press, 1980.

Legarda, Benito J., *After the Galleons: Foreign Trade, Economic Change and Entrepreneurship in the Nineteenth Century Philippines*, Manila: Ateneo de Manila University Press, 1999.

Rodrigo y Alharilla, Martín, "From Periphery to Centre: Transatlantic Capital Flows, 1830-1890," in A. B. Leonard, and David Pretel (eds.), *The Caribbean and the Atlantic World Economy: Circuits of Trade, Money and Knowledge, 1650-1914*, Basingstoke: Palgrave Macmillan, 2015, pp. 217–37.

Tone, John Lawrence, *War and Genocide in Cuba, 1895-1898*, Chapel Hill: University of North Carolina Press, 2006.

Warren, James Francis, *The Sulu Zone, 1768-1898*, Singapore: Singapore University Press, 1981.

Yun, Lisa, and Ricardo Rene Laremont, "Chinese Coolies and African Slaves in Cuba, 1847-74," *Journal of Asian American Studies*, 4, 2 (2001), pp. 99–122.

CHAPTER 14
THE ENVIRONMENT
Josefina Gómez de Mendoza

The environment of the Iberian Peninsula is characterized by a number of features: a substantial water scarcity occurs in most of the land due to the limited and variable rainfall; numerous mountain ranges limit all types of exchanges across boundaries; and great biodiversity and high quality of landscapes. The last two centuries have witnessed large hydroelectric developments and massive reforestation programs.

Following the crisis of 1898, Spanish elites became increasingly concerned with fully exploiting their country's natural resources by changing "the geography of the motherland." These policies focused primarily on interbasin water transfers, which benefited the most productive agricultural regions. In any case, it was during the Franco dictatorship when, due to a combination of authoritarianism and fast economic development, that most of the landscape transformations took place.

Conservation policies based on the American model of delineating national parks were launched in Spain in 1916, relatively early in relation to other European countries. Policy evolved throughout the twentieth century, with more attention paid to geology than to ecological diversity. In the early twenty-first century, more than one fourth of Spain is protected, partly due to the role of the regional governments, and it is the largest contributor of protected lands to the Natura network of the EU. Current problems focus on planning and management of the protected areas.

Intense urbanization and the abandoning of the rural areas due to depopulation took place later but more intensively than in other Western European countries. With the exception of Madrid, most urbanization took place in the coastal areas, and was associated with tourism development along the Mediterranean coast. The high rates of urban coastal development represent a threat to the conservation of natural resources, in particular of land, water, energy, and biodiversity. Overall, the natural environment of Spain has suffered greatly from the accelerated urban development, and the time has come to identify novel policies for the correct management of the present status.

Changes in the image of Spain's natural resources

The political and social crisis that took place in Spain in 1898 brought about a movement of profound national reform, known as "*Regeneracionismo*" (see Chapter 15) which included a change in the way Spaniards viewed the geography of their homeland. The long-standing positive view of Spain as a fertile and naturally well-endowed country (*Laudes Hispaniae*) was replaced by a negative and pessimistic one, emphasizing the poor soil quality of the Iberian Peninsula. Lucas Mellado's *The Ills of the Homeland* (1890), which claimed that 45 percent of the country's land was unproductive and only 10 percent fertile, is an outstanding example.

This "geographic" pessimism gave rise to a great volume of literature, but implicitly involved a program of reaction: as Segismundo Moret, minister of the interior, put it in 1883, "there is a need to redesign the geography of the country to resolve [simultaneously] the agricultural and social questions."

Two qualifications are necessary. First, such pessimism was not unique to Spain. Following its defeat by Prussia in 1870, France underwent a similar, albeit less acute, experience; the French Third Republic attempted to attenuate this dejection with an image of "*la terre nourricière*," of a balanced nature and a pleasant physiognomy that rose above any regional differences and provided the country with a national identity. Secondly, this pessimism was not shared in Catalonia; the geographic literature of the Catalonian *Renaixença* is much kinder in relation to the generosity of the land and the labor of its people.

Among all the negative factors, it was the country's relief, which hindered transport, and the uneven and irregular rainfall, which received most attention. Santiago Ramón y Cajal, who won the Noble prize for Physiology in 1906, said that "Spain is a vast stretch of sterile terrain surrounded by a narrow strip of fertile land."

Climate and orography account for the torrential nature of many of the rivers on the Iberian Peninsula, which eroded the soil, leaving slopes bare and giving rise to what was known at the turn of the century as an authentic "*mal de piedra*" (stone disease). If we add to this the deforestation resulting from abusive logging and numerous fires, one can understand why some authors got carried away, employing an exaggeratedly negative rhetoric, speaking of "the skeleton of the homeland." "Trees were felled to sow wheat, and now there is no wheat and hardly any trees," according to the writer Julio Senador in his book *Castilla en escombros* (the Rubble of Castile). This title may seem melodramatic, but it accurately reflects the environmental and social awareness of the middle classes, who were demanding that politicians address the situation.

If the fundamental problem was the aridity of Spain, the solution was irrigating the land and planting trees, making water and forests productive in order to promote the nation's wealth (as was said at the time) and to deal with poverty and with it the entire social situation.

Natural resources: Water and forests

A secular cycle of grandiose hydraulic policies

The obsession with water was deeply rooted in Spain and gave rise to the 1820 Draft Law on Roads and Canals of the Kingdom, which contains the famous declaration: "not one drop of water should go to the sea without paying the tribute it owes to the land." Mendizábal, the minister responsible for the 1837 disentailment (see chapters 3, 25), said something similar: "Spain will not be wealthy as long as the rivers flow into the sea." The 1866 and 1879 Water Laws established the principle that surface water was public property as well as the system for granting use rights to individuals.

The end of the century brought a new idea that the State now had the technical capacity, as well as the social and political motives, to carry out a vast hydraulic policy. Joaquín Costa, one of the most influential figures of the Regenerationist movement, submitted a program for agrarian development based on irrigation to the 1880 Congress of Agriculture: he proposed establishing "an arterial hydraulic system" throughout the country. In 1892 he summarized his program of regenerationist reforms "that expresses in figures the whole economic policy the country must follow in order to be redeemed" under the name of hydraulic policy. At the start of the twentieth century, when Rafael Gasset, a staunch pro-hydraulic development politician, took the post of minister of Agriculture, Industry, Commerce, and Public Works, a General Plan of Irrigation Channels and Reservoirs was set in motion (1902): the first of a series that would end with the General Plan of Hydraulic Works (GPHW), approved in 1933 during the Second Republic.

Prior to this, in 1926, the Hydrographic Syndicate Confederations (HSC) (Confederaciones Sindicales Hidrográficas) had been set up in large river basins, a pioneer experience in Europe, patterned on similar water agencies such as the Tennessee Valley Authority. These regionally based public corporations with some autonomy from the Government integrated the agricultural, industrial, and energy interests existing in the Spanish parts of a river basin— the Portuguese areas were not included. This entailed a pact among the sectorial interests of the territory. The HSC, which still exist, have the autonomy to plan and manage the basins. Ramón y Cajal expressed the trust placed in the hydraulic regeneration by comparing it to a national education program: "To intensely cultivate the barren terrain of our land and of our minds, saving it for the prosperity and progress of the nation, all the rivers that are lost to the sea, all the talent that is lost to ignorance."

This early twentieth-century program of hydraulic regeneration had three important features. The first one involved a conception of economy of nature: there was an unequivocal attempt to develop and intensify croplands while respecting the natural order of the land use (for instance, forested areas should not be cleared). This, therefore, is a vision closer to the philosophies defending the harmonies of nature, a natural order that includes humans, rather than a view based upon ecological balance, a more dynamic concept that refers to the balance in relations between living beings and their environment. In the nineteenth century, numerous naturalist scientists were determined to recognize, systematize, and map nature's elements, but it was not until the first decade of the twentieth century when ecological science was initiated in Spain.

This respect for natural order brought about an initial disagreement among forestry engineers regarding the order of priorities. While the foresters maintained that there was first a need to reforest the mountain headwaters of the rivers in order to prevent the reservoirs from filling up with earth, the civil engineers defended the urgent need to build dams. Gasset put an end to this argument by stating that pressing social needs—hunger in the countryside—could not wait for reforestation, a period he termed "geological time."

The third question related to the territorial and regional options of the water policy, and the possibility of a plan for the whole national territory. In the 1902 Plan, the reservoirs were selected on the basis of cost in relation to irrigable area. This meant giving priority to the Peninsula's inland environments, the two Castiles and Aragon, which had the most extensive irrigable areas, to the detriment of the eastern coastal environments, which were smaller but more efficient. As has been stated, the creation of the HSC intended to provide a regional solution, although in reality, the only operational one before the Civil War was in the Ebro valley. The 1933 National Plan of Hydraulic Works recovered the unitary and national character of the hydraulic policy, but tended to favor the Mediterranean, as this was the classical irrigation area and presented greater potential for production. This was immediately criticized as not truly national, but rather "only Mediterranean."

Unlike other areas of economic activity, during the Franco dictatorship there was no slowdown or interruption in developing new water supplies. On the contrary, the 1940 National Plan of Hydraulic Works (NPHW), which resuscitated the republican projects (perhaps without all their social, ethical, or pre-ecological drive), was in force up to 1985. It established an ambitious three-phase plan that gave priority to the construction of reservoirs for electric power and irrigation. The results were spectacular. The second half of the century saw the construction of reservoirs on the headwaters of the Peninsula's big rivers, the Ebro, the Duero, the Tagus, and the Guadiana. In 1933, there were 187 dams; the number had increased to 267 in 1950; and in 2015 there were 1,200 dams, 350 of which are large reservoirs mostly for irrigation and hydroelectric production.

A total of 1.23 million hectares of Spain's land was irrigated in 1900; by the early twenty-first century, this had increased to 3.7 million hectares, which represents 7.4 percent of the total area. One-third of this corresponds to historical irrigation systems; another third is the result of the hydraulic works conducted mainly in the second half of the twentieth century. The remaining third corresponds to private property irrigated with groundwater, with overexploitation in the cases where extractions exceed the sustainable recharge. Extraction of water from aquifers has increased tenfold throughout the twentieth century, and over 75 percent of this water has been used for irrigation. Due to the magnitude and scope of the irrigation modernization programs, Spain is now being compared to Israel, as it is the second country in the world with the highest proportion of its irrigated area devoted to drip irrigation. The environmental effects of hydraulic works—sediment deposits, nonpoint pollution, erosion of river beds, transformation of riparian vegetation, impacts in the landscape—have not been sufficiently studied, but there has been even less research on the social impacts of the relocation of local populations from the areas to be flooded by reservoir construction with minimum financial compensations under Franco's authoritarian regime.

Forests: Public property and mass reforestation

Modifications to forests and their uses have also had a huge environmental impact on the Iberian Peninsula. Following the 1855 civil disentailment (a belated Spanish version of the enclosure of common land), State's forestry engineers fought to prevent the sale of the most valuable forested areas to private individuals who intended to use it for logging. They believed in the ecological ("cosmological" was the term used at the time) function of forests, above all in relation to hydrologic functions. In order to prevent the sale of forests, they created the Catalogue of Public Utility Forests (PUF). The Catalogue did not include surfaces with holm oak and cork oak, and therefore the *dehesas*, or open woodlands (mostly of communal or municipal ownership), were not protected from sale to private individuals. The importance of this measure may be perceived from the fact that today most of the protected land is currently classified as PUF.

The second half of the twentieth century was also a significant period of reforestation. During the Second Republic (1931–36) a law on State Forest Heritage (*Patrimonio Forestal del Estado or*—PFE) was enacted, not only for protection, but also for production, and was based on planting of short-rotation species. As in the case of hydraulics, the Franco dictatorship continued, and even extended, the Republican initiative, and in 1939 a Reforestation Plan was approved. After the Civil War, the plan included a provision for the reforestation of six million hectares, both for protection and for production. Thus, the PFE initiated an intense reforestation process which in many cases astonished the FAO: over three million hectares were reforested from the 1940s to the 1970s, at an average rate of 100,000 hectares per year.

The result was dramatic ecosystem changes with landscape alterations and significant socioeconomic repercussions. Assigning large areas for reforestation contributed to the eviction of the inhabitants of villages flooded for the construction of reservoirs. Sometimes these processes reinforced each other. In the reforestation process of the 1940s and 1950s, quantity prevailed over quality; it was a real "crusade" or "national reconquest," in the highly ideological words of the time.

Hydrological-forestry objectives clearly underlay most reforestations in inland, Mediterranean, and southern Spain where, in most cases, medium—or slow—growth pines were used, which shows that at least at the start, short-term timber production was not intended. On the contrary, in Spain's Atlantic and Cantabrian mountains and on the coasts, fast-growth species, such as eucalyptus, for the production of timber and cellulose were preferred. This contradiction, which has been denounced by scientists and environmentalists since the 1980s, had quite an effect upon public opinion. In 1991, surprisingly, the SFH and the State Forest Management Authority were consolidated into the Institute for Nature Conservation (ICONA): in other words, the organism in charge of reforestation came to manage conservation—clearly a sign of change. ICONA operated until 1991, when its forests came under the jurisdiction of the regional governments.

Evolution toward criteria of sustainability and resource management

Reservoirs and pine forests constituted two major instruments of development of the Franco era and are part of its legacy. However, starting in the 1980s, the spread of ecological ideas led to the questioning of both hydraulic and forestry policies. Post-Franco democratic governments reduced the predominant role of the State, which characterized the Franco period. The 1987 Bruntland Report on sustainable development commissioned by the United Nations called for more conscious resource management. As has been said, this change of direction is perhaps initially more evident in forestry, as criticism grew of this prodigious reforestation, which on the other hand had not been totally mindful of the diversity of environments or of the dynamics of ecosystems. Moreover, restrictions were placed upon public-use forest lands, without affecting private forests—the vast majority—whose "Protection Forests" (the equivalent of the MUP under private ownership) have not really been classified.

Reforestation today has little to do with the old regenerationist dream of replanting the mountains as natural environments belonging to that "forest region" within the territorial order that was believed to adapt to the laws of nature. Nowadays the aim is to sustainably manage vulnerable areas and species suffering from poor management. Forest fires have become one of the biggest problems, as well as the context in which the planet's tensions have been expressed. Perhaps these fires are not more numerous, but they are much bigger as a result of rural depopulation and nature tourism, which attracts city people who are quite unaware of the risks or the delicate balances involved within the forests. As for reforestation, the situation has been inverted: for instance, in the replanting of agricultural lands, implemented as one of the measures of the EU's Common Agricultural Policy, it is precisely the abandoned croplands that are planted.

The regulatory framework has also changed. The first Forestry Law of the democracy came in 2003, replacing the Franco's regime's. On paper, it promoted the principle established by the United Nations in 1997, that forests form part of the concept of sustainable development and that there is therefore a need to ensure their conservation, protection, restoration, and enhancement, and to comply with their multiple environmental, economic, and social functions. In 2006, a specific reform of the law prevented reclassification of forests that had been burned as urban land for development until a period of thirty years had elapsed. In 2015, a conservative government once again included in the law exceptions to this prohibition based on "urgent necessity" (another opportunity for corruption), which has drawn much criticism from environmentalists, who claim that the new law is insufficiently protective of the environment and that it conceals speculative interests.

The last few decades of the twentieth century also saw the emergence of a critique of long-standing ideas about water, a topic that has always constituted good politics, that is, worthy of being promoted by the State, regardless of the cost. It has been shown that infrastructure built with public money has provided cheap and abundant water to certain social and economic groups in specific territories and that huge amounts of water and financial resources have been transferred to landowners in certain areas. Moreover, the system of concessions for agricultural purposes is much more opaque than for urban and residential use.

The 1985 Water Law (which substituted the hundred-year-old 1879 Law) brought a change, albeit timid, in the basic philosophy. Based on a consideration of water as a scarce resource, current policy focuses on rationalizing use and management in relation to the environment, and attempting to meet demand rather than increasing supply, as had occurred up to the end of the last century. Furthermore, the public domain was extended to include groundwater resources as well as surface waters.

Since then, legislation and planning initiatives have reflected changing parliamentary majorities, and the lack of a long-term water policy. European Union policies, such as the Water Framework Directive (2000), a real milestone in resource planning in that it prioritized the good ecological condition of waters, as well as respect for environmental flows, have also had an impact. One recurring issue has been the "water wars" between regions providing water, such as Castilla-La Mancha and Aragon, and those receiving it, such as Catalonia, Murcia, and Valencia. In 2001, a conservative government promulgated a National Hydrological Plan that continued these transfers, but they stopped in 2005 due to the new socialist administration, which invoked the EU directive's principle that prior to any transfer, there was a need to optimize resources in each basin and to sustain flows to guarantee water quality. Since returning to power in 2011, the conservatives have restored the transfers while using the habitual environmental rhetoric. One thing has become clear: it is not possible to equate the old philosophy of the water agencies (confederations) for an agreement on production and use with the Integral Basin Management that the EU directive foresees. Indeed, this was drawn up with a focus on central and northern Europe, and it ignores critical issues, which are specific to southern Europe, such as drought management and the realities of water conservation under water scarcity. In any case, one thing is becoming increasingly obvious on observing the study of this secular cycle: we need to learn how to cope with water scarcity, combining emerging technologies with socioeconomic and institutional measures specifically adapted to the Spanish situation and with a long-term view.

Protected Natural Areas

Nature conservation: From alpine mountains to biodiversity

Spain is a country of great environmental and landscape variety, containing four of the nine terrestrial biogeographic regions and three of the five marine regions of the European Union. Over a quarter of its surface area—27.2 percent—is protected by one or another category of Protected Natural Areas (PNA), and Spain is the country that provided the biggest area to the EU's Natura 2000 network of core breeding and resting sites for rare and threatened species, and some rare natural habitat types, 18.9 percent of the total. Spain's history of conservation began early, as will be seen, but declarations intensified in the last third of the twentieth century, as the governments of the autonomous regions created by the Constitution of 1978 became involved and the PNA regional networks were created. Marine protection took much longer, but in the last few years, 29 Special Protection Areas for Birds (SPA) as well as ten Sites of Community Interest (SIC) have been designated. Conservation criteria have varied throughout the last century, and the Spanish PNA catalogue, in particular for National Parks, clearly reflects these changes and, consequently, the history of conservation in Spain. Initially, greater attention was paid to protecting high-mountain areas, but at the end of the twentieth century, criteria almost exclusively referred to biodiversity.

Conservation began in Spain in 1911 and was closely associated with protecting national monuments. The National Parks Law of 1916 was based on the US model of national parks and two years later the first two parks: Covadonga in the Cantabrian mountains, and Ordesa in the Pyrenees in Aragon, were created. In accordance with the American criteria, these parks were conceived as spatial reserves in which exploitation was prohibited or restricted in order to preserve and make known, in the words of the law, "the natural beauty of their landscapes, the wealth of their fauna and flora and their geological and hydrological particularities." Uses were thus limited to culture, recreation, and pedagogy which, from the start, involved problems with private owners and pointed to the need to acquire public lands.

During a brief second stage, from the 1920s to the beginning of the Civil War, it was decided to forego creating any more parks in favor of smaller "Sites of National Interest," which came to some Mediterranean and coastal areas, although not as yet on biological grounds. It was not until the 1950s that any more national parks were established: two volcanic parks in the Canary Islands, Teide on the island of Tenerife and Taburiente on La Palma island in 1954. A third, Timanfaya on Lanzarote, was added in 1974. Meanwhile, in 1955 another mountain park was incorporated, Aigües Tortes y Lago de San Mauricio, in the Pyrenees of Catalonia. The first wetlands parks came later: Doñana in Western Andalusia in 1969 and the Tablas de Daimiel, a continental wetland in La Mancha in 1973.

Atlantic mountains and forests were protected in Spain prior to the wet and Mediterranean environments, or to put it another way, geological and forestry criteria outweighed biological or ecosystemic ones. I believe that this preference is explained both by the inherited romantic conception of nature and its archetypal landscapes, and by identity-related and patriotic sentiments.

The first National Parks (1918): Nature, education, and patriotism

The appreciation for landscapes was introduced into Western culture by late-eighteenth- and early-nineteenth-century Romanticism. The Romantic conception of landscape involves an aesthetic experience as part of knowledge. The geographer Alexander von Humboldt, one of the great theoreticians of the concept of aesthetic mediation of knowledge, wrote that humankind and nature could not be conceived as separate realities: "The external physical world is reflected as in a mirror in the moral interior world."

The modern experience of nature comes from unique, demarcated landscapes, above all the mountain summit and the primeval forest. Nobody put it better than Jean-Jacques Rousseau: "No plains, however beautiful, ever seem that way to me. I need torrents, rocks, fir trees, black forests, mountains, difficult paths to follow; I need to pass along terrifying precipices." Notwithstanding the literary differences in quality, the Marquis of Pidal, promoter of the Spanish national parks stated: "A landscape without trees, apart from ugly, is uninteresting." Geology, forests, and abysses are therefore the principal forms of romantic sensibility.

This Romantic conception of nature and knowledge of one's own landscapes took time to spread throughout Spain in the nineteenth century, but in the last third of the century, two related events contributed to a more rapid appreciation of Spain's landscapes and to attributing educational and regenerating qualities to them. In the first place, philosophy of nature, quite unknown at the time, was incorporated into Spanish thought by the Krausists and the *Institución Libre de Enseñanza* (ILE) (Free Institution of Teaching), which was established in 1876 (see Chapter 16). The ILE made education one of the bases of the regeneration needed by Spain, and it placed direct contact with nature at the center of its educational project. The "institutionalists" contributed greatly to modernizing the cultural appreciation of Spanish landscapes. In his article "Landscape" (1886), Francisco Giner de los Ríos, one of the founders of the ILE, as well as its principal promoter, exalted "the purifying contact of nature"; in the same article he was quick to defend what he called "geological aesthetics" as, according to him, "all landscape is geology." José Ortega y Gasset (see Chapter 32) would also evoke landscape's educational dimension years later by stating: "Landscape is a pedagogue."

The second event was the emergence of identity-based national regeneration movements, especially the *Renaixença* in Catalonia (see Chapter 10). Landscape took on an historical significance, thereby enhancing its cultural value. For Catalan cultural nationalists, Montserrat was the very symbol of the nation. "The mountain of Montserrat means the Catalan nation" wrote Victor Balaguer. Many mountain regions gained prestige on being considered as a Spanish (or Catalonian or Valencian) Switzerland. To put it another way: while Spanish landscapes were identified and valued, a tacit acceptance arose with regard to reserving the category of "national interest" for those landscapes that were most comparable with the European ones–mountainous landscapes.

Covadonga and Ordesa complied with all the prerequisites: a park in the mountains and another in a valley, said the promoters. The only European precedents were those of the League of Picturesque Germany and the Engadin and Gran Paradiso parks in Switzerland, "fragments of the alpine heart of the homeland," hunting reserves rather than territorial ones. The promoter of Spain's first national park was an aristocrat, a great hunter and a mediocre politician, Pedro Pidal, the Marquis of Villaviciosa de Asturias.

The opening of the Covadonga park was made to coincide with the anniversary of the battle of Covadonga (722 CE), which in traditional historiography was considered to constitute the first act of the "Reconquest" of Spain from the Arabs. But Covadonga and Ordesa were also the preferred places of the romantic naturalist discovery, and of mountain climbing. The parks complemented each other: Covadonga, a mountain park, with summits delimited by deep ravines whose greatest feature is the imposing high-mountain limestone rock formation; Ordesa a valley park, carved by two glaciers, majestic and serene, where forest and rock alternate in perfect harmony: this was how they were described when they were declared as national parks. "Authentic sanctuaries of nature," said Pidal: "Doesn't art have its sanctuaries? Why shouldn't there be sanctuaries for nature?"

As has been pointed out, the early declaration of national parks in the United States involved love of nature, exaltation of the fatherland and religion. In his book called *Les figures paysagères de la nation* (the nation's landscape figures), François Walter (2004) shows the extent to which the images of the landscape and the references to it were widely mobilized throughout Europe in order to construct national identities. Unlike parks in the United States, which did serve as models, but in which the concept of wilderness predominated, in Europe nature was rarely separated from its aesthetic, ethical, historical, and patriotic aspects. Thus, at the start of the twentieth century, a museum-like concept of nature was applied that classified monuments and natural sites according to the model of architectural monuments, in accordance with the laws on historical heritage and protection of artistic wealth. The creation of the first national parks (Sweden 1909, Switzerland 1914 and Spain 1918) was thus justified by the patriotic dimension. Covadonga, the "cradle of the Spanish nation," responded in this way, according to the authorities at the time, to a simultaneous work of science, education, and patriotism. Thus, landscape and environment constitute effective instruments for creating heritage. This is seen in the zoning process, the demarcation of reserves, provided these do not conflict with ownership rights. The initial nature conservation policy we have just summarized therefore simultaneously contains elements of modernity and of stale tradition. These contradictions are well reflected in a phrase by the Marquis of Villaviciosa: "Giner de los Ríos, the pedagogue, used to take his pupils to the Picos de Europa mountains. King Alfonso XIII, the politician, set an example for the Spanish people by visiting the Gredos mountains. The archbishop of Tarragona showed the people of Aragon the way to the Ordesa valley, which he visited. Pedagogy, Politics and Religion are in harmony."

The slow road toward ecosystemic representativeness

The reason why no new parks were created between 1918 and 1954 is related to conflicts over land ownership. Indeed, from the political and legal perspectives, the owners of the land included in the park have always been reluctant to accept the restrictions involved; in the case of Covadonga (which has greatly extended and is now called Picos de Europa) there has been, and still is, resistance.

During the 1920s and the Second Republic (1931–39), the scientist, geologist, and geographer Eduardo Hernández-Pacheco (for the first time, not a politician) was in charge of managing the Parks Department. He preferred to diversify conservation, making it more representative of the country's ecological and landscape diversity. Additionally, he defended park management by the State, accessibility for respectful tourism, promotion of the wealth of the populations included, and dissemination of culture, all of this while respecting owners' rights. In order to enhance diversity in the protected areas, he preferred to create Natural Sites of National Interest, smaller reserves subjected to fewer restrictions. Around twenty Sites were declared of national interest prior to 1936: mountains continued to predominate but large karstic landscapes, those formed by the dissolution of rocks such as limestone and offering featuring caves, such as the Ciudad Encantada in Cuenca, were included. So were lagoons and the "residual botanic formation" of the Palmeral in Elche.

Particularly noteworthy is the case of the Guadarrama Mountains, in the Iberian Central Range just north of Madrid. The landscapes of Guadarrama were a particular favorite of the members of the ILE and in 1886 they founded the Society for the Study of Guadarrama, to which geologists, botanists, zoologists, and geographers belonged. Guadarrama became the place of choice for the Institution's pedagogic and reformist project. If this area was not declared a national park in the first few decades of the nineteenth century, it is doubtlessly because there was a preference for the parks in the north of the Peninsula, for the aforementioned reasons. In the 1920s, when the time seemed to have arrived, ownership-related issues prevented integral protection, which was limited to the handful of sites considered to be of greatest interest. Guadarrama would be declared a National park only in the early years of the twenty-first century.

When the process of creating national parks resumed in the 1950s, it was oriented in a totally different manner. The 1957 Forest Law put the parks under the jurisdiction of the forestry administration, the so-called Council for River Fishing, Hunting and National Parks. And as this was a moment at which tourism was becoming more important, the Ministry of Tourism assumed an increasing level of influence. As has been mentioned, in 1954 the first two volcano parks were declared in the Canary Isles, due to their touristic and morphological values; the Taburiente Park followed them on Fuerteventura Island in 1974. In 1955, the Aigües Tortes y Lago de San Mauricio Park completed this trio of mountain parks, in this case due to its granite structure. The Mediterranean mid-mountain remained unclassified, and Doñana park, was not declared until 1969, and Tablas de Daimiel, a continental wetland, until 1973. Doñana, in southwestern Spain, one of Europe's first biological reserves, was made a national park in 1969. As far back as 1910, two British hunters, Abel Chapman and Walter Buck, contributed to the myth of the locale with their book *Unexplored Spain* (1910). In this frontier world, they exalted the exoticism of its African nature, the splendor of its sterility, its lovely desolate landscapes and its oases. The long delay in making it a national park was due to the priority given to the alpine stereotypes, and to the fact that it was considered to constitute an unhealthy landscape. From the hygienist and colonizing points of view prevailing at the time, it would have been more valuable to drain it and put the land to productive uses. Projects for draining marshes began in the middle of the eighteenth century and continued for two hundred years. They were associated with initiatives for the eradication of malaria, but also involved agrarian reform, and were generally supported by the local population, healthcare officials and, subsequently, tourism promoters. The following is an interesting example of the contradictions arising in environmental policy: in 1918, the same year in which the first two national parks were created, the Law on Draining of Lagoons, Marshes, and Swamps was promulgated. Doñana had been subjected for a long time to damaging actions from the ecological point of view. Decisions regarding this great Andalusian park were slow, and it became necessary for the highest European authorities to join forces with Spanish ornithologists and zoologists. In the 1950s, the zoologist Francisco Bernis pioneered the protection of Doñana's true values, and opposed reforestation with exotic species, demanding drastic changes in protection policies. Doñana was saved, but other significant lagoons, such as Antela in Ourense, La Janda in Cadiz, or la Nava in Palencia, were not.

Natural heritage, biodiversity, and regional PNA networks

The 1975 Law on Protected Natural Areas entirely modified the definition of PNA, establishing "the existence of primal ecosystems that have not been substantially altered by human penetration, exploitation or occupation" as a prerequisite. This clearly biology-based inflexion was confirmed by the Law on Protected Natural Areas and Wild Flora and Fauna (1989), which established ecosystemic representativeness as a classification criterion and which heralded the decentralization of the network, promoting the status of Regional Nature Park (RNP) as being governed by the regional authorities. The biological National Parks of this generation are the subtropical *laurisilva* forests in Garajonay Park on la Gomera island (1981); the Cabrera archipelago (1991) as an example of a marine ecosystem, and Cabañeros Park (1995) in Toledo and Ciudad Real, representing (at last) Mediterranean ecosystems. In recent years, the size of some parks has been considerably enlarged, for instance, Picos de Europa Park (previously known as Covadonga and changed to avoid the patriotic connotation) and Ordesa y Monte Perdido. In 1999, the Sierra Nevada National Park was declared, Andalucia's first mountain National Park; the process involved conflicts relating to competencies between the Andalusia regional government and the State. To date, the regional governments have shown different kinds of attitudes and sensitivity in relation to PNA's. But, as a whole, it should be pointed out that the area classified as protected has been greatly enlarged, to over four million hectares, with a predicted area of six and a half million hectares, 12.5 percent of the country's territory. Some regions, such as Andalucia, under the auspices of European regulations, plan to declare up to 25 percent of their territory as Sites of Community Interest. The general criteria involve biodiversity and sustainable development, but also territorial identity and construction of regional landscape identity. Many sites and monuments have been transformed into RNP and Natural Sites of National Interest, and all the national parks have a pre-park perimeter falling within the jurisdiction of the regional authorities. In response to international provisions aimed at preventing loss of diversity, in 2007 Spain promulgated the Natural Heritage and Biodiversity Law, explicitly intended to maintain essential ecological processes and basic vital systems, to conserve biodiversity and geodiversity, to secure resource sustainability, to inform citizens, and above all, to ensure that environmental law prevails over territorial or sectorial law. The law still mentioned the "beauty of landscapes," but it has joined the European Landscape Convention promoted by the Council of Europe, which defines landscape as "part of the land, as perceived by local people or visitors, which evolves through time as a result of being acted upon by natural forces and human beings." Everything can be a landscape, not only outstanding ones; they are simultaneously natural and cultural, and peoples' perception is an important factor. Meanwhile, two more episodes should be added to this history of the first few decades of the twenty-first century. On the one hand, in 2014 a new National Parks Law was passed, which undoubtedly brings order, but also introduces some exceptions to the prohibition on providing land for urban development inside some parks. On the other hand, two more parks have been included in the National Network, which currently comprises fifteen. First, the National Park of Monfragüe (2007), which is the first one in Extremadura and was included due to its Mediterranean forests and its *dehesas*. Secondly, the Cumbres (Summits) del Guadarrama National Park (2013), whose adhesion fulfilled the dream of the members of the ILE and of the opinion of most intellectuals. Conceived almost one century before, in the years of rapid economic growth, it was subjected to development for urbanization and winter sports.

The urban environment

Spain's population became much more highly urbanized over the course of the twentieth century. While in 1900 only 32 percent of the people lived in towns of over 10,000 inhabitants, by 2000 this figure had risen to over 76 percent. Throughout the century, Spain's population increased by twenty-two million inhabitants, eighteen million of which have become concentrated in cities with populations of over 50,000 inhabitants. This process was based upon a system of towns that were already consolidated half-way through the last century and which generally belonged to a model of compact Mediterranean cities; these were historical towns which, until the middle of the nineteenth century, were surrounded by city walls; nineteenth-century planned expansions; and as a final element, working-class suburbs that grew along roads. In the second half of the twentieth century, Spanish cities acquired very different layouts, with the appearance of large peripheral and metropolitan areas and a rapid process of urban sprawl.

Urbanization was accompanied by processes of declining population in many provinces, largely due to migration to industrial cities, and especially Madrid, Barcelona, and Bilbao (see Chapter 19). In addition, there has been a spectacular increase in the populations on the coast, and any map therefore shows this greater demographic density along Spain's 10,000 km of coastline, above all on the Mediterranean coasts and the islands. Apart from other factors, this growth is undoubtedly the result of sun and sand tourism, which continues to be the dominant modality in Spain.

Hygienist town planning: Internal reform extensions and outskirts

At the start of the nineteenth century, Spain's cities were still enclosed within their city walls and were quite unhealthy. As the population grew, cities became crowded, extending along a tortuous labyrinth of an urban layout, with narrow, badly ventilated streets and no sanitation infrastructure with garbage accumulating in the streets. The housing problem was dire, due to a lack of land, much of which belonged to nobles and the Church estate, and which was off the market. All the testimonies coincide. For example, in 1860, Ildefonso Cerdá, one of the founders of modern town planning and inventor of the word urbanism, described Madrid as "a labyrinth, with narrow, tortuous, unhealthy, winding streets that, in some parts were inaccessible, even on foot."

In these conditions, the Development Ministry at the time, with its corps of civil engineers, and the big city councils, with their architects, urgently addressed the question urban renovation. This model was based on Baron Hausmann's opening of wide streets (percées) in Paris, although Spanish town planners were careful to insist that dwellings could not be demolished without rehousing the population in dignified accommodation. In 1861, a draft law appeared for the "Renovation, Sanitation, Expansion and other improvements" for the population: a global conception that considered both the existing city and the expansions thereof, as well as the services required. For the old part of the cities, planners considered draining of land, suppression of unhealthy accommodation or neighborhoods, construction of drainage systems, and ventilation for blocks of houses.

Priorities in Spain, however, were very different. Urban expansions, known in Spain as *ensanches*, got priority over reform works in historic cities. There was a lack of public funding, and the new private investors preferred to invest in the new city. The law passed in 1864 was now only a Law on City Expansion. Under the auspices of this law, many cities were enlarged, most notably, Cerdá's Barcelona Ensanche, one of masterpieces of modern town planning, the more modest Madrid Expansion, and that of Bilbao. But the reality differed greatly from the liberal idea of the expansion, which was conceived as a way of relieving the crowding of the old town centers, as well as a more egalitarian and balanced town-planning model. Cerdá himself drew up an economic project that involved charging property gains taxes for town-planning uses but it was never carried into effect.

In the last third of the nineteenth century and the first third of the twentieth, landowners retained land in the new *ensanches* for speculation: it took a long time for it to be occupied, and this process was partial and oriented. All this did not help to improve the situation of the historical town centers. On the other hand, peripheral land was used to house the new, immigrant population; these were the so-called outskirts, extensions for housing for low income population, spaces with absolutely no respect for town-planning regulations, growing in synch with demand, usually following the roads exiting the city, without restrictions and occupied by cheap housing for workers.

All this did little to relieve problems of overcrowding and disease. Madrid was not equipped with public service water until 1858, when Queen Isabel II inaugurated a canal, a first result of a dramatic public work of canalization of mountain waters. In 1899, an official report described horrendous scenes of misery and deprivation in Madrid, with the working classes struggling for survival, a situation that was potentially explosive. Mortality rates in the big cities were estimated at 40 per thousand, and there were repeated—and lethal—epidemics, especially of cholera, which was always more frequent in poor neighborhoods than in the middle-class areas. The year 1895 saw the appearance of the law on Sanitation and Internal Enhancement of Big Cities. Projects at the end of the century therefore hailed back to the start of the century: demolishing substandard housing, building large roads, ensuring water supply to houses, building pavements and drainage systems, improving the railway network, and building ring roads and boulevards. It was only in the first third of the twentieth century, with the approval of the 1924 Municipal Statute, that the councils were able to implement these reforms.

Urban sprawl: The environmental problems of the diffuse city

Spanish cities changed significantly over the course of the nineteenth century; they changed even further during the twentieth century, and especially during the second half of the century when urbanization intensified in a belated process similar to other parts of Europe (see Chapter 19). By the 1970s, city centers became demographically stagnant, whereas their metropolitan and regional areas grew. It was at this time that the Spain's urban model started to undergo a change: from the compact Mediterranean city, comprising complex quarters for residential use that were functionally mixed and stable, to an abrupt shift to the diffuse city, to an urban explosion involving low-density urban single-family units, connected by an extensive network of roads for motorized traffic. In a certain manner, it was a copy of the British or American model in a country with very little experience of single-family housing units located far from the center. The new model is therefore based on automobiles, on single-family houses, and on mortgages, in an economic model entailing easy bank loans, traffic, low interest rates, all of which promoted the economic bonanza from the 1990s to 2008, and which involved astronomical private indebtedness. In these years, there was a high level of urbanization, but little good town planning.

There has been a sustained and irreversible process of creating what geographers call artificial land. Between 1987 and 2006, artificial land urban housing, industrial zones, shopping centers, roads, etc., has increased by 51.7 percent, from 1.3 percent of the territory to over 2 percent. According to the *Atlas of Urban Areas in Spain*, the 79 cities with populations of over 100,000 inhabitants have shown an increase in artificial land of 43.7 percent in the last nineteen years, well above the 15 percent increase in population. This is highly significant and expresses the change in the territorial model of urban areas: there has been a much greater increase in houses built than the rate at which the population has increased, in some cases, from twice as much to fourfold. Some of the numbers are staggering: the increase in the new average annual artificial area is 27,666 ha/year (i.e., 76 ha per day) and, taking 2005 as the reference, the years 2000–05 saw 15 percent of all construction in the country's history.

The most intense relative growth rates were in the metropolitan areas of Madrid, along the radial motorway network and the ring roads, with the incorporation of some of the nearby provincial capitals. On the coast, the rate of construction quadrupled between 1987–2000 and 2000–05. In less than one generation, almost half the Mediterranean coast (43 percent) has become artificial. Since the crisis, which began in 2008, and the bursting of the real estate bubble, there has been a notable slowdown in construction, but the effects thereof are clearly visible.

This intense occupation of the territory for residential uses has had environmental, economic, social, territorial, urban, and landscape-related consequences. From the economic and social perspectives, the territorial model of extensive occupation favors fragmentation and segregation and loss of social cohesion. But above all, these processes of low-density dispersal occupation of the territory in the urban, metropolitan, periurban, and tourist areas involve an exponential increase in mobility, mostly involving private automobiles, with the resulting construction of new transport infrastructures, generally high-speed and oversized, almost always at the expense of the taxpayer; there is also a greater need for facilities and services.

This diffuse development and the resulting oversized road networks also have numerous negative environmental effects: loss of biodiversity, barriers preventing circulation of species, destruction of habitats and ecological corridors, loss of accessibility to fragments of habitat and of territory. This is all highlighted by studies investigating indices of connectivity and fragmentation. This kind of development also involves the waterproofing and sealing of enormous areas of land, which distorts the hydric cycle and involves waste of water and energy. The urban structure and its buildings are big consumers of energy and water and cause big emissions of carbon dioxide.

Let us add to all this insularization of our natural areas. Naredo (2010) put it graphically: "The sea of more or less natural rurality that still existed in the 1950s and which contained some urban islands, has become a metropolitan sea in which a few islets of nature survive, and are generally submitted to some status of protection."

There has also been an important collateral effect. Cities constitute one of the greatest heritages we possess. Together with the process that has urbanized, rather than create cities (with social life in the streets, mixed functions, public open spaces, and social cohesion), historic city centers have experienced two other processes: first, gentrification, and then a tourist explosion in historical and monumental areas, which are in danger of becoming theme parks for foreigners. The emergence of web-based services such as Air BnB has exacerbated this problem, especially in Barcelona.

It is true that in recent years environmental consumption has been partly reversed or at least has stabilized (partly as a consequence of the financial crisis of 2008): for instance there has been a drop in average water use and in the production of garbage, along with an increase in the facilities for the mechanical and biological treatment thereof. It is also true that public and citizen strategies are now more careful, and that the indicators of all the environmental rates used for cities have been multiplied and perfected in relation to the initial formulations, such as carrying capacity and growth limitations. The annual editions of the *Environmental Profile of Spain* edited by the environmental public administration highlight this. But, as the European Union warns, there are time lags between a decrease in pressure and the reflection thereof upon the environment. It does not bode well that in Spain, as the economy is just getting back on its feet (although the crisis is not yet over), the building industry is resuming its activity again without guarantees of sustainability.

Further reading

Burriel, Eugenio L., "Empty Urbanism: The Bursting of the Spanish Housing Bubble," *Urban Research & Practice*, 9, 2 (2016), pp. 158–80.

Garrido, Alberto, and M. Ramon Llamas, *Water Policy in Spain*, London: CRC Press, 2009.

Gómez Mendoza, Josefina, and Nicolás Ortega Cantero, "Interplay of State and Local Concern in the Management of Natural Resources: Hydraulics and Forestry in Spain (1855-1936)" in Anne Buttimer, and L. Wallin (eds.), *Nature, Culture, Identity*, Netherlands: Kluwer Academic Publishers, 1999, pp. 137–44.

Gómez Mendoza, Josefina, "The persistence of Romantic Ideas and the Origin of Natural Park Policy in Spain," *Finisterra. Revista portuguesa de Geografia*, XXXIII, (1998), pp. 19951–63.

López-Gunn, Elena, "Agua Para Todos: A New Regionalist Hydraulic Paradigm in Spain," *Water Alternative*, 2, 3 (2009), pp. 370–94.

Moral Ituarte, Leandro del, "Governance of Large Hydraulic Infrastructure in Spain: A Historical Approach," in Tapio Katko, Petri S. Juuti, and Klaas Schwartz (eds.), *Water Services Management and Governance. Lessons for a Sustainable Future*, IWA Publishing, 2012, pp. 43–52.

Ministerio de Agricultura y Medio Ambiente, *Environment profile of Spain* 2012. <http://www.magrama.gob.es/es/calidad-y-evaluacion- ambiental/publicaciones/pae2012englowresolution23-4-2014_tcm7-328424.pdf>

Romero, Joan, Carme Melo, and Dolores Brandis, "The Neoliberal Model of the City in Southern Europe: A Comparative Approach to Valencia and Madrid," in Jörg Knieling, and Frank Othengrafen (eds.), *Cities in Crisis. Socio-spatial Impacts of the Economic Crisis in Southern European Cities*, New York: Routledge, 2016, pp. 79–93.

Swyngedouw, Erik, *Liquid Power: Contested Hydro-Modernities in Twentieth-Century Spain*, Cambridge, MA: MIT Press, 2015.

CHAPTER 15
CULTURE
Rafael Núñez Florencio

The complex ideological construction we call culture is based on an intricate web of influences and interrelations. In the case of modern Spain, it is crucial to keep in mind that at the end of the eighteenth century, the country broke out of a lengthy isolation. During the nineteenth century, thousands of travelers crossed the Pyrenees and their experiences and observations were the ingredients that went into the most successful and longest lived cultural construct of the period, the Romantic image, one which would cover the country's reality like a skin. This was the only Spain many foreigners would ever know.

The persistence of this perspective makes it easy to understand modern Spanish culture through preconceived ideas and commonly held stereotypes. Spaniards were assigned characteristics which were the polar opposite of those attributed to people from the more advanced countries of Western Europe leading to the paradox that one of the westernmost countries on the continent would be widely seen as being "the East": a backward place populated by people who were fanatical and violent, but also proud, happy, and alive (curiously, during the early modern period, Spanish culture was seen as ascetic, serious, and religious). To this day, for millions of tourists, Spain remains the country of sun and fiesta.

Any attempt to understand Spanish culture as emanating from an unchanging national essence would produce nothing more than clichés. This chapter avoids such approaches, preferring to explore various aspects of that culture empirically and to demonstrate that, as in other European countries, Spanish culture of the nineteenth and twentieth centuries went through various phases, following the historical development of the country as a whole. Far from being something monolithic, modern Spanish culture has been—and continues to be—marked by great contrasts and important geographic and generational diversity.

Backwardness and upheaval: The romantic imprint

The myth of a romantic Spain, at once backward but full of spontaneity and vitality, and the antithesis of bourgeois Europe, was forged in the first third of the nineteenth century. Spain was a country of profound contrasts, best exemplified by the paintings of Goya: the love for liberty depicted in its popular uprising against Napoleon contrasted to its submission to the Inquisition and the despotism of Fernando VII. The "romantic" label thus represents this stereotype, a country of monks, warriors, bandits, gypsies, and bullfighters. Spain, and its archetypes *Carmen* and *Don Juan*, became the setting of passion: love and death intertwined.

When war with Napoleonic France broke out in 1808, the legacies of the great artists of the Enlightenment were alive and well in. Many of them, like Gaspar Melchor de Jovellanos and Leandro Fernández de Moratín, were still at the height of their creative productivity. Goya himself, considered a flagship figure in Enlightenment Spain, continued painting until his death in 1828. Other figures straddled two eras as well, such as José María Blanco Crespo, better known as Blanco White (1775–1841) or the poets Alberto Lista (1775–1848) and Manuel José Quintana (1772–1857).

Scholars have been breaking down the previously powerful barrier between the Age of Reason (the second half of the eighteenth century) and Romanticism (the first half of the nineteenth century) and have created the concept of Pre-romanticism. This approach has challenged the established dichotomy of reason versus emotion, but has also demonstrated that the roots of the Romantic Movement lay in the Enlightenment, with the works of Jean-Jacques Rousseau being an important point of connection. Some Spanish Enlightenment authors, Meléndez Valdés and Jovellanos, for example, began to exhibit traditionally romantic themes, such as introspection, melancholy, an appreciation for nature, and nostalgia in an explicit way. Even the most overly romantic themes, such as obscurity, death, the cemetery, and the macabre, are mentioned in some of the key works of the previous period, including José Cadalso's *Noches lúgubres,* published posthumously in 1789–90.

The myth of romantic Spain was something else that emerged from the eighteenth century. In 1782, Nicolas Masson de Morvilliers's article "Espagne" in the first volume of the *Géographie modern*, published in Paris, included the negative assessments of Spanish culture that were to play a crucial role in the Spanish intellectual debate during the next two centuries. Spain was, he wrote, "like those weak and disgraced colonies that endlessly need the protecting arm of the metropolis: it's got to be helped with our arts, our discoveries; it even resembles the desperate ailing diseased that without consciousness of their condition reject the help that life presents." Spain lives in an "embarrassing lethargy": art, sciences, and commerce are inexistent; "Spain lacks mathematicians, physicists, astronomers, naturalists" Spaniards are "indolent, lazy and apathetic" the nation is a "pygmy country" and "poor within its treasures" overall, "Spain is probably the most ignorant country in Europe."

Masson de Morvilliers's criticism was nothing more than a personal and highly debatable opinion but even so, it did not fail to drum up controversy. It revived the old question of Spanish decadence that, once again, would be at the forefront of Spanish intellectual debates throughout the contemporary age. The political and cultural factions engaged with rationalist reforms had an image of the country not so different from that of Masson de Morvilliers. In 1822, the liberal Blanco White, in exile in London, published his *Letters from Spain* in which he portrayed Spain as a nation characterized by sectarian violence, economic underdevelopment, and ideological—religious—fanaticism.

This was essentially the same portrayal as that made by the greatest Spanish cultural figure of the period, Francisco de Goya, who also lived his final years outside of Spain and died in 1828 in Bordeaux. Goya's style of painting evolved throughout his lifetime, and although he focused much of his work on the Spanish people, nobility, members of the government, and royal family, it is the distinct aesthetic and style of painting that he developed in the last years of his life that is of relevance here.

Ever mindful of the pulse of his time, in 1814, Goya painted *La carga de los mamelucos* and *Los fusilamientos del Tres de Mayo*—generally known as the *Second of May, 1808* and the *Third of May, 1808*—depicting the uprising of the Spanish people against the French invasion (see Chapter 2). In his engravings titled *Los desastres de la guerra* (The Disasters of War) (1810–15), he powerfully portrays the barbarity and cruelty of that war, and wars in general. In addition, the group of paintings known as *Pinturas negras* (Black Paintings) (1819–23), fourteen mural paintings embody the most atrocious facets of the human condition with painful sincerity and without contemplations. Other compositions from this period explore the topics of madness, witchcraft, murder, and cannibalism.

Goya's work counters a portrayal of the misery of Spanish life with a compassionate attitude toward the weak, and a celebratory air toward freedom fighters. The Spanish are portrayed as fanatic and cruel but also as brave and heroic, capable of facing an exceptional force in defense of their principles. This last aspect is what visitors to post–Peninsular War Spain emphasized: the sleepy nation denounced by Masson de Morvilliers was not only alive and well, but also capable of great feats. Romantic writers from various countries, such as Victor Hugo from France, Lord Byron from Great Britain, and Washington Irving from the United States, made Spain the protagonist of their work.

Ironically, Spanish Romanticism itself would take longer to develop, its first major figures emerging only in the 1830s: the playwrights Duque de Rivas (1791–1865) and Juan Eugenio de Hartzenbusch (1806–1880) and poet José de Espronceda (1808–1842). By far the most interesting writer of this period is Mariano José de Larra (1809–1837), whose work covered a variety of genres, but who remains best known for his satirical articles on the Spanish way of life written under the pseudonym of *Fígaro*. These are still considered the best portrayal of Spanish life from the first half of the nineteenth century. Other writers, most notably Ramón de Mesoneros Romanos (1803–1882), developed a particularly Spanish type of satire known as *costumbrismo*, which focused on national stereotypes and traditions.

The best of Spanish Romanticism arrived later, emerging in the second half of the century. Gustavo Adolfo Bécquer (1836–70), author of the legendary narrations (*Leyendas*) and the popular poetry (*Rimas*), enjoyed great acclaim and popularity during this period. The most enduring product of Spanish Romanticism has been José Zorrilla's (1817–93) *Don Juan Tenorio*. First performed in 1844, this retelling of the story of the seducer, or Don Juan, was the most important play of the Romantic period in Spain and it continues to be produced today.

Spanish Romanticism also found room for women writers, and three women had success at this time: Rosalía de Castro (1837–85), who wrote in Gallego as well as Spanish; Carolina Coronado (1820–1911) whose poetry included denunciations of the new liberal order for leaving women under "the yoke of their sex"; and Cuban-born Gerturdis Gómez de Avellanada (1814–73), a writer whose plays, novels, and poetry took her into the literary and social elites of Madrid. Gómez de Avellanada also published magazines directed specifically at women: *La Ilustración. Álbum de las Damas*, which appeared in 1845, would be, she wrote, "the best literary review that has been published in Spain."

Stability, progress, and nationalism

Spain saw political stability and economic growth in the second half of the nineteenth century, which led to social and cultural modernization and made the growing nation more "European" and less "romantic" (see chapters 3, 4). As a whole, Spain became modernized and adjusted itself to the standards of the old neighboring nations of Western Europe. Although foreigners refused to recognize it, Spain was no longer the "oriental," poor, and romantic country they so loved.

As cities broke through their ancient walls and expanded into new *ensanches* (see Chapter 12), urban social and cultural life took on a new vigor, aided by the spread of societies, cultural centers, *casinos, cafés,* and other meeting points, a development which would pick up speed as the century drew to its close. Cafes turned into meeting points where people from literary or political circles of all denominations could exchange ideas or conspiracies. In Madrid, certain cafés (*Fornos, Colonial, Oriente, Gijón*) would become representative of the ebullient political and cultural scene of the period. This urban and bourgeois environment of professionals, journalists, politicians, artists, and men of letters proved open to new ideas from across Western Europe. Positivism found a niche in Spain, although with more resistance than in other places, and the weight of Catholicism in Spanish culture continued to hold strong. The two most important thinkers of the mid-nineteenth century were the traditionalist Juan Donoso Cortés (1809–53) and the priest Jaime Balmes (1810–48). Spanish universities stagnated under Thomist philosophy, a dogma that distanced itself from reality and had an antiquated and theoretical mind-set, distant from modern science.

The renewal of pedagogy and universities in general—a fundamental issue in the emerging "Silver Age"—arrived in unexpected ways. In 1843, a Spanish professor, Julián Sanz del Río (1814–69), obtained a scholarship to study in Germany. There he came in contact with the philosophy of Karl Krause and he became its fervent supporter. Though Krause was a secondary intellectual figure in Germany and his metaphysics was not compatible with modern science, Sanz del Río constructed an eclectic system that emphasized the power of reason, defended liberty of thought, incentivized research, and supported educational innovation, all of this within the strictest of humanist ethos.

This was a revolution for Spain at the time, whose political and institutional representatives ordered a full-blown persecution of Sanz del Río when he set forth to install such principles. This persecution also affected his colleagues, collaborators, and disciples such as Fernando de Castro (1814–74), Nicolás Salmerón (1838–1908), and Francisco Giner de los Ríos (1839–1915), the latter of whom played a crucial role in the renovation of Spanish pedagogy, leading a reformation movement that became crystalized in the *Institución Libre de Enseñanza* (ILE), an institution for the educational freedom.

The years of the Democratic Sexennium (1868–74) ushered in a hope for improvements, but soon these hopes were frustrated (see Chapter 3). The Restoration which followed reverted to a hard line. In February 1875, the government issued the Orovio Decree, named after the minister of Fomento, Manuel Orovio, forbidding any teaching that did not adhere to Catholic doctrine. Some professors from the Universidad Central de Madrid were dismissed for not respecting the decree or resigned in protest. Giner de los Ríos was among them, and far from giving up his ideals, he created the idea for an alternative pedagogical movement to the university that was closing its doors to him. Thus the ILE was founded, without any doubt one of the most profound and longer lasting movements for cultural renovation in the Spanish society.

Other enthusiastic defenders of freedom and pedagogical renovation joined him: Gumersindo de Azcárate (1840–1917), Augusto González de Linares (1845–1904), Joaquín Costa (1846–1911), Manuel Bartolomé Cossío (1857–1935), Adolfo González Posada (1860–1944), and Pedro Dorado Montero (1861–1919), among others. Giner's legacy outlived him, and most of the notable thinkers or schools of the time came into contact with *institucionismo* (ILE) at some point. Throughout the twentieth century the seed of the ILE would bloom into projects, schools, and centers that would be decisive in Spanish cultural life, including the Junta de Ampliación de Estudios, the Instituto Nacional de Ciencias Físico-Naturales, the Centro de Estudios Históricos, the Museo Pedagógico Nacional, la Residencia de Estudiantes, the Instituto Escuela, la Residencia de Señoritas, and the Misiones Pedagógicas.

This process of educational renewal sprang from the frustration and the incapacity of the Spanish progressive elites to change established institutions. Some intellectuals were tempted by politics, either as republicans or in the emerging Socialist Party. Other politicians close to the ILE had already held responsible positions, such as Eugenio Montero Ríos (1832–1914) or Segismundo Moret (1833–1913). Committed republicans and militant republicans were many, from Salmerón to Rafael María de Labra (1840–1918). From the socialist ranks, Julián Besteiro (1870–1940) and Fernando de los Ríos (1879–1949) developed their activities during the twentieth century. Despite this movement, the theoretical weakness of Spanish socialism never sprouted an important Marxist theorist (See chapter 30).

The weight of conservative and traditionalist ideas in Spanish society continued to be significant into the twentieth century. It was commonplace to directly associate "Spanish" with "Catholic." Those who did not follow the official doctrine of the Church were catalogued as "Bad Spaniards," "traitors," or "foreign sympathizers." The most brilliant scholar of the period, Marcelino Menéndez y Pelayo (1856–1912), wrote a monumental eight-volume *Historia de los heterodoxos españoles* (1880–82) which catalogued an exhaustive array of "deviations" and "dissidents" throughout history: Jews, Protestants, those inspired by French ideologies, and liberals. The subject of ideological controversy to this day, his work became inscribed in the process of nationalization that Spanish culture underwent in the late nineteenth and early twentieth centuries.

The process of nationalization was furthered in other spheres as well, notably in history painting. Large-scale works replayed the history of Spain from an epic and stereotyped perspective (*glorias patrias*), including pieces like *La conversión de Recaredo* (1888) by Antonio Muñoz Degrain (1840–1924), *La rendición de Granada* (1882) by Francisco Pradilla (1848–1921), *Isabel la Católica dictando su testamento* (1864) by Eduardo Rosales (1836–73), *Los comuneros de Castilla ante el patíbulo* (1860) by Antonio Gisbert (1834–1901), and *La rendición de Bailén* (1864) by José Casado del Alisal (1830–86), to name but a few. Not all paintings of the era had to subscribe to the genre, but one of the best artists of the time, Mariano Fortuny (1838–74), knew how to reconcile historical frames with a very modern "orientalist" gaze in his paintings of North African landscapes and characters.

Sculpture was undergoing a similar process, made evident in the multiple works by Mariano Benlliure (1862–1947) or Aniceto Marinas (1866–1953). Within the context of conservative nationalism, artist Ricardo Bellver (1845–1924) built a monument to the devil, a highly controversial project. The sculpture called *El ángel caído* (1885) can be found in Retiro Park in Madrid. Historicist recreation was also popular in architecture with the advent of diverse "neos": Neo-Romanesque, Neo-Gothic, and *Neo-Mudéjar* (Moorish Revival). Many of these sculptors, and none more than the Catalan Benlliure, devoted much of their effort to producing the large number of monuments to political leaders which came to adorn Spanish cities in this period. The massive monument to Alfonso XII in the Retiro which was inaugurated in 1922 is the outstanding example.

Spanish arts, then, could not escape the strong influence of a national idiosyncrasy (see Chapter 36). The works of two of the great composers of the time, Isaac Albéniz

(1860–1909), author of *Iberia* (1905–1908), and Enrique Granados (1867–1916), author of *Danzas españolas* (1892–1900) and *Goyescas* (1911), were a testament to this idiosyncrasy. The *Zarzuela* and the *Género Chico* (light plays with music) also represented the national alternative to Italian opera. The *Castizo* musical movement enjoyed terrific success and the audience's favor held steadfast for a long time. Its importance cannot be overstated, as many of its pieces have formed a part of the Spanish collective memory for many generations. Some representative works include *El barberillo de Lavapiés* (1874) by Francisco Asenjo Barbieri (1823–94), *La verbena de la Paloma* (1894) by Tomás Bretón (1850–1923), *Agua, azucarillos y aguardiente* (1897) by Federico Chueca (1846–1908), and *La revoltosa* (1897) by Ruperto Chapí (1851–1909).

The second half of the nineteenth century is often characterized in the literary tradition as seeing the triumph of Realism followed, in the last decades, by the transformation into Naturalism. Spanish Realist literature presented a brilliant list of novelists (in fact, the novel became the genre par excellence of the nineteenth century). Among them, Juan Valera (1824–1905), José María de Pereda (1833–906), Emilia Pardo Bazán (1851–1921) (see Chapter 28), and Armando Palacio Valdés (1853–1938) stood out as national treasures. Nonetheless, most agree that the greatest novel of the period was *La Regenta* (1885) by Leopoldo Alas. Under his pseudonym *Clarín* (1852–1901), he masterfully depicted life in the provincial city of Oviedo, including the influence of the Catholic clergy over bourgeois women, during the Canovist Restoration (see Chapter 18).

Benito Pérez Galdós (1843–1920) is perhaps one of the best novelists of the period in any language. Galdós wrote an immense number of books: from the series *Episodios Nacionales* (a set of 46 historical novels describing the history of Spain from the Battle of Trafalgar to the Restoration) written between 1872 and 1912, to novels like *Doña Perfecta* (1876), *La familia de León Roch* (1878), *Fortunata y Jacinta* (1887), and *Misericordia* (1897). In its entirety, the work of Galdós is the most complete and penetrating portrayal of Spanish life during the Restoration. Galdós went on to become a sort of restoring force for the Spanish literary scene at the beginning of the twentieth century, with his anticlerical *Electra* (1901), which was received with great acclaim and also generated considerable protest (see Chapter18).

From pessimism to splendor: "The Silver Age"

The period from the end of the nineteenth century to the outbreak of the Civil War in 1936 is widely seen as one of the most glorious moments for Spanish culture, a "Silver Age" second only to the "Golden Age" of the sixteenth and seventeenth centuries. Even as the country reeled from the disastrous defeat at the hands of the United States in 1898, the colonial war in Morocco, and the emergence of mass politics (see Chapter 4), new groups of writers known as the Generation of 1898, the Generation of 1914, and the Generation of 1927 elevated Spanish literature to the levels it had known in the days of Cervantes and Calderón de la Barca. Essayists like Miguel Unamuno and José Ortega y Gasset (see Chapter 32) and, above all, the poet and playwright Federico García Lorca, rose to national, and even international, prominence. In the world of painting, Pablo Picasso, the quintessential universal Spaniard, began to work from Barcelona, at the time the hub of a great cultural renaissance, before further developing his artistic career from Paris, the capital of Western art at the time. Although literary and artistic pursuits flourished in Silver Age Spain, the role of the sciences and universities also grew in this period.

Historians tend to pinpoint 1898 as the beginning of the twentieth century in Spain, but in terms of culture, this date is as contested as the debate on Romanticism discussed above. About a decade before the famous *Desastre del 98,* many among the nation's elites knew that Spain needed profound reforms in order to overcome its backwardness and succeed in implementing a new "regeneration" (in economical, educational, social, political matters). The term made such an impact that almost all public projects in Spain during the following decade were labeled "regenerationist" (*regeneracionista*).

Regeneracionista theorists overstated the evils of the nation in the hopes of accomplishing transformation on all fronts. The challenge at hand, they claimed, was not a temporary crisis, but a deep structural problem. They framed their arguments in terms of decadence, which had already become second nature in political debate by that point, and degeneration, an intellectual fashion shared across western and central Europe. According to them, the trajectory of Spanish history since the sixteenth century had been in permanent decline. Using the fashionable biological terms of the era, Spain was a decrepit nation, ailing, agonizing, or, as Francisco Silvela would mention in an important article, "lacking a pulse."

Already in 1890, the geologist Luis Mallada (1841–1921) had drawn a devastating panorama of the Spanish situation in *Los males de la patria* (see Chapter 14). It seemed obvious that the defeat of Spain in the war against the United States and the loss of Cuba, Puerto Rico, and Philippines, the remnants of its once-great colonial empire, was interpreted as a confirmation of this dramatic diagnosis and only intensified that sensibility behind it. In the two years after 1898, a so-called disaster literature flourished, including such titles as *El problema nacional* (The National Problem) by Ricardo Macías Picavea (1847–), *Del desastre nacional y sus causas* (On the National Disaster and Its Causes) by Damián Isern (1852–1914), to name only two. These works pointed to solutions for overcoming Spain's multiple problems (employment, discipline, organization, efficiency, instruction, morality), but emphasized the evils of Spain, and inevitably concluded that the country was beyond cure. They described its history of mistakes, failures and losses as well as its contemporary shortcomings. In this manner, the empiricist criticism became metaphysics: the problem was not the situation of Spain in a particular era, but Spain as such and the Spaniards themselves. Thus the "problem of Spain," which would occupy the minds of Spanish intellectuals throughout the twentieth century, was created.

Due to the depths of its criticism, the vehemence of its attitude, and the ambition of its objectives, *Regeneracionismo* was bound to fail. Its greatest representative was Joaquín Costa (1846–1911), author of *Oligarquía y Caciquismo como la actual forma de gobierno en España* (1902), and a tireless activist who died in bitterness as he saw all his aspirations frustrated. Pessimism became a common denominator of elites who aspired to have the country succeed as a prosperous Western European nation. This radical negativity was highlighted even further among youth, though paradoxically this skeptical and hypercritical attitude was compatible with an explicit attraction toward "deep Spain" (*España profunda*): the Castilian plateau, its scenery, and its inhabitants. These younger figures became known as the "Generation of '98" (a term coined by *Azorín* in 1913) but historiography and literary criticism now prefer the label the "Crisis of '98" in the aim of drawing a more comprehensible timeline of the era.

The so-called youths of '98—some, like Unamuno, who was born in 1864, were no longer so young—shared many things, especially the radical criticism of the condition of their country at that moment, but they also had many aesthetic and ideological differences. One of its most skeptical members, Pío Baroja (1872–1956), wrote a diversity of novels of unmatched value. The trilogy of *La lucha por la vida* (1904) and *El árbol de la ciencia* (1911) are the most representative. Similarly, José Martínez Ruiz, known as *Azorín* (1873–1967) was the author of exquisite and refined prose who specialized in the poetry of small things: *Las confesiones de un pequeño filósofo* (1904), and *Castilla* (1912). The aforementioned Ramiro de Maeztu followed a path of conservative ideological radicalization, seen in his *Defensa de la Hispanidad* (1934). Unamuno, along with Ortega y Gasset, was one of the most important philosophers of the period: his strictly philosophical works were matched by his equally impressive breadth of writings, including essays and narratives, poetry, and theatre. Some examples include *En torno al casticismo* (1895) and *Del sentimiento trágico de la vida* (1913).

The greatest dramatist of the period was without a doubt Ramón María del Valle-Inclán (1866–1936). He was a peculiar character who not only wrote some of the most impressive plays of the time (*Divinas Palabras*, 1919; *Luces de Bohemia*, 1924), but also coined the term *esperpento* to refer to the systematic deformation of reality, which in his opinion, was necessary for characterizing the grotesque character of Spanish reality. In poetry, the most outstanding figure was Antonio Machado (1875–1939), who recreated the Castilian landscape with melancholic sensitivity in his *Campos de Castilla* (1912). The long list of '98ers was contrasted by a group of more aesthetic poets, successors of the Nicaraguan Rubén Darío, who were called modernists: among them, Manuel Machado (1874–1947) and Juan Ramón Jiménez (1881–1958), winner of the Nobel Prize for Literature in 1956. The contrast between the Youth of '98 and modernism was no longer accepted neither historically nor in literature.

In part due to the theorizing of José Ortega y Gasset (1883–1955)—without a doubt the most relevant and influential figure of the first half of the twentieth century—the cultural life of this period is often considered the point of origin from which successive generations of intellectuals sprang, including the generations of 1914, 1927, and 1936. In contrast with the Generation of 1898, for example, the generation of 1914 tends to be more vital and optimistic, more European, and more scientifically oriented. As well as Ortega himself (see Chapter 32), this generation included the doctor and humanist Gregorio Marañón (1887–1960), writers Ramón Pérez de Ayala (1880–1962) and Ramón Gómez de la Serna (1888–1963), and the future president of the Second Republic, Manuel Azaña (1880–1940) (see Chapter 33).

The authors of '27, defined as a relatively homogenous group for the homage they paid to the great Golden Age poet Luís de Góngora (1561–1627), were the generation of great poets: Pedro Salinas (1891–1951), Jorge Guillén (1893–1984), Gerardo Diego (1896–1987), Dámaso Alonso (1898–1990), Vicente Aleixandre (1898–1984) (winner of the Nobel Prize for Literature of 1977), Luis Cernuda (1902–63), Rafael Alberti (1902–99), and, above all, Federico García Lorca (1898–1936), the most widely read author in Spanish contemporary literature and the best known internationally. Lorca masterfully united the popular lyricist sensibility (*Romancero gitano*, 1928) with surrealism (*Poeta en Nueva York*, 1930), and was a fantastic dramatist that expressed like no one else the anguish of Spanish life in works such as *Bodas de Sangre* (1933), *Yerma* (1934), and *La casa de Bernarda Alba* (1936), which continue to be staged around the world in the twenty-first century.

Dividing Spanish history into these fixed generations, however, can be problematic, making it impossible to capture the complexity and diversity of Spanish cultural life during this brilliant period. Scientific investigation, for example, experienced spectacular developments. In 1906, Santiago Ramón y Cajal (1852–1934) received the Nobel Prize for Medicine for his pioneering work in neurology. Ramón y Cajal's achievements were little less than heroic because he conducted his research in a hostile environment, almost isolated, with nearly no resources. Nonetheless, slowly but surely, things started to change. Universities and other educational centers underwent a period of strong activity, due in part to the impulse provided by the ILE and its dependent organizations, such as the Council for Development of Scientific Studies and Research. Never before had so many Spanish students traveled abroad to complete their studies, and many of the most important scientific and cultural figures of the day, including Marie Curie, Albert Einstein, Henri Bergson, and Le Corbusier, visited Spain. Laboratories and research centers were created, although the outbreak of the Civil War interrupted their work. For example, Severo Ochoa (1905–93), who would win the Nobel Prize for Medicine in 1959, began his career working in the lab run by Doctor Juan Negrín (1892–1956). In fact, Negrín himself had studied in the United States before becoming professor of physiology at the Universidad Central in Madrid. He gave up his scientific career for politics and wound up as prime minister of the Republic during the last two years of the Civil War.

Another problem with the panoramic view is the difficulty of acknowledging the literary, artistic, and scientific explosions that occurred in the provinces. Spanish intellectual and cultural life did not revolve around events in Madrid, although everything that happened in the capital had major resonance.

Regions with their own languages experienced cultural revivals (see Chapter 10). Catalonia experienced the most important process of cultural renovation, with different characteristics from those in the rest of the country. The phenomenon known as *Renaixença* had its roots in the middle of the nineteenth century, and *Oda a la patria* (1833) by Bonaventura Carles Aribau (1798–1862) is often regarded as its starting point. Throughout the nineteenth century, this romantic cultural resurgence was colored with nationalist vindications (*Jocs Florals*), giving way to some political demands for self-recognition and autonomy against Madrid's centralism, which made it difficult to dissociate the cultural from the political. Some key figures in this field include Jacint Verdaguer (1845–1902), author of two epic poems in Catalan, *L´Atlàntida* (1876) and *Canigó* (1886); and Joan Maragall (1860–1911), author of a varied assortment of works (poems, essays, articles, etc.).

In part as a consequence of the crisis of '98, the beginning of the twentieth century saw nationalist sentiment take hold, and an impressive culture boom emerged in most fields. The Catalan capital of Barcelona underwent a moment of splendor between the two International Expositions of 1888 and 1929. Modernism in the architectural field reached its greatest heights with the works of Lluís Domènech i Montaner (1850–1923), Josep Puig i Cadafalch (1867–1956), and, above all, Antoni Gaudí (1852–1926). Many of their best works were houses commissioned by the city's economic elite. If today Barcelona constitutes a tourist attraction of the first order, it is to a great extent thanks to the many masterpieces they created.

Sculpture too lived a moment of splendor, but it was in the field of painting where the greatest creative outbursts happened, and particularly the works of those who gathered in the tavern *Els Quatre Gats*, among them Santiago Rusiñol (1861–1931) and Ramón Casas

(1866–1932). Pablo Ruiz Picasso (1881–1973), a young man from Malaga, was already showing promising talent with works such as *Les demoiselles de Avignon* (1907), although his oeuvre would not reach the shine and renown until his move to Paris. The energies of the Catalan culture of the era were prolonged in the movement called *Noucentisme,* led by the thinker and essayist Eugeni D´Ors (1881–1954) and extending to the most varied domains of culture, from literature—where Josep Pla (1897–1981) shone—to music, such as the great cellist Pau Casals (1876–1973).

The "Silver Age" of Spanish culture offered a tremendously diverse panorama that is difficult to depict in a few pages. Its breadth spanned from the international acclaim and, eventually, the Nobel Prize for Literature awarded to José de Echegaray (1832–1916) in 1904 and Jacinto Benavente (1866–1954) in 1922 to the Ibero-American Exposition of 1929 in Seville. Vicente Blasco Ibáñez (1867–1928), a writer who did not fit comfortably into any of these "schools," also won international acclaim with best sellers such as *Blood and Sand* (1908), which was made into four movies, including one directed by the author in 1916 and another starring Rudolph Valentino in 1922. Blasco Ibáñez was also an important political figure, leading the Valencia-based republican *Blasquista* movement whose success was largely based on the pioneering newspaper *El Pueblo*, for which he wrote vast amounts of material.

This period also saw a boom in the publication of literary reviews and periodicals devoted to culture and politics, with titles such as *Germinal, Vida Nueva, Gente Nueva, Electra, Helios,* and *Alma Española,* among others. Ortega y Gasset was a promoter of the two most influential political-cultural publications, *España* and *Revista de Occidente.* Great newspapers like *El Imparcial* and *El Sol* paid increasing attention to culture. Other important magazines of the era such as *Litoral, Verso y Prosa, Cruz y Raya, Octubre, Ultra,* and *La Gaceta Literaria* (1927–31), gave the literary avant-gardes exploring the diverse "isms" (futurism, surrealism, dadaism, creationism, ultraism), a platform for experimentation and diffusion. *La Gaceta Literaria* was edited by Ernesto Giménez Caballero (1899–1998) who became one of the founders of Spanish fascism and a defender of the Franco dictatorship.

Aside from the literary realm, other arts also lived glory days during this time: painter Darío de Regoyos (1857–1913) depicted this glory in his series *Black Spain*, for example; Julio Romero de Torres (1874–1930) painted Sensual Spain with female nudes; José Gutiérrez Solana (1886–1945) specialized in *Sinister Spain*; while Ignacio Zuloaga (1870–1945) remained the most characteristic representative of *Profound Spain*, and Joaquín Sorolla (1863–1923) achieved international acclaim as a flagship figure of *Luminous Spain*. Most of all, although Picasso developed his works from Paris, his topics and paintings were always genuinely Spanish.

The contributions of Juan Gris (1887–1927) to Cubism were also noteworthy, and were countered by two great exponents of the renovation in sculpting, Julio González (1876–1942) and Pablo Gargallo (1881–1934), who also unfolded a great part of their creative work in Paris. Cultivated music also reached its highest peaks under the wing of Manuel de Falla (1876–1946) and Joaquín Turina (1882–1949), although this also became an expansionist period for another more popular sort of music, the *Zarzuela*. In 1939, this would come to a head with Joaquín Rodrigo's (1901–99) composition of one of the most melodic and widespread tunes of Spanish music, the *Concierto de Aranjuez*. And in Luis Buñuel (1900–83), Spain produced one of the first great figures of the artistic medium which would come to dominate the twentieth century, the cinema.

The impact of war

The Civil War brought this flourishing cultural renaissance to a crashing halt. Most writers, artists, and scientists left Spain for exile. García Lorca had been murdered by a Falangist hit squad early in the Civil War. Those who lived remained in a sort of "internal exile." Early Francoism (1939–59) was characterized by repression and cultural closed-mindedness, but this soon gave way to extensive economic development, which allowed Spain to open its doors to foreign tourists under the slogan "Spain is different" (see Chapter 7). For millions of visitors, Spain became a country of happiness and amusement. Even Spaniards compensated for the state of the nation by immersing themselves into the world of soccer and the international successes of their beloved Real Madrid. In opposition to this growing popular culture, a new high culture developed that was radically anti-Francoist.

Leaving aside the cost of human suffering and lives, the destruction of material goods and the economic repercussions, the outbreak of war brought about the abrupt stop to all the cultural activities: educational projects, scientific investigations, art exhibits, literary activities, and cultural life in general. The Spanish Civil War was a total war in the modern sense, affecting not only the soldiers but also the entire population. In short, war conditioned everything. There was no possibility for cultural activity beyond propaganda: the limited artistic or literary activity available served one cause or another (posters and murals calling for mobilization, propaganda-ridden films, manifestos, politicized congresses, compromised art, militant literature). Perhaps the only exception to the political servitude of intellectual activity toward immediate politics is Picasso's *Guernica* (1937), not only the best artistic piece about the Spanish war but also a universal declaration of the horrors of war in general. But then Picasso was in Paris, far removed from the war itself.

The failure of the revolt of the armed forces commanded by General Franco left Spain broken in two: each party wielded great brutality in order to hold control of their areas, pursuing with force not just the enemy but also any suspicious parties. Artists, writers, scientists, and intellectuals prepared to leave the country, escaping from threats against their work and their lives. Some, including Baroja, Marañón, and Ortega y Gasset, came very close to be executed. Others were not as lucky. Ramiro de Maeztu was shot to death in Madrid in 1936, while Unamuno, died in horror in Salamanca on December 31 that same year, after having heard the founder of the Legion Millán Astray scream: "Long live death! Die intelligence!," a preamble of the *cleansing* that was about to happen in the "new Spain." The poet Miguel Hernández (1910–42), one of the most spontaneous voices of poetry of the 1930s, died in jail as a youth. Others, such as the poet José Hierro (1922–2002) and the playwright Antonio Buero Vallejo (1916–2000), suffered similar penalties but survived and became prime examples of the cultural resistance under the rule of Franco.

The first years of the new regime were characterized not only by its relentless repression and the installation of a doctrine inspired by fascism, but also by a mixture of militarism, traditional conservatism, and Catholicism (see Chapter 7). The most orthodox fascists, such as the poet Dionisio Ridruejo (1912–75), felt betrayed and eventually distanced themselves from the regime. The most important intellectuals of the 1940s were ideologues for *Franquismo*, including Antonio Tovar (1911–85) and Pedro Laín Entralgo (1908–2001). Even the most important publication of the period, the magazine *Escorial* (1940–50), shyly opened its doors to the most conservative end of the liberal culture of the previous period.

Laín himself advocated explicitly for the drawing of a bridge with the past in his essay *La generación del 98* (1947). When he wanted to reformulate the famous topic *El problema de España* (1949), he found a violent response from one of the regime's spokesmen, Rafael Calvo Serer: *España sin problema* (1949). Thus, the enthusiasm gave way to indifference or criticism as shown by the trajectories of the important authors of the time, poets Luis Felipe Vivanco (1907–75) and Luis Rosales (1910–92), novelist Gonzalo Torrente Ballester (1910–99) and philosopher José Luis López Aranguren (1909–96), among others. Some would end up perched on symbols of the democratic opposition during the latest breaths of Franco regime.

Meanwhile, many other academics, researchers, or creators would go about their works in silence, fighting difficulty in a sort of internal exile. Not all of them, however, found the same conditions. The most prominent among them enjoyed the advantages of public recognition and begrudging tolerance from the regime. Such is the case of those who came back from foreign lands to restart their activities in Spain, like Ortega y Gasset, Marañon, and the historian Ramón Menéndez Pidal (1869–1968). Pidal, for example, took up old projects that were ultimately realized, such as the many volumes of the magnificent *Historia de España*. Other authors had considerably fewer advantages, such as philosopher Xavier Zubiri (1898–1983), a conservative but unconnected to Franco regime; the thinker Julián Marías (1914–2005), disciple of Ortega; the anthropologist Julio Caro Baroja (1914–95), author of an extensive oeuvre, or the most recognized Catalan-language poet, Salvador Espriu (1913–85).

Despite the fact that even under Franco and the severe censorship of the regime, cultural vitality was unstoppable, a large part of the cultural production of the era was generated in exile outside Spanish borders, especially in France, Mexico, and Argentina, countries that hosted waves of Spanish emigration. Just as the United States benefited from receiving the many Jews and others fleeing Nazi Germany, these countries benefited from the presence of so many outstanding Spanish creators and intellects. Mexico's premier academic institution, the Colegio de México, was largely created by Spanish exiles. The vast majority of Spanish authors remained in exile for many years, and many of them eventually died abroad or did not return until the 1970s.

The majority of scientists who had worked so arduously to set the basis of research in the previous period were exiled for a long time, from physicist Arturo Duperier (1896–1959) to chemist Enrique Moles (1883–1953); philosophers like José Gaos (1900–69), Juan David García Bacca (1901–92), María Zambrano (1904–91), and José Ferrater Mora (1912–91); historians Américo Castro (1885–1972) and Claudio Sánchez Albornoz (1893–1984); writers Arturo Barea (1897–1957), Ramón J. Sender (1901–82), and Max Aub (1903–72), author of a monumental piece about the Spanish war in six volumes, *El laberinto mágico* (1943–68). Luis Buñuel, likely the best Spanish filmmaker of the twentieth century, developed his career in Mexico and France. Salvador Dalí (1904–89), the most acclaimed Spanish painter of the twentieth century after Picasso, created the largest part of his oeuvre outside of Spain.

Inside the country, an important change occurred in the mid-1950s. The "generation of the 50s" refers to a group of famous poets and novelists that renewed Spanish literature in those years: among them short-story writer Ignacio Aldecoa (1925–69), poets José Manuel Caballero Bonald (1926), Carlos Barral (1928–89), and Jaime Gil de Biedma (1929–90) and novelists Juan Goytisolo (1931), Juan Marsé (1933), and Luis Goytisolo (1935), to cite but a few. Literary milestones in this period included the novels *Nada* (1944) by Carmen Laforet (1921–2004), *El Jarama* (1955) by Rafael Sánchez Ferlosio (1927) and *Tiempo de Silencio*

(1962) by Luis Martín-Santos (1924–64), this last one considered by the critics to be one of the best portrayals of Spanish society under Franco. Within a more popular type of literature *Los cipreses creen en Dios* (1953), the first of a series of four works by José María Gironella (1917–2003) that depicted a less Manichean description of the civil war, had a great impact.

But in literature, the two greatest authors of the period were Camilo José Cela (1916–2002) and Miguel Delibes (1920–2010). The first, a Nobel prize winner in 1989, author of *The Family of Pascual Duarte* (1942) and *La Colmena* (1951), two essential works of the narrative panorama of the Spanish twentieth century. (Interestingly, Cela also worked as a censor for the regime in the 1940s.) The second, Delibes, published his striking first book, *La sombra del ciprés es alargada* in 1947, and later portrayed the misery of the rural world (*Las Ratas,* 1962) and the unhappy lives of the common people (*Cinco horas con Mario,* 1966).

Hostility toward the regime in almost all cultural sectors intensified during the 1960s, and continued to increase until Franco's death. Economic development and improvement in the quality of life spurred demands for freedom. Universities were full of young students studying Marxism in hiding and increasingly taking to the streets to face police. Spanish tourism also saw a boom, skillfully sold by the regime with the slogan "Spain is different," a slogan which once again made reference to the Spanish romanticism. The Franco regime sold a particular brand of popular Spanish culture, among which was the stereotyped *flamenco* and the bullfights as typically Spanish activities. Lola Flores (1923–95) and Manuel Benítez or *El Cordobés* (1936) became the archetypical representative of the folkloric Spain that was popularized by Manolo Escobar (1931–2013) with a *Pasodoble* that would become famous over the world: *¡Y viva España!*

Thus for millions of tourists, Spain became, culturally speaking, a comfortable destination of beach, sun, *paella, sangría,* bullfights, *flamenco,* parties, and *siestas*. As in the nineteenth century, Spain was considered a backward country, one in love with itself. This could not have been further from what the cultural elites of the moment, increasingly opposed to the decrepit regime, felt. More than ever, cultural manifestations of any sign were strongly politicized.

The movies of the country's important directors, among them the works of Juan Antonio Bardem (1922–2002), Luis García Berlanga (1921–2010), and Carlos Saura (1932), stood as testament to these changes. These were reinforced by the refreshing theatre of *Els Joglars* (Albert Boadella, 1943); the songs of Joan Manuel Serrat (1943) and the Catalan *Nova Cançó* of Raimon (b.1940) and Lluís Llach (b.1948); the literature of the combative Manuel Vázquez Montalbán (1939–2003) and the cold and exquisite prose of Juan Benet (1927–93). Even those who created art that distanced itself from political controversy, like painters Joan Miró (1893–1983), Antoni Tapiés (1923–2012), Antonio Saura (1930–98); sculptors Pablo Serrano (1908–85), Jorge de Oteiza (1908–2003), and Eduardo Chillida (1924–2002), did not miss the opportunity to display their work and themselves as anti-Franco.

Freedom, Europeanism, modernity

The end of the Francoist dictatorship allowed Spain to reintegrate itself wholly into a developing Europe. In 1992, international celebrations (especially those of Barcelona and Seville) presented the world with a prosperous, free, and modern country. Culturally, the Madrid *movida,* a heterogeneous countercultural movement headed by the cinema director

Pedro Almodóvar, found great acclaim worldwide. The turn of the twenty-first century has seen Spain become a vital and attractive country, one which, culturally speaking, has proven its literary and artistic prowess, but which was not made great strides in its contributions to philosophy, science, technology, and research.

After the death of Franco, the transition to democracy allowed the country to regain freedom and begin a shift toward modernization, a shift that led to its integration with the rest of Europe (see Chapter 8). From the beginning of the twentieth century, so-called Europeanization (political, economic, and cultural integration to Western Europe) had been the ideal of Spanish elites. Those objectives were met with relative ease in a very short span of time.

The years of transition were not free of setbacks or controversy. The return of liberty generated unrealistic expectations that soon led to frustration: a so-called disenchantment, poignantly symbolized by a film of the same title (1976) by Jaime Chávarri which portrayed the family of poet Leopoldo María Panero. Shortly thereafter, a sentiment of general frustration erupted, depicted in the stories of Rosa Montero (1951–) titled *Crónica del desamor* (1979) and in the extensive *Carvalho* series of detective novels (1972–2004) by Vazquez Montalbán. This sentiment swiftly became a hedonistic and provocative frenzy known as *La Movida*—the "Madrilenian move"—that later extended into other Spanish cities, a youth movement of counterculture and eclectic profiles capable of integrating the vanguard with traditionalist and *Castizo* elements.

The "Madrilenian move" was a form of protest, a generational manifestation, and a way of life. Although it was not an organized movement, it had pointed means of diffusion, such as the magazines *La Luna de Madrid* and *Madrid me mata*; the television program *La Edad de Oro,* and its flagship venues, the *Rock-Ola* and *La Vía Láctea* nightclubs, together with direct and indirect support from the Madrid city council that was presided at the time by a veteran Marxist, "the old professor" Enrique Tierno Galván (1918–86). One of the most popular writers of the moment, Francisco Umbral (1932–2007), gave it an aura of prestige. From the artistic point of view, the *movida* expressed itself through painting, photograph, graffiti, fashion, short stories, film, and, above all, through music, with multiple bands that lived their heyday and downfall in the span of a few years, among them *Alaska y los Pegamoides, Nacha Pop, Kaka de Luxe,* and *Radio Futura.*

The most representative and universal figure of the movement became the film director Pedro Almodóvar (1949–), author of films which enjoyed immense success in Spain and around the world. Almodóvar started making movies as an amateur, with films like *Pepi, Luci, Bom y otras chicas del montón* (1980), and in time became one of the most valued Spanish directors due to his international acclaim and his institutional recognition (including two Oscars). Almodovar's influence goes beyond his own many films: Many of the actors who have worked with him—known as Almodóvar´s boys and girls—have become international stars in their own right: including Antonio Banderas (1960–), Javier Bardem (1969–), and Penélope Cruz (1974–).

The world reflected by Almodóvar through his films is very Spanish in the traditional sense—bulls, Catholicism, folk songs (*coplas*)—but at the same time this world has a modern gloss, an expressive freshness in which unbelievable situations coexist with a continuous dose of calculated provocation. All this has made the Spanish director stand as an ambassador and cultural representative of "new Spain": with the appreciation of foreign onlookers, a renovated Spain has emerged, one brought up to date, without having left behind the Spain of old.

In the new democratic Spain, 1992 constituted the culminating moment in the country's international recognition: that year the Olympic Games was held in Barcelona, the Universal Exposition in Seville, and Madrid was named cultural capital of Europe. During the time between the last decade of the twentieth century and the first years of the twenty-first century, Spanish culture and its representatives reached unprecedented prestige. Its representatives have come from a myriad of disciplines, some of whom include architects Rafael Moneo (1937) and Santiago Calatrava (1951); painter Miquel Barceló (1957); cardiologist Valentín Fuster (1943); poet Pere Gimferrer (1945); musicologist Jordi Savall (1941); sociologist Manuel Castells (1942); philosopher Fernando Savater (1947); geneticist Antonio García-Bellido (1936); opera singers Plácido Domingo (1941), Monserrat Caballé (1933), and José Carreras (1946); biologist Francisco José Ayala (1934); guitarist Paco de Lucía (1947–2014); innovative cook Ferran Adrià (1962) and his mythical restaurant *El Bulli*; singer Julio Iglesias (1943); oncologist Mariano Barbacid (1949); tailor Adolfo Domínguez (1950); paleoanthropologist Juan Luis Arsuaga (1954), writers Javier Marías (1951), and Antonio Muñoz Molina (1956).

As this randomized list indicates, the Spanish culture and language (headed by the prestige of the Cervantes Institute) that is projected and sold abroad today with the commercial claim "made in Spain" has its strong and its weak points. On the one hand, the minority presence of female names persists. Although the feminist movement has provided a boost in the last decades, there is still a long path for women to tread in order to obtain full-fledged public visibility and to conquer areas of power in institutions. Only six of the forty-six members of the Royal Spanish Academy are women, for instance. Similar numbers can be seen in other cultural centers. As the title of a famous movie by José Luis Garci (1944–) indicates, this is a "pending subject" in Spanish society and culture.

After the Civil War the Franco regime had persecuted languages other than Spanish although as time went on the prohibitions were lifted and gave way to a relative unofficial permissiveness. Starting in the 1960s, and especially during the regime's last years, the use of these languages, and especially Catalan and Basque, became one of the most recognizable symbols of resistance to the regime. The *nova cançó*, with figures such as Raimon (1940–) and Lluis Llach (1948–), was one outstanding example.

The Constitution of 1978 proclaimed "Spanish or Castillian" as the shared language of all Spaniards but gave "co-official" status to the languages of the autonomous regions: Catalan in Catalonia, Basque in Euskadi, and Galician in Galicia. This facilitated the flourishing of these languages, although not to an equal extent. The expansion of Catalan has been the most spectacular example. It enjoyed the benefit of a long and distinguished cultural tradition as well as the support of powerful cultural industries (many of Spain's most important publishing houses are located in Barcelona). Much of the Catalan media: radio, television, and magazines adopted Catalan as their standard language. This was also a politicized assertion of identity and greater autonomy from Madrid, the national capital. Newspapers were a partial exception. On the other hand, many Catalan-language novels, poems, plays, and movies had no political connotations at all. The government of Catalonia also imposed an educational policy known as "linguistic immersion" which required students to be educated in Catalan, something which has been the source of ongoing controversy.

The powerful growth of Catalan has produced political conflicts with traditional Spanish centralism, but it has also provoked an internal conflict between the proponents of the so-called Països Catalans who see much of Mediterranean Spain as a Catalan-speaking zone and people in the Valencian Community who see their language as distinct from Catalan.

Euskadi and Galicia have also experienced similarly complex conflicts, although these have been shaped by the specific economic, cultural, social, and political circumstances of these regions. The government of Euskadi has certainly tried to strengthen the Basque language but it has had to deal with two problems: the fact that Basque is a rural language which is radically different from the country's other languages and that it was much less widely spoken, especially in the cities. Despite being a politically conservative region, the government of Galicia has worked to increase the teaching of Gallego in the schools and its use in culture in general without producing the same kind of political conflicts as in Catalonia.

Overall, the flourishing of languages other than Spanish has been a positive development, enriching the country's cultural diversity. At the same time, it has been a continuous source of political controversy which has contributed to its not being widely accepted in the rest of Spain.

History continues to weigh down the current state of Spanish culture. The country highlights a myriad of artistic and literary activities, now extended into adjacent areas such as gastronomy, fashion, and design, but continues to be highly deficient in areas such as scientific research (save for some very specific areas like bio-sanitary investigation), applied science, technology, the hard sciences, and philosophy. The universities enjoy a generous system of self-government and have multiplied in recent years with administrative decentralization: they are also enormous bureaucratic centers filled with endogamy, incapable of accomplishing revitalization or connecting to the business world. At the time of writing, there was not a single Spanish university on the list of the 100 best universities in the world.

Continuous and failed reforms have produced a deteriorating system of public instruction and it shows mediocre results in international reports. Although Spain is now a modern and advanced country—far from its romantic roots—Spanish culture continues to be perceived by millions of tourists annually through the long-standing stereotypes: bulls, flamenco, Catholic pomp (Holy Week) and above all, great parties: Fallas in Valencia, Seville's Holy Week, Pamplona's Saint Fermin, etc. In the meantime, peripheral nationalisms in Catalonia, the Basque Country, and Galicia work to build a cultural identity that is original, distinct, and alternative to the Spanish one. Even in the twentieth century, the weight of history and political interference has not led Spaniards to recognize themselves in their so-called cultural symbols.

Further reading

Colmeiro, José F., *Spain Today: Essays on Literature, Culture, Society*, Hanover: Dartmouth College, 1999.

Gies, David Thatcher, *The Cambridge Companion to Modern Spanish Culture*, Cambridge: Cambridge University Press, 1999.

Gracia, Jordi, and Miguel Ángel Ruiz Carnicer, *La España de Franco (1939-1975). Cultura y vida cotidiana*, Madrid: Síntesis, 2004.

Jordan, Barry, *Spanish Culture and Society: The Essential Glossary*, London: Arnold, 2002.

Mainer, José-Carlos, *La Edad de Plata, 1902-1939. Ensayo de interpretación de un proceso cultural*, Madrid: Cátedra, 1987.

Rodgers, Eamonn (ed.), *Encyclopedia of Contemporary Spanish Culture*, London: Routledge, 2002.

Sánchez, Antonio, *Postmodern Spain: A Cultural Analysis of 1980s-1990s Spanish Culture*, Oxford: Peter Lang, 2007.

Smith, Paul Julian, *Contemporary Spanish Culture: TV, Fashion, Art and Film*, Cambridge: Polity, 2003.

Stanton, Edward F., *Culture and Customs of Spain*, Westport, CT and London: Greenwood Press, 2002.

Treglown, Jeremy, *Franco's Crypt: Spanish Culture and Memory Since 1936*, New York: FSG Books, 2013.

CHAPTER 16
INTELLECTUALS

Santos Juliá

Translated by Christopher G. Cunningham

Miguel de Unamuno was probably the first person in Spain to use the term *intellectual*. He underlined it as a noun in a letter he sent to the president of the Council of Ministers, Antonio Cánovas del Castillo in November of 1896 in which he urged clemency for his unfortunate friend, Pedro Corominas, an anarchist sympathizer who had been condemned to death following a terrorist attack in Barcelona. The Dreyfus Affair in France, which began in 1894, with Emile Zola's famous *J'Accuse* (1898) and, above all, Maurice Barrès's searing response the next month, brought the term into general use. And in 1899 Ramiro de Maeztu could hail its appearance without envisioning the fate that this new personage would acquire in the twentieth century. He wrote that "the intellectual has appeared and before his inscrutable gaze the lie cannot prevail." This was how those literary figures, publicists, and professors began to identify themselves as intellectuals with each other and before the public: a number of men who were there so that the lie would not prevail, or in other words, who were there to defend universal values. Self-invested with the authority they derived from that defense, the intellectuals set about making abundant use of the weapons made available to them from their profession: writing and speaking, newspapers, and public lectures.

These first intellectuals came to be known as such through joining friendship groups like the one called "the three": after Azorín, Pío Baroja, and Maetzu. As in the case of the indefatigable Miguel de Unamuno, they went on to sign manifestos or publish protest articles in newspapers and participate in public forums opposing this or that subject. They did not care for the idea of formal groupings, and they did not even take on the task of publishing reviews or establishing their own periodicals. Nor did they show any great political coherence as they very rapidly moved from socialist and anarchist discourses to reactionary and conservative positions. They spent little time on political and social questions. Rather they spoke unceasingly of the State and society, mostly in derogatory terms. Frightened by the mobilization of the masses (see Chapter 17), they doubted the people's political capacity and broke with the liberal tradition of their predecessors by inventing a narrative of the history of Spain; not as that of a fallen nation that would regain its strength when the people recaptured their freedoms, as the romantics and the liberals believed, but as a dead nation that awaited the day of resurrection. The immediate consequence of these actions was a deep hostility toward the politicians and toward politics in general, and the hope and invocation of the strong man in his multiple guises that filled publications at the end of the century: a guardian of communities, a prudent and restrained strongman, a brilliant man, a benevolent tyrant, a hero, a superman, an iron surgeon, a redeemer, a sculptor of nations.

Such was the intellectuals' baptism. They identified with the term *intellectual* when they started to sign protest manifestos against one thing or the other, as they did in France around the Dreyfus affair and in Spain over the Montjuich verdicts of 1896. But some time needed to elapse before the term "protest" would become linked to that of "intellectual" in a mutually identifiable way. It happened for a simple reason, the resolution of one of the crises that highlighted the political life of the Restoration period that carried Eugenio Montero Ríos to the presidency of the Council of Ministers in June of 1905. At first glance it is surprising that "the protest of the intellectuals," spread across the front pages, would spring from such a routine motive, removed from the defense of universal values and fundamental rights normally linked to the actions of the intellectual. But when the protest text is examined, it makes clear the intellectuals' exemplary character and the way they understood the role they should play in the mid-1910s of the twentieth century.

This first collective protest by intellectuals counted Benito Pérez Galdós at the head of a list that included many names from the world of culture: Vicente Blasco Ibáñez, Pío Baroja, Azorín, Ramón Pérez de Ayala, and Ramiro de Maeztu, Luis Morote, Manuel Ciges Aparicio, and Ramón del Valle-Inclán. It showed, above all, their pride at being part of the intelligentsia's elite. They were guided in their actions by what they understood as their own lofty and pure values, and the moral anguish that came from pondering a people passive before their political leaders. They rebelled, therefore, as surrogates for the people who were unable to express their discontent. And if the motive for the rebellion was entirely altruistic, it was no less valid. The intellectuals rose up invested with a sense of supreme judicial legitimacy. They did not call the people to action; neither did they propose an organized campaign, nor demand clean elections. They were simply protesting the formation of a government headed by someone judged responsible for the 1898 Treaty of Paris, which ended the Spanish-American War, and for having the audacity to name his son-in-law as minister. They expressed their condemnation in a signed judgment that they took to the newspapers that would communicate it to the public.

A few more years were needed before this intellectual protest, both spoken and in writing, would vanish from the debates in the *tertulias* (Social gatherings) and the press before protest was revived as a continuous action sustained in one way or another by an association of intellectuals. With time and some further events, the perception of the relationship between the intellectual and the masses changed from that which had been previously based on the involvement and role of intellectuals during the crisis at the end of the century. The intellectual then felt insecure in his place in society, his former preeminence threatened for the sole reason of being an artist or writer of merit, surrounded by the ignorant masses, anguished by the decadence of the nation and the degeneration of the race. He emphatically affirmed his independence and, at the same time, his separate superiority. Save for sporadic occasions he did not feel part of a social class, self-assuredly assembling resources in order to take action. As a result, he put full faith in the written or spoken word, but would reject any effort toward organizing.

This changed beginning in 1909, a crucial year for the perception the intellectuals held of themselves and of politics (see Chapter 18). Not coincidentally, it would once again be Maeztu who expressed it in the most urgent terms. "From July 1909," he stated in the *Ateneo de Madrid*:

We knew that the Spanish revolution had begun to operate independently of our intellectual classes. One grew pessimistic, on balance, about the outcome achieved up to then by the intellectuals' involvement in the public sphere. In one part there were a few achievements, but more than that, the conspiracy of praise took a more lamentable turn than the conspiracy of silence: we cried out and the response was to call us distinguished, discreet and industrious; we raised our cry to a howl and they labeled us as remarkable, and prominent.

When they stopped shouting and took a look at their surroundings, "things continued to be the same as before." Some gave up the struggle, some—like Maeztu himself—retired to be with their thoughts, others ended up renouncing their roles in order "to live the rational life." The protest had ended without achieving anything.

But at this juncture the masses started the revolution. It was time, therefore, to think again about who the intellectuals were and what their purpose was. And Maeztu pointed out that the intellectuals were starting to emerge in Spain now not "as meteorites fallen from the sky and monsters from the natural world, but as a systematic means of linking one to the other in an ideal chain of teachers and disciples." The young Spaniards who began graduating from European universities would shape the new generation of intellectuals to which Maeztu referred. They were supported financially by the *Junta para Ampliación de Estudios* and on their return home, they obtained appointments as university professors, or distinguished positions in their chosen professions. Many of them had a technical education and benefited from a firmer institutional base than the men of letters who arrived in the capital in search of fortune and glory. Moreover, Maeztu stated, these new intellectuals would soon have a sure guide in the emerging star whom they invited to take charge and lead them forward—José Ortega y Gasset (see Chapter 32).

Ortega would quickly become the "thinker" of this privileged, youthful minority. They learned German, English, or French, expanding their studies outside of the country thanks to a policy of scholarships. These new people did not see themselves as degenerate nor did they enjoy entombing themselves in the cemeteries, just the opposite. Theirs was not the introverted view of Spain that Unamuno desired, a land "peopled by fakirs curled up in the sun and hirsute dervishes with scratching staffs, absorbed in pondering the enigma of death," but rather, in the words of mathematician Julio Rey Pastor, a "vigorous and optimistic generation unreservedly engaged in the joy of life," a generation determined to work tenaciously in order to win "the inclusion of Spain into the international community." Before the Great War they had all visited France, Germany, or the United States. It would not be surprising then that this generation who called themselves "new," identified with the Allies and confronted, in what was called a civil war of words, the rampant Germanophilia of the traditional media. And immediately after it became commonplace for European scientists to give courses and lectures in Madrid and Barcelona which, in the middle of the 1920s, had become regular stops on the international conference circuit. The flow of visitors was constant as was that of the Spaniards who kept in permanent contact with foreign research centers. The visitors discussed mechanics, geometry, histology, and physics and relativity. And those Spaniards who returned these visits did not recount the stories of the Alhambra, but discussed the structure of matter and its magnetic properties. In truth, as Thomas Glick pointed out, beginning in 1910 there started to emerge in Spain a limited but very active scientific community who were used to meeting with foreign scientists of the very highest caliber.

These were the people whom Ortega addressed in his stand against the old politics. In announcing the creation of the League of Spanish Political Education, Ortega was joined in signing the prospectus by Manuel Azaña (see Chapter 33), future Socialist cabinet minister Fernando de los Ríos, and the famous criminologist Constancio Bernaldo de Quirós, among others. And in the impactful lecture in which he denounced the old and proposed the new, the emphasis would no longer be on protest, but on action. Political action was taken as the work of political parties and it was to give way to action directed at creating "organs of social service, culture, technology, mutual aid and life, in other words, humanity in all its forms." Ortega did not disdain politics, nor did he wish to intervene in them, but in agreement with his perception of the weakness of Spanish civil society, the new class, as a select minority, had to shoulder the burden of rebuilding society by organizing themselves so as to educate the masses.

The debate around this issue of this new intellectual class ought to have led to the creation of a coalition, or a political party capable of substituting the two dynastic parties, a debate that Joaquín Costa had stirred up toward the end of the century. Instead, it ended with the intellectuals turning their backs on any form of organization. Ortega offered a clear reply: it was not the time to engage in politics with the aim to "win power." It was not power or the government that mattered, but the invention of a scheme that would replace social confusion with a more effective State. Ortega postponed the urgency to conquer institutions in favor of organizing the select minority into their areas of expertise: the rebuilding, in deference to the emerging professional class, of an all-encompassing and national dialogue that would legitimize the great task of educating the masses.

The announcement of the League of Political Education, the conference "Old and New Politics," the magazine *España*, the newspaper *El Sol*; these were the consequences of the emergence of this new intellectualism in public life. Those who were very young in 1898 thus affirmed their own identity, clearly distancing themselves from the generation that carried the weight of that disastrous year. Theirs was the first generation that studied in foreign universities and, as a result, they replaced national self-absorption with a European preoccupation. Most did not return as *literati*, but as university professors, teachers, medical doctors, engineers, scientists, and lawyers. Unlike their predecessors, they quickly gained a sense of community and became conscious of themselves as forming an elite. They criticized the literary class, who were otherwise admired, for their egotism and exhibitionism. They showed no aversion to organizing; quite the opposite, they had felt the need to organize as a consequence of their situation. Without discounting newspaper articles, they also busied themselves in writing political books, and promoting publications and publishing houses directed at the whole of the professional classes. They did not suffer the ideological fluctuations of their elders. They were liberals, or new liberals who, after flirting with socialism, ended up identifying democracy with republicanism. Few had passed through an anarchist or revolutionary phase in their youth. They never detested the city, they considered politics as a form of inevitable destiny, and it did not occur to them to renounce democracy. They built their discourse predominately as a variation of the great metaphor of the two Spains, official and actual, old and new, that provided a rhetorical figure in order to encourage a mobilization that would open the pathways to a participatory process.

While in Madrid, men of letters protested and the professionals formed short-lived leagues of civic education, in Barcelona those who around 1890 had occupied leadership positions in the atheneums and other cultural societies began campaigns in support of the Catalan language or Catalan civil law. It is difficult to understand, in spite of their lament for the ruined state of the nation, their rejection of politics, their anti-parliamentarianism, their fears of liberalism and of the overwhelming presence of romantic elements in their discourse. They resembled a Catalan version of the Spanish Generation of '98. They did not reject the past, they did not present themselves publicly as if none before them had spoken or written anything, as if history only began with them. Moreover they were determined to act, to intervene in public life in a collective manner through cultural centers. They wanted to be considered as the ones who would continue the task of recovering the lost fatherland which had been evolving since the early nineteenth century (see Chapter 10). They were there to rescue an identity, that of great medieval Catalonia. But in doing so they did not wish to waste any material conveyed by those who before them had taken the same path, although without having reached this goal.

This younger generation, then, did not need to brand their elders with the stigma of old age, or boast of breaks with the past or new beginnings. On the contrary, in order to regain the lost nation, they avidly read everything that had been written or recounted from years before. If one had to personalize and synthesize a history rich in intersections, initiatives, coalitions, and excisions, it would be necessary to cite the likes of the politician Enric Prat de la Riba, the architect Josep Puig i Cadalfach, and Luis Duran i Ventosa, all born around 1870. They could read with equal benefit the left-wing federalist Valentí Almirall, the canonical traditionalist and subsequent Bishop of Vic, Torras i Bages; or Joan Maragall, the modernist poet; all of whom were born between one and three decades earlier. They did not just read them, but participated with them in public functions, shared with them responsible positions in different associations, and felt deep affection toward them.

They met in private institutions and collective settings with politicians, industrialists, priests, and jurists. There emerged from these gatherings the characteristic type of Catalan nationalist intellectual who was completely estranged from their contemporaries in the Generation of '98. These intellectuals were no mere literary figures, lawyers, architects, and medical doctors who could be upset about the ills of the country in the way that others were. Rather, they were people whose concerns for their country translated into professional and enhanced collective action from a rich network of cultural institutions created for this very purpose. The number and variety of institutional meeting spaces are notable; not just *tertulias*, nor chats in cafés, but meetings at associations, centers, literary clubs, leagues, unions, within political parties, and cultural and recreational societies with their rules, their formalities, their fees and boards of directors. What the men of letters wrote; the houses and palaces that the architects built, or the churches and monasteries that they restored; the court cases the lawyers defended were all directly related to what they did in the institutions they ran to recover the Catalan nation. They were not just ideologues or moralists, nor did they limit themselves to protest. They worked to awaken a nation that they judged to be asleep and to set it moving toward reclaiming its authentic self. Their rhetoric is not comprehendible if one only sees it as an evolution of almost predetermined ideas culminating in a final synthesis. They were, on the contrary, statements that were built on a common ideal and, therefore, as the collective mission of the national community, activities, and interests that did not always coincide.

If Catalonia was the intellectual vanguard that worked to awaken the slumbering nation, the Great War would be the charge that ignited wider aspirations and regional and national demonstrations among the new professional class. In 1915, Blas Infante published *El Ideal Andaluz*. By 1919 in Córdoba, *el Manifiesto Andalucista* revived the idea of abolishing central power and having a free Andalucia. Shortly before, *Unió y La Joventut* brought out a *Declaració valencianista* in defense of the notion that the Valencian people possessed a strong individuality evidenced by their own language, racial traits, and a common history and economic conditions. In this context, there appeared in Lugo "the first explicitly collective affirmation from the Galician nation," in a manifesto approved by the Assembly of delegates from the *Irmandades da Fala*, which met in Lugo in 1918. In the Basque Country, Jesús de Sarría launched the review *Hermes* that, in its first issue, vindicated the part that the Basques had had in the history of Spain. And from the Castilian deputies in the Cortes there emerged a *Message from Castile* sent to the Government in the form of a reply to the *Bases for Catalan Autonomy* approved by the Mancomunidad of Catalonia.

Intellectuals of the protest, intellectuals of the leagues of public education, intellectuals organized to create the nation or awaken the sleeping nation; these were three different kinds of intellectuals, three different ways in which intellectuals were involved in the public sphere. They were very active when in the first issue of the magazine *Nosotros* on May 1, 1930 some youths who felt a part of another generation affirmed that Spain had entered a period of historic crisis. It was a crisis that had not been opened with the fall of Primo de Rivera the month before (see Chapter 5). It came from far in the past and now it only remained to recognize that "the crisis is before us" and that now one had to "look to the future." Thinking back on the year 1930, Rafael Cansinos recalled in his memoirs that politics absorbed everything. The only topic of conversation was the crisis of the regime, and half measures were not possible: "The people want the Republic. Now there is no room for formulas of reconciliation. This is the truth. Today's popular saying is that 'we must redefine ourselves'. One has to state clearly if he is with the Monarchy or against it." A year earlier, Antonio Espina, obsessed by the encounter of the 3 with the 0, and convinced that in previous centuries when faced with this same encounter humanity had given birth to great currents of thought and culture, such as neoclassicism, and the *Discourse on Method* of 1630, rationalism, and the encyclopaedism of 1730, the Romantics, *Hernani*, the sentimental Europe of 1830, asked: What will our challenging 1930 have in store for us? We do not know, but what we do know is that we "have to redefine ourselves." The politicization of the culture was on the move and it became necessary to pick a side and embrace the "people's cause."

Taking sides did not disturb the slumber of the writers and artists of previous generations. Until the mid-1920s it was a matter of a select minority, a spiritual aristocracy taking up the mission of awakening and guiding the masses in creating society and the nation in a new light. But the ups and downs of politics, together with their pretension of having an influence left the intellectuals to ponder the question of whether or not they should "become involved in politics." It was at this point that the road began to divide. Ortega, for one, drew back. As he wrote in *Imperativo de intelectualidad* in 1922, the intellectual in order to exercise his influence "over the future destiny of Spain should not make it his intention in the first place." Five years later he wrote that the intellectual does not feel the need for action. On the contrary, he judges action as an annoyance best to be avoided. The intellectuals are those rather rare kinds of men for whom "it is unnecessary to be involved in anything," because it is enough that they be who they are.

But not everyone agreed to abstain from political life. As the 1920s went on, the intellectual's perception of his role underwent a radical transformation. European politics were going through a period of great confusion: the dictatorship of the proletariat controlled Russia, first in its Leninist and later in its Stalinist version; Mussolini rose to power in Italy, while liberalism and democracy were looking bankrupt. In Spain a dictator began to encounter problems with the university world. Something had to be done. The intellectual could not live on the sidelines becoming a kind of priest of art for art's sake. Art must engage life, acknowledge it, and express its problems by siding with it. The young intellectuals, like everyone, had to define themselves and get involved. No one said as much, but the image of the committed intellectual who uses his pen to serve ideas had taken hold. For certain, there was a surfeit of ideas in 1930: liberalism, democracy, fascism, socialism, communism, and anarchism, and the intellectuals had to choose among them. The new generation of Antonio Espina, José Díaz Fernández, Maria Zambrano, Ernesto Giménez Caballero, Ramiro Ledesma, Ramón Sender, Francisco Ayala, Rafael Alberti, and José Bergamín were impelled to opt for one or the other. Some chose fascism, others communism, and still others the Republic or socialism.

And there was also no lack of those who did it for the faith and the Catholic Church, such as the canon of Granada cathedral, Rafael García y García de Castro, who asked himself in 1934: "What do we understand by intellectuals?" The reply from this ambiguous figure was worthy of a history treatise or theory: "For some time this name has been in fashion and it has been applied without exception to writers of ideas and those with marked leftist tendencies." For a cleric of the 1930s, the term intellectual had once been attributed to leftist writers, an idea full of meaning since it gathered in a single word everything that opposed what was national, Christian, and Spanish. There was nothing strange, therefore, "in these days of unrest and tumult, with barricades in the streets and Parliament caught up in shameful, pugilistic hatred, self-indulgence and blasphemies," that "intellectual" raised in the canon's mind "the scene of apocalyptic desolation, the opening of the well of the abyss from which spews forth smoke that obscures the sun and locusts that lay waste to the earth."

The intellectuals had indeed succeeded in drawing Spanish culture close to the then predominant cultural currents of Europe. That Europeanization for which Costa had clamored and which Ortega turned into a recruiting device was now in the throes of a rapid secularization. If some of the loudest intellectuals of the Generation of '98 anguished over the tragic sorrow of life—Unamuno wrote a famous essay with this title—those who came after them drew attention most of all to the joy of their own lives. This was apparent in Ortega's case; in those who came later, those from the Residencia de Estudiantes who came later, among them Federico García Lorca, Alberti, Luis Buñuel, and Salvador Dalí, it was a provocation. In spite of the overwhelming presence of the Church with its dense network of educational institutions which entrapped the spirit of the middle class, it is surprising just how secular the dominant culture was among those generations in the first third of the century. The Church had lost the working class a long time ago, but its influence among the middle class that played a leading role in the so-called Silver Age of Spanish culture was truly null and void.

What concerned the men of the Church, nevertheless, was not so much the distancing from religion that those foreign-influenced leftists had achieved, as with the social influence that they attributed to "the representatives of knowledge" and the position of cultural power that they had achieved while Catholics remained at the margin, "without participating in the governance of the State." This was a perception shared by the intellectuals of the two great currents of political Catholicism that had watched, perplexed, and disorientated, the proclamation of the Republic. The first started as traditionalists and Alphonsists (pro-Alfonso XIII), and ended up by joining Acción Española (*Spanish Action*). Maeztu appears again together with Eugenio Vegas, José Maria Pemán, and Pedro Sainz Rodríguez. They took it for granted that the enemies of religion and of the nation had gone about occupying all the posts from which they could spread among the public views that contradicted those of the Church.

Oral and written propaganda, the press and university professorships remained "in enemy hands." All the means of power had been peacefully surrendered to the revolutionary leaders. The second group, the *accidentalistas*—for whom the question of monarchy or republic was less important than the actual content of the laws—, who emerged from social Catholicism at the beginning of the century and from the National Catholic Association of Propagandists, could hardly be distinguished in this matter from the traditional monarchists. A manifesto signed by, among others, José María Gil Robles, and Franco's brother-in-law Ramón Serrano Suñer, proclaimed that while Catholic thought had been absent from Spain for a quarter of a century, enemy forces, inspired impiously by relativism and evolutionism had been able to prepare first an intellectual campaign, and later a practical one. Their triumph was evident in their dominance of the institutions, the administration, the press, the possession of power, the university, the street, and the barracks.

Whatever their point of departure, Catholic intellectuals were convinced that after half a century of absence from the field of thought, the enemy had taken all the positions. Nevertheless, if the simple fact of the proclamation of the Republic had shown to one and all the depth of the damage inflicted on religion and the fatherland by the intellectuals, its very existence ought to serve as an incentive to awaken Catholic intellectuals from their placid slumber that they had been in since the time of Cánovas. The Republic, in other words, needed to be understood as Ángel Herrera would have it, as a *felix culpa*: the "fortunate persecution that is giving rise to this magnificent reaction among Catholics in all of the country." It was a type of whip sent by God with the dual goal of punishing one's own for their indolence and timidity, while also calling them to action in order to "fight like valiant crusaders until the last trench."

This guilt would not be completely redeemed until Catholics woke up and took action. At this point once again the positions of the two main hotbeds of Catholic intellectuals of the 1930s and 1940s were not far apart. The men of Acción Española saw their mission as a kind of conquest, a crusade that would restore the great Spain of the Catholic Kings and the House of Austria; the start of a new Reconquest. No one should shrink before the final outcome of the call to action. In such a state of affairs, Catholics enjoyed a "right of rebellion." The men of Acción Popular shared the very same siege mentality and vision for the task ahead: a recapturing of ground foolishly lost to the enemy. It was necessary to publicize modern Catholic thinking, to launch oral and written campaigns, to fight in the vanguard of the counterrevolution, and to put an end to the desolate parenthesis that ecumenical thinking had had in Spain for twenty-five years. It would be, in accord with the manifesto of its intellectuals, a reconquest that ought to bring about a renaissance. The proposals for action that emanated from the intellectual circles of the two great currents of Catholic politics were illustrated by terms like war, crusade, and reconquest.

Indeed, the Catholic intellectuals whether monarchists or *accidentalistas* shared something more than the diagnosis of the situation. To begin with, they agreed that the enemy had dominated the field. Their enemy had a generic name: the intellectuals, whether traitorous or misguided as Pemán saw them, or a more specific one: the Institución Libre de Enseñanza (see Chapter 15). It was, as they all claimed, the cancer that corroded the University; a sect that carried out an anti-nationalist campaign whose aim was to destroy religious ideas; a nest of freemasons and foreign sympathizers, which proposed to de-Catholicize Spain. There was an urgent need to wake up and take action, to do battle in every area of the public arena to regain lost ground. In the end this action had to be organized by circles and societies that would urge their members to act in solidarity. And in this nothing differentiated the nucleus of intellectuals in Acción Española, all of whom sought from those affiliated with Acción Popular to be able to fight in the vanguard of the counter revolution.

It is this decision to take the offensive in an organized and collective way in order to gain positions of power from to impose their political will that differs radically from all preceding notions of what it meant to be an intellectual. They fought and following a war they conquered all power, eliminating the enemy as much as they could in the process. They went forward with the "brutal mutilation" of the university. And in their desire for "the summary execution of the noble Institution," on the way they took control of everything, from professorial chairs, to magazines and newspapers to the ateneos. (university). As a consequence of the "abundant emigration" of intellectuals during and at the end of the Civil War, "in Spain only the Catholics remained, those who expressed such things openly, and those who wisely kept silent on the question," recalled José Luis López Aranguren writing in 1969. This was the same Aranguren who twelve years earlier amused himself with the idea that during a quarter century Spain had witnessed a real Catholic spring. Practically all of the writers of his generation—the so-called Generation of 1936, those who were mobilized during the Civil War—were able to say: "We have been Catholics." Catholics then were everywhere, but Catholics who were divided, as Dionisio Ridruejo, who was a fascist, a Catholic, and an intellectual, put it between the narrow minded and the more tolerant.

What he meant was that while some Catholic intellectuals were prepared to tolerate other Spanish intellectual traditions—socialists, democrats, liberals, or secularist—many others were not. These were positions which their colleagues, and even friends, from the 1920s had advocated during the civil war. They included high-quality magazines and reviews such as *Hora de España* which published the public lecture read by Arturo Serrano Plaja in the name of a group of young writers and artists at the 2nd Congress of Anti-Fascist Writers for the Defense of Culture held in the summer of 1937. Here those young intellectuals explained that they were as soldiers fighting in the trenches as "the Youth of the Republic."

One issue they had to confront was the relationship between art and politics, especially after September 1936 when the Communists held powerful positions in the Ministry of Public Instruction and Fine Arts. They had before them the example of the intellectuals and artists of the Soviet Union who had put themselves at the service of the great proletarian party, but the writers and artists who defended the cause of the Republic possessed a long tradition of independent work that was reflected in one of the most extraordinary undertakings of the three years of the Civil War: the Spanish Pavilion at the International Exposition of 1937 in Paris. The work of the architects Luis Lacasa and Josep Luis Sert, it featured in front of its main façade the Column by Alberto (Sanchez Pérez) formally entitled *El pueblo español tiene un camino que conduce a una Estrella* (the Spanish people have a road which leads to a star). There also were sculptures by Picasso, *Cabeza de mujer*, and *Dama oferente* (*Femme au vase*); the statue of a Catalan peasant women, *La Montserrat*, by Julio González; and sculptured stone heads by Emiliano Barral, Joan Miró's mural *El Payés catalán en revolución* (*The Reaper*) and Alexander Calder's *Mercury Fountain*. Most famous of all was Picasso's mural *Guernica*. The Spanish Pavilion and its compendium of exhibits symbolized this singular moment that Spanish architecture, sculpture, and painting experienced during the years of the Republic and which would have their literary equivalent in the immortal *Elegía español* (Spanish Elegy) by Luis Cernuda.

To paraphrase Cernuda, the "old spring" had to wait a long time to weave its charm anew over that immense body, now trampled on, destroyed; quite literally thrown by the Catholics into the flames of hell. Meanwhile in Spain, the narrow minded and the more tolerant debated in the shadow of the eternal theme of Spain as a problem: what to do with traditions that fell victim to the Civil War? Might they be liquidated as un-Spanish, as anti-Spanish or anti-fatherland manifestations as justified by the Opus Dei intellectuals like Rafael Calvo in *Arbor*? Or might their reintegration be possible after a thorough exercise to purge them of any devious tendencies, as sought by some Falangists. Laín and Ridruejo made this case in the pages of *Escorial*.

In the meantime, the intellectuals who had been the splendid protagonists of the fittingly named Silver Age searched for some way to become organized after the defeat (see Chapter 15). In exile they launched magazines like *España Peregrina*, *Revista de Catalunya*, *Realidad*, and *Las Españas* among many others to foster new associations such as happened in 1940, when exiles founded the *Unión de Profesores Universitarios en el Extranjero* in Mexico. This group made themselves known through a Declaration signed in Havana on October 3, 1943. The Spanish Republic's cause, they wrote, was identical to that of the Allies during the Second World War, and they expressed their faith that the Allies' triumph would permit Spain to recover its sovereignty in order to be able to contribute to building of a new world order. It was signed by professors with diverse ideological and political affiliations such as Pere Bosch Gimpera, Afredo Mendizábal, Fernando de los Ríos, María Zambrano, José Giral, and Luis de Zulueta.

The course of the World War, the subsequent isolation of Spain, and the apparent weakness of the Franco regime; the creation by socialists and republicans of the Junta Española de Liberación; as well as the liberation of France in the summer of 1944, were some of the motives that pushed the Spanish Communist Party to reorganize the Alliance of Ant-fascist Intellectuals under the name of Union of Free Intellectuals. Historian Manuel Tuñón de Lara, one of those responsible, recalled a Memorandum delivered to the open embassies in Madrid. It contained conclusions in keeping with a program of demands that included the restoration of the law and civil rights to the Spanish people, the return of the emigrants, the international recognition of the people's right to elect the regime of their choice, and the entry of the democratic Spanish state into the UN. All of these made clear their attachment to the government of the Republic.

In the end, it was all in vain. Franco stayed in power and the failure of the democratic-liberal tradition was complete. The tripartite diplomatic note from the United States, the United Kingdom, and France of March 4, 1946 counseled the peaceful resignation of Franco, the abolition of the Falange and the formation of an interim government "under which the Spanish people would have the freedom to determine their preferred kind of government and to elect their leaders." It guaranteed to Franco that the three signatories had "no intention" of intervening in Spain's internal affairs. After a series of resolutions on the Spanish question, the UN General Assembly proposed the exclusion of Franco's government as a member of international organizations and the recall of ambassadors given the fascist origins and nature of the regime. At the same time, the whole world made it clear that neither the democratic powers, nor the Soviet Union, nor the United Nations had the slightest intention of recognizing the republican institutions, nor would they expel Franco from power. The Spanish question would need to be resolved by the Spaniards themselves.

In the end, after so many frustrated hopes, everyone understood that Franco was not going to be replaced either by a monarchy emerging from the bowels of his regime, or through the restoration of a republic. Franco was there to stay until he died. This fact was confirmed in the summer of 1953, when the United States and the Vatican signed lasting accords with the regime that signified its definitive consolidation of power.

For intellectuals, it was now necessary not to remain prisoners of the past if the aim was to open a pathway to a future democracy. It became necessary to close the door on the Civil War, starting in university settings and among the intellectuals, and to accept that the future could not be built under the persistence of civil war conditions, the unending division of Spaniards into victors and vanquished that was at the heart of the dictatorship (see Chapter 7). In a manifesto addressed to Catalan youth from Barcelona in 1956, the historian Jaume Vicens Vives declared that "the Civil War has ended." The document added that Catalan youth "find that the heavy inheritance of those unfortunate events is completely alien to them. They do not recognize either winners or losers." A feeling of detachment with respect to the Civil War was mirrored in similar, but more expansive terms in the document *Testimony of the Generations Distant from the Civil War*, a singular composition produced by a circle of young Catalan intellectuals, including the novelists Juan and José Agustín Goytisolo, who came together between 1950 and 1954 around the magazine *Laye*. This long text affirmed, as a first sign of identity, that none of them "has been able to participate even in a minimal way in the social structure that was imposed on the country after the worthless fratricidal slaughter" even though the young grew up in a "mythological climate of cultural reverence for the man sent by Providence to save Spain."

The year 1956 was not just any year in the history of the Spanish intellectuals. In February, a student rebellion at the University of Madrid provoked what the British ambassador Ivo Mallet defined as a serious crack in the monolithic structure of the regime. Evidence that the Falangist Spanish University Union had ceased to be a political force came with the first suspension of rights supposedly recognized in the Fuero de los Españoles. This was the explicit, conscious deletion of the dividing line that the regime had imposed between the victors and the vanquished. Of no less importance was a government crisis that would not end for another year. Some youthful Spaniards stated their views in a manifesto on April 1, the anniversary of the founding of a regime "that has not been able to integrate us into an authentic tradition or propel us toward a common future of reconciliation with Spain and with ourselves . . . we the sons of the victors and the vanquished." These university students and graduates including Enrique Múgica, Javier Pradera, Ramón Tamames, and Javier Muguerza, clearly showed the emergence of a new political subject who demanded a restoration of the rights of freedom of expression and association, and the democratization of university organizations. The Civil War was reduced to the status of a useless event which, as a group of young people from Valladolid wrote in yet another manifesto, it was necessary to "consign to oblivion" as it could obstruct the roads to the future.

The news that something had shifted in Spain, the publication of these manifestos in the newspapers of parties with organizations in France and in Mexico, found an immediate response among intellectuals in exile. A Frente Universitario Español (FUE) was formed in Mexico this same year. The acronym—FUE—was chosen deliberately, to preserve continuity with the Federación Universitaria Escolar from the years of the Primo de Rivera dictatorship and the Second Republic. Its principles affirmed that "the past Civil War placed a heavy burden of collective responsibility from which no sector of Spanish society can consider itself exempt, rather than completely loading it on the shoulders of the enemy." Even in exile, the Civil War, now twenty years in the past, had suffered a profound transformation. This had consequences for "the immediate situation," with the express refusal to "recall, elevate or heap scorn on the affairs of arms." It could not be any other way. Achieving a "future solution" could not be based on "any restoration of erroneous or mistaken historical trajectories." "We must be rid of the War," the Frente Universitario Español also affirmed as if responding to those in Spain who considered the War as over. In fact, this group of intellectuals proclaimed a "complete break from the errors of the past" and immediately followed this declaration with a proposal to build a future that is reinforced by "our best popular traditions adapted to the economic and cultural developments of our times."

The portrayal of the Civil War that spread among the new generation of intellectuals in Spain and in foreign exile—aptly named the Generation of '56—was a project for the future that would soon be shaped into a political strategy which would have a long life. The Communist Party defined its approach as one of national reconciliation whose objective consisted in opposing the dictatorship with a common front of democratic forces. The intellectuals took on new roles. Notwithstanding age, or political origin, their ranks grew thanks to the use of the right to petition recognized by the regime itself. They were able to reclaim fundamental rights of assembly and free expression, the freedom for the incarcerated to participate in strikes, the ability to protest against torture, and the demand for amnesty. It was what one of the young promoters of the February 1956 movement, Javier Pradera, called "the signed struggle": manifestos or petitions that extended a language of freedom and democracy and carried the signatures of intellectuals, without attention to age or political profile. It was unique in that a fellow traveler of the Communist Party was able to agree with a former member of CEDA or an old Falangist with a liberal, always under the shadow of some eminent personality respected by all, such as Ramón Menéndez Pidal, who directed respectful letters to the authorities in power.

This all came together in activities that would occupy all of the decade of the 1960s, beginning with the miners' strikes in Asturias and the encounter in Munich in 1962. And the trend continued until well into the 1970s, with new or revived magazines in which the signers of those earlier petitions or denunciations would evaluate and propagate a new democratic language. These publications included *Cuadernos para el diálogo*, *Serra d'Or*, *Triunfo*, *Destino*, *Aldebarán*, and more. Their content covered conversations between Castilians and Catalans on the future shape of the Spanish state: would it be a federation, a confederation, or a set of autonomous regions? Debates swirled around the question that Dionisio Ridruejo had formulated in 1961, and that had been reiterated by Communist leader Santiago Castillo in 1965: "after Franco, what?" The protests and mobilizations were motivated by the conditions of exclusivity, the trials before the Tribunal of Public Order, the jailing of workers and university students, torture, and press censorship (see chapters 7, 17). So it was in the 1960s, a time of too many rich people, of too many people mobilized in meetings, forums, and assemblies until it all exploded amid the outcry that marked the first steps in the transition to democracy and the demands for freedom, amnesty, and statutes of autonomy. In all of these cases, the presence of a signature on the bottom of a manifesto, or the stirring up of the once tranquil professional colleges, especially the bar societies, led to heavy fines. That would be the way of doing things for the protesters of those days. Perhaps there were no great intellectual luminaries in the style of the first third of the century, but there still was a bountiful representation of those self-styled intellectuals from the professions, and the worlds of literature and the arts. Even with the consolidation of democracy they never stopped participating in demonstrations, forums, and rallies such as those organized against the continued membership of Spain in NATO or against the Iraq War, to cite two noted recent examples.

What has happened in recent years to this figure, the intellectual, that emerged with its own name in the last years of the nineteenth century and at the end of the twentieth was the subject of a great deal of talk about its silence, even its demise? So far the twenty-first century has provided us with a false impression. It confuses the disappearance of great intellectual figures from the protest movement on the scale of an Unamuno, or of a select minority of intellectual leaders such as an Ortega, or of the intellectual committed to a political party or the State, as kinds of fellow travelers, with the end of the intellectual as a category. However an overview of today's state of affairs suggests the contrary, that if those images of the intellectual have disappeared, the intellectuals continue to exist, and even thrive, in other guises. If one compares the Paris daily *Le Monde* of fifty years ago with that of today, for example, one notices the absence of intellectual involvement then and the superabundance of such activity now.

Every day the press, whether in hard copy or, as in recent years, in digital form, offers us analysis, reasoned protests, professions of faith, samples of indignation that arrive from professors, engineers, doctors, lawyers, economists, and civil servants as if—and this is key to the question—the work of the intellectual had been democratized. Rather than disappearing, intellectuals have multiplied and diversified while at the same time tending to limit the scope of their messages to subjects of which they have, or believe they have, specific knowledge. They no longer pretend to speak for the voiceless, or even less to be the light that guides their way in the dark; they only wish to contribute together with others of the same background to the debate on those matters for which they feel competent, conscious that this is the only way to enrich the public sphere in a democracy. The intellectual has become an expert.

But there is something more than the multiplication intellectuals as critical observers of politics and society in print, the media, and internet blogs, a change in image due to the expansion of democracy and the end of Communism. In Spain, during the long years of the Franco era, the predominant image of intellectuals was that of the dissident. They could originate from the Catholic world, as was the custom in the older generation, or from a secular culture which was common among the youth participating in the 1956 rallies and even more so some ten years later among university students who launched the union of democratic students. The intellectual was someone who professed to be against power, against all power, a perspective which was almost always linked to a certain degree with a Marxist view of society and history. Aranguren himself had proclaimed that, except on very rare occasions, the intellectual's political place is always on the left.

This meant that the discovery of the full horror of the Soviet gulags and the simultaneous discrediting of the Marxist canon, combined with profound changes in the intellectual field and its relation to the way power is exercised in democracies, a redefinition of what intellectuals are and what was expected of them, was needed. It was no longer enough to limit oneself to cultivating suspicious thoughts about the things went on beneath the surface of politics and which really explained the existence of a perverse configuration of society. The triumph of democracy, the end of socialism, the rejection of determinist paradigms, the critique of an anti-humanist ideology, the significance of events; all contributed to the decline of a type of intellectual who owed his excellence to a conscious understanding that he was in the secret depths of history. The links between politics and democracy had to be reconsidered and the forms of public debate reinvented, with an acceptance of some level of eclecticism, the acknowledgment of the plurality of points of view, the certainty that no one had the last word, and a recognition of fragility of one's own views. This then caused an immediate and perplexing reaction, a kind of uncertainty over the role of the intellectual that was somewhat reflected in the wave of discontent that so many Spanish intellectuals, writers, and artists, experienced during the transition to democracy and what they considered its disappointing results: a transition without a rupture, a transition imposed by the *franquistas*, a transition that had swept away the utopias, a transition built on the gravestone that entombed memory as José Vidal-Beneyto wrote in *El País*.

All this happened on the eve of the rapid expansion of the internet, a development whose full implications remain unknown. Today two decades after the death of the intellectual was announced, there are daily initiatives that restate old demands, voice new claims, or formulate proposals to face new problems. These usually come from associations, forums, foundations, or professional programs with clear mandates to engage in public debates dealing with the particular interests of the "collectives" to which they belong: geographers, economists, judges, cleaning staff, ecologists, teachers at all academic levels, and researchers; a variety of backgrounds that are reflected in the diversity of their goals. These collective intellectuals are replacing the individual ones of the past.

Intellectuals have had a visible presence in many areas in recent years. These include mobilization against world poverty, the defense of a living shoreline, the demand for democratic renewal, the proposal to reactivate the Spanish labor force, the protection of the Galician language, land unification in Castile, letters written in support of science and research, demands for legal action to preserve our historical heritage, the exit from the euro zone to maintain economic and monetary sovereignty, the opposition to the eviction of tenants, displays of solidarity with a judge, support for this or that party, indignant protests against corruption, or against the "regime."

The abundance and diversity of this new role suggest that the World Wide Web has served as an instrument for mobilizing groups, associations, and platforms which on occasion become the basis for the creation of new political parties. The most significant example has been the 15M movement with its circles and assemblies from which have evolved gatherings and political parties, including Podemos, poised to directly intervene in the political system (see Chapter 8). In this way, against the apocalyptic fear of a humanity composed of atomized and alienated individuals glued to television sets as predicted by illustrious social and political scientists at the end of the twentieth century, the so-called social media have not only been instrumental in multiplying the signatures on petitions. They have also summoned people to take to the streets and demonstrate in defense of all those things for which debating is not enough and for which action is necessary. There is always an intellectual in the front row, on condition, of course, that he/she is media savvy. This reality was highly visible in the last few years of José María Aznar's government with demonstrations against globalization, the management of the Prestige oil spill debacle, the war in Iraq, and the March 11, 2004 terrorist attacks in Madrid.

There have been more such demonstrations since the start of the economic crisis with no indications that this will change in the future. There will be declarations followed by street demonstrations and the reading of some manifesto against the government cuts that are hurting public education and the funding of research, development, and innovation; in defense of the arts, of a museum or a conservatory of music, or in defense of the welfare state and of public services, especially health; against the privatization of hospitals; for the right to choose, and for the right to housing without evictions. Alongside demands from specific groups, a new consciousness of citizenship has emerged which protests against institutionalized corruption, against a system of political parties transformed into a kind of cartel, against the electoral law, against Spain's stagnant democracy. This simply expresses disaffection for the present political system, without knowing for certain how to replace it, except for the already real demand for a democracy, the kind of democracy that more than a few are determined to conquer in the streets.

Further reading

Aguilera Cerni, Vicente, *Artistas españoles contemporáneos. La postguerra. Documentos y testimonios*, Madrid: Servicio de publicaciones del Ministerio de Educación y Ciencia, 2 vols., 1975.

Amat, Jordi, *Els 'Coloquios Cataluña-Castilla' (1964-1971). Debat sobre el model territorial de l'Espanya democràtica*, Barcelona: Publicacions de l'Abadia de Montserrat, 2010.

Aznar Soler, Manuel (ed.), *El exilio literario español de 1939*, Barcelona: GEXEL, 2 vols., 1998.

Brihuega, Jaime, *Manifiestos, proclamas, panfletos y textos doctrinales. Las vanguardias artísticas en España, 1910-1931*, Madrid: Cátedra, 1982.

Casassas, Jordi (ed.), *Els intel.lectuals i el poder a Catalunya (1808-1975)*, Barcelona: Pòrtic, 1999.

Fuentes Codera, Maximiliano (ed.), La Gran Guerra de los intelectuales, *Ayer. Revista de Historia Contemporánea*, 91 (2013).

Gracia, Jordi, *Estado y cultura. El despertar de una conciencia crítica bajo el franquismo, 1940-1962*, Barcelona: Anagrama, 2006.

Gracia, Jordi, *La resistencia silenciosa. Fascismo y cultura en España*, Barcelona: Anagrama, 2004.

Juliá, Santos, *Historias de las dos Españas*, Madrid: Taurus, 2005.

Juliá, Santos, *Nosotros, los abajo firmantes*, Barcelona: Galaxia, 2014.

Mainer, José-Carlos, *La Edad de Plata (1902-1939). Ensayo de interpretación de un proceso cultural*, Madrid: Cátedra, 1981.

Mesa, Roberto (ed.), *Jaraneros y alborotadores. Documentos sobre los sucesos estudiantiles de febrero de 1956 en la Universidad Complutense de Madrid*, Madrid: Editrial de la Universidad Complutense, 1982.

Muñoz Soro, Javier (ed.), Los intelectuales en la transición, *Ayer. Revista de Historia Contemporánea*, 81 (2011).

Picó, Josep y Juan Pecourt, *Los intelectuales nunca mueren. Una aproximación sociohistórica (1990-2000)*, Barcelona: RBA, 2013.

CHAPTER 17
SOCIAL MOVEMENTS
Ángeles Barrio Alonso

Translated by Isadora B. Norman

A historical synthesis of social movements in modern Spain leads us to reflect on the nature, origins, and factors conditioning collective action within a historical process which can be divided into at least three consecutive stages. The first of these, the "classic stage," which coincides with the establishment of liberal rule and the dissolution of the *ancien régime* and continues to the final years of the nineteenth century, was an era of profound transformations in the social order, when popular movements were mainly focused on conquering liberal citizenship rights within the framework of the nation (see chapters 1–4). During the second stage, from the turn of the century until the end of the Franco dictatorship, popular movements aimed to conquer social rights, and collective action—either informal or oriented toward formalizing power structures and rights—alternated between that of an apolitical nature and the demobilization which characterized the Restoration period, and the intense politicization which occurred during the Second Republic; this trend toward politicization ebbed once more during the first years of Francoism to reemerge again at the end of the dictatorship (see chapters 4–7). During the third stage, since Franco's death, under the political pluralism of the democracy, social movements seemed to leave the leadership of collective action to political parties. At that time, alternating political forces and integration into European institutions, elements which lend stability, returned mobilization to specifically social terrain, more in favor of "cultural" rather than political goals. Since 2008 however, unease generated by the global economic crisis has yet again led to a shift in trends, and social protest and mobilization once again converged with politics (see Chapter 8).

Mobilization and protest during the first era of liberalism: People/Nation and liberal citizenship

Throughout the dissolution of the Old Regime and the establishment of liberalism in Spain, collective action was aimed at reclaiming representative rights and political participation on behalf of the "excluded"—the working class, laborers, uprooted peasants, and women. These movements took on several different forms, of varying intensity, often encouraged by factions and parties willing to turn them to their advantage. They also generally coincided with periods when *progresismo* (progressive liberalism) won out over the conservative liberal *moderantismo*. The liberal Spanish nation, based on the Catholic monarchy and *moderantismo*, frequently compelled radical and democratic liberals to resort to insurrection and popular mobilization, through urban "juntas" and military coups (known as *pronunciamientos*). In 1820, Riego led an uprising which declared the reestablishment of the liberal Constitution of 1812; in 1836, sergeants at La Granja declared themselves against Maria Cristina's Regency and the limited political rights granted by the Royal Statute of 1834, once again demanding a return to the constitutional order established in 1812; in the summer of 1854 the insurrection which led to the Progressive Biennium was also declared by *pronunciamiento*, to great popular appeal. Finally, in 1868 in Cadiz, Admiral Topete, along with Generals Serrano and Prim, paved the way for a revolution which, in September of that same year, would send Isabella II into exile and inaugurate a six-year period of democracy known as the *Sexenio Democrático*.

At that same time, the matter of dynastic legitimacy after the death of Fernando VII gave rise to Carlism, an intense and long-standing anti-liberal and anti-revolutionary movement which spread mainly in the north of Spain. Carlism gave rise to three consecutive armed conflicts—from 1833 to 1839, from 1846 to 1849, and from 1872 to 1876—in which, with the support of the Catholic Church and taking tradition as their banner, much of the peasantry uprooted and made penniless through policies of expropriation, sought to settle their scores with liberalism.

During the first half of the nineteenth century, in addition to military uprisings and armed conflicts, there were also civilian insurrections, revolts, anti-tax riots, strikes, assaults on excise tax offices and warehouses, damage to crops, and attacks on convents. These *"bullangas"* or "disturbances," as they were called at the time, were the manifestations of feelings of injustice, premodern manners of protest which drew on elements of traditional behavior. Mobilization was disparate, tumultuous in some cases, characterized by widespread furore, without clear leadership, and occurred in cycles with other movements, such as those of the Catholics, anticlericals, or students. Incidents of anticlerical violence during that period, such as the assaults upon priests and friars in July 1834 in Madrid or the burning of convents in several cities in the summer of 1835, inspired by the anti-Carlist movement and encouraged by the progressives, correspond to these cycles. Nevertheless, it was not until the intensification of these movements during the *Sexenio Democrático* when open confrontation between conservatives and moderates, on the one hand, and liberals, democrats, and federalists favoring freedom of religion and the defense of secular society, on the other, became apparent. Later, during the Restoration, when Spanish Catholics following the commitment of the Papal encyclical *Rerum Novarum* (*Of New Things*) (1891) to "re-Christianize" society, took the public stage with furious propaganda campaigns protesting against the liberals' timid attempts at secularization, anticlericalism returned in force. From 1901 to 1910, all of José Canalejas' attempts to submit religious associations and orders to ordinary laws, control their size and assets, and secularize some aspects of education failed. The religious question had become a matter of national concern (see Chapter 18).

As in other European countries, in Spain secularism, civil rights, or freedom of thought, managed to articulate a kind of interclass mobilization which coincided in timing, once again, with the advance of progressivism. Some episodes of student mobilization, such as Saint Daniel's Eve in Madrid in 1865 which produced fourteen casualties, or when many students joined the military uprising at the San Gil barracks in 1866; or clashes between liberals, conservatives, and Carlists at universities like Zaragoza, Salamanca, Oviedo, Granada, Valladolid, Seville, or Valencia—were not mere street brawls. Their defense of universal values such as tolerance and reason, in connection with the radical and democratic liberalism represented by republicanism, in turn fueled a fledgling feminist movement. By the turn of the century, during the pivotal period surrounding the wars in the colonies, feminists joined forces with the abolitionists, anticlericals, pacifists, and anti-militarists, creating links between different hotbeds of activity which had popped up in traditionally liberal cities such as Cadiz, Malaga, and Valencia, with propaganda campaigns designed to invade the public arena. When compared with the British suffragist movement, the echoes of the early Spanish feminist movement were quite limited; nonetheless, it did manage to introduce the "woman question" into the wider debate on rights and freedoms (see Chapter 11).

However, the true protagonists of the opposition movements and protests were the working classes and the peasantry. Their actions took diverse forms. There were Luddite-type uprisings—in 1821 textile machinery was destroyed in Alcoy, Tarrasa, Segovia, or Avila; in 1835 the Bonaplata factory in Barcelona was set on fire; or in 1854 the so-called war of the *selfactinas*, or self-acting spinning machines. There were partial conflicts and strikes that, in terms of liberal "respectability," were considered subversive. The breakup of the manorial system had already upset the status quo in the rural sphere and labor deregulation, especially the abolition of the guilds in 1833 had ended the protection offered workers by the guild and support systems provided by the Church under the Old Regime. Workers attempted to find alternatives through friendly societies, cooperatives, and resistance in order to negotiate hourly wages with employers, joining forces to support each other. Nevertheless, as trade unions were illegal, the survival of labor organizations was entirely dependent upon the goodwill of the civil governors; taking advantage of political changes during the Progressive Biennium, the first workers' rallies in favor of the right to unionize took place.

The Catalonian textile industry was the epicenter of a general strike in the summer of 1855 which centered on the right to unionize, and where different liberal factions competed to attract workers to their respective causes. Demanding the legalization of trade unions in order to be able to undertake collective bargaining was not a revolutionary "cause"; in fact, in May textile workers had presented a proposal backed by more than thirty thousand signatures on the matter to the government. However, the violence of events over the summer put an end to the manifestly legal approach espoused by the budding unionization movement. Government indifference and the lack of social legislation led to the radicalization of the protest movement amid a process of progressive degradation of worker's rights, in which the installation of machinery and new production techniques lowered skilled workers' wages to the same level as those of the unskilled, and in which frustration with the lack of reforms and the few opportunities for social mobility for the working class were on the rise. This situation was exploited by political leaders to prepare the revolution which took place in September 1868, in circumstances where economic crisis had worsened the already precarious living conditions of the working class.

The so-called Glorious Revolution of September 1868 was not the result of waves of social protest but rather a political decision made by a coalition comprising the Liberal Union, Progressive and Democratic parties, to overthrow the Bourbon dynasty. Civil mobilization appeared in the form of the numerous popular revolts which followed the revolution and the classic "junta" format across the country. Protests against the tax burden and riots against the tax on basic necessities (known as the *impuesto de consumos*), including incidents of burning tax offices, customs houses, and government-licensed tobacconists, forced governments to eliminate some of these taxes and duties. The workers' movement, incapable of articulating a large-scale mobilization, setting up barricades or leading the uprising, was not a key player, as shown by its absence in the revolutionary power structure. Instead, the revolution was made by the "people," an image of the assimilation of lower classes by the middle class, which takes place in revolutionary contexts, and where national sovereignty tends to blur together with popular sovereignty.

What followed—including the brief imported monarchy of Amadeo of Savoy and the First Republic—was, despite its brevity, a period of great political and institutional change. Freedoms were expanded, such as freedom of education and religion (although the separation of Church and State, contemplated in the projected constitution of 1873, was never enacted); rights were recognized, including for example, the right to unionize; universal male suffrage and trial by jury were instituted. Therefore, when, in June of 1873, the presidency of the Republic passed to the leader of the federal republican party, Francisco Pi y Margall, whose defense of social rights had led to his enormous popularity with the working class, many workers, sympathetic to the federal party, believed they had lived to see the myth of the worker's republic converted in reality. The cantonal rebellion which broke out that summer in Alcoy, Cartagena, Loja, Ecija, Alicante, Orihuela, Sagunto, Valencia, Cadiz, Malaga, and Béjar, was a grassroots movement which aspired to enact, from the municipal level, the age-old dream of decentralization and solidarity preached by the federalists. But when Pi y Margall, incapable of neutralizing the "die-hard" federalism in the cantons, resigned, barely one month after taking on the presidency, the dream vanished. The "moderate" Nicolás Salmerón managed to put down the uprisings in the most rebellious cantons until he too, amid great pressure, was forced to resign. In September, the presidency was taken on by "Unitarian" Emilio Castelar, and finally, with the surrender of the canton of Cartagena in January 1874, the Federal Republic met its end.

What, in E. P. Thompson's terms, was a plebeian experience of proletarianization in which the "people" became a "class" extinguished any expectations of democratic change represented by the idea of "republic" for the working class. During this process, the arrival in 1868 in Spain of the First International (International Workingmen's Association) in the person of Giuseppe Fanelli, an Italian activist and follower of the Russian anarchist Mikhail Bakunin, proved decisive. Laborers' associations in Madrid, Barcelona, and other parts of the Mediterranean coast, and Andalusia, established the *Federación de la Región Española,* FRE (the Spanish Regional Federation of the IWA), and held their first congresses. In 1872, when the rift between supporters of Marx and Bakunin in IWA became known, the Madrid branch separated to create a new Marxist federation, which in 1879 would give birth to the Spanish Socialist Workers' Party (PSOE) (see Chapter 30).

In the summer of 1873, coinciding with the uprisings in the cantons, an extremely radicalized labor conflict occurred in Alcoy, which was the Federal Committee of FRE headquarters at that time. The conflict was brutally quashed and FRE declared illegal. The events at Alcoy had a huge impact and promoted the ideological migration of many workers from federalism to anarchism, where they easily settled in thanks to shared ideas and values. The internationalist movement during the Restoration managed to rebuild the *Federación de Trabajadores de la Región Española*, FTRE (Workers´ Federation of the Spanish Region), but their possibilities for action where limited by the new regime's unyielding position on social rights.

The FTRE maintained the legalistic stance characteristic of the Bakuninists, who were both federalist and collectivist, especially in Catalonia. In Andalusia, however, where Errico Malatesta and Peter Kropotkin's theories and propaganda tactics had spread, anarchism was starting to become nearly a "religion" among agricultural workers. Amid poor harvests in the fall of 1882, the First International's hostility toward the rural bourgeoisie led Sagasta's liberal government to harshly put down a series of conflicts. Empowered by the supposed existence of an underground organization, *La Mano Negra* ("The Black Hand"), local authorities had free rein to disband unions and round up and arrest fieldworkers en masse on the grounds that they had started fires and damaged crops. Fifteen people were sentenced to death, of whom six were eventually executed. The *Mano Negra* incident was highly controversial at the time, and the hypothesis of a police conspiracy supported by local authorities was backed by some members of the press who were critical of the government for attempting to pacify the Andalusian countryside by meting out punishments to make an example of workers associated with the First International. In any case, this repression put an end to the FTRE, which disappeared almost completely. Ten years later, in 1892, a riot in Jerez protesting low wages which resulted in an urban uprising was brutally put down by the Army, with no clemency for those convicted, marking a turning point in the type of rural mobilizations carried out up until that time.

In the countryside, where the ties binding communities together were strong and the wide-open expanses served to soften, to a certain extent, imbalances in social relationships, archaic communal modes of protest endured, including torching the fields and destroying agricultural equipment and buildings. The repertoire of urban collective action, on the contrary, had modernized and mainly aimed to get the attention of public opinion. The 1887 Law of Associations, which enshrined the right to freedom of association, made the creation of unions possible; the socialist Unión General de Trabajadores or UGT (General Workers' Union) was formed the following year. Thus, in the same way that republicans made banquets into acts of affirmation and fraternity, workers also took their celebrations into the public arena in order to extend their networks of sociability, identity, and brotherhood, which proved to be just as efficient as party propaganda and publications. Thus, the founding myths of working-class culture were formed, through commemorative rituals and celebrations, such as the Paris Commune, the Chicago martyrs, or 1 May, which began to be celebrated in the 1890s, and were the best examples of public acknowledgment of class.

The crisis of national consciousness and the struggle for social citizenship at the dawn of the twentieth century

The loss of the colonies in 1898 marked Spain's transition from the nineteenth to the twentieth century. It was a shock to the national consciousness for which the Spanish political elite, unaware of the challenge the war against the United States meant for construct of national pride, were totally unprepared. With public opinion stirred up by campaigns in the working-class and republican press against the power of the Catholic Church and criticism from intellectuals blaming the Church for the country's backwardness and ignorance, anticlericalism reemerged with a vengeance and took to the streets in new ways, not only in newspaper editorials or political rallies. One clear example were the protest marches spurred in a number of cities following the showing of Benito Pérez Galdós play *Electra*, in which Catholics and anticlericals often came to blows.

Secularization and education, as alternatives to paternalism, were demands of a burgeoning feminist movement. While still a small minority, the movement was increasingly active in demanding equal rights with men and fighting against political marginalization. By formulating distinctive visions of the role of women, their actions transcended the then normal circuits of republicanism, laicism, and free-thinkers. The anti-militarist movement also resounded with the urban middle class, which like the working poor, did not share the patriotic enthusiasm which bolstered the Crown and the Army during the war in Morocco.

Therefore, when members of the reserve forces shipped out from the port of Barcelona in the summer of 1909, it sparked a wave of popular indignation which triggered a revolutionary uprising. The *Semana Trágica* (Tragic Week) marked a turning point in mobilizations and collective action. The reaction to the casualties being sustained in the Moroccan campaign in the face of a markedly inferior enemy had provoked protests in many cities. In Barcelona, *Solidaridad Obrera* (Worker's Solidarity), a federation of workers' associations which would shortly thereafter drive the creation of CNT, the main anarchist union, called for a general strike on July 26. The strike soon spread to nearby towns, communications went down, the first barricades were erected on the streets, and workers and the forces of public order clashed.

The *Semana Trágica* was a popular revolt with no visible leadership which returned the spirit of 1873 to the streets, and where those most active in the attacks on armories and warehouses, fires at convents, and other acts of iconoclasm were women and children. However, while it shared some of the typical characteristics of the traditional *bullanga*, this was not just a mere explosion of popular irrationality, but rather a mélange of traditional and modern forms of protest, of riots, and general strikes. Its expansion throughout Catalonia and its impact in other Spanish cities point to complex causes, feelings of exclusion among the working class which sparked a reaction of collective disobedience to the State. The unpopularity of a war which the rich did not fight and the indifference of a government which adjourned the *Cortes* to avoid criticism from the opposition added fuel to the fire of an anticlerical discourse which steered popular ire against religious orders, convents, and charitable organizations, rather than against employers, banks, or factories. Responsibility for the rioting was blamed on republican radicals, *Catalanistas*, and anarchists, and retaliation was harsh. In addition to more than seventy fatalities and five hundred injured, more than one hundred buildings were burned and uncountable cases were brought to trial. In the end, five people were sentenced to death, more than fifty to life in prison, as well as numerous other shorter sentences for imprisonment and banishment. The refusal of Antonio Maura to commute the death sentences of Francisco Ferrer Guardia, an anarchist publicist and the director of the *Escuela Moderna* (Modern School), considered to be the ideologue behind the revolt, provoked an international campaign sympathetic to his cause—one of the first of its kind. Popular outcry over Ferrer's summary execution was made evident by the shouts of "Maura, no!," which echoed through the streets of many Spanish cities (see Chapter 4).

Through a process similar to that in other European countries, by the beginning of the twentieth century the workers' movement had definitively left behind the "spontaneity" of earlier times. The leading role in protests now belonged to organizations. While membership figures were low compared to those of Great Britain, Germany, France, and Italy, the "old" workingmen's associations had become "unions" and had modernized labor conflicts. Although the socialist syndicates, faithful to UGT's moderate approach, defended "regulated strikes," associations with anarchist leanings had adopted new "direct action" tactics stemming from revolutionary syndicalism in Italy and France. Under the pompous name of "general strikes" many local strikes were organized during those years in Barcelona, Seville, Gijón, Córdoba, Huelva, and other cities. And as employers began to organize in response, these conflicts became increasingly radicalized. With the constitution of the great anarchist syndicate, the *Confederación Nacional del Trabajo* or *CNT* (National Confederation of Labor) in Barcelona at the end of 1910, the problematic process of articulating a unionization which would continue to be characterized by mobilization and struggle reached its peak.

In spite of Spain's official neutrality, the First World War signified a deep shock for a society undergoing profound changes (see Chapter 5). The War upset the rules of world trade and allowed the industrial and business elite—banking, mining, shipping, or metallurgy benefited the most—to grow effortlessly rich through overproduction in a replacement market which Spain's neutrality offered them. On the other hand, the middle and lower classes suffered the effects of massive inflation. All attempts to tax capital gains and earned income ran up against resistance from the local oligarchies which dominated provincial governments, with the result that modernizing government administration was made impossible due to lack of resources. Campaigns "in favor of basic needs," as they were called at that time, took place all over the country to protest price increases, the popular response to the inability of the government to deal with the rocketing cost of living. Discontent, regardless of interclass hostilities, on this occasion was in response to a weak State, incapable of responding to the demands of a society immersed in change.

The response of Spanish political forces to the First World War was the split into supporters of the Allied cause and the Central powers, a division which reflected their support for or opposition to greater democracy in Spain itself, and which also divided Spanish public opinion. And in an atmosphere of patriotism stirred up by the Great War, the nationalist movements which, since the crisis of 1898, had begun to form in Catalonia and the Basque Country—and to a lesser extent in Galicia—became more assertive. In the so-called neutrality rally held in Madrid in May of 1917, Antonio Maura defended the official stance of neutrality, but in an equally multitudinous "left-wing" rally, held barely one month later amid an atmosphere of enthusiasm for the allied cause, Alejandro Lerroux and Melquiades Álvarez, among other intellectuals and republican leaders, openly called for a "republic," resulting in a number of incidents. The call for a parliamentary assembly to demand constitutional reform, which was to have been celebrated in Barcelona on July 19, 1917, was banned by the government and it was the first step in a process which had brought together the divergent political forces which made up the opposition—republicans, socialists, *Catalanistas*, etc.—as well as the unions, and which led to the organization of a national general strike in August.

The strike, however, was a failure everywhere but in areas such as Vizcaya or Asturias, where more intense union mobilization managed to confer some cohesion to the disturbances, which were eventually brutally repressed by the police and the Army. The failure of August 1917, along with the impact of the Bolshevik Revolution, was decisive in moving the working-class unions to be increasingly skeptical when faced with the possibility of collaboration, both among themselves and with "bourgeois" political parties, and in rekindling their mission of social transformation, as was evidenced by the mobilizations launched in the winter of 1918–19.

Unionization had seen unprecedented expansion, not only in terms of class-oriented unions, but also for free trade unions, businessmen's organizations, and Catholic associations. It was no longer just skilled workers who joined unions and marched in protest: ordinary laborers, fieldworkers, shop assistants, merchant sailors, the liberal professions, disgruntled members of the armed forces, or business owners all organized unions or other types of collective organizations and together established formal and informal networks in the defense of their class, group, or even their gender. One clear example were the feminist associations formed by women from the working and middle classes and by intellectuals: among others, the *Asociación Nacional de Mujeres Españolas* or ANME (National Association of Spanish Women) was created in 1918, and in 1921 the *Cruzada de Mujeres Españolas* (Spanish Women's Crusade)—increasingly active in mobilizing against the Church and the government.

During the wave of conflicts and strikes known as the "Bolshevik triennium" that rocked Andalusia between 1918 and 1920, there was none of the millenarianism and the redistribution of lands that had marked the earlier peasant revolts, but rather demands for better labor contracts. Hundreds of strikes, not only in the countryside but also in provincial capitals and in the cities, led by workers from a wide variety of trades and sectors, which included both traditional transgressive acts and new trends of socialization, effective propaganda campaigns, mass meetings, and boycotts, could not be considered merely a spontaneous revolution headed by irate peasants; rather it was coordinated collective action in favor of union dues, municipal reforms, and negotiated solutions to improve crops and productivity.

The strike at Barcelona Traction Light and Power Company, known as *La Canadiense* because its head office was in Toronto, in 1919 had also called for union recognition, the absence of which was an insurmountable obstacle for the efforts by *Instituto de Reformas Sociales* (Institute for Social Reform) to make labor relations less conflictive. The conflict, which began as a very localized walkout over the firing of several unionized workers was, thanks to actions planned by CNT, soon transformed into a general strike which left the city without water, power, or transportation for several days. Although the local authorities and government representatives attempted to seek a negotiated solution and the liberal government leader, Romanones, even declared the establishment of the eight-hour workday, the CNT's success was too much of an affront for the military powers to handle. As it proved impossible to reach an agreement in which the strikers could return to work without suffering retaliation and the anarchist prisoners were set free, the CNT called for a general strike, and the trade associations responded with a lockout. The government collapsed, constitutional rights were suspended, and a state of war was declared in Catalonia, followed by repressive actions against union headquarters and the most active CNT militants.

Spanish governments were incapable of passing legislation on collective bargaining or recognizing unions as entities with legal rights. They were unable even to respect the guidelines on labor law set out by the International Labor Organization to which Spain, as a signatory to the Treaty of Versailles, belonged. Instead, they chose to provide support, sometimes tacit sometimes explicit, for the anti-union policies of the Spanish businesses which had been creating their own national organizations. The result was further violence and terror, especially in Barcelona, where the scene of what was known as *pistolerismo*, a "war" between hired guns bankrolled by the business associations and CNT militants, littered the streets with corpses (in the first six months of 1923 alone, 53 were reported dead and 102 injured in a range of attacks including 23 robberies, 11 bombings, 22 shoot-outs and two accounts of arson, among other, minor, violent incidents).

In March 1922, the battle moved to Madrid when anarchists assassinated the prime minister, the social Catholic Eduardo Dato. Prior to that, in June 1921, a reckless and disastrous military maneuver at Annual in Morocco, which led to the deaths of ten thousand Spanish soldiers, once again mobilized Spanish society against the war. Parliamentary debate regarding Annual, verbally violent, and very polarized between those supporting "impunity" and those bent on persecuting the "responsible parties," translated into public opinion scandalized by the role of the Army—and even the King himself—in Spain's management of the Protectorate (See chapter 5).

The solution to the legitimacy crisis affecting the regime was the now-classic military coup. This *pronunciamiento* was instigated by General Miguel Primo de Rivera in September 1923. Primo enjoyed the consent of the King, who interpreted the move as a simple change in government, and the support of landowners and the business-owning bourgeoisie. Faced with no response from public opinion, the coup aimed to put an end to misgovernment, social subversion, and the threat presented by separatist movements.

Mass mobilization and formal protest in the 1920s and 1930s

Primo de Rivera's coup d'état, which established a military dictatorship and ended more than fifty years of constitutionalism and parliamentarianism, reduced opportunities for protest and opposition. Although a great admirer of Mussolini, Primo de Rivera used his own public presence to legitimize his rule in the eyes of Spanish society through passionate support for patriotic citizenship. This was a mobilization based on citizens' responsibilities toward the fatherland rather than their rights, which took the form of demonstrations and parades sponsored by the Patriotic Union, the dictator's own political party. In the absence of elections and customary constitutional freedoms, such as peaceful protest and freedom of association, and with censorship of the press in place, dissent was manifested in symbolic ways to avoid police control, or through methods typical of underground resistance, civilian and military plots and conspiracies to overthrow the regime, which all amounted to nothing.

With the CNT declared illegal, anarchist groups which had sprung up in the face of repression during the Barcelona *pistolerismo* soon reactivated both individual attempts and conspiracies. This was the case of an unsuccessful attack on the Barcelona shipyards in November of 1924. The *Solidarios* (Sympathizers, in Spanish), whose best-known members were Juan García Oliver, Buenaventura Durruti, Francisco Ascaso, and Rafael Torres Escartín, were blamed for the assassination of Cardenal Soldevila in June 1923, the robbery which took place in the same year of the Banco de España in Gijón, and the failed attempt on the life of Alfonso XIII in Paris in 1926. Perhaps the most significant development was the creation of the *Federación Anarquista Ibérica* or FAI (Iberian Anarchist Federation), a group made up of activists who revitalized the earlier anarchist tradition of insurrection which had always been present in libertarian political culture.

However, the anarchists were not the only ones who opposed Primo de Rivera. From 1925, when the continuity of the dictatorship was institutionalized through the Civil Directorate, opposition increased incessantly among sectors that had originally lent support to the regime, and conspiracies multiplied. The "*Sanjuanada*" (named after St. John's Eve) of June 1926, involved republicans like Melquiades Álvarez, conservatives like Sánchez Guerra, and military men like Valeriano Weyler. In November of that same year *Estat Català*, Françesc Macià's radical Catalanist group, which was in exile in France, prepared their youth strike force, the *escamots*, to cross the Pyrenees. Intellectuals and students had been the first to organize resistance to the dictatorship and decry the lack of freedoms at universities. Disciplinary measures against professors enraged students in Madrid who took over Faculty buildings, boycotted the dictator's public appearances, and participated in a number of incidents. This led one of their leaders, Antonio M. Sbert, to be punished and expelled. Repression against Sbert, who had founded in 1927 the *Federación Universitaria Escolar* or FUE (University Scholars'

Federation) a nonpartisan but declaredly anti-dictatorship student union, triggered protests and unrest which were repeated in universities all over Spain in 1929 and which led to closures due to the threat they posed to the Barcelona International Exposition. Once classrooms were restored to order, in January 1930 a general strike halted university activities and forced Primo de Rivera, lacking support and utterly alone, to step down shortly thereafter.

Forms of protest had been renewed and radicalized during the Dictatorship. Spanish civil society had mobilized in favor of the right to exercise citizenship and demand political change. The uprising at the Jaca garrison in the name of the republic in December 1930, which led to the summary execution of the ring-leaders, Captains Fermín Galán and Ángel García Hernández, had an extraordinary impact on public opinion. The peaceful proclamation of the Second Republic on April 14, 1931, as the result of municipal elections, was the denouement of a period in which social movements coincided to put an end to the Monarchy. The Second Republic, a democratic regime committed to the modernization of the country and reforming the State, offered greater opportunities for mobilization and protest; however, reforms soon brought to light underlying conflicts between the masses, anxious for progress, and upper classes who feared the changes implied in the "historical" realization of the republican dream.

The republican-socialist coalition which governed between 1931 and 1933 brought in significant changes in a number of areas as well as overseeing the creation of a new, democratic constitution (see Chapter 5). The Republic also saw new levels of political and social mobilization. On the right, Catholics mobilized politically as never before. Union mobilization was equally intense, with strikes and labor conflicts multiplying—more than 1,100 strikes were reported in 1933 alone. These actions were increasingly politicized and radicalized, but there were also trade association lockouts, uprisings, and local, urban, and rural riots, episodes of iconoclasm, and varied examples of political violence. The CNT, whose syndical philosophy of mobilization and combat was now up against the arbitration policies brought in by socialist Minister of Labor—and former UGT leader—Francisco Largo Caballero, found the justification for the anti-system approach favored by the "die-hard" anarchists in the repression suffered by the unions during the strikes. In January 1932, with the uprising in the Alto Llobregat region of Catalonia, the CNT initiated a wave of rebellions, walkouts, and land takeovers, especially in Andalusia, La Mancha, and Extremadura. The most notorious was the Casas Viejas incident of January 1933: a very minor agricultural strike which pitted protesters against the police wound up with a village devastated, 20 civilian casualties including strikers, the elderly, women, and children, several dozen injured and the death of three civil guards. The reaction included a parliamentary investigation into the conduct of Manuel Azaña's government. These anarchist insurrections ended in December 1933 with the attempted attack on the Congress building intended to prevent the center-right majority elected the previous month from forming a government.

Once the governing coalition with the center-left republicans was broken off and the November 1933 elections brought the center-right to power, the Socialists also turned to insurrection. They were particularly concerned about the new Catholic *Confederación Española de Derechas Autónomas* or CEDA (Spanish Confederation of Autonomous Right-wings), which they mistakenly identified as fascist, from entering the government. In order to do so, they sought out the support of other working-class and left-wing forces, launching the *Alianzas Obreras* (Workers Alliances)—a sort of agreement on strikes, which the anarchists did not wish to join, chastened by their experiences in December of 1933—and took the usual step of preparing a plan for revolution. Secret meetings and other clandestine activities like building up stocks of weapons occurred all throughout the summer of 1934. The plan consisted in calling for a general strike as soon as CEDA members entered the cabinet and that is exactly what happened early in the early morning of 5 October when the new government, with three CEDA ministers, was announced.

As an openly advertised revolution, with a mix of utopian and pragmatic objectives, October 1934 was a failure. In Madrid, confusion among the leadership diminished the effectiveness of the protests, and in Barcelona, where Lluís Companys, president of the Generalitat, proclaimed the Catalonian State within the Spanish Federal Republic, the rebellion was rapidly quashed. In industrial and mining regions of the Basque Country, union mobilization kept the strike alive for a few days. In Asturias, where the Workers Alliance had incorporated socialists, anarchists, and communists, the radicalization of the rank and file, especially among the miners, overpowered the leadership of the movement and kept the dream of self-determination and a social federalist revolution going until, finally on October 20 the army put it down. More than 1,300 deaths, 3,000 injured, nearly 30,000 arrests, and 20 death sentences (although only two were carried out) weighed heavily on public opinion, which considered that the suspension of Catalonia's autonomy, the disbanding of socialist controlled town halls, massive layoffs at businesses, closure of union headquarters, and even the arrest of Azaña, who just happened to be in Barcelona when the revolt broke out, and the trial that followed, could be considered the government's revenge. The brutality of the repression, particularly in Asturias, transformed the October revolution into a legend for the working class, and ended up returning to haunt the government.

Nonetheless, the experience of that October institutionally weakened the Republic, giving new para-fascist right-wing organizations the chance to resort to violence, as was the case of Ramiro Ledesma and Onésimo Redondo's *Juntas de Ofensiva Nacional-Sindicalista* or JONS (Unions of the National-Syndicalist Offensive), or the *Sindicato Español Universitario* or SEU (Spanish University Union), with ties to José Antonio Primo de Rivera's *Falange Española*. This moved the Socialists to return to a revolutionary rhetoric with turned out to be decisive in the Popular Front's victory in the February 1936 elections. The mobilization which took to the street in the spring of 1936, with direct and indirect clashes between organized right-wing groups and labor activists was extremely violent—more than one hundred and fifty leftists died, more than seventy on the right, and a score of police officers as well. Even so, this street violence in no way justified the military and civilian plot which led to the military uprising on July 18, 1936.

The reaction to the coup of one part of Spanish society, with citizens taking to the streets and demanding the government to arm them to defend the Republic, marked the official recognition of earlier forms of mobilization, in a country now divided into two. In republican Spain, where the coup d'état did not take hold, a spontaneous revolution broke out. There were new revolutionary local governments. Union and party militias were the seed which grew into an army made up of volunteers who, along with the officers who remained loyal to the Republic, were put in charge of military action on the front. Behind the lines, the revolution took the shape of collectivization and other ways of organizing production and consumption. In the countryside, where in an extension of agricultural reform, more than 150,000 families took part, and in the factories, the service sector and the transportation industry, collectivization was a way to forge forward toward the ideal of worker control and the abolition of private property.

The women who participated very actively at the front and behind the lines encountered the struggle led by antifascist organizations, like the communist-leaning Agrupación de Mujeres Antifascistas (AMA) or the libertarian-leaning Mujeres Libres, which offered the opportunity to exert some degree of feminine leadership (see Chapter 6).

The war gave free reign to hostilities among different social actors which appeared in all aspects of public life, at the same time transcending to individuals' private lives, leaving no one untouched. In the regions of Spain under rebel control there was a violent counterrevolution designed to eradicate all traces of republicanism. The first victims were military personnel loyal to the Republic and civilians, who in some way, shape or form represented activists from left-wing, republican, socialist, communist, nationalist or CNT unionist parties. The number of victims behind the lines approached 100,000 dead, in addition to 50,000 executions after the end of the war. Other groups, such as civil servants, including teachers, were victims of systematic purges—more than 7,000 teachers were removed from their classrooms—due to their links to the ideology of the Republic.

Nor was violence absent in Republican Spain, especially anticlerical violence—around 7,000 clergy fell victim to socialist and anarchist furor—with the usual incidents of iconoclasm, blasphemy and irreverence, which were nothing less than a vengeful response to an institution which, ever siding with the powerful, now sanctioned the rebels' war against the Republic as a "Crusade."

From dictatorship to democracy: Demobilization, opposition, politicization, and depoliticization

Franco's victory over the Republic put an end to all possibility of protest or opposition which, during the early years of Francoism, was limited to anarchist and communist guerilla activities in the hills in Asturias, the Spanish Levant, and Aragon, in rural areas of Catalonia, Andalusia and Castile, and in cities like Madrid, Barcelona, or Bilbao. The *maquis,* as they were called, carried out attacks, sabotage, and even bombings, put them in the dictatorship's crosshair's which, throughout the forties, made them subject to brutal and systematic repression. More than 2,000 guerillas were shot down, leaving only a few isolated cells which disappeared completely in the 1950s.

Starting in the fifties, migration, economic development, and the rise of foreign tourism brought significant changes to Spanish society (see Chapter 7). These, in turn, gave rise to new forms of mobilization. In the case of women, the Catholic version of femininity, based on high birthrates and subordination, instigated by the government under the auspices of Catholic Action and the *Sección Feminina*, began to be put to the test thanks to the first strikes and protests over wage inequality. The opposition, while still limited to the inner circles of clandestine organizations, revealed a significant shift in attitude, a loss of fear, an affirmation of gender. Something similar was happening among youth and students, groups which had swung from the militancy of the final years of the Republic to complete depoliticization. Thanks to the crisis of authority spurred by the tide of generational change, these sectors began to mobilize against the regime through nonpartisan collective action which demanded an end to SEU and free and democratic union representation. The riots at Madrid's Universidad Central in February 1956 resulted in Rector Pedro Laín's resignation and the dismissal of

Education Minister Joaquin Ruiz-Jiménez, who had represented an extremely brief period of liberalization in the politically and intellectually stifling atmosphere that predominated in Spanish universities at the time. The most radical students opposed to the dictatorship, including future political leaders and opinion-shapers like Enrique Múgica, Javier Pradera, and Ramón Tamames, who came from families embedded in the regime's elite.

During the 1960s, women, middle- and lower-class students were able to attend university thanks to scholarships. Enrollment swelled and staff numbers grew through the hiring of young professors with precarious contracts—the PNN—whose presence, just like that of new students, revolutionized obsolete university faculties. These were all decisive factors in the definitive intensification of opposition to the dictatorship. Radicalization, especially stemming from incidents like the 1965 expulsion of Professors Enrique Tierno Galván, José Luis Aranguren, and Agustín García Calvo in Madrid, or Manuel Sacristán in Barcelona, politicized activities during the seventies when the student movement joined its democratic demands with those of the workers.

In the fifties, the labor movement remained limited to a few protests and walkouts at large companies in industrial and mining regions—between 1956 and 1958 there were several strikes calling for a minimum wage, an eight-hour workday and unemployment insurance in Catalonia, the Basque Country, Madrid, or the mining zone of Asturias. Labor mobilization intensified, however, after the collective bargaining law passed in 1958, which while lacking freedoms and rights, introduced collective labor agreements. The big strikes in 1962 and 1963 in the coalfields of Asturias and Leon, Puertollano and Riotinto, or in cities like Cartagena, Vigo, Ferrol, Valencia, Zaragoza, and Madrid called to attention the appearance of a "new working class" which had extended its repertory of actions. Within the official union movement, amid such an atmosphere of high spirits, the first *Comisiones Obreras* or CCOO (Workers' Commissions) emerged as a "grass-roots" alternative and managed to get the government in a corner.

Unlike the historic union organizations UGT and CNT, they were not underground groups, and during the sixties the CCOO transformed into a social movement within the official Francoist unionization structure. Although ideologically heterogeneous, in 1966 they declared themselves in favor of democracy, and shared the philosophy of national reconciliation put forth by the Communist Party, which was increasingly present within the commissions. Although the regime levied the usual repressive actions, conflict continued to spread until in 1969 the *Comisiones Obreras* were declared illegal and in 1969 a state of emergency was declared. Far from dwindling, labor conflict to grow. If there had been five thousand strikes from 1964 to 1974, there were over three thousand in 1975 alone.

After Franco's death in November 1975, protest increased even further (see Chapter 8). The year 1976 was an especially virulent year in terms of protests and retaliation. In the cities, which had grown rapidly and often without adequate services, local neighborhood associations emerged, which became a sort of school for democratic participation, pluralism, and consensus. Veiled support from opposition parties was one of the keys to success as it allowed for avoidance, in many cases, of detection by the police. Feminism also experienced a great leap forward with the establishment of different organizations, such as the *Movimiento Democrático de Mujeres* (Democratic Women's Movement), an independent front open to different ideologies although with strong communist leanings; the *Asociación Democráctica de la Mujer* (Women's Democratic Association), a subgroup which split off from the first; the group Women and Socialism; or the *Frente de Liberación de la Mujer* (Women's Liberation Front), which operated through unified programs and took to the streets to call for legal equality, proposing reforms, which affected women's private lives, like the legalization of contraceptives, the decriminalization of adultery, or the right to abortion.

Workers, students, women, neighborhood associations, nationalists, each demanded democratic rights and freedoms from a dying regime. It was the dawning of "new social movements," which represented the changes which Spanish society had undergone, and in the face of which the Francoist elite itself considered breaking their paralysis to seek out democratic alternatives after the death of the dictator.

During the process of the democratic transition, however, these social movements started to become less explicitly political. As happened elsewhere in Europe, mobilization became more "cultural" and disconnected from the political stripes of the government in office. The Constitution of 1978 formalized the legal framework which had joined feminism and transition—from 1977 to 1978 contraceptives were legalized and adultery was decriminalized, in 1981 divorce was legalized, and in 1985 abortion was allowed in some circumstances—, relegating debate over feminism to a more theoretical than political arena.

Transnational rhetoric made inroads in the environmental, which emerged quickly but remained limited to a small minority. Peace and anti-military movements, on the other hand, were politicized in the anti-NATO debate, especially due to the referendum on Spain remaining in the organization overseen by Felipe González's Socialist government in 1986, which divided the Spanish left that until then had traditionally been opposed to NATO. Something similar happened with the conscientious objector movement and the draft dodgers. This was directly related to the structure of the military, inherited from the Dictatorship, a model which was not modified until 1997, when compulsory military service for men over age 18 was abolished. Mobilization in favor of individual rights was especially active among gay rights organizations, led by the LGBT collective, which called for an end to discrimination based on sexual orientation and supported cultural liberalization. Homosexuality was decriminalized in 1986 and in 2005 Spain became the third country in the world to legalize same-sex marriage.

Spanish society, nevertheless, remained sensitive to certain political causes. If the protest marches in 1981 against the failed 23 February coup d'état had seen hundreds of thousands of Spaniards take to the streets in defense of the Constitution and democracy, rejection of ETA's terrorist activities would institutionalize the use of the red ribbon or "white hands" in the 1990s and an expression of collective condemnation of their killings. In 2004, when the Popular Party (PP) government aligned the intervention in Iraq defended by George W. Bush and Tony Blair, it also provoked a massive reaction of public opinion against a war which took on a political profile as a result of the terrorist attack on March 11 in Madrid, and the government's controversial handling of the matter.

The economic crisis which began in 2008 has generated a transnational movement of indignation. In Spain, this has taken on a specific form known as 15M, a movement created after 15 May, when a demonstration that included a variety of mobilizations turned into a cosmopolitan protest with international echoes. The slogan *"no nos representan"* ("they don't represent us"), expressed the discontent of the middle classes in the face of corruption and the austerity measures taken against the crisis and demanded a real, more transparent, and participatory democracy. The anti-eviction movement, a response to the fact that more than 350,000 families were evicted from their homes between 2008 and 2014 for defaulting on their mortgages, has led Spaniards to seek out alternatives and has sparked political debate on the nature of the crisis and its social consequences.

The emergence of new left-wing political groups in the aftermath of 15M, like Podemos (We can), Barcelona en Comú (Barcelona Together), En Marea (The Wave) in Galicia, Compromís (Compromise) in Valencia, or the spread of the center-right, anti-Catalanist party Ciudadanos (Citizens) from Catalonia to all of Spain, is evidence of the change in the party system passed down from the Transition and new styles of political competition.

Further reading

Álvarez Junco, José, "Movimientos sociales en España: del modelo tradicional a la modernidad postfranquista," in Enrique Laraña and Joseph Gusfield (eds.), *Los nuevos movimientos sociales. De la ideología a la identidad*, Madrid: CIS, 1994, pp. 413–42.

Castells, Manuel, *Redes de indignación y esperanza. Los movimientos sociales en la era de internet*, Madrid: Alianza, 2012.

Cruz, Rafael, *Protestar en España. 1900-2013*, Madrid: Alianza, 2015.

De la Calle Velasco, Maria Dolores, Manuel Redero San Román (eds.), *Movimientos sociales en la España del siglo XX*, Salamanca: Ediciones de la Universidad de Salamanca, 2008.

Ortiz Heras, Manuel (ed.), Dossier "Movimientos sociales y culturas políticas en la construcción de ciudadanía: la transición española," *Alcores*, 14, 2012, pp. 13–138.

Pérez Garzón, Juan Sisinio, *Contra el poder. Conflictos y movimientos sociales en la Historia de España. De la Prehistoria al tiempo presente*, Granada: Comares, 2015.

Quirosa-Cheyrouze, Rafael (ed.), *La sociedad española en la Transición. Los movimientos sociales en el proceso democratizador*, Madrid: Biblioteca Nueva, 2011.

Rivera, Antonio, José María Ortíz de Orruño, and Javier Ugarte (eds.), *Movimientos sociales en la España Contemporánea*, Madrid: Abada, 2008.

Romanos, Eduardo, "Epílogo. Retos emergentes, debates recientes y los movimientos sociales en España," in Donatella Della Porta, and Diani, Mario (eds.), *Los movimientos sociales*, Madrid: CIS/ Editorial Complutense, 2011, pp. 315–46.

CHAPTER 18
RELIGION
Julio de la Cueva Merino[1]

At the dawn of the modern era, religion in Spain was embodied in a categorical statement enshrined in the Constitution of 1812: "The religion of the Spanish nation *is, and ever shall be*, the Catholic Apostolic Roman and only true faith; the State shall, by wise and just laws, protect it and prevent the exercise of any other." Despite the forcefulness of this constitutional declaration, two hundred years later, fewer than a fifth of all Spaniards consider themselves "practicing Catholics" while more than one-quarter identify themselves as "nonbelievers," "indifferent," or practitioners of "other religions." The events that bridge early-nineteenth-century Catholic Spain and the secular Spain at the start of the twenty-first century constitute the focus of this chapter, which attempts to explain the nonlinear process that linked an initial state of affairs in which the Catholic religion was absolutely dominant to the current situation of religious recomposition characterized by the advance of secularization and a plurality of beliefs. However, this is not a teleological tale of inevitable decline. Rather, these pages seek to provide an account of the centrality and relevance of the Catholic religion—and the debates and conflicts surrounding it—to the configuration of Spanish politics, culture, and society over the course of the last two centuries.

Catholicism, nation, and liberal revolution (1808–74)

As the Old Regime was coming to an end in Spain (see Chapter 2), the Catholic religion provided the main framework within which the daily lives of individual Spaniards and society as a whole played out. The Catholic Church itself was an enormously rich and powerful institution that owed its prosperity to the income produced by its immense agricultural holdings, its urban properties, mortgage loans, and tithes. Its power came, in part, from this immense material wealth, but also from its close association with the Catholic monarchy, its monopoly over the instruments controlling thought and customs, the large number of clergy (70,840 priests, 53,098 monks and friars, and 24,471 nuns in 1797), its dense network of religious, charitable, and educational establishments, and its immense spiritual influence. At the beginning of the nineteenth century the Catholic religion was omnipresent in Spain. Religious symbols and buildings dominated both the urban and rural landscapes. The sound of the church bells marked the hours of the day; Sunday obligation indicated the passing of the weeks; the rhythm of the year adjusted to the liturgical calendar. The important moments of personal and family life were ritualized according to the prescriptions of the Church and the most momentous occasions of community life were accompanied by religious celebrations. Mass—with its

[1]Research for this chapter was financed by the Junta de Comunidades de Castilla-La Mancha, Project PPII-2014-020-P.

corresponding sermon—, the annual obligation to confess and take communion at Easter, the practice of various devotions, belonging to confraternities, the processions, popular missions, and many other religious manifestations, all contributed to reinforcing the centrality of Catholicism in the individual and social conscience. When the Spaniards had to fight against the French in the War of the Pyrenees (1793) or the War of Independence (1808–1814), the confrontation was to a large extent understood as a religious crusade.

Given the shared construct shaped by this social and cultural landscape it was perfectly understandable that the nation would identify itself with Catholicism and be intolerant of any other religion, as established in the Cadiz Constitution. In fact, the same principle of religious intolerance was contained in the constitutional charter adopted in Bayonne in 1808. In the case of Cadiz, liberal legislators considered it absolutely natural that the sovereignty hitherto invested in a Catholic king be transferred to the Catholic nation as a new political subject. However, the same article that sanctioned the confessional nation attributed to it—and therefore to the state—responsibility for protecting religion. In other words, it recognized the right of the civil power to intervene in ecclesiastical affairs in order to reform the Church.

Reforming the Church involved changing its discipline and organization in addition to transforming the structure of its relationships with the civil authorities by constructing a separate religious sphere subject to the higher interests of the State. Here the liberals converged with eighteenth-century Jansenist and regalist traditions and projected them toward the future through a series of measures that would stay in place until the early 1840s. These measures included freedom of the press (which permitted anticlerical criticism), the end of the Inquisition, the expulsion of the Jesuits, the suppression of most male and some female religious communities, the abolition of tithes and, finally, the disentailment of assets belonging to the clergy. These measures, which would also lead to a rupture in diplomatic relations with the Holy See in 1836, brought about, in the words of historian William Callahan, "the destruction of the Old Regime Church."

Indeed, the once almighty Spanish Catholic Church was reduced to a state of weakness from which it would take a long time to recover. It had not only lost a large part of its economic foundation and a growing number of its clergy—in 1860 the number of clerics and nuns had dwindled to 63,000 from more than 148,000 in 1797—but also had to impotently witness the weakening of the influence it had exercised over society. Anticlerical criticism of ecclesiastical vices was widely disseminated in printed texts and from theatre stages, while at the same time some progressives were advocating religious tolerance, something supported by the more advanced democratic and republican groups. By the middle of the century, most of them had abandoned their earlier blind faith in the unquestionable Catholic unity of the country and were espousing freedom of religion.

The Church's position was further damaged by its adherence to an increasingly staunch anti-liberalism. Although the first Spanish liberals all considered themselves Catholics and included a notable number of priests, starting in 1812 other Catholics, again including many priests, had declared themselves radically opposed to liberalism, defending absolute monarchy and the supremacy of the Church. This would become the predominant position inside the Spanish Catholic Church. It was strengthened by, on the one hand, the condemnation of liberalism in Rome that culminated in the encyclical *Quanta Cura* and the accompanying *Syllabus of Errors* (1864) issued by Pope Pius XI and, on the other, national events that fueled a dynamic of confrontation between the Catholic and liberal camps reflected in various armed conflicts including the Carlist Wars (see Chapter 3). Over the course of these hostilities, the Legitimists took up the banner of defending Catholicism and a number of clergymen supported the Carlist cause, even going so far as to take up arms. This, in turn, intensified liberal anticlericalism at times to the point of highly violent sporadic actions such as the so-called slaughter of the friars in 1834 and 1835. These events occurred in the context of the First Carlist War and involved the death of 75 Jesuits and other members of religious orders in Madrid at the hands of rioting mobs in the first year and a similar number of regular clergy in Barcelona and other towns in the second.

Despite these tensions, Catholicism continued to constitute the primary framework of significance for the immense majority of Spaniards. Moreover, once the political waters calmed and moderate liberals took power in 1844, the Church began its slow recovery. *Moderantismo*—the Spanish variant of doctrinaire liberalism—offered conditions for Church-State understanding so favorable that the Church could not afford to pass up if it wished to rebuild within the new liberal order. The Concordat of 1851 signed between Spain and the Holy See was the best illustration of the rediscovered harmony, with its first article reaffirming that "the apostolic Roman Catholic religion, which, to the exclusion of any other cult, continues to be the sole religion of the Spanish Nation, shall be preserved always in the dominions of Her Catholic Majesty, with all the rights and prerogatives." The Concordat also guaranteed that public education at all levels would conform to Catholic doctrine. Article 29 permitted the gradual reestablishment of religious congregations, although its ambiguous wording would lead to conflicts later on. The secular clergy, in turn, would begin to be paid by the State. It appeared that the alliance between throne and altar was recovering some of its old luster.

However, in the convulsive nineteenth century, peace never lasted long enough, at least for the Spanish Catholic Church. The first shock came during the 1854–56 biennium with a new disentailment of clerical assets and a declaration freedom of religion in the constitutional project of 1856, which never actually came into effect. The challenge posed by the 1868 revolutionaries (see Chapter 3) was more serious and long lasting; after deposing Queen Isabel II, they accused her—among many other things—of having facilitated the recovery of clericalism. The Constitution of 1869 recognized freedom of religion although, interestingly, it did so while also acknowledging the premise that being Spanish was synonymous with being Catholic: "the public or private exercise of any other form of worship is guaranteed to all foreigners resident in Spain . . . *If any Spaniards profess a religion other than the Catholic*, all that the last clause provides is applicable to them." Despite this affirmation of religious freedom, the most advanced liberal sectors represented by republicanism continued to be convinced that freedom of thought and the secularization of the State deserved a more radical solution. This could have been achieved with the Constitution of 1873 drafted after the proclamation of the First Spanish Republic, which expressly included the separation of Church and State, but was never promulgated. The challenge to Catholic hegemony was not limited to constitutional texts; during the Sexennium, a large number of secularizing measures were adopted. Most updated the measures approved in the 1830s, including the expulsion of the Jesuits and suppression of religious communities. However, others like the introduction of civil marriage in 1870 were completely novel. Along with the laws, displays of street anticlericalism took place, some of them spontaneous, some of them led by the local authorities.

It is difficult to assess the extent to which the conflictive episodes of the Sexennium and the decrease in ecclesiastical power over the course of the century fomented secularism in the society. A dearth of studies makes it difficult to assert anything with certainty, although some signs indicate a decline in religious practice during those years, at least in urban areas. However, the attitude of a small minority that ostensibly broke away from Catholicism is less ambiguous. Some members of this minority declared themselves free-thinkers, while others broke with the Church to follow a liberal Catholicism influenced by Krausist philosophy and still others embraced Protestantism. In fact, for Protestant churches, the constitutional proclamation of religious freedom in 1869 provided the opportunity to break into Spain and establish small communities around the country, many of which endured in the memory of evangelical church members, with some exaggeration, as the second Spanish Protestant Reformation.

The reaction of Catholics to what was seen as the loss of religious unity came swiftly. The Association of Catholics, established in 1868, undertook a mobilization movement that manifested itself in various initiatives including the successful collection of more than 2,800,000 signatures against freedom of religion (Catholics were less adverse than liberals to mobilizing women and bringing them into the public sphere). In the political arena, Catholics made their voices heard through the moderates and Carlists whose ranks gave temporary refuge to the so-called neo-Catholics, followers of Juan Donoso Cortés, who understood Catholicism as the best prophylaxis against revolution. In 1872 a new Carlist war began. However, as it progressed, the hope of many Spanish Catholics was not invested as much in the triumph of the Legitimists as in the restoration of the monarchy in the person of Alfonso XII.

Restored Catholicism and its discontents (1875–1931)

The reestablishment of the monarchy inaugurated a long period known as the Restoration (see Chapter 4), during which the Spanish Catholic Church was able to undertake its own restoration. This ecclesiastical recovery was possible thanks to the mutual support between the Spanish Catholic Church and the new regime devised by Antonio Cánovas de Castillo. Cánovas knew that the Church's cooperation was needed to ensure the stability of the monarchy of Alfonso XII and give it legitimacy both against the Carlists, who were presenting their political project as the only truly Catholic one and were still at war in 1875, and against revolutionary threats from the left, whose potential had been demonstrated in the immediately preceding years (see Chapter 17). The Church, in turn, also feared revolution and in this respect, it was willing to accept a highly moderate liberal regime like that of the Restoration as the "lesser evil." Moreover, the Church yearned for the security guaranteed by State protection and was not about to spurn it. In short, the politics of *ralliement*, or the acceptance of liberal regimes promoted by Pope Leo XIII, would end up confirming the merit of the direction that the Spanish Church was taking.

Both the Conservatives, represented by Cánovas del Castillo and the Liberals, heirs to the old progressives, agreed to participate in a new understanding with the Church, at least until 1900. This was helped by the Constitution of 1876, which tolerated the practice of other religions with some conditions while it affirmed Catholicism as the official religion of the state. While the formulation did not initially satisfy either the Church, because it did not reestablish the "Catholic unity" of Spain, or the progressives, because it did not maintain freedom of religion, in practice it pleased everyone in the end. Not surprisingly, in this atmosphere of cordiality between the parties that alternated power as part of the "*turno pacifico*" and the Church, the political forces (Carlists and Integrists) who called themselves "Catholic" and were also loudly anti-liberal had almost no real support. It is also noteworthy that when attempts were made in the 1880s to create a unitary confessional party, the Catholic Union, to channel the political action of all Spanish Catholics (like the German *Zentrum*), it dissolved into Cánovas' Conservative Party.

The weakness of the Catholic political forces in no way implied the withdrawal of the Catholic religion from the political sphere. In fact, Catholicism permeated the political culture—or perhaps, political cultures—of the Spanish right, from conservatism to traditionalism. While a secular conception of the Spanish nation had irrevocably made its way into the wide spectrum of left-wing politics, rightists continued to identify the nation with Catholicism, which they saw as the very essence of nationality. This conviction was best expressed by the prolific Catholic writer Marcelino Menéndez Pelayo in 1882 when he asserted that "Christianity gave its unity to Spain" and famously added, "Spain, evangelizer of half the globe, hammer of heretics, light of Trent, sword of Rome, cradle of St. Ignatius of Loyola...; this is our greatness and our unity: we have no other." This formulation summarized the essence of so-called National Catholicism. While historians have understood this term to mean different things, for the Restoration period, historiography has seen National Catholicism as a political culture that proclaimed the consubstantiality of religion and the fatherland and recognized the role of the Church in directing society. However, unlike the integrism of the traditionalists, it was characterized by possibilism, which allowed for conditional acceptance of the liberal regime, as well as an active interest in the capitalist modernization of the country. It should be added that the identification of nation and religion also characterized the definition of the emerging substate nationalisms, although much more strongly in the Basque than in the Catalan case (see Chapter 10).

In any case, politics was not the principal avenue chosen by the Church to achieve its material reconstruction and the recovery of its spiritual influence over society. Politically speaking, it was enough to know that it enjoyed the favor of the State and the privileges that came with being the official church. In this propitious situation, for example, the Church soon managed to ensure that all of the Spanish dioceses once again had a bishop, something that had not been the case since 1868. The number of the secular clergy, who took charge of the parishes, where they had primary responsibility for pastoral care, holding services and administering sacraments to the people, quickly increased to 45,000, (including some 13,000 seminarians) and stayed there until the end of the period. Although this number was high, their distribution was irregular, with high ratios of priests per inhabitant in the northern half of Spain and rural areas versus low numbers in the south and urban areas.

The numbers for regular clergy, women and men, were much lower, but what was even more remarkable was their spectacular growth. While in 1860 there were only 1,863 monks and 18,819 nuns, in 1931 the former group numbered 20,000 while the latter exceeded 80,000. The religious congregations were the Catholic Church's shock troops in its drive to recover the terrain lost during the century. Thanks to their numbers motivation, and the generous donations they received, they were able to establish a presence in very diverse areas, two of which stood out among the rest: education and charitable work. Many congregations, both male and female, founded schools, and many others, largely female, administered charities. For decades an important part of the Spanish population received their education in religious schools: not only the sons and daughters of the bourgeoisie, who clearly preferred this type of institution, but also boys and girls from other social classes. These were not the only activities to which the monks and nuns devoted themselves: the men, especially, could also be found administering their own churches, in competition with the parishes, leading missions, managing associations of the faithful, and publishing books and journals.

However, they did not reach the people only through education, charity, preaching, and social activities. They needed to reach them through imagination and emotion as well, an enterprise in which the Church was a master. As in the past, the services, liturgy, sermons, and sacraments constituted the basic pillars of the relationship between the Church and its followers. Popular or local religion, from humble town pilgrimages and festivals to the magnificent processions for Corpus Christi in Toledo and Holy Week in Seville, also continued to be extraordinarily important. Whether modest or grandiose, public demonstrations of piety were constant in every town. Two devotions conveniently promoted by the hierarchy were especially favored by Catholics in those years: the Marian devotion and the cult of the Sacred Heart of Jesus. Both were universal devotions, but they allowed for particularly Spanish readings. The veneration of the Virgin Mary could be adapted to a multitude of regional or national sentiments—the Virgins of Pilar, Covadonga, Begoña, Montserrat, and so forth—and the version of the Sacred Heart of Jesus for home consumption promised his reign in Spain "with more veneration than anywhere else." Both also made it possible to develop the community dimension of worship and to cultivate a more intimate pious space.

The Church's insistence on recovering its influence over society was generally rewarded with success, although it was a mixed success. Again, the dearth of studies in this area makes it difficult to evaluate accurately the level of religious practice, but the evidence suggests that it was high among the upper and middle classes across the country and very high among peasants in the north and center of the Peninsula. Religious observance among peasants in the south and urban workers, especially in the large cities, was lower, in part because the Church was incapable of designing an efficient pastoral strategy in these areas.

The one social group that was distinguished by its piety was defined not by class, but by gender: women. For this reason, historians talk about a "feminization of religion" in the nineteenth and a good part of the twentieth century—and not only in Spain. The transmission of faith at home; attendance at pious acts; even the composition of congregations (as seen in the growing number of nuns), were all undeniably female. It is thus not surprising that nineteenth-century Spanish literature featured the recurring presence of female characters like Ana Ozores, the protagonist of Clarín's novel *La Regenta*, who were overcome by religious emotion.

In any event, Spanish Catholicism during the Restoration gave the impression of having recovered exceptionally well from the breakdown it underwent during the most difficult years of the liberal revolution. Its institutional presence and spiritual influence were comparable to that of the Old Regime, but there were important differences deriving from the presence of a number of modern elements. First—as time would tell—Spanish Catholicism was not necessarily incompatible with modernity, but adopted elements of modernity for its own purposes and adapted to modernity to achieve its own ends. Secondly, the importance that religion regained in Spain was not an exception—the cliché of "Catholic Spain"—in the Western context; indeed the period between the mid-nineteenth and mid-twentieth centuries has been interpreted in recent studies not as a time characterized by the "decline of religion" but as a sort of "second religious age" around the world.

The impressive vigor of Catholicism during the Restoration naturally upset some people. Or perhaps it would be better to say that the overwhelming public presence of official Catholicism did not stop certain groups—some of which have already been mentioned—from expressing or increasing their dissent. These included participants in the Institución Libre de Enseñanza; people who identified with free-thinking; people who met in Masonic lodges; and people who hoped to secularize the State and society from a position of political militancy, mainly republicanism, but also anarchism and socialism. Other groups cultivated heterodoxy, whether religious "modernism," Protestantism, or the new spiritual forms that were extremely popular during the *fin-de-siècle* like spiritualism and theosophy.

Around 1900, discontent with Catholic dominance was mobilized in the form of anticlerical collective action. The reasons for this mobilization were related to the atmosphere of fear in the secularist press resulting from the spectacular recovery of ecclesiastical power in the preceding decades that manifested itself, most notably, in the growth of religious orders. It was also connected to the state of shock induced by the "disaster" of 1898 (see Chapter 4) and the consequent search for who was responsible for the state of national decline that had led to it. It had to do, in short, with a mix of international factors—the desire to emulate the secularism of the Third French Republic—and national ones—the formation of a new Conservative cabinet which was accused of clericalism, the marriage of the Princess of Asturias with the son of a prominent Carlist, the premiere of *Electra*, an anticlerical drama by Benito Pérez Galdós—all of which introduced a cycle of protest that would last until 1910. This protest occasionally assumed violent overtones, the outstanding example being the so-called Tragic Week in 1909 during which more than eighty religious buildings were burned in Barcelona. During the first years of the twentieth century, the Liberals led by José Canalejas again assumed their commitment to secularization and undertook some political initiatives aimed at limiting the privileges of the Church. However, if there was one political force that truly embodied the secularist enthusiasm of those years, it was republicanism, which made anticlericalism a key element of its discourse and an essential feature of its political culture. In truth, anticlericalism constituted a common feature among the various leftist groups, that is, republicans, socialists, and anarchists.

The counterpart to early-twentieth-century anticlerical mobilization was Catholic mobilization, which took a defensive position in the face of the renewed onslaught of secularism. The recurrent self-representation of the Church as a tower beleaguered by its enemies found new grounds to assert itself in Catholic discourse. The mobilization of Spanish Catholics had actually already really begun in the final years of the nineteenth century with the organization of national Catholic conferences and the development of still modest Catholic social action, designed to respond to the challenge posed by the working-class problem (this was part of a general Catholic initiative prompted by Pope Leo XIII's encyclical *Rerum Novarum*). Now in the twentieth century, Catholic collective action was intensifying, serving its counter-secularization objectives with a modern repertoire of mobilization, holding meetings and demonstrations, establishing local electoral platforms, publishing newspapers, including the national paper *El Debate*, and developing a Catholic associative network. The expansion of a denominational associative movement, which included powerful groups like the National Association of Catholic Propagandists founded in 1909, contained an interesting paradox: in the very clerical Catholic Church, the role assigned to the laity, both men and women, was becoming increasingly important. This group of associations would be integrated into an umbrella operational structure called Catholic Action, which had existed in a generic sense since the early twentieth century and was definitively organized in 1926 following the model proposed by Pope Pius XI for the universal Church.

This resolute Catholic opposition managed to thwart the successive secularizing reforms proposed during those years and in the battle between clericals and anticlericals, the former were victorious. A powerful symbol of this victory was the gesture made by King Alfonso XIII in 1919 when, in front of a colossal monument erected in the geographical center of Spain, he consecrated the nation to the Sacred Heart of Jesus. Four years later, the dictatorship of General Primo de Rivera came into power, foreshadowing the Franco dictatorship in its patronage of a Christian regime for the nation. The triumph of Catholicism, however, was more apparent than real; the incipient secularization of Spanish society continued to advance while anticlericalism and secularism survived as fundamental elements of leftist political culture.

The secular republic in peace and war (1931–39)

While the nineteenth century began with an unequivocal constitutional affirmation of the eternal Catholicism of the nation, the debate over the Republican Constitution of 1931 resonated with another assertion that highlighted the rashness of that pronouncement: "Spain has ceased to be Catholic." These words were expressed by Manuel Azaña, then Minister of War and soon-to-be Prime Minister of the Republic (see chapters 5, 33). Azaña represented the commitment of republicans and socialists to a secular state model. In fact, secularization of the state and further secularization of society (the "revolution of consciences") formed an essential part of the program of the reformists who came into power in April 1931. Their project was reflected in a constitutional text that separated Church and State, deprived the Church of public financing, dissolved the Company of Jesus, subjected religious acts outside churches to governmental permission, introduced divorce, made secularism compulsory throughout the educational system, and mandated the approval of a law that would prohibit religious congregations from teaching. When this legislation, the Law of Confessions and Religious Congregations, was passed in 1933, Spain became one of the most secular states in the West.

A more secular state, yes, but was Spain a more secularized society as well? It is difficult to confirm the extent of the latter, although some clergymen like the Redemptorist, Father Ramón Sarabia, agreed with Azaña, concluding that Spain was no longer as Catholic as the Church claimed. The hidden side of this secularization was decline in religious observance, while the most visible side was seen in the spectacular increase in anticlerical mobilization, especially among the lower classes. This mobilization was reflected in both oral and written propaganda and in boycotts of the Church's use of public space, and was usually supported by the local authorities, for example in the case of banning religious processions. In other instances, anticlerical protest was clearly violent in nature: the burning of monasteries in May 1931, the murder of 37 clergymen during the October Revolution of 1934, and more than 800 attacks on religious monuments and buildings and thirty assaults on ecclesiastics during the violent spring of 1936.

Spanish Catholics did not react to the challenge posed by the Republican regime in a unified way. Although it is likely that a good number of Catholics voted for republican candidates in the 1931 municipal and general elections, after centuries of alliance with the monarchy and with full awareness and fear of the secularization program of the republicans the Spanish Catholic Church as an institution viewed the Republic with understandable concern and notable distrust. However, these fears did not result in frontal opposition to the Republic and, indeed, the strategy adopted by the majority sector of the Spanish Church—led by papal nuncio Federico Tedeschini, Cardinal Vidal i Barraquer, and the secular leader Ángel Herrera Oria—was characterized by its pragmatism and consideration of the accidental nature of forms of government. Thus, they showed respect for the Republic and negotiated with the Republican government to achieve the best possible conditions for the Church. When negotiations were unsuccessful, Church officials agreed to operate within the law to defend the interests of the institution.

Generally speaking, the most important tool at the service of the ecclesiastical hierarchy was Catholic Action, which became very active during these years. On the political front, their primary instrument was the Spanish Confederation of Autonomous Rights (CEDA), a heterogeneous political coalition that made the defense of the Church its primary policy. The CEDA won the general election in 1933 although without the majority needed to form a government. Its electoral success was the fruit of three decades of Catholic mobilization and the irrefutable demonstration that the Catholic Church had adopted the ways of modernity, in this case modern mass politics. In October 1934, the CEDA entered the government.

In opposition to these "accidentalists," other Catholics, the most prominent of them being Cardinal Pedro Segura, Archbishop of Toledo, decided to confront the Republic from the outset. Segura was sent into exile by the government in July 1931 and forced by the Vatican— eager to ingratiate itself with the Republic—to renounce his episcopal see shortly thereafter. He was not the only prelate who had to leave the country. The Bishop of Vitoria, Mateo Múgica, accused of collusion with Carlism, was also forced into exile. Indeed, traditionalism or Carlism provided one of the political spaces where Catholics who were unwilling to compromise with the Republic found accommodation. The other nucleus that brought anti-Republican Catholics together was so-called Alfonsinism, the supporters of the deposed King Alfonso XIII. In the cultural society Acción Española and the political magazine of the same name, they proceeded to reformulate Spanish National Catholicism in a deeply fundamentalist way. It would be these two groups, the Alfonsists and the traditionalists, which began to consider the legitimacy of an armed insurrection in the defense of religion.

The armed uprising took place from July 17 to 18, 1936 and although it was not initially done in the name of religion, it soon took on the character of a religious crusade (see Chapter 6). Similarly, the revolutionary movement that hit the Republican rearguard assumed violently anticlerical, when not directly anti-religious, overtones. More than 6,700 members of the Catholic clergy, including bishops, priests, seminarians, monks, and nuns, were killed. The diocese of Barbastro in Aragon lost almost its entire clergy while others like Lerida, Malaga, and Toledo had to face losing nearly half of their priests. In Catalonia, more than 2,000 priests died violently, while more than 1,000 suffered that fate in the city and province of Madrid. Most of these crimes were committed during the first six months of the conflict, when the power of the Republican state was at its weakest. The ecclesiastics who survived the killing but were unable to flee to the other zone spent the rest of the war in hiding or, at least, concealing their clerical status.

Murder was not the only violent anticlerical practice. Throughout the Republican zone, churches were burned or used for profane purposes. Perhaps even more significant is the fact that churches and monasteries were the only buildings subjected to revolutionary anger. When they were not setting fire to entire churches, they burned or destroyed the objects in them, from pews to holy images. Other iconoclastic acts included mocking images, profaning consecrated hosts, parodying the Mass and processions, exhibiting mummified corpses, deliberately using blasphemy and removing religious references from proper names, place names, and daily language. The perpetrators of these acts of personal aggression or iconoclasm were members of leftist political or union groups or their sympathizers who had interiorized an anticlerical identity and been taught to see the clergy and the Catholic religion as formidable enemies of the people and the revolution.

As a consequence of the violence and the government's frightened passivity, religion went underground across the entire Republican zone and was not officially reestablished during the war. The only exception was in the Basque Country where the autonomous government was in the hands of the Catholic Basque Nationalist Party; this was the only area where Catholics fought extensively on the Republican side. Except in the Basque case, for the duration of the Civil War in the Republican zone, the long sought-after secular Spain was achieved in ways that were brutally expeditious. Almost nothing remained of the age-old presence and hegemony of the Spanish Catholic Church.

The Franco regime: National Catholicism in power and in decline (1939–75)

While the Spanish Catholic Church was being humiliated in the Republican zone, in the Nationalist zone it was the object of unlimited adulation and exaltation. The three-year-long coexistence of a persecuted Catholicism on the one hand and a triumphant Catholicism—when not complicit in another persecution—in the same country highlighted the fact that the Spanish Civil War was to a large extent a religious war. As noted above, the insurgents soon adopted the definition of the belligerent enterprise as a "crusade." Catholicism constituted the mortar that bound the broad mix of positions that brought the rebel soldiers together. An interpretation of the Republic's secularizing measures as "religious persecution," combined with news of the "martyrdom" of priests in the Republican zone, guaranteed early Catholic mobilization in favor of the Nationalist cause. This mobilization received the backing of bishops in the form of individual documents, most significantly Archbishop Pla i Daniel's September 1936 pastoral letter *The Two Cities*, as well as a *Joint letter of the Spanish bishops to the bishops of the whole world concerning the war in Spain* in July 1937. The progressive recognition of the New State by the Holy See thanks to the intermediation of the Archbishop of Toledo, Cardinal Isidro Gomá, was also very important. In the meantime, widespread religious demonstrations inundated churches and streets during the war and immediate postwar period in an atmosphere of religious pride.

Relations between the Church and the Franco regime were not only woven together through liturgical rites and declarations, but also through legal arrangements that turned the Spanish state into one of the most Catholic in the world: the secular legislation of the Republic was repealed, the Church was given countless prerogatives—including significant control over education—and, following a series of partial agreements, a new Concordat was signed between Spain and the Holy See in 1953 that solemnly confirmed the established privileges of the Spanish Church and Catholicism's status as the religion of the State. Moreover, the Franco regime seized every opportunity to affirm its commitment to Catholicism in the Fundamental Laws approved between 1938 and 1967, and Franco himself took part, such as when he stated in 1946 that "the perfect state is for us the Catholic state." Around that time as well, the characterization of the Franco regime as a Catholic regime became the cover that allowed the state to distance itself from the fascist powers with which it had been allied during the Second World War and reclaim its place in the West (see Chapter 7).

National Catholicism—or the union of state, nation, and Catholicism—thus constituted a basic minimum of the official rudimentary ideology of the Franco dictatorship, shared by all the groups that sustained it. However, this term has also been used more specifically to denominate one of the two primary political projects promoted by the State: an ultra-Catholic project with origins in *Acción Española* that would come into conflict with the Fascist-Falangist project. The situation was made even more complex by the presence of another important group of Catholics who began to collaborate politically with the regime in 1945 and to fill ministry positions: the "official" Catholics who formed part of Catholic Action and the powerful National Association of Catholic Propagandists.

The collaboration of these men with the dictatorship was part of a general strategy of the Spanish Catholic Church, as in 1875, to take advantage of the possibilities offered by the political system to restore and win back society. This was another face of National Catholicism, one that corresponded to an ecclesiastical project to install a Christian regime in Spain, in other words to make Spanish society officially Catholic. The highly anticipated restoration of the Church involved recovering financial means, including those contributed by the State, constructing and reconstructing churches and other buildings, and recruiting seminarians and novices to fill the ranks of the decimated clergy. While the number of diocesan priests and seminarians grew substantially, it never surpassed the 1930 numbers (26,000 seminary students in early 1966 and fewer than 9,000 novices in 1959).

The number of members of religious orders, however, reached an absolute record in the history of modern Spain with 31,000 monks and friars, and 97,000 nuns in 1971. This army of ecclesiastics, both regular and secular, put itself at the service of the Catholic recovery of Spain, a particularly urgent task given the visible disaffection of an important portion of population during the years of the Republic and Civil War. The tools they used were not new: broad control over the educational system with a practical monopoly of secondary schools; an inescapable religious presence in institutional care and the army; ownership of the media; the organization of popular missions; often compulsory attendance at religious events; an iron grip on morality; and ecclesiastical participation in the organs of censorship. One final tool and agent of this recovery—along with the clergy—was, again, Catholic Action, which became extraordinarily important during these years, especially through its specialized movements that sought to introduce the Church into particular environments. In this respect, a number of organizations like the Catholic Action Workers' Brotherhood (HOAC) and Catholic Youth Workers (JOC) were created to evangelize the particularly difficult working-class world.

By the 1950s, however, it was already possible to detect signs that foretold the limitations of ecclesiastical National Catholicism. On the one hand, the favor and protection provided by the regime were more ambiguous than they appeared. Certainly, the Church received maximum institutional and symbolic recognition and important benefits regarding education and the control of morality, but in exchange it made concessions that weakened its autonomy. For instance, the Head of State appointed bishops to fill vacant sees and the Church lost (to the Falange) some of the tools that had allowed it to model the population and orient it to its ideal of a *Societas Christiana*, including the unions, youth associations, and the possibility of having its own political party. The situation was particularly resented by some in the Catholic hierarchy, who felt it was excessively subordinate to the State. On the other hand, it was during this decade that the first "self-criticism" of the National-Catholic model appeared. While still in the minority, these critical voices belonged to members of the clergy and laity who were concerned about the evident failure of the official strategy to win back society, unfocused paternalism in the treatment of social questions and the isolation of Spanish Catholicism from the international reformist trends that resulted in the Second Vatican Council (1962–65).

When this council was convened in Rome it was a catalyst for the universal Catholic Church, and much more so for the Spanish Catholic Church. As is widely known, Vatican II constituted an *aggiornamento* or "bringing up to date" for Catholicism, its reconciliation with the modern world and its commitment to the respect for fundamental rights and freedoms, including religious freedom. The conciliar doctrine came into direct conflict with the very bases of Spanish National-Catholicism and came up against a wall of incomprehension both on the part of the Spanish ecclesiastical hierarchy and the Franco authorities, who were reluctantly obliged to pass a Law on Religious Freedom in 1967 due to the paradoxical need to adapt the restrictive Spanish legislation, which had initially been designed to satisfy the Church, to the progressive demands of the council. On the other hand, the majority Catholic group inside the Franco governments during the 1960s was no longer Catholic Action but Opus Dei, a secular institution with a conservative ideology founded before the war by the Spanish priest Jose María Escrivá de Balaguer. The state ministers who belonged to the group agreed to guarantee the survival of the regime by rationalizing the state administration and modernizing the country's economy.

Economic modernization and the processes of social change in the 1960s and 1970s, in fact, constituted the context in which the Church distanced itself from the Franco dictatorship. In the 1960s, dissidence with respect to the regime essentially occurred within the rank and file of the laity and clergy, part of which was quite actively involved in the social struggles of the period and, in the Basque and Catalonian cases, in the respective national movements as well. Moreover, the activities of these Catholic groups made it possible to open up spaces for debate and participation that contributed to the return of civil society and, in turn, later facilitated the success of the Spanish transition to democracy. In these circumstances—and for the first time in the history of Spain—Catholicism and the right ceased to constitute a perfect equation as many Catholic activists began to join the left as part of the anti-Franco opposition. This growing social and political commitment clearly caused tension, not only the foreseeable tensions with the authorities but also tensions inside the Church between an increasingly politicized base and a largely pro-Franco hierarchy. The product of these intra-ecclesiastical tensions was a crisis that affected Catholic Action between 1966 and 1968, resulting in the reorganization of the movement and the dissolution of its most committed groups.

It was now too late to maintain intact the status quo that connected Spanish Catholicism to the dictatorship. To begin with, in the coming years, the anti-Franco commitment of both laymen and priests would continue to deepen. Moreover, what became known in the historiography as the "uncoupling" (*desenganche*) of the Spanish Catholic Church from the

Franco regime was beginning to reach the hierarchy. In this case, the impetus came from Pope Paul VI himself, who was unwilling to maintain the alliance between the Church and a regime so out of line with conciliar doctrine. Finally, from a more practical point of view, it did not seem wise to join the fate of the Catholic Church in Spain to that of a dictatorship whose demise seemed imminent if only because of the advanced age of its dictator. The "uncoupling" strategy was the responsibility of papal nuncio Luigi Dadaglio and Bishop Vicente Enrique y Tarancón. To that end, Tarancón was named cardinal in 1969 after being appointed Archbishop of Toledo and later made Archbishop of Madrid and President of the Spanish Episcopal Conference in 1971.

This reformist atmosphere in the Church manifested itself in an exemplary manner in the Joint Assembly of Bishops and Priests held in 1971, which revealed the desire on the part of a majority of the clergy to adapt to a changing society and make a break with the authoritarianism of National Catholicism. Moreover, the Church expressed its clear desire to revise the Concordat and receive greater autonomy from the State, including the right to select its own bishops. Now that the Church as an institution appeared to be taking a critical position, occasions for tension with the regime's authorities and Franco himself multiplied. The most famous was the "Añoveros case," named after the Bishop of Bilbao, who was ordered into exile by the government, which was angered by his defense of the cultural rights of the Basque people. Thanks to an opportune threat of excommunication, which would have affected Franco himself, the government withdrew its threat. This case highlighted the paradox of the Spanish Catholic Church's final split with a regime that, over the course of its prolonged existence, had made the defense of Catholicism a key element of its raison d'être.

From unanimity to plurality (1975–2015)

Franco died a faithful child of the Catholic Church, although this Church was no longer the institution for which the crusade that began in 1936 had been waged. His death marked the beginning of a new historical period both for Church-State relations and for the Spanish population (see Chapter 8). The great social transformation—with its corollary secularization and religious pluralism—sparked by the economic and cultural changes of the 1960s accelerated as recovered political liberties grew. However, unlike other moments in the history of Spain, the departure of a clerical regime was not accompanied by a massive swing of the pendulum in religious policies or the emergence of anticlericalism. One immediate reason for this lay in the pact that underpinned the transition, which affected religion and many other areas. Another was the favorable effect for its public profile of the Church's internal renovation, its uncoupling from Franco and its renunciation of a direct political role in the new situation. Another far from negligible factor was the large number of former Catholic activists and non-Catholics who had fought alongside them in the anti-Franco struggle into the ranks of the left. Finally, thanks to the secularization process underway since the previous decade, a significant portion of Spaniards were now indifferent to religion instead of passionate about the institution— whether for or against—as their elders had been.

Church-State relations were regulated during the Transition—and continue to be so today— by a series of agreements that replaced the 1953 Concordat: a "basic agreement" in 1976 in which the King renounced his participation in the process of appointing bishops and four "partial agreements" in 1979 that regulated various specific questions, including education, always of great importance for the Church. These agreements guaranteed that all public primary and secondary schools would offer Catholic religion in conditions "equal" to other subjects. The partial agreements were negotiated at the same time as the drafting of the Constitution of 1978, which confirmed the right to religious freedom and the nondenominational nature of the State in a framework of "cooperation with the Catholic Church and other confessions."

Generally speaking, the governments that came into power before the early twenty-first century inherited this spirit of understanding with the Church, despite occasional conflicts. When they did occur, these conflicts were related to State management of issues regarding morality and education, which were particularly sensitive for Catholics. For instance, the legalization of divorce in 1981 upset the Church and the institution opposed the decriminalization of abortion under the Socialists in 1985. The Catholic protest against the education regulation implemented by the Socialist governments, which was seen as a threatening state intervention, was also energetic. In practice, the new legislation helped to stabilize private religious schools, since it provided public funding for subsidized charter schools (*colegios concertados*). On the other hand, the Spanish Catholic Church accepted the agreements signed between the State and evangelical, Jewish, and Muslim communities in 1992 with little difficulty.

The context of Church disapproval during this time was not only the accession of the traditionally secular left to power, but also the beginning of a new stage in the existence of the universal Catholic Church. After John Paul II became Pope in 1979, a process was launched to review Council Vatican II in terms of religious restoration. It was as if the Church was suffering from vertigo on the road to modernity and decided to withdraw into itself. Once again, it saw itself as a bastion under siege from the forces of secularism and moral relativism and again, its mission consisted of fully defending its space and recovering its lost terrain. In Spain, this counter-secularization project meant renewing the composition of the episcopate and clergy in harmony with the new directives from Rome. This new campaign was supported by both existing Catholic movements like Opus Dei and so-called new movements like the Neocatechumenal Way and Communion and Liberation as well as the confessional media. Additionally, in the political sphere, the most conspicuous sector of Spanish Catholicism once again turned to the right, now represented by the Popular Party (PP), as its natural ally.

The main issues mobilizing Catholics in the late twentieth and early twenty-first centuries were schooling, the family, and questions regarding sexual and reproductive morality. They also found inspiration for their battles in the memory of the clergy and laypeople killed during the Civil War, whose beatification as martyrs was revived during John Paul II's papacy. The Spanish Catholic Church, which was historically used to social and cultural hegemony, did not come to feel comfortable in a context of pluralist democracy and a secularized society. Ecclesiastic belligerence redoubled in 2004 when the Socialist Party, now led by José Luis Rodríguez Zapatero, returned to power and only began to retreat after the 2011 electoral victory of the Popular Party, which was considered more amenable to ecclesiastical demands. In any case, the true turning point for Spanish Catholicism toward more tolerant positions may be the accession of Pope Francis to the papal throne in 2013 and his changes for the agenda of the Catholic Church.

Whether because of the Church's drift toward more fundamentalist positions in the 1980s or because of its desire to recover its former identity amid the so-called historical memory project in the early twenty-first century (see Chapter 22), the Spanish left abandoned the religious consensus of the Transition and reintroduced secularism in its public demonstrations and programs. In this respect, the Rodríguez Zapatero governments firmly supported the autonomy of the state vis-à-vis the Catholic Church, knowingly approving reforms that would arouse strong responses from the institution: expanding and facilitating legal abortion, legalizing same-sex marriage, and adding a course, Education for Citizenship, to the school curriculum that was seen by Catholics as an unacceptable intervention in the right of parents to make decisions about education. To the left of the Socialists, both established political groups and newly emerging ones, acted and spoke in an even more radically secularizing way which at times verged on outright anticlericalism. In the general elections of December 2015, all the left-wing parties from the PSOE to Podemos ran with programs advocating the secularism (and not just the anti-denominationalism) of the Spanish State, to the point of advocating the reform of the Constitution and the revision or the denunciation of the 1979 agreements between the Church and State. It appears that the old religious cleavage that has traditionally separated the right from the left in Spain has not yet disappeared.

However, Spanish society no longer was—and no longer is—the one that had gone through that first and limited wave of secularization in the late nineteenth and early twentieth centuries, one of whose more striking manifestations was anticlericalism. Neither, of course, was it the unanimously Catholic society that it had been in an even more distant past that some had wanted to reconstruct in more recent times. As in other Western societies, a second wave of secularization between the 1960s and 1980s profoundly upset the religious landscape in Spain. The reach of this wave was quite broad, to the point of secularizing Spanish society. However, unlike the earlier wave, this distancing from religion did not manifest itself as opposition to the Church, but as disinterest in its practices, norms, and dogmas. For instance, in 1988 only 41 percent of the population said that they were practicing Catholics versus 83 percent in 1965, although 81 percent still declared themselves Catholic as opposed to 98 percent in 1965. In the last two decades of the twentieth century, then, a society that had abandoned the practice of Catholicism still continued, on the whole, to maintain its Catholic cultural identity.

In the twenty-first century, religious change has gone in two directions. On the one hand, the number of people who call themselves Catholics or practicing Catholics has continued to decline. This is most significant among young people, only half of whom say they are Catholics and only 10 percent practicing Catholics, while 26 percent say they are agnostics or atheists. In this respect, it is quite significant that in 2008, for the first time ever, more Spaniards got married in civil ceremonies than in Catholic ones. In 2015, there were three times more civil marriages than ecclesiastical ones. The dizzying speed of secularization among young people is resulting in a remarkable process which sociologists call "exculturation": the loss of Catholic roots in their culture and identity. At the same time, the mass arrival of immigrants over the last two decades has resulted in an expansion of religious pluralism never seen before in Spanish modern history (see Chapter 19). In 2010, there were a million Muslims and a million and a half non-Catholic Christians in Spain, of whom 900,000 were Orthodox Christians.

Over the course of two hundred years, Catholicism has generated consensus among Spaniards, but its status in society has also often been a source of conflict. In any case, the Catholic religion has always influenced the political agenda in one way or another, has been preeminent in social life, and has defined the identities of Spaniards, for or against it. Only recently, beginning in the 1970s and as a consequence of secularization, has Catholicism lost the central role it had long enjoyed. Consequently, the present and future religious landscape in Spain is characterized by a plurality that includes a Catholicism that is still in the majority, though in decline, growing religious indifference—if not open atheism—among the youngest generations and the increasing incorporation of followers of other faiths into Spanish society. Be that as it may, without understanding the role played by religion, it is impossible to understand the history of Spain over the last two centuries.

Further reading

Boyd, Carolyn (ed.), *Religión y política en la España contemporánea*, Madrid: CEPC, 2007.

Boyd, Carolyn, *Historia Patria: Politics, History, and National Identity in Spain, 1875-1975*, Princeton: Princeton University Press, 1998.

Callahan, William J., *The Catholic Church in Spain, 1875-1998*, Washington, DC: The Catholic University of America, 2000.

Callahan, William J., *Church, Politics, and Society in Spain, 1750-1874*, Cambridge, MA: Harvard University Press, 1984.

Cazorla-Sanchez, Antonio, "Did You Hear the Sermon? Progressive Priests, Conservative Catholics, and the Return of Political and Cultural Diversity in Late Francoist Spain," *Journal of Modern History*, 85, 3 (September 2013), pp. 528–57.

De la Cueva Merino, Julio, "The Assault on the City of the Levites: Spain," in Christopher Clark and Wolfram Kaiser (eds.), *Culture Wars. Secular-Catholic Conflict in Nineteenth-Century Europe*, Cambridge: Cambridge University Press, 2003, pp. 181–201.

Guia, Aitana, *The Muslim Struggle for Civil Rights in Spain: Promoting Democracy through Migrant Engagement, 1985-2010*, Brighton: Sussex Academic Press, 2014

Lannon, Frances, *Privilege, Persecution, and Prophecy: the Catholic Church in Spain, 1875-1975*, Oxford: Clarendon Press, 1987.

Planet Contreras, Ana I., "Spain," in Jocelyne Cesari (ed.), *The Oxford Handbook of European Islam*, Oxford: Oxford University Press, 2014, pp. 311–49.

Thomas, Maria, *The Faith and the Fury: Popular Anticlerical Violence and Iconoclasm in Spain, 1931-1936*, Brighton: Sussex Academic Press, 2013.

CHAPTER 19
MIGRATIONS
Aitana Guia

The modern history of Spain is a history of movement and migration. Yet historians, many of whom privilege settlement over mobility, have been slow to incorporate the concepts of mobility studies into their analyses of the country's history. Looking at migratory movements allows us to glimpse a history of Spain from the margins, to hear the voices of those who in the past have been expelled from the national body. Migration, both voluntary and involuntary, has been a regular occurrence in Spain. Involuntary or forced migration occurs when people are forced to flee their country of birth to avoid persecution, imprisonment, or death. Today we call these people refugees, but in the nineteenth century they were known as exiles (or *emigrados* in Spanish), a term that originally referred to people fleeing the French Revolution, but which has since been applied to anyone fleeing political or social persecution. Voluntary migrants, also called economic migrants, are people whose movement is triggered by lack of economic opportunities in their place of birth; many decide to either move within their own country or cross national borders in an attempt to improve their life prospects. The term "voluntary" helps to differentiate these people from those who must leave to avoid the threat of violence or death, but this distinction downplays the fact that poverty can be as much a threat to a person's life as physical persecution. Increasingly, migration scholars try to analyze the mixed motivations that trigger human movements. Both forced and voluntary migrations help to explain the political, social, and economic evolution of modern Spain.

This chapter explores Spaniards' internal migrations, the movement of Spanish exiles and economic migrants to Latin America and Europe, and also the movement of foreigners to Spain. Rather than adopt a geographical or chronological organization, it discusses mobility according to the reasons that triggered these various movements. It looks at the various forced migrations that punctuated Spain's modern history, as well as the many voluntary migrations, both internal and external, that have shaped the country's history.

Recurring forced migrations

Amparo Batanero left Spain in the spring of 1937 with 455 other children on the French ship *Mexique*. Batanero was five years old at the time; she traveled with four of her five siblings, who were seven, nine, eleven, and twelve years old. With her father on the frontlines of the Civil War, her mother thought it was better to spare her children from certain death in Madrid (she kept only her three-year-old with her). When these child refugees reached the Mexican port of Veracruz on June 9, thousands of people cheerfully awaited them, and the other ships sounded their sirens as a gesture of welcome; according to the national daily *El Excelsior*, "Mexico [had received] its new sons." Batanero built a life in Mexico, and she would not return to Spain until

1960, as a twenty-eight-year-old mother of five. Many children in her situation had difficult lives; many were never reunited with their parents.

Political exile became a common feature in the era of revolution and counterrevolution inaugurated by the French Revolution. People whose thinking went against the status quo, such as Polish and Italian nationalists, or German and Finnish socialists, were forced to flee within Europe or to the Americas, sometimes more than once. Though estimates vary, some historians argue Spain has lost as many as nine hundred thousand people to exile since 1808. If we consider that the country had 11.6 million people in the 1822 census, and 23.7 million in 1930, the loss of nearly a million people for purely political reasons—in addition to millions of others for economic reasons, as discussed below—indicates that the country has not been able or willing to properly care for its people. Historical research on exile in modern Spain suggests that the largest population movements coincided with the second absolutist restauration under Ferdinand VII (1823–33) and the Spanish Civil War (1936–39) (see chapters 3, 6). In nineteenth-century Spain, around two hundred thousand people were forced into exile. Between 1936 and 1939—a span of only four years—the number is six hundred and fifty thousand. While it is tempting to see in these numbers confirmation of Spain's black legend, we should remember that political exile has been a recurring theme all over Europe.

Writer Mariano José de Larra highlighted in 1835 that "it doesn't matter how liberal one is, whether in the process of emigrating, returning, or getting ready to emigrate again, the liberal symbolizes perpetual movement, is the sea with its eternal ebb and flow." Spain experienced a two-part exodus of liberals during the nineteenth century. The first migration coincided with the absolutist restoration between 1814 and 1820, and saw over twelve thousand liberals and pro-French supporters, mostly public servants and advocates of enlightenment ideals, flee to France. Geographically, linguistically, and culturally close to Spain, France has been the preferred destination for Spanish political exiles for centuries. The second episode, the so-called Ominous Decade of absolutist rule that followed the failed Liberal Triennium (1820 to 1823), triggered the exile of 48,000 people—again, mostly to France, but also to Portugal, Italy, Great Britain, the Netherlands, Algeria, and even the United States (see Chapter 2). Afterward, there was also a smaller but ongoing exile of liberal elites, including Generals Baldomero Espartero and Juan Prim (see Chapter 29). In fact, the revolutionary pact among Progressives and Democrats that led to the 1868 Glorious Revolution against Isabel II was signed by exiles in 1866 in the Belgian city of Ostend. While some of these liberals, such as the writer Blanco White, or General Espartero, went to Britain, 77 percent—many of whom lacked the means to travel further—stayed in France.

On the other side of the political spectrum, Carlists (supporters of a rival faction of the Bourbon dynasty) fled Spain on three separate occasions during the nineteenth century. The first came after the 1839 Convention of Vergara, which ended the First Carlist War (1833 to 1839). Historians estimate that the number of Carlists in France during this period peaked in 1840 at about thirty-six thousand. Carlist exiles also went to Algeria, Morocco, Tunisia, and Egypt; others decided to join the flow of economic migrants leaving for the Americas after 1870. With the end of the Third Carlist War (1872 to 1876), twenty thousand people left once again for France. The cycle of Carlist exile would soon close with the amnesty of February 1876, but it would open again seventy years later with the Civil War, as conservatives, monarchists, and traditionalists were forced out of Republican-controlled areas after 1936.

When they hear the phrase "Republican exiles," most people think of the massive flow, into France and across the Atlantic, of refugees from the Spanish Civil War. But Republicans, along with anarchists and socialists, were intermittently forced into exile throughout the late nineteenth and early twentieth centuries, from the end of the First Republic in 1874 to the establishment of the Second Republic in 1931. During this period, the experience of exile had a significant impact on the political culture of Republican supporters. They organized themselves in secret societies and conspiratorial meetings; they carried on clandestine activities along the French border; and they worked to establish political and social organizations in their countries of exile. Under Manuel Ruiz Zorrilla, Paris became the epicenter of the Spanish radical diaspora. Republican, anarchist, and socialist exiles acquired valuable transnational experience in revolutionary activity in France, where revolutionaries from Russia or Italy were also gathered. But France was not the only destination for these people; during this period more than one hundred thousand exiles, mostly anarchists, left for Algeria as well.

While historians have debated the number of people who fled Spain at the end of the Civil War, a consensus is forming around the figure of 450,000. By the beginning of April 1939, most of them (about 430,000) were in France. By 1944, a further 162,000 had left the country; of these, 140,000 went to France, 8,800 to Africa, 19,000 to the Americas, 891 to Russia, and 2,000 to other parts of Europe. By region of origin, 36.5 percent came from Catalonia and 18 percent from Aragon, but many of them were internally displaced persons from other regions of Spain who found refuge in Republican-controlled areas as the war progressed.

Our understanding of the sociological profile of these exiles is based on a 1939 census by the Servicio de Evacuación de los Republicanos Espanoles (SERE) of 278,000 males in French refugee camps. These numbers fail to account for those male refugees with the means to circumvent the camps, as well as women, who comprised 41 percent of the total adult refugee population.

We know that 32.75 percent worked in the primary sector. The overall percentage of primary-sector workers in Spain at the time was 45.51, which means primary-sector workers were underrepresented within the male refugee population. This can be explained by the difficulty these workers may have had in finding the means to leave. By contrast, 48.94 percent of the male refugee population worked in the secondary sector, compared to only 26.51 in the overall Spanish population. This overrepresentation can be explained by the large support for Republican ideas found in this sector. Approximately, 18.31 percent worked in the tertiary sector (compared to 27.98 percent for the overall population). The underrepresentation of tertiary workers can be partially explained by their ability to escape camps or travel to other destinations. While the middle and upper middle classes, including many intellectuals, were able to leave for the Americas, the Republic's most modest supporters, including many anarchists and communists, were forced to remain in Europe. Many were particularly vulnerable after the onset of the Second World War.

The Republican exodus to Latin America, estimated at between twenty and twenty-five thousand in Mexico alone, was abetted by a shared linguistic and cultural tradition, but these factors alone did not guarantee a smooth transition. Certainly, many professors, journalists, writers, and other professionals were able to develop their careers in Spanish-speaking countries, but varying conceptions of nationalism, lukewarm support by some host governments, economic difficulties, and even ideological conflicts among Republicans themselves, weakened the exiles' ability to act as a single group, and thus better protect their most vulnerable members. And even though the Republican diaspora in Mexico is rightly known for the achievement of its artists, such as the writer Max Aub and the painter Remedios Varo, or the caliber of its academic institutions, such as the prestigious university research center Colegio de Mexico, intellectuals made up less than 1 percent of the total number of Spanish exiles.

Republican exile was further triggered by the dictatorship of Francisco Franco. The last time Spaniards had to flee their country for political reasons occurred during this period, in the early 1960s, when students, intellectuals, Basque nationalists, members of the Communist Party, and politically active workers had to flee Franco's police at a time when torture and the death penalty were still the norm. They were unable to return until the amnesty of 1977, two years after Franco's death.

Some groups, such as women and children, have slowly started to get the scholarly attention they deserve. Between August 1936 and October 1937, 32,017 children were evacuated from Spain, particularly from the north, of whom 20,266 were eventually repatriated. 456 of these children, Amparo Batanero among them, were rescued by an initiative of Mexican president Lázaro Cárdenas. They were known as the "Children of Morelia" for the city that welcome them. Notwithstanding official support, these children had difficult lives; since it was assumed they would soon return to Spain, they were not allowed to be adopted by Mexican families. As it happened, decades passed before most would see their families again. Siblings were separated and very few had educational opportunities. When government support eventually dried up, some became street children. Batanero would become an advocate for the Children of Morelia, who only received financial compensation from the country that had abandoned them during the presidency of José Rodríguez Zapatero (2004–11).

With the exception of some prominent figures, like the Communist politician Dolores Ibárruri (known as "La Pasionaria"), who went to Moscow (see Chapter 34), or the writer María Zambrano, who lived in Cuba, Puerto Rico, Italy, France, and Switzerland, the experience of women has too often been overlooked in studies of forced migration. We know from some studies that 41 percent of all the refugees from the Civil War were women, and that 80 percent of these women were housewives with no source of income. To the misery and difficulties that came from exile, these women also had to deal with a lack of education and professional training—not to mention a lack of gender equality in general.

Exiles have also sought refuge in Spain; while their numbers have not been as high as those leaving, their ideological backgrounds have been diverse. From supporters of the old regime escaping the fury of French revolutionaries, to Italian liberals fleeing absolutism in the early 1820s, French clergy escaping persecution in the lead up to the 1905 separation of church and state, and European Jews escaping the Nazis, Spain has been a temporary place of refuge for many. A significant in-flow of political exiles was also triggered by the imposition of dictatorships in Chile, Uruguay, and Argentina beginning in 1973. Between ninety and one hundred and thirty thousand of these people found refuge in Spain, mostly in Madrid and Catalonia. Not surprisingly, the largest refugee group was from Argentina, whose dictatorship began after Franco's death in 1975. Refugees to the country had to find work and residency permits and fight to get their education recognized in a Spain that was not yet a signatory to refugee conventions.

More recently, refugees from various conflicts in Africa, the Middle East, and even Europe have sought safety in Spain. In 2014, most of these people were from Syria, Ukraine, and Mali, three countries in the midst of civil war and military uprisings. According to the Spanish Commission to Assist Refugees (CEAR), 3,614 people asked for refugee status or international protection from Spain in 2014; 44 percent obtained it. This figure lies between Hungary's ridiculously low acceptance rate for the same year (9 percent) and Sweden's much more generous example (77 percent).

Voluntary migration

1. Bread with onion: Rural-to-urban migrations

Francisco Candel was born in Casas Altas, in the Spanish-speaking interior of Valencia, in 1925. When he was two years old, his parents moved to Barcelona and settled in a shanty town in the hills of Montjuic, an experience he would later use as inspiration for his 1957 novel *Donde la ciudad cambia su nombre* (Where the City Changes its Name). Though he had only a primary-school education, Candel became an influential journalist and writer.

Migration was central to Europe's industrialization in the nineteenth century. The formation of a general labor market triggered internal migrations from rural areas to more developed economic centers like Madrid, Barcelona, and the Basque Country. But while this trend began in the nineteenth century, and increased in the first third of the twentieth century, internal migration assumed massive proportions after the Spanish Civil War.

Some historians argue that between 1900 and 1960, rural-to-urban migration was as high as seven million people. The most significant decades would be 1921–30, 1941–50, and 1951–60. In the last decade alone close to two million Spaniards moved from rural to urban areas. But this movement was highly uneven. Out of Spain's fifty provinces, forty were net senders while only ten were net receivers. And of these ten, the provinces of Barcelona and Madrid received 43 and 39 percent of migrants, respectively, while the Basque Country welcomed 14 percent; combined, the other provinces represented only 4 percent. In other words, Barcelona, Madrid, and the Basque Country—or 4 percent of Spain's territory—absorbed 96 percent of its internal migrants between 1951 and 1960.

In trying to explain these numbers, scholars sometimes use the so-called push pull theory. In every migratory movement, there are push factors that encourage people to leave and pull factors that attract people to particular destinations. While this theory alone cannot explain exactly who decides to move, when they decide to do it, and why they favor some destinations over others, it can help to explain the context in which humans exercise their agency and embark on a migratory journey. In modern Spain, the main factor that pushed people out of rural areas was lack of employment—particularly for women, who were the majority of these migrants. Employment in rural areas, such as it was, was limited to subsistence agriculture and seasonal labor; this was reduced even further by the growing use of machinery on farms. Moreover, a lack of education, health, and commercial or professional services also encouraged the movement to cities.

A key feature of these migrations was a change of occupation. While most rural migrants came from agricultural backgrounds, city life meant working in construction, factories, or services. But the move to a city also involved crossing cultural and ethnic barriers that could otherwise hinder migrants' integration. Barcelona, one of the provinces to receive the largest percentage of migrants in the 1950s, had a different language and culture that, in spite of Franco's attempts to erase and prohibit it, was still an integral part of its identity. The speed with which internal migrants arrived in the region, along with their being Spanish speakers and having different customs and religious referents, created tensions between old and new Catalans. Ethnic Catalans called this the "migration of the Andalusians." They claimed these migrants "had not known spoons" (because they were too poor to make soup) and that their diet was limited to "onion with bread." It was in this context that Candel wrote *The Other Catalans*, in which he attempted to lessen ethnic Catalans' fear that the newcomers would dilute their language and culture. In Spain, "internal" movement could even involve a change of continents. Such was the case for migrants from the mainland to the country's colonial territories in North Africa, where Spaniards lived at the mercy of colonial wars, decolonization movements, and possibly finding themselves in the position of having to head back across the Mediterranean.

2. Searching for El Dorado? Economic migrations to Latin America

Clara González was born in the Panamanian city of Remedios in 1898. She was the daughter of David González, an Asturian who had immigrated first to Cuba and then to Panamá. Her indigenous mother from the Ngäbe or Guaymí people of Chiriquí died when she was young and Clara sought female role models in the nuns of Saint Vincent de Paul. David worked as a carpenter and store clerk, but he never made enough money to go back to Spain, pay the mortgage he had placed on his family land, and reconnect with the children he had left behind. Clara would become a primary-school teacher, and after returning to university, the first woman in Panama to graduate from law school. Her fight for women's rights led her to found the National Feminist Party in 1923. In 1946, Clara was elected member of the National Assembly and, although eventually defeated, became the first woman to run for the vice-presidency.

Spanish migration to the Americas was not new in the modern period. Already in the sixteenth century, the Spanish crown granted fifty-five thousand visas to its overseas territories. Most people left from Andalusia, Extremadura, and Castile. The migration of colonial administrators and army officers, businessmen, and clergymen came to an end with the nineteenth-century independence of most Spanish-American colonies (except for Cuba and Puerto Rico) (see Chapter 13). Colonial migrations promoted by the crown were replaced in the nineteenth century with the migration of laborers and their families, until the 1850s much of it illegal. For example, many of the newcomers to Cuba or Puerto Rico were farm laborers, indentured or free, from the Canary Islands or rural areas of the Iberian Peninsula. While for a time, independence slowed the movement of Spaniards to Spanish-speaking America, economic migrants did not wait for the resumption of diplomatic ties to start a new life on the other side of the Atlantic. Landowners in these newly independent countries realized they needed labor to develop their economies, and they looked for agricultural workers in the poorest areas of their former colonizer. Venezuela and Uruguay favored sturdy laborers from the Canary Islands; Argentinian sheep producers favored Basque shepherds. Between 1830 and 1865, the number of Spaniards that left is estimated at three hundred and fifty thousand. In the middle of the nineteenth century, most Spanish emigrants preferred Spanish possessions in

Cuba and Puerto Rico or Brazil, but by the 1860s the great majority of Galicians were headed for Argentina.

In the great migrations of the 1870s to the onset of the First World War, Spaniards were not the only Europeans to leave the Old World for the New, and nor were they the largest group. This massive movement was triggered by a great demand for labor in both North and South America, and it was facilitated by the advent of faster and cheaper ships that used coal instead of wind. Reliable and affordable transportation also allowed American agricultural commodities, such as grains or meats, to enter European markets. In turn, this triggered a drop in similar products on the continent, which made redundant agricultural workers more likely to contemplate immigrating to the Americas. Such people depended on the personal networks by which migrants shared information—on desirable destinations, or how to navigate the journey safely—with their families and friends.

European migration also brought new figures to the fore, such as transportation promoters and emigration agents; these people facilitated and encouraged movement by earning a cut for every person that left for the Americas. Intermediaries sold ship tickets and gave credit to those individuals or families that could provide capital goods as collateral. The spread of information and available means for financing the journey opened the Americas to larger sectors of the society that, decades before, could not have even imagined such a move. Clara's father was one of those Asturians who mortgaged family property to finance his American journey.

Almost forty million Europeans immigrated to the Americas in this period; one in twelve were Spaniards. 1912 saw the largest number of Spaniards—240,000—leave for the Americas in a single year: this was more than had left for the Americas in all of the seventeenth century. When we look at the passenger lists of those bound for Argentina, we see that two-thirds of the total number came from the underdeveloped areas of Galicia, Castile, and Andalusia; the remaining third came mostly from Catalonia and Asturias. The Canary Islands, together with Galicia, was the area of Spain that sent the highest number of emigrants to the Americas. While Canary Islanders concentrated in Venezuela, Galicians were the largest group in Argentina. Most of the other migrants went to Cuba, Argentina, and Brazil. In Cuba, Spaniards were the largest European group; in Argentina, second after Italians; in Brazil, third after Italians and Portuguese. Some of these migrants partook of two separate migrations: the one that brought them initially to one of these three American countries, and then another that took them to Chile, perhaps, or Colombia, or another destination where they hoped they would have better opportunities. After the late 1950s, new destinations—Venezuela, and to a lesser extent Uruguay, Mexico, Chile, and the United States—emerged, but overall, the number of immigrants going to the Americas declined.

Spaniards worked as laborers in the coffee haciendas in Sao Paolo, in the grain or cattle ranches in the Argentinian Pampa, or in the sugar cane plantations in Cuba. Others joined local workers in building the Panama Canal, though the Spanish government prohibited immigration to that country after 1907 to protect its citizens from unsanitary and inhumane working conditions. Some Spaniards stayed in cities and worked in construction, transportation, or domestic services. They also opened small businesses. By 1920, 80 percent of Cuba's corner stores were in the hands of Spanish families.

Women comprised 23 percent of the total number of immigrants, though they were spread out unevenly. While in Argentina, female migrants made up 33.3 percent of new arrivals, in

Cuba they were only 15.5 percent. These women are usually studied as "dependent migrants," part of familial movements in which agency resides with men; the women follow later, to achieve family reunification. But the fact that many women followed this pattern did not stop them from being labor migrants. Family reunification did not limit women to the domestic sphere—on the contrary, for those families that made a living by running small grocery stores, for example, women's work was a crucial part of family income. Moreover, a significant percentage of female migrants were single. For instance, of the many thousands of women to emigrate from Galician ports, 67.25 percent did so on their own. They worked as domestic, service, or agricultural laborers.

During this time, the great migration was perceived by politicians in Spain as a disgrace—a reflection of a malfunctioning economy that was unable to provide for all citizens, yet another sign of the so-called decadence that had manifested after 1898 in the "disastrous" loss of the colonies of Cuba, Puerto Rico, and the Philippines to the United States. Indeed, large-scale migration represented a loss for Spain. In migration theory, this is known as "brain drain" for the country of departure and "brain gain" for the country of destination. The idea is that the country of departure has invested resources in an individual, for education (even if only primary), for health, for employment; once that person leaves, this "investment," along with any potential return, is lost. Yet these losses were offset by the huge remittances that Spanish migrants sent home during this period. From 1906 to 1910, annual remittances from Latin America were between 250 and 300 million pesetas. If we consider that the total sources of revenue for Spain amounted to just under 2.3 billion pesetas in 1906, then remittances went a long way toward balancing finances and activating the economy.

Contrary to the popular image of the impoverished migrant—forced to flee Europe, never to return—are the *golondrinas* (Sparrows), workers who left for the Americas and traveled back and forth depending on economic opportunities and family needs. There were also *Indianos*, or *Americanos*, native Spaniards who left for the Americas and made it rich, returning with a fortune they later used to start businesses or lead ostentatious lives. Miguel Viada Buñol was one such *indiano*. A marine merchant who made it big in Cuba, he promoted and financed the construction of a rail line between Barcelona and his birthplace, the nearby city of Mataró, in 1848, the first in mainland Spain. Another famous *indiano* family, the Vidal Quadras, left the Catalan city of Sitges for Venezuela and Cuba at the turn of the nineteenth century. They returned a few decades later, opened a bank in Barcelona, and became an influential family in business, politics, and art. But return migration was not limited to those who made it big: as many as 60 percent of Spaniards who left between 1882 and 1935 returned—though not to the same areas they had left. Despite the economic difficulties that sometimes forced Spaniards to leave, it implied a certain privilege to have a country to return to.

3. Going north and moving up: Economic migrations to Western Europe

Eliseo Rosende and Elva Expósito met and married in Le Locle, Switzerland. Both had left Galicia in the 1960s to find work and start a new life in central Europe. Eliseo headed to Lausanne, where he worked in a restaurant for years without proper documentation; when a factory in Le Locle offered him legal work, he did not have to think twice. Elva left Spain with a cousin, and she too worked in a restaurant before finding a job in one of Le Locle's clock factories. Their two daughters, Beatriz and Madalena, were born in that city, and they managed to study despite the fact that, until the 1990s, Swiss law prohibited the children of immigrants without permanent residency from attending public schools. Beatriz studied political science and became a union organizer, while Madalena earned a PhD. Nobody among their immigrant friends and neighbors imagined these daughters of Galician farmers would go so far.

Though Spaniards had already begun migrating to France in the nineteenth century, the economic frenzy that occurred after the Second World War prompted many more to set their sights on the rapidly developing economies of Western Europe. Some historians argue that 3.5 million Spaniards moved to France, Germany, and Switzerland. Many returned; others stayed. Some migrated legally—225,000 to France, 380,000 to Germany and Switzerland—but hundreds of thousands of workers, like Eliseo Rosende, left Spain illegally. Some of these people were regularized in their country of destination after some time, which only tended to skew the numbers involved. For instance, the French census of 1968 stated that the number of Spaniards in the country was around 610,000—or three times the number of official emigrants there.

Spaniards' economic migration to Western Europe began in the early 1950s, saw significant growth after 1961, and petered out after host countries closed their foreign-worker programs in the face of widespread unemployment after the 1973–74 oil crisis. These migratory patterns show that the connection between economic development in one's country of origin and the decision of thousands of migrants to leave is more complex than just poverty or lack of opportunity: it goes far beyond a simple push-and-pull explanation. While the movement of Spaniards to Western Europe coincided with the period of the Spanish economic miracle—when industry, economic development, higher salaries, and better living standards came to the country after 1959—these benefits were regionally uneven and slow to take shape. The reasons for individual Spaniards to leave thus remained in place.

Postwar economic migration was not an isolated Spanish phenomenon. Around 8 million Italians, Portuguese, Greeks, Yugoslavians, Turks, Moroccans, Algerians, and Tunisians also partook of this temporary economic opportunity. Italians, Spaniards, and Portuguese were often part of a dynamic some historians have called the Latin migration system. Italians would arrive first, followed by Spaniards, who would replace them in their jobs; Italians could then move up the economic ladder in their host country or return home to an improved economy. After a while, Portuguese would arrive and replace Spaniards in a similar fashion. In contrast to the late 1970s, European countries were hungry for cheap labor in the immediate postwar period. But this demand was accompanied by stringent requirements: host countries preferred young, healthy males. As a result, by 1968 only 26 percent of all Spanish workers in France were female, and in Germany two years later, women comprised 29.4 percent (though these numbers were higher than in Spain itself, where women made up 21.6 percent of the labor force in 1964 and 24.7 percent in 1975). In some countries, such as Germany, Spaniards—both male and female—were concentrated in the industrial sector, but in other countries their options were more diverse; in Switzerland, for example, a quarter of male Spaniards worked in construction, followed by industry and hospitality. 38 percent of women worked in hospitality, while 14.5 percent worked in domestic services. Spaniards in France worked mainly in agriculture, whether for the entire year or for just a few months during the wine, beet, and rice harvests. Between 1962 and 1974, as many as one hundred thousand temporary workers brought in the harvest in France each year.

Sending and receiving countries signed bilateral agreements to regulate this movement, and they created particular organizations in charge of selecting migrants. Germany signed agreements with Italy in 1955, Greece and Spain in 1960, Turkey in 1961, Morocco in 1963, Portugal in 1964, Tunisia in 1965, and Yugoslavia in 1968. The migrant-labor programs initiated with these agreements were temporary in design. Western European countries did not want to attract permanent residents, with the diverse cultural and social needs that their young families would entail. They preferred single men who would work for a short period of time, usually two years, and then return home with their earnings. When these workers returned to Spain, they did not settle in the same underdeveloped areas they had left, but rather in one of the country's rapidly growing cities. As a result, the areas that had produced these migrants in the first place never recovered from the demographic hemorrhage of the 1950–70s.

Was this migration perceived as a disgrace, as the transatlantic migration had been at the turn of the century? Franco and many of the other authoritarian leaders whose citizens had left (António de Oliveira Salazar in Portugal, the Colonels in Greece, King Hassan II in Morocco) were actually delighted to bid farewell to a population for which their economies could not provide; these people could become disenchanted and turn against their rulers if they remained at home, so migration worked as a sort of safety valve to control an idle and youthful population. And by facilitating family reunification in those countries that allowed for it—France for instance—the Francoist administration was also able to save on the cost of education, health, and social insurance. Migrants' remittances, as we have seen, were also viewed as a source of hard currency. Indeed, historians estimate that they covered between 17 and 30 percent of Spain's trade deficit between 1960 and 1973. The Francoist administration, via the Spanish Institute for Emigration, even organized a banking transfer system to facilitate, promote, and control migrants' remittances.

As Figure 19.1 shows, the oil crisis of 1973–74 initiated a downward trend in the migration of Spaniards and an increase in those returning home. Not only were these Spaniards able to find work at home, but many were able to move away from the hardest and most poorly paid jobs, such as greenhouse pickers or domestic servants, since these were now being filled by international immigrants. However, with the onset of the world recession in 2008, the period of prosperity brought on by Spain's entry into the EU in 1986 was revealed to be an exception rather than a rule. According to the National Statistical Institute, almost 1.5 million Spaniards were living abroad in 2009; by 2015 this number had ballooned to almost 2.2 million, a 46 percent increase in just six years. Mostly young and educated Spaniards were leaving the northern provinces of Asturias, La Coruña, Pontevedra, and Orense, the Canary Island of Santa Cruz de Tenerife, Madrid, and Barcelona. Every single year from 2009 to 2015, more women left than men, albeit not by a large margin. Most of these immigrants were of working age and, judging by the increase in minors abroad, many were bringing their children with them. In some cases, people whose parents and grandparents migrated to Switzerland in the 1960s and returned home to have families, have once again set their compasses north.

Climbing Fortress Europe: The making of multicultural Spain

Domingo Antonio Edjang Moreno was born in Torrejón de Ardoz, Madrid, in 1977. His Equatorial Guinean father was a military man working in the nearby base. His mother, from

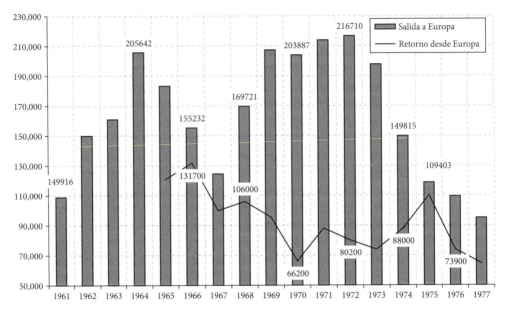

Figure 19.1 European and transatlantic migration from Spain, 1960–77.

the poor region of Extremadura, was an ethnic Spaniard. Edjang, better known as the political rapper El Chojin, ruminates on the place of race in contemporary Spain: "When your dad is black, your mother is white, and you are somewhere in between them, you learn naturally that the amount of melanin is unimportant." How did Spain go from a country that sent millions of its citizens abroad to one that looks up to El Chojin, the son of internal and international migrants?

Migration to Western Europe began declining in the early 1970s; it was largely over by the time other European countries closed their guest-worker programs in the wake of the oil crisis of 1973–74. For more than three decades, from 1974 to 2008, Spaniards, now rooted and prosperous, forgot that they had once been a country of exiles and migrants. A booming construction sector, cutting-edge agribusinesses, and a growing tourist industry attracted unprecedented levels of international migration from the mid-1990s to the onset of the economic recession in 2008. While in 1981, the 198,042 foreign-born migrants in Spain comprised just 0.52 percent of the total population by 2010 the numbers had risen to 5,747,734 people and 12.2 percent of the total. (It has since dropped to 10.7 percent, or about 5 million people.) One-third are from Latin America, particularly Ecuador; European migrants make up another third, of which Britons and Romanians are predominant. The oldest and largest immigrant group from one single country is from Morocco.

Becoming a country of immigrants did not come easily. While Spaniards themselves were intimately familiar with exile and migration, they lacked experience with incoming migration control and integration programs. In fact, the country's first immigration law, approved in 1985, on the eve of Spain's entry into the European Economic Community—the precursor of today's European Union (EU)—the following year, was aimed at policing foreigners without any provisions for social integration. The law enshrined privileges for some migrants while ignoring others. It assumed, for example, that some immigrants, due to their "cultural affinity" with Spain, were more likely to integrate and thus deserved longer work and residency permits, and these same immigrants were granted easier access to citizenship (the normal residency requirement of ten years lowered to just two). This group included migrants from Latin America, Andorra, the Philippines, Equatorial Guinea, and Sephardic Jews. Some were included because they shared linguistic and religious customs with the majority of Spaniards; others—namely Sephardic Jews—were included as a symbolic restitution of a historic crime (the expulsion of Spanish Jews in 1492). And yet the same criteria could easily be applied to Moriscos, Spanish Muslims forced to convert after the Christian conquest of Iberia, and expelled altogether between 1609 and 1614, but who were nonetheless ignored by the law. People from Spain's former colonial territories, such as the Philippines and Equatorial Guinea, were included, while incomprehensively, people from Western Sahara or Spanish Morocco were not. An impartial observer is forced to conclude that the Spanish Parliament intended to hinder the arrival and integration of populations from these Muslim-dominated countries that, using the government's own criteria, could also claim "cultural affinity" with Spain.

With Spain joining the EU, Western Europeans began immigrating to the country in large numbers, and citizens of the former Eastern Bloc followed as their countries joined in the early twenty-first century. Brits and Germans make up part of the large "Sun migration" to Spain. These groups enjoy legal status, usually have money to buy property, and are either retired or working for their own fellow nationals. They interact little with locals, but they are not resented to the same degree as other immigrants because they are perceived to be net contributors to the economy. The 2016 Brexit referendum put the future status of the more than 300,000 citizens of Great Britain living in Spain in doubt. Backlash against Eastern Europeans has been more intense, because most are traditional economic migrants, but also because of their different ethnic and religious backgrounds. By 2004, when most Eastern European countries had joined the EU, there were already hundreds of thousands of Eastern Europeans living and working in Spain. Their countries' entrance into the EU made it easy for them to legalize their situation and become politically engaged citizens. In the province of Castelló, for example, immigrants amounted to 18.6 percent of the population in 2010; 49.5 percent of these where Romanians. In local elections, their votes have been courted with questionable enticements by the entrenched Popular Party elite.

Most immigrants have had to navigate a complex and unreliable bureaucracy and fight to obtain two separate types of permits, one to work, the other to reside legally in the country. Since Spain did not have an official system to import immigrants, as in Canada or Australia, most people who wanted to remain in Spain overstayed their tourist visas or arrived illegally after a costly, and dangerous—often deadly—crossing of the Mediterranean. Between 1985 and 2005, the lack of legal means to reach Spain created massive pockets of undocumented workers who were employed in the country's thriving underground economy. But Spanish politicians' lack of experience with immigration policies, compounded by a failure to acknowledge the benefits of immigration and the need to ease tensions between old and new Spaniards, made for poor immigration management. Spanish governments have had to offer "exceptional" regularizations in the form of amnesties of illegal aliens in 1985, 1996, 2000, 2001, 2003 and most recently, in 2005. Other European countries have pressured Spain, Italy, Portugal, and Greece to stop relying on such regularizations, and to find other ways to deal with the ongoing influx of irregular migrants. The Spanish government has responded with a new procedure based on "rootedness." This is defined as having been in the country for three years, demonstrating a one-year job contract, and family ties with other immigrants—or citizens—legally residing in Spain. It has functioned unevenly at best.

While many scholars argue that regularizations represent top-down affairs decided by governments according to the economic needs of employers, this is a reductionist view of how a government deals with political pressure from civil society. Churches and NGOs have long demanded a radical transformation of the situation of undocumented migrants, and migrants themselves, organized in social movements and engaged in such acts of civil disobedience as hunger strikes and church and university occupations, have lobbied hard to place their demands on the mainstream political agenda. For example, one of the largest regularizations, which granted legal status to 230,000 people, was implemented in 2001 by a Conservative government that had adamantly opposed it. It was called the "regularization by rootedness" (*arraigo*), and it was forced on the government after a nationwide immigrant-led mobilization of undocumented migrants demanded access to legal status and the improvement of work and residency conditions it would provide.

Another push for fundamental rights on the part of undocumented migrants occurred in Ceuta and Melilla between 1985 and 1987. These two North African towns have been under Portuguese and Spanish control since the fifteenth century, but independent Morocco has contested these claims repeatedly. For most of the cities' history, they were military outposts with little civilian and commercial development, but during the twentieth century their populations almost doubled; by the time Spain had reestablished democracy, these cities had become complex settler outposts best described as borderlands. Even though today it is hard to imagine—with Ceuta and Melilla surrounded by two barbed wire fences constantly monitored by police—the borders between these cities and their surrounding territories have been porous for most of their history. By 1985, Melilla's population was composed of two-thirds European descendants with Spanish citizenship and one-third Muslim, most of whom were undocumented workers from nearby Morocco. With the immigration law of 1985, the Spanish government considered these people foreigners, and asked them to apply for new work and residency permits. Yet the Muslim population in Melilla refused; most of them had either been born in the city or had lived there for years—longer, in fact, than the ten consecutive years necessary for the granting of Spanish citizenship. For two years, the (nativist) local government and the government in Madrid refused, but eventually they were forced to accede: tens of thousands of citizenship applications were thus granted, ending the conflict and securing a clear pro-Spanish majority in both cities—at least for the time being.

In Latin America, Spanish immigrants benefited from cultural and racial privileges; in Western Europe, despite widespread racism against southern Europeans, they enjoyed either legal migration or frequent and easy regularizations due to the fact that their labor was a sought-after commodity during the economic miracle. Yet non-European immigrants to Spain have faced a backlash from ethnic Spaniards. While violent outbursts have been limited to the Catalan town of Terrassa in 1999 and the Andalusian town of El Ejido in 2000, the social perception of immigrants as equal neighbors has been slow to trickle down into the Spanish imagination. It has been particularly difficult in those regions, such as the Basque Country or Catalonia, where nationalist projects demand cultural assimilation; in such a context, other languages and religions are perceived as threats to the survival of the nation. In "Rap vs. Racismo," a song by thirteen Spanish rappers and DJs, MC and producer Nerviozzo raps: "Dude, you're not a racist, you're an idiot/ . . . Nations disappeared long ago and borders are really only the surfaces of our skin, which is why our grandchildren will all be shades of brown/ . . . Coward, if one day you are made to face your demons you will see that they're white, like you are." Similarly, El Chojin's "N.E.G.R.O." questions a society that cannot seem to recognize its own inability to identify and deal with racism among its people: "No, ladies and gentlemen/ this way, there is no option to find solutions/to the alleged problem of people of different races living together/in a society that likes confrontation/if you're black, you're going to have to deal with racism/on top of all the other problems, and worse of all your society will deny it/and say, Spain is racist? Come on, don't exaggerate!"

Exile and migration: Striking a balance

Some historians argue that the expulsion of cultural elites throughout Spanish history is one of its defining features, a crucial part of the Spanish experience. This tradition of exile and expulsion has long been used as evidence of Spain's black legend. But historians must be careful not to project a single, essentializing cause for the many episodes of exile in the country's past. Some argue that these were triggered by intolerance, parochialism, and lack of interest in, even disdain for, foreign ideas and movements. While these cultural explanations may have been correct in some cases, they still need to be tested against concrete ideological, economic, and political causes for the events they purport to explain. That exile has been common in modern Spanish history is hardly in doubt. But a more difficult question is why and to what end? We cannot explain exile movements without making reference to the misuse of institutional power to expel enemies and the backlash among those persecuted groups that this entailed; not coincidentally every Spanish monarch since 1808, with the exception of the current Felipe VI, were exiled at some point or, as in the case of Amadeo I, came from a foreign dynasty, and quickly abdicated and abandoned the country. The doctrinal and ideological influence of the Catholic Church also encouraged exile movements, most obviously under the Inquisition, and later, during the Spanish Civil War.

As for its consequences, the constant expulsion of enemy political factions hindered elite continuity, and led those who remained in Spain to perceive foreign influences as threats. But there is a tendency to link exile with (a failed) modernity, and rootedness with tradition. This reductive and binary view needs to be reconsidered. Migration theory has been good at tracing the numbers of people who move and the amount of money these persons send back to their families, but more recently, scholars have been trying to understand the nonmaterial benefits that migration involves for the country of origin. Scholars call these "social remittances," which refers to the skills and knowledge that migrants and exiles bring with them when they return home. Spanish society has clearly benefited from the social remittances of returning exiles. For instance, Spaniards in the United States helped shape the perception of the United States as the cradle of liberty and progress; similarly, Spanish liberals in Europe came in contact with cultural romanticism and, after Ferdinand VII's death, brought it back to Spain.

But important questions remain: how influential have these social remittances been in modern Spain? Why have exiles and migrants not been able to have a deeper impact on Spaniards' awareness of their country as a country of migrants? In the nineteenth century, exile was seen as a constant of political life. This idea slowly faded at the end of the century, but it came back with the massive Republican exodus brought about by the Civil War. The limits of exiles' influence, and the causes and consequences of their experience, needs to be explained in its proper context. For instance, Republican exiles included a great contingent of politicians, intellectuals, and artists, and yet these people were prohibited from influencing Spanish political and cultural debates by both distance and Francoist censorship. By the time Franco died in 1975, the intellectual figures of the Republican exile had become relics of a past that thirty-six years of Francoism had largely destroyed; the actual circumstances and timing of events hampered Republican exiles' ability to contribute to the restoration of democracy in Spain.

There are various ways of interpreting massive departures. The optimistic view of migration recognizes its great potential: people who were destitute are able to earn money and gain new skills in other countries, which in turn act as sources of regeneration for the region or country of origin. This kind of thinking underlies a shift in wealthy countries from foreign aid to development projects led by migrants. Since migrants originate in underdeveloped countries, and are versed in these cultures and languages, who better to bring back skills and technology transfer from donor countries? By contrast, a negative view of migration views the departure of young, able, ambitious, and educated citizens as a collective national failure. While the "best" men and women leave and help build other societies, the people left behind have to contend with oppressive structures—for instance, the clergy in Andalusia, or the Mafia in Sicily. If the escape route that migration offers was not there, these people would be forced to improve their places of origin. Of course, the decision to migrate sometimes does trigger phenomena that can adversely affect one's place of origin. But both the optimistic and the pessimistic views of migration and exile are defined as a zero-sum game, in the same way the brain drain/brain gain theory works. Recently, migration scholars have started looking at these phenomena from the point of view of brain circulation—the idea that a person's skills and contributions are not completely lost by their country of origin, nor gained solely by their country of destination. Take for example the activism in favor of the Spanish Second Republic on the part of Clara González, a Panamanian woman whose only connection with Spain was her Asturian father.

If we look at the journeys of migrants themselves, we are forced to agree with other historians that modern Spaniards have been privileged. Of course, this does not mean that their movements were devoid of hardship, humiliation, or personal tragedy, but Spanish migrants and refugees nonetheless benefited from being white and having places to go to that were culturally and religiously familiar. Some historians even consider the movement of Spaniards to Latin America a "privileged emigration," in the sense that, despite the harsh circumstances that forced them to leave in the first place, a large part of this group was able to improve their socioeconomic situations. Indeed, their shared language and religion, relics of a colonial past, allowed Spaniards in Latin America to transfer their white privilege to mixed societies imbued with racial prejudice.

The same argument, with some provisos, could be made for Spanish refugees. To be sure, hundreds of thousands of Republican exiles ended up in concentration camps in Southern France; the tens of thousands that Franco refused to repatriate ended up perishing in Nazi concentration camps such as Mauthausen. But overall, Spanish refugees and economic migrants have enjoyed imperial, religious, and ethnic privileges when it comes to their movement around the world. The generosity of Mexico and other American countries in welcoming Republican exiles right after the Great Depression was paralleled only by Western countries welcoming

Communist refugees after the Second World War. Such instances of ideological solidarity are of course quite rare.

Both the memory and the reality of Spaniards' economic migration to Latin America and Western Europe have faded in the democratic period, but the renewal of Spanish emigration since 2008 is nothing new. Rather, it is a resurgence of old currents and dynamics, ones that never really disappeared, but were simply waiting for an economic downturn to reemerge.

Further reading

Antolín, Pablo, *International Migration Flows: The Case of Spain (1960-1988)*, Oxford: University of Oxford, 1994.

Bover, Olympia, *Migration in Spain: Historical Background and Current Trends*, Bonn: Forschungsinstitut zur Zukunft der Arbeit, 1999.

Faber, Sebastiaan, *Exile and Cultural Hegemony: Spanish Intellectuals in Mexico, 1939-1975*, Nashville: Vanderbilt University Press, 2002.

Guia, Aitana, *The Muslim Struggle for Civil Rights in Spain: Promoting Democracy through Migrant Engagement, 1985-2010*, Eastbourne, UK: Sussex Academic Press, 2014.

Lillo, Natacha, *La petite Espagne de la Plaine-Saint-Denis: 1900-1980*, Paris: Autrement, 2004.

Moya, José C., *Cousins and Strangers: Spanish Immigrants in Buenos Aires, 1850-1930*, Berkeley: University of California Press, 1998.

Nunez Seixas, Xose M., "History and Collective Memories of Migration in a Land of Migrants: The Case of Iberian Galicia," *History & Memory*, 14, 1 (2002), pp. 229–58.

Soo, Scott, *The Routes to Exile: France and the Spanish Civil War Refugees, 1939-2009*, Manchester, NY: Manchester University Press, 2013.

Zepeda, Karla, *Exile and Identity in Autobiographies of Twentieth-Century Spanish Women*. New York: Peter Lang, 2012.

Association of the 1937 Basque Refugees Children: http://www.basquechildren.org/

Zontini, Elisabetta, *Transnational Families, Migration and Gender: Moroccan and Filipino Women in Bologna and Barcelona*, New York: Berghahn Books, 2010.

CHAPTER 20
THE STATE
Diego Palacios Cerezales

States are elusive objects. From the viewpoint of international relations, states have diplomats and armies, wage wars and sign peace agreements. From the standpoint of the citizenry, states embody a political center, encompassing government and public administration. States have an imaginary component—as they represent the political expression of a human community—but they are also material—a network of organizations that enforce obligations (taxes, conscription, hygienic measures, etc.) and provide public services, from security to road building, from healthcare to scientific research. States define boundaries: in the first instance, territorial borders with other states, but also boundaries deciding who is a citizen and who an alien, and between the sphere of its own activities and that of civil society. This chapter explores the historical formation of the state in Spain since the nineteenth century, looking at the development of territorial administration, civil service, tax collection, public expenditure, public services provided, and at changes in the rights and obligations that have composed the relationship between citizens and state.

Before the nineteenth century, the government spent most of its revenue on the military. As in any other European country, the Spanish state was not much more than a tax-collecting machine paying for an army and a navy and claiming the royal justice as the highest court of appeal. Subjects enjoyed some public utilities, such as postal communications and a few royal roads, but these were conceived as internal improvements for the royal administration itself, not as services to the population. In addition, the reach of royal administration was limited. In many instances, the church, the nobility, cities, guilds, and other bodies had powers that the nineteenth century would consider part of the exclusive remit of the State. The Catholic Church collected its own taxes—the tithe—and controlled an important chunk of the justice system—the Inquisition—whereas in one-third of the territory local lords, not crown-appointed judges, dispensed justice. In addition, in eighteenth-century Spain there was no common framework of law and administration. People from some regions and in certain professions; noble landowners did not pay land tax; some offices belonged to families that had purchased them in the past, and certain trades were monopolized by guilds and cities. As in other Old Regime European societies, each region and social group had its own privileges and customs, and there was no clear-cut distinction between the sphere and the state and that of civil society. Pablo Olavide, a reforming official of the late eighteenth century, described Spain as a

> body composed of other and smaller bodies, separated and in opposition to one another, which oppress and despise each other and are in a constant state of war. Each province, each religious house, each profession is separated from the rest of the nation and concentrated in itself... [Spain is] a monstrous republic of little republics which confront each other because the particular interest of each is in contradiction to the general interest.

In face of the powerful presence of these smaller and self-regulated bodies, some historians have claimed that until the nineteenth century, the royal administrations of Western Europe were not proper states. From this perspective, officials such Olavide, who tried to reinforce the power of the crown, could be described as state-builders. They aimed at putting the lands and populations under a shared law, shared weights, and measures, the abolition of customs barriers between regions, and the definition of a common framework of rights and obligations toward the crown. That clarity, so dear to the Enlightenment, would allow the pooling of human and material resources, the equitable distribution of sacrifices and the introduction of desired reforms such as unified national markets. Royal officials had also long harbored greater ambitions. They wanted the crown to transcend its sovereign roles—international and dynastic competition, internal order, supreme legal authority—to become the center of a project for human and material development that would provide prosperity and happiness, in tandem with increasing the Crown's income and thus aggrandizing Spain's international status. This project of active and uniform government clashed with traditional political culture, which cherished the privileges and customs peculiar to the different elements federated under the crown: medieval kingdoms and principalities, cities, communities, guilds, estates, religious confraternities, military and religious orders, the church itself.

Since the seventeenth century, successive institutional reforms provided fragments of a would-be national administration, but these usually superimposed themselves over the preexistent patchwork of privileges and customs. Localism, privileged groups, and the veneration of tradition, resisted reform. Amid the upheaval caused by the Napoleonic invasion, the 1812 constitution proposed a common system of government and administration that would override previous arrangements, but it was not until the 1830s that the durable triumph of liberalism over absolutism would allow for a full-fledged national reform turning the king's subjects into equal citizens with the same rights and obligations (see chapters 2, 3).

Territorial unification

Following the death of Ferdinand VII—the last absolute king of Spain—in 1833, undersecretary of state Javier de Burgos brought about the division of Spain into 49 provinces. Burgos was an admirer of the enlightened ministers of Charles III who, during the second half of the eighteenth century, had devised a comprehensive collection of reforms which they were unable to fully accomplish. He had also worked for Joseph Bonaparte during the Napoleonic occupation of Spain and esteemed the centralization and rationalization the French administration had attained after the Revolution. The division of the kingdom into provinces of roughly equal size facilitated the coherent administration of the space and the population, while their capitals would centralize the provision of administrative services, from tax collection to secondary education, from justice to economic development. The reform sought an "efficacious" and "quick and simultaneous" administration, led by agents that "would know the local needs and means." Burgos' goal was "the omnipresence of the administration . . . removing at once the thousands of obstacles and promoting, with a single and enlightened impulse, great prosperity. Those charged with doing this must form a chain which starts with the head of the administration and ends with the last local policeman."

By 1833, the reorganization of the territory was seen as more urgent than ever. The upheavals of the previous three decades—the 1807 French invasion, the subsequent war, the exile of the administrative elite that had collaborated with Joseph Bonaparte (including Javier de Burgos himself), and the swings between constitutionalism and absolutism—had left the machinery of government and taxation in tatters. The loss of most of the American empire, furthermore, had caused a grave fiscal problem, as these colonies had provided one-third of the public revenues during the eighteenth century (see Chapter 13).

De Burgos' reforms represented the triumph of the ideas of uniformity and active government dear to enlightened absolutists, but also of that of the sovereign nation, closer to the liberals' taste. After the protracted set of reforms usually called the "liberal revolution" (1812–74) provinces and municipalities would become sections of the national administration, and a clear distinction between state and civil society would emerge. According to the reformers, once the little reducts of privilege and rivalry were destroyed, a free market coupled with enlightened government would release social energies hitherto crippled by outworn institutions and archaic policies.

The 1833 territorial administration destroyed the spatial expression of the old regime and replaced it with an understanding of Spain as a nation-state, a unified territory in which all citizens and land would be subjected to the same code of law. Old kingdoms such as Castile or Valencia, and the principality of Catalonia, were now divided into provinces, most of them taking the name of their capital city. For example, Barcelona, Gerona, Lérida, and Tarragona would still appear in the maps as forming Catalonia, but these four new provinces would not share a common civil administration. [Starting in the late nineteenth century, this vision would be challenged by the emergence of nationalist movements in Catalonia, the Basque Provinces, and Galicia (see Chapter 10).] The provincial map reorganized metropolitan Spain, including the Canaries and the Balearic Islands; Philippines, Cuba, and the remaining overseas dominions, in contrast, would be subject to special laws—consolidating a difference between the government of the metropolis and that of the colonies that had not been so clear-cut during the eighteenth century. The 1833 reform consolidated a provincial map which was going to be the backbone of the state. The provincial division also marked a drive toward homogeneity and centralization that endured until the establishment of regional governments—in 1978.

The 1833 reform also represented the blending of enlightened reformism and liberalism that would preside over the construction of the state during the nineteenth century. Governing elites during the reign of Isabella II agreed on a general set of principles and ideas: the preeminence of the nation, equality of civil rights (for men), representative government, and separation of powers. These beliefs provided coherence to the subsequent legal codification and institutional assemblage of the state. On the other hand, as the implications of these reforms would never be fully pursued, the dissonance between principle and reality would fuel the criticism of the liberal state at the end of the nineteenth century.

The preeminence of the nation meant that church and nobility lost the power to tax and impart justice, functions that now fell under the exclusive remit of the state. It also implied that all public offices would belong to the nation, hence putting an end to the sale of jobs, the monopoly of the nobility over some offices and the inheritance of local magistracies. The principle of equality, embodied in the provincial structure, in turn entailed equal taxation and recruitment. Land in the hands of noblemen, the Church, and other privileged

Map 20.1 Territorial division of Spain after 1833.

bodies—hitherto largely exempt from taxation—was now, in theory at least, at the reach of the taxman. In fact, most Church land was declared "goods of the nation" and sold to cover the government's debt. Finally, the separation of the legislative, judicial, and administrative powers reshaped the whole organization chart of the state. In the old regime, regional courts (*audiencias*) and intendants coordinated policy, collected taxes, and imparted justice. Now, the administrative and judicial branches of the civil administration would rely on two separate hierarchies of officials. The triumph of liberalism was not absolute. Some champions of the old regime and regional difference tried to revive privilege, having some success in the case of the Basque regional privileges (*fueros*) and, due to the slowness of legal codification, in the preservation of local and regional civil law, especially in Catalonia.

Agreement on general principles did not prevent liberals from disagreeing over some key issues, disagreements that provoked tensions between the 1820s and the 1870s. There were two competing approaches to the relations between citizens and the state which produced two contrasting institutional projects, one more "civic" and one more "bureaucratic." According to the civic ideal, the citizens themselves should control, and even perform, most public services: for the policing of property and security, there would be a citizen militia; for the dispensation of justice, jury service; for the ordinary government of the provinces, elected representatives; for the collection of taxes, local boards would be in charge. Civic involvement was understood as a virtuous element of the political system and as key to preventing the development of a too-powerful and autonomous royal administration, always keen to encroach on a citizen's freedoms, and his purse.

In contrast, some other liberals feared the "civic" state as a burden and a recipe for anarchy. They did not relish the idea of constant involvement: why would a busy merchant want to dress in militia uniform and patrol a highway once a week if some taxes would pay a professional police? Why would he want to lose his time in jury service if a trained judge could dispense justice? Moreover, what about the transformation of local councils and provinces into political bodies: would having these headed by central government appointees not produce a better coordination of policy?

Disputes between these two models of state, along with the related question of the extension of voting rights, were central to the constant political upheaval that lasted up to the 1870s (see Chapter 3). In general, the Moderate Party advocated a bureaucratic state while the Progressives championed citizen militias (*Milicia Nacional*) and elective local councils. Progressives and Moderates changed the constitution every time a revolution or a *pronunciamiento* got them into power; in accordance to their models of state, they also changed the nature of the local councils—from elected bodies to delegate sections of the central administration—and organized and dissolved the *Milicia Nacional*.

During revolutionary situations such as those of 1842, 1854–56, or 1868–74, many militia units and councils became political bodies that defied central government guidance and rejected taxation and recruitment. Hence, even Progressive elites came to resent the lack of collaboration of these "bedrocks of political freedom." In the end, these experiences undermined the project of a civic state and led to the triumph of the bureaucratic approach.

Bureaucratization came coupled with centralized political control. Javier de Burgos had imagined state bureaucracy as a well-ordered hierarchy of dutiful civil servants promoting production, commerce, and knowledge. As many projects do not survive contact with reality, the heads of the provinces, soon-to-be called civil governors, became key resorts for the political control of the provinces. They were named by the central government and turned into a cog of party politics, supervising local councils, and favoring the incumbent's party electoral triumph.

Building the state (1833–50)

Whereas the 1833 territorial division set the blueprint for the organization of the national administration, major reforms in 1844 and 1845 set up two additional long-standing cornerstones of the Spanish state: the liberal tax system and the Civil Guard. Ministers Alejandro Mon and Ramón Santillán simplified the previous tax administration. The new system was a partial success, as it assured a steady intake of revenue, but it contained a key flaw that made it less efficient than similar models in France and Italy. In this peculiar area of administration, the Moderates, in good measure representatives of the landed interests, preferred civic involvement over professional bureaucracy: they blocked the development of a land survey and gave the control of taxation to local boards formed by the richest taxpayers, who, unsurprisingly, were interested in concealing their wealth from the state. The state became a blind tax collector. It had no systematic knowledge of the extent, productivity, and ownership of the sources of wealth—farms, workshops, factories, cattle, or arable land. For the rest of the century, the rich undertaxed themselves, overtaxed small farmers, and concealed wealth. This reliance on the wealthy impaired the ability of the state to develop as an autonomous force, making many believe that Spain was in the hands of an "oligarchy." Besides, as population grew and some sectors of the economy became more productive, the inability of the state to monitor this growth prevented a concomitant growth of public revenue. Being blind to internal wealth, the machine of taxation was alarmingly unproductive: between 1850 and 1890, for each peseta the Spanish government invested in tax and customs collection, it only harvested six. In France the figure was fourteen.

Neither the new tax system nor the sales of Church land allowed for a sustainable budget and public debt became the chronic problem. In fact, in 1851, 1882, and 1899 Spain partially defaulted on its debt. International creditors complained vociferously, but unlike Greece and Egypt, Spain was able to maintain its fiscal sovereignty, an indication that nineteenth-century Spain was still a sizable power, despite its marginality in international politics and its comparative poverty.

While the core of Europe saw industrialization takeoff and the big powers engage in a new round of colonial expansion, Spain grew more slowly. Whereas in 1830 Spanish GDP per capita was 80 percent that of France and Britain combined, by 1900 this figure was only 54 percent (see Chapter 9). Spain was comparatively poor indeed, and this poverty explains in part the inability of the state to fulfill its own promises. Universal education had been decreed since 1812, but the lack of resources of local councils, which had to pay for the primary schools, meant that by 1900 one in two Spaniards was illiterate, compared to one in six Frenchmen or one in thirty Britons. The construction of roads, channels, railways, and seaports was also trumpeted as a priority, but this was done late and with important budgetary constraints. In fact, the Ministry of Development (Fomento), established in 1847, spent only 9 percent of the national budget between 1850 and 1890, while 27 percent was spent paying debts, 7 percent on pensions, and 25 percent in maintaining the army and the navy. France and the Netherlands, in contrast, spent around 15 percent of comparatively bigger budgets on infrastructure development. Slow growth, slow change, and slow institutional development may depict Spain in the nineteenth century, but growth, change, and institutional development did indeed happen.

The iconic Civil Guard was created in 1844. This paramilitary constabulary was initially deployed following the principal roads, and by the 1850s it had arrived in most of the provinces. The building of barracks and the frequent presence of two uniformed men (the *pareja*) on the roads and in villages provided a new dimension to the physical projection of the state across the country—which in many localities had hitherto been reduced to the visit of the postman. The Civil Guard allowed the state to provide a new set of services to the population: crime-fighting, finding lost cattle, and helping in case of fire or any other disasters. All classes could seek help from the Civil Guard, but during social conflict landless peasants and workers resented it as the hard fist of landowners and industrialists.

The paradox of a military constabulary being "civil" in name reveals two additional tensions that bedeviled the construction of the Spanish administration: the tension pitting a professional civil service against spoils and partisanship, on the one hand, and that pitting civilian against military administration on the other.

Internationally, the success of the French *gendarmerie* and police and the British "bobbies" had made the creation of a professional police one trademark of modern administration. In Spain, some ministers dreamed of a civilian force that would take policing duties from both the civic militia and the army. On the other hand, the Duke of Ahumada, the founder of the Civil Guard, feared the politicization and indiscipline of the constabulary in the event of the guards being subordinated to the provincial civil governors. To those who pointed out that British policemen were civilians and did not usually carry firearms, it was answered that the "level of civilization" of the Spaniards did not allow for such niceties. The partisans of a paramilitary police won the tug-of-war: the recruitment and discipline of the constabulary was handed to the Ministry of War and, in order to avoid local influence, officers and men could not be natives of the districts in which they served: instead of being a civilian force within the community, the Civil Guard became a projection of the abstract force of the state and was often considered an army of occupation.

The militarization of the police increased the encroachment of the military into the structures of the state. Spanish militarism became identified not only with the participation of the army in revolutions and *pronunciamientos*, but also with the militarization of the policing of protest. During the Carlist Wars, the captains general—regional heads of the army—were routinely in charge of internal order and once peace came they refused to hand over their power. In face of social protest, the army affirmed its autonomy by refusing its subordination to civil authorities. Instead, if deemed necessary to restore order, the captain general proclaimed a state of war, conducted military operations, and tried strikers and rioters in military courts. Between 1843 and 1851 the military executed at least 140 civilians in Barcelona and in the summer of 1855, courts-martial pronounced 20 death sentences in Valladolid, after a wave of bread riots that had become highly politicized.

A slow expansion (1850–1900)

Many critical voices depicted the Spanish civil service of the mid-nineteenth century as mere a source of spoils for patronage. "In Spain the state is a pool of government jobs and a flock of traders called political parties," wrote Timoteo Alfaro in 1861. Every time the government changed, civil servants lost their jobs and were replaced by new appointees. The insecurity of jobs affected local, provincial, and national administrations alike. It was common to complain that this produced low professionalism and provoked revolutions. The former civil servants were known as *cesantes*, a clientele that waited for a new political reversal to get hold of a government salary and a future pension. The *cesantes* were a common enough type to be included in the 1843 *constumbrista* work *Los españoles pintados por si mismos* (The Spaniards as they See Themselves).

While a spoils system was the rule, it was not the full picture. Since the eighteenth century the complexity of some policies had led to the constitution of technical bodies requiring highly qualified personnel, namely mining and civil engineers. In addition, producing skilled civil servants and professionals was one of the priorities of the Ministry of Development, which had founded engineering, technical and veterinary schools, and provided scholarships since the 1830s.

These state-employed engineers avoided party patronage by developing a guild-like status within the public service. They became self-regulated Administrative Corps *(cuerpos de la administración)* that recruited their members among the best students of the engineering schools. These groups ensured the continuity of many policies through the changes of government. By 1855 the Ministry of Development employed 30 forestry, 64 mining, and 152 civil engineers. Most of these were based in the provinces and were assisted by a handful of lesser officials.

The state also gained visibility in these years. The incremental presence of distinctive state buildings—barracks, post offices, courts, road mender's houses, as well as of men in uniform such as soldiers, *carabineros* (customs police) civil guards, postmen, and *peones camineros* (road menders)—embodied the state and created a national landscape that provided internal coherence and external differentiation. For international travelers, the variations in the officials' uniforms became one of the most common signs of having crossed the border.

Other than these uniformed corps, by 1848 the state paid 12,400 public servants, from judges to janitors. Of these, one in four resided in Madrid. The rest worked in the provincial administration: from 75 in the small province of Logroño to 452 in Barcelona. The vast majority of government's personnel were male. The 1855 budget, in fact, mentions only 10 women—the *matronas* of the customs service who searched women in the main ports and border crossings. Many other women, mostly nuns, served in hospitals, schools, and welfare institutions, but these were run by local councils.

The growth and professionalization of the civil service also allowed for the state to take over some areas of activity that hitherto had been left in the hands of the Catholic Church, until then the only organization that reached every parish. After the 1868 revolution the civil register of births, deaths, and marriages was established, and the civil code recognized civil marriage. This was just one of the many areas of conflict between church and state, as Catholicism, in addition to being the only religion allowed in Spain, sought to retain its control over the cemeteries, the rites of passage, the commemorations' calendar, education, and the use of public spaces for religious ceremonies, such as processions. The Church also retained its internal *fuero*—the right to try clergy in church courts, out of the reach of the state—and tried to expand the religious orders and to emancipate them from the restrictions imposed on civil associations. These areas of disagreement were never resolved and conflict sparked every time a more liberal government tried to expand the reach of the state and encroach on Church privilege (see Chapter 18).

Nevertheless, thanks to the civil register and the establishment of statistical services, the state began to have more reliable data for taxation, recruitment, and planning purposes, even if the key land survey was not completed until the mid-twentieth century.

The number of public servants grew steadily, reaching 76,000 by 1913, of whom six in seven worked outside Madrid. In addition, it is worth noting that, as local councils and provincial boards were in change of many central government policies—from military recruitment to public health—the state did not act only through the direct involvement of its officials. Local councilors, municipal employees, and social elites, who peopled the provincial boards of agriculture, charity, health, education, and public works, took part in the implementation of state policy, negotiating its rhythm, depth, and boundaries.

There were several initiatives to professionalize the civil service starting in the 1850s. Prime Minister Juan Bravo Murillo—whose motto was "more administration and less politics"—defined civil service categories and clear career paths, linking some jobs to demonstrable merit, skill, or experience. In 1866, General O'Donnell decreed the immovability of civil servants, a radical alternative to the spoils system, but as this favored his own appointees the decree was discontinued once he fell from power. In any case, during the following decades recruitment for the qualified jobs was increasingly done by means of competitive state examinations, known as *oposiciones*. The top-ranked candidates of the *oposiciones* also acquired a special status as members of a *cuerpo de funcionarios* (civil servants)—with rights and obligations closely defined by law. From the 1870s onward there were *oposiciones* for the judiciary, professorships in university and secondary education, postal and health services, prison guards, factory and customs inspectors, tax officials, state lawyers, diplomatic posts, auditors, and public notaries. Every time the central government took over an area of activity, such as schoolteachers in 1901, *oposiciones* became the usual means of recruitment and promotion. This system was fully institutionalized by Maura's 1918 law, which fixed the statute of the civil servant.

Oposiciones brought about administrative stability and guaranteed a minimum of professional skills, but also brewed a powerful corporative tradition within the Spanish civil service. Critical voices would say that once a civil servant got a job for life, he had no incentives for good performance. The *oposiciones* also became a national institution that changed the relationship of many educated Spaniards to the state. Patronage did not disappear, but many good jobs were now open to hardworking students who did not enjoy political connections. Thousands of candidates perused the official journal looking for the next round of public examinations, studied and rehearsed the exercises for months, even years, craving to become civil servants.

The state in society

Nineteenth-century Spaniards had a kaleidoscopic experience in their dealings with the state. Through regulations, law, courts, police, roads, the privatization of communal lands, postal service, military obligations, elections, taxes, education, and opportunities for employment, the state became a growing presence. Many of the experiences were shared with other Europeans , such as the imposition of the metric system in the 1860s, which displaced half a dozen regional measures that contemplated a myriad of local variances, or the international system of official time.

Taxation and military service made many citizens perceive the state as an imposition, but other policies represented an expansion of life chances and career opportunities. Health policy had begun to take shape since the eighteenth century through hygiene regulations and the maritime control of international epidemics. Since the 1830s *cordons sanitaires* became more professionalized, thanks to the maritime and border patrol of the *carabineros*. In addition, provincial health boards headed by government-employed doctors guided the local councils in the implementation of sanitary policies. Hygienic measures were relatively cheap, but effective: cemeteries were built—the dead had hitherto been buried within the parish church—houses were whitewashed to control epidemics, and drinking water was channeled to public fountains to assure supply and quality. All these measures had a noticeable impact on the containment of infectious diseases. By 1850 epidemics had become shorter and more localized.

Since 1837, the obligation for a doctor to issue death certificate before any burial took place and the recording of the causes of death allowed for meaningful health-related statistics: life expectancy, child mortality, and causes of death, facilitating international comparison and public debate. The existence of reliable numbers helped public health activists to demand action from the government. The activity of the state, hence, empowered civil society. Health officials had promoted vaccination against smallpox since the beginning of the century, but actual implementation was uneven and depended on the active involvement of dedicated doctors. The 1880s were a turning point in this regard, as the poorer councils began to fulfill their obligation to hire doctors, midwives, pharmacists, and veterinarians. Smallpox vaccination finally became near universal and local health authorities more systematically controlled stagnant waters, livestock, and other suspected sources of infection.

Any black-and-white depiction of the relation between state and citizenry misses many shades and exceptions. Great segments of the population did not live peacefully integrated under the cover of the state. The authorities were supposed to act in accordance with the law, and the law to emanate from the representatives of the people; but for most of the population that did not read the press or the official Gazette, the law was nothing but what the officials did, which they often resented as the tyrannical imposition of a "foreign" and nosey official, even when it was well intentioned. Vaccination was often mistrusted as the source of new epidemics. Even death certificates and cemeteries were violently resisted in some mountain parishes up until the 1840s, as some communities resented government interference in long-established sacred rituals. Resistance to the state was visible in the dodging of every kind of statistical query, in tax and draft riots and in the resistance to the privatization of communal lands.

As states do not exist in a void, but are part of society, the growth of the state also empowered some groups and individuals and increased the dependence of others. In a society that was mainly rural, illiterate, and poor, local elites enjoyed a gatekeeper position between the central state and their communities. Stigmatized as *caciques* (tribal chiefs) by their critics, they were crucial to the local government, to the success of taxation, and to elections. They negotiated the conditions of their collaboration with the state and championed the channeling of public investment to their localities. *Caciques* could mobilize the state on their behalf, such as the Civil Guard to protect property, but they also provided recommendations for jobs and sheltered their *protégés* from taxation and military recruitment.

Comparative studies have shown that equity is a crucial element in nurturing patriotism—the disposition to contribute to the common expenses of a political community. In Spain, everybody agreed that neither taxation nor military service were equitably distributed, making the circumvention of obligations socially acceptable. Military service was supposed to touch all male youngsters in good health, but this obligation could be avoided by paying a sum or finding a substitute. As a result, only the lower classes served as soldiers, fueling resentment against the draft. This limited the nation-building effects that a more equal recruitment had in other European countries: "A military service that was avoided by the rich could not be considered *patriotic*: how to preach *sacrifice for the patria* if not everyone is a soldier?" The awful reputation of the army was summed up by the description of conscription as a "blood tax" levied on the poor. Draft evasion was common during the second half of the nineteenth century; so too were draft riots, and in 1909 the resentment exploded in Barcelona: the shipping of troops to colonial war in Morocco triggered a revolt across the city, the so-called Tragic Week (see chapters 4, 21).

The control of social protest was another contact point between state and society. The militaristic trends described in previous pages did not wane with the development of the civil administration. Between the end of the Third Carlist War in 1876 and Primo de Rivera's coup in 1923 there were only two years in which constitutional guarantees were respected all over metropolitan Spain. Every other year there was at least one province in which riots or strikes led the military to step in. In addition, as the civil guards were soldiers, they had the privilege of extending military jurisdiction over the people they dealt with. Whenever village riots and strikes led to clashes with the constabulary, the detainees were tried by military courts. This contrasted with neighboring France and Portugal, where the soldiers and gendarmes used in riot control always handed the detainees to the civilian judiciary.

Historians have been puzzled by the conundrum of militarism. How did the Spanish army conquer such a predominant role in the structure of the state? Does this militaristic trajectory in the nineteenth century explain the two long spells of military dictatorships in the twentieth century—Primo de Rivera's (1923–30) and Francisco Franco's (1939–75)? One long-standing answer points to the combination of the army's political role with the underdevelopment of the civilian administration. This thesis has merit, but, as we have seen, the civil service grew and became more complex and pervasive during the second half of the nineteenth century and, as explained later, these generals did not prevent the further development of a full-fledged civil administration.

The nationalist turn at the beginning of the twentieth century

Whereas the nineteenth century saw the establishment of the basic parameters of the modern state, during the twentieth century the scope of state activities grew and most of the population began to have a more constant and direct relation to public authority. It is fair to say that, despite the differences, all the main political alternatives of the twentieth century, from *regeneracionismo* to republicanism, from Francoism to democratization, cherished the state as the tool of choice for breaking with existing institutions and practices which, according to the peculiar views of each alternative, hampered "development" and "modernization."

The turn of the century coincided with a nationalist and protectionist turn in economic policy that increased state intervention and participation in the economy. In this respect, Spain was taking part in a common European trend. The public sector was not new. During the eighteenth century, the state had established some *manufacturas reales*—factories producing luxury goods and war material that also provided training in foreign production techniques. Many closed at the beginning of the nineteenth century, while the prevailing economic ideas led to the privatization of those that survived. This did not mean, however, the end of the public sector. The Ministry of War owned factories producing military equipment and the state retained a monopoly over products that could be heavily taxed, such as gunpowder, tobacco, and lotteries. Tobacco production was leased to private contractors and produced 14 percent of government revenue between 1850 and 1890, more than customs. As Spanish law gave the state ownership of subsoil rights, mining was also a key activity. Some mines were exploited by the state, but many others were leased to private investors or used to back public debt. After the 1880s, the nationalist turn led the government to protect some heavy industry deemed strategic for development and defense purposes, through loans, protective tariffs, and tax credits. In 1908, the government auctioned shipbuilding for the Navy to Spanish companies.

The so-called social question also changed the outlook of the state during the turn of the century. Population growth, urbanization, and industrialization, even if they were not as vast as in other European countries, changed the human landscape. Living and working conditions in the new industrial areas were appalling, and many workers embraced socialist and anarchist ideas (see Chapter 17). In 1883, the cabinet sponsored the organization of the Social Reform Commission, a consultative body that enquired into the living conditions of the working classes and proposed legislation. In 1903, this commission was revamped as the Institute for Social Reform and got more weight, becoming a quasi-ministerial body, which, in addition to proposing workers' protection legislation, supervised the enforcement of factory acts and promoted pension and welfare schemes. In 1901, a newly created Ministry of Education took over primary schools from the local councils, increasing investment and giving an important boost to the provision of schooling.

Despite the steady increase in public spending, at the beginning of the twentieth century government's share in the Gross Domestic Product was less than 10 percent, at a time in which France, Britain, or Germany were spending between 15 and 20 percent. These being richer countries, the percentages represented a bigger slice of a much bigger pie.

Spain did not take part in the First World War but the conflict had a huge economic, social, and political impact on the country (see Chapter 5). The example of class collaboration toward the war effort in France, Germany, or Britain, coupled with that of the successful mobilization of the private economy for a common goal, allowed for a reassessment and reinforcement of the projects that favored a steering role for the state in the economy and in social relations. In 1916, a department for the eventual mobilization of civilian industries was created, setting the framework for a policy of planning and coordination that would be vastly expanded during the Primo de Rivera dictatorship.

General Miguel Primo de Rivera's coup d'état represented a new breed of militarism. While previous governments had sought to increase the autonomy of the civilian administration from military involvement, now the army presented itself as the depository of the energy needed to guide modernization. In 1908, for example, Antonio Maura had presided over the professionalization of the urban police. A school of policing opened to promote the use of scientific methods of investigation and a system of internal promotion allowed the more gifted policemen to rise within the ranks. Reversing these trends, the dictatorship reserved the higher posts in the police for army officers.

The dictatorship's elite saw themselves as *regeneracionistas*. They wanted to put an end to traditional clientelistic practices and to liberate the energies of the nation, but at the same time, they saw the state as the guiding light of economic development. Competition, they thought, damaged the social order. The sheltering of the national economy from international competition and the coordination of production and markets became key policies. State banks were created to facilitate credit for industrial and commercial investment and new fiscal monopolies were established. CAMPSA, the new state oil monopoly, became one of Spain's biggest enterprises. In the name of "harmonious growth," existing businesses were shielded from competition by requiring government approval in order to open new factories. Authorizations, credits, tax rebates, and other privileges were part of the operation of big companies. Lucrative businesses became dependent on the protection and favor of the state. This created new links between private interests and government that often led to corruption and, at least, shrank field of action of these investors and entrepreneurs with no privileged connections to the political elite.

Harmony also implied the collaboration among social classes. A heavy hand was used against strikes, and the anarchist CNT was banned, but the Socialist trade union (UGT— *Union General de Trabajadores*) was recognized as a legitimate workers' representative and invited to take part in industrial arbitration.

Another pillar of the dictatorship's development policy was direct investment in public works. Roads and railways were built and improved, while dam-building symbolized a future of well-irrigated lands and plentiful electricity. Finally, it is worth noting the expansion of tourism policy. Since 1905, government had promoted Spain as a tourist destination, but it was the dictatorship that created a public agency for this and kick-started *Paradores de Turismo*—a network of state-owned hotels located in historic buildings and destinations.

Finally, education remained a keystone of the modernization project. Eight thousand new elementary schools were built between 1920 and 1930 and the number of both teachers and of pupils grew by 20 percent. On the other hand, education got a more ideological tone directed at patriotic indoctrination. Speaking Catalan and Basque in school was forbidden, religious and moral education were reinforced, and military drill for boys was introduced into the curriculum.

A republican state? (1931–36)

The republican experiment (1931–36), as Adrian Shubert has suggested, can be interpreted as an extension of the civil power of the state, replacing private power by public power. Republican governments acted aggressively to take primary education from the hands of the Church and to subordinate military institutions to civilian law. Agrarian reform, another key policy, represented the assertion of the state's right to change property relations in the name of the public good. It also threatened to break the control over local life exercised by the landed elite.

The change of regime was not traumatic for the civil service and the police. Despite some purges among the plainclothes police, continuity was the norm. At the same time, as clashes between demonstrators and police had been seen as signs of the illegitimacy of the former regime, the new authorities sought to offer a new republican and democratic style of policing that would heal the relationship between popular classes and state. New riot units, the unfortunately named Assault Guard (*Guardia de Asalto*), were meant to change the way force was used during collective conflict. Instead of wielding cutlasses and Mauser rifles, they were to use rubber truncheons. *Asalto* men were also lavishly motorized and were meant to be deployed quickly to prevent the escalation of conflicts. *ABC*, a conservative newspaper, was impressed after their first intervention in Madrid: "never before had we seen guards being cheered during a repressive action."

The deployment of the Assault Guard was meant to displace the Civil Guard from the more populated areas and help convert it into a more civilian-dependent force. In addition, the establishment of a regional government in Catalonia was accompanied by the subordination of the local garrisons of the Civil Guard to the *Generalitat*, symbolizing the end of centralism.

The policing reforms of the two first years of the Republic did not survive the subsequent upheavals. First, the urge to count on *Asalto* as a loyal republican force against anarchist insurrections led to it being transformed into a heavily armed force strong enough to replace the army and the Civil Guard for the policing of violent protest. Then, the change of government in 1934 and the aftermath of the Asturias revolution were accompanied by a counterreform in the Civil Guard, recentralization, and the militarization of *Asalto*. The policing model became a contested issue, as political polarization affected both the loyalty of the police and its ability to control disturbances without heating up social conflict.

The new state (1939–75)

Whereas the Second Republic sought to extend the reach of the state, it was the *Francoist* dictatorship that replaced it after three years of civil war that more thoroughly realized that intention. The regime undertook a sweeping purge of the civil service, cleaning liberals and socialists from its ranks and providing jobs for loyal Francoists. Spain became a unitary state again, putting an end to the short spell of autonomy enjoyed by the Basque Country, Catalonia, and Galicia.

The new policing model was uncompromising. Franco's army had won the war and it claimed its prize: in 1941 a new, fully militarized urban constabulary—the Armed Police (*Policía Armada*)—widely known as the "grays" (*grises*) for the color of their uniform, emerged from the ashes of Guardia de Asalto and was meant to be "a political police at the service of a totalitarian state." The police system was completed by a political brigade within the plainclothes investigative police who became infamous for their brutality.

The faith in the virtues of war-like mobilization and the Catholic project of overcoming class conflict through corporatism, already tested by Primo de Rivera, found new life under Franco's oversight and the Falangists' fascist enthusiasm. During the 1940s and 1950s the government sought to foster a strong national economy autonomous from dealings with the world economy (see Chapter 7). Agriculture was controlled through fixed prices and marketing boards. The state turned also into an active investor. In 1941, an Institute for National Industry (INI) was put in charge of developing heavy industry, which in time included the production of cars for mass consumption. The state also nationalized public services, as telephones and railways, and companies that produced strategic goods or provided massive employment, but which were not profitable such as coal mines. The INI became Spain's biggest industrial holding and many inefficiencies until the 1980s it was a synonym for Spain's industrialization.

The Franco dictatorship finally realized the objective of universal male conscription. The tightening of the draft provisions had been noted since the 1910s and the length of the service—two years—made it a central experience for a great share of the male population. For many poor Spaniards, becoming a soldier was their first opportunity to travel, learn a trade, or make connections to people living in other regions of the country. The knowledge and networks acquired in the ranks facilitated later migration to the city. In addition, many women were conscripted into social work for a year though the Sección Femenina. This had similar empowering effects, even if the proportion of participants was much lower.

A new device came to link the Spaniards to the state for good: the national identity card (Documento Nacional de Identidad or DNI). Since the 1850s heads of household got a document from the town council, the *cédula* personal. It was mainly used for electoral identification and recorded only name, address, place of birth, profession, and marital status. The authorities had to rely on trusted witnesses to confirm that the bearer of the *cédula* was its owner. In 1943, the police took charge of issuing DNIs, which came to link every citizen to a number for life. Both the card and the central inventory recorded personal information, a picture, and a sample of fingerprints. From then on, the state could certify by objective means the identity of all adult Spaniards. The DNI became the true mark of individual identity, endorsed by the state.

Spaniards born during Francoism experienced universal education, military and social service, internal and international migrations, national broadcasting—from 1956 to 1990 the only television station in Spain belonged to the state broadcaster RTVE—and a pervasive state that conducted all official business in Castilian (see Chapter 7). This thick fabric of experiences cemented an idea of the nation shared widely across classes and provinces. The national landscape was not consensual, being felt as an imposition by speakers of minority languages, but many Spaniards lived it as a natural frame of reference, a solid reality that was later to be shattered by the regional devolution that followed democratization.

In 1950, new police recruits were still instructed that they were not serving under the rule of law. "In foregone times, the liberal doctrine demanded an excessive respect for procedural and juridical guarantees," explained Colonel Francisco Rodriguez, security director, to new police recruits, "[but] you are the political police of the state and you have to serve this sole politics . . . Franco, Franco, Franco!" This militant interpretation of state functions remained alive throughout Francoism and justified countless instances of police brutality against defenseless citizens. Yet, the machinery of government was complex and during the 1950s important sectors of the dictatorship's elite strove to subject the state to the law. For many modernizers within the regime, administrative reform constituted a controlled path to modernity that could avoid the risks of political liberalization.

By the 1960s, as the increasing complexity of society and the international context was apparent, the government recruited a new crop of technically able civil servants. Devotion to Franco alone was no longer a sufficient qualification. A new generation of well-trained officials, described by Santos Juliá as "a group that distinguished between service to the state and service to the government," entered the administration. The professionalization of the higher echelons of the public service, staffed during the 1960s by young civil servants who had not fought in the Civil War, meant that future democratization would not need a wholesale transformation of public administration.

Even the police took an active part in this transformation. In 1960 the "091" police phone service was inaugurated in Madrid and Barcelona—symbolizing that the police were at the service of citizens, ready to go wherever called. In 1969, in turn, new riot units specialized in using nonlethal weapons, such as tear gas, rubber bullets, and truncheons, reduced the use of firearms in the control of collective protest. The police was still heavily militarized, but looked to advanced democracies for models. Some officers even dared to propose a professional police ethos. In 1972, the monthly *Policía Armada* magazine analyzed the infamous Castilblanco 1931 massacre—the lynching of four civil guards during a rural strike. Instead of rehearsing the well-known tale of red hordes and honorable martyrs, the article argued that the violence resulted from a failure in the planning of the intervention. Careful planning and more training were the answer, not intransigence and brutality.

Many key movements for democracy emerged from within the ranks of the state itself. This was clear in the education sector, but also in the civil service. At the end of 1974, 500 top officials signed a petition asking for "a democratic state in which public authority would come from the people." A small and clandestine Military Democratic Union (UMD) even began to operate within the police and the army. Less than one year after Franco's death, in October 1976, a manifesto advocating political neutrality circulated among policemen. Two months later, several thousand policemen and civil guards shocked the government by demonstrating in Madrid, asking for demilitarization and the same health insurance and pensions as civil servants. During the transition to democracy, however, pro-democracy movements within the police were less visible than the terror of far-right activists closely connected to some sectors of the army and the same police. Security forces were heavily strained by ETA killings, which targeted 171 army and police men between 1978 and 1980, and some engaged in a dirty war against the left and Catalan and Basque separatists. Brutal police interventions such as those of Vitoria in 1976—five strikers dead—and Pamplona and Basauri in 1978, when police rioted and caused havoc, also showed that the political authorities did not have full command of the police. Nonetheless, the pro-democracy movements within the army and the police became a key pool of allies democratic reformers could count on to smooth the change of regime without totally losing the control of the situation.

A European social state under the rule of law (1975–present)

The Moncloa agreements of October 1977 were the blueprint for the democratic reform of the state, enshrined in the 1978 constitution (see Chapter 8). These included a deal regarding a more comprehensive system of welfare, which increased the employers' and the state's share of the costs. Furthermore, the agreements included an overhaul of the whole tax system, which still followed the principles of the 1845 reform: a new income tax, to be complemented in time by a value-added tax. The tax reform led to a steady increase in public revenue in the 1980s and allowed the state to finance generous welfare reforms.

The Moncloa agreements also dealt with the thorny issues of militarism and policing. The army lost its power to project its jurisdiction over civil society—in 1977 alone 124 civilians were convicted by military courts—while a police reform was announced. The "protection of citizen's rights" and subordination to "international agreements" and "Western standards" were enshrined as the guidelines for the future.

Police reform came even before the approval of the constitution: the rank-and-file soldiers of the Armed Police were transformed into civil servants, the force was renamed National Police and the civil governors were given greater powers over it. This new brown-suited police also replaced the Civil Guard in every town of more than 20,000 inhabitants. Police change—from gray uniforms to brown—was meant to make the democratization of the state visible. Even so, by 1980 the public's attitudes toward the police were still heavily influenced by political alignments. According to one survey done in 1981, most left-leaning Spaniards still resented the police as a Francoist legacy and did not feel that "the police was there for their protection," while most of those with rightist leanings did.

After the approval of the 1978 constitution, the democratization of municipal governments, regional devolution, and integration into the European Economic Community were the three main processes that redistributed state power. The constitution granted autonomy to the "historic" regions of Catalonia, Galicia, and the Basque Country. By the mid-1980s, the process of regionalization had consolidated 17 Autonomous Regions *(Autonomias),* each governed by a parliamentary government (see Chapter 10). Regional governments gradually took powers from the central state, including health and education. Since the 1990s, most of the services the Spanish citizens receive were delivered by local and regional administration. The other side of the coin is that everywhere except the Basque Country and Navarre, fiscal powers are mainly in the hands of the national government. After the 2008 financial crisis,

Map 20.2 Territorial division of Spain after 1978.

this situation provoked a debate about the fiscal irresponsibility of spendthrift regional governments that please their constituencies without the burden of having to tax them. The debate pitting patronage against professionalism has also emerged again, as local corruption is often attributed to the enormous pool of jobs that mayors and regional governments have at their disposal.

Regional autonomy also affected the policing map. Demilitarization of police was completed in 1986, when the all-civilian National Police Corps (CNP—Cuerpo Nacional de Policia), which was to wear a blue uniform, absorbed both the brown *"nacionales"* and the plainclothes police. But the most symbolic change was brought about by the creation of regional and local police forces, the Basque *Ertzaintza* (Public Guard) and the Catalan *Mossos d'Esquadra,* which took over responsibility for general patrol and security duties during the late 1980s and the 1990s. These forces ended the regular presence of Civil Guards and national policemen on the roads and streets of these two regions. The visual projection of the central state through the uniforms of the police, which had marked the national landscape since the deployment of the Civil Guard in 1845, was over.

Military service remained mandatory during the first two decades of democracy, but Spain was now an urban and schooled society, and stripping conscription of many of the empowering features it had had during previous decades. In 1984, the right to refuse military service on grounds of conscience was recognized and time in the ranks could be replaced by an alternative social service of longer duration. In 1989, one in twenty recruits declared themselves conscientious objectors; during the 1990s, the numbers skyrocketed to one in two. This massive rejection of conscription—mostly non-coordinated despite the visibility of the antimilitaristic movement—shattered the recruitment system and overcrowded the social services, which were unable to find use for the more than 70,000 objectors a year. Finally, in 2001, conscription was suspended and the army professionalized. This put an end to a long-lasting and pervasive point of contact between the state and the population. Even so, the *fiestas de quintos*—festive rituals of passage to male adulthood that had sprouted all over rural Spain in parallel to the acceptance of universal conscription since the 1910s—survived the end of military service. This may highlight the complex interpenetration between state development and the self-understanding of local communities.

With the end of conscription, mandatory civic duty was reduced to the draft of citizens for managing the voting stations during election days and to jury duty. On the other hand, the obligation to attend school was reinforced. During the nineteenth century, where education was available, children were obliged to attend school between the ages of 6 and 9. The leaving age was raised to 12 in 1909 and 14 in 1964. Democratic Spain followed the tendency and the age was set at 16 in 1999, the government thus forcing every child to undergo 10 years of schooling.

The entry of Spain to the European Community in 1986 and the European Union in 1993—which granted European citizenship—meant that Spain had to open its markets to the rest of Europe. It also gave more arguments to those who favored the privatization and dismantling of the largely inefficient state industrial sector. Spain also renounced some degrees of sovereignty, as the Euro replaced the peseta in 2002 and legislation and policy had to be adapted to imperatives decided in Brussels. This had many effects. On one hand, European legislation and courts empowered some civil society groups, such as nature protection organizations. On the other hand, Europeanization accelerated the trend to ever-increasing penetration of state-sponsored regulatory practices through society, conditioning everyday life and eroding local custom. Bullfighting has survived, except in Catalonia, but during the 1990s, bans coupling hygienic and moral concerns abolished many instances of violence against animals during local *fiestas*. Sanitary legislation, in turn, has deeply altered traditional forms of food processing and selling, and has even transformed the rituals of the rural tradition of festive pig slaughtering.

The history of the Spanish state over the last two centuries fully belongs to a common tale that encompasses developed Europe. Yet, key concerns of this story, such as the forces pitting centralization against regionalism, public versus religious schooling or the professionalization of the civil service against patronage, remain contentious in Spain. The universality and depth of welfare provisions, consensual since the transition to democracy, have been challenged by privatization policies and spending cuts at the beginning of the twenty-first century. This is an area of dispute that may shape future relations of the citizenry to the state, as "welfare nationalism"—and not ethnic or constitutional concerns—has been identified in some surveys as the strongest link of many Spaniards to the national community. The loopholes in the fiscal system, in turn, are again a contested issue. The decrease in the tax revenue after the 2008 crisis, three times bigger than the shrinking of the GDP, revealed that the Spaniards were much more prone to hide their wealth from the state than most other Europeans.

Despite some recurrent themes, four decades of democracy and prosperity have changed the parameters of the debate about the state. The military regional governments were suppressed in the 1990s, the military was professionalized and now seems duly subordinate to civilian authority. Hence, militarism appears to be a closed affair. At the same time, the state has attained an unprecedented ability to penetrate society and produce change—at least when coupled with social demand and democratic support. The distance between two examples may summarize this transformation of state capacity. In 1766, the government's attempt to ban the long capes and broad-brimmed hats worn by *madrileños* was blocked by the famous *Esquilache* riots. In contrast, a 2011 ban on smoking in bars and cafés swiftly and without resistance transformed routines that until then had seemed deeply rooted.

Further reading

Álvarez Junco, José, *Spanish Identity in the Age of Nations*, Manchester: Manchester University Press, 2011.

Blaney, Gerald. "Keeping Order in Republican Spain, (1931–36)," in *Policing Interwar Europe*, Gerald Blaney (ed.), Basingstoke, NY: Palgrave, 2007, pp. 31–68.

Cardoso, José Luís, and Pedro Lains, *Paying for the Liberal State: The Rise of Public Finance in Nineteenth-Century Europe*, New York: Cambridge University Press, 2010.

Comín, Francisco, *Historia de la Hacienda Pública (2 Vol.)*, Barcelona: Crítica, 1996.

Macdonald, Ian R., "Spain's 1986 Police Law: Transition from Dictatorship to Democracy," *Police Studies*, 10, 1(1987), pp. 16–20.

Martinez Navarro, Ferrán, and Esteban Rodríguez Ocaña, *Salud Pública en España. De la Edad Media al Siglo XXI*, Granada: Escuela Andaluza de Salud Pública, 2008.

Moral Ruiz, Joaquín del, Juan Pro Ruiz, and Fernando Suárez Bilbao, *Estado y Territorio en España 1820-1930: La Formación del Paisaje Nacional*, Madrid: Los Libros de la Catarata, 2007.

Pro Ruiz, Juan, and Manuel Rivero, *Breve Atlas de Historia de España*, Madrid: Alianza, 1999.

Shubert, Adrian, *A Social History of Modern Spain*, London: Routledge, 1992.

Vincent, Mary, *Spain 1833-2002: People and State*, New York: Oxford University Press, 2007.

CHAPTER 21
WAR AND THE MILITARY[1]
Geoffrey Jensen

Since Napoleon's invasion in 1808, Spaniards from all walks of life have felt the effects of their country's politically powerful armed forces, while also suffering through foreign and civil wars. During the nineteenth century the Spanish military faced Napoleon's armies, took part in devastating civil wars, and fought in colonial conflicts in the Americas, the Pacific, and Africa, while prominent army officers intervened regularly in politics. During the first quarter of the twentieth century the Spanish army waged a long and costly war in Morocco, which in turn had significant consequences in Spain itself, and the Spanish occupation of parts of Africa lasted until the 1970s. Like the rest of the country, the military was torn apart by the Civil War of 1936–39. It then served as a bulwark of Franco's dictatorship until his death in 1975. Even thereafter it remained a source of political concern, most noticeably during the transition to democracy. As a fighting force, a social body, and a political and cultural agent, the military has left a deep impact on modern Spain. Conflicts over military service and the composition of the officer corps have featured prominently throughout this period, as this chronological exploration of the roles of the military in Spain's modern history will illustrate. Other key themes include the army's role in politics, its internal structure, and its relation to ordinary Spaniards.

The war against Napoleon and the origins of a modern national army, 1808–14

The Spanish army did not earn many laurels in the war against Napoleon. Without the intervention of British forces under the command of Sir Arthur Wellesley (later the Duke of Wellington) and the irregular fighters who brought the word *guerrilla* into the modern lexicon, Napoleon might well have triumphed in Spain. The causes of the Spanish army's difficulties were manifold, including a chaotic wartime political climate, disagreement about the form and function of the armed forces, and widespread intervention by the *juntas*, or councils, that sprang up all over Spain. This period marked the first use in history of the word *liberal* as a political term, but in spite of the high-minded liberal principles expressed in the Spanish patriots' famous 1812 Constitution of Cádiz, the realities of wartime Spain meant that the historic document had scant influence on the nature of guerrilla warfare, although its idealization of the citizen-soldier and the people's militia would contribute to later military reform attempts.

The war began with a popular uprising against French occupation, immortalized by Goya in his famous painting of the May 2, 1808 insurrection in Madrid, and elements of

---

[1]Thanks to Fernando Puell de la Villa and Sasha D. Pack for commenting on an early draft of this chapter.

the Spanish army joined the uprising from the beginning. But in most regular battlefield encounters the Spanish army did not do well, the early victory in July 1808 at the Battle of Bailen notwithstanding. The army's success at Bailen, moreover, paradoxically weakened its political position within Spain, as some *junteros* falsely attributed the French defeat to irregular volunteers, who were actually few in number and played no role in the battle's outcome. But junteros used a romanticized version of the battle as an argument for privileging the citizens' militia ideal over the regular army.

The Spanish military's difficulties in the war had other causes as well. The quality of the rank-and-file soldiers was low, the army lacked sufficient cadres, and the officer corps was professionally divided. The Spanish cavalry was especially weak. When the war against Napoleon began, some 100,000 French troops were already inside Spain's borders, and among the major European powers Spain had the unique misfortune of not enjoying a period of truce at any point between 1808 and 1813 in order to rest and refit its army. The country began the war already battered by recent conflicts with Portugal, revolutionary France, and Britain, which had decimated the Spanish navy at Trafalgar in 1805. To make matters worse, the French already occupied the capital city of Madrid when the war began. And much of the Spanish high command, including many captains general, were sympathetic to the French. In spite of its failure to win more battles, the Spanish army joined the guerrillas and the British army to form a trinity of effective opposition to the French. All three elements were necessary to expel Napoleon from Spain, and the Spanish army's contribution to this tripartite effort was greater than is usually acknowledged. Indeed, Spain's army may have actually caused more French casualties than the guerrillas or the British, who normally get most of the credit.

Yet the guerrilla fighters would go down in Spanish history as the heroes of the war, for understandable reasons. After the Spanish victory at Bailén, the regular army's major battlefield successes were few and far between, whereas the difficulties the guerrillas posed for the French were well known, and they allowed Spain to lay claim to its own liberation. The guerrillas also made an undeniable strategic contribution to the French defeat by causing serious logistic and security problems and greatly complicating military occupation in general. They tied down so many French troops, who had to guard vital supply lines and other potential guerrilla targets, that French commanders could not concentrate the forces necessary for a decisive victory against Wellesley's army. The guerrillas also received much postwar acclaim because of their ostensibly patriotic motives and the idealized perceptions of the "people's war" they waged. Such perceptions complemented nascent Spanish nationalism, and they fit well within the wider European Romantic movement (see Chapter 15).

In both military and civilian Spain, moreover, the irregular war against Napoleon set the stage for the creation of a "guerrilla myth," with long-lasting military, political, and cultural consequences. The myth not only supposed that the guerrillas had liberated Spain by waging a popular and unified nationalist war, but it also identified the typical Spaniard as a "natural" guerrilla fighter. The influence of the guerrilla myth lasted well into the twentieth century, and served ideologues from across the political spectrum. In the eyes of the left, the guerrillas fought for the liberal-nationalist values associated with the 1812 Constitution of Cádiz, while for conservatives the guerrillas were defenders of traditional Catholic and monarchical values against secular foreign invaders. Such idealized visions of guerrillas and people's war seldom corresponded to reality.

Admittedly, French secularism and brutal occupational policies provoked some nativist resistance, and there were certainly instances of patriotism around which a modern concept of national identity would form. The wartime abolition of the nobility requirement for entry into the officer corps, for example, coincided with the taking up of arms by nobles alongside artisans, agricultural workers, and others of more common background. Foreign commentators, from the famous military theorist Henri de Jomini to Napoleon himself, would subsequently portray the Spanish people as having united in a people's war, and the strategic importance of the guerrillas and their contribution as symbols to modern Spanish nationalism are undeniable.

Nevertheless, many guerrillas were just groups of bandits fighting for their own interests. The devotion of these guerrillas to "the people," as far as such devotion existed at all, was overwhelmingly local, and because of the guerrillas' brutality they were actually unpopular among many civilians. The most effective guerrillas did not fight in the armed bands that rose up independently in the chaotic conditions of French-occupied Spain, but rather in units incorporated into the regular Spanish army. The wartime rise of some of these soldiers, including farmers, Catholic friars, and the illiterate poor, to high ranks made the army the first meritocratic profession in Spain. Overall, though, the nationalist and liberal ideals associated with the Constitution of Cádiz had scant influence on the guerrillas, even if aspects of the Spanish armed resistance resembled a people's war.

Yet the Constitution should not be ignored either, for this justly celebrated milestone of Western liberalism tackled head-on fundamental questions about military organization and power that would haunt Spain for well over a century. It reflected the same uneasiness about a standing regular army that the founders of the United States had felt a few decades earlier and it also revealed the lingering influence of the pacifism seen in some influential Enlightenment writings. Accordingly, it called for the establishment of a National Militia, under the control of the Cortes, or parliament. Manned by citizen volunteers who had to meet certain income requirements, this new armed force was to be independent of the traditional King's Army.

Thus even though the constitution's language reflected the liberal-nationalist ideal of the nation in arms, in concrete terms it rejected truly national military service or even allowing all social classes to volunteer for its militia. This contradiction revealed a quandary that would hinder attempts to reform the Spanish army until well into the twentieth century. Proposals to institute a draft would often be tempered by the more pragmatic reluctance of politicians—including liberals—to allow young men from their own social classes to be drafted. Spaniards were well aware of the poor conditions in many barracks, ongoing provisioning woes, and the fact that service overseas often meant death through combat or disease. Thus subsequent attempts by military reformers to develop a mass, national army or truly democratize military service would be tempered by laws allowing for exemptions. Some of the legal ways to avoid the draft during the nineteenth and twentieth centuries included paying a fee in lieu of serving or hiring a substitute. Spain was not exceptional in this regard; France would not institute a truly universal male draft until after 1870, and a century later young men in the United States could avoid being sent to Vietnam by enrolling in universities. But in so underdeveloped a country as nineteenth-century Spain, the disproportionately heavy price paid by the poor was particularly harmful over the long term, exacerbating social conflict and civil-military relations. And the inequities of military service certainly did not improve military effectiveness, as some army officers lamented.

The reaction and revolution, 1814–33

Far removed from the miseries of the rank-and-file, the political protagonism of a relatively small number of army officers during the nineteenth century has received the most attention from historians. Since the early eighteenth century Spanish military officers had regularly held political positions, and civilians had come to accept the monarch's right to appoint army officers to certain public functions. In fact, most military officers considered the possibility of assuming such political roles to be an inherent part of their profession. The war against the French, however, brought with it a new level of political protagonism, and later in the century generals would decide the rise and fall of governments and could even become the country's de facto rulers as regents of the crown.

The return of King Fernando VII to Spain after the French defeat in 1814 set the stage for this kind of military intervention in politics (see Chapter 2). The army now had twice as many generals as when the anti-French uprising had begun, and the officer corps had swollen to around 16,000 men, of whom only one-quarter were needed now that the war was over. In light of the bankruptcy of his treasury, Fernando decided to reduce the size of the peacetime army. Three-quarters of the army were demobilized, which meant that some 440 generals, almost 10,000 other officers and around 150,000 rank-and-file soldiers lost their income and were sent home. Most of those who remained on active duty ended up living in precarious conditions in camps at the foot of the Pyrenees Mountains.

In the political sphere, once back in power Fernando rejected the liberal ideals of the Constitution of Cádiz, returning Spain back to absolutism. Accordingly, he purged the officer corps of liberal elements and reinstated the nobility requirement for entrance into the officer corps. Eventually, however, he went so far as to alienate an increasing number of even those officers who had survived the purges. Budget cutting decrees in 1817 that described the army as a "useless and harmful" institution made clear to officers the king's lack of appreciation for their calling, even though they had fought to restore him to the throne not long before. It is hardly surprising, then, that many military men were open to overtures by liberal politicians who wanted to curtail his absolutism and force him to reinstate the Constitution of 1812.

This military liberalism had already taken root in the officer corps, at first tentatively during the eighteenth-century Bourbon reforms, and then more deeply during the War of Independence. During this conflict many officers from the old Bourbon army became casualties or retired, and others went with Napoleon's brother Joseph into exile in 1814. At least some of the 4,000 Spanish officers held captive in France during the war were undoubtedly exposed to French liberal ideas while there, bringing them back to Spain after the war ended. Moreover, in August 1810 the requirement of noble status for entrance into the military academies was dropped, resulting in an increase in the number of academy entrants of non-noble background during the war.

In the meantime, the wars of independence in Spanish America meant more soldiers would probably be sent there, a likelihood that liberal activists were quick to exploit. The anti-Fernando officers joined civilian politicians on the issue, seeking to attract soldiers by promising to get them out of overseas service. Finally, on January 1, 1820 officers in Cádiz destined for Buenos Aires rose up against Fernando VII's absolutism (see Chapter 2). After failing to extinguish the slowly spreading rebellion, the king ceded to the liberal demands, eloquently expressed by Major Rafael del Riego, and pledged to follow the constitution that he had earlier rejected. The uprising became known as a *pronunciamiento* after Riego used the term as he harangued troops during the 1820 uprising.

The *pronunciamiento*, in which a leading military figure "pronounced" on behalf of a political group in order to overthrow the existing government, became Spain's only viable instrument for effecting regime change during much of the nineteenth century. The general pattern was for the initial uprising to be followed by similar actions in different regions of Spain, eventually leading to the fall of the Madrid government. *Pronunciamientos* could take place in the name of any of the major political parties, as leaders of distinct ideologies all found making alliances with military representatives to be Spain's only open avenue for political change.

More immediately, Riego's *pronunciamiento* had various consequences for the military: he and his fellow liberals forced the king to restore the constitution, to remove the requirement of noble status for aspirants to the officer corps and to reinstate previously purged officers. But the increasing politicization of the corps that accompanied the *pronunciamiento* in fact clashed with the army's interests, because the political platform of Riego's liberal allies called for an army at the service of the national will, civilian administration of government, and a citizens' national militia, which would in effect rival the regular army. Such conflicts between political programs and professional military interests would continue to characterize civil-military alliances in the era of *pronunciamientos*.

The liberal government that Riego installed did not last long and was overthrown in 1823 by a large French army. Riego, who tried unsuccessfully to organize resistance against the return to absolutism, ended up forsaken by his soldiers, who sensed better than he the shape of things to come, and then sent as a prisoner to Madrid. Condemned to death, he was hanged along with 11 political allies. It was neither the first nor the last time in nineteenth-century Spain that an attempted overthrow of the government ended badly for its protagonists.

After Riego's defeat in 1823, the king threw out the constitution once again and reinstated most of his former absolutist policies, forcing intellectuals and other liberals—civilian as well as military—into exile. Riego subsequently became the most important martyr of the liberal cause and the march, the Himno de Riego, its anthem. Fernando also established a new armed force, the Royalist Volunteers. In retrospect, it is easy to see how this move reflected the changing perception of military politics. Whereas in 1820 the liberals had established a national militia because they feared the regular army was too conservative, in 1823 absolutists created their own alternative to the army because they perceived it as a liberal threat, and Fernando contracted mercenary forces from Switzerland and France. He would soon figure out, however, that a regular force built around a tightly controlled professional officer corps provided more stability than any militia ever would.

In the meantime, in Peru the victory of pro-independence forces in the Battle of Ayacucho (December 9, 1824) marked the definitive end of Spain as a colonial power in South America, a major turning point in the dramatic decline of the country's international status (see Chapter 13). In spite of Spain's decline on the global stage, however, the army's overall situation actually improved after 1823, as Fernando now understood the importance of keeping his officers happy albeit under close political control. He closed military academies for fear that they had become hotbeds of liberalism and freemasonry, but he also made sure that officers and their soldiers did not go unpaid. From 1826 on he appointed War Ministers with relatively reformist outlooks (the *aperturistas*), although he also continued to crack down hard on dissidents from the political left as well as the right. Indeed, his military policies helped create an army capable—in spite of a poor start and some serious setbacks—of surviving a devastating civil war the following decade, when the threat to Madrid would come from the far right rather than the left.

In the meantime, the corporatist character of the military profession grew, thanks in part to the opening up of the officer corps to non-nobles that had taken place in fits and starts since the War of Independence. Fernando reinstated the requirement of noble status after Riego's defeat in 1823, but it would be replaced in 1836 by a *limpieza de sangre*, or "blood purity" test, in which aspirants to the officer corps had only to prove their pure "Christian" origins. The anachronistic nature of this "race"-based test—usually associated with the Inquisition— notwithstanding, it opened up the officer corps to a wider social spectrum. (This regulation would remain in effect until 1865).

Indeed, Spanish military culture would change considerably during the nineteenth century, as common class origins ceased to be the main unifying force for the officer corps. Specialized centers for officer education, the introduction of academy entrance exams, and a standardized system of promotions, assignments, and retirements would all came together to create, as Puell de la Villa writes, "a sense of shared professional identity, of belonging to a unique collective." These institutional characteristics made the officer corps "much more solid and exclusive" than it had been during the eighteenth century, when social class alone had been the dominant shared characteristic of army officers.

The First Carlist War, 1833–40

The Spanish army's first major conflict after Napoleon's defeat, the First Carlist War (1833–40), broke out over the question of who would succeed Fernando VII, who died in late September 1833 (see Chapter 3). It pitted the regular army, which defended the right of Fernando's daughter Isabel to assume the throne, against his brother Carlos and his supporters, known as Carlists. The war's sociopolitical impact was as deep as it was broad, ushering in a profound radicalization of popular politics. As Mark Lawrence writes, when the seven years of war finally came to an end, "hundreds of thousands of soldiers and militiamen and hundreds of thousands of civilians besides, had been schooled by violence into exercising political consciousness for the first time." As collective bodies, moreover, soldiers would intervene directly in politics during the war, thereby determining election results. The war would also bring about the political rise of one of Spanish military history's most remarkable characters, Baldomero Espartero, to whom we will turn below.

At the war's outbreak, however, the politics of the army were basically under control. Most officers, regardless of any natural conservative inclinations they may have held, proved willing to fight for the new queen, the three-year-old Isabel II, and her mother María Cristina, who served as regent until Isabel came of age. The officers remained loyal in large part because of the efforts Fernando had made during the last years of his life to keep his officers and their soldiers content. As he had learned from the uprising of 1820, treating the army badly could have dangerous consequences. Thus before his death he had made sure that army officers received a steady and secure income, which for most outweighed political convictions. Setting the stage for the ascension of his daughter to the throne, he had devoted additional resources to the military, increased promotions, and weakened the segments of the military most likely to cause trouble for his dynastic line. Officers' willingness to support his daughter's dynastic cause may have also stemmed from appeals to their traditional, gender-based sense of honor to act as gentlemen and defend Isabel and María Cristina. In any case, military officers' inherently conservative mentality lacked the strong religious component of civilian conservatism then, which the Carlists embraced. Army officers' willingness to fight the ultrareligious Carlists may have stemmed as well from memories of how the most anti-liberal, reactionary elements of the Church had supported Fernando VII during and after his return to the throne in 1814, when had had carried out policies especially prejudicial to the army.

The bloodiest civil war in nineteenth-century Europe, the First Carlist War affected all parts of Spain, taking more lives per capita than the Spanish Civil War of 1936–39. Total casualties on the government side (including wounded and missing in action) numbered some 175,000. The Carlists probably lost at least an equal number of soldiers. Given these figures, it is not surprising that the army underwent significant changes during the war against the Carlists. Most visibly, both sides' forces grew dramatically. The need for soldiers in the Isabeline army (also known as the *Cristino* army, for the regent María Cristina) was so great that it had to institute nine wartime drafts, calling up a total 370,000 men. In comparison, during the entire eighteenth century the total number of draftees to the Spanish army had numbered only around 75,000, and even during the War of Independence the figure had reached around 250,000. For the officer corps the war brought with it a wave of promotions, and it only grew after the peace terms allowed for the incorporation of Carlists into the regular army.

The realities of war for the common soldiers were of course rather different than for officers, but for the rank-and-file too the Carlist War marked a key phase in the long-term transformation of the Spanish army from a force of career, professional soldiers at the service of the crown to a mass citizen army constituted to defend the Spanish nation. The Carlist soldiers were volunteers who fought, at least in theory, for a cause and leaders in whom they believed in return for regular pay and provisions; laws did not dictate their recruitment. But in the Isabeline army a more modern, legally defined system of draft lotteries developed, anticipating what was to come (see Chapter 25). In short, the professional, career soldier characteristic of the eighteenth century was becoming the "temporary soldier" ("*soldado de reemplazo*"; literally "replacement soldier") of the nineteenth, theoretically drawn from all of Spanish society.

Unlike in France, however, where the French Revolution had caused an abrupt rupture in the military ways of the Old Regime, in Spain the shift in how the state manned its military evolved over a long and complicated historical period in response to changing military needs. In the late eighteenth century, Prime Minister Manuel Godoy had initiated some military reforms, and during the War against Napoleon the politicians at Cádiz had introduced new solutions to the problem of manning the military. The Carlist War then brought with it a demand for massive numbers of soldiers, necessitating repeated waves of conscription, and the conflict also forced the Madrid government down an increasingly liberal path. The widespread violence, economic suffering, and related social and political turmoil of the war included violent resistance to military service, which became a major preoccupation for political and military leaders of all stripes. In spite of the strong social resistance to wartime military service, however, the reality of repeated military drafts, along with an inundation of the public sphere with the language of constitutional liberalism, lead to a growing internalization of the idea of military service—of a *contribución de sangre*—as a natural component of the modern, liberal state. By 1868, 90 percent of the army would consist of draftees. This was a far cry from 1789, when 90 percent of the army had been made up of professional, career soldiers.

Of course, the theoretical acceptance of the idea of national military service did not translate perfectly into reality. As in many other countries, laws allowed families with sufficient resources to evade military service by setting the price for exemption within the reach of the middle classes. The leftist *Progressives* may have defined the liberal philosophical underpinnings of military service, but the *Moderates* often put it into practice. Hence, however much the middle classes accepted the notion of a constitutionally mandated draft, in practice their politicians passed legislation allowing draftees to buy a substitute to serve in their place. The inequities of military service would trigger protests and political turmoil—sometimes on a massive and violent scale—for many years to come.

In the officer corps, the Carlist War fostered a new, shared mentality among those who fought together. The consequences of war—including the deaths of some 5,000 officers— greatly increased promotions. Although those who received new commands were a varied bunch, including students, members of the Provincial Militia, and soldiers who had risen up from the ranks, many came to share liberal political sympathies. Juan Prim is an outstanding example (see Chapter 29). The intensely conservative Catholicism of their enemies fostered a shift toward anticlericalism among many officers, whose views began to converge with the political platform of the Progressive party. In particular, the officers fighting in the northern campaigns felt abandoned by the Moderate-dominated government in Madrid, whose inability to pay them in a timely fashion did not help. Some even came to flirt with radical theories of legal rebellion, arguing that the army, because of the diverse social strata it brought together, constituted a democratic institution. The generals fighting at the front, moreover, became more conscious of the political power they held, since the government needed them to defeat the Carlists. Only after the government sent more resources to General Baldomero Espartero's forces in the north did he resume his offensive campaign that led to the Carlist collapse.

Espartero (1793–1879), one of the most outstanding figures of modern Spanish military history, had already gained considerable fame. A commoner who had become an officer during the war against Napoleon and a decorated combat veteran of the War of Independence and Spain's last colonial war in South America, by the final stages of the Carlist War he had become the most famous living military figure in Spain. A lifelong devotee of the monarchy, he tended toward liberal politics, eventually allying himself with the Progressives, even though at the conclusion of the Carlist War the rival *Moderates* also offered him their top leadership position. After a *pronunciamiento* in 1840, he took over the position of regent from María Cristina, mother of the still-underage Queen Isabel II.

The "Regime of the Generals," 1840–68

The regency of Espartero marked the beginning of what became known as the "generals' regime," which lasted until the Revolution of 1868. During this period a small number of prestigious military figures dominated the government, becoming in effect full-time politicians. These so-called *espadones* (literally "broadswords") acted as party leaders rather than as representatives of the military as a whole (see Chapter 3). As the Spanish military historian Fernando Puell de la Villa has observed, the conversion of leading military figures into professional politicians actually did more harm than good to the officer corps as a whole. In spite of the high positions of an illustrious few, most officers during this period saw their social status and real income fall, and they avoided direct intervention in politics. For this reason, it is misleading to affirm that "the military" or "the army" dominated Spanish politics in the nineteenth century. Instead, the generals' regime was detrimental to the army as a collective body, and the vast majority of officers fared no better on an individual basis either. Furthermore, sociopolitical developments did not help the army's fighting ability, which saw its focus shift more toward maintaining domestic order than defending the country from foreign enemies. In the words of another Spanish military historian, the army threatened to become more of a "great body of armed bureaucrats" than an organization of war-fighting professionals.

At the national level, Spanish politics took on a militarist appearance simply because the status of the *espadones* as high-ranking army officers was fundamental to their public identity and effectiveness. The need for political parties to have a respected military leader distinguished Spain from most other European countries. Even if they did not act in the interest of the army as a whole, moreover, the effects of their actions certainly had far-reaching consequences for it. An especially corrosive problem for the army was how each successful *pronunciamiento* brought with it a mass of promotions meant to reward political loyalty. This practice in turn exacerbated the growing problem of the top-heavy nature of the army, which had started during the war against Napoleon and worsened with each subsequent conflict. In the early nineteenth century there was one officer for every 20 soldiers; by 1868 the ratio was 1:5, and in some units the ratio reached 1:1!

Espartero soon discovered the perils of the army's special interests. The officers who served him in wartime now expected his support, but an army of 200,000 men was hardly necessary after the Carlists surrendered, and it was also expensive. Yet mass demobilization would bring economic misery, especially among the many young officers who lacked the 25 years of service necessary to receive a pension. Given the state of the national budget, however, Espartero and the Progressives felt compelled to reduce the regular army by almost 80,000 men, although they also expanded the National Militia, where they got most of their political support. Rising dissatisfaction in the army led to two military uprisings against Espartero. The first, an audacious plot that involved attempting to kidnap the queen failed, but the second, organized by *La Orden Militar Española*, anti-Espartero secret society based in France and financed by the deposed María Cristina, succeeded in July 1843. The victors, led by Generals Ramón María Narváez and Leopoldo O'Donnell, dissolved the National Militia but promoted all officers in the regular army to the next highest rank. The number of generals rose from 584 to 647. Although Narváez implemented various necessary reforms and has been credited with creating the modern Spanish army, the continued policy of gaining loyalty through promotions was not good for the army. After O'Donnell staged his own successful pronunciamiento in 1856, all officers were again promoted by one rank. At the same time, moreover, O'Donnell sought to reduce dissatisfaction among draftees by reducing their length of service.

This reduction in the length of service revealed how much common soldiers preoccupied military leaders. Indeed, officers worried throughout the nineteenth century about how the inequities of military conscription fueled anti-militarism among the poor. The Carlist War had alleviated somewhat the extreme economic misery that rank-and-file soldiers had lived with since 1814, as peace allowed Spain to regain some of its financial footing and some military leaders—Narváez in particular—sought to keep soldiers content and thus under control. Most army sergeants during this period were dedicated professionals who had risen to their positions through skill and hard work. The backbone of modern armies, sergeants are a crucial link between officers and their soldiers, socially and operationally. During Spain's many years of war they had seen their pay increase, and the possibility was open to them of receiving commissions and entering the officer corps, even if rising above the rank of major was highly unlikely. But during the so-called generals' regime sergeants became increasingly dissatisfied with their professional outlook, as peacetime conditions reduced their opportunities for advancement. In times of political turmoil, the inclination toward more radical politics that some sergeants shared with their soldiers, paired with the attempts by radical political movements to turn both groups into revolutionaries, thus destabilized the army and, consequently, the country as a whole. This threat would manifest itself most dramatically in the run-up to the Revolution of 1868 (see Chapter 3).

In the meantime, General O'Donnell built up support for his regime by involving Spain in various overseas adventures between 1858 and 1863 (see Chapter 13). These military actions failed in the end to improve the grand strategic position of the country or enhance its international prestige, with the possible exception of the Moroccan campaign. But for a time, at least, the imperialist activity helped him win support from many Spaniards, including the kind of traditional conservatives who by nature rejected his brand of populist nationalism, associated with the secular liberalism they despised. The Moroccan campaign, which O'Donnell personally commanded, was especially effective, for it provided the perfect opportunity to invoke Spain's historic wars against the forces of Islam, thereby appealing to religious conservatives, while simultaneously employing the liberal language of the "civilizing mission." The name the Moroccan campaign assumed in Spain—"the War of Africa"—reveals much about the propagandistic value of the conflict, which was really just a limited response to attacks by Moroccan tribesmen around Spain's North African city of Ceuta.

Glorious Revolution, Restoration, and war at home and abroad, 1868–1909

Soon christened the "Glorious Revolution," the overthrow of the monarchy began in September 1868 with a naval mutiny in Cádiz (see Chapter 3). Generals Prim, Francisco Serrano, and other opposition military leaders soon gained the allegiance of much of the army, and Serrano's forces defeated loyalists at the Battle of Alcolea, resulting in the queen's exile to Paris. During the following months the Cortes searched for a replacement for Isabel, settling on the Italian prince Amadeo of Savoy in November of 1870. His reign would last until early February 1873, when Spain became a republic. The First Republic did not solve Spain's problems, however, and in late 1874 military men would again bring about regime change, this time restoring the monarchy.

Two major wars further complicated this tumultuous period. Just weeks after the Glorious Revolution began, an uprising in Cuba marked the beginning of what would become known as the Ten Years War. Predictably, the corresponding rise in military manpower needs affected the poor most of all. Moreover, the 1866 bankruptcy of companies that sold insurance guaranteeing to pay the fee for exemption from military service left policyholders suddenly vulnerable to the draft, further radicalizing the political climate.

Another Carlist War, lasting from 1872 to 1876, only worsened the usual controversy over military service and greatly complicated military politics. By the time the Carlists surrendered, the army had fought successively in the name of King Amadeo I, five different presidents of the First Republic (including General Serrano) and King Alfonso XII, who at the start of 1875 restored the Bourbon dynasty to Spain (see Chapter 4). Moreover, the radical policies of the First Republic caused many officers to cross over to the Carlists, where they remained until the Bourbon Restoration. It did not help that in February 1873, in the midst of the Carlist and Cuban wars, the First Republic decided to suppress the draft and create an all-volunteer army. It then established a new militia, the "Volunteers of the Republic." The latter attracted far fewer men than hoped, and many of those who enlisted—including some Carlists—did so in order to stir up trouble.

Catalan nationalism also reared its head. In March the provisional government of Barcelona demanded control of the forces in the east in return for withdrawing their demand for Catalonia's independence. After Madrid ceded, the Barcelona political leaders then replaced the regular force with a volunteer militia. Unlike their counterparts in Madrid, they went as far as to reject the incorporation of soldiers from the regular army into their new militia. Predictably, serious problems with insubordination, desertion, and officer loyalty further hindered the war against the Carlists. In the summer of 1873, the army also had to fight against a left-republican, Cantonalist rebellion inspired in part by the Paris Commune. Finally, in late 1874 General Arsenio Martínez Campos overthrew the Republic and brought the Bourbon monarchy back to Spain under Isabel's son Alfonso. Not surprisingly, the politics of many officers had shifted to the right during this tumultuous period.

With Alfonso XII as king and Antonio Cánovas del Castillo as its chief political architect, the Restoration (1875–1923) ended the era of *pronunciamientos*. But the disappearance of overt political intervention by army officers did not eliminate the political influence of the military, regardless of Cánovas' efforts to civilianize public life. Following the example of Bismarck's newly unified Germany, he introduced the figure of the "soldier-king" to Spain. Although the new regime's use of the soldier-king concept strengthened military loyalty to the government, by bolstering the crown-military relationship, he set the stage for later problems, especially after Spain became more involved in Morocco.

In return for not intervening directly in politics, the army was largely left to its own devices. The officer corps turned inward and became more of a closed community separate from civil society, while military bureaucratization, corporatism, and use of the army to put down civil strife all increased. However, much the Restauration had reduced direct political intervention by individual military figures, it had also fostered the growth of an "incipient *praetorianism*," or tendency by officers to intervene in politics to protect their institutional interests.

The Spanish army's next major conflict, fought against Cuban *independentistas* who rose up in 1895, ended with the victorious intervention of the United States in 1898 and Spain's loss of Cuba, Puerto Rico, and the Philippines. Marking the definitive end to Spain's once-great empire in the Americas and the Pacific, the so-called Disaster of 1898 provoked much nationalist soul-searching among civilians and military men alike, not to mention enormous human and material losses. Thanks to inadequate training, administrative incompetence, material shortages, and widespread disease, the Spanish army in Cuba experienced major setbacks, while the customary unfair conscription policies made the war more unpopular at home, especially among the poor. Predictably, the number of draft dodgers (*prófugos*) rose dramatically after 1895, eventually making up one-quarter of the annual quota. Spanish strategy and tactics became notably more effective with time, especially after General Valeriano Weyler assumed command in Cuba in 1896, but the human costs and political price of his actions were devastating. His strategy of *reconcentración*—involving the forced resettlement of civilians into concentration camps—had genocidal consequences, killing one-tenth of Cuba's population. Not surprisingly, it also provoked outrage abroad and political opposition in Spain. After his recall to Spain in 1897 and the US invasion the following year, the fate of the Spanish army on the island was sealed.

During this period army officers became increasingly disenchanted with liberal parliamentary government, which they blamed for steering the country on its disastrous course, and they grew even more protective of their corporate interests, unable to see how their own resistance to military reform had contributed to the army's difficulties in Cuba. Officers perceived—with some justification—that politicians and the media had unfairly made the army the scapegoat for a military defeat that had many causes, and they felt that their sacrifices went unrecognized. They manifested their dissatisfaction collectively by attacking newspaper offices and, more significantly, pressuring to expand the military's legal jurisdiction over civilians, including those who insulted "military honor." Many officers also began to see in North Africa a potential place of national and professional redemption.

Morocco, the *Juntas de Defensa*, and the *africanistas*, 1909–31

Although the North African enclaves of Ceuta and Melilla had been part of Spain for centuries, since the last part of the nineteenth century political, commercial, and military figures had expressed interest in expanding Spanish occupation in the area. In 1909, the army's involvement in North Africa heated up when Madrid sent ill-prepared soldiers to act against Moroccan tribesmen threatening a railroad connecting Spanish-owned mines and Melilla. After a major ambush caused over a thousand Spanish casualties, including around 180 deaths, the government called up reserves, including some 500 men who had already completed their military service and did not expect to be called up again. The resulting protest triggered the so-called Tragic Week of bloody rioting and widespread strikes in Barcelona, bringing down the national government. Once again, the issue of military conscription had loomed large in a key chapter in Spanish history (See chapter 17).

After Spain and France imposed a colonial protectorate upon Morocco in 1912, the Spanish army slowly fought to gain control of its zone, a process that only widened social and political fissures at home. The Moroccan campaigns sowed discord within the army as well. The rise of a relatively small group of officers, the so-called *africanistas*, who gained rapid promotions through combat merit in Morocco, stoked the resentment of the many officers based in Spain, who felt left behind and thus favored basing promotions strictly on seniority instead of combat merits. Although army politics were immensely complicated and groups did not always fall neatly into one group or another, in general many peninsula-based officers found their voice in political pressure groups calling themselves *Juntas de Defensa* (and later *Comisiones Informativas*). The political power of the *Juntas* peaked around 1917, when they pressured the government to alter national policy on their behalf. The crisis they provoked greatly debilitated the Restoration political system (see Chapter 5).

Then another military development, this time on the battlefield, dealt a new blow to the regime. In the summer of 1921 the Spanish army suffered at least 8,000 casualties near Anwal (*Annual*), Morocco, in the worst defeat of any colonial army in twentieth-century Africa. The debacle, largely a product of poor command decisions and occupational methods, flawed strategic direction from Madrid and the skills of Riffian leader Muhammad Abd-el-Krim el Jatabi, played a key role in General Miguel Primo de Rivera's decision to seize power in 1923 and establish a dictatorship. Although the dictator initially angered *africanistas* with talk of abandoning Morocco, he soon reversed his position. In 1925, as part of a joint Franco-Spanish operation, the Spanish military staged a large-scale, combined-arms amphibious landing at Alhucemas (Al Hoceima) Bay that helped lead to Abd-el-Krim's defeat. The operation made clear how much the Spanish military had improved since the disaster at Anwal, even earning the praise of French war hero Marshal Philippe Petain. But the corresponding fame and influence of its *africanista* heroes did not bode well for Spain's political future.

The Second Republic, Civil War, and the Franco Dictatorship, 1936–75

Most officers were indifferent or moderately supportive of the Second Republic at its founding in April 1931. But Republican leader Manuel Azaña's sweeping military reforms alienated many officers from the new regime, despite the indisputable need for drastic change (see chapters 5, 33). The army was top heavy and its structure outdated, with the disproportionate amount of money dedicated to officer salaries draining away resources that could have helped modernize and improve it. Aspects of Azaña's military policies were flawed, and his arrogant attitude earned him enemies. But no meaningful military reform could possibly have pleased everyone in the officer corps, and the volatile political climate—in which Azaña suffered fierce and frequently unfounded attacks—only made his job harder. Nor did it help that some high-level, influential military figures suffered professionally because of his decisions—including Francisco Franco, the most famous of the *africanistas* (see Chapter 35).

Well aware of Spain's history of military intervention in politics, Azaña harbored doubts about the loyalty of some generals and rewarded those whom he trusted. Political considerations could thus affect military rank under Azaña's leadership of the War Ministry, a practice that subsequent governments of the right and the left would continue. Top *africanistas*, many of whom were skeptical of democracy and civilian rule, were especially sensitive to perceived slights.

In the meantime, the governments of Spain's first democracy employed the army for internal repression more frequently than at any other time in its history, essentially turning it into a political instrument. Many officers viewed with dismay the growing social and political disorder in the country as a whole, unfairly blaming all problems on the left. Equating their own interests to those of Spain as a whole, many saw themselves as national redeemers. The Spanish Civil War began in July 1936 when a group of generals rose up against the Republic, gaining the support of crucial elements of the army. Within months General Franco assumed military and political command of the rebel forces (see Chapter 6).

The Republican political leaders in Madrid faced a difficult situation, as the leftist militia volunteers who reacted most energetically against the military rebellion instinctively distrusted all professional officers, even those who remained loyal to the Republic. Almost all of the militias—anarchist, socialist, Catalan, Basque, "Trotskyist," or other—resisted centralization, with the important exception of the Communists. Although the Republicans fared badly on the battlefield during the early weeks of the war, a surprisingly efficient militia system developed, thanks largely to good staff work. The Communists, whose strong influence on Republican military policy stemmed from the USSR's large contribution of military aide and personnel, favored incorporating the militias into a unified, communist-dominated regular army with traditional standards of organization, rank, discipline, and training.

On the battlefield, the Republican forces suffered from an insufficient number of capable, experienced officers. In some cases, officers who began the war as captains were commanding divisions or corps within months. The most famous example of a meteoric rise in rank was Vicente Rojo, who went from being a newly promoted major at the war's onset to general and chief of staff in less than two years, commanding Republican forces at the massive Ebro offensive in 1938. Like many top Republican leaders, he was an excellent staff officer, although he lacked the field leadership experience of many of his Francoist counterparts. At the lower command levels, the Republicans sorely needed more experienced noncommissioned officers (NCOs) and junior officers, especially in the artillery corps. Most rank-and-file soldiers on both sides fought not for ideological motives but because they were drafted, although Franco did a better job of providing for his soldiers and even incorporating prisoners of war into his forces.

Although not without discord, Franco's side unified its command structure much earlier and suffered from less internal political dissension (see Chapter 6). Furthermore, the rebel leaders were almost exclusively *africanistas* who had fought extensively in Morocco, where many of their officers and NCOs had also acquired valuable combat experience. Franco also benefited enormously from the use of Moroccan mercenaries and the contributions of Nazi Germany and Fascist Italy in personnel and materiel, which was of better quality than what the Republicans received from the Soviets. The attitudes of other great powers and the international climate of appeasement favored the insurgents as well. On April 1, 1939 Franco declared victory.

When Germany unleashed the Second World War the following September, the Spanish army was in terrible shape, and Spain never officially joined the Axis, in spite of Franco's clear sympathies. Nevertheless, his regime orchestrated the sending of tens of thousands of Spanish volunteers, some in name only, to fight in the Blue Division for Nazi Germany on the Eastern Front. (On the other side, many Spanish exiles served in De Gaulle's Free French forces and the Resistance, and were among the first Allied soldiers to enter Paris after its liberation.) After the war, Franco's reorganization of the armed forces made it clear that he favored the political stability of his dictatorship over military effectiveness. So while he succeeded in keeping the military under control, severe problems in materiel, staffing, and operational abilities persisted for decades. Although the 1953 military agreement between the United States and Spain brought with it some material improvements, in the late 1960s the army remained the institution least touched by the modernizing wave that had finally hit the country.

Nevertheless, the beginnings of a "military transformation" were underway, bolstered by the reform project of Lieutenant General Manuel Díez-Alegría. General Manuel Gutiérrez Mellado gave subsequent impetus to the reform efforts, and the military transformation culminated with the January 5, 1984 passage of the Organic Defense Law, affirming civilian control over the armed forces and improving coordination among military commanders. The military certainly remained a concern as Spain democratized after Franco's death, especially during the failed coup attempt of February 23, 1981, involving a handful of generals and other officers from the army and Civil Guard. But the Spanish military as a whole remained steadfastly loyal to the Constitution while the renegade Civil Guardsmen held parliament hostage for 18 tense hours, and the vast majority of officers shared the rest of the country's sense of relief when the coup's leaders stepped down at King Juan Carlos' order. To be sure, many officers shared with the coup's protagonists the perception that Spanish society failed to appreciate the military lives lost to terrorism during the transition to democracy, and some doubted the viability of democratic government in Spain. But this did not mean they approved of the coup, and the officer corps accepted the Supreme Court's sentence against its military protagonists without the kind of public protests or resistance that would have occurred at many other times in Spanish history. Paradoxically, under Franco's dictatorship the Spanish military had become less interventionist than at any time in its modern history, thereby facilitating the last thing the dictator himself had wanted: the country's transition to democracy.

The Spanish army's form, function, and composition also changed significantly after Franco's death. In 1982 Spain officially joined NATO in spite of serious misgivings on the part of a good number of Spaniards. Shortly thereafter the new Socialist prime minister Felipe González reversed his earlier opposition to NATO membership, and in a 1986 referendum Spaniards elected to stay in the organization, thanks in no small part to González' pledge to resign if the country voted otherwise.

With major structural changes in the armed forces still in progress, in late 1988 the United Nations Secretary General requested that Spain join a team of foreign military observers in Angola, ushering in a new era in the history of the Spanish army. In spite of its relatively small size, the military has remained active on the international scene ever since, operating in the Balkans, Latin America, Haiti, Africa, Iraq, Afghanistan, and elsewhere. With the exception of Spain's participation in the occupation of Iraq after the US-led invasion of 2003, the military has consistently enjoyed ample public support for its actions abroad, especially its peace-support and humanitarian missions. The Spanish mission in the Balkans beginning in October 1992, which occurred as women were becoming increasingly visible in the armed forces, played a particularly important role in altering the public image of the army. Women, who first gained entrance to military academies in 1988, have come to make up 12 percent of Spain's military personnel, which is one of the highest proportions of any European army.

The new image and functions of the army coincided with a fundamental change in its composition. Like many of its European counterparts, it moved away from universal male conscription during this period, transforming into an all-volunteer force. The potent argument that a small, professional, well-trained, and technologically adept force would be more effective than a mass army of draftees helped propel this change, as did political opposition to the draft and the ever-rising number of conscientious objectors. At the very end of 2001, nearly two centuries after the Cortes of Cádiz had instituted conscription, Spain held its last military draft.

These changes have not always gone smoothly, but there is no question that Spain has come closer than ever to achieving what military reformers since the nineteenth century have wanted: a truly modern army, fundamentally comparable to its European counterparts. The biggest challenges the military faces, such as figuring out how to live up to international commitments and defend the country on a paltry budget, are hardly unique in Europe. The army lacks the kind of political sway that it held for much of the nineteenth and twentieth centuries, but few Spaniards, whether civilian or military, would choose to return to the days of *pronunciamientos*, the generals' regime, or dictatorship. Perhaps because of this, along with the humanitarian character of most of the current military's missions and the absence of conscription, Spanish perceptions of its armed forces have become remarkably positive. Paradoxically, a strong pacifist streak and a profound reluctance to commit to policies that might lead to war characterize Spain in the early twenty-first century, but, as opinion polls attest, its military has become one of the country's most respected institutions.

Further reading

Alpert, Michael, *The Republican Army in the Spanish Civil War*, Cambridge: Cambridge University Press, 2013.

Álvarez Junco, José, *Mater dolorosa: la idea de España en el siglo XIX*, Madrid: Tauris, 2001.

Balfour, Sebastian, *Deadly Embrace: Morocco and the Road to the Spanish Civil War*, Oxford: Oxford University Press, 2002.

Bowen, Wayne H., and José A. Álvarez (eds.), *A Military History of Modern Spain: From the Napoleonic War to the International War on Terror*, Westport, CT: Praeger Security International, 2007.

Boyd, Carolyn P., *La política pretoriana en el reinado de Alfonso XII*, Madrid: Alianza, 1990. (Revised and expanded version in Spanish of *Praetorian Politics in Liberal Spain*, Chapel Hill: University of North Carolina Press, 1979.)

Esdaile, Charles J., *Fighting Napoleon: Guerrillas, Bandits and Adventurers in Spain, 1808- 1914*, New Haven: Yale University Press, 2004.

Graham, Helen, *The Spanish Civil War: A Very Short Introduction*, Oxford: Oxford University Press, 2005.

Jensen, Geoffrey, *Cultura militar española. Modernistas, tradicionalistas y liberales*, Madrid: Biblioteca Nueva, 2014. (Revised and expanded version in Spanish of *Irrational Triumph: Cultural Despair, Military Nationalism, and the Ideological Origins of Franco's Spain*, Reno: University of Nevada Press, 2002.)

Lawrence, Mark, *Spain's First Carlist War, 1833-1840*, New York: Palgrave MacMillan, 2014.

Matthews, James, *Reluctant Warriors: Republican Popular Army and Nationalist Army Conscripts in the Spanish Civil War, 1936-1939*, Oxford: Oxford University Press, 2012.

Payne, Stanley G., *Politics and the Military in Modern Spain*, Stanford: Stanford University Press, 1967.

Payne, Stanley G., *The Spanish Civil War*, New York: Cambridge University Press, 2012.

Seidman, Michael, *Victorious Counterrevolution: The Nationalist Effort in the Spanish Civil War*, Madison: University of Wisconsin Press, 2011.

CHAPTER 22
THE POLITICS OF MEMORY[1]
Paloma Aguilar and Clara Ramírez-Barat

The Spanish transition has been often presented as one of the most peaceful and successful democratic transitions and praised as model to follow. The traumatic memories of the population after a brutal civil war and a long-lasting and cruel dictatorship were not easy to overcome. According to many authors, the basis for the peaceful and successful stabilization of democracy in Spain was precisely the decision to leave the past behind. However, in recent years, different voices have been claiming that the Spanish transition was not as exemplary as it has been portrayed, mainly because it failed to provide justice, truth, and proper reparations to the victims of Francoism, and because it left certain institutions inherited from the dictatorship untouched. Moreover, it was neither a peaceful process; indeed, political violence was present throughout the democratization period.

Many of those who now hold this critical view, such as left-wing political parties and victims' associations, also claim that it is necessary to correct these gaps. Moreover, some human rights and victims groups have resorted to international jurisdiction as means to obtain what they have not been able to get in Spain. The conservative political parties (mainly the People's Party: Partido Popular, or PP)—which considers that arrangements of the Spanish transition are untouchable and is clearly against any digging into Franco's past—oppose these positions. So does the Spanish Catholic Church, which has systematically avoided asking for forgiveness for its active support of the Francoist side during the Civil War and its connivance with the dictatorship. Even though the Spanish Church has actively promoted beatification of its victims during the war, it claims that it is a great error for the Francoism victims to dig into the past. As far as the Spanish society overall is concerned, according to various surveys conducted by the *Centro de Investigaciones Sociológicas* (CIS), the most important Spanish institution for survey data, the popular endorsement of the exemplarity of the Spanish transition seems to be slowly diminishing according to the generational change. Also, in 2008, the majority of the Spanish population seem to be favorable with the idea of passing a law to deal with the memory of the past. In general terms, there is a strong association between the critical evaluation of the Transition and the demand for more justice to the victims of Francoism.

This chapter provides a brief summary of the politics of memory and transitional justice (TJ) in Spain since Franco's death in 1975 until today. The first section focuses on the first years of the democratic period until the creation of the Association for the Recovery of Historical Memory (*Asociación para la Recuperación de la Memoria Histórica*, ARMH) in

---

[1]This text is a very summarized and updated version of P. Aguilar and C. Ramírez-Barat, "Reparations without truth or justice in the Spanish case," in N. Wouters (ed.), *Transitional Justice after War and Dictatorship. Learning from European. Experiences (1945-2000)* (Antwerp-Oxford: Intersentia, 2014). We thank Intersentia for having authorized us to publish this revised version.

2000. The second section deals with what we have called the "post-TJ period," which started in 2000, reached a peak in 2007 with the approval of the so-called Law of Historical Memory (hereafter, LHM), and continues today. Finally, some conclusions are presented.

Before proceeding, it is important to provide definitions of two central concepts. The first is historical memory. Although memory is something which pertains to individuals, the terms "collective memory," "social memory," and "historical memory" have been applied to the ways in which various groups of people share "memories" of important historical events and in which invoking these memories can strengthen the connections among them. In some contexts, the term "historical memory" can also imply demands for reparations for past violations of human rights which, it is claimed, have been deliberately silenced, and the recognition of the rights of victims, whose testimony is given special weight as a source of historical truth. This is the case of "historical memory" associations and laws.

The second concept is transitional justice. This refers to a complex of measures, some judicial, some not, which consist of programs for economic and symbolic reparations, truth commissions, initiatives to recover the memory of victims, institutional reforms and purges of the bureaucracy. Such measures have been applied in a number of countries, especially during transitions to democracy, to try and deal with the violations of human rights or crimes against humanity committed under a dictatorship or during extended conflicts. To the extent that such measures aim to defend the rights of victims and condemn the perpetrators, their driving goal is to contribute to the promotion of civic confidence and the strengthening of democracy.

Early memory policies and TJ (1975–2000)

The Franco dictatorship began to be dismantled upon the death of the dictator in November 1975 but the legacy it had left behind still loomed large. According to the latest rough estimates, the Republican repression caused around 50,000 deaths during the Civil War and Francoist repression caused around 130,000 deaths, including an estimate of the 30,000–40,000 executions after the conflict. Between 1936 and the postwar period, around 367,000 to 500,000 political prisoners passed through almost 200 concentration camps. At the end of the war, Spain's prison population was approximately 270,000, while between 1940 and 1945 around 10,000 persons were deported to Nazi camps. During the conflict around 30,000 children on the Republican side were sent abroad, many of whom never returned; while after the war hundreds of thousands went into exile, though a significant number of them returned in the next years. After a very exhaustive purge, thousands of people were forbidden from returning to their former jobs. Moreover, the Francoist regime denied economic support to war veterans, mutilated, widows, and orphans of the defeated side, and only the relatives of the victims of Republican repression were allowed to exhume bodies from common graves. In contrast, those who fought or sympathized with Franco's forces were widely honored, given a preferential treatment in employment, granted compensation measures and pensions, provided with health care benefits, and given economic support to exhume the bodies of their family members from mass graves and to bury them properly.

Political change in Spain came through a very long process of negotiation between the reformist sectors of Francoism and the different political forces of the democratic opposition (see Chapter 8). Soon after the dictator's death some partial and limited amnesty measures for political prisoners were adopted invoking the spirit of "national reconciliation". The first law approved by the Parliament after the democratic elections of June 1977 was precisely an Amnesty Law, supported by all political parties except Franco's heirs in the Alianza Popular, which led to release to the few remaining political prisoners. The law also made it easier for those who had been expelled from their jobs for political reasons to regain them, or if they were beyond working age, to receive the pensions they would have been entitled to had they not been expelled. However, in its criminal dimension, this very broad amnesty applied not only to the violent actions committed by the groups opposing the dictatorship, but also all the rights violations committed by the officials of the regime. Many still consider this law as the quintessence of "national reconciliation" in Spain, but for others it is the main obstacle to undertaking a real process of TJ process.

The decision not to undertake punitive measures against human rights perpetrators was accompanied by several measures to provide material compensation for the defeated. From 1976 until 1984, seven laws were passed providing some form of economic support or/and rehabilitation to different categories of beneficiaries from the Republican side (including war wounded, widows, orphans, and members of the Military and of the forces of public order). They were not part of a comprehensive policy aimed at dealing with the past and were not intended to provide justice. In general terms, these policies recognized the unequal treatment that was provided to the defeated, and offered them the same rights that had already been given to the victors. Only later did they address the victims of the dictatorship. Indeed, it would only be in 1986 that one of the most important gaps of the Amnesty Law was finally filled, when the members of the Democratic Military Union (UMD) who had received sentences under Francoism were reincorporated in the army. The fact that it took nine years after the Amnesty Law to adopt such measure reveals the power that the military retained during the first years of democracy. Finally, in 1990 the General Budget Law offered compensation to those who had spent time in Francoist prisons for the first time.

These were the only TJ measures during that period. In contrast Spain saw none of the measures: trials, vetting, restitution of individual property, truth-seeking, and symbolic reparations, which were typical in countries that democratized more recently.

Memory irruptions and post-TJ policies (2000–15)

After the implementation of these limited measures, Spanish politicians respected the tacit agreement of leaving the thorniest aspects of the past behind, which was the basis of the "national reconciliation" for many years. However, decisions to sidestep history tend to be revised, and memory irruptions are inevitable with the passage of time. In fact, since the mid-90s and, particularly, since 2000 Spain has witnessed the emergence of a post-TJ process that has transcended the institutional arrangements established during the transition. This development can be explained by a number of factors.

To begin with, generational change has proved to be a crucial variable. The "third generation" after the war, that has brought this issue to the forefront of the public sphere has grown up under a stable democracy, is devoid of the guilt and fears of their predecessors, and feels more comfortable with the international legal framework and with the language of human rights. Part of this generation of "grandchildren" believes that challenging the institutional arrangements made during the Transition will not destabilize Spain, and considers that the time has come to provide public visibility and justice to the victims of Francoism. This does not mean that the former generations were totally passive with respect to the past; in fact, the first cycle of exhumations of republican victims took place after Franco's death and was undertaken by the first and second generation in a hostile environment. However, these exhumations had a more private character and, with few exceptions, did not receive media attention. Importantly, many people from these older generations, particularly in small villages, remained silent because of the enduring trauma and fear.

Secondly, the ARMH, which was established in 2000, as well as various other organizations established in recent years, in most cases by families of victims of the war, have strongly advocated the recovery of the "silenced" memory of the Republican victims. ARHM in particular has promoted many successful exhumations all over Spain, and a handful of initiatives vindicating the recovery of the memory of the victims of the Civil War and Francoism that have played a key role in shedding light on the regime's repressive machinery and in raising awareness, at both the national and international levels, about the existing lacunae in terms of victims' reparation in Spain.

Thirdly, a strategic political turn took place in the Spanish Workers' Socialist Party (PSOE) after it lost power in 1996, following 14 years in office during which the legacy of past was mostly ignored. When the conservative PP took office under José María Aznar, the leftist, Catalan, and Basque nationalist parties tried to stigmatize it for its Francoist roots. This process was particularly active between 2000 and 2004. The initiatives presented or supported by the PSOE during that period established a precedent difficult to ignore when it later regained office in 2004. The fact that the PSOE, lacking a parliamentary majority, needed the support of parties that were much more determined than it was to drive to these issues, especially Izquierda Unida (IU), and Esquerra Republicana de Catalunya (ERC), also helps explain the important policies that were approved after 2004.

Fourthly, the evolution of international human rights and international criminal law frameworks and the lobbying efforts of INGOs such as Amnesty International, as well as international institutions such as the United Nations, the Council of Europe, and the European Parliament, have proved to be very relevant as well. Following the work of the Committee of Enforced Disappearances, the official visit to Spain in January of 2014 of the UN's Special Rapporteur on the promotion of truth, justice, reparation, and guarantees of nonrecurrence, increased the pressure on the Spanish government. The report issued after this visit highlighted the great distance existing between the government and victims' groups, and called on the government to revise the Amnesty Law and adopt a series of measures to provide justice to the victims of the Civil War and Francoism.

Finally, the importance of fortuitous events, such as anniversaries of the Civil War and the Second Republic, should not be underestimated. A particularly crucial one is what has been called the "Pinochet effect": the consequences of the detention in London in October 1998 of the Chilean dictator—on the initiative of the Spanish judge Baltasar Garzón.

1. Measures approved from 2002 to 2015

On November 20, 2002—date of the anniversary of Franco's death—the Constitutional Commission of the Congress of Deputies unanimously approved a declaration stating that "no one could feel legitimated in using violence with the aim of imposing political convictions and establishing totalitarian regimes," and urging the government "to develop an integral policy of recognition for those exiled as consequence of the Civil War." Only one year later, during the celebration the 25th anniversary of the Constitution, the Congress organized an act of tribute to the victims of the dictatorship. The homage was not endorsed by the PP, the governing party at the time, which claimed that the opposition parties were breaking the agreement reached in 2002, according to which if the PP, for first time in its history, was to "condemn Francoism," the political left would have to accept in turn "never to use this topic again for political confrontation." Only some weeks earlier, the PP had also opposed an initiative submitted by a Basque nationalist party, Eusko Alkartasuna (EA), and endorsed by the PSOE among other parties, requesting that the government assist and provide recognition to the victims of the Civil War and the dictatorship, facilitate access to the archives containing information about the war, support the exhumation of mass graves, and reassess the pensions of the "children of the war."

The PSOE came to power following the elections in March of 2004. Only two months after Jose Luis Rodríguez Zapatero started his presidency, the Congress approved a proposition requesting the government to undertake a study regarding the legal situation of the victims of the Civil War and the dictatorship's repression, and to advance proposals for ameliorating their economic situation. The motion also urged the government to facilitate access to private and public archives containing relevant information on the repression, and to submit a draft bill of solidarity with the victims who suffered personal harm during Franco's regime while trying to exercise the civil liberties that would be later recognized in the Constitution. In response, the government appointed an Inter-Ministerial Commission chaired by the vice-president, charged with submitting recommendations on the matter before the end of the year. Parliament also began to receive a large number of petitions on issues such as increasing of the pensions being received by children of war, the improvement of access to health care for those who were still living abroad, and the transfer back to Barcelona of the documents that were seized in Catalonia after the Civil War by the Franco regime and kept in the General Archive of the Spanish Civil War in Salamanca. Finally, in 2006 the Congress approved a bill proposed by IU symbolically declaring 2006 as the "year of historical memory."

On July 28, 2006, the Inter-Ministerial Commission submitted two reports to Parliament, one regarding the situation of the victims and one on archives, as well as a draft law. This initiated a difficult negotiation process between the PSOE and the rest of the political parties. While the PP manifested a strong opposition to the law, the leftist groups and some human rights and victims' organizations criticized its shortcomings. The bitter debates in Parliament soon spilled into the media, involving many public figures and academics. Despite all this, the average Spaniard was hardly involved in the discussion.

The law was finally passed on October 31, 2007 with two parties voting against it: the PP and ERC which, although it had initially been one of its main promoters, finally refused to endorse the law because it didn't declare the trials of the Franco era null and void. Law 52/2007, "which recognizes and expands the rights, and establishes measures in favor of those who suffered persecution or violence during the Civil War and the dictatorship," more widely known as the Law of Historical Memory, established the framework for the implementation of memory politics in Spain. It regulates, broadly speaking, four different issues: reparations, the exhumation of mass graves, the removal of Francoist symbols, and the question of access to archives.

2. Reparations

The bulk of the articles of the law establish different compensation measures and recognize some categories of beneficiaries that were not included in previous reparatory laws. It also standardizes some situations that, until then, were being addressed in different ways by the Autonomous Communities. An interesting novelty of the law is that it granted reparations for those who died while "defending Spanish democracy" between January 1, 1968 and October 6, 1977.

In terms of symbolic reparations, the law declares all the tribunals that were created on political, ideological, or religious grounds during the Civil War and the dictatorship illegitimate. Additionally, it recognizes the right of the victims of such courts to obtain a "declaration of reparation and personal recognition," issued by the Ministry of Justice. This measure was highly contested, for many were expecting that the law would declare the sentences of the Francoist tribunals null and void. Another fundamental symbolic measure was the granting of Spanish nationality both to the members of the International Brigades and to the descendants of those who were forced into exile between July 18, 1936 and December 31, 1955. In 2011, the Senate approved a long-standing demand of the memory associations: that those who had disappeared during the Civil War and the dictatorship were to be included in the civil registry as deceased.

3. Mass graves

The location of mass graves and the identification of the remains of those who were killed during the war and its aftermath was another of the key issues regulated by the law. This was important not only because it had constituted one of the major demands of victim associations since 2000, but also because until today there has not been any official attempt to locate and identify the thousands of bodies that remain buried all over the national territory. While civil society associations had been particularly active in the location and exhumation of mass graves, this activity had been mostly carried in an ad hoc and private manner. Consequently, many families have not only had to provide funds but also surmount administrative and legal challenges to gain access to the places where the burials are located. The law tackled the issue along three lines: the commitment of the government to draft a protocol for the exhumation of the remains; the elaboration and publication of a national map of mass graves; and the establishment of a program to provide economic support for such activities. However, the Law still left the task of exhuming and identifying the remains in the hands of civil society, something victims' associations and human rights groups strongly criticized.

In December 2008, the government passed a law establishing an Office for the Victims of the Civil War and the Dictatorship that, among other tasks, was mandated to elaborate a protocol of scientific and interdisciplinary action for the exhumation of mass graves and the elaboration of an integrated map covering the national territory of the inhumation sites. A still-incomplete map of mass graves was made available online in May 2011 but hasn't been systematically updated since then. An exhumation protocol was approved only in September, after a four-year delay. The idleness of the central government contrasted, however, with the approach to this issue taken by several Autonomous Communities, especially Catalonia, Andalucia, Navarra, and the Basque Country.

While the law did not recognize state responsibly for the exhumation of Civil War mass graves, it did establish some provision for economic support. Starting in 2005, the Socialist government issued an annual call for applications to associations, foundations, universities, among others, for grants with the general aim of "promoting the recovery of the collective memory and the moral recognition of the victims of the Civil War." The grants served to finance a variety of projects including the compilation of censuses of the disappeared, exhumations, celebration of tributes, compilation of documents and oral testimonies, production of documentaries, celebration of exhibits and publications. This support was sharply reduced when the PP returned to power in 2012 and completely eliminated the following year. This explains why associations are now resorting to crowdfunding to go on with the exhumations.

4. Removal of symbols

The removal of symbols commemorating the Francoist repression, except where such symbols have artistic or religious relevance, was another measure contemplated in the law. Although the PSOE government undertook measures to remove a significant number of symbols, this provision has not been applied consistently across the country, and there has been a strong resistance in some municipalities to remove monuments and change the names of the streets. The leftist parties, ERC, IU, and ICV, have repeatedly raised this concern in the Parliament.

Among the symbols of the Francoist past, none matches the Valley of the Fallen where Franco is buried in significance. The complex is a basilica, a monastery, and a massive grave holding the remains of 33,847 victims of the Civil War. The LMH provided that the Valley of the Fallen "shall not be used to celebrate political rallies," while an additional disposition states that "the Management Foundation of the Valley of the Fallen will include in its mandate to honor and rehabilitate the memory of all those who died during the Civil War or as the result of the posterior political repression." On May of 2011, the Council of Ministers created an "Expert Commission for the Future of the Valley of Fallen" chaired by the Ministry for the Presidency. Five months later, the Commission submitted a report with several recommendations, all of which, except for one concerning the relocation of Franco's remains to a private cemetery, were agreed upon unanimously. More than four years after the submission of this report, however, not a single recommendation has been implemented. On the contrary, in May 2013 the PP government announced a project to restore the portal of the basilica where Franco was buried. In 2014, the PSOE presented a proposal in the Parliament to resuscitate the expert report on the Valley and promote the necessary actions to reform and provide the monument with new meaning but the PP used its absolute majority to defeat it claiming that the Valley is a peaceful place conceived to gather all those who died during the Civil War.

5. The archives

The final set of issues regulated by the LMH relates to the preservation of and access to private and public archives that contain information about the war. To date, three steps have been taken in this direction. In 2008, access to death certificates from the civil registry was regulated. The next year, the government passed a royal decree regulating the Military Judicial Archives and, finally in November 2011, a decree regulating the access to the State Archives. Before the general elections of November 2011, the Socialist Defence Minister promoted the declassification of around 10,000 documents from the Judicial Military Archives dating from 1936 to 1968; however, in May 2012, the PP announced the cancellation of the process alleging potential diplomatic conflicts. In any case, a crucial obstacle for obtaining information on Francoist repression is the Law on Official Secrets (*Ley sobre Secretos Oficiales*), which regulates the access to archives and official documents. This norm was passed by the dictatorship in 1968 and, with very few amendments made in 1978, remains in force. Finally, the law established the setting up of the Documentary Center of the Historical Memory and the General Archive of the Civil War, and declared such collections part of the national documentary and bibliographic heritage. Located in Salamanca, the Center hosts a notable collection of materials relating the war and the Francoist repression.

6. Judicial initiatives

Disappointed with the evolution of the process, in December 2006, five organizations of families of people who disappeared during the Civil War and under Francoism presented several claims at the National High Court (*Audiencia Nacional*). According to the proceedings issued by the Prosecuting Judge, Baltasar Garzón, on October 16, 2008, these claims denounced "alleged crimes of illegal detention under the framework of a systematic and preconceived plan to eliminate political opponents through multiple deaths, torture, exile, and forced disappearances from 1936, during the years of the Civil War and the postwar, that took place in different geographical spots of the Spanish territory." While the Prosecutor of the AN considered that the alleged crimes were covered by the Amnesty Law of 1977, Garzón declared himself competent to investigate 114,266 disappearances, stressing that the facts had never before been judicially investigated in Spain. With this move he was admitting the claims presented by twenty-two families of disappeared persons formally accusing 35 members of the Francoist leadership and authorizing the exhumation of nineteen mass graves.

This decision came as a big surprise to many, as the possibility of opening judicial proceedings against Francoism had never before been seriously considered. In addition to triggering an important reaction in Spanish public opinion, Garzón's action acquired another dimension when the ultra-right-oriented trade union, Manos Limpias, presented a complaint against Garzón for intentionally issuing an unjust judgment before the Supreme Court that lead to the opening of a proceeding against the judge. On April 24, a widespread demonstration supporting Garzón was organized in more than twenty cities. Significantly, these demonstrations turned into the first massive mobilization in homage to the victims of Francoism. The issue also acquired an international dimension when, two weeks later, the body governing the judiciary in Spain suspended Garzón. The story made the international media and several human rights organizations declared their public support for the judge. In Spain, memory associations and prominent figures of the legal profession strongly expressed their concern.

The trial against Garzón started on January 24, 2012. As some commentators emphasized, the proceedings made it possible for the families of victims of the Civil War to have their cases heard in a courthouse of Spain for the first time. A month later, the Court cleared Garzón of the charges of abuse of power while declaring that he had misinterpreted the law, thus ending any possibility of further investigation of the alleged crimes in Spain. Following this sentence, the Supreme Court ruled in favor of the competence of local courts to decide the mass grave issue. It also stated that while the families of those buried in the mass graves could request exhumations for identification purposes, the alleged crimes could not be considered crimes against humanity. As a consequence, from that moment on, the legal power to exhume mass graves would depend on the decisions of individual courts instead of following a national policy. The situation became even more adverse for the families of the victims when the European Court for Human Rights refused to hear the first claim regarding a Civil War disappearance ever brought before it on the grounds that it had been presented too late. A breach seems to have opened recently, however, when a local judge in Soria admitted, for the first time in Spain since the Garzón trial, a case for Francoist crimes.

The closure of Spanish (and European) judicial venues triggered a radical change in the strategy as victims associations looked overseas to Argentina for alternative jurisdictions to pursue justice. Things took then an unexpected turn in September 2013 when, following a procedure that was presented to the federal court in Buenos Aires in 2010, the judge in charge of the case, María Servini, decided to officially request the extradition of four members of the Francoist security forces, including two who are still alive, under charges of alleged torture. This case, which involved crimes allegedly committed in the 1970s, raised the hopes of victims groups and was a catalyst to greater coordination in their stance against impunity. After a long proceeding in which the PP again showed its clear opposition to the use of the courts to correct the abuses of power of Francoism, in April 2014, the National High Court denied the extradition of the two alleged perpetrators to Argentina, although it did invite the opening of a case in Spain. Even so, Judge Servini continued with the proceedings, traveling to Spain in May 2014 to gather testimony from four victims of Francoism. Five months later she requested the extradition of Twenty more former officials of the Franco regime, including Eight former ministers. The PP government once again rejected the extradition. A week later four experts from the UN, the special rapporteurs on Extrajudicial or Arbitrary Killings, Torture, and Promotion of Truth, Justice, and Reparations, together with the president of the Working Group on Enforced Disappearances, issued a joint statement stressing that the decision not to extradite implied denying the right of victims to truth and justice, and again requesting that the Spanish government either judge or extradite. Following this statement, a group of 28 senators belonging to all political parties except the PP presented a document in the Senate requesting the creation of a Commission to study and implement the recommendations included in both the Special Rapporteur Special Rapporteur on the promotion of truth, justice, reparation, and guarantees of nonrecurrence and the Working Group on Enforced Disappearances.

Finally, another important development in the judicial arena is the issue of the so-called stolen children. In one of the decisions Garzón issued in 2008, he drew attention to a "systematic plan" for the removal of children of Republican families, whose parents were considered "ideologically" inadequate to raise them, dead, in exile, detained, or disappeared. Once removed from their families, the children would come under state supervision and their names would be changed. According to Garzón, who estimated that there were around 30,000 such cases, these would not only constitute crimes against humanity not covered by the Amnesty Law of 1977, but, as he argued, most of the victims would still be alive. Accordingly, he requested the State Prosecutor to investigate the crimes, punish those responsible, and compensate the victims.

On November 5, 2010, three local courts referred the cases back to the AN, considering that the crimes fell under its jurisdiction, since they constituted crimes against humanity. Although the AN Prosecutor considered that the Court did not have the competence to investigate these crimes, the pressure exercised by the *Plataforma Grupos Afectados de Clínicas de toda España de la Causa de Niños Robados* (Platform of Hospital Groups from all over Spain Affected by the Case of the Stolen Children), which had gathered documentation of more than 300 cases of disappeared children, led him to request that the Ministry of Justice create an office to coordinate the demands of the affected persons. The case entered in a new phase when a second group, the *Asociación Nacional de Afectados por Adopciones Irregulares* (National Association of those Affected by Irregular Adoptions, ANADIR), presented a claim before the State Prosecutor, reporting around 261 cases of children allegedly stolen in private and public hospitals all over Spain between 1920 and 1990. They accused the professionals of these centers, many of which were administered by the Catholic Church, of deceiving the mothers by telling them that the children had been born dead, and then giving them illegally to adoptive parents.

The proceedings in this second case started in March 2011. By June there were 849 investigations open all over Spain. In April 2012, the government announced its intention to create a census of those affected by this particular situation. (Still in a design phase, the census will allow both parents and children looking for their biological relatives to cross reference information.) In October 2012, a judge established for the first time that the crime of stealing children is not subject to the statute of limitations. This decision was seconded by the State Prosecutor, who elaborated a policy on how to deal with these cases that was distributed to all public prosecutors. In September 2013, the association *Todos los Niños Robados son También Mis Niños* (All Stolen Children are also my Children) presented a judicial complaint joining the Buenos Aires lawsuit and the case was still open by the end of 2015.

7. Social initiatives

During the first twenty-five years of democracy, the politics of "national reconciliation" prevailed. In the political sphere this meant avoiding the thorniest aspects of the Civil War and the Francoist repression, while in the social sphere only very low profile initiatives took place. Throughout this period, Spain centered all its efforts in the economic modernization of the country and the stabilization of the new democratic system.

However, as time passes by and new generations enter in to political life, the repressed memories of the traumatic past have a tendency to reemerge. Indeed, in the past 17 years the violent legacy of the Civil War and the dictatorship has strongly erupted in the public sphere. Starting in 2000, when families of the victims began to organize themselves and managed to insert their demands in the political agenda of some of the leftist and nationalist parties, Spain has witnessed a gradual irruption of its most recent and tragic history. The "movimiento memorialista," a solid nation wide associative movement, although one which is also very fragmented and often strongly resisted, has emerged and reverberated in the public space in the form of films, books, research projects, and photography or history exhibits about the war and the dictatorship. There have also been public initiatives, particularly in regions such as Andalucia, the Basque Country, and Catalonia, which have further bolstered this movement.

The perseverance of the families of those who suffered the repression of Francoism, and especially their struggle to locate, exhume, identify, and rebury the remains of their loved ones, has played a fundamental role in moving this process forward. According to the most recent official figures, between 2000 and 2012, more than 300 mass graves were exhumed and more than 5,700 bodies found. Within the same process, and partly supported by the existence of public subsidies since 2005, there have also been an increasing number of initiatives to vindicate the memory of the victims through symbolic means in streets, squares, and cemeteries all over the country.

Parallel to this recovery of memory, the most recent developments in Spain have also clearly articulated a message of recognition that was absent before. However, and in spite of the important steps taken, the LMH contains very important gaps, above all the failure to include the possibility of annulling Francoist sentences or to institute a coordinated. It is thus not surprising that since 2008 some political groups have been presenting new—though unsuccessful—proposals before the Parliament seeking to advance the agenda of the memorial movement. Likewise, the fact that Garzón is the first person to have been tried in a matter related to Francoism is more than telling. Since 2012, victims' associations have been seeing how the combination of political change and severe economic crisis has interrupted, and even reversed, some of the steps that had already been taken. Among the first measures adopted by the PP government, for example, were the closing of the Office of Attention to Victims of Civil War and the Dictatorship and the elimination of the entire budget assigned to the LHM. Importantly, while there have been an increasing number of public statements acknowledging the human rights violations committed during the war and the dictatorship and/or the suffering of the victims, at the national level, the PP has not yet publicly condemned the Franco dictatorship in an explicit manner. In fact, in May 2013, the PP government was still the only party voting against a parliamentary initiative aiming at establishing July 18, the day on which the Civil War began, as the "day of the condemnation of Francoism."

The refusal of the Spanish state to satisfy some of the victims' demands is not only increasing the social pressure in favor of truth and justice but also facilitating the creation of new organizations such as the *Coordinadora contra la Impunidad del Franquismo*, which includes more than 30 associations; the *Plataforma por la Comisión de la Verdad sobre los Crímenes del Franquismo*, which includes more than 100 groups; and *Red Aqua*, which brings together all associations and individuals supporting the criminal process in Buenos Aires. Although the existence of collective platforms pursuing common goals constitutes a very important step in the memory movement, their survival is uncertain given its long history of fragmentation and internal confrontation.

The consensus of the transition in question

The political elites who oversaw Spain's transition to democracy considered that the priority was to stabilize the new regime in a country that, four decades after the end of the Civil War, was still traumatized by the memory of the conflict—vividly evoked in the mid-1970s by high levels of political violence. As a result, they decided that the politics of "national reconciliation" were the best means to achieve stability. At the same time, the way in which the transition to democracy took place in Spain, with the reformists of the Franco regime playing a leading role in its architecture and the military exerting important pressure, made punishing those responsible for the atrocities committed or the radical reforms of certain institutions unthinkable.

The need to overcome the traumatic memory of the Civil War and the Francoist repression, the desire to leave behind the historical spiral of revenge, the absence of a strong social demand for accountability, the lack of international pressure against impunity at that time, and, finally, the need to appease ETA terrorists and its supporters help explain the approval of an ample Amnesty Law in 1977. The importance of this law lies in the fact that all crimes by the parties in conflict (both during the Civil War and under the dictatorship) were forgiven, a gesture that was presented as the foundation for the reconciliation among Spaniards. Even today, the symbolic power of this gesture remains so strong that, contrary to the post-TJ developments that have taken place in many other countries, in Spain the prospects for the annulment of this law are extremely low. Many Spaniards still consider the Amnesty Law, together with the Constitution, the cornerstone of the Spanish democracy. The result is that a law that was initially proposed to release the few remaining political prisoners of the dictatorship, and to provide reparations to its victims, has ended up being impeding the judicial investigation of the truth and granting impunity to human rights perpetrators.

After two decades in which the young democracy was consolidating, and during which the only TJ policies adopted consisted of a fragmented and incomplete reparations scheme, this status quo slowly started to be questioned with the creation of a series of victims and families of the victims associations around 2000, which began to be supported by some of the leftist political parties. The high visibility obtained by the exhumations these organizations carried out made it impossible to go on ignoring Francoist terror and the deep wounds it had left in Spanish society. The images of the remains of victims piled up in common graves all over the country were received with a mixture of horror and surprise both in Spain and abroad. Nobody seemed to suspect that such a modern and prosperous European country, which had been internationally praised as an example for its democratization process, could, after more than 60 years, still hide so many thousands of skeletons spread across fields, caves, ravines, and wells.

All of this, together with the new political climate after the general elections of 2004, crystallized with the approval in 2007 of the first comprehensive LHM of Spanish democracy. Using more a memory than a truth or justice-based approach, the law contemplated a varied set of issues including some reparations policies, the removal of symbols of the authoritarian past, and the conservation of and access to archives. While it should be acknowledged that the LHM provided a strong impetus to the recovery of memory in Spain, its implementation has been problematic and important gaps and obstacles remain. The moderate position of the PSOE when in office has not been particularly helpful in giving impetus to this process. The political and media polarization around these issues helps to understand the apparent inhibition of a Spanish society cautious about dealing with the past, even if, according to surveys, it is mostly in favor with the provisions of the law. The defeat of the Socialists by the PP in 2011 led to the complete stalling of state action on the politics of memory. While many victims groups and human rights organizations continue to criticize the shortcomings of the law, the PP government has consistently refused to look back to the Civil War and, especially, the dictatorship, or to support the demands of the victims.

In the social realm there seem to be two contradictory impulses. On the one hand, the lack of political and judicial wills to attend the most pressing claims of the victims has contributed to fostering the creation of some unitary platforms within a movement that has traditionally been deeply divided. And, in some cases, it has also contributed to the radicalization of their demands. In fact, at the time the LHM was being debated in Parliament, most victims associations would have been satisfied with the annulment of Francoist trials, the development of a state-led exhumation policy, and the conversion of the Valley of the Fallen into a museum devoted to the victims of Francoist repression. Garzón himself, as he has often explained, did not seek to place the Francoist perpetrators in the dock, but to bring out the truth of the highly repressive nature of the regime. However, frustration has propelled victims associations to go beyond their initial demands: Some of the plaintiffs in the Buenos Aires proceedings seek criminal justice for torture committed by perpetrators who are still alive on victims who are alive as well.

On the other hand, the general weakness of the Spanish civil society, and of the memory movement in particular, has been an important obstacle for advancing in TJ policies. These negative effects have been multiplied by the lack of sensitivity among the majority of Spanish judges to the recent developments in international human rights law and to the principles of universal jurisdiction. Whereas human rights advocacy has proven to be a crucial determinant of human rights prosecutions in other countries, the late and scarce support provided by legal experts to the associations for the recovery of historical memory has been crucial for understanding its lack of visibility and strength in Spain, although this began to change with the creation of Rights International Spain in 2010. These groups' long struggle has been able to keep the process alive, although progress has been slow. The recent renewed and stronger pressure of the UN, which seems to have taken hold in all the political parties except the PP, seems to indicate that new developments will unfold in the future, particularly if the PP loses power.

Further reading

Aguilar, Paloma, *Memory and Amnesia: The Role of the Spanish Civil War in the Transition to Democracy*, New York: Berghahn Books, 2002.

Aguilar, Paloma, "Transitional or Post-Transitional Justice? Recent Developments in the Spanish Case," *South European Society & Politics*, 13, 4 (2008), pp. 417–33.

Aguilar, Paloma, and Clara Ramírez-Barat, "Amnesty and Reparations Without Truth or Justice in Spain," in Nico Wouters (ed.), *Transitional Justice and Memory in Europe (1945-2013)*, Cambridge: Intersentia, 2014.

Blakeley, Georgina, "Evaluating Spain's Reparation Law," *Democratization*, 20, 2 (2013), pp. 240–59.

Davis, Madeleine, "Is Spain Recovering its Memory? Breaking the Pacto del Olvido," *Human Rights Quarterly*, 27, 3 (2005), pp. 858–88.

Encarnación, Omar, "Reconciliation after Democratisation: Coping with the Past in Spain," *Political Science Quarterly*, 123, 3 (2008), pp. 435–59.

Encarnación Omar, *Democracy Without Justice in Spain: The Politics of Forgetting*, Philadelphia: University of Pennsylvania Press, 2014.

Escudero Rafael, "Road to Impunity: The Absence of Transitional Justice Programs in Spain," *Human Rights Quarterly*, 36, 1 (2014), pp. 123–46.

Gil Gil, Alicia, "Spain as an Example of Total Oblivion with Partial Rehabilitation," in Jessica Almqvist and Carlos Espósito (eds.), *The Role of Courts in Transitional Justice: Voices from Latin America and Spain*, New York: Routledge, 2011.

Golob, Stephanie, "Volver: The Return of/to Transitional Justice Politics in Spain," *Journal of Spanish Cultural Studies*, 9, 2 (2008), pp. 127–41.

Jerez-Farrán, Carlos, and Samuel Amago (eds.), *Unearthing Franco's Legacy: Mass Graves and the Recovery of Historical Memory*, Notre Dame, Indiana: University of Notre Dame, 2010.

Sánchez-Cuenca, Ignacio, and Paloma Aguilar, "Terrorist Violence and Popular Mobilization: The Case of the Spanish Transition to Democracy," *Politics & Society*, 37, 3 (2009), pp. 428–53.

Tamarit, Josep M., *Historical Memory and Criminal Justice in Spain*, Cambridge: Intersentia, 2013.

CHAPTER 23
SPAIN IN WORLD HISTORY
Scott Eastman

Spain's modern history, especially its trajectory during the long nineteenth century, extending from the Age of Revolution to the outbreak of the Great War, fits uneasily into an emerging paradigm of world history. Historian Patrick Manning has shown how an interconnected multipolar system characterizes a globalized history, essentially replacing an older model based upon civilizational nodes—virtually isolated and insular units that developed at a remove from one another. Whether seen in terms of economics or culture, a civilizational model emphasized regional differences rather than interplay and communication. In the last thirty years, world historians increasingly have shone light on the multiplicity of connections across continents and cultures.

Atlantic history, like world history, places larger trends and movements—transregional and transnational phenomena—ahead of local particularities. The state itself is not the unit of analysis, as diaspora, disease, and economics shape many of these narratives. Commodities, from sugar and silver to human beings, often seem to take center stage in such accounts. Christopher Columbus, sailing under the banner of a Spanish monarchy recently unified by Ferdinand and Isabel, first brought sugar to Hispaniola as early as 1493. Within two centuries, slavery and the slave trade, and its reciprocal relationship to sugar cultivation, in many ways underpinned the entire Atlantic system. By 1700, there were fewer than a million European settlers in the New World, but over two million enslaved Africans had been forced to labor in these growing European colonies. The experiences of slaves, sailors, and immigrants also represent an important part of the turn toward more inclusive and comprehensive histories. Coinciding with the rise of subaltern studies and postcolonialism, Atlantic history and world history decenter a story that traditionally has given more agency and value to the West than to the rest. In attempting to recover previously marginalized voices and historical actors, both individual and collective, Dipesh Chakrabarty insists that historians must rethink modernity and the idea of politics in order to broaden notions of a political sphere. He writes that Europe itself should be provincialized. Thus it is more important than ever to place smaller polities as well as peripheral nation-states into a truly globalized, world historical framework.

Many contemporary textbooks and monographs, however, continue to relegate modern Spanish history to a few terse lines, in spite of the fact that the Hispanic Enlightenment and early Spanish liberalism had a great impact on Europe and the Americas. The word *liberal* was first used to denominate a political faction, or party, in the context of the constitutional revolution that shook peninsular Spain and Spanish America in the early nineteenth century, and the term *guerrilla* warfare originally described the dispersed, irregular conflict in Spain from 1808 through 1813 (see Chapter 2). A different kind of cultural nationalism grew out of these struggles, incorporating religion into a new form of political identity. Spaniards, alongside so many others, took part in the great wave of European immigration that occurred between 1820 and 1930. While over 50 million men, women, and children crossed the Atlantic, over 4 million hailed from Spain, with many choosing Argentina and Cuba as their final destinations (see Chapter 19). For a plethora of reasons, nineteenth-century Spanish history merits a fundamental reconsideration in light of world history and its emphasis on connectivity.

The Spaniard Julián Juderías coined the term "leyenda negra," or Black Legend, in 1914 to describe the atavism and backwardness of his nation. Spain's turn-of-the-century public figures turned inward in order to explain the perceived decline and decadence of the state. Spanishness had become a fraught commodity, more closely associated with religious fanaticism and the horrors of sixteenth-century colonialism than with a great commercial empire spanning the globe. Additionally, Spain appeared isolated from major events in European history such as the revolutions of 1848 and insulated from ideological changes like the spread of communism. This sense of decline was compounded by the failure of the mid-century attempts at empire building under Leopoldo O'Donnell's Liberal Union (see Chapter 13). Twentieth-century Spain, shorn of the remnants of its American empire, did not participate in the Great War or in the Second World War. The country remained largely agricultural, with close to two-thirds of its labor force tied to production on the land. Spanish citrus and wine exports grew in the early 1900s, but industrialization lagged behind nations like France and Britain. Swiss and French companies helped to expand export-oriented agriculture, including olive oil. Had Spain become detached from the vanguard of successful, modernizing European nations? What part did it play in contributing to nineteenth-century global history? By exploring the ideas of prominent intellectuals, from Emilio Castelar to Joaquín Costa, as well as the ways in which the state represented itself to the outside world, we can see how Spanish perceptions and attitudes shifted decisively from a global orientation to a focus on internal dynamics and developments.

The definitive loss of most American territories by 1825 combined with the subsequent "disaster" of 1898 consigned Spain to permanent status as a lesser power. To outsiders, observed Juderías, Spain seemed to be defined by an older identity couched in sixteenth-century terms, lacking the progressivism exhibited by its more dynamic neighbors. Concurrently, many Spaniards turned away from what had been a decidedly imperial gaze to interrogate their interior, essential qualities that supposedly made up the indelible Spanish national character. Their views continue to resonate in history books today. This chapter will assess imperial, intellectual, political, and cultural history, but it will tell a different story and reach different conclusions. Spain will be portrayed as a typical nineteenth-century European state that saw its imperial ambitions in large part thwarted by rivals like Britain and the United States and suffered the vagaries of civil wars and ideological battles that played out across Europe and the Atlantic world. Spain also possessed a strong and influential liberal tradition and grew its economy slowly and steadily as it embraced industrialization, much like other developing countries and regions at the time. Inserting these narratives into the larger scope of world history serves as a corrective to earlier texts that tend to present British, French, and German histories as exemplary of the nineteenth-century European experience.

Between 1808 and 1813, Napoleon's troops occupied most of the Iberian Peninsula, incorporating the kingdoms of Spain and Portugal into a European polity that extended from the Grand Duchy of Warsaw in the east to Naples, the Confederation of the Rhine and Holland in the northwest. A modest group of officials and churchmen promulgated the French-inspired Constitution of Bayonne as the law of the land. Nonetheless, by 1812, an independent, modern, liberal Spanish state had been conceived that would stand as a beacon of freedom for other like-minded actors. In the course of the war with France, Spain underwent a profound political transformation that many saw as a harbinger of future political movements and mobilizations, beginning with the uprising in Madrid on May 2, 1808. Juntas, committees formed in times of crisis, governed in the name of the monarch and organized resistance against the French. The "general revolution" against Napoleon, predicted Álvaro Flórez Estrada in 1810, will "change the entire political system of Europe" and will therefore cement Spain's legacy as the most important nation on the continent. Soon, Spaniards elected deputies from almost all its territories, from the Philippines and the Caribbean to the peninsula, to serve in the newly consecrated Cortes. Spain's nascent political faction that had established a new government in the midst of brutal warfare and had written the Constitution of 1812 soon came to influence revolutionaries from Russia and Greece to Portugal, Brazil, and Mexico. Thus Flórez Estrada's words seemed prophetic from the vantage point of the early 1820s, during Spain's second attempt at constitutional governance, the Liberal Triennium of 1820–23. Karl Marx subsequently lauded Spanish representatives who had come together in Cádiz, the one city that remained outside the French orbit during the entirety of the War of Independence. He wrote:

> The circumstances under which this Congress met are without parallel in history. While no legislative body had ever before gathered its members from such various parts of the globe, or pretended to control such immense territories in Europe, America and Asia, such a diversity of races and such a complexity of interests—nearly the whole of Spain was occupied by the French. . . . From the remote angle of the *Isla Gaditana* they undertook to lay the foundation of a new Spain. . . . How are we to account for the curious phenomenon of the Constitution of 1812, afterward branded by the crowned heads of Europe, assembled at Verona, as the most incendiary invention of Jacobinism?

The resulting constitutional document, first published on March 19, 1812, was, according to Marx, truly "a genuine and original offspring of Spanish intellectual life, regenerating the ancient and national institutions, introducing the measures of reform loudly demanded by the most celebrated authors and statesmen of the eighteenth century." Many histories gloss over the fact that Spaniards from the peninsula to the Americas welcomed the inauguration of constitutional governance, promulgating the Constitution of 1812 in Spanish Florida, New Spain, Peru, and of course in Cádiz, along with many other Spanish territories. A deputy to the Cortes, the Conde de Toreno, while taking issue with many of its central planks, including the uniformity and inflexibility of a document written for European as well as American provinces, called it modern Spain's "first blueprint of liberty." It symbolized the beginning of a path toward modernity, with liberal provisions such as the inclusion of Spanish-American and indigenous men as full citizens with voting rights and the abolition of the seigniorial regime. By 1813, the hated Inquisition also had been dismantled. On the other hand, unlike the radical Condorcet, who had advocated on behalf of women, free blacks, and slaves during the French Revolution, few spoke out in favor of rights for women or men of African descent in Spain.

Progressives, known as *exaltados* in the lexicon of the early 1820s, looked to the Constitution of 1812 as a paragon of justice and a model for a reinvigorated liberal government after the absolutist interregnum of Ferdinand VII between 1814 and 1820. The revolutions of 1820, with notable sparks from Madrid to Naples, Piedmont, and Sicily, drew strength from the

Hispanic tradition of constitutionalism as an early iteration of internationalism sought to tear down the remnants of the Old Regime. The Russian poet Aleksandr Pushkin compared the revolutionary conflagrations of Spain, Naples, Greece, and Russia, as all had been ignited by revolt in the Pyrenees. Yet most of these proved to be short-lived affairs, with the Holy Alliance and a restored monarchy in France putting an end to radical politics in Spain and the Austrian borderlands. The Decembrists in Russia, echoing the rhetoric of Spanish liberals, likewise appear as a blip on the radar rather than a sign of things to come in the autocratic east.

At the same time, Spain's international influence clearly waned with the strife and turmoil in Spanish America that began with the enlightened priest Miguel Hidalgo's *Grito de Dolores* in 1810. A mere two years earlier, Spanish-Americans had been unanimous in declaring in favor of the monarch Ferdinand VII, held hostage in France. Uncertain over their status as a viceroyalty in French-occupied Spain as war dragged on, however, Americans began to air grievances both old and new, and autonomist sentiment coalesced in New Spain, New Granada, and the Río de la Plata. While the opening of the Cortes allowed peninsular and American Spaniards to build a new representative political system, factions in America already had moved away from the umbrella of the Spanish Monarchy. Venezuelans wrote their own constitution and declared independence in 1811. Stung by the refusal of peninsular deputies in the Cortes to grant natural rights and citizenship to men of African descent, many *pardos*, or free blacks and slaves in New Granada, supported insurgent movements against the Spanish. But by 1815, the civil wars that had begun in New Spain and in New Granada died down, and even Simón Bolívar, who would be renowned as the Liberator of South America, expressed concern over resurgent Spanish forces. Events in the Río de la Plata, today's Uruguay and part of Argentina, galvanized momentum against the restored government of Ferdinand VII and his discredited absolutist policies. Although an earlier movement in 1810 had surged in the name of the captive monarch, his nullification of the Constitution of Cádiz in 1814 had fractured loyalist sympathies in the New World, as many favored a liberal administration in the metropole. In 1816, a congress held in the city of Tucumán declared the United Provinces of the Río de la Plata independent from Ferdinand and cut ties with Spain. American identities, from Chile to Mexico, were consciously constructed to elide connections to the motherland and to resuscitate memories of despotic and arbitrary government. Bolívar compared Spain to an unnatural stepmother with whom all ties should be severed. Bolívar even solicited British help when it appeared that the Spanish had taken the upper hand. Despite this, later Latin American literature celebrated insurgent victories like that of José de San Martín in 1818 at Maipú, Chile by connecting them to indigenous resistance against conquistadores in the sixteenth century. Bolívar's triumphs, accordingly, avenged the Inca Atahualpa's destruction at the hands of the Pizarro brothers (although loyalists won most of the battles in Peru prior to 1824 and their final defeat at Ayacucho). Spain had lost its great power status at the Congress of Vienna in 1815, and this was confirmed when the regime of Ferdinand VII was not invited to participate in the 1818 Congress of Aix-la-Chapelle by the great powers, although the ongoing warfare in Spanish America and the status of its colonies were to be discussed. In a successive international conference held in Verona, a meeting of the Quadruple Alliance—composed of Austria, Britain, Prussia, and Russia—sanctioned the restoration French government to send troops, referred to as the 100,000 sons of St. Louis, to quash the remnants of Spanish liberalism and the revived Constitution of 1812. In an ironic turn of fortune, just twelve years later during the First Carlist War, close to twenty thousand Belgian, British, French, and Portuguese auxiliaries supported the Spanish government in their struggle against counterrevolutionaries largely based in the north who clamored in defense of throne and altar.

By 1829, with Ferdinand installed in power after the 1823 French invasion quickly put down the liberal regime, Spain had organized an ill-fated expedition in Cuba under Brigadier Isidro Barradas to reconquer independent Mexico. In hindsight, argued Prime Minister O'Donnell in 1860, the mission was poorly conceived and poorly executed, premised as it was on the belief that reunification would not be opposed by the majority of Mexicans. Such illusions capture the myopia of governing officials who ignored or brushed aside the rise of new national identities strongly grounded in an anti-imperialist ethos. Between 1827 and the early 1830s, for example, the Mexican government passed a series of expulsion orders to purge the remaining Spanish expatriate population. This sentiment continued to simmer, especially as Spain was slow to initiate diplomatic relations with its former colonial holdings—Mexican independence was recognized only in 1836 under the auspices of the Constitution of 1812. Falling back on the metaphor of the mother and child, deputies to the Spanish Cortes lamented that the Americans had reached the stage of education and maturity that allowed them to break with the motherland and establish their independence (which of course they had done in 1821). Peruvian relations were not opened until 1879. The expulsion of colonial representatives from the Cortes in 1837 exacerbated the tendency to look inward rather than embrace a pluralistic identity.

Spain's involvement with the institution of slavery and extensive economic ties to Cuba and Puerto Rico presented a conundrum for the liberal political class. On the one hand, Spain officially renounced the slave trade in a series of treaties between 1815 and 1822 with Britain. Yet merchants expanded the scope of their activities with the withdrawal of European competitors from commercial engagement in slavery, and many individuals and companies benefited tremendously through the 1860s. Catalan, Basque, and Cantabrian merchants established successful enterprises that had ties to the slave trade, and family members would go on to found major international businesses that continue to operate today like the Banco Bilbao Vizcaya Argentaria (BBVA). Spain actively took part in what some historians have referred to as the Atlantic world's "second slavery," a period that saw the number of slaves imported to Cuba surpass the total sold in all of Spanish America between 1521 and 1773. According to Christopher Schmidt-Nowara, over 766,000 slaves were sold in Cuba between 1791 and 1867, while approximately 700,000 were imported from the sixteenth through the late eighteenth centuries. Spanish Cuba was the global leader in sugar production by the 1820s and was able to increase output to 40 percent of the world's sugar by 1870 with the massive expansion of slave labor. Slavery and industrialization went hand in hand, and most mills were completely or partially mechanized by the 1860s. Railroads were built in Cuba before tracks were laid in Spain. These economic successes did not come without a price, as a loose alliance of Creoles, free people of color, slaves, and even British abolitionists, all opposed to the slave trade, rebelled in 1843. The Escalera conspiracy certainly provided some of the material for the 1969 film *Burn!* (directed by Gillo Pontecorvo and starring Marlon Brando), as Creoles had been encouraged to fight for political independence with the support of a British consul in Havana in order to secure the abolition of the slave trade and of slavery. The Spanish under Captain General O'Donnell, however, cruelly suppressed the uprisings and exiled, tortured, and killed leaders and participants alike. Spain did not bow to pressure from US presidents Polk and Pierce in 1848 and 1854, respectively, to sell the island (President

Adams had offered to buy Cuba as early as 1825). Instead, officials propped up the Cuban slave system while presiding over the abatement of Puerto Rican slavery in the 1840s until its official abolition in 1873.

Mid-century intellectuals like Emilio Castelar, who would later serve as President of Spain's First Republic in 1873, decried the activities of slave traders and worked toward abolition. Grounded in the new logic of positivism and Hegelian notions of historical progress, he published manifestos promising a democratic future as well as a possible union with the old empire, notably Mexico. Though no revolutions rocked the Iberian world in 1848, radical figures like Fernando Garrido and Nicolás María Rivero founded the Democratic party a year later to advocate for republican causes such as universal manhood suffrage. With politics opening up in Spain, Progressives came to power in 1854 and continued to push back against the more conservative 1845 constitution that had followed on the heels of civil war in the 1830s (see Chapter 3). This generation of men and women established economic organizations, arts groups, and scientific associations to achieve meaningful and lasting reforms for the benefit of the nation, including a Spanish Abolitionist Society in 1865. Castelar's career provides a glimpse into the complicated relationship between their liberal ideals, race, and imperialism in the second half of the nineteenth century. And just as the Cádiz Constitution of 1812 brought about significant changes within Spain and exerted an outsized influence across southern Europe and the Americas (it was even briefly revived in 1836 in both Spain and parts of Cuba), Castelar's ideas were influential as well as controversial in terms of empire and identity. While Spain's nineteenth-century imperial ambitions have not received much attention from historians and have been dismissed in textbooks, as they were stifled and did not lead to long-lasting occupations, the wars of O'Donnell's Liberal Union government were not insignificant. Designed to recapture a sense of national honor and dignity and to stimulate foreign trade and investment, Spain's expansionist plans from 1857 through 1863 must be understood as part of Europe's second wave of imperialism that crested by the end of the century with much of the world under European military, political, and cultural domination.

Spanish liberal imperialists focused on North Africa as the centerpiece of their strategy to bring back an age of imperial glory. Under the heading "Our Destiny in Africa," in the 1859 periodical *Chronicle of the War of Africa*, Castelar pondered questions of civilization and modernity through the prism of ongoing military engagements. Much like the British statesman Arthur Balfour denigrated contemporary Egypt as a land of former greatness that in more recent times had been dominated by a succession of absolute rulers, Castelar portrayed Africa as an impenetrable wall, closed to all progress, a land littered with the bodies of former conquerors. He preached that civilization would not remain enclosed in Europe and America; rather, the modern world inexorably extended outward in order to achieve universal rights and justice. He juxtaposed a people infused by Christian ideals and liberty against populations enslaved by their own ignorance in cities on the other side of the Mediterranean. Just as the Russians naturally looked to civilize the East, he wrote that Spain, at the westernmost point of Europe, had a unique mission to bring civilization to Africa.

In fact, the Spanish government had maneuvered to carry the mantle of progress from Vietnam to the Americas as well as Africa in a series of conflicts that would mark the high point of Spain's mid-century imperial ventures. The French and Spanish governments used the pretext of the murder of a Spanish Catholic missionary in 1857 to send an expeditionary force to Annam, part of today's Vietnam. Many believed French ministry propaganda that the soldiers would be welcomed as liberators. Alongside a larger French contingent, close to fifteen hundred men from the Army of the Philippines fought in Tourane (Da Nang) and Saigon in operations that ultimately led to a French occupation. Spain received little more than a share of the indemnity forced upon the defeated Vietnamese Emperor. An expedition was launched in 1858 to colonize the island of Fernando Póo and the Rio Muni region (Equatorial Guinea) in sub-Saharan Africa. More importantly, Spain invaded the northern reaches of Morocco in October 1859 because of continued unrest and skirmishes in and around their outpost at Ceuta, a city still held by Spain today. Local pirates and smugglers based around the other Spanish presidio of Melilla, close to the Algerian border, contributed to the instability of the region. In order to quell these disturbances and with the goal of expanding their territorial bases in northern Africa, the government sent in 45,000 troops and took the key strategic town of Tetuán in early February 1860. Despite long marches and a cholera outbreak that threatened to overwhelm the hospitals of Ceuta, the nationalist press pushed for additional conquests. Many argued that Tangier and Fez would be the next targets. Spaniards read news from the battlefronts on a daily basis, as a telegraph line now connected Iberia to Africa, and reports circulated that both Jews and Moors, the catchall term for North Africans, had received the Spanish troops as liberators. Spain hailed the general in charge of the campaign, Juan Prim, as a national hero (see Chapter 29).

The relative success of Spanish arms in Morocco, which was given the vainglorious moniker of the War of Africa, had a contagious effect on diplomats and politicians and contributed to a growing jingoism in the peninsula. Almost immediately after the taking of Tetuán, plans were being laid for another effort to seize Mexico and discussions were underway to annex the volatile Dominican Republic. But triumphalism was tempered by the fact that the Spanish government, in response to British pressure in particular, ended the war in Morocco before further conquests could be undertaken and agreed to settle for a temporary occupation of Tetuán and a large indemnity to be paid out by the Moroccan sultan. The Treaty of Wad-Ras, signed in 1860, also provided Spain with a future base of operations around an older, abandoned port used to send expeditions to the Canary Islands in the early sixteenth century. In the twentieth century, this enclave of Ifni would be disputed by Spain and Morocco prior to and during the Moroccan independence struggle.

In spite of the fact that the War of Africa produced little in the way of tangible results or conquered lands, Spanish diplomats and Cuban officials moved toward Dominican annexation by the end of 1860. The Dominican president in particular appealed to Spain to reclaim its territory due to ongoing hostilities with Haitian rebels allied with disenfranchised Dominicans on the disputed border between the two countries. The conflict was exacerbated by the fact that the Dominican Republic had been taken over by its neighbor for more than two decades between 1822 and 1844, and many held strong anti-Haitian sentiments. Furthermore, the emerging doctrine of scientific racism provided ideological ammunition to Spanish imperialists who denigrated Haitians and maintained the facile view that all Dominicans, regardless of race and class, wanted to return to the Spanish fold and receive military and economic aid. Consuls in Hispaniola perpetuated these views, and even convinced British and French diplomats that this was true. So by March 1861, Spanish and Dominican officials confidently proclaimed the merging of the Dominican Republic with the Spanish Monarchy, and Queen Isabel signaled her approval. Dominican cities drew up official documents of approval in a kind of referendum on annexation. Yet many marginalized men and women, along with liberals who had been conspiring against the authoritarian president, expressed reservations and an abortive uprising took place that spring. What began as isolated incidents snowballed into all-out rebellion in 1863 that some called a veritable race war. Brutal counterinsurgency tactics only served to alienate communities caught up in the warfare and radicalized the rebels.

The Spanish also used political and economic machinations to justify occupation of the Mexican city of Veracruz in December 1861. The British and French helped to lay siege to the port as a means to force the Mexican government to pay its outstanding debt obligations. Citizens of the three nations were owed millions of dollars, and foreign bondholders had not received payments from the Gadsden Purchase, Mexico's sale of land to the United States in 1853–54. General Prim, charged with overseeing the movement of troops from Cuba, appeared to be an ideal candidate for the job, especially as he was married to a Mexican heiress, Francisca Agüero González. Yet the French could not be held in check in Vietnam or in Mexico, and in both cases, the Spanish lost out due to the Machiavellian Napoleon III. Spain did not receive any territorial concessions in Vietnam after the Treaty of Saigon was signed, and the Spanish withdrew from Mexico in April 1862 as it was clear to all involved that the French were planning a large-scale invasion and were prepared to bring a foreign emperor to take the Mexican crown. By the summer of 1862, after soldiers were retired from Tetuán because Britain had helped Morocco to pay down its indemnity, Spain had lost much and gained little from its imperial wars.

Two years later, a scientific expedition that had sailed from Spain in 1862 to collect detailed geographical information and specimens of New World flora and fauna seized Peru's Chincha Islands. Just as Spanish forces had landed in Veracruz in order to force Mexico to pay its creditors, a Spanish squadron had taken the islands, known for guano deposits, in order to coerce Peru into paying its debt to Spain. Used as a fertilizer, guano had become one of the most important export commodities in Latin America. Because Spain had underestimated the strength of Peru's economic base and military, their vessels were unable to win a decisive naval battle at the mainland port of Callao in 1866.

To make matters more difficult for the embattled Spanish government, a revolution broke out in September 1868 that dovetailed with a major rebellion in the Caribbean a month later (see chapters 3, 29). Queen Isabel was forced into exile and a retinue of generals, led by Prim, and Progressive politicians, including Castelar, seized power. In Cuba, Creole planters in the eastern provinces of Puerto Príncipe and Santiago de Cuba, falling behind their better financed rivals in the west and faced with an increased tax burden, led the revolt against the Spanish. They spoke of equality and gradual emancipation, but did not clarify their exact goals in regard to the pressing issue of slavery. Although unsuccessful, the insurgents precipitated political and social movements that would bring about the abolition of slavery by 1886. Emancipation occurred in fits and starts over eighteen years, quite unlike what took place in the United States after the Civil War. The 1870 Moret Law freed children and slaves over the age of sixty. Practiced more in the breach than in the letter, the law nonetheless ushered in a formalized and gradual process toward emancipation in which slaves increasingly participated. In 1880, the Spanish Cortes pushed forward the issue by creating a system of *patronato* to soften the blow of abolition to come eight years later. Slaves took advantage of the legislation to fight legal battles over the intent and scope of the new laws. Enslaved litigants brought large numbers of cases to the juntas convened to preside over questions of self-purchase, the proper registration of slaves, and the orderly manumission of children and those over 60.

In 1870, Spain found itself relegated to the margins of great power diplomacy even though a dispute over the Spanish crown lay at the center of a simmering European conflict. Liberals in Madrid had been seeking a suitable royal to replace Isabel II. Officials made overtures to the Portuguese and the Italians as well as the Prussians, and in consultation with Napoleon III's France, Spain was on the verge of accepting the Hohenzollern candidate Prince Leopold. But because of the controversial publication of the Ems dispatch, in which Otto von Bismarck released an abridged text exposing a rift with France over the Spanish throne, the French initiated hostilities against the Prussians. Isolated from the brief but consequential war that led to German unification, the Spanish government subsequently invited Italian King Victor Emmanuel's second son, Amadeo, to take the throne in November 1870.

Spanish identity, in flux since the beginning of the century and disputed in political and intellectual circles, lacked a clear anchor and symbolic grounding during these years. In the 1870s, the country established a short-lived republic and sent Amadeo packing, again fought a Carlist war and faced down rebels in Cuba. Spaniards increasingly looked inward for inspiration and for ways to express their supposed distinct national traits and characteristics. One venue for such demonstrations was the world's fair, the first of which was held in London in 1851. Spanish artists and architects constructed an image of exoticism for visitors that vacillated between pavilions evoking Castilian imperial grandeur and those highlighting Andalusian folklore, bullfighting, and flamenco. The contribution to the 1867 exposition featured a stuffed bull penetrated by *banderillas* and a sword. Although Spain lagged behind in terms of literacy and manufacturing, Spanish educational exhibits won more awards than any other except the host nation in Philadelphia in 1876. The Spanish managed to win a gold medal in 1878 with their Mudejar architecture that for most visitors appeared to be a careful reproduction of the Alhambra. Interestingly, the church and expressions of Catholic identity did not feature prominently in Spanish exhibitions at the time.

Joaquín Costa, who came from a peasant background in Huesca, Aragon, was selected to work at the 1867 Universal Exposition in Paris as an apprentice laborer, and his nine-month stay in France made a great impression on him. He criticized Spain's self-representation as a nation of bandits and bullfighters that hearkened to a history of vice and scandal. What then made Spaniards distinct in an age of nationalism, imperialism, and Darwinism? Many intellectuals, like Azorín and Miguel de Unamuno, projected the ideal of a spiritual, mystical Spanish consciousness that they traced back to the Reconquest. Unamuno insisted that eternal Spain lived on in the present day through art, literature, and culture. At the same time, he claimed that the decadence of the Habsburgs accounted for the strength of the Inquisition and the vitality of the Counter-Reformation; for Azorín, Habsburg decadence and a neglect of agriculture had led to the chronic problems of the *latifundia* that had weakened economic development. Such understandings owed a great deal to the works of Rafael Altamira and Francisco Giner de los Ríos, who had articulated notions of a romanticized "spirit of the people" that contrasted with the decadent economic policies of the seventeenth-century Habsburg dynasty. Subsequent writers such as Salvador de Madariaga built upon such tropes in arguing that the psychological center of the archetypal Spaniard—the soul—determined that their lives would be animated by passion and emotion. Of course, this could be interpreted as a justification for Spain's underdevelopment and malaise, but it also reified an essential and timeless view of Spanish identity.

A nascent sense of regionalism came into conflict with Spanish nationalism as well (see Chapter 10), as evidenced by debates at the world's fair held in Barcelona in 1888. While schools could not by law teach Catalan or languages other than Castilian organizers pushed a localist agenda that seemed to showcase Barcelona's industrial capacity and to uphold the values of Catalan identity. To counter this, the Spanish government brought in myriad examples of regional culture and folklore from all parts of Spain as a celebration of the "patria chica" throughout the peninsula. These divisions within Spain foreshadowed the political polarization evident by the twentieth century. Valentí Almirall, one of the leaders of the Catalan movement, opined that most of Spain was not ready for modern progress. Influenced by French positivism, he bemoaned Spanish decadence. Tracing it to the history of the Reconquest and to the importance of religious and military values, he maintained that Castilians had become indifferent and ignorant, especially with the establishment of the Inquisition in the late fifteenth century. And thus Spain passed from "barbarism to decadence, without passing through the light of civilization." His contemporary, Pompeyo Gener, wrote that "Spain is paralyzed by a necrosis produced by the blood of inferior races" and by the fact that the Inquisition and the Crown expunged free-thinkers from Spain, leaving as residue "fanatics, serviles, and imbeciles." Gener, with a proto-fascist sensibility, pleaded for a "scientific dictatorship" under a "Darwinist Cromwell" to stimulate science and industry. This would help the "diverse Spanish races" but would not come at the cost of republican liberty, which would be upheld. His thought, similar in some ways to the scientific thinking of Costa, shared little with early Spanish liberalism and exposed deep rifts across Spain's regional landscape.

There were a number of key differences between the thinking of the *doceañistas*, the liberals infused by the spirit of 1812, and those influenced by the German philosophical tradition of Krausism by the end of the century. Karl Christian Friedrich Krause had been a somewhat obscure German philosopher who sparked a great deal of interest in Spain for advocating a secular form of education, especially in the sciences, while also adhering to a moral and spiritual ideal not unlike that of Georg Wilhelm Friedrich Hegel or Leopold von Ranke. Costa, impacted by Krausism, believed that the state should be subordinated to the interests of society. He was not an idealist and focused on concrete issues such as common law and the ways older legal systems could be adopted and even maintained in the modern age. Finally, he departed from Hegelianism, and the idea of an ineluctable form of progress taking shape, and rather believed that the state could play a role in actively advancing change and progress. He argued that in many parts of Spain liberty did not exist as such, because a large part of the population remained enslaved to nature. In others, they were tied to the land and agricultural production. Spain had become decadent over three centuries, he sighed, and the Spanish people faced a kind of spiritual poverty. To liberate them, then, the state had to embark on a series of initiatives, from constructing dams and canals to irrigation projects. By 1883, Costa had taken an active interest in empire building as another means of economic development and helped to sponsor a national congress on colonialism—the Spanish Congress of Colonial and Mercantile Geography.

Costa justified his positions with nationalist and economic arguments based on historical precedent. In contrast to those who interpreted Spain's early nineteenth-century history as a success story, a morality tale, or even a war for independence, *fin-de-siècle* intellectuals like Costa were less sanguine about their forebears. He presented Spain's struggle to maintain its once-great empire in economic terms. The proponents of protectionism in Cádiz had closed off American merchants and had denied them the benefits of free trade, he thundered. Unlike Bismarck, who could base his policies on decades of economic integration vis-à-vis the German Customs Union, Bolívar had no similar basis upon which to construct a Pan-American state. Spanish and even Spanish-American politicians had failed to make political unification the culmination of economic union. Costa attempted to balance his particularly negative views of early liberalism and the waning of Spanish power with a more positive assessment of Spain's late-nineteenth-century fortunes. He saluted men like Argentine leader Nicolás Avellaneda for praising modern Spain's influence on Latin America and for having stimulated the development of science, scholarship, and character. Writing in his 1884 work *Juridical and Political Studies*, Costa enthusiastically cited Colombian journalists lauding Spain, for instance, and he pushed for renewed commercial contacts with American ports to reinvigorate industry from Catalonia to Valencia and Andalusia.

Hispanic solidarity was strengthened in the face of consistent aggression by other powers. In 1885, Germany made clear its pretensions to annex the Caroline Islands and Palau, which it claimed Spain had abandoned. This caused an anti-German outburst in Spain. The Pacific islands were linked to its historic interests in the Philippines and thus to sixteenth-century conquests. Although Spain kept the territories after the matter was submitted to Pope Leo XIII for arbitration, it was obvious that the United States represented the gravest threat to Latin American sovereignty and to Spanish possessions in the Caribbean and in the Pacific. Anti-Americanism offered a road toward reconciliation between Spaniards and Spanish Americans. The advent of Hispanism, epitomized by the establishment of the Ibero-American Union in 1885, coincided with the idea of a racial bond between what many referred to as members of the Latin race (some suggest it reached its apogee with the 1929 Ibero-American Exposition in Seville). The publication of the Madrid-based journal *La Raza Latina* between the years 1874 and 1887, with correspondents reporting from Mexico to Uruguay, testifies to the importance of the concept. In contradistinction to the emergent ideal of racial purity in Germany, Spanish anthropologists and scientists said that the Spaniard originated from a racial alloy, a blending of the different peoples who had mixed in the Iberian Peninsula. This fusion resulted in a superior people endowed with strength and moral rectitude—qualities visible from Spanish America to the Mediterranean islands of Sicily and Corsica that had been part of the Habsburg realms. In line with their colleagues in Britain and France, anthropologists established the first anthropological society in Spain in 1865 followed quickly by the founding of an archaeological museum and an ethnographic institute in Madrid that featured Spanish colonial art and artifacts.

The twenty-fifth anniversary of the landing of Christopher Columbus in the Bahamas on October 12, 1492 sparked renewed interest in Spanish America and Spain's historical legacy in the New World. Even Columbus' body had been at the center of recent controversies between Spain and the Dominican Republic after the Santo Domingo cathedral announced the discovery of his remains in 1877. During the commemorations, sponsored in large part by the Ibero-American Union and its influential intellectual and political membership, debates hinged on ideologies both past and present. Conservatives tended to point to the religious aspects of the period and the glory of the former empire, as liberals focused on anticlericalism and secular inquiry that had brought Spaniards and Americans together in the nineteenth century and would continue to do so in the future. Delegates from Latin America, Spain, and Portugal attended congresses in Madrid and throughout the peninsula as a counterpoint to the Chicago World's Fair and the celebration of Columbian heritage in the United States. They passed resolutions advocating women's education and spoke out on social issues, but they also consciously constructed a sense of *hispanismo* in contrast to what they viewed as a materialistic and corrupt Anglo-American identity. Conversely, the Filipino writer José Rizal grounded notions of national difference in earlier, preconquest cultures and spoke of a burgeoning sense of remoteness from Spanish identity. This sentiment crested during debates over the planning of the 1887 Philippines Exposition in Madrid, described by some as a representation of primitive Filipino savagery. Of course, these exhibits simultaneously justified the ideal of the civilizing mission. Criticisms of the exoticism on display—complete with native villagers presented for gawking European visitors—gave rise to a sense of fraternity among many colonial intellectuals. Concurrently, nineteenth-century Puerto Rican and Cuban scholars looked back to indigenous *boricuanos* and *siboneyes* (Tainos) as the founders of their respective nations. This served as a direct riposte to conservative Spanish academics like Marcelino Menéndez y Pelayo, who plainly stated that islands like Puerto Rico and the Philippines had no history.

Cuban nationalist José Martí responded to those who would disparage the Americas by repeating the mantra of the Black Legend—that decadence had become an inherent aspect of being Spanish. Although he had studied in Spain, he lost faith in peninsular republicans who had reinstated colonial deputies to the Cortes in 1878 after the Pact of Zanjón ended the Ten Years' War in Cuba but did not provide an avenue toward freedom and independence. To make matters worse, in the early 1890s, Cuba did not enjoy the same privilege of universal manhood suffrage, granted in Spain in 1890. A proposed plan of autonomy for Cuba fell flat when the government became involved in Melilla, one of Spain's north African enclaves, in 1893. With twenty thousand troops deployed, the prime minister sidelined Cuban affairs and ended debate over Antillean issues in the Cortes. One of the first rebel flags to fly in Cuba read "Long live colonial autonomy!" Soon, however, leaders, many of whom had served in the Ten Years' War, embraced calls for outright independence.

Close to 200,000 Spanish troops saw action in the warfare between 1895 and 1898, fighting against the tens of thousands soldiers of the Cuban Liberation Army. By 1898, the Cubans had the active support of US forces, including the famous American volunteers led by Theodore Roosevelt. Diseases such as yellow fever also took a terrible toll. In addition to the tens of thousands of soldiers who perished, close to 170,000 Cuban civilians died, many in "reconcentration" efforts to move rural populations into protected cities. Known as the "butcher," the general behind the idea of forced relocation, Valeriano Weyler, embarked on what can only be called total war. Scorched-earth policies and atrocities were committed on all sides, devastating the island's economy. In the Philippines, secret societies, millenarian agitation, and nationalists inspired by the martyrdom of Rizal undermined Spanish legitimacy between 1896 and 1897. The yellow press in the United States jumped on the bandwagon as well, recycling the idea of the Black Legend that dated back to the sixteenth-century Bishop Bartolomé de Las Casas. In 1895, the *New York Times* ran an editorial reminding its readers of Spanish cruelties that dated back to the War of Jenkins' Ear in 1739 and to the conquest of the Americas. Untold crimes were committed and millions of lives were lost, the writer noted, citing the claims of the eighteenth-century historian William Robertson as well as Las Casas. Of course, Spanish national character remained imbued with the qualities of a persecuting race. In return, Spanish and Latin American newspapers caricatured the Yankees as pigs and derided their foreign policy and expansionist designs. The United States declared war in February and April 1898 and quickly defeated the Spanish in Manila and in Santiago, Cuba, respectively. By the Treaty of Paris of December 1898, Spain sold the Philippines for $20 million; Cuba, Puerto Rico, and Guam had been ceded to the United States. Two weeks later, they sold off their other Pacific islands to Germany. The United States had essentially replaced Spain as the dominant colonial power in the Pacific and the Caribbean with military actions that seemed to anticipate the Roosevelt corollary to the Monroe Doctrine.

While US diplomats smugly called the Cuban conflict a "splendid little war," Spanish intellectuals considered the events of 1898 a great disaster that demanded soul-searching, introspection, and ultimately regeneration. Declarations of sympathy came from Latin Americans like Rúben Darío, who spoke of fraternal bonds between the Hispanic *raza*. Many scholars now insist that the period should be interpreted as an ideological crisis that had far-reaching repercussions in terms of national identity and the trajectory of liberal politics. But the loss of the last of Spain's major colonial possessions did not precipitate a significant financial upheaval nor did a political crisis that threatened the continuity of the state ensue. Within the intellectual realm, a multiplication and fragmentation of discourses occurred due to the crisis of positivism, as the Generation of '98 grappled with the rise of the working classes, democratization, popular protest, and the strengthening of Catalanism and Basque nationalism. Troop deployments to the colonial theatre in Morocco in 1909, after the discovery of rich deposits of iron and lead in the north in 1906, incited rioting and anticlerical violence rather than a populist rhetoric of mobilization. War in the Rif lasted seventeen long years and exacted a major financial toll on the state. Thus in the aftermath of the Spanish-American War, only the initial conquest itself remained as a potential unifying signifier of collective identity in Spain. Terminology was inverted so that the "discovery" of America came to symbolize a rediscovery of an interior Spanish identity, consecrated as the *Día de la Raza*, or Day of the Race, October 12, an official holiday by 1918.

In both urban and rural areas by the twentieth century, competing ideologies and political polarization were indicative of the globalized conflicts that plagued Europe from the Great War through the Depression era and the Cold War, and Spain's Civil War was in many ways a pan-European struggle. One of the only nonbelligerents in both of the world wars, Spain may have moved toward isolationism and autochthonous development, but it could not inoculate its citizens from the struggle between fascism and authoritarianism on one side and liberalism, republicanism, socialism, and communism on the other. By the 1980s, however, a largely bloodless transition to democracy—a watershed in Spanish and European history—presented a model for many Latin American states in the process of moving away from military rule. While Spain's position in the world has moved far afield from imperial hegemon, an enduring Spanish legacy, from its Catholic roots and linguistic heritage to its political culture, continues to be felt around the globe today.

Further reading

Earle, Rebecca, *The Return of the Native: Indians and Myth-Making in Spanish America, 1810–1930*, Durham, NC: Duke University Press, 2007.

Eastman, Scott, and Natalia Sobrevilla Perea (eds.), *The Rise of Constitutional Government in the Iberian Atlantic World: The Impact of the Cádiz Constitution of 1812*, Tuscaloosa: University of Alabama Press, 2015.

Inman Fox, E., *La invención de España*, Madrid: Cátedra, 1998.

Pozo Andrés, María del Mar del, "The Bull and the Book: Images of Spain and Spanish Education in the World Fairs of the Nineteenth Century, 1851-1900," in Martin Lawn (ed.), *Modelling the Future: Exhibitions and the Materiality of Education*, Oxford: Symposium, 2009.

Schmidt-Nowara, Christopher, *Empire and Antislavery: Spain, Cuba, and Puerto Rico, 1833-1874*, Pittsburgh: University of Pittsburgh Press, 1999.

SECTION THREE
INDIVIDUALS

CHAPTER 24
FERNANDO VII

Emilio La Parra

Translated by Kevin Chrisman

On May 30, 1789 King Carlos IV summoned the Cortes to swear in his successor, Prince Fernando as Prince of Asturias. The oath of the heir of the thrown, a symbol of the continuation of the dynasty, was one of the most traditional and important rites in European monarchies. It was particularly important in Spain where, unlike in other kingdoms, there was no ceremony of coronation or consecration of the king. Spanish kings were sworn in, not crowned. The sumptuous and solemn ceremony which took place on September 23, 1789 in the church of San Jerónimo de Madrid was accompanied by other equally colorful celebrations which lasted several days with the enthusiastic participation of the full court, government authorities, the population of Madrid, and many foreigners who arrived for the occasion. In the fall of 1789, with the revolution already underway in France, it seemed that the monarchy and the traditional in Spain were enjoying a moment of glory. Four decades later, however, in 1833, the solemnity of the oath-taking of Fernando VII's successor, Princess Isabel, was sullied by the absence of a substantial part of the royal family and important figures, such as the Archbishop of Toledo and the absence of the unanimous acclaim of the people for the Princess of Asturias as in the past. By the end of his reign, the Old Regime model inherited by Fernando VII had ceased to exist.

Born on October 14, 1784, Prince Fernando suffered from health problems throughout his childhood. Subjected to a monastic life, deprived of entertainment, and sidelined from public life, he was reduced to an insignificant role in the court. His teachers, most of whom were clerics, were not men of highest merit of the Kingdom, and although some demonstrated the capacity to perform their tasks, the education the prince received was far from excellent. But he was not ignorant, nor did he despise the world of culture. Continually concerned about building his library, he acquired a sufficient knowledge of French to translate texts from that language. His curiosity to learn about the economic state of the Kingdom in person was reflected in his travel diaries. Following the tradition of his father, he was interested in the plastic arts, and the creation of the Prado Museum was due to him. However, the image conveyed by his contemporaries was that of a common man lacking in grandeur, given to familiar relationships with servants, fond of crude language, and more concerned about popular amusements than scientific and artistic innovation. Addicted to nights out in search of wanton love affairs, he was also imbued with a religious piety verging on the superstitious. People who dealt with him have presented him as weak-willed, easily influenced by his close relatives, and—as his mother and Napoleon said of him—"hypocritical, extremely distrustful, timid and cowardly, and incapable—according to Lord Holland—of feeling affection for others, including his parents, who corresponded in kind." Withdrawn to the point of apathy when facing difficulties, if the circumstances were favorable he was able to impose himself on others and dominate them, showing just how despotic and cruel he was, and how willing to do anything to satisfy his egotism.

Ferdinand's marriage in October 1802 with María Antonia de Nápoles signified a radical change in his life. Under the influence of his wife he became interested in politics, but since he was forbidden this activity, he did everything in secret, by intrigue. Assisted by a group of aristocrats and clerics which we can call the "faction" or the "Fernando party," Fernando and his wife had as their principal objective to end the disorder and eliminate the abuses and vices produced—they claimed—by the despotic government of Manuel de Godoy, an upstart without merit who had inexplicably risen to a lofty position. However, their real motive was that they feared that Godoy would obstruct Fernando's access to the throne. The Fernando party also sought to end Godoy's reformist policies, increasing the weight of the aristocracy in the government and safeguarding the ecclesiastical immunity that was threatened by regalist policies.

Given his close relationship with the monarchs—he was widely rumored to be the Queen's lover—and the source of his power, any action against Godoy impacted the kings and, therefore, was a risk factor for the Spanish monarchy, which was in a critical situation at the start of the nineteenth century. Spain was going through serious economic difficulties that caused widespread discontent, while also being subjected to strong pressure from Napoleon— since 1796 Spain and France were formal allies—that greatly conditioned its foreign policy and fully committed it to war against England.

Far from reforming the monarchy, the activities of the Fernando party aggravated its problems. Their offensive against Godoy began in the field of public opinion, through a propaganda campaign inspired by the proceedings that took place during the French Revolution, that was founded on the dichotomy between Good and Evil, embodied respectively by Fernando, the virtuous and innocent Prince, and Godoy. But the darts that they threw against him hit the sovereigns, especially the Queen. One particular project financed by Fernando himself stands out in this regard: the elaboration of several dozen illustrations that painted Godoy mercilessly in an indecent tone, although in reality the Queen, who was presented as the one responsible for elevating *el Choricero* (the "thief") and, therefore, ultimately to blame for all the misfortunes of the Kingdom, bore the brunt of the attack. Furthermore, her guilt was not blamed on error or political contingency, but on her sexual depravity; it was, therefore, a product of her will. The central theme of the satire left no room for doubt: Godoy had climbed to the top because it gave the Queen *ajipedobes*, an obscene neologism that was to be read from right to left (*Sebo de pija*). This vulgarity leaves no doubt about how far Prince Fernando was prepared to go to satisfy his ambitions. (It is also evidence of how sexuality could be used as a powerful weapon against publicly prominent women. Isabel II would also be the target of such attacks.)

In their campaign to do away with Godoy (and with the interference of the Queen in the government), Fernando's supporters devised a plan to denounce his crimes to Carlos IV and obtain, at the same time, the support of Napoleon. To achieve the latter they requested the hand of a lady from the family of the French Emperor for Fernando, who had been a widower since 1806. Alerted by several reports, on October 27, 1807, the date of the signing of the Treaty of Fontainebleau with Napoleon, the King ordered that the rooms of the Prince of Asturias be searched and part of the conspiracy was discovered. Fernando was arrested and legal proceedings known as the Trial of El Escorial were opened to determine the facts. Fernando confessed to everything, but only fragments of what had occurred became public, through two real decrees published in the official Gazette of Madrid. In the first, the King mentioned, without relating the details, an operation to dethrone him and alluded to the involvement of his son. In the second, Carlos IV forgave the Prince and ordered the trial of the rest of those implicated in the conspiracy to continue. The royal decree included two letters from Fernando addressed to his father and mother in which he admitted to a "serious crime" and begged their forgiveness.

Unaware of what happened, public opinion judged it unlikely that the Prince of Asturias participated in an operation to overthrow the King and interpreted these events as a maneuver by Godoy to denigrate the "innocent Prince," victim of the ambition of a despot and the depravity of the Queen. Thus, the failure of the conspiracy, at first glance a victory for Godoy, was turned into a success for Fernando, who was clearly victorious in the battle for public opinion. In addition, Fernando thought he had obtained the support of Napoleon, for after Carlos IV denounced the participation of the French ambassador in the plot, the Emperor replied angrily: "From today on, I take the Prince of Asturias under my protection."

After the events of El Escorial, *los fernandinos* (pro-Fernando) were in an excellent position to try a new assault against Godoy. The opportunity was provided by the attempt to move the court to the south of the Peninsula as a precaution against: any unexpected action by the French troops, who since October 1807 were entering Spain, officially to attack Portugal as part of the provisions in the Treaty of Fontainebleau. Fernando and his supporters forcefully refused to make the trip. On March 17, the population of Aranjuez, where the royal family was in residence along with Godoy, joined by people from the surrounding villages brought in deliberately, attacked Godoy's residence and took him prisoner. To silence the voices that called for Godoy's head for treason, on March 19th, Carlos IV abdicated in favor of his son. *Los fernandinos* described the event, known as the Mutiny of Aranjuez, as a spontaneous action by the people, heroically willing to clean up the monarchy. (Liberals later adhered to the main lines of this interpretation.) In reality, the mutiny was organized by the individuals of the court and members of the nobility closest to Fernando, with the considerable involvement of the French ambassador.

Fernando VII commenced his reign dominated by two obsessions: to do away with Godoy and to guarantee the backing of Napoleon. He found no problems with the first, as Godoy was definitively removed from politics, but he failed with the second as Napoleon did not recognize the new King of Spain. Fernando subordinated everything to getting Napoleon's recognition and, as a result, paid little attention to governing beyond stopping Godoy's planned reforms and satisfying the aspirations of the aristocracy and the clergy, while obediently accommodating the will of the Emperor. As a result, French troops consolidated their control over the northern half of the country and, without the consent of the new King, moved into in Madrid. When the Emperor announced he was going to Spain to reaffirm the alliance, Fernando VII left the capital on April 10th to meet him. The trip ended in Bayona, where Napoleon was waiting, already thinking about replacing the Bourbon dynasty with his own.

Napoleon managed the transfer of the Spanish Crown with relative ease. On May 6th, Fernando relinquished the Crown to his father, Carlos, who had also come to the city, and he, in turn, relinquished it to Napoleon two days later. One dynasty had replaced another. Without giving Fernando the title of "Majesty," Napoleon designated the castle-palace of Valençay as the residence of Fernando, his brother Carlos, and his uncle Don Antonio. "The Spanish Princes," as they were called by the French Imperial authorities, passed the War of Independence there until their departure on March 13, 1814.

Submission to Napoleon, accompanied by the cowardice and the mistrust of others associated with his character, marked Fernando's conduct during his stay in Valençay. He complied without resistance with the orders he received; he repeatedly refused to consider the plans of escape which were put to him; he wrote to Napoleon congratulating him for his victories in Spain and to his brother Joseph for assuming the Spanish throne while doing nothing to contact the Spaniards who fought in his name. In his memoirs, French Foreign Minister Talleyrand wrote that "the only thing one can say about the Spanish Princes" during the five years they spent in Valençay, "is that they lived."

In late 1813 there was an unexpected turn. Faced with the relentless hounding by the international coalition, Napoleon urgently needed to end the war in Spain to move the troops fighting there to other fronts. He negotiated a treaty with Fernando VII which was signed in Valençay on December 11th of that year. For the first time, he recognized him as King and promised he would return to Spain with "the same authority that his father had." With the prospect of ruling as an absolute monarch, Fernando accepted the treaty even though the Cortes did not ratify it, and despite the categorical rejection by England, Spain's main ally in the war. Following Napoleon's advice, he embarked on a trip to Spain. His arrival in Gerona on March 24, 1814 was received with enormous enthusiasm by the population. The return of the "innocent Prince" symbolized Spain's victory over Napoleon. Thus, Fernando returned greatly strengthened in the public's perception. He was the "legitimate" king, facing the "intruder" José Bonaparte and the "tyrant" Napoleon.

The crisis of the traditional Spanish monarchy, to which Fernando had greatly contributed while he was Prince of Asturias, had been resolved in his absence by the Cortes of Cádiz, which had transformed Spain into a constitutional monarchy (see Chapter 2). But Fernando and his entourage did not accept this solution and they interpreted that the general desire of the Spaniards was to see the king enjoy full sovereignty, without the limitations established by the Constitution of 1812. The promise received from Napoleon at Valençay and the demonstrated antipathy of Wellington, who was the supreme commander of the Spanish-British allied troops, toward the work of the Cortes, paved the way to repealing the Constitution, declaring the decisions of Cortes of Cádiz void and restoring the absolute monarchy. Fernando VII announced this in Valencia in a manifesto dated May 4, 1814, the prelude to a coup d'état perpetrated and prepared in accordance with the usual procedures (intrigues, secret negotiations, and an intense propaganda campaign).

Fernando never accepted a representative political system, whatever its form, nor did he comply with the Constitution. However, in 1820, after the Riego rebellion, he was forced to swear allegiance to the Constitution of 1812, although he immediately encouraged all types of operations against it, including the formation of armed bands. During the nearly four years the constitutional regime remained in place (from January 1820 to September 1823), he considered himself a prisoner of the liberals and deprived of his royal prerogatives. Spain was, he told other European monarchs whose help he requested to change the regime, dominated by "anarchists" and "republicans" who hated the King and threatened his life and that of his family. This sense of personal insecurity, mixed with a visceral hatred for the liberals and constitutionalism, characterized his reign.

In 1823, Fernando VII overthrew the constitutional regime for the second time. As in 1814, he counted on the support of an important part of the Spanish population, especially the clergy, but he needed external help to realize his goals. In 1814, he benefited from the initial impulse from Napoleon. He also had the help of Wellington, although in his case more from omission than from action. (The British hoped for the establishment of a monarchy close to the English model, but despite being informed about the preparations for a coup against constitutionalism, they did nothing to prevent it.) Armed with a mandate from the European powers who met at the Congress of Verona, the French intervened in Spain in 1823, sending the so-called Hundred Thousand Sons of San Luis to put down the revolution. On both occasions, the Spanish absolutists were unable to overcome the constitutionalists by themselves, and if the final results were ultimately unfavorable for the latter, the former did not enjoy a complete victory, even though they did everything in their power to restore the *ancien régime* (Old Regime) in its entirety. That was made clear in symbols and rituals and in the rhetoric of numerous official measures in the two stages of the absolute reign of Fernando VII (1814–19 and 1823–33) and in the social measures. But as Miguel Artola has noted, the resulting political system did not respond completely to the monarchic model of the *ancien régime*. Instead, it produced a shift in the center of power which became concentrated in the hands of the King and a small number of ministers and advisors directly under him. The old Councils were distorted; although the work of Cortes of Cádiz was repealed, the ruling class did not recover their jurisdictional rights that had been abolished in 1811; and for all the talk about the "alliance between the Throne and Altar," regalist policies subordinating the Church to the Crown continued.

As in other European monarchies in the post-Napoleonic era, the restoration in Spain did not mean then, a return to what had existed before the French Revolution, but the birth of a new political era. But unlike what happened in other places, where a constitutional order very favorable for the Crown was established, in Spain every trace of the representative system was eliminated and everything was based on the will of the king who exercised his power more freely than his predecessors and did not tolerate anything that could impede it, even when it came to counterrevolutionary demands. A paradigmatic example of this is the Inquisition, a symbol of the *ancien régime* that was abolished in 1808 by Napoleon and in 1813 by Cortes of Cádiz. Fernando VII restored it in 1814 because he considered it necessary in order to persecute the liberals. When the constitutional government of 1820 removed it again, the King did not restore it in 1823, despite many requests that he do so, especially from the clergy. By this time, the King had other means of control and repression, among them the police which, unlike the Inquisition, a mixed ecclesiastical and civil tribunal, depended entirely on the monarchy. International pressure against the hated tribunal also weighed heavily on the royal decision.

In short, the political system created by Fernando VII was characterized by the unfettered exercise of royal power, marked by a counterrevolutionary spirit and the systematic practice of harsh political repression. There was no compromise with liberalism, nor will to make peace. Fernando VII tried to erase the root ideas and the work of the revolutionaries—"remove them from the midst of time," he said in his Manifesto of May 4, 1814. Liberals faced prison or even death, and those who could went into exile (see Chapter 26). (England and France were the most welcoming destinations, although some also went to the newly independent republics in South America.) Before, in 1813, supporters of King José had done the same thing. Political exile and the many failed attempts of the liberal refugees to rally the Spanish population against absolutism became one of the most significant features of the reign of Fernando VII. Others, no less important, were the loss of most of the American colonies—another sphere in which

Fernando's only answer was the use of force—and the notable decline of Spain's international position.

Despite the harshness of the repression, the purge of the administration, and the consolidation of the privileges of the clergy, voices were soon raised against the King. Most were clergymen demanding more firmness against liberalism and the establishment of an absolutely theocratic system. Cornered by the liberal opposition and right-wing royalists, and facing a grave economic and social crisis, the King cleared the way for a reform project to modernize his administration. Some of the measures were significant [the creation of the Council of Ministers and the Ministry of *Fomento* (Development), a new mining law, and the Code of Commerce], which were products of circumstances, aimed to guarantee the survival of Fernando's regime, but there was no attempt to bring about political change, as the king never relinquished his absolute power (See chapter 2).

These reforms neither pleased the liberals, nor satisfied the ultraroyalists. Taking advantage of the discontent of farmers and artisans, in 1827 the latter organized a movement in Catalonia that threatened to spread to other parts of the country. This rebellion of the *Agraviados* or *Malcontents* (Discontented), as it is known, abounded in criticism of the government and even of the King himself, who was accused as being incapable of defeating the enemies of religion and the Throne. After trying repression and getting meager results, Fernando VII decided to visit Catalonia personally. The trip, which was extended across the north of Spain, was a rousing success. On his return to Madrid in August 1828, he had recovered much of his lost popularity and the most moderate royalists forged the illusion that channels for political participation would be opened and systematic repression ended. Royal policies did not change a bit, however.

One of the biggest problems for Fernando VII, the one which became the biggest of them all toward the end of his life, was that of his succession. His first three wives: María Antonia of Naples (1802–06), Isabel of Braganza (1816–18), and María Amalia Josefa of Saxony (1819–29), left him no heirs. (The second wife had had a daughter who died when she was not even two months old.) His fourth wife, his cousin María Cristina de Borbón, who he married in 1829 amid great popular enthusiasm, had two daughters: Isabel and Luisa Fernanda, but no son. In March 1830, months before the birth of the first child, who would later reign as Isabel II, Fernando VII issued a document called the Pragmatic Sanction. This abolished the Salic law, which the Bourbon dynasty had brought to Spain in 1713, and restored the Castilian inheritance law, which allowed a woman to inherit the throne if she had the best claim without being passed over for men with weaker ones. The King justified his decision by mentioning that it had been decided in the Cortes in 1789 that had sworn him Prince of Asturias, although the decision was never made public. The ultraroyalists were categorically against this, and declared themselves firm supporters of the King's brother, Carlos María Isidro, whose reactionary position was well known. Moderates and liberals supported it. They believed that with the death of the King, which given the state of his health would come sooner rather than later, María Cristina would govern as Regent with no other option than to consolidate the throne of her daughter than allowing political change and opening the way for the return to constitutional government. The measures taken by María Cristina, when due to the King's illness in 1832, she assumed control of the government: the reopening of the universities and a decree of amnesty that, although very restrictive, permitted the return of a considerable number of liberal exiles, confirmed them in this belief.

After 1830, Spanish politics took place in an environment marked by agitation, provoked by the division between those who were called *carlistas*, defenders of Carlos María Isidro's right to the Throne, and the *isabelinos* or *cristinos*, supporters of the future Isabel II. The fracture was evident in the royal family and in the court, giving rise to a number of bizarre events, such as the abolition and enactment for the second time of the Pragmatic Sanction, changes in government, and surprising negotiations to combine the rights of Isabel with Prince Carlos. Together with the news about the formation of Carlist circles and the discovery of weapons in churches and convents, there emerged different kinds of rumors, one about the formation of a Carlist regency which was preparing uprisings in different parts of the country, others about the maneuvers of suspicious individuals (liberals) carrying out political innovations destined to restrict the rights of the throne, as a notice distributed to the top military commanders at the beginning of 1833 claimed.

Aside from the question of the succession, the liberals protected by the environment created in Europe by the revolutionary movements of 1830, persevered in their attempt to reestablish the constitutional system in Spain. All of them, however, failed and most of those who were involved were sentenced to death. The most famous were the cases of Mariana Pineda and General Torrijos, both of whom, along with Rafael de Riego, who had been executed following Fernando's restoration in 1823, were made into symbols in the struggle for freedom, being later called "martyrs for freedom" by the liberals.

After suffering from serious health problems for several months, Fernando VII died on September 29, 1833. His widow, María Cristina, assumed the role of regent during the minority of her three-year-old daughter Isabel II, but Don Carlos firmly declared his right to rule. This confrontation, which was about much more than who would succeed to the throne, led to a civil war that would last more than seven years.

Further reading

Cevallos, Pedro, An Exposure of the arts and machinations which led to the usurpation of the Crown of Spain, and of the means pursued by Bonaparte to carry his views into effect, [S.l.], London: Stockdale: 1808.

Esdaile, Charles J., *The Peninsular War: a new history*, London: Allen Lane, 2002.

Fehrenbach, Charles W., "Moderados and Exaltados: the Liberal Opposition to Ferdinand VII, 1814-1823," *The Hispanic American Review*, 50, 1 (1970), pp. 52–69.

Fontana, Josep, *De en medio del tiempo. La segunda restauración española, 1823-1834*, Barcelona: Crítica, 2006.

Izuierdo Hernández, Manuel, *Antecedentes y comienzos del reinado de Fernando VII*, Madrid: Editora Nacional, 1963.

Jakóbczyk-Adamczyk, Patrycja M., *Allies or Enemies. Political relations between Spain and Great Britain during the reign of Ferdinand VII (1808-1833)*, Frankfurt am Main: Peter Lang Edition, 2015.

Kolli, Baron Charles L., *Memoirs of the Baron de Kolli, relative to his secret mission in 1810 for liberating Ferdinand VII., King of Spain, .. from captivity at Valençay ..*, London: Treuttel and Würtz, 1823.

CHAPTER 25
FRANCISCO ARANGO Y PARREÑO
Vicent Sanz Rozalén

Francisco Arango y Parreño is one of the people who are essential to understanding the process that transformed Spain's colony of Cuba into one of the most prominent slaveholding territories in the nineteenth-century capitalist world. While most of his political activity took place before 1808, his legacy turned him into the organic intellectual of the slaveholding sugar planters for decades afterwards.

From the moment of his death and for the rest of the century, he remained in Cuban memory. The poet and journalist Ramón de Palma wrote a hagiographic sketch in 1838. In 1865, the centenary of his birth, the Sociedad de Amigos del País de La Habana, an institution he had helped found and which he ran, commissioned a homage from two of his descendants, and in 1883 another descendant wrote an article in which he placed him among the most illustrious Cubans, describing him as "a practical advocate of progress." In a very different time, one of his goals was to minimize the role Arango y Parreño had played in stimulating the island's slave economy.

Francisco Arango y Parreño was born into a well-placed Cuban creole family. His grandfather, Pedro Arango Monroy, was a military officer, merchant, and shipowner from Asturias who arrived in Havana in 1680. Eight years later he was Contador Mayor del Real Tribunal de Cuentas, an important official in the financial bureaucracy, and from then on the Arango family would remain part of the economic, social, and political elite of the island. His father, Miguel Ciriaco Arango Meireles, was a colonel in the militia and held a number of key positions in the government of Havana, including that of mayor. In the 1760s he acquired a sugar mill in the region of Regla.

In November 1751, Miguel Ciriaco Arango Meireles married Juliana Margarita Parreño y Espinosa and Francisco was born fourteen years later. After studying humanities at the elite Jesuit Real y Conciliar Colegio de San Carlos y San Ambrosio in 1781 he entered the Law School of Havana's Real y Pontificia Universidad de San Gerónimo and graduated five years later. His keen mind soon brought him the Chair of Royal Law at the University. Early in 1787 his family sent the newly minted lawyer to Santo Domingo to represent them in a case brought by the heirs of the Marqués de la Real Proclamación in which they claimed the return of a position in the Havana city's government which his son, who had died in 1773, had transferred to Francisco's uncle, Manuel Felipe de Arango. The Court decided in favor of the Arangos but the decision was appealed to the Council of the Indies in Madrid.

Arango was granted permission to travel to Spain to continue to represent his family's interests. He was 22 and it was his first trip to the Peninsula. He enrolled in the Real Academia de Jurisprudencia de Santa Bárbara so that he would be qualified to practice law in Spain. In the imperial capital he had the benefit of advice and assistance from the Count of Buenavista, a second cousin, and the Count of the Santa Cruz de Mopox. He also began to build a web of contacts in the Court.

In June 1788 the Havana city's government named Arango its agent in Madrid, a position previously held by the Count of Buenavista. He also received detailed instructions about what he was expected to achieve in his interactions with the imperial authorities. He was now the principal representative in Spain of the slaveholding sugar aristocracy. That same year he would also receive the title of lawyer from the Councils of Castile and of the Indies, the two most important bodies in the Imperial government. He now had the qualifications to act in his family's behalf in the case against the Marqués de la Real Proclamación and, appearing before the Council of the Indies in 1789, he won it.

Arango would soon have an opportunity to act before the decision-making centers of the Court. The contract held by the Liverpool-based British Company Baker and Dawson to provide slaves for Spanish America was coming up for renewal, a question of immense importance for Cuban sugar planters and mill owners. Arango, who had an ongoing correspondence with Felipe Alwood, the representative of the British firm in Cuba, followed the instructions he received from Havana. There were plenty of complaints about low quality and high price of the slaves, but, afraid that they might be left without any supply at all, the Cuban sugar elites supported the renewal of the contract, although they did raise the possibility of individuals being permitted to engage in the slave trade to counter a possible shortage.

On February 6, 1789, Arango submitted his report on the contract to Antonio Valdés, Secretary of the Navy, who had been charged with bringing the matter to the Junta de Estado. The report was characterized by the marked influence of "reformed mercantilism," the idea that allowing free trade within the Empire would produce both a bigger market for Spanish products and lower prices on items coming from the colonies. Stimulating the economy of the colonies should, it said, be "the secure foundation" of the power of the State, and this would be achieved by promoting "absolute freedom" of commerce and the opening up of the slave trade. A royal decree of February 28, 1789 left the contracts with foreign merchant houses intact although, with the goal of increasing the export of colonial products, it also authorized subjects of the Spanish monarchy to engage in the slave trade. This was Arango's first action defending Cuban sugar interests, but his role in achieving a positive result was much smaller than he claimed, or than many scholars would later claim. In the end, all he did was to follow instructions and take advantage of the circumstances.

At this time Arango attempted to take advantage of the reorganization of the bureaucracy to get a position in the colonial administration. He failed, even though he had the support of the powerful Minister the Count of Floridablanca, but the attempt left him with valuable experience of the ins and outs of the workings of the administration, developing a good relationship with Diego de Gardoqui, the influential Secretary of the Council of State who had been Spain's first ambassador to the United States, and developing his skills at building the networks which would help him achieve his goals.

The slave revolt which shook the French colony of Saint Domingue in August 1791 provided Arango with another opportunity to promote his ideas about the practical political economy of colonialism and slavery. The first reports about the revolt reached Cuba on August 25 and were sent from there to Spain, arriving in Madrid on November 18. That same day, Arango received a letter from the Havana city's government explaining the fears that these events were causing in Cuba. The situation was particularly problematic because the Council of State was due to meet in three days to come to a decision on the renovation of the slave trade contracts. If fears of a slave revolt spread they might endanger the outcome.

It took Arango only one day to write his essay *Representación hecha a SM con motivo de la sublevación de esclavos en los dominios franceses de la isla de Santo Domingo* (representation to His Majesty on the occasion of the slave rebellion in the French colony on the island of Santo Domingo). Here Arango set out his thoughts on the causes of the rebellion and its implications for the Spanish monarchy, and for the island of Cuba in particular. One had to look at the "French misfortune" through a "political lens," he wrote. The event was frightening, but it also offered an opportunity: Saint Domingue was the largest and most profitable producer of sugar in the world and if its production disappeared it would leave a hole in the Atlantic and global economies which Cuba, as a colony, should not hesitate to fill. In Arango's view the French only had themselves to blame: their way of administering their colony and treating the slaves there had provoked the rebellion.

As Rafael Marquese points out, the Saint Domingue slave revolt forced Arango to develop a theory of the historical experience of Spanish slaveholding which could dispel fears of a possible uprising in the Spanish colony. It was crucial to influence the discussion which was going to take place in the Council of State and convince the decision makers that the radically different character of the institution of Iberian slavery meant that what was happening in the French colony could never happen in Spanish colonies. Both "social practice" and the "legal framework" of Spanish Law protected slaves from the abusive behavior of their owners; this was a benevolent perception of slavery in the Iberian world which contrasted with the violence which characterized slave societies in French territories. Arango's project emphasized, as Ada Ferrer has noted, that by adopting the appropriate measures Cuba could become the new Saint Domingue without turning into a new Haiti, that is without the danger of slave revolts. The role of the state was to provide vassals with the means for enriching themselves which would, in turn, enrich the state. Increasing the material prosperity of Cuba, turning it into a model colony, would be to the benefit of the metropolis. But none of this could be achieved, Arango emphasized, unless the freedom to engage in the slave trade announced in the Decree of February 1789 were extended and the Cuban slave system strengthened.

In his conclusions, Arango offered to set out his project in greater detail. This would be the starting point for his celebrated and influential *Discurso sobre la agricultura de La Habana y medios de fomentarla* (discourse on the agriculture of Havana and how to stimulate it) which Arango gave to Eugenio Llaguno, the Secretary of the Supreme Council of State on January 24, 1792. Arango even had the nerve to send an original copy directly to King Carlos IV.

The *Discourse* offered a historical survey of the reasons why Cuba had yielded such limited returns to Spain and set out the policies which needed to be implemented in order to develop the island's wealth. Arango's ideas about slavery had a fully Atlantic dimension: French, British, and Portuguese colonies became the points of reference for avoiding mistakes and adopting effective policies. His sole goal was to promote the interests of the Havana sugar elite by turning the island into the greatest sugar emporium in the Atlantic world. Rather than Adam Smith's *The Wealth of Nations* (1776) with its "invisible hand" of the market, Arango's inspiration came from the practices of the plantations and the sugar mills and adaptation to the principles of colonial mercantilism. Sugar and slavery were the watchwords which would guarantee the successful working of the Colonial Pact: the profitability of the sugar plantations and mills worked by slaves would underpin the loyalty of the colonists to the Spanish Crown.

Arango's ideas were put forward to the Council at its meeting on February 20, 1792 in a proposal from Gardoquí and almost all of them would be accepted: promoting the technological development of sugar processing, reducing taxes, and increasing the freedom to trade in slaves. The Council also approved the creation of a new institution, the Committee for the Protection of Agriculture, which Arango had designed with himself in mind, and gave its permission for him to undertake a trip to study the functioning of the economic systems, the organization of production and commerce, colonial administration, and the use of slave labor in various parts of Europe and the Atlantic world.

In 1793 Arango was named Honorary Judge of the High Court of Santo Domingo and Appeals Judge in the Real Consulado de Comercio of Havana, the official body which controlled all trade. And once the Finance office gave the go ahead on September 22, he made plans for his journey to take up his new job on the other side of the Atlantic and undertake his study mission. He left Aranjuez in March 1794, traveled through La Mancha and Andalucia to reach the port of Cádiz where he boarded ship with the Count of Casa Montalvo. After stops in Portugal and England he headed across the Atlantic, toward Barbados and Jamaica. The journey came to an eventful end early in 1795 when Arango's ship sank off the southern coast of Cuba. He survived and arrived in Havana with valuable knowledge about the most appropriate and valuable varieties of sugar cane, the best types of soil for cultivating it, and the application of steam power to processing the juice.

From this moment on he would act with unceasing energy to create the structures that would allow the sugar elite to realize their ambitions—and to allow his own fortune to grow. In Havana he would encourage the activities of the La Real Sociedad Patriótica de Amigos del País (Royal Patriotic Society of the Friends of the Country), an institution devoted to promoting economic development of which he was to serve as president in 1797 and 1798, and its publication, the *Papel Periódico*. He would serve as Perpetual Trustee of the Real Consulado and would create the Committee for the Protection of Agriculture. He would also develop a close relationship with Luis de las Casas y Aragorri, Governor and Captain General of the island after 1790, who made him his private advisor, and with José Pablo Valiente y Bravo, the Intendant of Finance. He and Valiente y Bravo also became partners in La Ninfa, a technically and commercially innovative sugar mill where 350 slaves worked. There were suspicions that they had bought it with money obtained through fraud related to special import licenses for flour from the United States. Arango would remain involved in this business in 1796 with Intendente Valiente, the Count of Santa Cruz de Mopox, and even Manuel Godoy, the Spanish King's prime minister.

Throughout the last years of the eighteenth century, Arango would never stop writing reports on all the measures the government took which could affect the interests of the Cuban planters. His already close relationship with the colonial authorities became even closer when a new Captain General, the Marquis de Someruelos, arrived on the island in 1799. By that time, Arango's personal estate was valued the impressive amount of 475,000 *pesos*.

In April 1803 he was part of a delegation which Someruelos sent to Sainte Domingue to negotiate the return of a loan the Spanish Crown had made to the French authorities to explore the possibility of a commercial agreement that would end the contraband trade among slaves from the French island to Cuba and try to recover the money seized by Toussaint L'Ouverture, the leader of the slave revolt. The delegation also had a secret mission: to assess the possibility of slavery being restored to the French colony after the likely victory of Napoleon's troops over the rebels and how this might affect Cuba. This led Arango to incorporate into his plans a strategic alliance with France, although this disappeared after the resistance to the Napoleonic invasion of Spain which began in May 1808 (see Chapter 2).

On September 1, 1803 Arango inherited the position of Regidor Alférez Real in the municipal government of Havana. He also renewed his acquaintance with the great scientist Alexander von Humboldt, whom he had met during the German's previous visit to the island in 1800. The two would become close correspondents from then on. In October 1804, the newly appointed Intendent of Finance and Director of the Royal Factory of Havana, Rafael Gómez Roubaud, commissioned Arango to prepare a report on ways of developing the tobacco industry on the island. Arango's proposals to end the state monopoly (*estanco*), plus Gómez Roubaud's suspicions that Arango had embezzled funds, provoked an intense dispute between the two men which lasted more than a decade. For a few months at the beginning of 1805 he would hold the office of Superintendent of Tobacco. That same year he applied to be accepted into the Order of Charles III but would be rejected until 1818.

The events of 1808 brought Arango to the center stage once again. The creation of Juntas in the Western Colonies worried the sugar planters greatly. On the theory that the best defense is a good offence, Arango and the planter elite decided to forestall a similar development on the island by creating a Junta Suprema de Gobierno (Supreme Government Committee), which would assume control of the key institutions and prevent developments which could threaten the planters' hegemony and the slave system. On July 26, 1808, the group issued a manifesto addressed to the Suprema Junta Central in Spain which immediately provoked intense controversy on the island. Groups opposed to Arango and his cronies took advantage of the situation to accuse them of provoking sedition even though this was the furthest thing from Arango's mind. Freedom from Spanish rule was not only unnecessary, it was also highly dangerous. Arango was not a liberal, and he was certainly not an advocate of independence, and the manifesto, which he wrote, stated unambiguously that "we are Spaniards." He remained what he had always been, an "enlightened patriot" who promoted ever stronger ties between the colony and the metropolis in the interests of both. In the end, the captain general rejected the idea of creating a *junta*.

In 1809 Arango resigned from his positions in the Real Consulado and the municipal government, although he would be named Honorary Judge of the Audiencia (High Court) of Mexico by the Regency which was governing Spain. From 1811 one of his principal concern, would be the question of slavery. When motions to study the possible abolition of slavery were presented in the Cortes of Cádiz, slave owners on the island were alarmed. Andrés de Jáuregui, the Cuban representative in the Cortes, and Arango's business agent in Spain, opposed them immediately. The Havana City Council, the Real Consulado, and the Real Sociedad Patriótica designated Arango as their spokesman and charged him with preparing a document arguing in favor of maintaining slavery. This document was presented to the Cortes on July 20, 1811. It argued that the Cortes did not have the legitimacy to make any decisions on the matter unless the slave owners' interests were represented. Once again, Arango took an Atlantic perspective and added new elements, pointing to developments in the United States and Great Britain. He rejected outright the idea that slavery could be questioned from a moral point of view and argued that the only relevant question was the economic one. In the end, the abolitionist proposals went nowhere.

As Arango's direct participation in the parliamentary debates became more important, in January 1813 he was elected as one of Cuba's deputies to the Cortes. His brief experience as a deputy ended when Ferdinand VII abolished the Cortes and the Constitution in May 1814.

The defeat of Napoleon and the consequent strengthening of British power created a new situation in the Atlantic as well as in Europe. Arango took advantage of the circumstances in

Spanish America to manage the question of Cuban loyalty effectively. Cuban sugar production generated considerable income for the Crown, he argued; it had to be protected and developed further. This required that slavery continue and be protected as this was the only way of ensuring social stability on the island. At the same time, the industry needed the government to take measures to reduce Spanish interference in Cuba's economic relations with the rest of the world. Achieving these objectives would be his main goal as a member of the Council of the Indies, the body which advised the King on all matters pertaining to the American colonies, which he joined in 1815. Arango was now working at the highest levels of the Spanish imperial administration.

In 1816, at 51 years of age, Arango finally married. His wife, Rita Quesada Vial, was a daughter of the third Count Donadío de Casasola. They had four children who were born between 1819 and 1823. In 1817 he was appointed to the Joint Committee to oversee the working of the treaty with Great Britain on the abolition of the slave trade. The Committee agreed that the trade would end in 1821 in return for compensation of 400,000 pounds from Great Britain. Internal and external pressures which made it harder and more expensive to sustain the slave-based economy had forced a new strategy: draw out the process of abolition and prolong the existence of the trade as long as possible.

Arango returned to Cuba in 1818. Just a year before the state tobacco monopoly had been abolished and, to the relief of the planters, who had been working Crown-owned land, the private ownership of the land where tobacco was grown would shortly be recognized. Arango took charge of the business' interests of his friend and partner, Intendent Valiente, and returned to the Real Consulado as its Prior. The return of constitutional government in 1820 (see Chapter 2) gave groups opposed to Arango and his network, posing as liberals, a new opportunity to criticize him.

The end of the Liberal Triennium and the restoration of absolutist government in 1823 saw Arango reappointed to the Council of the Indies. He was also appointed to the Junta Real para la Pacificación de las Américas (Royal Committee for the Pacification of the Americas). The following year he was named Intendant of the Army and Superintendent of Finance for Cuba and was decorated with the Great Cross of the Order of Isabel the Catholic. Even so, his public and political activities became less significant as he devoted his energies above all to developing curricula for the island's schools.

The new national and international circumstances, including the increasing influence of abolitionists in Great Britain, led Arango to rethink the bases of the defense of slavery. In May 1832 he wrote his *Representación al Rey sobre la extinción del tráfico de negros y medios de mejorar la suerte de los esclavos coloniales* (representation to the King regarding the extinction of the slave trade and ways to improve the lot of slaves in the colonies). Here he proposed that the slave trade be abolished under the supervision of the slave owners themselves and be replaced by another form of forced labor similar to medieval serfdom which would ensure that the planters had all the workers they needed. The importance of this work lies in the new perspective on slavery Arango adopted in the new context and the effects this would have on the slave economy. He ignored any moral or ethical questions about slavery; for him it was purely a question of economics and labor relations. As the world got more complicated, it was essential to find new legal mechanisms that made it possible for the sugar barons to continue to enjoy a workforce which was both cheap and completely under their control.

In 1834 Arango was appointed to the chamber of Próceres (Senate) under the new Estatuto Real (see Chapter 3), but his health prevented him from traveling to Madrid to be sworn in. At the same time, he was granted the noble title of Marquis de la Gratitud. He died in Havana in 1837 at the age of 73.

Francisco Arango y Parreño represented the power of the Havana-based slave-owning oligarchy in the power structure of the Spanish empire at the end of the Old Regime and the transition to the new liberal order of the nineteenth century. His written works established the foundations for a new structure of slavery and the plantation system in the capitalist societies of the Atlantic world. He would be one of the foremost champions of what has been called the "second slavery," which integrated slave labor into the process of accumulation and reproduction of the economic relations of capitalism. Historian Allan Kuethe's pithy summary of Arango's life and legacy is an apt one: "He could have been another Bolívar, but he died a royal bureaucrat."

Further reading

Corwin, Arthur F., *Spain and the Abolition of Slavery in Cuba, 1817-1886*, Austin: University of Texas Press, 1967.

Ferrer, Ada, *Freedom's Mirror: Cuba and Haiti in the Age of Revolution*, New York: Cambridge University Press, 2014.

Grafenstein, Johanna von, "The Atlantic World at the Time of the Haitian Revolution: The Point of View of Francisco de Arango y Parreño," in Renate Pieper and Peer Schmidt (eds.), *Latin America and the Atlantic World (1500-1850). Essays in honor of Horst Pietschmann*, Köln: Bölhau Verlag, 2015, pp. 351–66.

Marquese, Rafael, Tâmis Parron and Márcia Berbel, *Slavery and Politics. Brazil and Cuba, 1790-1850*, Albuquerque: University of New Mexico Press, 2016. (First edition, Portuguese, 2010).

Schmidt-Nowara, Christopher and Josep M. Fradera (eds.), *Slavery and Anti-slavery in Spain's Atlantic Empire*, New York and Oxford: Berghahn Books, 2013.

Tomich, Dale, "The Wealth of Empire: Francisco Arango y Parreño. Political Economy, and the Second Slavery in Cuba," *Comparative Studies in Society and History*, 45, 1 (2003), pp. 4–28.

Zeuske, Michael, "La sacarocracia cubana y los inicios del ciclo revolucionario burgués en España. El papel de Francisco Arango y Parreño," in Alberto Gil Novales (ed.), *La revolución burguesa en España*, Madrid: Universidad Complutense de Madrid, 1985, pp. 277–85.

CHAPTER 26
JUAN ÁLVAREZ MENDIZÁBAL
Mark Lawrence

Juan Álvarez de Mendizábal (1790–1853) was one of a handful of great outsiders who shaped nineteenth-century Spanish politics. Like Baldomero Espartero, Juan Prim (see Chapter 29), and Francisco Pi y Margall, Mendizábal came from a relatively undistinguished family background, very different from the scions of noble families who furnished the ranks of both progressive and moderate parties. Most strikingly, his lineage was Jewish in origin. Given the Spanish tradition of prejudice toward descendants of the "new Christians," Juan's family took care to change their surname from the Jewish-sounding "Méndez" to the Basque-sounding "Mendizábal."

By the turn of the nineteenth century the Mendizábal family had developed one of the greatest commercial houses in Cadiz, Spain's most bourgeois and least clerical city and cradle of the liberal revolution (see Chapter 2). These facts alone would make Mendizábal a worthy case study in nineteenth-century Spain, not least because Mendizábal himself stressed his plebeian origins whenever these proved politically useful. Catapulted into power by the liberal revolution of September 1835, Mendizábal warned the Cortes that as he was a "son of the people" without any aristocratic blood in his veins, he would face more obstacles than any other minister. Sonorous monologues were the norm in the Spanish Parliament, but, as this chapter will show, Mendizábal's rhetoric at least underscored his achievements with regard to the grand projects of disentailment and militarization undertaken during the crisis months of the 1830s' liberal revolution (see Chapter 3).

Mendizábal was much more than a demographic anomaly. The skill in commerce he showed from a young age made him ideally placed to play a key role for the Patriot forces during the Peninsular War. As treasurer to the Patriot Army of the Centre, Mendizábal learned the inseparable bonds linking finance with politics. The ending of the war in 1814 coincided with the return of Ferdinand VII and his abolition of Spain's first attempt at constitutional government, and Mendizábal returned to his commercial interests in Cadiz. But his support for liberalism remained undimmed as the contacts which he had nurtured with the Valencian Beltrán de Lis family during the war flowered into reciprocal godfatherhood of each family's children.

Mendizábal's move to Madrid in 1817 propelled him into the underworld of liberal conspiracies against Fernandine absolutism, and by the autumn of 1819, Mendizábal had become treasurer to the Riego plot to revive the rule of the Constitution of 1812. The success of the Colonel Riego's revolution of 1820 unleashed a veritable *empleomanía*, or unrestrained competition for government jobs, which proved an impossible burden on a virtually bankrupt economy. But unlike most revolutionaries during the Liberal Triennium (1820–23), Mendizábal was uninterested in achieving public office, and instead continued his commercial activities in his native Cadiz. Yet his close contacts with Riego and other revolutionary leaders proved highly lucrative all the same, and Mendizábal's financial skill was pressed into service once more in the capacity of army treasurer. Funds were sorely needed by the liberal regime which had become increasingly beleaguered by a population alienated by economic reforms and receptive to the appeal of armed counterrevolution.

Although the revolutionary army managed to suppress most royalist guerrilla bands by the spring of 1823, it showed far less willingness to offer resistance to the invasion of a regular army comprising French and émigré Spanish troops. The French "100,000 Sons of St Louis" allied with the Spanish "army of the faith" in sweeping all before them. In stark contrast to the enduring belligerence offered to the French by Patriot forces during the Peninsular War, in 1823 constitutional armies offered token resistance at best. Mendizábal's native Cádiz was the major exception, as it withstood a three-month siege by the counterrevolutionary armies. Mendizábal, who throughout 1823 had already been serving as treasurer to the revolutionary Army of Andalucia, was fully stretched organizing supplies for the maritime city and its defending garrison, no small feat given that the rest of Spain was in the grip of counterrevolution and Britain alone among the great powers looked upon Spain's second liberal experiment with any degree of kindness. Once the city fell on September 23, 1823 and King Ferdinand reclaimed his absolute powers, Mendizábal like so many other constitutionalists fled into exile. Royalist mobs ransacked his house and daubed its walls with the words "house of blacks" (casa de negros), a popular slur describing liberals' corrupted souls.

Fleeing to Gibraltar and then to Britain, Mendizábal joined a generation of liberal leaders who escaped the violent counterrevolutionary repression in Spain and lived out a decade of their lives in exile. Sentenced to death in absentia, Mendizábal rebuilt his life as best he could under the gloomy skies of London. His travails ranged from a spell in a debtors' prison to being the toast of the Hispanophile Whigs and Spanish exiles who regularly met at Holland House, a center for literary and political life. Mendizábal's skill at securing finance for the cause of liberalism in Iberia placed him at the right hand of the exiles' leader, Francisco Espoz y Mina. Like other exiled liberals, Mendizábal relied upon his Masonic contacts as a network for survival and for the international business of liberal revolution.

During the "Ominous Decade" (1823–33) of restored absolutism, the regime of Ferdinand VII maintained repression by creating Spain's first modern police state underpinned by a large reactionary militia called the Royalist Volunteers. The first target for Fernandine vengeance was the liberal movement. Riego was publicly garroted and several others who survived abroad were summarily executed upon being captured reentering Spain (usually via doomed but dramatic coastal incursions). The second target for the Fernandine regime was arguably more subversive in nature. For the "Carlist" faction of theocrats (defenders of Carlos María Isidro's right to the Throne) and ultraroyalists Ferdinand VII was not reactionary enough (see chapters 2, 24). Ferdinand's death in September 1833 and the Cristino (supporters of the future Isabel II) takeover of the army and state provoked a Carlist insurgency which turned into Spain's bloodiest modern civil conflict, the First Carlist War of 1833–40.

Spain's turmoil should be placed in its European context. Even though liberal revolutions had been suppressed across southern Europe in the early 1820s, the cause of liberty was revived by the dynastic dispute in Portugal which erupted into civil war in 1828. Though "civil," this war was decided by international intervention, as the liberal side of Dom Pedro (pedristas) by 1834 defeated the absolutist forces of Dom Miguel (miguelistas), thanks largely to British supremacy at sea and international volunteers fighting on land. Crucially, Mendizábal acted as agent for a huge loan funding the pedrista war effort. Until Ferdinand's death produced a revolution in Spain's foreign policy, the Spanish government supported the *miguelista* side, and the British faced considerable diplomatic pressure not to allow Spaniards to serve the cause of Dom Pedro. Two months before Ferdinand's death, Madrid was assured that "with the single exception of Mendizábal, agent for the *pedrista* loan, Dom Pedro is rejecting repeated offers by Spaniards to enter his service and the British forces at Oporto have instructions to report the arrival of all Spaniards entering at this city."

Mendizábal's financing of both *pedrismo* and a failed invasion of émigré liberals across the Pyrenees in 1830 earned him such notoriety that in 1834 he remained in a select company of exiles refused amnesty by the Cristino regime. When amnesty was finally offered later that year, Mendizábal was still nominally in the service of the victorious constitutional queen of Portugal; he was also busy in London arranging funding for the British Auxiliary Legion. This force, along with more seasoned volunteers from the French Foreign Legion and from Portugal, formed the armed wing of the Quadruple Alliance intervention in support of Cristino Spain against the Carlists. As the Cristino war effort went from bad to worse, the government in Madrid faced inexorable pressure to liberalize its political institutions. Responding to an initially limited invitation in July 1835 to join the beleaguered *Moderate* government, Mendizábal made his way to Madrid. He witnessed at firsthand the provincial risings, anticlerical outrages, and tax strikes that would lead to the September "revolution of the juntas" and the downfall of the *Moderate* government of Count Toreno. As Toreno fled to France ahead of assassination threats, in September Mendizábal became Spain's first *exaltado* prime minister since 1823.

Mendizábal's twelve years in exile had made him the most Anglophile of Spanish liberals. His cosmopolitan nature became the butt of innuendo from his *Moderate* opponents and the subject of vitriol from the Carlists. The Carlist press described Mendizábal as a Wandering Jew bent on looting the Spanish Church as collateral for Jewish financiers in the City of London. Certainly, Mendizábal admired Britain as a country where centuries of evolving liberty stood in stark contrast to the abuses of executive power in his native Spain. Upon accepting the premiership in September 1835, Mendizábal wrote to the Queen-Regent alluding to Magna Carta and the Bill of Rights as historical inspiration for radically expanding government policy of suppressing Carlist-ridden monasteries. He often wrote to the British ambassador, George Villiers, that the tragedy of civil war might yet seal an enduring Anglo-Spanish alliance, fulfilling the missed opportunities of 1814 and 1823. As the civil-military relations deteriorated in Cristino Spain over the course of 1835–36, Mendizábal complained to his detractor, General Fernando Fernández de Córdova, Commander-in-Chief of the Army of the North, that political adversaries in Spain could not remain on decent terms like in England where "fair play reigned in politics."

Yet once in office, Mendizábal realized that Britain was part of the problem as well as the solution to Spain's Civil War. Mendizábal came to power at the moment of acute crisis. The war caused government debt to balloon out of control, owing to the 600,000,000 *reales* annual cost of maintaining the army, and (from 1835) the almost 100,000,000 *reales* per year for the foreign auxiliary legions, resulting in an annual structural deficit of 300,000,000 *reales*. By 1835 state expenditure had risen from a prewar annual average of 700 million *reales* to around 990 million, and by 1837, this annual sum would rise exponentially to 1,900 million. New sources of income were secured via forced taxes, the revenues from Cuba's booming sugar trade, and loans from abroad (mainly from British banking houses). But the September 1835 revolution diminished revenues as the hated consumption taxes were suspended in many cities and the juntas proved unable or unwilling to restrict imports of cotton goods from Britain. The ensuing layoffs of cotton workers in Catalonia threatened to tip the balance of the Principality—hitherto divided between the Cristino coastal plain and the Carlist far west—in favor of the enemy as the Carlists proved skilled at exploiting economic discontent.

Luckily, Mendizábal enjoyed long-standing contacts with the Paris and London bourses which afforded him better terms of credit than any other Spanish prime minister could have obtained. But he also faced constant pressure from Ambassador Villiers to accept a free-trade agreement with Britain in return for a substantial loan. For his part, Mendizábal wanted a more generous British loan whose proceeds would gradually be paid off by the proceeds of customs receipts, a very different proposal from outright free trade. The two men could not reach a compromise and adverse reports in the pro-Carlist section of the British press embarrassed Mendizábal and by January 1836 he dropped his proposal. Even though British military and financial support continued to give Britain the hegemonic foreign policy role in Spain (much to the chagrin of France, the other Great Power signatory to the Quadruple Alliance), Mendizábal now realized that an end to the civil war could only be reliably sought from inside Spain. This in itself was a controversial viewpoint, as certain sections of liberal opinion, especially among *Moderates*, had been clamoring for formal military intervention by France as a way to bring the Carlist Basque Country to heel (ironically in much the same way that the French-led invasion of 1823 had ended Spain's second liberal experiment). But Mendizábal understood the moral defeat inherent in a liberal victory secured by foreign intervention and resolved instead to maximize the considerable domestic resources of Cristino Spain.

Mendizábal's first achievement was the resurrection of central government control over the regional juntas behind the September revolution. Even his *Moderate* detractors credited him with success in his policy of "forgetting, respecting, revising, repairing and reforming." Under the mantra of "Liberal Union," Mendizábal deployed great tact in taming the revolutionary juntas, as all juntas except Andújar (which sponsored a revolt in Andalucia) accepted being redesignated as "Committees of Armament and Defence" with watered-down powers ultimately under central government authority. The Liberals' paramilitary force, the Urban Militia, which had been in some of the thickest fighting against the Carlists, was renamed the "National Guard" and its recruitment and powers expanded in an effort to relieve some of the burden of the regular army. A wave of liberal patriotism, some genuine and some contrived, swept across Cristino Spain. Public officials "volunteered" cuts to their salaries for the duration of hostilities, liberal students waived their exemptions from conscription, and women's circles organized relief for war wounded and orphans.

Mendizábal seized this brief atmosphere of good will to impose a crash program of militarization. But conscription was traditionally hated by Spain's popular classes whom four decades of imperial, national, and civil wars had taught that a rich man's war was always a poor man's fight. Three rounds of conscription of 25,000 men each had already been enacted since the start of the Carlist War. But in September 1835 Mendizábal introduced an unprecedented levy of 100,000 men. All males between 18 and 40 years were liable to be drafted, free exemptions being given only to the disabled, only sons, clergy, and veterans. Well-to-do draftees could purchase exemption with the "blood tax" of 4,000 *reales* (or 1,000 *reales* accompanied by a healthy horse). For those without wealth or friends in authority, conscription was a very real threat. Yet barely half of the 100,000 sent to reinforce the Army of the North actually reached the front, as desertion and sickness over the winter of 1835–36 exposed the reality behind Mendizábal's Liberal Union propaganda, and relations between the prime minister and General Fernández de Córdova, accordingly grew worse.

Despite Cristino victories in July 1835 at Mendigorría and the first siege of Bilbao, the Cristino front thereafter was everywhere in retreat. The Carlists blockaded the provincial capitals of Bilbao, San Sebastián, Vitoria, and Pamplona, cities which from the summer of 1835 were virtually all that remained of Cristino-held territory in the Basque Country, and they even began dispatching guerrilla-style expeditions beyond the River Ebro. General Fernández de Córdova demanded more men and regular supplies before committing to an offensive and Mendizábal demanded that the Commander-in-Chief show initiative in order to justify reinforcements. This civil-military crisis completed the irreconcilable division in Spain's liberal movement. Divided since the Triennium and exile into *Moderates* and *exaltados*, Spanish liberals under Mendizábal's premiership split into two recognizably modern parties of *Moderates* and *mendizabalistas* (from 1836 known as *Progressives*), leaving radicalized leftist elements in the semilegal underworld of the National Guard (from September 1836 called the "National Militia") and secret societies.

Mendizábal in power exasperated many of his erstwhile champions, not least Ambassador Villiers who despaired at how he insisted on occupying the ministries of Foreign Affairs, War, Marine, and Finance in addition to the premiership. Such multitasking ensured that poorly delegated subordinates exercised the initiative by taking Mendizábal's liberalization policies in sectarian directions. Waving aside accusations of presiding over leftist mob rule, in January 1836 Mendizábal won a vote of confidence and dissolved the Cortes in order to convene new elections which would be held under a much broader franchise than those hitherto allowed under the highly restrictive Royal Statute of 1834. Mendizábal's campaigning for the March 1836 elections showed the degree to which he had retained provincial support since the days of the September juntas. He was elected in no fewer than eight different constituencies and chose to represent his home city of Cadiz.

Even though Mendizábal was returned to power, a renewed crisis in civil-military relations saw the Queen-Regent dismiss her radical prime minister and appoint the Moderate Javier Istúriz in his place. But Mendizábal was out of power for less than four months. In the August 1836 "Mutiny of La Granja" the army toppled the Istúriz government and forced María Cristina to appoint a Progressive administration. Between September 1836 and August 1837 Mendizábal occupied the portfolio of Finance Minister in a term associated with his most enduring legacy: the famous ecclesiastical confiscation laws (known in Spanish as *la Desamortización*: "disentailment") which targeted Spain's monastic properties (see Chapter 18).

The need to disentail Spain's huge ecclesiastical lands had long been a reformist cause in Spain, even before the liberal party actually existed (serious attempts to release the grip of "dead hands" on Spanish land stretch back to the 1760s). Enlightened opinion viewed with disdain the entailed property of the Church which could neither be bought nor sold and which seemed not to be dedicated to the most productive uses. But in 1836 the Carlist War gave the matter added urgency for two reasons, one financial and other related to public opinion. First, it was clear that neither a foreign loan nor renewed extraordinary taxes would be sufficient to balance the budget, and still less to reduce the national debt. Thus the prospect of auctioning confiscated church property in return for payment in cash or in government bonds promised both to restore state finances and to give buyers a material interest in the victory of the liberal revolution against the Carlist menace. Second, Cristino public opinion had become increasingly anticlerical in response to the well-known religious claims of the Carlists and the individual defection of so many priests and monks to the enemy cause. The Cristino government had already expelled the Jesuits in July 1835 and army officers had begun closing Carlist-ridden monasteries and convents and expelling clerics on their own authority.

Given this anticlerical climate, Mendizábal faced no difficulty getting laws approved abolishing the tithe (which was replaced by a smaller tax controlled by local authorities), suppressing all religious houses containing fewer than twelve residents, and effectively placing most property belonging to the secular and regular clergy on the market (even though relatively little property as yet changed hands). This onslaught on the corporate power of the Church was motivated by a spirit of anticlericalism but not anti-Catholicism. Even though Mendizábal's *exaltado* biographer celebrated the disentailment as a long overdue measure against clerics who were a "mob of parasites, living ghosts and dying visions," it was the political, not the moral, power of Catholicism which so vexed liberals like García Tejero. There were no known atheists in Spain at this time and Mendizábal himself devoutly raised his children as Catholics and condemned the "immorality" in gender relations produced by the Carlist War.

Alongside Mendizábal's disentailment, in August 1837 came the final and definitive abolition of feudal jurisdiction in Spain. Noble landowners were turned into capitalist property owners and their rights to territorial ownership theoretically opened up to legal challenge by villagers (even though few challenges were successful). Cristino victory in the Carlist War ensured that Mendizábal's liberal settlement prevailed. The guns of the paramilitary Civil Guard (created in 1844) kept property in the hands of its lawful if not always rightful owners.

Mendizábal's legacy was therefore controversial on both the left and the right of political opinion. Carlists, right-wing Moderates, and later Neo-Catholics condemned Mendizábal's assault on religion and traditional property rights. The doctrinal Spanish voice of counterrevolution during 1848, Donoso Cortés, observed that Mendizábal's property revolution had been carried out in a manner that proletarianized the poor. Mendizábal's policy was criticized on the left, too. In 1836 Álvaro Flórez Estrada thought that nationalized property should solve the problem of the rural dispossessed, inoculating them against Carlism by distributing lands on cheap and renewable 50-year leases. Mendizábal himself realized the social shortcomings of the property revolution and campaigned in the 1846 Cortes elections on a platform of redistributing land to Carlist War veterans. The benefit of hindsight allowed twentieth-century Marxists to regard the disentailment as a tragically missed chance of democratizing Spain via the creation of mass landownership. Spain was compared unfavorably with the "success" of Revolutionary France and aligned with the baleful example of the Prussia of the Junkers. Whatever the legacy of disentailment—and it should be noted that some research in the 1990s presented a more optimistic interpretation of the property revolution— we must remember the circumstances in which it arose. The brutality of the Carlist War created popular anticlericalism, and the struggle for survival gave Mendizábal no time to prepare a better scheme.

Mendizábal had no further opportunity to perfect his revolutionary settlement. After serving as Finance Minister during the dying months of the Espartero Regency in 1843, he fled into exile during the Moderate counterrevolution the following year. In France he was bankrupted by his failed business ventures, but he was rescued by the Moderate amnesty of 1846 which permitted him to return to Spain. In 1847 Mendizábal was elected as a Cortes deputy once more, and he saw out the remainder of his life as the parliamentary leader of the right-wing faction of the Progressives. In 1849 a new party of the left, the Democrats, was founded, comprising left-wing Progressives, republicans, and even some socialists. Mendizábal's politics, like those of most Spanish radicals, grew more moderate with age, but his death in November 1853 came soon enough to preserve his legacy as one of the founding fathers of *progresismo*. Ten thousand people attended his funeral. A Progressive-dominated parliament voted in April 1856 to erect a statue to him, but their fall from power meant that it was not erected until the Revolution of 1868. Fittingly, it stood in a square in Madrid which had been the site of a disentailed convent.

Mendizábal's statue met a grim fate at the end of another civil war one hundred years after the one which made him famous. One of the first symbolic acts following Franco's victory march into Madrid in 1939 was the removal and destruction of Mendizábal's statue from "Progress square" and the renaming of the location after a famous cleric. This act more than any other demonstrates how Mendizábal, the colorful outsider, personified the tragic division of modern Spain.

Further reading

Borrow, George, *The Bible in Spain*, London: John Murray, 1843.

Burdiel, Isabel, *La política de los notables: moderados y avanzados durante el régimen del Estatuto Real (1834-1836)*, Valencia: Edicions Alfons El Magnanim, 1987.

Christiansen, Eric, *The Origins of Military Power in Spain, 1800-1854*, Oxford: Oxford University Press, 1967.

Garcia, Tejero Alfonso, *Historia político-administrativa de Mendizábal*, Madrid: Ortigosa, 1858.

Janke, Peter, *Mendizábal y la instauración de la monarquíia constitutcional en España (1790-1853)*, Madrid: Siglo XXI, 1974.

Lawrence, Mark, *Spain's First Carlist War, 1833-40*, Basingstoke: Palgrave, 2014.

Marichal, Carlos, *Spain, 1834-44: A New Society*, London: Tamesis, 1977.

Montojo, Juan Pan, "Juan Alvarez y Mendizábal: El Burgués Revolucionario," in Isabel Burdiel and Manuel Perez Ledesma (eds.), *Liberales, agitadores y conspiradores: biografías heterodoxas del siglo XIX*, Madrid: Espasa Calpe, 2000, pp. 155–82.

CHAPTER 27
COUNTESS ESPOZ Y MINA

María Cruz Romeo Mateo

Translated by Abril Liberatore

In 1922, writer Emilia Pado Bazán published a brief biographical sketch of her fellow Galician, Juana María de la Vega (1805–72). She wrote that the Countess Espoz y Mina—a title she had received in 1837—"could not be understood by those who saw her merely as a writer or a thinker: politics was her calling, and passion for the liberal cause was her life mission." She was right. The life trajectory of the countess is one of a woman who enthusiastically crossed the line separating public and private life, pushed social boundaries, and contributed to the triumph of progressive liberalism in the Spain of Isabella II (see Chapter 3). How was she able to pursue this political vocation in a society that labeled political women "degenerate subjects of feminine nature"? How did she nurture her liberal passion throughout her life? Who was Juana Maria de la Vega? What type of woman was she? What type of woman did she want to be and did she become?

Juana María de la Vega came from an enlightened, liberal, and relatively well-off family. She was born in 1805 in La Coruña to a family that had become wealthy by doing business in Cuba and trade in the Americas. Her father, Juan Antonio de la Vega, became involved early on personally and financially in the liberal and patriotic cause of 1808, and from then onward, his life was tied to the liberal cause. The political back and forth in Spain forced him into exile to Portugal between 1815 and 1817, an opportunity which allowed him to build personal and political networks which grew to transcend regional and national borders.

The future countess grew up in a household that valued the need to raise women out of ignorance. No expense was spared in her education, which was impressive for the time. The concept of regenerating society through liberal political thought was mirrored by the belief in the regeneration of the individual through values such as reason, utility, work, responsibility, and autonomy. She made these qualities hers and many years later, in her memoirs, she called her education as a youth "her most prized patrimony." This patrimony allowed her to uproot any notions of women as inferior, and she firmly believed that educated women had the capacity to improve societal problems. In this regard, her family life was the first place where she developed her role and outlook as a woman.

The liberal and enlightened life of the Vega family also fomented a view of marriage as a consensual union, not an arranged one. Juana Maria decided on Francisco Espoz y Mina. By the time of their courtship in 1821, he was the highest military authority in Galicia of the liberal political order which had returned in 1820. It was a marriage chosen freely by both parties, but there was a great difference in their ages, education, and social status. Juana was 16 years old when the engagement was announced, an educated young lady from a commercial family. On the other hand, General Espoz y Mina was a mature man of 40, with limited formal education who had been raised in rural Navarra. The War of Independence offered him access to the military and his liberal beliefs allowed him to climb the military hierarchy and develop an immense popularity. "It was love," the countess wrote many years later, "and a firm enthusiasm for the new patriotic institutions" that led them to marriage.

Three essential components followed the countess throughout her life: love, liberty, and patriotism; and her passion for these three ideals allowed her to consistently criss-cross between sentiment and reason; between the private and the public; between masculine and feminine. They also brought her significant life experiences. From 1823 to 1834, she became involved with her husband's conspiratorial activities during his years in exile in England and France, and in 1841, she accepted a position with the new progressive regime as governess to Queen Isabella II and her sister, a post she held until 1843. She would also maintain a salon in her home at La Coruña, which became the nucleus of the failed coup of 1846 against the existing Moderate regime. She was involved in the relations between Galician progressives and the party leadership in Madrid. She promoted social reform and material and educational aid. Finally, she wrote one of the most impressive collection of memoirs and autobiographies of the nineteenth century. For the countess, there was no contradiction between her love for her husband, who had passed away in 1836, and her defense of the liberal fatherland. These were the foundations for a private and public life devoted to service and her commitment to the political culture of progressive liberalism. This was her great political passion: the triumph of progress.

When in the middle of the nineteenth century, she wrote a collection of memoirs that would not be published during her lifetime and which retold her experiences until 1834, the year she returned to Spain from exile, and her achievements in her position as royal governess, she developed a unique identity which did not quite fit the stereotype of the "domestic angel," a stereotype that took hold among respectable societies in the second half of the nineteenth century (see Chapter 11). Instead, her image was a paragon of private and public virtues, including her loyalty and devotion to her husband; her maternal abnegation; her ability for sacrifice; her devotion to the liberal cause; her defense of the good of the nation over party interests; her commitment to charity as a civic obligation and as a logical outcome of the social image as the mother. This was not the image promulgated by the ideology of domesticity as it resolutely transcended the ascription of the woman to the private sphere.

Furthermore, her public image did not coincide with the countess' own self-image. The contemporary press propagated an image of her as respectable, maternal, and domestically oriented woman. Her public interventions were always presented as those of a righteous yet tender widow who loved her late spouse, of her patriotism, and of the evangelical zeal which made her the "protecting angel" of the poor and the socially marginalized. Juana María de la Vega never rejected this image, and in fact she cultivated it, although she never gave in to the liberal model of femininity. Quite the opposite: her life trajectory is an excellent example of the opportunities individuals have to shape and sometimes transform dominant cultural discourse.

The countess' opportunity for action and thought were rooted in the liberal revolution, her experiences as a British exile and her progressive liberalism. She was raised in a politically, socially, and culturally tumultuous world. The Spanish world of the first decades of the nineteenth century was one searching for the sexual order that would define liberalism and for the meaning of the concept of "woman." In general, liberalism shared the idea of the different but complimentary nature of the sexes, but beyond this there were alternative visions of gender, especially with regard to the education, intellectual capacity, and public perception of women. In short, there was no *one* liberal public discourse that defined normative feminine identities. Raised in a liberal household that valued feminine education and the fostering of reading and writing, Juana María de la Vega quickly became integrated in the progressive political culture which sought to find a balance between the rationality and intellectual capacity of women and their domestic nature.

Exile was a significant experience in the life of the Countess Espoz y Mina, as she wrote in *En honor de Mina. Memorias íntimas* (In Honor of Mina: Intimate Memoirs). When the liberals were defeated again in 1823, she moved to England where she and her husband lived in a humble flat near London, which quickly became a gathering place for Spanish exiles and a headquarters of liberal emigration. Most exiled Spanish women tended to lead a discreet and reserved life, but this was not the case for Juana María. She never strayed too far from political activity and records indicate that she was the real author of her husband's memoirs, *Breve extracto de la vida del general Mina* (A Brief Excerpt of the Life of General Mina), which were published in 1825. As secretary to her husband on several occasions, she was responsible for his correspondence with other Spanish and foreign conspirators. She also developed her own smaller circle of political allies, which included men who would become important figures of Spanish political history. As can be seen by her writings, the countess clearly enjoyed both moral and political authority.

Her life as a political exile did not occur in a closed family or private world. For her, this uprooting became an opportunity to learn a second language as well as new customs and values that were different from those she had held until then. She had an active social life and could often be found attending receptions and visiting writers and poets. Without a doubt, her intellectual horizons grew as a result. After her return to Spain as a widow, she traveled to England often, and always spoke highly of the country and its culture.

England fed her love of liberty and showed her opportunities available to women in the field of philanthropy. The future countess had arrived in a country with a rich history of formal associational life, particularly of societies directed at alleviating poverty and disease and educating the lower classes. Although it was a masculine world, women had an active role in administering alms. When her husband died, she returned to her hometown and resolved to replicate there the structure of charitable associations. In 1838, she founded the La Coruña Women's Association and acted as director of the group until her death in 1872. The Association, the clearest reference point for the modern conception of welfare in Spain, took care of orphaned children and the sick at the Hospital de la Caridad.

Her progressive political culture was also behind this personal determination. This imagined a political and social order based on the gradual and orderly expansion of the public sphere through the guided and controlled integration of the popular classes and the women of the middle classes. Her indubitable elitism ironically incorporated a call to the people and a discourse on gender that sought to expand the public spaces open to women as an indispensable step toward progress. In contrast to moderate liberalism, progressivism valued the education of women as much as their civic activism in fields that did not contradict their supposed maternal essence. In this sense, philanthropy projected a social maternity and the qualities that were attributed to women's nature: love, sacrifice, and abnegation, into the public space.

The Countess Espoz y Mina made these progressive ideas her own at the same time as she had a hand in defining them. On the one hand, she did not question the sexual hierarchy on which liberal society was based. On the other, she defended philanthropic activism against conservatives who sought to limit or control it. As opposed to other women writers of the 1840s and 1850s, such as Gertrudis Gómez de Avellaneda or Carolina Coronado, who constructed a feminine voice that challenged the limits of domesticity and denounced the contradictions of liberal universalism, Juana María de la Vega represented herself as a "defenseless lady," a middle-class woman who had realized the respectable, liberal domestic ideal.

Nevertheless, her philanthropy had an openly political goal: the regeneration of society according to progressive ideals: a liberal order that espoused progress, happiness, the nation, and the people. Her work on this project went above and beyond the norm for women who engaged in benevolent work. In addition to her intense and long-lasting welfare work, she took charge of organizing social assistance at the local and regional levels. Her philanthropic model was based on independence from public powers and religious authorities, the active role of civil society, and the participation of women. For her, it represented an opportunity to engage publicly as a feminine subject who was capable, responsible, and respectable.

This project was not simply about educating the poor, although she founded schools for children and adults. It was not simply about curing disease, although she also served as a supervisor at the Hospital de la Caridad. It was not simply about reinstating the outcasts of society either, but she founded, along with Concepcion Arenal, a society responsible for the care of imprisoned women. It was not simply about protecting the living conditions of those on the margins of society, but she served as a patron for a housing cooperative in Madrid. And it was not simply about fomenting professions, but before her death she created a foundation that funneled its income toward the creation of a theoretical and practical school of agriculture. All this was very important in the Spain of the 1850s and 1860s, but the ultimate goal of the Countess Espoz y Mina was much more ambitious: she aimed for complete societal reform. As she wrote in a letter published in the press in 1865: "I am convinced that one of the greatest advantages we can give to our people is to disseminate among them the knowledge that they unfortunately lack." Educating the people would lift them from misery, allow for their integration in the progressive public sphere, and would simultaneously instigate progress across the nation. Spain could become another England thanks to the work of an exemplary elite of progressive men and women. Her project was also about social reform that engaged with humanism and the Christian political economics of the Viscount Alban de Villeneuve Bargemont, whose work she translated and published in 1862 in an article titled "Private Welfare".

Contrary to some of the other writers who criticized the liberal project of natural differentiation between the sexes, the Countess Espoz y Mina never made peace with the moderates who ruled Spain after 1843. There was never any ambiguity regarding her politics: she was a lady of progressivism through and through who worked incessantly for the success of her political beliefs.

The countess achieved public notoriety when the regency of Espartero named her *aya* (governess) of Isabella II in June of 1841, with the aim of helping educate her as a constitutional queen. Why was she chosen for this role? On some occasions, this assignment has been explained as an expression of official recognition toward her husband, who had died in 1836 as a popular hero for his military career against the French, the absolutists, and the Carlists; it has also been explained as a result of her wide networks of political relationships, woven years earlier by her father and her husband. As she wrote, it was her "political ideals" that made her the ideal person to shape, in the words of a progressive leader, another Queen Victoria. These ideas were inspired by the liberalism of her parents, but were not simple copies of her father's or husband's progressivism. The former, suffering from degenerative paralysis, returned from exile with his daughter in 1834 before the formation of the Progressive Party; and the liberalism of the General Espoz y Mina had a focus on the military and personal power, one which the countess silenced and smoothed over in her memoirs and in her *Memorias del general Espoz y Mina*, which was eventually published in 1851–52, the only work she published in her lifetime. Her personal progressivism was more civic based, and challenged the concentration of power in one person.

The countess was raised in progressive politics, not so much due to her parents as to her life experiences between 1820 and 1834, due to her personal trajectory and the friendships she developed while in exile. In early 1840, months before the summer revolution that ended the regency of Maria Cristina, she maintained a correspondence with many significant progressive leaders in which they discussed the future of the nation. José María Calatrava, prime minister in 1837, wrote: "I know that I don't need to explain to you the issue of elections in that province. You know very well that the issue is vital. Things are at a point that if we lose the battle, revolution seems to me inevitable. The short sightedness of these people is unbelievable to me." We do not know what Juana María's response was. But the very existence of this letter, and others like it before she was appointed governess, points to the political socialization of the countess and her early influence in matters far beyond what gender discourse prescribed, such as the election of deputies, and her role in a patrician liberalism that did not shy away from the danger of revolution.

The Countess accepted the revolution that brought Espartero and other renowned military men to power in September 1840. The Queen mother lost her political authority and the guardianship of her daughters and went into exile. One of the main concerns of the new progressive regime was the education of Isabella II, who was only 11 years old. This task was given to the "old glories" of the liberalism of Cádiz, Agustín de Argüelles, and Manuel José Quintana, who convinced the countess to accept the post of *aya* in July 1841, and later the post of lady-in-waiting in October 1842, which she retained until the fall of Espartero and the entry of the Moderate General Ramón María Narváez into Madrid in July 1843.

She aimed to raise the young Queen according to what she saw as the "civilization of the century," embodied in the idea of progress and confidence in the virtues of the middle classes or, as she wrote, in the social group that belonged to "the class of the people and not the aristocracy." Progress and virtue were the foundation of a humanist and Christian notion of society, one that distinguished men (and women) for their merits and qualities. She was exceptionally critical of the world of privilege, of decadence and obscurantism, and she believed that the middle classes were intelligent, hardworking, charitable, and honorable. It was this imagined world of middle-class respectability which she sought to introduce into the palace, the symbol of all she condemned.

In line with these beliefs, she sought to teach the Queen the rights and responsibilities of a constitutional monarch. She spoke with her about the sacrifices made by the nation in the name of liberal institutions and the Throne. She explained what real power represented in a modern world, that the authority of kings was rooted in the love of their people, and that her basic function was thus to cultivate the love of her nation, a love that the countess identified with its moral, intellectual, and material progress. As a result, she worked to convert the Queen to her brand of Christian humanism and social reformism. For Juana María de la Vega, the monarchy needed to be an institution committed to the good of the nation. The task of educating the queen was a way to create a progressive Queen, one infused with the ideals of constitutional liberty, of social reform and progress, and of the moral values of the middle class: an entrepreneurial queen dedicated to bettering society, paralleling the example set by the middle classes.

The education of Isabella II was a matter of great political importance. "The battle for the queen," as the political struggle for control over Isabella II was called, marked relations between the two streams of Spanish liberalism, the moderates and the progressives, and the Countess Espoz y Mina found herself in the middle of the conflict. Palace intrigues, the opposition of the servants loyal to María Cristina, and the moderates' attempt to "rescue" the Queen and her sister from their progressive caretakers by force in October 1841 indelibly marked the life of the countess at the Royal Palace.

Immediately after leaving the position there, she recorded her experiences in a volume entitled *Apuntes para la historia del tiempo en que ocupó los destinos de aya de S. M. y A. y camarera mayor de Palacio* (notes for the history of the time spent as Governess to Her Majesty and Head of the Palace Household), which was published by the Congress of Deputies in 1910. The *Apuntes* are a defense of her actions and those of her party against the accusations from the Palace and the moderates that the Queen and her sister were held hostage, separate from their environment and their mother, as well as against the critiques from some progressives who opposed Espartero. In it, the countess places responsibility for the failure to produce a new Queen Victoria on the absolutist and obscurantist environment of the court, and the tensions that divided the progressive party following the creation of the one-man Regency under Espartero. As opposed to what she wrote in the *Apuntes*, likely because she thought to publish them some day, on a few handwritten cards which have been preserved in her personal archives she wrote a piece entitled "On the Political Situation in Spain," in which she blames the divisions among the progressive factions and the "ruin of the Regency" on the French government, the weakness of the English ambassador; the weakness of Espartero's last government; and most of all, the progressive leaders Manuel Cortina and Salustiano de Olózaga, who had surrendered themselves to the hands of their enemies, the moderates. She could trust only in "the Spanish people," who "are slow in understanding political bad faith, but who, more condemn that offence more than any other."

When the revolution against Espartero succeeded, the countess resigned from her position, but she did not stop believing in the Spanish people and she did not abandon her passion for politics. Returning to La Coruña, her house and her salon were transformed into informal centers for the patronage of progressives, their conspiracies and their friendships. She was watched closely by the moderate authorities in 1846 when the coup in Galicia, which had been organized by Progressive groups and young intellectuals connected to a discourse defending Galician interests, failed. Almost ten years after that failed attempt to depose Narváez, she continued to defend its "patriotic goal." It is not clear how deeply involved she actually was, but her solidarity and her involvement with these types of activities between 1843 and 1854 was undeniable. Her personal archive contains a confidential note from a hypothetical "Central Provincial Committee" which she envisioned being established in Galicia had the 1848 revolution succeeded.

How could a woman with her political credentials develop this philanthropic profile, publish the *Memorias* (of which she was the true author), and avenge the image of her husband in the press during the 1860s? The countess stood on three privileged pillars: the court, the Progressive Party, and the philanthropic sector.

The memory of her years with Isabella II kept her admiration for the Crown alive and, with time, her respect and affection for the Queen grew. Her stance on the middle class connected with the idea of a strong "exemplary" Crown. The countess was received by the Queen and her husband on numerous occasions, including the royal visit to Galicia in 1858, and the Queen was involved financially in several of the countess' charitable projects. She enjoyed the support of the monarchy: in 1862 she was named Vice-protector of Welfare, and the cooperation she received from, with authorities in Madrid, Cuba, and the Philippines during the 1860s, is testament to the support she enjoyed from the monarch.

She also cultivated personal and political relationships with progressive leaders in Madrid and La Coruña. In a poorly structured political system, communication between different networks was essential for the health of the party, especially during elections. Educated since childhood in the culture of letter writing, the countess maintained frequent contact with many progressives. Personal relationships mixed with political issues: the development of the party in the city; hopes of triumph; and the convenience of choosing leaders outside the province; and the aptitude of local candidates unknown in Madrid. It was the highest level of politics to which a woman could aspire in the mid-nineteenth century, and it was also the personal and familiar brand of politics of liberalism. If progressist politicians anxiously awaited the countess' letters it was not solely out of friendship. She had her own symbolic capital: the protection of the monarchy and her close relationship with the popular sector through her philanthropy, and the party used it to their advantage when needed. Her charitable work also garnered her sympathy among respectable rungs of society, who saw her simply as the "guardian angel of the unfortunate."

The Countess Espoz y Mina never challenged the sexual order of liberal society, but she took advantage of the discourse on gender and its paradoxes to present herself as a capable individual who pushed respectable middle-class femininity to its limits.

Further reading

Burguera, Mónica, *Las damas del liberalismo respetable*, Madrid: Catedra, 2012.

De la Vega, Juana, *Apuntes para la historia del tiempo que ocupó los destinos de Aya de S.M. y A. y camarera mayor de palacio*, Madrid: Boletín Oficial del Estado, 2014.

De la Vega, Juana, *Memorias de la Excma. Sra. Condesa de Espoz y Mina*, Madrid: Hijos de M.G. Hernández, 1910.

Durán, José Antonio, *Juana de Vega, la gran dama del primer progresismo español*, Madrid: Taller de Ediciones J.A. Durán, 2005.

Romeo Mateo, María Cruz, "Juana María de la Vega, condesa de Espoz y Mina (1805-19872). Por el amor al esposo, por amor a la patria", in Isabel Burdiel and Manuel Pérez Ledesma (eds.), *Liberales, agitadores y conspiradores. Biografías heterodoxas del siglo XIX*, Madrid: Espasa Calpe, 2000.

CHAPTER 28
EMILIA PARDO BAZÁN
Isabel Burdiel

In order to appreciate the historical importance of the life and work of Emilia Pardo Bazán (1851–1921) it is essential to consider the way the novel, and culture in general, can help understand the tensions produced by the socioeconomic and political changes that Spain experienced in the second half of the nineteenth century and the first decades of the twentieth. This was a crucial period in the construction of the nation-state, the process of nationalization of Spaniards—of women as well as men—and in the definition of the challenges of democracy and authoritarianism as responses to what has been called the emergence of mass politics, with its redefinition of the concept and practice of citizenship (see Chapter 4).

Pardo Bazán was both the most cosmopolitan intellectual of her generation and Spain's nineteenth-century "grande dame of letters." During the second half of the century, along with figures such as Benito Pérez Galdós and Leopoldo Alás, *Clarín*, she played a decisive role in the construction of the country's cultural sphere and literary canon. During her lifetime, her works were translated into a vast number of languages, including Japanese. She wrote some of the canonical novels of Spanish literature, such as *The House of Ulloa* (1886) and *Mother Nature* (1887), and made a decisive contribution to public discussion of literary naturalism and what a genuinely Spanish literary tradition might look like.

She was a multifaceted figure: journalist, critic, historian of literature, writer of stories, and playwright—the only field in which she was not successful. She was also a successful literary entrepreneur who created a magazine and a publishing house which were trailblazers in introducing Spanish audiences to the greats of contemporary Russian literature as well as to cutting-edge European debates on feminism through translations of the works of John Stuart Mill and August Bebel. One of the most original aspects of her intellectual trajectory was precisely the way she inserted feminism into the Spanish cultural and political debates of the second half of the nineteenth century, using the word openly and helping make it respectable in a way no other writer of her time managed. She achieved this both through such works of fiction as *Memoirs of a Confirmed Bachelor* (1896) and key interventions in the public sphere, for example her 1889 article on "The Spanish Woman" in London's *Fortnightly Review* and her celebrated speech, "The Education of Men and Women" to the 1892 Hispanic and Portuguese American Pedagogical Congress.

At a moment when celebrity culture was taking root in Spain, when a large and eager public combined admiration for artistic or literary achievement with an interest in the private lives of cultural figures, Pardo Bazán carefully managed her image as a writer and a famous woman, becoming both an agent of this change and one of its objects. She was a woman full of paradoxes: she was passionate and radically anti-sentimental, she was daring and scathing in her judgments, and she relished controversy. She managed to be a Catholic and a feminist, a militant Spanish nationalist and a convinced European, a Carlist, a Regenerationist, an anti-liberal, and an iconoclast. She was a traditionalist who was fascinated by science, a humanist, and an unapologetic elitist, modern and anti-modern. It was as if her works and her life competed with each other to see which could be more subversive of the established model for how to be a *respectable* woman writer. Her public persona, no less than her novels and literary criticism, embraced all the manifestations of what was problematic about the modernity of the Restoration.

Emilia Pardo Bazán grew up in a family environment which permitted her to develop her intellectual and emotional faculties in ways that were unusual for a young woman of her time. Her father, José Pardo Bazán, was a *hidalgo*, a minor nobleman from Galicia, who was economically well off and enjoyed a highly respectable social position. His relatives included a number of well-known liberals as well as a sympathizer with the regime of Joseph Bonaparte who had translated Voltaire. A Progressive as a young man, he was elected to the Constituent Cortes of 1854 and 1869 as a member of that party. Emilia had memories of the great *Progressive* leader Salustiano Olózaga visiting the family's homes in Galicia and Madrid. José Pardo Bazán shared the Progressive belief in an orderly and controlled expansion of the public sphere which would turn the middle classes into the backbone of a modern nation and open the door to the participation of the lower classes.

Progressives also had innovative ideas on marriage, coming to see it as the union of two equals by mutual consent in which educated women played a fundamental role. By educating capable and virtuous citizens, they would cross the boundaries separating the public and private spheres. This was a good description of José Pardo Bazán's wife, Amalia de la Rúa. She came from as prestigious a family as his, one which boasted liberal writers and journalists as well as a number of military men. Throughout her life, she served as Emilia's powerful guardian angel, always encouraging her and supporting her ambitions. Another important figure in her early life was the Countess Espoz y Mina: Emilia's mother was involved in her philanthropic activities and she allowed Emilia the run of her impressive library in La Coruña (see Chapter 27).

The Pardo Bazán family was rich and supported the Progressives; it was also deeply Catholic, although these two commitments would become increasingly difficult to balance as the "culture wars" between liberalism and Catholicism heated up in the second half of the century (see Chapter 18). Finally, along with pride in her social class, adherence to Christian morality and tolerance for all *respectable* political opinions and literary interests, Emilia's father left her with a credo that combined his Progressive and Catholic faiths: "If they tell you that there are things which men can do but women cannot, reply that it is a lie because there cannot be separate moralities for the two sexes."

Frustrated by the unbending exclusivism of the Moderates, José Pardo Bazán was one of the many Progressives who welcomed the Revolution of 1868 which removed Isabel II from the throne. He was also one of the many who were panicked by the political and social conflict that marked the *Sexenio Revolucionario* (see Chapter 3). These years were a turning point for the Pardo Bazán family as they were for nineteenth-century Spanish liberalism as a whole. Emilia's father could not abide the radicalism of the times and when the Cortes Constituyentes approved the freedom of religion he resigned his seat in parliament and, like many others of his social class, withdrew into private life until the Bourbon Restoration. As a reward, he was given the Papal title Count of Pardo Bazán. Still, his liberal instincts had not been entirely extinguished: when in 1875 the government punished a number of university professors for their Krausist beliefs, he expressed his support for them.

Emilia was also the child of this historical turning point and the profound damage it did to the liberalism of the earlier part of the century. It is no coincidence that her first great novel, *The Tribune* (1883), is the story of a female revolutionary, an intelligent but uneducated, honest, and passionate woman who worked in the tobacco factory of La Coruña, who is betrayed by a gentleman. The year 1868 was crucial for her personal life as well: as she put it in her autobiography: "I got married, I dressed as a woman, and the September Revolution broke out." She was 17 and it was an arranged marriage. Her husband, José Quiroga de Deza, also came from a *hidalgo* family, but one with strong Carlist sympathies which Emilia soon adopted. Against all the stereotypes, her husband gave her the space to grow intellectually, respected her and even, according to legend, never stopped loving her. He certainly provided her with a degree of freedom unheard of for the period and he dropped out of her life in a civilized way when they argued over Emilia's desire to go beyond merely being a writer to get involved in unfeminine political controversies and become a professional intellectual. They began to live apart in the mid-1880s and, although there was never a legal separation, in 1890 he provided the legal documents that allowed her to control the money she earned from her writing, something which, as a married woman, she would not have been able to do otherwise.

Unlike other contemporary women writers, Emilia made this decision without doubts, fears, or concerns about her identity. Rather, she made it with passion, the will to overcome obstacles and to be herself. From the first, Emilia Pardo Bazán presented herself as a versatile intellectual who believed in talent and hard work and was determined to break down the conventional barriers between high and low culture. When her great friend and mentor, the Krausist intellectual Francisco Giner de los Ríos, warned her of the risk entailed in abandoning serious work in favor of writing novels she told him:

> Here is what I believe: he who has the disposition to write should do so, starting small but aiming at more; making mistakes but also getting things right; in whatever style they can, plain or fancy, high or low; about serious topics or frivolous ones, as his temperament dictates; without aiming for perfection or believing himself above the rest; respecting taste and decorum but with a certain verve; without waiting to arrive at an exact philosophical, aesthetic or other criterion which can never be achieved. You don't believe this and this is where we differ.

When she published her book *La Cuestón Palpitante* (The Burning Question) (1883), her thoughts on the way modern novels should be written, it provoked considerable controversy and made her name, even though the couple of novels she had written to that point had not made much of an impact.

There were existing models for writers: erudite and isolated or tormented bohemian. Pardo Bazán rejected them in favor of becoming a professional and a businesswoman who promoted her works and sought out the intellectual networks and institutions she needed in order to succeed. These included the Circles and Atheneums of the cultural high society of the time, the universities and, above all, the Academy of the Spanish Language. She achieved it all except for being chosen a member of the Academy but she even turned the three rejections (in 1889, 1891, and 1912) to her advantage. A number of members supported her candidacy and their letters are much more interesting than the run-of-the-mill misogyny of her opponents. Moreover, the way in which she handled these rejections further strengthened her public image and forced the Academy to state explicitly that it had rejected her because she was a woman. She proclaimed that she would be a "perpetual candidate" and years later wrote that this was "a special case in which the struggle was worth more than victory."

Naturally outgoing, Pardo Bazán never wanted to lock herself away or adopt the puritanical and timid attitude to the world that other women writers, afraid of the negative moral judgments to which public women were still subject, adopted. Her attitude stood in stark contrast to solemn seclusion and the puritanical manners, dress and personal style of the Countess Espoz y Mina, the prestigious social reformer Concepción Arenal (1820–93), or the sorrowful poet Rosalía de Castro (1837–85), and many of her contemporaries were unable to deal with it. From very early on Pardo Bazán realized the sexist trap facing a woman who acquired a reputation for seriousness by rigorously respecting the social expectations of domesticity, modesty, and lack of ambition. She chose a busy social life and a "flamboyant" wardrobe, and never hid her ambition for literary glory. She was a regular at the great aristocratic salons of the day as well as running a highly prestigious *tertulia* (intellectual gathering) of her own in both Madrid and La Coruña. She was also well known for her passion for lace and spectacular hats. As a result, for years she was said to be erratic and superficial. She was also said to be, and here the absolute lack of any sentimentality in her work probably played a role, "a male talent" and to have "a manly attitude." Her great contemporary *Clarín* said that she "writes in a manly way and produces like a man."

There was one role which she absolutely refused to play, which she could not abide, and against which she fought all her life and in all her works: the "domestic angel" of liberal, bourgeois culture (see Chapter 11). This is a stereotype she repeatedly demolished in her books. *Her* female protagonists are not punished with tragedy or death as they are in Tolstoy's *Anna Karenina* (1877) or Pérez Galdós' *Tristana* (1892). To judge by her correspondence with Pérez Galdós, with whom she had an affair, she destroyed the expectations that he along with so many other male writers prescribed for their female protagonists in her life as much in her work. Indeed, she was more than happy to turn the usual roles on their head, as she did in this letter to him: "I have always held myself back with you out of fear of causing you physical harm. . . . I have always thought of you the way robust husbands think of their delicate wives."

Pardo Bazán never accepted the image of the solitary woman writer condemned to a loveless life of solitude, shut away with her pen in an attic, removed from the world, and perhaps even a bit crazy. Nor did she cultivate the image of the fearless Amazon of letters, although many tried to ascribe it to her. When at the end of her life someone asked her if she found writing easy she replied: "Indeed, if it weren't I wouldn't write. Writing is not like mining coal." This way of projecting herself in society, of openly and joyously defining herself as a *famous woman*, was perhaps her most subversive trait. It would be hard to find another woman writer of her generation anywhere in Europe who matched her in the difficult task of what Mary Jo Margadant has called "creating a female 'I' intelligible to the public."

Pardo Bazán's "female I" remains a puzzle to this day. Scholars continue to disentangle the combinations of social elitism and marked anti-liberalism with a deep concern for the "social question," and of the feminism and Catholicism she brandished as the cornerstones of her identity. Some have seen her strong Catholicism and her social and political elitism as inconsistent with her attempt to create a modern woman, but this assumes a necessary conflict between religion and modernity, not to mention the democratic nature of early feminism. Indeed, historians have recently come to see that in Catholic Europe, and in Spain in particular, religion provided a useful vocabulary for expressing early feminist ideas. If we reject these positions we can appreciate her Catholicism, and elitism, as well as her criticism of many aspects of modernity not as inconsistencies but as the intellectual tools and the language she had available to articulate her keen sense of injustice at the inequality between the sexes.

Pardo Bazán's Catholicism was an underlying form of social, moral, and intellectual orientation which played different roles at different times in her life. First of all, it was a fundamental part of her self-fashioning as the great lady of Spanish literature. One of her responses to the controversy surrounding *La Cuestón Palpitante* was to go to Rome to request the Pope's approval for the book. Second, Catholicism was a form of personal spirituality which represented a historic victory over "barbarism," generally identified with the Muslim world, and which provided men and women with a shared moral conscience. It should be noted, however, that she spoke more often of "Christianity" than "Catholicism" and was fully prepared to criticize the Catholic Church in her books, especially for endorsing a gender order that so hurt women. Finally, for Pardo Bazán, Catholicism formed an essential part of Spanish national identity, a key element of social cohesion and a link between the elite and the people in the nation's march toward progress. It was also a response to the long-established view of Spain, widely held among foreigners, as a backward, almost Oriental place, a view that she knew well from her travels in France and always tried to combat.

The question of religion connects to that of social class. Pardo Bazán was an open social and political elitist; after inheriting her father's Papal title in 1908 she signed all her correspondence Countess of Pardo Bazán and worked hard to get a new and more important title for her son. At the same time, she was also a hybrid, moving repeatedly between liberal and conservative political circles as well as aristocratic, intellectual, and social ones.

Emilia Pardo Bazán always lived between two shores, a powerful demonstration of the shortcomings of a view of the past based on simple dichotomies such as modernity and progress or liberalism and reaction. What is clear is that she was very critical of the liberalism of her time but this did not make her a reactionary, someone who always looked on the past as a time better than the present. She was too intelligent and cultured for that. She knew that every historical period contained a number of different tendencies, that these were often in conflict with each other, and that there was no single ideology of progress. There were the remnants of the old world and the promises of the new and the interesting space were the tensions between them. There was tradition and progress but neither was exempt from criticism. She could look at the past, the old aristocratic order that had been destroyed by the emergence of modern capitalism, nostalgically but never romantically. The "natural" and harmonious rural society that reactionaries talked about was a myth, as she made clear in her great novel *The House of Ulloa*, but the world that had replaced it was no less unjust, much less stable, and ruled by corrupt elites who lived in fear of the people.

This dark side of progressive liberalism, the "twisted timber" of its ideas of liberty and equality, are is constant themes of her work. In her novels, essays, speeches, and newspaper articles she returned again and again to the question of the role of the new elites, of how they would live up to their responsibilities, confront the anxieties of the modern world, and mold and lead a new, modern Spain that remained true to its traditions while becoming truly European. This is where her analysis of the "woman question" fits in. Whether it was her recognition that it was a basic problem of national moral, political, and cultural regeneration or whether her keen awareness of the differences in independence and social power between the men and women of the new elite which allowed her question the system as a whole, she ended up calling into question the narrative of inevitable progress that was shared by liberals of all stripes. She made it clear that in giving men ever greater political rights and in accepting the sexist approach of contemporary science, liberals had put women in a less advantageous position than ever before because they had created an unprecedented breach between the masculine public sphere and the feminine private sphere. Her work made a substantial contribution to the debate over the entry of the "masses" into politics as well as to the complex relations between liberalism and first-wave feminism at what she saw as a crucial crossroads in the creation of the modern Spanish nation. This was a process which involved the novel and literary criticism as well as more formal means of nationalization coming from the state, and as an intellectual and a famous woman, Pardo Bazán was at the very center of public discussion.

Hers was a distinctive voice. It was neither the conservative one reaffirming the traditional role of women as guardian of the essence and honor of the fatherland, nor the progressive liberal, radical, or even socialist one of the citizen-mother. Rather, it was a voice that denounced the hierarchical difference between the sexes and proposed instead a strong and active role for women in the construction of the Spanish nation. In her view, true progress and true equality could only come from the full recognition of individuality and difference. Individuality was crucial: equality that ignored it led to what she saw as the authoritarian tendencies of liberalism and democracy. Women would only be truly equal when they were allowed to be as different from each other as men were already. This extended to motherhood. She had three children herself and was quite happy as a mother, but she didn't see motherhood as defining a woman's identity. Her statement "all women conceive ideas but not all of them conceive children" was far ahead of its time. It was this ability to conceive ideas, to make the common sense of her time a topic for discussion, and to create characters who were complex and original—starting with her own public persona—that made her nineteenth-century Spain's "grande dame of letters."

Further reading

Acosta, Eva, *Emilia Pardo Bazán. La luz en la batalla*, Barcelona: Lumen, 2007.

Bravo Villasante, Carmen, *Vida y obra de Emilia Pardo Bazán*, Madrid: Revista de Occidente, 1962.

Faus, Pilar, *Emilia Pardo Bazán. Su época, su vida, su obra*, La Coruña: Fundación Barrié de la Maza, 2003.

Kirkpatrick, Susan, "Emilia Pardo Bazán: La ambigüedad de una mujer moderna," in Manuel Pérez Ledesma e Isabel Burdiel (eds.), *Liberales eminentes*, Madrid: Marcial Pons, 2008, pp. 376–85.

Lejárraga, María, "La feminidad de Emilia Pardo Bazán," in Alda Blanco (ed.), *A las mujeres: Ensayos feministas de María Martínez Sierra*, Logroño: Instituto de Estudios Riojanos, 2003, pp. 133–40.

Pardo Bazán, Emilia, "Apuntes autobiográficos," prólogo a *Los Pazos de Ulloa* (1886.) *Obras completas* II, Madrid: Biblioteca Castro, 1999, pp. 5–57.

Pardo Bazán, Emilia, *La mujer española y otros escritos*, Madrid: Cátedra-Feminismos, 1999. (Edición de Guadalupe Gómez-Ferrer)

Pardo Bazán, Emilia, *The House of Ulloa*, London: Paperback, 2016.

Parreño, Isabel, and Juan Manuel Hernández (eds), *Miquiño mío. Cartas a Galdós de Emilia Pardo Bazán*, Madrid: Yurner, 2013.

CHAPTER 29
JUAN PRIM
Gregorio de la Fuente Monge

One of the distinguishing characteristics of Spanish liberalism was the political prominence of military men as party leaders. Juan Prim (1814–70) was, along with Baldomero Espartero and Ramón María Narváez, a model of the nineteenth-century Spanish liberal military officer and prominent political leader.

The Carlist War and colonial endeavors in the 1860s allowed Prim to make a brilliant military career. He took advantage of this to build a parallel political career as a member of the Progressive Party which, after a number of ups and downs, culminated with his leadership of the Revolution of 1868. As head of the Provisional Government he oversaw the drafting of a new constitution and the election of a new monarch, Amadeo of Savoy, but his assassination cut short the most promising attempt to democratize Spanish political life during the nineteenth century (See chapter 3).

Juan Prim y Prats was born in the Catalan city of Reus shortly after the end of the Napoleonic War. He came from a relatively humble family: his mother was the daughter of small shopkeepers and his father was a soldier and failed notary. Prim himself was a poor student who did not finish high school and who, for lack of any other options, wound up working in his father's office. The Carlist War saved him from obscurity: in 1834 he joined the Tiradores de Isabel II, the volunteer unit his father commanded. His bravery and innate leadership abilities brought him a rapid series of promotions and in 1837 he was awarded the rank of captain, which allowed him to command regular troops. By the end of the war he was a colonel and had been twice decorated. Politically, he leaned toward the Progressives.

The revolution of 1840 opened a period of three years of Progressive government (see Chapter 3). Prim had not been involved, but he was able to get elected to parliament for his home province in February, 1841. As a deputy, he voted against the proposal for a one-man Regency; defended Catalan textile interests; and was critical of the clergy, who he saw as Carlist sympathizers. The bombardment of Barcelona in November 1842 brought about his complete break with the Espartero regency. He spoke out strongly in Parliament and when the government refused to issue him a passport, he traveled to France under a secret identity where he met with the Moderate exiles who were conspiring against the regime. This was the first of what would prove to be a number of such conspiracies in which Prim participated.

He returned to parliament following the elections of 1843 and as the Regency entered its final crisis; Prim spoke forcefully against it, even launching a fierce attack on Espartero himself. When the Regent closed Parliament, Prim returned to Reus where, on May 30, he helped launch an uprising against Espartero. It was a failure and Prim was forced to abandon the city with 500 men. He went to Barcelona where he put himself at the orders of the local revolutionary committee, which promoted him to brigadier general and tasked him with defending the city. He forced the government forces to withdraw and then helped push them back toward Madrid and their final defeat at Torrejón de Ardoz on July 22. Two days later, at the head of 4000 Catalan volunteers, Prim entered the capital behind Narváez and the other leaders of the revolution. The head of the provisional government, General Serrano, recognized Prim's contributions by confirming his promotion to brigadier and naming him Count of Reus and Viscount of Bruch.

Prim was still a young man—he was only 28—but he was already a General with two noble titles who enjoyed the esteem of his countrymen. This meteoric ascent suggested a promising political career, but the future would be much more complex and difficult than the past.

In August 1843 Prim was sent to Barcelona as military governor. The government hoped to use his prestige there to head off protests against its failure to respect the promise that Serrano had made to hold a meeting of the Central Revolutionary Junta. Prim failed to convince the Barcelona Progressives, many of whom were on the Democratic, and even Republican, wings of the party, and they in turn denounced him as a traitor. When the Jamancan revolt broke out on September 2, Prim dealt with it in much the same way that Espartero had dealt with Barcelona the previous year: with brute force. When militiamen insulted him he supposedly shot back, "o caja o faja"—either a coffin or a general's sash. He withdrew his troops from the city and watched as it was bombarded for two weeks before surrendering. Prim got his "faja," a promotion to field marshal, but at the price of seeing his popularity in Catalonia destroyed.

The next years would be difficult. Prim had been party of the conspiracy against Espartero but he always considered himself a Progressive. In October 1844, he was implicated in a conspiracy against Narváez and condemned to six years in prison on the Mariana Islands in the Pacific, although he was pardoned the following year at his mother's request. He spent two years in exile before an amnesty allowed him to return to Spain in 1847. The government considered him to be politically untrustworthy and got him out of the way by sending him to Puerto Rico as captain general. He held the post for only a year but earned himself a reputation for his racism and his brutality in dealing with slaves, embodied in his *Bando contra la raza Africana*—Edict of the Black Race. The edict imposed severe punishments for any crime committed against people or property by people of African ancestry as well as closely regulating their social activities. Using fear of the influence of the French Revolution in the Caribbean as an excuse, he even went so far as to help put down a slave revolt in the Danish colony of Santa Cruz. The King of Denmark gave Prim a medal but the Spanish government was less impressed: he was convicted of numerous violations of the law and banned from holding office in the colonies for three years.

Prim spent the next six years traveling in Europe and renewing his contacts with Barcelona Progressives. He was also able to revive his political career, getting elected to Parliament in 1850, 1851, and 1853. Prim sought to regain the prestige he had enjoyed in Catalonia until the events of 1843, and one of his most important speeches in these years criticized the government's harshness in dealing with Catalonia, which remained under a state of siege. "For how long do we have to be treated like slaves?" he asked. "Are we or are we not Spaniards?" Even though he was willing to criticize it, Prim was also very adept at not going beyond the narrow limits the government was willing to allow. And the government was still unprepared to trust him entirely: when the Crimean War broke out in June 1853, he was appointed head of the Spanish military mission sent to observe the conflict. The posting gave Prim the opportunity to widen his European contacts, including meeting Napoleon III in Istanbul, as well as learning about modern warfare. He turned his observations into a book, *Memoir of a Military Trip to the Orient* (1855), which earned him international prestige.

Prim's mission in the Crimea meant that he missed the Revolution of 1854 that brought Espartero and the Progressives back to power but he soon returned to Spain. Lord Howden, the British Ambassador in Madrid, described the 40-year old Prim as "young, brave, eloquent, unprincipled, insolent and restless." Prim once again ran for Parliament. In his electoral manifesto he called for "a monarchical constitution with all the guarantees of a republic." He also announced his support for a number of reforms, most of which were part of the Progressive program: suffrage for all Spanish men who were literate or paid a small amount of tax, bringing back the National Militia, ending conscription, suppressing the hated "consumo" tax, subordinating the clergy to the State, a new disentailment, the construction of railways and free, or at least "inexpensive" elementary education. He was elected in 1854 and again in 1855.

In his role as deputy, he supported Espartero and defended the high tariffs which protected Catalan industry against demands for free trade, but as a soldier he was a firm believer in defending national honor when it was offended and public order when it was challenged. During a brief stint as captain general of Granada he fought the Berbers who had attacked the city of Melilla, an action which brought him yet another promotion. And when General O'Donnell launched a coup in July 1856, attacking Parliament, dissolving the Militia, and mercilessly putting down Progressive and democratic resistance, Prim's primary concern was to retain the confidence of the Queen and to protect his political future. He approved O'Donnell's reactionary policy of public order which privileged the principle of authority over the freedom of citizens. Liberty and order were two sides of the same coin, to be sure, but his understanding of the relationship between the two was much closer to that of his Moderate adversaries than of his supposed Progressive allies.

Any hopes Prim had of an influential role in the new regime quickly disappeared. In October the Queen replaced O'Donnell as head of government but she replaced him with the old conservative standby, and his longtime enemy, Narváez. Their antagonistic relationship soon surfaced again: Prim published a letter which was deemed to lack the respect due to the authorities and he was sentenced to six months internal exile in Alicante. When he was again elected to Parliament in 1857, this sentence was commuted to residence in France.

The year 1858 looked more promising. On the personal front, his wife gave birth to their first child. Politically, Narváez was dumped in favor of the more moderate O'Donnell who was able to govern for almost five years, a record for the nineteenth century. O'Donnell achieved this by bringing together the widest possible range of liberals in his new Liberal Union party. Prim was one of many Progressives, pejoratively called "resellados"—turncoats—, who were attracted by the possibilities of advancement this offered.

This certainly worked for Prim, at least for a while. Immediately after the new government took office in July 1858, the Queen named him a senator for life. His biggest break came the following year, when O'Donnell launched Spain into the so-called War of Africa in Morocco. O'Donnell himself had overall command, but Prim was in charge of the first reserve division with which he won the battle of Los Castillejos on January 1, 1860, a victory which was soon immortalized by the painter Mariano Fortuny. He was then given command of the Second Army Corps, which included a battalion of Catalan volunteers raised by the Diputación of Barcelona, with which he achieved two additional victories, at Tetuán and Wad-Ras, which forced the Sultan of Morocco to sue for peace.

The war provoked an unprecedented wave of enthusiasm across Spain which brought great prestige to the Liberal Union government. The army also took advantage by staging victory parades, including one in Madrid in which Prim was the star. He was now a national hero and would quickly be turned into a legend by writers and artists such as Victor Balaguer, Pedro Antonio de Alarcón, Fortuny, and others. The Queen rewarded him by making him a grandee of the first class with the title Marquis of los Castillejos. From Madrid he went to the French spa town of Vichy where he was feted by Napoleon III.

Prim returned to Spain in September 1860: in Catalonia he received a hero's welcome in Figueras and Gerona before arriving in Barcelona. There, in the presence of Isabel II, he was celebrated as glory of the nation and commander of the Catalan volunteers. Then, in Reus, he was hailed as the town's greatest son and given a series of banquets which lasted for two weeks. In his speeches, Prim took care to describe himself as a "good Catalan," always ready to fight for his Queen, "the glory of the fatherland and the honor of the Catalan people." This victory tour finally allowed Prim to distance himself from the events of 1843, which had cast such a cloud over his popularity in Catalonia.

Soon afterward, Prim was sent back to America. The Spanish, French, and British governments had decided to send a military expedition to Mexico to ensure that the Mexican government paid its debts to their investors and in November 1861 Prim was named Spain's ambassador and military commander. When he arrived in Havana, Prim learned that General Serrano, the captain general of Cuba, had already taken troops to Mexico and seized control of the customs house of Veracruz. Following O'Donnell's instructions as well as the terms of the treaty, Prim refused to intervene in internal Mexican conflicts and limited himself to seeking a negotiated solution. In this he was helped by his personal contacts with the Mexican Minister of Finance, González Echeverría, uncle of Francisca Agüero González, the wealthy Mexican woman Prim had married in Paris in May 1856. Prim and the Minister were also involved in a family business which they sold at this time, making a huge profit. Prim came from a poor family and both his repeated trips abroad and his growing taste for luxury meant that he had always had money problems. His marriage eliminated them.

Along with his British counterpart, Prim refused to support Napoleon III's plans to impose a monarchy on Mexico and when he received word that the government of Benito Juárez was prepared to satisfy Spain's demands, he declared his mission accomplished. When Prim ordered his troops back to Havana, Serrano, who wanted to cooperate with the French in making Maximilian of Habsburg emperor of Mexico, blocked his attempts to remove Spanish troops from Mexico. Prim responded by transporting them on British ships.

Before returning to Spain, Prim went to the United States, which was then in the middle of its Civil War. He met President Lincoln and observed the Army of the Potomac; he went away much impressed with the country's military capacity and even more convinced that his decision to withdraw from Mexico had been the right one, even though it had cost him the friendship of Napoleon III. But when he returned to Spain, Prim found himself at the center of a political controversy. Under pressure from the French government, sectors of the Spanish press, the Moderates, and even some members of his own party, O'Donnell censured Prim for his conduct. On the other hand, Isabel II demonstrated her support by accepting his invitation to stand as godmother to his daughter, who was baptized in the royal palace.

Prestigious and popular, and enjoying the support of the Queen, Prim decided that the moment had come to break with the Liberal Union and patch things up with the "puros," the Progressives who had remained in opposition and who had lacked a military leader since Espartero's withdrawal to his home in Logroño in August 1856. He was, he said, the

Progressives' best chance to be called to power and the party leadership agreed. The formal reconciliation took place in March 1863 at the house of Salustiano Olózaga, the party's leading parliamentarian. There were still problems. When the Progressives decided to protest the government's restrictions on campaigning by boycotting the elections, Prim at first refused to go along. However when his attempts to convince the Queen to change course failed, he changed his mind. Despite Prim's hesitations, and there would be more, the Progressives—and democrats—would use electoral boycotts as a way of challenging the legitimacy of the regime.

At a crucial banquet in May 1864 Prim declared that the party would come to power "one way or another." This statement made him the leader of the branch of the party which advocated a military uprising, *pronunciamiento*, to force the Queen's hand and call the Progressives to power, and from this point on he would be involved in a number of conspiracies. The first came in August 1864; it failed dismally and earned him arrest in the provincial city of Oviedo. Following two more failures in 1865 he fled to France although he was amnestied by the government. Back in Madrid he met various times with O'Donnell, again the prime minister, and with Isabel, but these conversations did not produce the result Prim hoped for: to be given the opportunity to form a government. In January 1866, he attempted another rising near Madrid but it failed and he was forced to flee to Portugal. This time the government would not be lenient: a military court declared him a rebel and sentenced him to death in absentia.

Prim was now a permanent exile and he watched from France as an uprising led by sergeants in the San Gil barracks in Madrid was brutally repressed by General Serrano: 66 sergeants were shot, newspapers closed, and hundreds of Progressives and Democrats forced into exile. In August 1866 he presided over a crucial meeting of these exiles in the Belgian city of Ostend. There they signed the Pact of Ostend in which they agreed to overthrow Isabel II and hold elections under universal male suffrage for a Constituent Assembly which would determine the future form of government: the constitutional monarchy the Progressives wanted or the republic the democrats desired. They also agreed to accept Prim as their leader and to use a new tactic, a *pronunciamiento* backed by a civilian uprising.

The first attempt came in August 1867 and it was another failure. Crossing the border from France, exiled military officers raised armed bands across Aragon and Catalonia. Prim was supposed to have joined them but he changed plans, sailing to Valencia and trying to provoke a revolt there. When this failed he returned to France and headed to the border but by the time he got there the movement had collapsed and he decided not to cross. Prim had issued a proclamation calling on Spaniards to rebel against "what exists" and offering them a democratic Constituent Cortes and such popular measures as the abolition of obligatory military service and the *consumo* tax but there was no *pronunciamiento* in the cities to support the civilian rebels. The Democrats felt they had been betrayed; some abandoned Prim while those who did not, never trusted him entirely. When O'Donnell died suddenly at 58 in November 1867 the bulk of his Liberal Union joined the revolutionary coalition. Prim now had the military allies he needed for a successful revolt.

Success finally came in September 1868. Prim led a coalition of Progressives, Democrats, and Unionistas which chased isabel from the throne and destroyed the Moderate regime. Along with Admiral Topete, he was at the head of a revolt by navy ships in Cádiz and issued the proclamation, "Long live Spain with honour" which called for "a provisional government which represents all the vital forces in the country, which ensures public order so that universal [male] suffrage will lay the foundations of our political and social regeneration." After defeating troops loyal to the Queen at the Battle of Alcolea, General Serrano, the commander of the revolutionary army, promoted Prim to Captain General, the highest rank in the Spanish army. As Isabel went into exile in France, Prim sailed up the Mediterranean coast, consolidating revolutionary positions in the cities. When he got to Barcelona, he was received by massive cheering crowds. On the day of the uprising, his portrait had been paraded through the streets of the city and a painting of the Battle of los Castillejos hung from the Balcony of the Diputación. In Barcelona, in Zaragoza, in Madrid, and elsewhere, Prim concluded his speeches with cheers for Liberty and National Sovereignty and with the slogan, "Down with the Bourbons," giving the revolution an unambiguously anti-dynastic goal.

Prim was given the post of War Minister in the Provisional Government headed by Serrano. With the Democrats excluded from the government, the revolutionary coalition soon collapsed. Most Democrats joined the new Federal Republican Democratic party, but a minority, known as the *cimbrios*, continued to support the Progressive project of a democratic monarchy. In January 1869, Spain had its first elections under universal male suffrage. Prim was elected in two districts, Madrid and Tarragona, and chose to represent the former. He also retained his position as Minister of War. The Progressives were the largest group in Parliament and, as their leader Prim played a major role in shaping the new regime. The new constitution made Spain a "democratic monarchy" with broad civil rights including, for the first time, religious freedom. When it was promulgated on June 1, 1869, Serrano became Regent until a new monarch could be selected. Prim replaced him as prime minister and formed a new cabinet, which included a few of the *cimbrios*.

Prim had retained the War Ministry and this presented him with four significant problems. The first was the war in Cuba, which had broken out almost immediately after the September revolution (see Chapter 13). The war, which would drag on for ten years, forced Prim to abandon his plans to grant the colony autonomy and his promise to abolish conscription. It also meant limiting the debate on the future of slavery in Puerto Rico. The second problem was the large number of anti-conscription protests prompted by the need to call up large numbers of men in 1869 and 1870. In Barcelona and Jérez, where there were major riots, Prim did not hesitate to use force. Third were the republican uprisings, especially the widespread insurrection in the autumn of 1869 which forced him to suspend constitutional guarantees. Finally there were the Carlist revolts in the summer of 1869 and 1870. His use of military force, combined with a Public Order Law and a new Penal Code, lost Prim much of his popularity among the lower classes but the Army remained loyal.

Prim's biggest task as head of government was to find a new monarch. In a famous speech to the Cortes he said that the Bourbons would "never, never, never" return to the Spanish throne. This eliminated three possible choices: Isabella's son Alfonso, the Carlist pretender, and the Duke of Montpensier, a member of the French Orleans family who was married to Isabella's sister, and who had considerable support among the Liberal Unionists although he was unacceptable to Napoleon III. But finding a replacement proved much harder than he had anticipated, as he later admitted in Parliament. The most popular candidate was the 75-year-old Espartero; the fact that he had no children and thus could not found a dynasty made him acceptable to many republicans. Espartero was not interested, and when Prim sent him a letter offering him the throne but not guaranteeing parliamentary support, he refused.

With no Spanish candidates available, Prim had to look for a king elsewhere in Europe, and this meant navigating the difficult waters of European diplomacy. Over a year and a half he sounded out King Victor Emmanuel of Italy about one of his sons; Ferdinand of Saxe-Coburg and Gotha, the widower of Queen Maria II of Portugal; and a member of the German Hohenzollern family. (This last possibility was manipulated by the Prussian chancellor Otto von Bismarck to maneuver Napoleon III into starting the Franco-Prussian War which paved the way to the unification of Germany.) In the end, Victor Emmanuel agreed to allow his son, Amadeo, to accept the Spanish throne. The Cortes approved on November 16, 1870.

The new king arrived at the Spanish port of Cartagena on December 28. The night before, as he was riding through the streets of the capital in his carriage, Prim was shot. He died of his wounds three days later. Suspicion fell first on the Republicans, then on Serrano and Montpensier, but the assassin was never found. Amadeo reached Madrid on January 2; en route to the Cortes to swear allegiance to the constitution he stopped to pray before Prim's body, knowing that he had lost his most powerful supporter, the statesman who had embodied the principles of Liberty and Order. Just over two years later, on February 11, 1873 Amadeo abdicated and Spain became a republic.

Further reading

Anguera, Pere, *El general Prim. Biografía de un conspirador*, Barcelona: Edhasa, 2003.
Diego, Emilio de, *Prim. La forja de una espada*, Barcelona: Planeta, 2003.
Donezar Diez de Ulzurrun, Javier, *Prim. Un Destino Manifiesto*, Bilbao: Silex Ediciones, 2016.

CHAPTER 30
PABLO IGLESIAS
José Álvarez Junco

Founder and president of the Spanish Socialist Workers Party (PSOE) and its union organization, the General Workers Union (UGT), as well as founder of its newspaper, *El Socialista*, Pablo Iglesias Posse was the embodiment of the social democratic sector of the workers' movement in Spain for the last two decades of the nineteenth century and the first two of the twentieth.

Born in El Ferrol, Galicia, in 1850, his early years were marked by the harsh conditions so characteristic of the lives of the lower classes of the period. When Pablo was nine his father died and his mother, hoping to get help from a relative who worked as a servant for a noble family, moved with him and his younger brother to Madrid. When they arrived, they learned that the relative had died and no assistance was forthcoming. The two boys were sent to Royal Hospice of San Fernando while their mother squeezed out a precarious living cleaning houses and doing laundry in the Manzanares River. The brother died there, but Pablo received his first education and began to train as a typesetter. When he was twelve he managed to leave the Hospice and get a job in a print shop. With his apprentice's wage, which was less than one *peseta* a day at first, and the money his mother made they were able to rent an attic and buy enough food to survive.

The trade he learned in the Hospice was crucial to the course of Pablo's life. Far from being industrial workers, typesetters were literate—their job demanded it—and highly skilled, a kind of labor aristocracy. They could also exert a lot of pressure: a strike could paralyze the press which was central to the country's political life.

Pablo was eighteen when the Glorious Revolution of 1868 took place and it proved an intensive experience for him (see Chapter 3). On the one hand, he took advantage of the classes for workers offered by the government to further his education, studying French among other subjects. On the other, through the typesetters' union he came into contact with the group which founded the Spanish section of the International Working Men's Association or IWMA (see Chapter 17). He published his first article, a denunciation of wars and their disastrous impact on the working class as the product of capitalism, in their newspaper, *La Solidaridad*. On May 2, 1870, the anniversary of the popular uprising against Napoleon in 1808 and often a day for anti-French outbursts in Madrid, Pablo participated in an event showing solidarity with French workers which was broken up by the semiofficial goon squads known as the *partidos de la porra* (parties of the truncheon). Around this time he was fired from his job, the first of a number of occasions this would happen.

Both Pablo's life and that of the nascent Spanish workers' movement were marked by the Paris Commune of 1871. The Cortes debate over whether the International should be banned was passionate and even apocalyptic in tone and the harshest and most extreme measures were threatened. The members of the Spanish section responded with manifestos and protest meetings in which they accused the republicans for repressing what the claimed was a workers' revolution. Pablo Iglesias chaired some of these events.

The repression of the Commune pushed many French Socialists into exile. One of them, Paul Lafargue, who was also Karl Marx's son-in-law, went to Madrid where he made contact with the group which published *La Emancipación*, to which Iglesias belonged. Lafargue warned them of the existence within the IMWA of a fraction made up of followers of the Russian anarchist Mikhail Bakunin which had rebelled against the leadership of the London-based Association's General Council of which Marx was a member. In fact, most of the leaders of the IMWA's Spanish section were clandestine followers of Bakunin, which meant that the *La Emancipación* group, which included Francisco Mora, Hipólito Pauly, Inocente Calleja, and José Mesa, who had translated the *Communist Manifesto* into Spanish, as well as Iglesias were a minority and found themselves expelled from the organization, even though the General Council supported them.

The two groups differed over theoretical issues, particularly whether after the revolution there should be a dictatorship of the proletariat—Marx's position—or whether all political authority should be abolished—Bakunin's. There were also two more immediate ones: should the workers' organization be centralized or have a federal structure and should it participate in electoral politics or not. On both questions, the Marxists backed the first approach and the Bakuninists the second. The IMWA split at its Hague Conference in September 1872 which expelled Bakunin and his followers. In Spain, however, things went differently: at a conference in Córdoba three months later, the "anti-authoritarian" and "anti-political" wing won. Meanwhile, the Democratic Sexennium continued its tumultuous course but the Internationalists, wrapped up in the bitter debates with the republicans, or "bourgeois left," paid little attention to the important political changes, and even revolutionary situations, taking place around them.

Two successive military coups in 1874 put an end to this period and ushered in the Restoration of the Bourbons under the leadership of Antonio Cánovas del Castillo (see Chapter 4). The IMWA was banned and for the next seven years the revolutionary labor movement disappeared. For his part, Iglesias limited his activities to the typesetters' union, the Asociación General del Arte de Imprimir, of which he became president. Then in 1879, in a tavern near the Puerta del Sol in the very center of Madrid, Iglesias and 24 supporters decided to found a political party, the Spanish Socialist Workers Party. Of these 25 men, 16 were typesetters, 5 were medical students, and four were artisans. There was not a single member of the industrial proletariat among them.

In 1881, the Liberal Party came to power and the political situation became less restrictive. With Iglesias as its president, a National Typesetters' Union was created and carried out a strike in Madrid. It was a success, although it brought Iglesias and several of his comrades a jail term.

Some more progressive members of Spain's elites were becoming concerned about labor issues and in 1883 the government created the Social Reform Commission to study the lives of the working class. Although the Madrid Typesetters' Union and the Socialist organization made powerful presentations to the Commission, Iglesias was skeptical of the possibility of any meaningful changes being made within the capitalist system. The social and protective laws of the social democratic state were too far in the future for them to see.

The year 1886 was a crucial year in Pablo Iglesias' life. On the personal side, his mother died. He was still living with her, even though he was now 36. After her death he moved in with his friends Juan Almela and Amparo Melià. Seven years later, their marriage ended and Pablo and Amparo became a couple. They would remain so until his death in 1925. On the public side,

1886 was the year in which the weekly *El Socialista* appeared. As he himself would later admit, it was only after this that Spanish socialism really began to exist. The degree to which the paper mimicked its French namesake was striking: Iglesias even had the very first issue delayed until he received the exact same type as it used! There was some debate among the leadership over the paper's ideological line, especially its intention to "combat all bourgeois parties and especially those with the most advanced ideas." Jaime Vera opposed on the grounds that it was useful to have good relations with sympathetic parties against the purely "reactionary" ones but Iglesias did not agree and imposed his view.

Two years later, both the PSOE and UGT held their first conference. Both meetings addressed the question of whether the organizations should be based in Madrid, the national capital, or Barcelona, the major industrial city and home to the largest number of industrial workers. Since 1881 there had been a Democratic Socialist Spanish Workers' Party in the city. Barcelona also had a long-lived newspaper, *El Obrero*, as well as a strong union, the Tres Clases de Vapor, which took pragmatic positions including cooperating with republicans. This last point aside, it shared a lot with the PSOE and UGT, but Iglesias' obsession for centralized control of the entire organization prevented any merger. The National Committee of the PSOE was established in Madrid and the UGT's moved there in 1899, after a decade in Barcelona where more than half of the country's socialists lived.

Both the party and the union languished for the rest of the century, with a membership which barely doubled the original number of 3,000, a third of whom were typesetters. Outside of Madrid and Barcelona, there were centers in Bilbao, where Facundo Perezagua had been active, and in Malaga, although failed strikes against the Larios company in 1894 did the Socialist organizations serious damage.

Spanish socialism in this period was very weak on Marxist theory. As Antonio García Quejido, one of the UGT's founders, would later admit, few of the early leaders had read the *Communist Manifesto* and even the most well-read had seen only a French summary of *Capital*, a few other short texts by Marx or Engels and the occasional French or Italian pamphlet. They produced almost no theoretical works of their own; aside from *El Socialista* there were some short-lived periodicals devoted to theory, like *La Nueva Era* and *La Lucha de Clases*. Debates about theory of any sophistication were few and far between, and except for a few historical works by Juan José Morato they did not even produce any analyses of the contemporary conditions of Spanish workers. All this made their attendance at the congresses of the Second International, which was founded in 1889, especially important. Without leaders who could speak other languages, the Spanish delegates were limited to presenting a report on the situation in their country and did not participate in the debates about the development of the international workers' movement. "We were there to learn," Iglesias once confessed.

The ideas of Iglesias and his group boiled down to a rigid "economism" based on a belief that Spanish society was fully capitalist, on the iron law of wages, and on a straightforward class struggle between workers and bourgeois. Socialists should take advantage of legal loopholes to get improved conditions; they should run candidates in elections, although only as a propaganda tool because the goal was to make the revolution, not to elect deputies; and above all they should work to strengthen their organizations and never put them at risk with "adventures" such as wildcat strikes or acts of violence. The political approach developed by Iglesias was far removed from that of the anarchists, who rejected legal activities and engaged in permanent confrontation, but it was also very different from the outright reformism of the

Tres Clases de Vapor, which thought that the system could be changed gradually; and above all from the republicans, who Socialists saw as a class enemy whose politics would produce nothing beyond merely formal political changes.

One outstanding feature of Iglesias' approach was his insistence on the moral regeneration and increased self-esteem of the workers. Material gains were not enough: Socialists had to fight against illiteracy, alcoholism, and fondness for uncivilized entertainments like bullfights. Socialist publications systematically contrasted the "cultured" or "emancipated" worker to the "coarse, vulgar" employer. There was an effort to create an entire Socialist culture which included propaganda meetings, plays, and reading groups, a culture which drew on models popular among the middle classes and avoided work produced by the cultural avant garde. It was a mentality dominated by an obsession for formality, austerity, hard work, and the absence of corruption. This stood in opposition to the "corrupt" clergy. It was also similar to the ideas of the Institución Libre de Enseñanza, although less than their strongly interiorized Protestant-style moral principles, for they were based on a cult of the collective, later symbolized by the Casas del Pueblo.

As moderate as it was, this approach ran head on into the authoritarianism and rigidity of Spanish politics and the rigidity of Spanish society, which had little room for social reforms and saw the demands of the workers more as an issue of public order than anything else. As a result, even so moderate and restrained a man as Pablo Iglesias frequently found himself in jail, often for months at a time. He was also the target of innumerous personal attacks, including a famous rumor about his wearing a luxurious fur coat which he had bought with the dues paid by party members.

One especially famous moment was May 1, 1890. At its founding congress the year before, the Second International had decided to declare this day for demanding the eight-hour workday. The Spanish upper classes were beside themselves with fear and many families abandoned the cities which were left under the control of the army. When the day came, in Madrid there was only one meeting, and not even in the streets, and a demonstration led by Iglesias which presented a petition to Prime Minister Sagasta.

The year 1890 was also an important year in Spanish politics because of the introduction of universal male suffrage. However, the resiliency of the *cacique* system meant that Spanish Socialists were unable to achieve the success of their counterparts in Germany, France, or Great Britain (see Chapter 4). At the end of the nineteenth century, when the German Sozialdemokratische Partei Deutschlands (SPD) had received three million votes and won a quarter of the seats in the German parliament, the PSOE had yet to elect its first deputy.

The 1890s were also the years of anarchist terrorism, "propaganda by the deed," in Barcelona, which culminated with an 1896 bombing which was followed by mass arrests, confessions extracted under torture, and the execution of five innocent people. The Socialists joined the protest campaign alongside anarchist and radical republicans. Something similar happened during the opposition to the Cuban War (1895), which brought Socialists together with federal republicans and the young intellectuals of the "Generation of 1898" (see Chapter 16). Even so, Pablo Iglesias refused to accept the usefulness of such collaborations. He condemned the war but as a matter of principle: the working class had no fatherland and war was the creation of capitalism. He didn't bother to analyze the specific causes of the conflict, nor did he feel any sympathy for the Cuban rebels, but, given the unpopularity of the war, the unjust draft system and Spain's defeat, even this superficial analysis was enough.

The defeat provoked a deep crisis in the Restoration system, but it would take the Socialists ten years to take advantage of it. A minority of leading figures, like Juan José Morato and Antonio García Quejido, argued openly for an electoral coalition with the republicans, and there were some sporadic and meager efforts to work together. In 1899 they and the federal republicans presented a joint candidacy in Madrid and in the next party congress the PSOE approved occasional alliances when liberties were at risk. In 1903, as the republicans were becoming more unified and winning more votes, Socialists from Madrid who favored collaboration began to study the possibility, but Iglesias remained an adamant defender of Socialist isolationism. "We will always see the Republicans as enemies," he insisted, "hopefully they will always see us, as representatives of the working class, in the same way."

The twentieth century opened with some major strikes, in Bilbao in 1901 and a general strike in Barcelona in 1902, which brought out some 80,000 workers and led to a hundred deaths. The reaction of the PSOE was to hold firm to its policy of not putting the organization at risk and not to support the strike. It did the same with a proposed strike against the rising cost of living in 1905.

Despite suffering from ill-health, Pablo Iglesias continued to write for *El Socialista*, travel the country making speeches, attend international conferences, and gather information about the living conditions of Spanish workers and the observance of Spain's first labor laws, on Sunday rest, women's and children's work, and workplace accidents. Still convinced that no real improvements were possible under capitalism, he denounced these laws as mere paternalism, but this did not stop him from doing what he could to ensure they were respected. He also agreed to take part in the Social Reform Institute which was created in 1903 and in which the PSOE was offered five of the six places designated for workers' organizations.

After years of trying, Iglesias was elected to the Madrid City Council in 1905. He gave well-researched speeches in which he denounced abuses, speculation, inadequate municipal services, and poor working conditions. The party and the UGT became increasingly concerned with fighting for short-term reforms and put less emphasis on revolution. And they grew, as the opening of the Madrid Casa del Pueblo in 1908 demonstrated. The impressive building offered a library, a cooperative store, medical insurance, and a hall which could be used for meetings, putting on plays and showing movies.

A new war, this one in Morocco, started in 1909. The protest campaign brought the socialists closer to the republicans, especially after the Tragic Week in Barcelona and the subsequent repression unleashed by the government of Antonio Maura. This included the execution of the anarchist educator Francisco Ferrer, which produced an international scandal. The slogan "¡Maura no!" became the rallying cry for the creation of a Bloque de Izquierdas (Left Bloc) which the socialists joined, along with republicans and even Liberals.

Iglesias had been jailed again and when he was released he called a meeting with his supporters to determine strategy. They decided that the drift toward authoritarianism finally justified moving closer to the "bourgeois" left which allowed the Bloc to become the Conjunción Republicano-Socialista, an electoral coalition with a program of social reform, democratic freedoms, the separation of Church and State, obligatory military service, and morality in public life. This was the most important decision Iglesias made in his life: it led to the election of 53 Socialist city councilors across the country in the municipal elections of December 1909 and, then, in the parliamentary elections of May 1910, to the election of Iglesias as the first Socialist deputy to the Cortes.

As a deputy, the Socialist leader maintained his harsh tone. From the first moment he made it clear that the PSOE had joined the Conjución in order to "overthrow the regime" and that it would respect the law "so long as the law allowed the party to grow" but that this respect would end "when the law did not allow it to realize all its goals." He also caused a scandal when he said that "in order to stop Sr. Maura from returning to power my friends are prepared to attack him." When shortly afterwards there was an attempt to kill Maura in Barcelona, the conservative press charged him with inciting it.

In the second decade of the twentieth century, Spanish socialism changed due to its coalition with the republicans but also because of the influence of progressive and politically oriented members of the middle class like Jualián Besteiro, Fernando de los Ríos, Luis Araquistáin, and Indalecio Prieto. At the same time, Iglesias' health continued to decline and after 1912 he no longer attended PSOE congresses although he kept control of things through his loyal supporters.

The First World War divided the party, as it did Spanish society as a whole, into supporters of neutrality and supporters of the Allies. Iglesias held the second view, which was clearly dominant at the 1915 party congress, which approved a motion that an Allied victory would create new opportunities for the workers' movement.

The war also provided a great stimulus to the Spanish economy, but at the cost of rampant inflation and the PSOE led the protests against the rising cost of living. These included a 24-hour strike in December 1916, the first time the UGT and the anarco-syndicalist Confederación Nacional del Trabajo (CNT) had ever acted together. They collaborated again, in August 1917, in a general strike which was put down by the army with hundreds of casualties (see Chapter 5). The members of the strike committee, including socialists Besteiro, Andrés Saborit, Francisco Largo Caballero, and Daniel Anguiano, were tried by a military court and sentenced to life in prison. They were released following the elections of December 1918 when the PSOE increased its number of deputies to six, including the entire strike committee.

In the last ten years of his life, his deteriorating health forced Iglesias to give up his political obligations. In any case, the complexity of the new conflicts: the crisis of the Cánovas system—with the fragmentation of the two main parties and the increasing intervention of the king—the European war, massive inflation, collaboration with the CNT, were beyond him. In 1918, Largo Caballero was elected as General Secretary of the UGT and Besteiro as vice-president of the PSOE; Iglesias retained the title of president of both organizations but he no longer wielded any real power.

Starting in 1918, the Russian Revolution was the central, and agonizing, issue for Spain's socialists. At first, the PSOE gave it a tepid welcome, congratulating the triumph of democratic and socialist ideals, but the Socialist Youth were very enthusiastic and the Madrid Socialist and Asturian Federations, as well as a number of key figures, supported the Third International. A special party congress to debate the question was held in December 1919 and a motion to delay a decision was approved by the very narrow margin of 14,000 to 12,800. A second special congress six months later voted to join the new Moscow-based International, but only if it respected the party's autonomy, something which the 21 Conditions set out by Lenin made impossible. The party then sent a two-man delegation to Russia but de los Ríos and Anguiano made conflicting recommendations. Finally, in April 1921, a third special congress rejected membership, but only after Iglesias had sent a letter strongly supporting this position. Following this decision the advocates for joining the Third International abandoned the PSOE to create the Spanish Communist Party (PCE). The debate had produced a schism in the working class, something which Iglesias found inconceivable.

The war in Morocco started up again in 1921 and Spain quickly suffered two disastrous defeats, at Annual and Monte Arruit. Iglesias and the PSOE campaigned against the war and their campaign brought the closure of the Madrid Casa del Pueblo and the arrests of a number of leaders, including his adopted son Juan Almela Melià. The demands by Indalecio Prieto that those responsible for the disasters be held responsible threatened not just the military but the King himself and contributed to the coup staged by General Miguel Primo de Rivera in September 1923. The PSOE and UGT both condemned the coup, but not too strongly: they said that they did not see it "with sympathy" and that they held out "no hope" for it, but they refused to join the general strike called by the anarchists and Communists. Those closest to Iglesias, like Largo Caballero and Besteiro, refrained from condemning the coup while Prieto, who was much more political, did so. Later, Largo Caballero and Manuel Llaneza, leader of the powerful Asturian coalminers' union, agreed to join the new corporative institutions created by the dictatorship.

Pablo Iglesias died on December 9, 1925. Vast numbers of people filed through the Casa del Pueblo to see the body of the man who personified Spanish socialism and then marched in the funeral procession for his burial in the secular cemetery. Nonsocialists like Miguel de Unamuno, José Ortega y Gasset, and the intellectuals of the ILE described him as a man who was honest and entirely dedicated to a cause, a rarity in Spanish political life. They were right, but Pablo Iglesias also had a less positive side, rigid, authoritarian, and jealous of his power in the institutions he had done so much to build.

Further reading

Martin, Benjamin, *The Agony of Modernization. Labor and Industrialization in Spain*, Ithaca, NY: Cornell University Press, 1990.

Meaker, Gerald, *The Revolutionary Left in Spain, 1914-1923*, Palo Alto: Stanford University Press, 1974.

Morato, Juan José, *El Partido Socialista Obrero. Génesis, doctrina, hombres, organización, desarrollo, acción, estado actual*, Madrid: 1918 (reed., Madrid: Ayuso, 1976).

Morato, Juan José, *La cuna de un gigante. Historia de la Asociación General del arte de Imprimir*, Madrid: 1925 (reed., Madrid, Ministerio de Trabajo, 1984).

Pérez Ledesma, Manuel, *El obrero consciente*, Madrid: Alianza, 1987.

Sassoon, Donald, *One Hundred Years of Socialism: The West European Left in the Twentieth Century*, London: I. B. Tauris, 2010.

Serrallonga, Joan, *Pablo Iglesias. Socialista, obrero y español*, Barcelona: Edhasa, 2007.

Tuñón de Lara, Manuel, *El movimiento obrero en la historia de España*, Barcelona: Laia, 1972. (3 volumes).

CHAPTER 31
FRANCESC CAMBÓ
Enric Ucelay-Da Cal

Catalans often stand out in Spanish politics like sore thumbs. They are always a part of the picture, somehow out of place, certainly not granted the importance that they attribute to themselves. Barcelona is Spain's "second city," a stubborn rival to Madrid's primacy as capital, perennially insinuating that better leadership could be had under a Catalan orientation in the face of the often heavy-handed supremacy of centralist guidance. Barcelona promises an alternative perspective to "Spain" as an idea, both more Mediterranean and more European than the faded memory of world empire that somehow Madrid seems to embody. Undoubtedly, the political figure that stands out in the twentieth century as the major spokesman for this sideways rereading of Spain, for its most radical, yet practical, reinterpretation was Francesc Cambó (1876–1947).

Posterity has not been kind to his memory. Perhaps this reflects his double role, as parliamentary head of Catalan nationalism for over twenty years and as a key figure in the most reformist wing of Spanish conservatism. In the end, he proved too Spanish for Catalan nationalists and too Catalan for Spanish nationalists, and his reputation has paid for it.

Cambó was born on September 2, 1876, the third son of seven children of a wealthy peasant family in the town of Vergés, in the northern Catalan region of Lower Ampurdán. Popular wisdom paints people from there as canny, clever, stubborn, and hardworking. Cambó certainly possessed all these traits.

Catalan inheritance law, which was different from that in the rest of Spain, gave everything to *l'hereu* (the "heir"), the eldest—ideally male—child. If there were enough money, younger brothers would get their studies as "liberal professionals" (lawyers, physicians) paid for, and were then expected to fend for themselves. Girls were married off with a dowry. If there were not enough family capital, then the younger brothers would be apprenticed to a trade, while the sisters stayed home, literally as "spinsters" (i.e., spinning and weaving in domestic production), and as unpaid domestic help. Such things were discussed and negotiated: a family council decided that Francesc was most likely to succeed and so, instead of inheriting the farm, in 1891 he was sent to study law at the University of Barcelona.

Cambó's student years were significant. He had to work at tiresome chores to make ends meet, but he also met the best and the brightest in the small Law Faculty. Some were sons of the city's solid bourgeois families; others were, like him, outsiders. He became one of the youngest members of the group which formed around Enric Prat de la Riba (1870–1917), whose background was similar to Cambó's. But the group also included big-city boys like Joan Ventosa Calvell and Lluís Duran Ventosa, as well as the architect from Mataró, Josep Puig Cadafalch. All studied law in the late 1880s and early 1990s, and they would make up the nucleus of Catalan political leadership for decades to come. Ironically, these top students, hard workers with the highest grades, coincided at the University of Barcelona with Sabino Arana, the founder of Basque nationalism and his younger brother (and often inspiration)

Luís. The Aranas were weak students and Sabino dropped out to pursue his political ideals (see Chapter 10).

Like the new Basque nationalism with which it coincided, Catalan nationalism was strongly Catholic, conservative in social matters, and extremely leery of electoral politics. Prat and Cambó changed all that; they distanced themselves from the hidebound "Catalanist Union"; sought to appeal to a wider range of opinions; set up a newspaper; and in 1901 created a political party, the *Lliga Regionalista* or "Regionalist League", that was happy to include well-known personalities—doctors, lawyers—on tickets for parliament and for the Barcelona City Council. What mattered was their opinion about the rights of the Catalan nation and its language. For the rest, they could be monarchists or republicans, devout Catholics or anticlericals. The *Lliga* was a highly effective example of single-issue politics, with a disciplined vote-getting machine capable of generating majorities because of low voter participation. By 1905, it could count on solid support in Barcelona city and province, and possible alliances in Girona; although it was far weaker in the provinces of Lleida and Tarragona, the party gave the image of "controlling" all Catalonia.

The *Lliga* proved enormously successful at modern mass politics, with a talent for propaganda that seemed guileless and for provoking fights, while apparently standing aside as if it had nothing to do with the blows that followed. Its satirical press, notably the *Cu-Cut* (Cuckoo), was merciless, especially attacking militarist opinion forming among army officers and mocking them on points of their sensitive macho pride following the disastrous defeat in the Spanish-American War (see Chapter 21). Finally, in late 1905, a group of officers in uniform attacked the offices of the regionalist papers, hurled the furniture out of the windows, and set the rubbish afire. Then they demanded that any "crimes" against the honor of Spain, its institutions, or symbols be dealt with in military, not civil, courts. Garrisons all over Spain telegraphed their backing. The liberal government in Madrid, traditionally linked since the previous century to the army, simply caved in. The result was a broad wave of protest that joined the extreme left and right, all those political forces that accepted some sense of Catalan "regionalism," and rejected the dynastic system and therefore faced the rigors of military justice for their speeches or publications. Prat saw the opportunity for a *Lliga*-led movement and in the 1907 elections *Solidaridat Catalana* (Catalan Solidarity) won a massive victory. For the first time, there existed in the Madrid Parliament an explicitly Catalan minority with a clear political presence. The natural leader of "the Catalans in Madrid" to negotiate with the reformist, conservative government of Antonio Maura was Cambó, who was then scarcely 31 years old. Just before the election someone fired on his coach and he was seriously wounded, giving him the aura of a martyr (the attack was blamed on the Radical Party, a pro-Spanish, Republican party with a strong working class following in Barcelona).

Despite his best efforts, Cambó was unable to get his Catalan Solidarity colleagues and the Spanish conservatives to agree on a "Home Rule" agreement, like that being touted for Ireland in British politics. The violent street protest which broke out in Barcelona against the colonial war in Morocco, the "Tragic Week" of July 1909, shattered Catalan Solidarity and revealed a split in strategic focus between Cambó and Prat. While Cambó had failed to achieve anything in Madrid, Prat, who had been in charge of the provincial administrative entity (*Diputación*) of Barcelona since 1907, increasingly emphasized the development of local institutions in Catalonia over parliamentary action in the capital, and thus created for himself the image of a potential "president of Catalonia."

Between 1909 and 1911, the *Lliga* experienced a hidden but bitter struggle between the partisans of the two men over the question of the appropriate type of collaboration with the Spanish state, although a truce and reconciliation were arranged. The *Lliga* was now clearly a diarchy, between Prat—who dealt with "*Catalunya endins*" (inside Catalonia)—and Cambó—who was in charge of "*Catalunya enfora*" (outside Catalonia). Cambó's task was to convince liberal Prime Minister José Canalejas to accept a coordination of services (or *Mancomunidad*, in Spanish; *Mancomunitat* in Catalan) among the "diputations" of the four Catalan provinces. Canalejas, who was undertaking a liberal reform program which was intended to take the fire out of republican demands, which were now backed by a rising Socialist Party and anarcho-syndicalist unions, saw the attraction of assuring Catalan parliamentary votes in the Chamber and the Senate by promoting the regional reform Cambó was after and agreed to a deal. There was one small problem: many liberal factions balked at following their leader and the debates dragged on during the 1911–12 session. Then everything was overturned when Canalejas was assassinated while looking in a bookstore window, literally on his way to the opening of the new parliamentary session. His successor, the Count of Romanones, had a good working relationship with Cambó, but he lacked the personality to overcome the dissent within the liberal ranks. The parliamentary debates continued through the 1912–13 political session and when summer vacations began it was evident that the "Mancomunidad bill" was going nowhere. When parliament reopened in October 1913, Romanones finally threw up his hands and resigned, in what would become a trademark gesture.

Constitutionally, it was the King's prerogative to appoint the next prime minister, but this time Alfonso XIII faced a very difficult situation. The custom was to invite the leader of the opposition to form a new cabinet which would be followed, a few months later, by one of the Restoration's "managed elections" which would produce the majority needed for efficient governance (see Chapter 4). But the left had not forgiven Maura for the repression in Barcelona in 1909 ("¡*Maura No!*" was the enduring slogan), and King Alfonso XIII hesitated, both from his own insecurity and from his conviction that party fragmentation would reinforce the power of the Crown by making it irreplaceable in any government change. He also disdained Maura personally. For his part, Cambó knew that the maximum Catalan representation—some 30 seats in the Chamber and Senate—would not produce any significant capacity for leadership without a breakup of the two-party system. In the end, Alfonso called on the conservative second-in-command, Eduardo Dato, to form a government. Maura exploded with rage and the conservatives split down the middle. As the Liberals were already a welter of "personalist" groupings with no common consensus, the Spanish Parliament ceased to be an effective legislative tool. Dato's solution was to extend vacations as long as possible and govern by royal decree, the method he used to create the *Mancomunitat* in mid-December 1913. Cambó had increased his influence by allying with the King, but achieving other key Catalan demands, like the creation of free port zones to take advantage of the First World War commercial traffic with neutral Spain, proved elusive.

Then a crisis of the political system gave Cambó his great opportunity. At the end of 1915, parliament rebelled, and dumped Dato and his system but the divided Liberals were not up to the circumstances. Spain had avoided getting involved in the First World War, but it was still dealing with a full-scale "little war" in the protectorate it had assumed in Northern Morocco in 1912. This conflict divided colonial officers, with rapid battlefield promotions, from garrison careerists, who demanded a regular system of steady advancement. The latter, having observed the success of army pressure groups in the Ottoman Empire in 1908 and Greece in 1909, as well as the Republican revolution in Portugal that overthrew the monarchy in 1910, challenged the government, civilian authority, and their own army chain of command. Two cabinets crumbled under militarist defiance before King Alfonso called on Dato, who used his usual methods, with an early dissolution of Parliament.

This was Cambó's potential moment of greatness. There was general consensus among all political opinion except die-hard conservatives that the 1876 Constitution was in need of major revision and in the summer of 1917 Cambó led a full-scale parliamentary protest, convoking an assembly of Catalan deputies and senators, who met in Barcelona and invited all their colleagues to a new assembly to demand constitutional revision. There was a favorable response, but also a sharp reaction from the Dato government, which used the police to break up the initial session of the new *Asamblea de Parlamentarios*. The militarists, until then on the sidelines, came down clearly in favor of Alfonso XIII and his conservative cabinet. Socialist and anarcho-syndicalist unions declared a general strike to back the parliamentarians, but the army crushed it. Everyone waited for the opening of Parliament in the fall, but instead of continuing with the constitutionalist initiative and despite enjoying considerable support, Cambó cut a deal with the King (news in September of the proclamation of a republic in Russia was a major factor in his decision; the Bolshevik takeover would come a week after Cambó's meeting with Alfonso). This was a potential watershed moment for Spanish history, but one which turned out to be a missed opportunity. Unlike Sweden, where that same autumn there was a liberal-socialist "Democratic breakthrough" which reduced the powers of the Crown and the influence of the military, Spain saw no meaningful political change. Cambó offered a "National Coalition Government" which gave the *Lliga* an outsized role in Spanish politics—and himself a seat in the cabinet which he held from March 1918 to November 1919—but which was incapable of serious reform.

Cambó gambled on an upsurge in regional nationalisms to advance reform but this did not materialize. In November 1919 he abruptly resigned as Minister of Development to confront the challenge to his leadership coming from republicans and new-style radical nationalists in Barcelona. As part of the widespread euphoria stimulated by President Woodrow Wilson's call for national self-determination, Catalonia lived its Wilsonian moment. There was a call for a real "Integral Autonomy" for Catalonia but faced with the hostility of the Paris Peace Conference, worker violence and militarist response in Barcelona, and the appearance of Catholic unions opposed to the rise of industrial unions in anarchist hands, this too fizzled out in early 1919.

Cambó returned to the cabinet as Finance Minister in 1921 as part of the emergency government formed by Maura following a military disaster in Morocco. He held this important Finance post until the cabinet broke up in March 1922 and there was general agreement that he had been responsible for major reforms. By 1923, however, Cambó was worn out politically and had to deal with Prat's successor as president of the Mancomunitat and Lliga strongman, the architect Puig Cadafalch, who was potentially open to possible collaboration with the militarists.

By then, Cambó had become a millionaire. Through his acquaintance with the slippery American-Belgian financier Dannie N. Heinemann, Cambó, and his law partner Joan Ventosa, also a *Lliga* leader, became the brokers for a deal that took the Argentine branch of the German AEG trust beyond the reach of Allied takeover by making it into a Spanish company. Money on that scale made Cambó a free agent in Spanish politics and gave him a cosmopolitan air that distanced him from the local bickering of Barcelona. In 1923 he was willing to resign from active politics and take a long and meditative cruise through the Eastern Mediterranean on his new yacht. He thought seriously, and wrote a lot: on early Italian Fascism (which he understood as a clumsy call for a stronger executive free of crown meddling in a liberal parliamentary monarchy); on Turkish and Greek nationalisms; and, after the coup d'état by General Primo de Rivera in September 1923, on the nature of dictatorship, and of the future of Spain and the Bourbon monarchy. Cambó was to use European terminology, a strong *liberal*, who wanted a representative government and regular elections, but he was *not* a *democrat*, and distrusted trade unions as well as the initial signs of welfare statism that was emerging in the 1920s. Instead, Cambó, who was in many ways a frustrated intellectual, trusted in the leadership role that the Catalan and Spanish intelligentsias in Barcelona and Madrid could play in promoting the development of Spain without sacrificing the country's regional and cultural complexity and diversity.

Cambó could ride out the Primo de Rivera dictatorship in comfort, even as the portly general, who in 1925 finally abolished the Mancomunidad, kept picking fights with him in the press. By way of silent reply, Cambó relied on his reputation as an international financier. In fact, however, he failed in this respect as well. Instead of picking off where the American engineer Frank S. Pearson, who had died on the *Lusitania* in 1915, had left the project for a vast makeover of Catalonia and Spain through hydroelectric power, Cambó attempted to corner the world market in cork, of which his native Ampurdán district was a leading producer. It did not quite work, and it points to a rural boy who made good and who could not quit, forget his roots.

Cambó basically counted on the intelligentsias to save the monarchy and conspired with Alfonso behind Primo's back to that effect. He also used his money for a cultural campaign: seemingly spontaneous manifestos, apparently unrelated cultural events—a Catalan-language page in the vanguard weekly *La Gaceta Literaria*, and then a show of publications in Catalan in the National Library in Madrid. His right-hand man, Joan Estelrich, a Mallorcan based in Barcelona, ran Cambó's cultural foundations and also took charge of ethnic minority contacts in Europe, basically to frustrate more radical proposals by Catalan and Basque nationalists. All these efforts put Cambó in the leading position for replacing the dictator when, finally, in January 1930, King Alfonso, under pressure from many sides, found the energy to dump Primo de Rivera.

Then it all fell apart, again. On the night train from Paris to Madrid, ready finally to take over, Cambó caught a sore throat. He checked with his doctor, who detected throat cancer. Since money was no object, Cambó decided for the best Harley Street in London had to offer. But he still had to deal with the invitation to lead government. He declined. Worse still, he did not explain his reasons. This had a powerful impact, and led to all manners of speculation, while the King had little recourse but to call on Dámaso Berenguer, a liberal general who had his confidence. An extremely cultured man (who, for example, spoke flawless English, most unusual in Spaniards), Berenguer was too cautious as a politician, especially as the figure expected to lead a major political transition without seriously rocking the ship of state. The slow-moving Berenguer quickly stumbled, and even monarchists refused to play by his rules. Furthermore, the monarchy's short-term future was complicated, as the heir presumptive suffered from hemophilia, and clearly was not destined to reign.

Cambó recovered from his cancer surgery and returned in the new year to present a new unitary cabinet with the *Lliga* participation, backed by himself and the liberal Romanones, although some Liberals had publicly taken pro-republican positions. Together with progressive conservatives, Cambó had to put together a new platform, the "Constitutional Center," as *the* political force to lead the rhythm of change. The new government, formed in February 1931, and led by the liberal Admiral J. B. Aznar, had a classic Cambó program, with everything the left offered, but presented in prudent terms. It promised an autonomy statute for Catalonia, among other liberties, to be realized without revising the constitution. It proved to be, however, a classic Cambó failure. There was an unexpected upset. A maverick separatist, with a complicated past (he was a former Spanish Army officer), Francesc Macià (1859–1933) returned from exile in Belgium after the new government was formed. Macià cobbled together a conglomerate of left nationalist and republican entities, and unexpectedly ran away with the municipal elections on April 12. Then, instead of waiting for the scheduled provincial administrative and national elections, he proclaimed a Catalan Republic and a Spanish Federation, which in turn led to the establishment of a Second Republic for all Spain in Madrid. The crowds in Barcelona festively chanted: "Long Live Macià, Death to Cambó!" Prudently, the defeated politician went into exile in France and returned in a visible way only in 1933.

By the time Cambó did return, Catalonia had been granted a degree of autonomy and Macià was president of the *Generalitat*, the Catalan regional government (see Chapter 5). While Macià was concerned only with Catalonia, even at the expense of other nationalities, Cambó favored Catalan-Basque sponsored coalitions of nationalists and regionalists. This meant that he tacitly supported the formation—at first, outside Catalonia—of the *Confederación Española de Derechas Autónomas* (CEDA), the powerful right-wing coalition created in 1933, which Cambó's Valencian allies joined. Cambó also attacked Macià's power base in the Catalan "governmental" party, the *Esquerra Republicana* (Republican Left), which was producing discontent as a sort of incipient "single-party" system in the Catalan regional parliament. He revamped the old, weathered *Lliga Regionalista* into a new, modernized *Lliga Catalana* in 1933, and succeeded in so shaking up the *Esquerra* in the November 1933 Spanish elections, that Lluís Companys, who had succeeded Macià when he died on Christmas Day and lacked his charisma, felt obliged to open the Catalan government to a broad alliance of the left.

In a Republican situation which had veered to the right, Cambó became one of the recognized senior statesmen of Spanish politics, able to balance between the younger head of the CEDA, the prickly José María Gil-Robles, the aged and now moderate Radical leader Alejandro Lerroux, and the President of the Republic, Niceto Alcalá-Zamora. The contradiction between Cambó's commitment to Catalonia and his commitment to Spanish national politics quickly emerged once again. Following the uprising of October 1934, the government suspended the *Generalitat* and put the members of the Catalan government in prison and Cambó found himself bitterly fighting former collaborators on the Spanish right who wanted Catalan institutions abolished. And as the political situation deteriorated further and the tensions increased, he came to terms with Companys and the *Esquerra* when the Catalan president came triumphantly out of jail and was restored to power in Barcelona in 1936. While he agreed with Gil-Robles in his active distrust of working-class revolutionaries, he had no special sympathy, or even trust, for the militarists in the Army.

When the Civil War began, Cambó did not immediately decide where to put his support. It was only once General Franco, who was the recipient of Hitler's military assistance, became

Generalíssimo of the "National Cause" in October 1936, that Cambó quit dallying and gave open support, financial and otherwise, to the insurgents. He continued to hope for some kind of monarchist solution, and perhaps briefly toyed with the idea of putting a member of the Italian royal family on the throne, but this proved to be a non-starter. When Franco forced the Falangistas, Carlists, and monarchists into the National Movement in April 1937, Cambó found that many of his old political friends had by now become enemies. He prudently sat out the Spanish Civil War in exile, mostly in Switzerland, but also around Paris and in and out of Italy.

After the fall of France to Hitler and Mussolini's entry into the Second World War, Cambó left Europe for Argentina, where he continued to wield significant economic power. Among other things, he controlled about half of the electricity of Buenos Aires. The Argentine capital was a jumpy place during the Anglo-German conflict, and got more nervous still when the United States entered the war in December 1941. Cambó's economic power made him of necessity a political figure, but his influence was undercut by scandals over his company's willingness to buy politicians to retain its contract. The Argentine political situation became more turbulent as the army, led from the shadows by ultranationalist officers like Colonel Juan Perón, took over. Cambó did not have any direct connections to Perón and he saw the rise to presidential power of the crowd-pleasing colonel as his worst nightmare, a cross of working-class demagoguery with power-hungry militarism. Despite his distaste for Franco and the fact that Ramón Serrano Suñer, Franco's brother-in-law and former political guru, with whom he had good relations had fallen from power in 1942, he decided to return to Spain and try one last comeback. He had made sure that Estelrich's initiatives in cultural politics respected the regime's rules, including its heavy censorship. He tidied up his personal life and married his companion, now that he had a grown-up daughter. The flight from Buenos Aires to Madrid had a necessary stop in Dakar, Senegal, which meant that he had to get an anti-malaria shot before leaving. He had a violent reaction to the vaccine and died in Argentina on April 30, 1947.

So, if he failed so often, why bother with Cambó? In purely Catalan terms, he represents a high point in the ebb and flow of Catalan nationalism. As the successful leader of a minority sector in parliament, Cambó pointed to ways for effective intervention in coalition politics. Seen in a broader perspective, however, he was perhaps *too* successful at building alliances, as this got in the way of his actually being able to effect those changes he felt were needed to make Spain work. His short-term mechanism of broad "unitary" or "national" governments, whether he was a member as in 1917–18, 1921–22 or whether he was just the guiding spirit as 1930–31, always pitted him against any real "democratic breakthrough" within the monarchy. Without demanding Catalan autonomy he would have lost his political base, but the primacy of this demand negated his capacity to maneuver as a conservative. Cambó was also thwarted by the political presence of the working class: he was too conservative to work with them and, in turn, they were too prone to extreme radicalization to want to come to any understanding with him. In some ways, his ideas eventually came to fruition in the very different context of the post-Franco transition.

Cambó wanted to revamp Spain as a multiple monarchy, like Austria-Hungary at the turn of the century or the British Empire and its Dominions just before the Great War. As Minister of Development, Cambó also paved the way for the completion of Spain's expensive railroad grid and as Finance Minister he established the working pattern for tariffs, basic to the always dangerous balance of agrarian and industrial interests in a developing economy. These were far-sighted policies but their real effects became visible only later, in the industrial and communications policies of the Franco regime after the mid-1950s, which tipped the balance to an urbanized, industrial society in Spain. By then, Cambó was dead but not forgotten, at least in Catalonia.

Further reading

Almendros Morcillo, Alfons, *Francesc Cambó: la forja d'un policy maker*, Barcelona: Publicacions de l'Abadia de Montserrat, 2000.

Buqueras, Ignacio, *Cambó*, Esplugues de Llobregat: Plaza & Janés, 1987.

Cambó, Francesc, *Memòries (1876-1936)*, Barcelona: Alpha, 1981. (A Spanish translation was published by Alianza Editorial, Madrid, in 1987.)

Cambó, Francesc, *Meditacions: dietari*, Barcelona: Alpha, 1982. (2 vols.)

Cambó, Francesc, *Llibres*, Barcelona: Alpha, 1984.

Cambó, Francesc, *Articles*, Barcelona: Alpha, 2007.

Cambó, Francesc, *Discursos i conferències*, Barcelona: Alpha, 2007.

Jardí, Enric, *Cambó: perfil biogràfic*, Barcelona: Pòrtic, 1995.

Pabónm, Jesús, *Cambó*, Barcelona: Alpha, 1952–1969. (3 vols.)

de Riquer, Borja, *Francesc Cambó: entre la Monarquia i la República (com les memòries s'acomoden a les circumstàncies polítiques)*, Barcelona: Base, 2007.

de Riquer, Borja, *Alfonso XIII y Cambó: la monarquía y el catalanismo político*, Barcelona: RBA, 2013.

de Riquer, Borja, *El Último Cambó, 1936-1947: la tentación autoritaria*, Barcelona: Grijalbo, 1997.

Ucelay-Da Cal, Enric, *El Imperialismo catalán: Prat de la Riba, Cambó, D'Ors y la conquista moral de España*, Barcelona: Edhasa, 2003.

CHAPTER 32
JOSÉ ORTEGA Y GASSET
Javier Zamora Bonilla

José Ortega y Gasset was, along with Miguel de Unamuno, the Spanish intellectual who had the greatest influence on public opinion during the first half of the twentieth century. His contributions to philosophy and his reflections on literature and the arts made him a leading figure in Europe's recent intellectual history. One of the great stylists of the Spanish language, during the 1950s he was a candidate for the Nobel Prize for Literature. In addition, from the beginning of the twentieth century through the Second Republic he was highly active politically, sometimes through organizations such as the Liga de Educación Política Española (League for Spanish Political Education) in 1913 and 1914 or the Agrupación al Servicio de la República (Group at the Service of the Republic) in 1931 and 1932, but above all through the press, where he was one of the most important voices in these years. His articles had a huge impact in the corridors of power and his influence among broader educated society was such that his public lectures frequently filled large theatres. Following the "Dreyfus affair" in France at the end of the nineteenth century, the intellectual who functioned as the conscience of a changing society, denouncing the abuses of power and seeking to influence politics, became an important figure. Ortega was the outstanding Spanish example (See chapter 16).

Ortega y Gasset was born in Madrid on May 9, 1883, the second of four children. His mother, Dolores Gasset y Chinchilla, was the daughter of Eduardo Gasset, owner of *El Imparcial*, the most important liberal newspaper of the time. His father, José Ortega Munilla, edited its prestigious literary supplement, *Los Lunes*. Eduardo Gasset was a liberal politician who had served as a minister during the reign of Amadeo of Savoy as well as one of the founders of the Institución Libre de Enseñanza in 1876.

After Eduardo Gasset's death in 1884, Ortega Munilla took on a leading role in the newspaper. It was widely said that one of his editorials could bring down a government. He became editor in 1900 and was on numerous occasions elected to Parliament for a "rotten borough." This was a common practice at the time, as it gave journalists parliamentary immunity. Ortega Munilla was also a well-known literary figure and was elected to the Royal Spanish Academy in 1902. As a result, Ortega y Gasset grew up in a house that was swarmed with people from Madrid's literary and political worlds.

José Ortega y Gasset learned to read in San Lorenzo de El Escorial, a town near Madrid where his family lived for long periods. He attended elementary school in Córdoba, where the family moved so that his mother could recover from heart problems in the warm climate of Andalucia and was then sent with his two brothers to a Jesuit high school in Malaga, where he was a boarder. After graduating in 1897, he went to the University of Deusto, a Jesuit school in Bilbao, to study law and philosophy, but he transferred to the Universidad Central in Madrid, graduating with a degree in philosophy in 1902. Law had been his father's idea; it was the ideal stepping stone to a political career, but José knew he wanted to devote himself to more intellectual pursuits. His long experience as a student in Jesuit schools made him a strong critic of their pedagogical approach and their religious formalism, and he expressed these views in letters to his parents, to his fiancée Rosa Spottorno, where he was particularly critical of their spiritual exercises, and in many of his later published works. In a review of the novel *A.M.D.G* which was set in Jesuit schools, he wrote that "it would be desirable to close the Jesuit colleges if only for a purely administrative reason: the intellectual inadequacies of the Revered Fathers."

He completed his doctorate in Philosophy in 1904 and the next year he went to Germany where he planned to learn more about idealism and use it as a corrective for what he considered the pernicious subjectivism which characterized Spanish thought. This was the first of three extended visits he would make to German universities between 1905 and 1911. The first was divided between Leipzig and Berlin; the next two were in Marburg. Here, in the work of Hermann Cohen (1842–1918) and Paul Natorp (1854–1924), he encountered the scientific objectivity he had been seeking. Marburg was also a university where Social Democratic thought, the so-called university socialism, was influential and the young Spaniard took it in enthusiastically.

Ortega y Gasset had published his first articles in the press in 1902 and soon was publishing pieces in *El Imparcial*, the paper his father edited. He did not get a free ride, however, and his father did not publish everything he wrote, especially when he increased his output in order to earn money to fund his stay in Germany. Ortega started with articles on literary questions but he was soon writing about politics as well. In 1907 he was fully engaged in the journalistic debates of the day. He crossed swords with major established intellectuals such as Marcelino Menéndez Pelayo, Joaquín Costa, Miguel de Unamuno, and Ramón de Maeztu, as well as with members of his own generation such as Gabriel Maura, son of Conservative leader Antonio Maura, with whom he discussed the future of liberalism. Where Ortega thought it should become more democratic and socially oriented, Maura argued it should become more conservative. Ortega's articles frequently contained criticisms of the government. One of his first articles, "Reform character, not customs," published in 1907, criticized Maura's Interior Minister Juan de la Cierva for proposing laws that prohibited certain popular customs while neglecting to build a single new school.

In 1908 Ortega helped found the journal *Faro* and two years later he helped found *Europa*. These were harbingers of the publishing initiatives which would be one of the hallmarks of his later career. These early magazines would be followed by more substantive undertakings: such as the magazine *España* (1915), the newspaper *El Sol* (1917), the *Revista de Occidente* (1923), and its affiliated publishing house, and a number of book collections for the important Espasa-Calpe publishing house.

After a year as Professor of Psychology, Logic, and Ethics at the Advanced School for Teachers, in 1910 Ortega won the Chair of Philosophy at Madrid's Universidad Central. The next year he again went to Marburg, but this trip differed from the previous ones in a number of ways. This time he had a fellowship from the *Junta para Ampliación de Estudios e Investigaciones Científicas* (Committee for Advanced Study and Scientific Research), and he was accompanied by his wife, who he had married a few months before, and the first of their three children was born in Germany. It was also different intellectually. He was now less averse to subjective approaches, which he had come to see as a perspective rather than as an error, and learned about Edmund Husserl's phenomenology, which began to play an important role in his own intellectual development, as his book *Meditaciones del Quijote* (1914) showed.

This book was published by the Residencia de Estudiantes, which was run by his friend Alberto Jiménez Fraud. Ortega had collaborated with the Residencia since its creation in 1910. It was closely connected to the educational philosophy of the Institución Libre de Enseñanza as well as to the program of "Europeanizing" Spain that was being put forward by the group of intellectuals known as the Generation of 1914. Many leading members of this group were involved in the Liga de Educación Política Española (League for Spanish Political Education), which Ortega launched in March 1914 with a lecture entitled "Old Politics and New." The League hoped to take Spanish politics in a new direction, one which was more liberal, more democratic, and with more social conscience—more "European" in short. It achieved little in the way of concrete results, but it led to the creation of an important new journal, *España*, which ran from 1915 to 1924. Ortega was the editor during its first year, and was followed by Luis Araquistáin and Manuel Azaña.

Years before, Ortega had had some dealings with Pablo Iglesias and the Socialist Party and with Alejandro Lerroux's Radical Party, and had written articles praising them. Now, he became directly involved in politics, joining the Reformist Republican Party of Melquíades Álvarez and serving on its executive committee. However, Ortega soon quarreled with Álvarez, whose positions regarding relations with the Liberal Party and the Restoration regime were more accommodating than his own. Disillusioned with direct political involvement, he attempted to cocoon himself in *El Espectador*, a one-man band of a journal in which he could write about whatever caught his fancy: art, love, truth, women. The original goal of publishing an issue every two months proved to be beyond even his abilities, although he did produce eight volumes between 1916 and 1934.

Ortega had stopped writing for *El Imparcial* in 1913. His criticisms of the Liberal Party, which on one occasion he had called a "national nuisance," had annoyed his uncle Rafael Gasset, who was a major Liberal politician as well as the principal owner of the paper. Ortega would not publish in what he called his "ancestral home" until 1917, when businessman Nicolás María de Urgoiti tried to take it over. The operation came to nothing after Ortega published an article on the political situation in which he claimed that everything was in ruins and called for a Constituent Cortes to draft a new constitution, which provoked King Alfonso XIII himself to intervene to prevent the deal from going through. Frustrated by this outcome, a few months later Urgoiti launched *El Sol*, which would soon became the most important paper in the country. For the next two years, the paper received virtually all Ortega's time and effort. It was also where almost all of his books, including the most famous one of all, *The Revolt of the Masses* (1927–30), were first published.

Ortega was already a well-known intellectual, but his articles in *El Sol* made him much more famous. He dissected the crisis of the regime, which the hot summer of 1917 had made evident. He proposed a program for government which included measures to improve the situation of the less well-off: a heavy inheritance tax, involving workers in management of companies, profit sharing and social security, reforming the constitution to make it more democratic, allowing true freedom of religion, and reorganizing the country's political structure by instituting sweeping administrative and political decentralization and creating self-governing regions.

His political work did not mean that he had abandoned his other interests. His articles brought the newest writing from Spain and Europe as well as the work of the artistic avant-gardes to the attention of the paper's readers. His sociological articles analyzed the emerging mass society which was creating what he saw as a new human type, "mass man," who was transforming the world in what he considered undesirable ways. His articles on philosophy set out his ideas on metaphysics, what he called "the new sensibility of our time."

Nor was Ortega's influence limited to Spain. He had already presented many of his philosophical ideas during his six-month visit to Argentina in 1916 (he would spend another six months there in 1928). In Argentina he was received as an intellectual giant, the representative of a new, modern, and European Spain, far removed from the usual Latin American stereotype of an imperial and backward country. Between 1911 and 1914 Ortega wrote for the Buenos Aires paper *La Prensa*; after 1923 many of his articles appeared in *La Nación* and were subsequently reprinted in a number of Latin American papers.

In 1923 he founded *Revista de Occidente*, which soon became one of the most prestigious cultural reviews in the world until it was shut down during the Spanish Civil War (it was very popular in Latin America, where it sold half its print run of 3,000 copies). Its pages were a "who's who" of Spanish and European writers, scientists, and philosophers: Sigmund Freud, Albert Einstein, Aldous Huxley, Bertrand Russell, Le Corbusier, Oswald Spengler, George Bernard Shaw, Virginia Woolf, William Faulkner, Thomas Mann, Franz Kafka, Joseph Conrad, Jorge Luis Borges, Federico García Lorca, and Rafael Alberti among many, many others. In addition to the review, Ortega started a publishing house with the same name where he continued the work he had started years before at Espasa-Calpe, introducing many of the latest literary, philosophical, and scientific innovations from Europe and beyond to the Spanish-speaking world.

Ortega returned from Argentina in 1929 to find Spain in the grip of Primo de Rivera's dictatorship (see Chapter 5). When Primo staged his coup in September 1923, Ortega, along with his collaborators in *El Sol,* thought it would sweep away the "old politics" he had criticized for so long. He soon realized, however, that the dictator was not making any effort to bring about a more democratic society, and he soon found that some of his articles were being censored by the regime. Many of his disciples begged him to speak out openly against the regime, and some even asked him to proclaim himself a republican, but Ortega had lost interest in political activism years ago. He declared that he was not one for joining political parties, although he never stopped trying to influence the country's political life through his writing. When the regime put down student demonstrations in the winter of 1929, Ortega joined some other professors in resigning his university chair, as well as the other public positions he held. Having lost his income, he decided to continue his teaching in the Sala Rex theatre in central Madrid but even with a steep registration fee of 30 *pesetas*—and half that for students—the venue was too small to accommodate the large number of people who wanted to hear his lectures on "What is Philosophy?" The course was moved to the Infanta Isabel theatre, which had seats for the nearly one thousand people who attended.

For the moment, this was the scope of Ortega's political engagement, but fast-moving political events—the fall of the dictatorship and the inability of the system to find a new solution—led him to speak out more forcefully. In November 1930, after the King had appointed General Berenguer to head the government, Ortega published an article which earned considerable international attention. In "The Berenguer Mistake" he argued that the errors that Berenguer had made while in power were less significant than the mistake the King had made in appointing him at all. The only solution was to create a new political situation, and he concluded by addressing his countrymen: "Spaniards, your State no longer exists! Rebuild it! *Delenda est Monarchia*" (The Latin phrase meaning "the monarchy must be destroyed" deliberately echoed the famous statement of Cato the Elder, "Cartago delenda est," during Rome's wars against Carthage).

Soon after this, Ortega returned to direct involvement in politics. Early in 1931 he joined with two other leading intellectuals, Gregorio Marañón (1887–1960) and Ramón Pérez de Ayala (1880–1962) to found the Agrupación al Servicio de la República which supported republican-socialist candidates in the municipal elections of April 12, 1931, elections which led to the proclamation of the Second Republic two days later. In June, Ortega was elected to the Constituent Cortes along with twelve other members of the Agrupación. As a deputy, he tried to prevent the new constitution from being a radical and partisan document, especially where religion and regional autonomy were concerned, but he became more and more disenchanted with the increasingly shrill tone of political debate and the measures taken by the government, which depended on the Socialists for its majority. In the fall of 1932, he again gave up on active political engagement and dissolved the Agrupación. When the right-wing CEDA won the elections of November 1933 he demanded that the party, which many saw as authoritarian, publicly proclaim its support for the Republic.

Ortega had returned to his university chair in 1930. His political activity during the Republic did not prevent him from teaching his classes and undertaking what he referred to as his "second voyage," continuing to refine and systematize his thinking. One particularly important intellectual stimulus was Martin Heidegger's 1927 book *Being and Time*. Ortega wrote many of his most substantial philosophical texts in these years: *About Galileo*, a university course he gave in 1933–34, *Meditación de la técnica*, *Principios de Metafísica según la razón vital*, *Ideas y creencias*, and *History as a System*. In these texts and others, Ortega y Gasset pushed even further his metaphysics of vital reason as a way of explaining the radical reality of the human life. Criticizing both classical realism and modern idealism, he rejected the conception of the static being that had been common to western philosophers since Parmenides: he argued that life is always a "being," a "becoming," a "task" from the past to the future. Against the agonizing and dramatic vision proposed by Unamuno and Heidegger, Ortega y Gasset saw life as freedom, something which must be exercised with a jovial and sporty spirit.

Ortega's "second voyage" was almost totally ended by the outbreak of the Civil War. Not fitting easily into either side, and fearing that his life was in danger from both, between 1936 and 1942 he was a nomad, enduring both economic and physical hardships. He fled from Madrid to France in August 1936, where he underwent life-and-death surgery for bladder and pancreatic conditions. He spent the entire war in Paris, but when the war ended in April 1939 he moved to Argentina to avoid the imminent European war that everyone expected. Even though his article "Concerning pacifism," published in the British journal *The Nineteenth Century* in 1938, had criticized the Republic, and even though his ideas had influenced such important figures in the Falange as Ramiro Ledesma Ramos and José Antonio Primo de Rivera, he knew that he would not be welcome in Franco's Spain.

This time, Buenos Aires was not as welcoming as it had been on his previous visits. The political climate had changed significantly—Peronism would soon be in power—and Ortega was also seriously affected by the conflicts within the Spanish community caused by their responses to the Spanish Civil War. Argentine universities had also been subject to a number of reforms which made them much less receptive to Ortega's philosophical approach. As a result he was unable to complete any of the projects he had in mind. He lived off lectures and teaching occasional courses, the royalties from his books and the articles he wrote for *La Nación*, but even this paper did not treat him as he expected and he broke off relations with it. These difficult circumstances did not prevent Ortega from continuing to develop his ideas, and he produced some of the most systematic statements of his mature philosophical thinking there.

By 1942 Ortega was tired of the situation in Argentina and decided to return to Europe. He also wanted to be able to see his grandchildren and to have closer contact with his friends and colleagues in Spain. Still unsure of his status in Spain, he and his wife moved to Lisbon. He decided to go to Spain in 1945 even though he knew that his failure to give the Franco regime a clear statement of support had earned him many enemies, especially among the Catholic press, which was not prepared to forgive his publicly proclaimed lack of belief or what it saw as his political errors. In spite of a powerful campaign against him in the press and the government's refusal to let him resume publishing *Revista de Occidente*, Ortega continued to believe that he could do something to continue the modernizing project he had started decades earlier. He accepted an invitation to re-inaugurate the Atheneum, one of Madrid's most important intellectual institutions, in 1946 and in 1948 he joined with his disciple Julián Marías in founding the Instituto de Humanidades (Humanities Institute), where he gave a number of important lecture series, including one on Arnold Toynbee's theory of world history. The Institute was an attempt to create a critical mass of like-minded professors outside of official institutions who could mold the younger generations in Ortega's philosophical principles. Even though Ortega's public lecture courses were a success, he never found the younger minds he was looking for.

Ortega found the hostile atmosphere in Spain tremendously disappointing. He closed the Institute and rarely made public appearances, although he continued to spend extended period of time in the country, especially during the summer. Pointedly, Lisbon remained his official residence until his death. From the late 1940s on he traveled widely, teaching, giving lectures, and receiving awards, among them honorary doctorates from the University of Marburg and the University of Glasgow. Starting in the late 1920s his work had been translated into numerous languages, and some of his books, and especially *The Revolt of the Masses*, became best sellers in Germany and the United States. He made his first trip there (to Aspen, Colorado) in 1949 as part of the celebration of the two hundredth anniversary of the birth of Goethe. He had already been offered a chair at Harvard, but turned it down, probably because he spoke English badly. Between 1949 and 1954 he once again spent long periods of time in Germany where he spoke on various questions, including the unification of Europe, an idea he had been promoting since the 1920s. He also continued to write and even picked up an old interest in art, with works on Velásquez and Goya.

In the summer of 1955, Ortega was diagnosed with terminal stomach cancer. His son Miguel, who was a doctor, made the diagnosis. He died in Madrid on October 18, 1955.

Further reading

Graham, John T., *The Social Thought of Ortega y Gasset: A Systematic Synthesis in Postmodernism and Interdisciplinarity*, Columbia: University of Missouri Press, 2001.

Gray, Rockwell, *The imperative of modernity: an intellectual biography of José Ortega y Gasset*, Universidad de California Press, 1989. (Ed. española en Espasa Calpe, Madrid, 1994.)

McClintock, Robert, *Man and His Circumstances. Ortega as Educator*, New York: Teachers College Press, 1971.

Ortega y Gasset, José, *The Modern Theme*, New York: Harper, 1961. (First edition translated by James Cleugh, London: The C. W. Daniel Company, 1931.)

Ortega y Gasset, José, *The Dehumanization of Art, and Other Essays on Art, Culture, and Literature*, Princeton University Press, 1968. (First edition translated by Helene Weyl, 1948.)

Ortega y Gasset, José, *Some Lessons in Metaphysics*, translated by Mildred Adams, Norton: New York, 1969.

Ortega y Gasset, José, *The Idea of Principle in Leibniz and the Evolution of Deductive Theory*, translated by Mildred Adams, New York: Norton, 1971.

Ortega y Gasset, José, *Phenomenology and Art*, translated and introduction by Philip W. Silver, NY: Norton, 1975.

Ortega y Gasset, José, *The Revolt of the Masses*, New York: Norton, 1993 (First edition, 1932).

Ortega y Gasset, José, *Meditations on Quixote*, translated by Evelyn Rugg and Diego Martín, introduction and notes by Julián Marías, Urbana: University of Illinois Press, 2000. (First edition, Norton, New York, 1961.)

Ortega y Gasset, José, *Toward a Philosophy of History*, Urbana: University of Illinois Press, 2002 (First edition, New York: Norton, 1941.)

Silver, Philip W., *Ortega as Phenomenologist. The Genesis of Meditations on Quixote*, New York: Columbia University Press, 1978.

Tuttle, Howard N., *The Dawn of Historical Reason. The Historicality of Human Existence in the Thought of Dilthey, Heidegger and Ortega y Gasset*, Nueva York: Peter Lang, 1994.

Zamora Bonilla, Javier, *Ortega y Gasset*, Barcelona: Plaza & Janés, 2002.

CHAPTER 33
MANUEL AZAÑA DÍAZ
Fernando del Rey Reguillo
Translated by Abril Liberatore

Manuel Azaña Díaz is considered one of the most important political figures of the 1930s in Spain. He was born in Alcalá de Henares, Madrid, on January 10, 1880, to an affluent and liberally minded family. As a youth, he was influenced by the teachings of his university professor, Francisco Giner de los Ríos. When he turned 20 in 1900, he defended his doctoral dissertation ("The Responsibility of the Masses," or *La responsabilidad de las multitudes*) with distinction. The question of the masses was of great interest to turn-of-the-century intellectuals, but Azaña rejected the stereotypes that were popular in his day and inflected his writing with optimism toward the engagement of the masses in the political sphere. He began publishing minor pieces in local papers, and grew to publish literary articles and theatre criticism in magazines like *Gente Vieja*. In 1902, he gave his first public speech, on freedom of association. In it, he defended the regulation of religious orders by the State, as well as the freedom of education for orders established with this goal. Even though Azaña argued for the supremacy of the State over the power of the Church, this represented a drastic distancing from the dominant anticlericalism of mainstream intellectual circles at the time. This speech, along with two others that followed, are testaments to a young thinker who concerned himself with the problems of his time, one prone to reformist stances and a staunch "accidentalist" with respect to forms of government, that is one for whom the question of monarchy or republic was less important than the actual content of the laws.

After this initial foray into public life, Azaña concentrated on his practice as a lawyer until 1911, when he returned to the public sphere. On February 4, he was invited by the Socialist Party of his hometown to participate in a conference amid the charged political context of the first crisis of the Restoration *turno* system created by the events of the "Tragic Week" of 1909. Azaña chose to focus his speech on what he called the "Spanish problem" and the role of the State. In doing so, he directly challenged the focus that other participants put on the school system (Francisco Giner, Joaquín Costa) and on higher education (José Ortega y Gasset). For Azaña, the key to change was the full democratization of the State: he called for taking control of the State away from the "greedy hands of the caciques" and for committing the State to societal progress. He also distanced himself from his colleagues by rejecting revolutionary tactics as political tool.

That same year, Azaña traveled to France for the first time to study French civil law at the University of Paris. Shortly after his return to Madrid, he successfully stood for a leadership position in the important intellectual institution the Ateneo as part of a list headed by the Count of Romanones (years later, in 1930, he would become the Ateneo's president). There he was able to develop his debating style in front of a loud and quarrelsome crowd. Above all, he brought stability to the institution, sorting out its finances, and building up its library's collection.

In 1913, Azaña and José Ortega y Gasset founded the League for Political Education, an organization that aligned itself to the Reformist Party founded by Melquíades Álvarez the previous year. By then, Azaña was a mature man; he adhered to a moderate liberalism founded in the transformative power of the law, a democrat with a commitment to social issues. He believed that political action should aim to bring about a parliamentary regime in which the sovereignty of the people was guaranteed. He also advocated a secular state, one that identified with cultural progress, social justice, and agrarian reform, all of which would be achieved without giving in to the temptation of revolution.

In 1915, Azaña began a long series of collaborations with the republican newspaper *El País*, including his initial discussion of military reform, a topic in which he developed a certain expertise, and to which he would often returned. His ongoing writing assignments, combined with an invitation to visit France by the Allies in 1916, led to Azaña's gradual radicalization, and ultimately he adhered to the Allied (and particularly the French) cause. In France, he continued to send articles describing his experiences to various publications, and he was quick to perceive the Great War as a portending profound shift in Spanish political life. In 1918, he decided to flex his electoral muscles, and made the decision to run for Parliament as a Reformist Party candidate in the Puente del Arzobispo district of Toledo. He was unsuccessful that year, and again in 1923. Nevertheless, he continued his explorations of the military question and developed the ideas which would underlay his reformist ideology during the Second Republic: the distancing of the military from the political realm; the limiting of military law to question of discipline; reducing the excessive number of officers; reducing periods of service, etc. Azaña studied French military organization in detail, always with the goal of modernizing the Spanish army in mind. France was the example to follow: a civil State that protected individual rights but also possessed an efficient and powerful military force. This was, for Azaña, the greatest lesson of the Great War.

The end of war reawakened in Spanish reformists the hope that the monarchy would at last accept their political program, in its own interest and due to the loss of prestige of the defeated autocratic powers. This hope led progressive intellectuals to call for the alignment of Spain with other European democracies, thus creating a nation worthy of forming part of a new world order. This would require the Crown to convoke a *Cortes constituyentes*, a special parliament to draft a new constitution, but this never happened. Dashed hopes led to frustration and an increased radicalization among sectors that had identified with the Allied cause during the conflict and had dreamed that their victory would guarantee a more just and democratic future for Spain. Amid these tensions, Azaña continued to distrust historic republicanism and he was unimpressed by the Socialist Party which was embroiled in a deep crisis caused by the departure of the groups which chose to join Lenin's Third International in 1919 (See chapter 30).

Under these circumstances, Azaña chose to distance himself from Madrid and moved to Paris on October 1919. From there he began to write for the cultural magazine *La Pluma*, which he founded and directed alongside his friend Cipriano Rivas Cherif. He headed the publication until 1923, when he became editor of the magazine *España*, which had been founded by Ortega y Gasset eight years earlier (see Chapter 32). During this time he also contributed to the Madrid dailies *El Imparcial* and *El Sol*.

The coup d'etat of September 13, 1923 led by Primo de Rivera was a turning point for Azaña: he became convinced that the monarchy was the primary obstacle to a democratized and modernized country. Unlike many other intellectuals, Azaña did not see Primo as a regenerator destined to undo the vices of the old guard. In 1924, he left the Reformist Party and declared himself a republican. He expressed his views in the clandestine manifesto entitled *Apelación a la República*, and in 1925 at the foundation of the Republican Action Party, which was promptly banned by the dictatorship. The party, however, served as a platform where Azaña built ties with similarly minded groups such as Lerrouxists, federalists, Catalanists, etc. He spent the ensuing years focused on his literary activities, which culminated in 1926 with the award of the National Literature Prize for his unpublished work *Vida de Don Juan Valera*. He wrote *El jardín de los frailes* the following year, which also received wide acclaim.

Azaña could have had no inkling of the political influence he would wield in the ensuing decade. In 1930, with the resignation of the dictator and amid increasing hostility toward the monarchy, Azaña was party to the San Sebastian Pact on August 17 and joined the revolutionary committee led by Niceto Alcalá Zamora which prepared to bring about the Second Republic. He spent months in hiding after the defeat of a republican military uprising in December 1930, but the popular mobilization following the municipal elections of April 12, 1931 which led to the proclamation of the Republic two days later saved him. Overnight he became Minister of War in the provisional government, and immediately set out to implement his reform program, aimed at combatting the evils of Spanish militarism and modernizing the army. Predictably, he raised the ire of a section of the military hierarchy, but his politics also received high praise from the Chamber of Deputies, the military press, and a large part of public opinion.

Few, including his cabinet colleagues, would have imagined that Manuel Azaña would go down in history as the embodiment of the Second Republic. But protected by the power of his words, his irrefutable logic, the depth of his thinking, and the clarity of his ideas, his political figure grew exponentially in the ensuing months. In October 1931, he was chosen by the Cortes to become head of government after Alcalá-Zamora resigned because of the heated debates on religious issues. Once the constitution had been enacted, Alcalá Zamora became president and gave Azaña the task of creating and presiding over the first constitutional government of the Republic. The new government would rely on an alliance of left republicans and socialists, with Lerroux's Radical Party in opposition. Azaña was steadfast in his belief that the installation of a democracy in Spain would only succeed if it integrated the working class into its institutions, and this became one of the keys to his political strategy. The weakness of the middle-class Republican parties was one motivation, but another, significant one was the fact that Socialists had played an essential role in the foundational coalition of the Republic, and that they had come out of the first legislative elections with the largest number of deputies. Azaña knew this, and he respected it.

And so, supported by leftist republicans and the socialists, the government launched an ambitious plan of reforms. Thanks to the military improvements already enacted by the provisional government, the plan foresaw profound changes in such important questions as agrarian reform, labor relations, the secularization of society, the decentralization of the administration, education, and the civil code (see Chapter 5). These changes would, it was hoped, make the new state key to the democratization of Spanish society. Such an audacious plan required the cooperation of the Socialists in order to bring stability and strength to the government's action; without them onside Parliament would have had to be dissolved. This did not constitute a change of regime but rather a profound transformation of Spanish politics and society. The republican alliance with the Socialists turned out to be more solid than their enemies had imagined and the results of its first months in office, as surprising as they were spectacular, angered centrist, and rightist republicans.

Azaña involved himself personally in the defense of the Catalonian autonomy statute; he understood the complexity of Spanish life and its construction as a collection of diverse identities. But resistance to this statute made the project a difficult one. It was finally passed on December 9, 1932, due only to the unexpected influence of the attempted coup d'état by General José Sanjurjo on August 10 of the same year. Its failure ultimately accelerated the passing of the statute after many months of heated debate both within and outside the Cortes. The Agrarian Reform Law was passed in much the same way. These two victories made that autumn the most successful period of Azaña's prime ministership.

The major changes undertaken during this period also gained him the unyielding opposition of most conservative political forces, such as Lerroux's Radicals, liberals, Catholics, and monarchists, as well as of the extreme left, like the anarchists and communists. The winter of 1933 saw the start of Azaña's political decline. His position suffered drastically from the tragic events at Casas Viejas in Cádiz in January of that year, when an armed insurrection launched by the anarchist CNT was met by armed police who left 20 people, mostly peasants, dead. Almost immediately, the conservative republicans and the Catholic right launched a campaign blaming Azaña's government, and him personally. The campaign led President Alcalá Zamora to lose confidence in Azaña, to his removal from office, and his rupture with the Socialists in September 1933. Azaña was now part of the opposition.

One thing worth paying attention to was Azaña's failure to realize the strength of the popular mobilization undertaken by Catholic political groups, which culminated in the creation of a new party, the Condeferación Española de Derechas Autónomas or CEDA (Spanish Confederation of the Autonomous Right). It was easy to assume that the Church had lost its dominant influence in Spanish society, and in a famous speech given during the constitutional debates, Azaña had gone as far as to say that "Spain has ceased to be Catholic." He could not have imagined, then, that under the banner of constitutional revision and in opposition to the socialist presence in government, Catholics would unite with the conservative republicans (headed by the Radical Party). By the time this became clear to Azaña, it was too late. His efforts to convince the Socialists to form a united front for the elections of November 1933 failed and the left suffered a terrible defeat. Azaña himself was elected only because Indalecio Prieto, a leading Socialist, had ignored party policy and included Azaña in the Socialist list for Bilbao.

Soon after the election, some on the Spanish left came to share the idea that violence was the only way of overcoming the fiasco. The socialists, feeling disconnected from the regime, adopted insurrectionist views and began to arm themselves. Although Azaña was quick to criticize the union of the Radical Party and the CEDA since he considered it contrary to the nature of the Republic, he made every effort to convince others that legality was the only way forward. His diaries, for example, recount the conversation he had on January 2, 1934 with the Socialist Fernando de los Ríos. The Socialist rank and file, especially in the countryside, was bearing the brunt of government policy, which was embodied in the phrase "Comed República"—Eat the Republic—and was becoming increasingly frustrated. Azaña insisted that this did not justify a socialist call to violence. He contended instead that the electoral failure and its consequences had to be rectified in that same sphere, and that insurrection would be catastrophic for Spain. For Azaña, it was unrealistic to believe that armed proletarians could overpower the army. He also worked to dissuade leftist Catalans from subverting Spanish law. But it was all in vain.

In response to the entrance of three CEDA ministers into the government in October 1934, leftist Catalan nationalists and socialists led an armed revolt. It caught Azaña in Barcelona where he had gone to attend the funeral of his friend Jaume Carner, who had been Finance Minister in his government. He had nothing to do with the insurrection and had in fact spent years speaking out against the use of violence. Nevertheless, he was detained and imprisoned in Barcelona as an alleged participant in the uprising launched by the regional government. He remained in prison until December 28, when the Supreme Court overturned the case and freed him.

Upon his release, and with a renewed allegiance to the power of the word in political action, Azaña put all his efforts into winning over popular support. His efforts yielded results almost immediately. In the ensuing months, he rebuilt his political capital by holding public meetings attended by thousands of spectators. He once again became the unavoidable point of reference for the forces of the left; with great effort and the help of his friend Indalecio Prieto, he even succeeded in winning over the socialists. In his speeches, he was very careful not to invoke the violation of democracy and legality. His great opportunity appeared in late 1935, when the President of the Republic ordered the dissolution of the Courts and called for new elections to be held on February 16, 1936. After arduous negotiations and overcoming the resistance of the Socialist group led by Francisco Largo Caballero, the leftist republicans, socialists, and communist decided to band together as a coalition with a program centered on amnesty for the accused of the October revolution, the revival of agrarian reform, the defense of Catalan autonomy, and social change. The Popular Front was born.

The rowdy electoral campaign produced a Popular Front victory and Azaña returned to his place as head of government. His sole objective became to resume the reformist politics that had been stalled since the elections of 1933, although circumstances obliged him to declare a state of emergency and establish censorship of the press. It is striking that in this moment of extreme tension, all of Spain saw in Azaña a savior of sorts, who would lead them out of a strained and difficult period. He had no problem accepting this responsibility, as he said in a famous speech in Parliament on April 15: "We have not come to preside over a civil war; rather, we have come to avoid it. But if someone provokes one, . . . our duty, honourable members, calmly and coolly, will always be on the side of the Republican state." This moderation was the most outstanding quality of the government he founded and led on February 19: composed exclusively of republicans, but supported in Parliament by socialists and communists, his electoral allies.

Azaña's good intentions could not avoid the tense parliamentary debates, the profound disruptions of public order, and the great social unrest which marked that spring. In this context, and with the votes of most of the parties that had previously united to depose Alcalá Zamora from the presidency, Azaña was named his replacement on May 10. At the same time, his attempts to incorporate socialists into a government to be led by Prieto were blocked by the increasingly radical Largo Caballero faction of the party. In this way, a tactic intended to strengthen the government actually ended up weakening it further at a time of open military conspiracy, intense union mobilization and ongoing violence on the streets. Without Azaña's presence, Parliament became increasingly dysfunctional and the country was left in the hands of a weak government led by his friend Santiago Casares Quiroga. Less than two months later, civil war broke out with the failed military coup of July 17.

For Azaña, the outbreak of war was a collective catastrophe, but also a truly personal ordeal. The President of the Republic was isolated in his official residence, with few visitors, eaten away by sorrow at his inability to do anything to stop the bloodshed. Faced with this tragedy, he was distressed and horrified, especially by the massacres carried out in the rearguard by forces that supported the government. In those weeks he was often tempted to resign. Upon hearing of the August 22 murders in the Model Prison, whose victims included Reformist Party leader Melquíades Álvarez, Azaña fell into a deep depression.

From the first few days of August, when it became evident that France and Great Britain would not supply arms to the Republic, Azaña knew it could not win the war. He was overcome with pessimism and a profound disappointment with his country. On September 15, he wrote in his journal: "In Spain, the democracy we once had ended with the outbreak of war; what has existed since then is not democracy. It is a revolution that has not yet gotten off the ground and has only produced chaos and an invasion by the unions which has failed after seizing and paralyzing the state and the government. Let us accept that democracy has failed; but as the monarchy failed dictatorship also failed and will fail again."

In October 1936, as the rebel army approached Madrid and with the agreement of the government, now lead by Largo Caballero, Azaña went to Barcelona. He stayed there until May 1937 but neither the national government nor the Generalitat paid him much attention. In those months he wrote his play *La velada en Benicarló*, a personal reflection on the war and its terrible consequences. Azaña became newly determined to get international, preferably British, mediation to put an end to the conflict: a peace with humanitarian ends that would spare Spain further sacrifices. What truly mattered to him was to achieve peace, but no one paid him much heed. He tirelessly instructed ambassadors and delegates to the League of Nations to reopen the door to negotiations but time and again he received a negative response from the Non-Intervention Committee, which prevented the participation of European democracies in the cause of the Spanish Republic. On November 4, 1936, four anarchist union leaders joined the government. Azaña was alarmed and vainly attempted to halt the decision. He was forced to sign the decrees after they were passed. Once again he considered renouncing the presidency.

But at the start of 1937, when it became clear that, against all odds, Madrid would resist the siege by rebel army and that war would be a long and costly one, Azaña took action once again. He concentrated his energies on finding a way to end the hostilities, forcing the intervention of democratic powers to oblige Germany and Italy to suspend their aid to rebel forces. The constitution of the Negrín government in May 1937 did little to change the situation or to further Azaña's initiatives, although the president was initially pleased with the solution to the crisis (see Chapter 6). The new government did nothing to realize the possibility of a negotiated peace and so the war raged on, as Negrín continued to believe that it could be won despite successive military defeats. For the new Republican strongman there were only two options: win or die. In the spring of 1938, Azaña decided he would no longer tolerate another year of war. He became convinced that he needed to provoke the end of the conflict, although he did not know when or how to so. There was no alternative to Negrín's policy, which did not include the possibility of capitulation, nor was there anyone capable of replacing him. Relations between Negrín and Azaña worsened. Furthermore, the possibility of an Anglo-French intervention was closed definitively when Chamberlain delivered Czechoslovakia to Hitler in September 1938. Negrín had always been right on one fundamental point: Franco would never accept an honorable negotiated peace, only complete, unconditional surrender. Franco's peace could only be one of vengeance, built on the annihilation of the enemy.

Despite his run-ins with Negrín, Azaña retained the presidency of the Republic until the start of 1939. When Catalonia was conquered on February 5, he left for exile in France alongside hundreds of thousands of Republicans who did the same to escape the advance of the Francoists. Despite the protests of Negrín and the communists, who continued to advocate war to the end, on February 27 Azaña surrendered at the Spanish Embassy in Paris, refusing to return to the country, as ordered by the head of the government. Azaña knew that France and Great Britain's acceptance of Franco was imminent, and this spurred his decision.

Taking refuge in a house in Collonges-sous-Salève on the border with Switzerland, surrounded by his loved ones, and gripped with increasingly poor health, Azaña dedicated himself to organizing his papers, preparing his works for publication, and writing even more. The outbreak of the Second World War two months later led his family to move south in search for refuge, and they settled in Pyla-sur-Mer on the Atlantic coast, 60 kilometers from Bordeaux. The German invasion of France in June 1940 caused Azaña great unease. On June 10, a large part of his family was detained by the Gestapo and sent back to Spain. Despite strong efforts by the American and Mexican embassies, and by Negrín himself, Azaña was unable to leave France. With some friends and family he took refuge in Montauban, a small town in the unoccupied zone under the control of the Vichy government. Amid pressures by police and Francoist authorities who demanded his extradition, Manuel Azaña died on November 3, 1940.

Further reading

Aguado, Emiliano, *Don Manuel Azaña Díaz*, Madrid: Nauta, 1972.

Azaña, Manuel, *The Vigil in* Benicarló, Rutherford, NJ: Fairleigh Dickinson University Press, 1982.

Alted, Alicia, Ángeles Egido and María Fernanda Mancebo, *Manuel Azaña: pensamiento y acción*, Madrid: Alianza, 1996.

Egido, Ángeles, *Manuel Azaña. El hombre, el intelectual y el político*, Madrid: Biblioteca Nueva, 2007.

Juliá, Santos, *Manuel Azaña. Una biografía política*, Madrid: Alianza, 1990.

Juliá, Santos, *Vida y tiempo de Manuel Azaña (1880-1940)*, Madrid: Taurus, 2008.

Marco, José María, *Manuel Azaña. Una biografía*, Madrid: Libros Libres, 2007.

Marichal, Juan, *La vocación de Manuel Azaña*, Madrid: Alianza, 1972.

Rivas Cherif, Cipriano, *Portrait of an Unknown Man: Manuel Azana and Modern Spain*, Rutherford, NJ, 1995.

Villena, Miguel Ángel, *Ciudadano Azaña. Biografía del símbolo de la II República*, Barcelona: Península, 2010.

CHAPTER 34
DOLORES IBÁRRURI, LA PASIONARIA
Rafael Cruz
Translated by Abril Liberatore

The life of Dolores Ibárruri covered the "short" twentieth century. She became a communist as soon as she heard the news of the triumph of the Bolshevik revolution (1917) and she would maintain this political affiliation until her death, which coincided almost exactly with the collapse of the Soviet Union (1991). Reflecting on her life in her *Memoirs*, she explained what this meant in personal terms: "I thought about being religious, and abandoned the faith. I wanted to be a schoolteacher, and I became a revolutionary propagandist instead. I dreamt of happiness, but I experienced difficulty in the most intimate parts of my life. I believed in victory, and I suffered terrible defeats with my people."

Ibárruri was born in 1895 in the village of Gallarta, in the Spanish-speaking part province of Vizcaya, an area teeming with British-owned iron mines. It was there that the Spanish socialists had organized the first major strikes in the Basque mines 1890 and 1892, and Dolores Ibárruri would witness the successive conflicts in the first decade of the twentieth century. At birth, Ibárruri's father registered her in the civil registry as Isidora, although on her baptism certificate she appears as Maria Dolores. Ibárruri finished her schooling at 15, and at 20 years of age, after working as a seamstress, a domestic servant, and a hotel clerk, she met and married the miner and socialist Julián Ruiz. Then she learned firsthand about the worker's resistance movement against the capitalist bosses, and when she discovered that the Church sided with the powerful, she began to question her Catholic beliefs. During the Holy Week of 1919, she published her first article "Hipocresía religiosa" (Religious Hypocrisy) in the publication *El Minero Vizcaíno* (Vizcayan Miner), using the pseudonym "Pasionaria" (Passionflower), a nickname which would remain attached to her for the rest of her life.

Those were years of intense social conflict in Vizcaya as in all of Spain. In Vizcaya, the newly created Communist Party of Spain (PCE) used violence to create its own political space in the face of the dominant Socialist Party and by 1920 most of the members of the Socialist Party of Sorromostro had joined the Communists. It was in this context that Ibárruri gave birth to her six children, only two of whom, Ruben and Amaya, survived into adulthood. Even though her husband had taught her about socialism and political activism, by the end of the 1920s they had grown apart significantly. She became a communist, explaining that she found it the "natural" way to explain and understand exploitation, inequality, and emancipation. She acquired her political commitment through her marriage, her union and political involvement with the socialists, and by her perception of the Russian Revolution of October 1917 as a model. These experiences forced her to rethink the injustices that were occurring all around her, and specifically the working conditions of miners and the living conditions of their families at home. From the simple equation "misery produces rebellion" to which she adhered all her life, she developed a more complex understanding: that it was a specific political experience, socialist and then communist, which made it possible to perceive the injustice faced by miners and their families.

In 1930, she was promoted to national leadership of the PCE, thanks in large part to her loyalty to the Communist leaders in Vizcaya, especially party leader José Bullejos, as well as her friendships with influential members, such as Communist International delegate Jacques Duclos. One year later, in 1931, she moved to Madrid and accepted an editorial position at the PCE newspaper *Mundo Obrero*.

The first governments of the Second Republic, however, did not tolerate the PCE's political activities, particularly the diffusion via newspapers of its uncompromising criticisms of the regime's activities. Many communist journalists ended up spending time in jail at one time or another because of their work and Pasionaria was incarcerated for almost 18 months. Around the same time she was buffeted by the party's internal divisions. When Bullejos and his entourage were replaced by José Díaz, Ibárruri was accused of supporting her deposed mentor and was forced by the new leadership to write and publish a "self-criticism" in the party's newspapers, a standard practice in the communist world at this time.

This led to an especially dark period in her life. As well as her imprisonment, she was far from Sorromostro and her children, and she suffered the effects of a deep distrust between her and the new party leadership. The communists were a marginal party in the Second Republic and her first experience as a parliamentary candidate for Asturias ended in defeat. At the end of 1933, however, the tide began to turn, and the PCE gave her an opportunity to redeem herself in the form of a trip to Moscow. There she met Stalin and she would retain an unbreakable admiration for the Soviet Union for the rest of her life. Her first experience of the Soviet Union reinvigorated her belief in communist ideology and gave her the energy to learn more about the Communist International and its strategies. As she wrote in 1934,

> I have learned something else. The idea of sowing potatoes has disappeared from my horizons. The idea of going to my garden tomorrow, to my hut, did not make me feel the weight of responsibility as intensely as one had to have it in these moments. Because this desire to rid oneself of responsibility so desperately made me unable to deepen my questions and study further, something I could no longer imagine. This didn't mean, however, that my homesickness for Sorromostro was completely gone.

Upon her return from the Soviet Union, the PCE put Ibárruri in charge of all political activities relating to mothers and women as head of the Spanish Committee of Women Against War and Fascism and the Pro-Working Class Children's Association. She also became an integral part of the Comintern's new Popular Front strategy of creating organizations open to leftist groups and individuals who shared the common goal of fighting Fascism. She was especially skilled at mobilizing communist allies and people from all walks of life with varied affiliations to the party, and her success drew on her public image as a grieving mother who was forced to send her two children to the USSR to be educated due to her unwavering commitment to her political and party life. In 1936, she was imprisoned again. Her female presence in a male-dominated political space, combined with her knack for oratory at public rallies and in the print media, ensured that in the ensuing years, she became one of the Communist Party's most active and influential members.

Pasionaria became well versed in the PCE's Popular Front doctrine, centered around the exaltation of the people and the defense of citizen's rights in the face of Fascism and the threat it posed to the rights already won and those still to be achieved. For the Party, the concept of the people was based on a number of moral values: honesty, sincerity, purity, righteousness, justice, humility, kindness, and strength, and the primary task of party members was the defense and diffusion of these values. At the same time, the very people it claimed to defend were constantly caught in opposition to the power of the oligarchy, a heterogeneous group of social forces whose moral makeup was the very antithesis to that of the people. This oligarchy was generally composed of cosmopolitan elites who did not share the traditions of the community and thus threatened its very position.

After her prison stay in 1936, Pasionaria was elected as a deputy for Asturias in the elections of February 1936 on the Popular Front ticket in which the Communists were junior partners to the Republicans and the Socialists (see Chapter 5). The election provided the ideal backdrop for her public persona, and she perfected her oratorical skills in rallies with her stirring speeches on injustice, the people, her calls for action, and a political and social alternative to the Republic which had been created in 1931. She continued this role during the Civil War, playing a key role in the creation and diffusion of numerous slogans two of which became famous around the world. The first, "They Shall Not Pass," was part of a speech she gave from the Interior Ministry on July 19, one day after the start of the war; the second, "the Spanish people would rather die on their feet than live on their knees," came in a speech she gave in Paris in September 1936 to generate French support for the Republican cause.

With the defeat of the Republic in sight, Ibárruri left Spain for Algeria on March 6, 1939, and after a brief stay, she settled in Moscow where she founded the radio station Radio España Independiente. In addition to defeat in the war, she had to endure the deaths of her beloved friends José Díaz and Pedro Checa and her son Rubén. The PCE was in exile in the Soviet Union, France, and Mexico, and shunned by the other parties of the Popular Front because of its support for the Hitler-Stalin Pact and its alliance with the followers of Juan Negrín, whose policies during the two years he headed the government of the Republic had lost him much prestige among the other anti-Franco parties (see Chapter 6).

The death of José Díaz in 1942 brought about an internal struggle for power, and two years later, the Communist International decided that Ibárruri should become of the leader of the party. At this point, her image as a charismatic leader was constructed highlighting her oratorical skills, her physical presence—including mourning clothes—her confident posture, and her convincing tone along with a contagious energy. The first biographies appeared, presenting her as a true representative of the Spanish people and the mother of the people, one who fought tirelessly for the oppressed.

After a brief stay in Paris, she traveled to Moscow for gallbladder surgery in 1948, and ended up staying indefinitely, far away from Paris where the Party's major political decisions were being made by Santiago Carrillo and his followers. In Moscow, she began the first of her memoirs, *El Único camino* (The Only Road), and she collaborated on the first official history of the PCE, as well as on a multivolume history of the Civil War. She wrote a lot, including the reports for the 1954 party Congress and numerous meetings of the Central Committee. The Communist press used her birthday as the occasion to reinforce her image as an exemplary popular figure and communist, recalling her multiple contributions to the fight against injustice and her capacity for suffering, such as the loss of her son Ruben, a Soviet soldier who perished during the Second World War, to illuminate the struggles of the people as a whole.

Ibárruri's personal misfortunes were followed by political ones during the 1950s. The death of Josef Stalin in 1953 was a blow for Ibárruri and the Communist Party, who considered him "the leader and master of all peoples," as the paper *Mundo Obrero* put it in March 1953. Khrushchev's "Secret Speech" at the XX Congress of the Communist Party of the Soviet Union three years later, in which he denounced the cult of personality built around the great leader as well as his many errors, caused even deeper struggles. Since meeting Stalin in the 1930s, Ibárruri had seen him as the personification of the Soviet Union which she so admired; the speech by his successor ended her faith in particular Soviet leaders if not in the idea of the Soviet Union itself, and she continued to support it even if she opposed specific policies of the new leaders, a position she demonstrated by traveling to Yugoslavia to meet the "renegade" communist Tito and supporting the PCE's criticism of the invasion of Czechoslovakia in August 1968.

Although Carrillo kept Ibárruri abreast of party policies throughout the 1950s, the two began to move apart. Carrillo had greater strategic vision and analytical capacity than she did and this allowed him to win control over the party's militants inside Spain as well as in exile. When she declared in a manuscript that she was the sole author of the National Reconciliation policy of 1956 she said that Carrillo was outraged over the slight. The last straw came when Carrillo and his supporters decided to call a Peaceful National Strike for June 18, 1959, and he informed her by letter only on March 4, after the decision had been taken. The Party leadership, he wrote, had decided to propose to the Socialist Party, the Christian Democrats, the Catalans, and other elements of the opposition to the Franco regime to undertake a series of "peaceful protest actions" which would culminate in a 24-hour general strike denouncing the regime's policies on June 18, 1959. The strike had minimal impact in Spain, although its effects were felt throughout the PCE. When Carrillo and other party leaders arrived in Moscow to see the Secretary General and to discuss the general strike, Ibárruri announced her resignation.

Ibárruri's resignation was a recognition of the growing physical and political distance between her and the real leadership of the Party which was based in Paris and centered around a group of younger people. The announcement of the general strike, and the fact that she had not been consulted, left no doubt as to her real role in the party leadership, or rather her lack of any real role. As Secretary General, all the Party's initiatives should have been under her control but this one had been taken without her even being consulted. At the 1960 Congress of the PCE in Prague, she was given the newly created title of "Party President" to clarify her subordinate position to Carrillo, who became Secretary General. At 64 years old, Ibárruri was probably PCE's best-known figure, but she enjoyed no real authority.

Stripped of her executive duties, Ibárruri's sense of responsibility to her party poised her to deal with two major setbacks in the ensuing decade. The first was the expulsion from the party in 1964 of the important young leaders Fernando Claudín and Jorge Semprún for deviations from the party line. While they emphasized that social and economic change in Spain had led most of the population to become politically passive, Carrillo and the majority of the party's leadership, Dolores among them, argued that the dictatorship was close to collapse and that a revolution that would do away with the vestiges of feudalism was at hand.

The second came four years later: the invasion of Czechoslovakia by Soviet troops under the Warsaw Pact. This setback took its toll on her. For the first time, she was forced to choose between loyalty to her own national party or to the Soviet Union, although she searched for a middle ground. She ultimately stood on the side of the PCE, a choice she made conscious of the problematic image this would give to the "anti-Communist rabble" of the West, one of a fractured socialist bloc, which would serve as a "poisoned arrow" for the prestige of the Soviet

Union among progressives everywhere. From 1968 onward, Ibárruri never discussed the Czech invasion privately, and she remained an ardent defender of the Soviet Union, mediating conflicts between the Spanish and Soviet parties. She was never fully able either to oppose the positions of the PCE or to change her views on the historical significance of the Soviet Union. Nor did she ever publicly endorse the Eurocommunism of the 1960s and 1970s, with its rejection of Leninist positions on revolution and the dictatorship of the proletariat.

Despite these developments, the image of Pasionaria remained the PCE's strongest symbolic resource. Her public image hinged on ideas of sacrifice, selflessness, and political intelligence, and the promulgation of this image was meant to claim those same qualities for the PCE as a whole. Her biographies were read like instruction manuals on how to devote oneself to the political cause, and she was often spoken of as a teacher and mother of all revolutionaries, the embodiment of the working class, and the incarnation of the virtues of the common people. On December 14, 1975, a mere two weeks after the death of Franco, the Party gathered in Rome for a public rally in her honor, which concluded with her cry, "See you soon, in Madrid!"

On May 13, 1977, after the legalization of the PCE a month earlier, Ibárruri returned to Spain after an absence of almost forty years. At 82 years of age, she was quickly elected as a member of parliament for Asturias, the same position she had held in 1936. The party executive took advantage of her public persona to extoll the struggles and the blood shed by all communists during the Franco dictatorship in a bid to increase votes. However, the Spain of 1977 was not the Spain of 1936, and electoral success demanded speaking to a range of social groups, not just the working class. In this context the sacrifices of Pasionaria and other PCE veterans were insufficient to attract the number of votes the party needed to become the dominant voice of the left in Parliament. Its 19 seats and 9 percent of the vote put it far behind the Socialists' 118 seats and 29 percent (see Chapter 8).

Ibárruri had difficulty functioning in the political world of post-Franco Spain. When her role as deputy was questioned by some party leaders from Asturias who said she was too old, she took their complaints as a slight and vowed not to be a candidate in future elections. Soon after, she aligned herself with her old rival Santiago Carrillo against his critics in the Basque Country and Madrid, and when his successor, Gerardo Iglesias, was criticized following the PCE's electoral disaster in October 1982, she defended him as well. She never understood Eurocommunism nor the abandonment of Leninism as a defining feature of the party. The PCE's change of direction, combined with her advanced age, exhaustion, and a cardiovascular illness, forced her out of active political life in the mid-1980s.

Following her return to Spain, the cult of Ibárruri's image was fed by the numerous interviews she gave, which were used for biographies of her life and work. She also published a second volume of her memoirs, which were less politically relevant but nonetheless well received, and a documentary was made of her life. Monuments were built in her honor, and her name graced the streets of cities governed by socialists or fellow communists. She died on November 12, 1989, and her funeral brought thousands of followers into the streets of Madrid.

Dolores Ibárruri was a fierce personality, energetic and enthusiastic for any activity she undertook, but in politics she found a means of expression and inspiration, and she did so as a woman in a male-dominated world. She was always very open about her successes as well as her failures: she was quick to reflect on her political and personal shortcomings, but always greeted others with a smile. She stood out for her physical appearance, her emotional speeches, and her tireless labor activism. As a political leader she lacked strategic ability and she never took the lead in determining party policy. On the other hand, her loyalty to the party's ideology and its leadership, whoever occupied the position of General Secretary, were remarkable.

Fellow Communist leader Armando López Salinas called her "the flesh of the people." In his view, the magic of Pasionaria was not that she *aligned* herself with the people, she *was* the people in its most genuine form. In the 1970s and 1980s, her actions represented the best of the party: her courage, nobility, dignity, sensibility, strength, solidarity, sacrifice, selflessness, and the unity of her principles, and her actions made her an example of how to live for and with the people. Ibárruri belonged to everyone. First and foremost, she belonged to the PCE, so much so that her life merged with that of the party from the start, and since 1985, the party included her as one of its founders in its literature. But she did not belong only to the PCE. At her funeral in November 1989, Julio Anguita, leader of the PCE, said: "we wanted you all to ourselves, but we see now that this can't be so." Ibárruri belonged to the people.

Pasionaria was imagined as a prominent member of a large family, a "tribe," as Raul Jucar wrote. She was the mother of the people, but also the sister, daughter, grandmother, and widow of the PCE, of the people, and of Spain. She was compared to the stars, the sun, the constellations. She was also compared to the great symbols of authority, a medieval queen for example, or of beauty, like the Venus de Milo or the Lady of Elche. She was imagined as a hero, one whose words "made our men into heroes." Comparisons were made with Spanish women of the past: Ibárruri is in the ranks of Rosalia de Castro, Mariana Pineda, and Agustina de Aragon. This is how the story of Dolores Ibárruri, La Pasionaria, was built.

Further reading

Biografía. Dolores Ibárruri, 'Pasionaria' Madrid: PCE, Comité Provincial de Madrid, 1938.

Bullejos, J., *La Comintern en España. Recuerdos de mi vida*, México, DF: Impresiones Modernas, 1972.

Camino, J., *Íntimas conversaciones con Pasionaria*, Barcelona: Dopesa, 1977.

Capellín Corrada, Maria José, *De la casa al compromiso político. Dolores Ibárruri, mito del pueblo. 1916–1939*, Madrid: Fundación Dolores Ibárruri, 1996.

Carabantes, Andrés, and Eusebio Cimorra, *Un mito llamado Pasionaria*, Barcelona: Planeta, 1982.

Carrillo, Santiago, *Memorias*, Barcelona: Planeta, 1993.

Cruz, Rafael, *Pasionaria. Dolores Ibárruri, Historia y Símbolo*, Madrid: Biblioteca Nueva, 1999.

Cruz, Rafael, "Pueblo, parapueblo y contrapueblo en 1931," in Javier Moreno-Luzón and F. del Rey (eds.), *Pueblo y Nación. Homenaje a José Álvarez Junco*, Madrid: Taurus, 2013.

Dolores Ibárruri, 'Pasionaria,' su vida, su lucha, México: Ediciones de la Sociedad de Amigos de España, 1938.

Falcón, Irene, *Asalto a los cielos. Mi vida junto a Pasionaria*, Madrid: Temas de Hoy, 1996.

Gallagher, Charles F., *La Pasionaria*, Hannover, NH: American Universities Field Staff, 1976.

Ibárruri, Dolores, *They Shall Not Pass: The Autobiography of La Pasionaria*, London: Lawrence R. Wishart, 1967.

Ibárruri, D., "Carta manuscrita," 9 January (Archivo del PCE, R-VI), 1934.

Ibárruri, D., *El único camino*. Prólogo de José Sandoval, Barcelona: Bruguera [1960], 1979.

Ibárruri, D., *Memorias de Pasionaria, 1939-1977. Me faltaba España*, Barcelona: Editorial Planeta, 1984.

Ibárruri, D. et al., *Historia del Partido Comunista de España (versión abreviada)*, París: Éditions Sociales, 1960.

Ibárruri, D. et al., *Guerra y revolución en España, 1936-1939*, Moscú: Editorial Progreso, 4 tomos, 1966–1977.

Morán, Gregorio, *Miseria y grandeza del PCE, 1939-1975*, Barcelona: Planeta, 1986.

Pamies, T., *Una española llamada Dolores Ibárruri*, Barcelona: Martínez Roca, 1976.

Semprún, Jorge, *Autobiografía de Federico Sánchez*, Barcelona: Planeta, 1977.

Sorel, Andrés, *Dolores Ibárruri. Pasionaria. Memoria Humana*, Madrid: Exadra de Ediciones, 1989.

Torres Ballesteros, S., "El populismo: un concepto escurridizo," in José Álvarez Junco (ed.), *Populismo, caudillaje y discurso demagógico*, Madrid: CIS, 1987.

Vázquez Montalbán, Manel, *Pasionaria y los siete enanitos*, Barcelona: Planeta, 1995.

CHAPTER 35
FRANCISCO FRANCO
Antonio Cazorla-Sánchez

Between the spring and summer of 1936, a young, ambitious, and politically compromised general faced a wholly unwanted dilemma. Francisco Franco (1892–1975) had been a darling of the Right since October 1934 (see Chapter 5). Thanks to his services to the government, and particularly to the War Minister, José María Gil Robles, he had risen to become Chief of Staff of the Army. He expected to maintain this professional prominence, but the victory of the left-leaning Popular Front in the general elections of February 1936 threw into disarray the Right's goal of driving the Republic in a conservative and even authoritarian direction. Moreover, the country entered a period of political and social turmoil and some of Franco's colleagues started to conspire to overthrow the new government and to install a military dictatorship. The nominal leader of this conspiracy was José Sanjurjo, who had been exiled in Portugal after his failed putsch attempt in 1932. This had made him the true idol of right-wing public opinion and the press, who often called him *caudillo* (leader). But the man in charge of the planning inside Spain was General Emilio Mola. During a secret meeting in March 1936 the conspirators invited Franco to join them. He refused to commit, but asked to be kept informed. Shortly afterward the government sent him to the Canary Islands as military commander of the archipelago. This was not the first time that Franco had had an ambiguous attitude toward political meddling, but now his fellow generals would not let him waver. Furthermore, he knew that the conspiracy was so broad that it would certainly split the Army. After much delay and many excuses, he committed himself only three days before the military rebellion was due to start, on July 18, 1936, and only after his colleagues had already started looking for a replacement. Remarkably, less than three months later, on October 1, 1936, Franco was elected leader of these same rebel generals.

How can we interpret what happened to Franco between July and September 1936? This question is crucial because his lightning ascent to the position of head of the rebel state would become central to the explanation of the meaning and mission of his life. Put differently, when Franco acquired supreme power, which he managed to transform during the Civil War into a personal dictatorship, hr had the story of his past and his rise to power rewritten. The emerging propagandistic interpretation of his life, which became the official truth in the following decades, presented a Franco who, since his youth, had been the providential *Caudillo*, the unique and undisputed leader of Spain, and who, in July 1936, simply met his destiny. For this supernatural reason he was acclaimed to his rightful position by the nation. With this discourse the propaganda of the nascent Francoist regime started to fuse the man, Franco, with the myth of the *Caudillo*. This myth was created by selecting and manipulating aspects of Franco's life before 1936, including inventing his role as the heart of the conspiracy that led to what would become known as the Movement of National Salvation. The reality, however, was at once less providential, more mundane and, at times, more sordid, than the dictator or his minions would ever admit. Franco's military career was made by the extraordinary circumstances of Spain's colonial wars. Born in El Ferrol (Galicia) into a military family, shortly before the country lost its empire in 1898, Franco became an adult when Spain was trying to gain a new empire in Morocco. He arrived there in 1912 as a nineteen-year-old officer who had recently graduated from the Infantry Academy toward the bottom of his class. Unlike in Spain itself, where promotion was dictated entirely by seniority and came slowly, in Morocco a rapid advance through the ranks was possible under the right conditions: good timing, belonging to the right unit, having the luck to survive, and having good patrons. Franco met them all. In 1912, Spain was reactivating its fight against the Moroccans. Two years earlier a system of promotion by battlefield merit had been introduced to encourage officers to go to Morocco. Franco joined the Regulares, a newly created shock unit of Moroccan mercenaries commanded by Spanish officers, which became the spearhead of most attacks. Franco was badly wounded in 1916, but he survived and was rewarded with a promotion to major. The founder of the Regulares, General Dámaso Berenguer, with the enthusiastic support of King Alfonso XIII, established a vast network of protégés in which Franco became incrusted. Franco's luck reappeared in 1920 when he joined the newly created Spanish Legion and the following year, when this unit played an important role in saving the city of Melilla after the Spanish army suffered a massive and humiliating defeat at Annual. By then Major Franco was a protégé of the king's new favorite, General Sanjurjo. Very soon, Franco himself became one of the monarch's darlings. In 1926, he was promoted to brigadier general and in 1928 was named director of the new General Military Academy.

In spite of what propaganda would later claim, Franco's dizzyingly rise through the ranks was not exceptional. Between 1912 and 1926, Berenguer, Sanjurjo, Mola, and Manuel Goded all saw their careers skyrocket, thanks to a promotion system which was overgenerous and, due to the king's meddling, deeply corrupt. These officers, often called the *africanistas*, had important supporters among Spain's social elites who made them the objects of frequent homages and acts of patronage. They were also celebrated by the pro-war press, which did not cease to glorify them as unrivaled warriors, *caudillos*, heroes, etc., who deserved even more rewards from an allegedly ungrateful Spanish society.

In 1936, many of these journalists would end up working for Franco's propaganda office, where they would bring their bellicose language, antidemocratic sociopolitical values, and class prejudices. These journalists did something else for their new master: they changed their own recollections of the war in Morocco. At the time they had lionized Sanjurjo; now it was Franco who they presented as the truest leader of the Army and obvious hero of Spain. In late 1936 and early 1937, they would also write the first official biographies, or rather hagiographies, of the emerging dictator. Along the way, the roles of Alfonso XIII, Generals Berenguer and Sanjurjo, and the other officers, as well as politicians such as Gil Robles, they had so lavishly praised in the past almost vanished from memory. Copying interpretive models already applied to Mussolini and Hitler, Franco's propagandists presented him as a product of his own genius, of God's will, and of the nation's need for salvation. A myth had been born, and with it history had died.

Until 1931 Franco had been a satisfied man. He was comfortable with the corrupt political system of the Restoration and with the monarchy. The arrival of the Republic changed all of this. The new Minister of War, and later Prime Minister Manuel Azaña put in motion an ambitious plan to revitalize the Spanish military, of which reducing the size and political clout of the army was an important part (see chapters 5, 21). These reforms included freezing and revising the merit promotions from which Franco had so benefited. Franco resented the country's new direction, but there was little that the young brigadier could or would dare to do. His former protector Sanjurjo, however, was both far more powerful and impetuous and in August 1932 he launched a poorly prepared coup which failed badly. On this occasion, Franco lay low, as he would continue to do so until the dramatic events of October 1934. During the Franco regime, his propaganda machine invented the myth of Franco as a general who was hated, feared, and persecuted by the Republic, and particularly by Azaña. This served to reinforce the image of the chosen, obvious to all, impending Savior of Spain being tormented by evil Marxists, atheists and Jews, but it was sheer nonsense: Franco's career did suffer, but no more so than those of many other officers. Azaña certainly did not fear him, although he had a healthy and warranted distrust of all *africanistas*. After the center-right won power in November 1933, Franco became an openly political general and his career again thrived: he was promoted to Divisional General in March 1934. In this period, the left, and particularly the Socialist Party, moved to radical positions and eventually prepared an ill-fated rebellion that took place in October 1934 in Catalonia and Asturias. Franco directed the military operations to quash the revolt in the latter, and his harsh policies, which produced almost 2,000 deaths among the revolutionaries, gained him both the admiration of the right and the hatred of the left. Rewards followed quickly. The following year, he was appointed supreme military commander in Morocco, and shortly after, in May 1935, Chief of Staff. In this position he served under the leader of the Spanish right, Gil Robles, then called by his filo-fascist followers *el JEFE* (the Boss). This was the man who, against all expectations, later failed to win the February 1936 elections. With this defeat, Franco's career entered a period of uncertainty that ended when he finally joined the July military rising.

In his first public proclamations after the revolt, Franco claimed that he was rebelling to save the Republic and the Constitution. This claim was dropped, and then hidden for the next forty years. Sanjurjo died in a plane accident during the first hours of the rising while attempting to return from his Portuguese exile. A few weeks later General Manuel Goded, a man who, had he survived, would have become Franco's main rival for power, was executed by the Republicans. In the meantime Franco's fellow conspirators had put him in command of the colonial Army of Africa. This was the only truly effective rebel force and guaranteed that his prestige rose as his troops advanced steadily toward Madrid during the summer of 1936. Franco also became the main recipient of Italian and German military assistance. When Hitler and Mussolini demanded a prompt unification of command among the rebels, it was thus only natural that in late September his colleagues decided to appoint him head of the nascent state and *Generalíssimo* of the rebel armies, although many assumed this was a temporary situation that would last only as long as the war continued. Franco used his newly acquired power to promote his image as an exceptional warrior, and God's chosen man to destroy the Republic and restore both religion and social order to Spain. He also profited from the prolongation of the war to consolidate his position. In April 1937, he unified the political forces on the Nationalist side into a single party under his command (see Chapter 6). General Mola, the last significant obstacle to total power, died in a plane crash in June 1937.

In January 1938, Franco formed his first regular government. By then it was obvious that he had accumulated enormous power; certainly more than any ruler in modern Spanish history. He was the *Caudillo*, or charismatic leader, Head of State, Prime Minister, *Generalíssimo* of the armed forces, and leader of the single party. In addition, there was not—and never would be—any constitution to limit his powers, which were more extensive than those of Mussolini and even Hitler.

When the war ended in March 1939, there was no question that Franco was the undisputed dictator of Spain. He had in his hands the possibility of healing the wounds opened by the Spanish Civil War and reconstructing a traumatized and materially shattered nation. He did neither. His subsequent actions, while they reinforced his personal power, only made both problems far worse.

The general population had suffered extensively from the violence and destruction of the war. Spaniards had lost loved ones fighting in both armies, as victims of bombardments or of political reprisals, and they had endured the loss of property, suffered scarcity, displacement, forced separations, etc. This collective pain created a widespread rejection of the war and a desire to see it end as soon possible. This sentiment benefited Franco's popular standing, especially after 1937 when it was obvious that he was winning the war and that his victory would mean peace sooner than later. But instead of peace, Franco's victory brought only revenge and more misery. Disregarding the fact that both sides had committed atrocities—and that the rebel side assassinated twice as many people as the republican side—the dictatorship gave a general amnesty to its supporters while embarking on a project of mass repression against those who had resisted it. As a result, perhaps another 50,000 people were executed in the postwar years while thousands died in the crowded prisons, victims of torture, neglect, hunger, and disease. Hundreds of thousands more spent years in prisons and labor camps. At the same time, pensions, public jobs, sinecures, and recognition were restricted to the survivors and relatives of Franco's supporters, the only officially recognized victims of the war (see Chapter 7). Spain was thus divided between the continuously praised victors and the excoriated losers of the war, all the while the Caudillo's propaganda machine and the Church lavishly praised Franco for his supposedly Christian policies that had resulted in the peace that reigned in the New Spain.

That particular peace guaranteed only a widespread socioeconomic misery that lasted well into the 1960s. Not only did Spain not follow the same democratic political pattern of most of Western Europe after 1945, it also did not experience the long period of economic prosperity and rising welfare the continent enjoyed after 1947. On the contrary, the Caudillo's insistence that Spain adopt an autarkic economic model combined with other harsh socioeconomic decisions—such as slashing salaries—condemned poor Spaniards to untold suffering and even death. From the end of the Civil War to 1945, perhaps 200,000 Spaniards died of hunger-related causes. For a country officially at peace, this was unique in twentieth-century Europe. Yet, the suffering of many was also the golden opportunity for those who had the connections and the means to exploit both cheap labor and the black market produced by economic incompetence. The regime tolerated these abuses, thus guaranteeing Franco the support of the propertied classes, including small farmers, who enjoyed the benefits of this situation (see Chapter 7). While the economy floundered, many Spaniards felt grateful to the *Caudillo* who had restored the social, economic, and cultural order and their personal prosperity threatened by the Republic.

Popular support for Franco went well beyond those who benefited from the spoils of war. This is a crucial and often ignored point. Aside from the appalling social conditions, what most concerned ordinary Spaniards in the postwar period was a possible return to civil war. This fear was accentuated by the ongoing world war. The dominant political value among the population then, and for many decades afterward, was "Never Again." This provided the context for the minting of yet another myth, the most powerful and popularly appealing of several successive myths: "Franco's Peace."

The Second World War started six months after the end of the Spanish Civil War. From the beginning, Franco's heart was with the Axis, and when Germany defeated France—and, it seemed, Great Britain—in May to June 1940, the Caudillo started to lose whatever caution had restrained him until that moment. He was convinced that the end of the conflict was near and he wanted to profit from the expected dismantling of the hated British and French empires. But he had a problem: Spain was exhausted and his army was in a pitiful state. Imitating Mussolini, he switched Spain's official position in the conflict from neutral to nonbelligerent. In reality, he wanted to intervene in the war paying a minimal cost. But since his resources were fewer than those of the Italian dictator, he had to wait longer, to the very last minute before England capitulated. That saved him, because that moment never came, and because after his meeting with Franco at Hendaye, just across the French border, on October 23, 1940, Hitler concluded that Franco was asking for too much while offering him mostly problems. Spain stayed out of the war for now, and Spaniards rested a little bit in their anxiety. But the Caudillo kept hoping for a German victory. After the Nazis invaded the Soviet Union in June 1941, he sent troops (the Blue Division, in which at least 45,000 men served) to fight alongside them on the Eastern Front. At the same time, his propaganda machine blasted the Allies, while the state apparatus and Spanish territory became a base of logistical support for the Axis. Luckily for the dictator, the Allies decided not to declare war on Spain.

For ordinary, poorly informed, and fearful Spaniards, what counted during the Second World War was not what Franco had tried to do (which they ignored or never knew about) but what they experienced: Spain did not became embroiled in the conflict and they did not suffer the horrendous destruction and the sociopolitical upheavals of the continent. The majority had always hoped that Franco wanted peace and when the regime started to moderate its pro-Axis line in 1944, the reality that Franco had been an ambitious and incautious but frustrated empire-maker was transformed in popular perceptions so that the Caudillo became Spain's main guarantee for peace, past and future. This is why, in 1945 and 1946, when the country was internationally isolated and the regime condemned, many apolitical Spaniards sided with the dictator. They preferred peace, even the existing miserable one, to the risks of foreign intervention and another war. Moreover, like other dictators of his time, Franco was already more popular than his regime, as people often blamed their problems on local authorities and on the ruler's ignorance of the problems and abuses. This was false, but it helped Spaniards cope with their daily lives and to maintain hope in a situation that was as daunting as it was often hopeless, particularly for the poor. In the meantime, aware that the alliance among the United States, Great Britain, and the Soviet Union was due to collapse, Franco waited for the storm to subside, even if this meant that his people's suffering was prolonged. He certainly did not suffer personally when Spain was excluded from the Marshall Plan in 1947. All this time, in his speeches and in the regime's propaganda, the *Caudillo* constantly reminded Spaniards of their fears of another war, reinforcing the insecurity of a society that both believed and was encouraged to believe that it was incapable of living in peace. Spain's trauma would always lay behind "Franco's Peace" and be the key of his hold on Spanish society.

The Cold War saved the regime from its mistakes, and particularly from its economic mismanagement. Government-backed loans from the United States started to arrive at the end of the 1940s and, in 1953, Spain and the United States signed a number of cooperation agreements. These included economic assistance, but at the price of the opening of US military bases and the installation of nuclear weapons on Spanish territory. Spain was admitted to the United Nations in 1955, but opposition to the regime in Europe kept it out of NATO and the nascent European Common Market. At the same time, Franco reinvented his public persona as an early, misunderstood anti-communist champion and defender of the Christian West from both Soviet aggression and from the continent's own self-inflicted moral decadence. Since the economy continued to sputter, the idea of Franco as the "Sentinel of the West" and Spain as its spiritual reservoir became a central topic of the regime's propaganda. These were ridiculous claims that barely hid the appalling socioeconomic conditions, the repressive nature of the regime, the dictator's international irrelevance, and the widespread contempt in which he was held.

Life for ordinary Spaniards got only marginally better during the 1950s, especially when compared to the much greater prosperity enjoyed by their European counterparts. But the regime's strict censorship meant that they were kept misinformed of real conditions at home and abroad, and particularly of the true reasons of their country's pitiful situation. Franco always blamed others for the difficulties that people experienced: the destruction caused by the "reds" during the Civil War; the pillage of Spain's gold reserves by those same "reds" to buy weapons from the Soviet Union; persistent drought; a supposed international blockade; the conspiracies of Spain's enemies (Republicans, Britain and France, Freemasons, even Jews); and so on. On the other hand, he always took personal credit for any real or supposed success and presented himself as the main source of authority on all topics. Nor did he have any problems in falsifying the record of his words or manipulating the data he used. At the same time, he persistently reminded Spaniards that questioning him would automatically lead to another war. He used both the public's disorientation and the suffering of the past for his own personal power, and in the process took hostage any expectations ordinary people might have for the future.

Conditions started to improve markedly after the much-belated 1959 economic reforms laid the bases for the spectacular growth of the Spanish economy during the 1960s and early 1970s (see chapters 7, 9). This period marked the nadir of Franco's popularity. Although millions still saw the aging dictator as a grandfather who cared for his people and had managed to deliver his long-prophesized progress and welfare, by the end of the 1960s, rising educational standards and other social changes had led a growing number of Spaniards to become dissatisfied with the authoritarian ways that so distanced Spain from most of Western Europe. Slowly, they increased the number of the roughly one-third of Spaniards who had never accepted Franco's regime. More and more frequently, students, workers, intellectuals, and artists, and even Catholic militants, publicly manifested their opposition to the dictatorship. Even though the majority of the population more or less passively still supported the *Caudillo* and feared the risks of political change, the regime proved incapable of mobilizing these loyal masses and creating a political project that would survive Franco.

The only response that the dictatorship had was repression, but this proved counter-productive as the rejection of violence was precisely the main political value that the majority of the population, loyal or not, still endorsed. The occasional killing and the more frequent incarcerations and beatings of opposition members only accelerated a process by which the regime was spilling blood and dying with the *Caudillo*. Furthermore, nobody seemed capable of replacing him and preserving the political structure that was almost indistinguishable from his persona. This included the future King, Prince Juan Carlos, a man who was unknown to the majority of the population and who was looked on with suspicion, and even contempt, by sectors of the political elite.

Franco became gravely ill in the summer of 1974. His conditions were many and the signs of one of them, Parkinson's disease, obvious. Although he partially recovered, this period of convalescence, when Juan Carlos temporarily replaced him as Head of State, helped Spaniards get used to the idea that the *Caudillo's* demise was fast approaching. There was a lot of uncertainty and foreboding among the general population and the elites, pro- and anti-Franco, about what this meant. In general, most Spaniards feared political instability and perhaps violence.

In October 1975, shortly after having sanctioned the execution of five opposition members convicted of terrorism, the *Caudillo* fell ill again. This only added more tension to an increasingly complicated political landscape. Two years before, in December 1973, Prime Minister Luis Carrero Blanco, the man Franco had designated to guide and keep an eye on the future King, had been assassinated by the Basque terrorist organization ETA. On April 25, 1974, the allied Portuguese dictatorship had been overthrown in an almost bloodless military coup. The Spanish regime, led by a very sick octogenarian general, seemed more isolated and anachronistic than ever before.

However, Spaniards' apprehensions—and many locals' and foreigners' dark forecasts—were not to be matched by events. When Franco died in the early hours of November 20, 1975, nothing happened. Some hurriedly conducted polls seem to suggest that a slight majority of the population felt saddened by his passing but also that the majority also declared itself calm and hopeful that things would turn out alright. The spell of fear that the *Caudillo* had cast over Spaniards for so long seemed to have vanished with the man's last breath. Admittedly, many Spaniards still had high regard, and even love, for him, but the majority agreed, in different degrees, that it was time to move on, without fear and without bitterness, toward a more inclusive future. In the following years, Spanish society became both democratic and better informed. This included coping with diversity, learning about the country's recent past and about the man who had ruled the country with an iron fist for almost forty years. In this century, only a small minority of citizens think that Franco's tenure was good for Spain; and no political party declaring itself his heir has been present in the nation's Parliament for decades. When in the early 2000s his statues were finally removed from public view, very few protested. Long before that, it was obvious that even if he had shaped Spain's history like no other modern ruler, the myth of the *Caudillo* had not survived the death of Francisco Franco.

Further reading

Cazorla Sánchez, Antonio, *Fear and Progress: Ordinary Lives in Franco's Spain, 1939-1975*, Oxford: Wiley-Blackwell, 2010.

Cazorla Sánchez, Antonio (ed.), *Cartas a Franco de los españoles de a pie*, Barcelona: RBA, 2013.

Fernández Duro, Enrique, *Franco: una biografía psicológica*, Madrid: Temas de Hoy, 2000.

Fusi, Juan Pablo, *Franco: A Biography*, London and Sydney: U. Hyman, 1987.

Losada Malvárez, Juan Carlos, *Ideología del ejército franquista, 1939–1959*, Madrid: Itsmo, 1990.

Moradiellos, Enrique, *Francisco Franco: crónica de un caudillo casi olvidado*, Madrid: Bilioteca Nueva, 2002.

Payne, Stanley and Palacios, Jesús, *Franco, A Personal and Political Biography*, Madison: University of Wisconsin Press, 2014.

Preston, Paul, *Franco. A Biography*, London: Harper Collins, 1993.

Reig Tapia, Alberto, *Franco 'Caudillo': Mito y realidad*, Madrid: Tecnos, 1995.

Rodríguez Jiménez, José Luis, *Franco, historia de un conspirador*, Madrid: Oberón, 2005.

Sánchez-Biosca, Vicente (coord.), *Materiales para una iconografía de Francisco Franco. Archivos de la Filmoteca*, 42–42 (2002–2003), 2 vols.

Sevillano Calero, Francisco, *Franco. Caudillo por la gracia de Dios*, Madrid: Alianza, 2010.

Tranche, Rafael R., and Vicente Sánchez-Biosca, *NO-DO. El Tiempo y la Memoria*, Madrid: Cátedra, 2000.

Tusell, Javier, *Franco en la Guerra civil: una biografía política*, Barcelona: Tusquets, 1992.

Viñas, Ángel, *La conspiración del general Franco y otras revelaciones acerca de una guerra civil desfigurada*, Barcelona: Crítica, 2001.

Zenobi, Laura, *La construcción del mito de Franco. De jefe de la Legión a Caudillo de España*, Madrid: Cátedra, 2011.

CHAPTER 36
MANUEL DE FALLA
Edward Baker

Cádiz was and still is Spain's most important Atlantic port. Founded more than 3,000 years ago by the Phoenicians, who called their settlement Gadir, in the eighteenth century it held the monopoly of Spanish colonial commerce, which experienced a notable revival in the second half of the century. During the Napoleonic Wars, Cádiz was the redoubt of liberal Spain, the seat of the Parliament which, in 1812, proclaimed Spain's first Constitution (see Chapter 2). As a center of shipping and commerce, Cádiz was, after Seville, the most important and wealthiest city of Andalusia, and it was both receptive to European music and, simultaneously, a common ground of popular musical currents from Africa, particularly the Maghreb, and Argentina— the tango is a creation of Cádiz and Buenos Aires, with Havana and the entire Caribbean basin in the middle. These influences were made manifest in *cante flamenco*, flamenco song, of which Cádiz was, along with Seville, Jerez and Malaga, a leading exponent.

Manuel de Falla y Matheu was born on November 23, 1876, into a prosperous family. His father, José María de Falla Franco, was in the shipping business and the family of his mother, María Jesús Matheu, was similarly well-to-do. They belonged by class and culture to a Cádiz bourgeoisie that was on the rise, and they lived in accord with their prosperity. Manuel's mother was a capable amateur pianist and his musical education began at home at a very early age. Until he was nine he did not study music outside the family confines but once he did he made great strides. In his twentieth year he was living in Madrid and studying piano and composition at the Royal Conservatory, where he crossed paths with Professor Felipe Pedrell, the composer and musicologist who was Spain's most influential musical nationalist. Pedrell argued that Spain's composers needed to study Medieval and Early Modern Spanish music, both liturgical and secular, as well as the measureless riches of the *cancioneros*, the popular song books.

By the 1890s, the Falla family's fortunes had suffered a grievous reverse and they moved to Madrid to be nearer to Manuel, who did his best to support them with music lessons. Indeed the family's penury motivated much of the young musician's early work as a composer— he turned out *zarzuelas,* that is, light operas, in the failed hope of making a living. In 1904, Spain's Royal Academy of Fine Art launched a musical competition that included a prize of 2,500 pesetas, an eye-catching sum, for the best one—act opera in Spanish, as well as one for piano. For the Academy project the young composer recruited a well-known librettist, Carlos Fernández Shaw, who had collaborated on the book for Ruperto Chapí's enormously popular *zarzuela, La Revoltosa*. In 1905, Falla presented his entry in the Academy's opera contest with *La vida breve* (A Short Life), a work that holds a special place in the composer's oeuvre because it is the first work that he fully embraced.

Falla was right to value it. From the outset, he had been working in an Andalusian musical idiom, with a marked presence of folklore and flamenco song. Andalusia holds a special place in modern Spanish culture. A synecdoche is a rhetorical figure in which the part stands for the whole, and in the nineteenth century and well into the twentieth, for both Spanish and European romantics, post-romantics, and neo-romantics, Andalusia stood as the synecdochic expression of Spain. A couple of musical examples can suffice. Isaac Albéniz's masterpiece, *Iberia* (1906–09), is a series of twelve piano compositions. Of the twelve, ten evoke Andalusia, only one, "Lavapiés," takes us to a popular quarter of Madrid, and the rest of Spain is all but shut out, save the reference to a *jota,* the northern dance and song in the opening piece, "Evocation," which also quotes an Andalusian motif. Claude Debussy's *Ibéria,* the second of three *Images for Orchestra*, begun at the same time as Albéniz's. Falla regarded it as Spanish. In an evocation of his friend and mentor he states that "without knowing Spain, or without having set foot on Spanish ground, Claude Debussy has written Spanish music" and sought to "concentrate on the evocation of Andalusia's spell."

In sum, "Spanish" music, in the context of early twentieth-century Europe, leaned forcefully toward an essentially—and often essentializing—Andalusian idiom. Indeed the lowest common denominator of that essentialization was a degraded typicality, a consumerist music hall Spain, the avoidance of which was an ever-present task for the best modern Spanish composers. In addition to his talent, intelligence, and taste, what saved Falla from those excesses was the influence of Pedrell, who cautioned repeatedly against falling into the pseudo-populist trap of the *andalucismo* and *flamenquismo* that filled Spanish theatres and music halls.

La vida breve is a melodramatic story of love, deceit, and death. The opera includes a flamenco song, an approximation of a *soleares,* a dramatic and moving core flamenco *palo*. It also has instances of Wagnerian chromatism and leitmotivs, for Falla's teacher, Pedrell, was one of Spain's earliest and greatest defenders of Wagnerian opera. The blacksmith repeatedly sings "*Malhaya quien nace yunque, en vez de nacer martillo*" (Unhappy is the man born a forge, instead of being born a hammer). More broadly, as Carol A. Hess observes, "the bulk of *La vida breve* relies on the Wagnerian practice of continuous music. More often than not, Falla places voice and orchestra on an equal footing, another procedure common in the work of Wagner."

La vida breve won the Academy's opera competition; in addition, Falla won the prize for piano, and with this stake he was able to help his family. But for a young Spanish composer living in Madrid and possessing Falla's talent and ambition, there was only one place to fulfill his promise: Paris. Falla set aside what remained of the money from the Academy competitions to finance the journey and he arrived in the summer of 1907, in the full flower of the *Belle Époque*. There, Albéniz and the pianist Ricardo Viñes, both longtime residents of Paris, befriended him, mentored him, and introduced him to the best Parisian musical circles—Debussy, Ravel, Dukas, and other composers, as well as the group of musicians and critics known as *les Apaches.* The idea of Falla, a painfully shy and intensely Catholic ascetic, being embraced by the Apaches, the musical Wild Men of Paris, is a paradox with mildly comic overtones, but thus it was.

For most of his Paris sojourn Falla lived a modest existence, although before his untimely death in 1909 Albéniz procured him a grant from King Alfonso XIII. The young composer stayed on in Paris for seven years, but when Europe went to war in August of 1914, he had no choice but to return to neutral Spain. That seven-year period was one of enormous growth. He absorbed everything from the impressionism of Debussy and Ravel to the early works of Igor Stravinsky, whose national-folkloric expressionism in ballets like *The Firebird* (1910), *Petrushka* (1911), and *The Rite of Spring* (1913) would deeply influence Falla's own ballets, in particular *El amor brujo*. But his actual works composed in Paris were few. He revised and completed the *Cuatro piezas españolas* (Four Spanish Pieces) for piano that he had begun in Madrid, and wrote the *Siete canciones populares españolas* (Seven Popular Spanish Songs), for voice and piano. Finally, he completely revised *La vida breve*, turning it into a two-act opera that was performed for the first time in Nice in 1913 and, shortly thereafter, in Paris itself. And that is the sum of his work as a composer in those seven Parisian years.

Nonetheless, it was in Paris that he conceived and perfected his fully mature musical project. For decades, Spanish modernizers in every area of cultural endeavor had posited a Spain/Europe antinomy: Europe was the source of wealth, power, knowledge, and modernity, whereas a woefully backward Spain stood at its periphery (see Chapter 15). Although this outlook was the basis of Spanish exceptionalism, there was nothing novel about it. In one or another version it was shared in those years by intellectuals from Italy, Greece, Turkey, Russia, and other countries on Europe's periphery. Within this framework, the task of the great Spanish creators of the roughly four decades prior to the Civil War of 1936–39 was to conciliate the deepest undercurrents of their nation's culture and Europe's most innovative tendencies. This is what Falla would achieve, thanks in no small measure to Paris, but he did so for the most part when he had left Paris behind.

It was the explosion of creativity in the following twelve years, from 1914 to 1926, first in Madrid and from 1919 in Granada, which would raise Falla to the stature of Spain's greatest modern composer and a creator of the first rank in European wartime and interwar modernism. In those years he composed *El amor brujo* (Love, the Magician, 1914–15), *Noches en los jardines de España* (Nights in the Gardens of Spain, 1916), *El sombrero de tres picos* (The Three-Cornered Hat, 1916–19), the *Fantasia Baetica* (Andalusian Fantasy, 1919), *El retablo de Maese Pedro* (Master Peter's Puppet Show, 1919–22), and the *Concierto para clave* (Harpsichord Concerto, 1923–26). Of these six works, the first four continued to cultivate the musical language of Andalusia, especially folklore and flamenco song and dance, whereas the final two stand at a great distance from Spain's South and represent a broader and perhaps a deeper understanding of the shifting terrain in which nationality and modernity were encountering one another.

Of the first four works, two were ballets. *El amor brujo* (1914–1915; 1925) and *El sombrero de tres picos* (1916–1919) have a number of things in common. Both are set in Andalusia and have recourse to Andalusian dance and song, both make use of voice, in each case a mezzo-soprano, and both story lines were created by writers who were intimately familiar with Andalusian culture. The scenario for *El amor brujo*, as well as that of *El sombrero de tres picos*, bears the signature of the playwright Gregorio Martínez Sierra, although the scenarios actually were written by his wife, María Lejárraga, who in fact wrote nearly all of Martínez Sierra's dramatic oeuvre. *El sombrero de tres picos* originated in the novella of the same title published in 1874 whose author, Pedro Antonio de Alarcón, was born in Guadix, in the province of Granada, where he grew up and was educated. This is the extent of the similarities of Falla's two ballets which are vastly different in story, tone, dance, and song.

El amor brujo aspired to plumb the depths of flamenco song and dance, whereas *El sombrero de tres picos* was folkloric and bucolic. The differences illustrate an essential aspect of Andalusia musical language. *Cante flamenco* shows strong folkloric influences, but *it cannot be assimilated to folklore*. This is particularly so at the level of performance. Traditionally, folklore tends to be rural, collective, and anonymous, whereas flamenco is a highly individualized. From the very outset of flamenco's consolidation as a musical corpus in the middle decades of the nineteenth century there were performers such as El Planeta, La Andonda, and El Fillo, who achieved wide recognition. *Cante* is also a fundamentally urban cultural phenomenon. It was in its origins the city music of extended, ghettoized gypsy families mainly from the left bank of the Guadalquivir river, especially Seville, Jerez, and Cádiz and the communities of the Cádiz bay. Thus, there was in this individualized urban music an innate tendency toward professionalization, a process begun in earnest in the 1860s and 1870s with the creation, first in Seville, then in all of Andalusia's major cities, as well as Madrid, of *cafés cantantes* specializing in flamenco. It is significant that at the very center of this process we find Silverio Franconetti, a *payo*, that is, a non-gypsy—his father was Italian—, and the first distinguished non-gypsy *cantaor*.

El amor brujo is among Falla's best-known works and is one of the most frequently performed. It's attraction stems in part from a rhythmic ferocity that has its roots in flamenco but also in Stravinsky's ballets of the period. The idea originated with the dancer and singer Pastora Imperio, who performed in the debut in Madrid in April 1915; the definitive version was presented in Paris in 1925. Given its proximity to flamenco song and the fact that it was written for mezzo-soprano, *El amor brujo* has often been performed, and to great effect, by *cantaoras* of the stature of Carmen Linares and Marina Heredia. It tells the story of the rivalry between two gypsy women, Candela and Lucía. As a child, Candela had been promised in marriage and indeed had married, but truly was in love with Carmelo. Lucía's husband killed Candela's husband, whose ghost haunts Candela. She attempts, night after night, to exorcize him by dancing with him. Candela learns through village gossip that her husband had been unfaithful and that his lover had been Lucía. Candela induces Lucía to attend her ritual dance and Lucía is spirited away by the ghost, leaving Candela free to be with Carmelo. If flamenco is melodramatic with tragic overtones, *El amor brujo* both fills that bill and adds a happy ending, albeit a melodramatic one.

El sombrero de tres picos is a bucolic idyll, but with an edge made of well-wrought satiric touches that separated it from the aforementioned degraded typicality, all of it informed both in dance and in song by Andalusian folklore. Falla's original version was a pantomime, *El Corregidor y la molinera* (The Magistrate and the Miller's Wife). The complete ballet version was commissioned by the great impresario Serge Diaghilev for his Ballets Russes, was choreographed by Léonide Massine and included the set, the drop curtain, and costumes designed by Pablo Picasso. It tells the tale of an elderly Magistrate who becomes infatuated with the young and pretty Molinera, and eventually is put in his place—and with him the *ancien régime*, symbolized by the three-cornered hat—by the handsome and courageous Molinero. The original pantomime was composed in 1916 and early 1917 and was premiered in April of that year, while the ballet with full orchestra had its premier performance in London's Alhambra Theatre in July 1919.

Falla's next two major compositions adhered to the musical language of Andalusia. *Noches en los jardines de España* (Nights in the Gardens of Spain, 1916) was a work for piano and orchestra inspired by his journey to Granada in 1915 accompanied by María Lejárraga. He had fallen in love with the city, particularly with the Alhambra and its gardens, and the exquisite impressionist chromatism of *Noches* is a faithful rendering of the composer's enchantment. The *Fantasia Baetica*—Baetica was the Roman name for the Guadalquivir and, by extension, for Spain's southern provinces—was commissioned by Artur Rubinstein, who premiered it in New York in February of 1920. It is musically and even physically a daunting work in which the piano is asked to mimic the guitar, in particular the *rasgueados*, the complex strumming of the flamenco guitar. Although the *Hommage pour le tombeau de Debussy,* his homage to Debussy, who died in March of 1918, was written for guitar, Falla wrote very little for the quintessential Spanish instrument. Nonetheless, the gravity of that brief salute to his Parisian mentor and friend stands at a very great distance from the dramatic violence and unforgiving percussive beauty of the *Fantasia* (the flamenco guitar is percussive by design; as distinct from the classical model, its very construction favors a percussive sound). That quality of the *Fantasia* was described by Ronald Crichton: "The *Fantasy* is an ABA form, B being very short. The mood of the outer sections is mostly harsh and percussive, with bitter snatches of *cante hondo* and passages which sound like Scarlatti rewritten by Bartók."

By 1919 Falla's parents were dead and his international reputation as a composer was very nearly consolidated. He had no reason to stay in Madrid and, along with his sister María del Carmen, who would accompany him for the rest of his life, he moved to the city of his enchantment: Granada. There he composed two more works that brought him further international renown, *El retablo de Maese Pedro* (Master Peter's Puppet Show, 1923) and the *Concierto para clave* (Harpsichord Concert, 1926). As a composer his explorations of Andalusian musical language were basically at an end, but his involvement with the music of his native land was not. In Granada he became an integral part of the city's *intelligentsia* composed of musicians, artists, writers, and intellectuals, in particular the family of Fernando de los Ríos, one of the leaders of the Spanish Socialist Party, a family that in turn was related by marriage to that of the young and immensely gifted poet and accomplished pianist, Federico García Lorca. It was Lorca who brought Falla into a project that he and several friends had devised—the Concurso de Cante Jondo, the Flamenco Song Competition. A cultural event of the first order and a decisive moment in the Spanish *intelligentsia*'s embrace of *cante* as high art, it took place in Granada in mid-June of 1922 in a setting of stunning beauty, the Alhambra. Falla and Lorca wrote introductory essays for the Concurso. Falla's essay, "Cante jondo," is a brief compendium that includes an "Analysis of the Musical Elements of *Cante Jondo*" and observations on the "Influence of These Songs on Modern European Music," especially in Russia and France, and well as a page on "The Guitar."

The Concurso, which was never repeated, was motivated by an ideology that is familiar to Americans because for many decades it governed our perception of Delta blues—purity versus commercialism, a compelling idea precisely because it contains a grain of truth. The idea of purity responds in large part to early twentieth-century intellectuals' primitivist fantasies, and in accord with them the Cante Jondo Competition was limited to amateurs. Nevertheless, the specific musical truth of commodification was brought home with great clarity in a newspaper article, "La proposición del *cante jondo*" ("What *cante jondo* proposes"), that Falla wrote in March of 1922 for *El Defensor de Granada*: "The severe melodic limits in which flamenco song develops have been crudely broadened; the modal richness of its ancient melodic range has been displaced by tonal poverty caused by the overwhelming use of the two modern scales, the ones that have monopolized European music for more than two centuries." In vivid contrast with the singing of masters such as Manuel Torre and Antonio Chacón, both of whom were in attendance at the Competition, the commercialized products to which Falla alluded were, again, the degraded typicality of music hall detritus.

This was Falla's last important statement, musical or otherwise, on flamenco in particular and on Andalusian music in general. At the time of the Concurso he was occupied with two masterpieces, *El retablo de Maese Pedro* and the Harpsichord Concerto, which explored

Spanish tradition in a modern idiom independent of the composer's Southern roots. In these remarkable works Falla explored other Spanish traditions, and with them a fresh conception of nationality and modernity. In the *Retablo* he turned to Spain's "Sacred Scripture," *Don Quixote*, specifically to Part II, Chapter 26, in which the knight errant enters the inn where a puppet show is about to be put on by Maese Pedro. The show takes as its theme a medieval *romance,* a poem from Spain's Carolingian ballad cycle—the episodes surrounding Charlemagne, Roland at Roncesvalles and, in general, the French *chansons de geste*, themes that Don Quixote knows intimately because they fill the romances of chivalry that have driven him mad. The ballad tells the story of Melisendra, taken captive by the Moors and held prisoner in Zaragoza, and her husband Don Gaiferos, who comes to free her from captivity. Here Cervantes played in the baroque manner with intersecting levels of representation—the puppeteer and his young *trujamán* or announcer/interpreter of events, the puppets, the audience, including Don Quixote, the truths and lies and ambiguities of stories. Falla embraced these different representations musically with the *trujaman*'s plainsong, the use of kettle drums and trumpets for the battle of the medieval Christians and Moors over Melisendra, and the jarring dissonance that accompanies Don Quixote's destruction of the puppets and theatre. For in his madness he has taken the puppet show for reality and has intervened in it to battle the Moors and free Melisendra. In doing so he destroys the marionettes and Maese Pedro's stage. The *Retablo* was first performed in Seville in early 1923 in a concert version with Falla conducting, and in the definitive version, marionettes and all, in Paris on June 25 of that same year. It was a resounding success there and everywhere it was played and went a long way toward consolidating Falla's international reputation.

Like the *Retablo,* the Harpsichord Concerto explores guitar and keyboard traditions of Early Modern Spain that go far beyond the musical idiom of Falla's native Andalusia. It also exhibits the neoclassicism that Stravinsky espoused in the 1920s. A work of surpassing intelligence, it lacks the charm of Falla's most cherished compositions and this surely accounts for what Hess has called its "bleak reception" since its first performances in 1926.

The *Retablo de Maese Pedro* and Harpsichord Concerto were the last important compositions that Falla would complete. The remaining twenty years of his life, until 1939 in Granada and until his death in 1946 in Alta Gracia, Argentina, were occupied with *Atlántida*, a work based on the Catalan cleric and poet Jacinto Verdaguer's epic about the myth of the lost continent of Atlantis. There is a sense in which Falla, in choosing this theme, was returning to a fantasy of his childhood in Cádiz involving the dramatization of Columbus's voyages. *Atlántida* is a scenic cantata with choruses, soloists, and a story line that tells of Atlantis, the parting of two continents, Europe and America, united again by Columbus's voyages of discovery across the Atlantic and the bringing of the Christian faith to the American heathen. The work was left unfinished upon Falla's death and was completed by his pupil Ernesto Halffter. Finished or unfinished, it was at a great remove from his finest moments. It is bloated, grandiloquent, and in its full extension, anywhere from an hour and a half to more than two hours, depending upon the version being performed, it may not contain much more truly compelling music than the roughly thirteen or fourteen minutes of the Harpsichord Concerto.

Falla's experience of the Civil War, the assassination of beloved friends, including Federico García Lorca, at the hands of Granada's Fascists, and his decision to leave Spain for Argentina shortly after the conclusion of the War, inevitably raise the question of the composer's political views. The subject has been and will continue to be examined from differing perspectives but it seems reasonable to state that Falla had no clearly defined political convictions. He was a fervent Catholic who moved comfortably in the world of modern secular European culture, to which he made lasting contributions and in which very few of his friends and associates shared his religious convictions. Accompanied by María del Carmen, he left Spain for Argentina not as a political exile in any ordinary sense—he could have remained in Spain unmolested—but because his country was now governed by Neo-Tridentine Catholics and Fascists, all of whom were vocationally homicidal. The War had crushed Falla's cultural and social world and there of was little or nothing left to keep him at home. Suffering from ill-health since the beginning the armed conflict in July of 1936, he lived for seven years in Argentina, mostly in Alta Gracia, where he died on November 14, 1946, just short of his seventieth birthday. María del Carmen returned with his remains to Cádiz, where he is buried in the crypt of the cathedral.

Further reading

Falla, Manuel de, *On Music and Musicians, with an introduction and notes by Federico Sopeña.* Translated by David Urman and J.M. Thomson, London and Boston: Marion Boyars, 1979.

Harper, Nancy Lee "Interpreting Manuel de Falla's *Fantasia Baetica: An Introduction and Masterclass.*" (2004), http://www.ibla.org/events/2005_wpta_publication.php4#nancy_l

Harper, Nancy Lee, *Manuel de Falla. His Life and Music*, Lanham, Maryland and Oxford: Scarecrow Press, 2005.

Hess, Carol A., *Manuel de Falla and Modernism in Spain, 1898-1936*, Chicago and London: University of Chicago Press, 2001.

Hess, Carol A., *Sacred Passions. The Life and Music of Manuel de Falla*, New York and Oxford: Oxford University Press, 2005.

Mitchell, Timothy, *Flamenco Deep Song*, New Haven and London: Yale University Press, 1994.

CHAPTER 37
PILAR PRIMO DE RIVERA
Inbal Ofer

The life story of Pilar Primo de Rivera (1907–1991) cannot be told separately from that of the organization that she founded and led for four decades—the *Sección Femenina de la Falange* (SF). Nothing exemplifies this fact better than the list of articles and obituaries that were published in the Spanish press following her death on March 17, 1991. Daughter of the former dictator Miguel Primo de Rivera and sister of José Antonio Primo de Rivera, founder of the Spanish Falange, she is mostly remembered today for her role in "redirecting" Spanish women into the service of Fatherland, Church, and Home. As the national leader of the SF she left behind her a monumental amount of documents, but only a few of them are of a personal nature. While several monographs published over the past two decades explore the workings of the SF, almost nothing has been written about the ways in which the private life, family background, and personal experiences of Primo de Rivera affected the vast organization which she headed.

Yet this shy woman, who often referred to herself as unattractive and lacking in charisma, was one of the most influential female political figures in twentieth-century Spain. Hiding behind the political legacy of both her father and her brother, she led an organization that evolved from a small right-wing splinter group in 1934, into the official women's organization of Franco's Spain in April 1937, seizing control over other women's organizations: the Spanish Syndicate for (female) University Students (SEU); the teachers and nurses' syndicates; and the Social Service for Women (*Servicio Social*). At its peak, immediately following the Spanish Civil War, there were more than 600,000 women in the SF.

The life story of Pilar Primo de Rivera, however, is central to the understanding of more than just the bureaucratic apparatus which she headed. It is also crucial to our understanding of an array of self-perceptions and identifications of a generation of Spanish women: middle class, well educated, and from conservative Catholic backgrounds. Born during the first two decades of the twentieth century, these women grew up against the background of the Rif War in the early 1920s and came into their own during the years of the Second Republic. While the first experience fostered in many of them an urgent wish for national regeneration, the second provided them with new professional, legal, and political opportunities and fashioned their aspirations as women (see Chapter 5). The Republican experience, however, also undermined some of the deepest convictions they held regarding morality and the desired political and social order for Spain. Those who, like Pilar Primo de Rivera, made their way into the SF would spend the rest of their lives attempting to reconcile the personal, political, and professional implications of these experiences.

Pilar Primo de Rivera was born in 1907, the child of a well-to-do military family in Madrid. Her mother died while giving birth to her sixth child. After her father lost power in 1930, he lived briefly in exile in Paris, passing away that same year. Pilar was raised by her two aunts. While her father instilled in her and in her siblings an intense sense of patriotism, her aunts kindled in them a deep religiosity. Following the footsteps of their father one of her brothers joined the Army and two opted for a political career. Fernando and José Antonio were killed during the Spanish Civil War. Another brother, Miguel, took a political post under Franco as the Spanish ambassador in London.

Primo de Rivera was 24 years old when the Spanish republic was proclaimed. Dionisio Ridruejo described her as a young woman "with little preoccupation for the way she looked. Agreeably timid, she still talked in a voice much like that of a little girl." According to historian María Antonia Fernández Jiménez, "she did not manifest any interest in following the [conventional] road leading to marriage, while at the same time lacking the courage to seek the sort of academic or professional training that would allow her to become [economically] independent." It was only in late 1935 that she received her nursing certificate, although she never had the opportunity to practice her new profession as she was already deeply engaged in what would become her life mission.

Five young women participated in the founding ceremony of the Spanish Falange, which took place at the *Teatro de la Comedia* in Madrid in November 1933: Pilar and Carmen Primo de Rivera (José Antonio's sisters), Ines and Dolores Primo de Rivera (the founder's cousins) and María Luisa Aramburu. José Antonio rejected their request to register as members of the Falange, refusing to include women within a movement which he envisioned as the spearhead of a future national-syndicalist revolution. Captured by the image of a new political life—politics as poetry, as José Antonio put it—the women insisted. Finally, a compromise was reached and all five, as well as two other university students (Mercedes Formica and Josefina Rodríguez Viguri), joined the Falange's Students' Union.

The SF, as an independent entity, was founded in the summer of 1934. From the moment of its establishment, the activities assigned to SF members were based on a highly traditional understanding of gender roles, but even prior to the Civil War a certain shift could be sensed. The Falange found itself relying more and more on the assistance of SF members in the diffusion of propaganda materials, smuggling weapons, and caring for political prisoners and for their families. Once the Civil War erupted the activities of the SF evolved to include an independent propaganda apparatus, regiments of nurses, and the *Auxilio Azul*, a clandestine organization which smuggled Falangists and churchmen from the Republican zone into Nationalist territory. All this was done within a highly structured organizational framework (similar to that of the Falange), which included delegates (or commanders) at the local, provincial, and national levels.

The Civil War was a monumental turning point for Pilar Primo de Rivera, as it was for an entire generation of Spanish men and women. It was during those years that her personal life became inseparably entwined with that of the organization she founded. Of all the events of the Civil War, the one that had the greatest effect on the Falange was the publication of the Decree of Unification on April 24, 1937. The decree merged all the political forces of Nationalist Spain into the *Falange Española Tradicionalista y de las JONS* and transferred control over all militia forces to the Nationalist army. While retaining the name Falange, this action in effect accomplished what José Antonio Primo de Rivera had warned against in a letter from his Alicante jail cell on the eve of the war. By the stroke of a pen General Francisco Franco emptied the original movement of all ideological content, turning it into the largest source of manpower for the newly formed Nationalist administration (see Chapter 6).

Ramon Serrano Suñer, Franco's brother-in-law, described Pilar Primo de Rivera's reaction immediately following the publication of the decree: "In a small apartment in the Plazuela San

Julian sat Pilar, like a high priestess, ready to offer any sacrifice to the memory of her missing brother. Through the apartment passed Falangists from all over the Spanish territory in order to express their embitterment and request orders."

Pilar Primo de Rivera's initial refusal to accept the Decree of Unification was the first step in a long and complex process which would establish her position as her brother's ideological successor within Nationalist Spain. This process started when the Falange's leadership first learned of José Antonio's execution in a republican jail in November 1936, a fact that was kept a secret from most of the rank and file. Under these conditions, Pilar acted to consolidate her position as the only legitimate interpreter of José Antonio's doctrine and as a focal point for sentimental identification with the missing leader. Her unrelenting and even ruthless efforts in this respect were best exemplified in the pursuit to integrate the original *Auxilio Social* into the SF during the final year of the war. This was done at the expense of Mercedes Sanz Bachiller—the widow of Falangist leader and founder of the JONS (*Juntas de Ofensiva Nacional Sindicalista*), Onésimo Redondo—who found herself removed from the organization she headed and politically marginalized.

Eight months after the unification, during the SF's Second National Congress, Pilar Primo de Rivera called upon members to accept the current political reality so that everyone could continue with the colossal project at hand—winning the war and building a New Spain. But her words also carried a heavy note of criticism: "Only the military and the Falange should have the right of veto in this difficult hour for the Fatherland . . . It is women most of all who must preserve the Falangist spirit and faith, since the others who understood this spirit are no longer amongst the living." These words were meant as a rebuff against those who, in Primo de Rivera's view, adopted the political label but not the true essence of José Antonio's doctrine. At the same time, the National Delegation was aware of the fact that in the power struggle taking place within the Nationalist coalition, the SF's survival and its leadership's ability to keep its own distinct interpretation of Falangism alive depended on its political usefulness to the newly evolving regime.

During the Civil War the SF developed a highly distinctive discourse that centered on the image of the *National Syndicalist Woman*. This discursive figure was shaped in constant reference to a variety of female historical models (such as Queen Isabel I la Católica and Santa Teresa of Ávila) as well as to the everyday experiences of SF members. Through this discourse, Pilar Primo de Rivera and other high-ranking SF members attempted to negotiate the tensions that their prominent presence and unorthodox lifestyle generated within a conservative and highly chauvinistic political system. Living as single women, wearing pants, exercising, moving unaccompanied through public spaces, and challenging Church authorities in matters relating to girls' education did not lessen their religious devotion. At the same time, the constant bickering with local Falangist leaders, criticizing some of the political decisions taken by the regime, and negotiating for more political and professional representation for women did not lessen their loyalty to General Franco or to the legacy of José Antonio.

In matters of both ideology and of gender relations it was Pilar Primo de Rivera who determined the SF's policy. Her personal background and the void left in her own life by the death of her elder brother and her mother were destined to shape the history of the organization which she led almost as much as the political climate in which it operated. In her autobiography, Primo de Rivera referred to her mother, Casilda Sáenz de Heredia, in the following words: "Hers was a Christian and heroic death, in keeping with the way she lived.

She very possibly knew she was going to die if she gave birth to that baby, but she no doubt felt she was abiding by her duty as a married woman, and this is what her conscience as a Christian dictated that she does . . . She would never have agreed to the legalization of abortions."

As historian Aurora Morcillo pointed out, the three texts which greatly influenced the construction of "femininity" in Franco's Spain were the sixteenth-century essay by Fray Luis de León *La perfecta casada* (The Perfect Married Woman, 1583), and Pope Pius IX's encyclicals entitled *Divini Illius Magistri* (On Christian Education, 1929), and *Casti Connubii* (of Chaste Wedlock, 1930). These writings reached a relatively large readership through their repeated publication and discussion in journals such as *Razón y Fe*, *Ecclesia*, or *Senda*. When using phrases such as "her duty as a married woman" and "her Christian conscience" in reference to her mother, Primo de Rivera must have been aware of the images she was evoking.

She was also aware that in the society in which she lived the only way to be a good wife and a good Christian was to live the life her mother had lived. But what if there was a way to avoid that life and still be considered a good Christian and a good Spaniard? What if she could find a way to fulfill her duty without being married? In the process of simplification, which canonical texts suffered under the Franco regime, it was all too easy to forget that Fray Luis de León had himself signaled an alternative when he stated that for women, the excellence of virginity was greater than that of marriage. In that respect the lifestyle of a high-ranking SF member provided the perfect solution, binding the women who chose it to a service of a higher cause and providing them with the perfect pretext for staying single: if the nuns Fray Luis de León had in mind when writing dedicated their lives to God, than SF members dedicated theirs to the Fatherland.

This notion received its official sanction in a decree published by Primo de Rivera in April 1938 where she stated that all SF members from the position of provincial leader up must be unmarried or widows without children, since "the situation of a married woman . . . is different from that of a single woman, who is completely free." Women were all assumed to have a nurturing side, which they had to access if they wished to explore their femininity to the full. However, nurturing did not necessarily mean a mother-child dyad. Pilar often encouraged SF members to think of their nurturing capacities in social terms. Even in cases when maternal relations were discussed specifically, this was often done as a model for wider social engagement. "Motherhood" was often discussed interchangeably with "spiritual motherhood," that is, the nurturing and fostering of other women, younger colleagues, and children who were not biologically one's own. The idea that women as a group had an inherent tendency to concern themselves with the welfare of others, and that this tendency was not necessarily expressed in terms of biological attachment, reopened the way to women's involvement in many walks of life—in the workplace and the community, as active and productive daughters of the fatherland.

Surprisingly enough though, being unmarried did not necessarily mean being single, and some high-ranking SF members, Pilar Primo de Rivera among them, at times had male companions. Primo de Rivera made only one mention of the great love of her life in her autobiography, and despite the fact that those brief words speak volumes they can easily escape the eyes of a reader who does not know what to look for: "During those times in Burgos, we often used to go to the Hotel Condestable, to get some word on the (progression) of the war. And it was there that we met a group of sailors, an event that, for some of us, was of transcendental importance. Later on we all went our separate ways, but for me at least, that meeting constituted the most important event of my life."

Primo de Rivera said enough for those who are aware of her longtime relationship with a captain of a Spanish submarine to know that she did acknowledge it, but even in 1983 she felt unable to directly discuss that "most important" event in her life. Exposing this relationship prior to 1975 would have cost both her public image and her political position. But the carefully guarded language she employed in her autobiography implies that perhaps there was an additional price to such a revelation: in light of her rejection of the more egalitarian gender codes that emerged with the transition to democracy, publicly exposing the contradictions between the SF's discourse and practice regarding chastity and morality would have left Primo de Rivera in an impossibly isolated position both socially and personally.

Religion was another factor that greatly influenced the SF's model of gender relations and defined its sphere of influence within the regime. Falangist doctrine concerning religion was rather vague. Most Falangists, especially the women, declared themselves to be devout Catholics. However, in his writings José Antonio was critical of all the too formalized nature of Spanish Catholicism, which suggests that he viewed the behavior of many clerics as problematic and responsible for the alienation of the Spanish working classes from religion. In search of a model that could accommodate her own experiences and her expectations for the SF, in late 1938 Pilar Primo de Rivera traveled to the monastery of Santo Domingo de Silos near Burgos. There she met with the Benedictine friar Justo Pérez de Urbel, who would become the SF's spiritual advisor. "Thanks to him," she wrote in her autobiography, "we entered a world which brought us closer to God. It was he who introduced us to the use of the missal, almost unknown then [in Spain]. Our religious formation followed the norms expressed [later] in the Second Vatican Council, and was always oriented towards the liturgies." The use of a Spanish "hand missal," which allowed all those present to follow the service; the position of the priest, who faced the women during Mass; and the insistence on the optional nature of Mass (except on Sundays) distinguished the SF from other Catholic women's organizations in the 1940s and 1950s.

As empowering as the SF's discourse on femininity might have been for its own high-ranking members, it is clear that the first generation of national leaders had come to realize that their elite status and access to central figures in the regime were the preconditions for their ability to continue their public work. Pilar Primo de Rivera's preferred channels of intervention included private appeals to the FET's General Secretary and intimate conversations with ministers' wives over afternoon tea. Correspondence with the Movement's General Secretaries (such as Raimundo Fernández Cuesta, José Luis Arrese, or José Solís) was always personal, direct, and firm. Meetings with ministers' wives, and with Carmen de Polo Franco, were viewed as a last resort when all other attempts to get through to the men had failed. Official receptions presented countless opportunities for solving problems (from budgetary issues to confrontations with ministers and Provincial Delegates of the FET), so the National Delegate carefully chose the ones she attended. She often referred to such social events as "part of the working day" and used to joke about the need "to go through life begging and learning to live off charity."

When the National Delegate identified the need for changes in policy, such as in the case of women's educational opportunities or professional and political representation, she sought out spaces within the existing legislation that would accommodate them. The 1961 *Law for Political and Professional Representation* and the 1966 amendment to that law are good examples. Discussions concerning the need for change in the legislation concerning women's political and professional rights took place within the SF as early as 1947. However, only a decade later did Primo de Rivera view the conditions as ripe for a change. The same tendency was witnessed concerning the SF's struggle to institute female physical education. While the organization created spaces where nurturing and exposure of the female body were acceptable, it did so by constantly seeking legitimization within official National Catholic discourse. Exercising and taking pride in the female body were advocated not in terms of personal gratification or self-fulfillment, but rather as an act of obedience to the God that created that body or in the name of service to the nation. It is precisely for this reason that the SF was viewed skeptically by the majority of Spaniards: while some people found it to be socially inclusive and culturally progressive to a dangerous degree, others felt it was conservative and backward, too middle-class in orientation and strongly attached to a chauvinistic and repressive regime.

This critical view of the SF persisted long after the organization itself and the regime it served were dismantled. The *Nueva Andadura Association* (ANA) was formed by Pilar Primo de Rivera and Adelida del Pozo in 1987 in order to unite former SF members throughout Spain and to conserve the SF's legacy. For its own members, however, it also performed an important social role. After the death of General Franco most SF members continued their work within a variety of public entities. This is not surprising considering their educational background and professional experience. But the easy way in which they resettled into the job market only highlighted their ideological and cultural isolation. For Pilar Primo de Rivera and many other former SF members, the ANA functioned as a surrogate organizational structure, a place where they could gather, discuss current issues and share personal experiences and memories with other women who had spent the majority of their adult lives in a manner similar to themselves.

In the post-Franco era there were at least two other Falangist veterans' organizations which had a significant female membership: *La Vieja Guardia* and *Plataforma 2003*. However, the ANA did not maintain close working relations with either of them. Following Pilar Primo de Rivera (who despite the changed political scene still saw herself as the sole authentic representative of José Antonio's doctrine) the ANA refused to take part in the majority of public events hosted by the other organizations. Nor did ANA members assist in their political campaigns. Andrea López, who headed the ANA in Madrid until her death in May 2006, commented on this lack of cooperation with a combined sense of pride and bitterness. As she told me in an interview on December 15, 2004:

> We always defined ourselves as *Joseantonianas* and our institutions kept a specific line. . . . There are many organizations and many Falanges (*muchas falanges*). But we have nothing to do with the other organizations. There are members of those organizations who take part in our activities. They are used to making quite a bit of noise (in political terms), but they know that such discussions can be carried out there, not here (at the ANA). We want no part of that (anymore).

While the relative isolation of the ANA also resulted from less prosaic reasons such as personal conflicts and the struggle over funds allocated to different veterans' organizations, the sense of alienation reflected in López' words cannot be dismissed offhand. This feeling of alienation is perhaps the clearest evidence of the conflictive and complex nature of the SF. In perceiving themselves as *Joseantonianas* (that is, as independent women, Falangists and Catholics), high-ranking SF members fought to reconcile which was irreconcilable.

The life story of Pilar Primo de Rivera attests to a combination of modernist and conservative practices and gender perceptions which existed side by side throughout an entire lifetime. The tensions between the elements of what was considered traditional feminine vocation and those embodying modernism were not resolved with the passing of time and the liberalization process undergone by Spanish society. In refusing to sacrifice any one aspect of their identity, Primo de Rivera and other high-ranking SF members constructed a "whole" that in the classic Fascist terminology was greater than the sum of its parts. But once it was severed from its base of political power and Spanish women were able to choose among a wider range of role models, it became clear that this "whole"—the organization and the discourse it upheld—had little appeal for the vast majority of Spanish women.

Further reading

Bergés, K., "Pilar Primo de Rivera – Cause Féminine, idéologie Phalangiste, strategies et enjeux politiques dans l'ombre du régime Franquiste," Thèse de doctorat, l'université de Toulouse-Le Mirail, 2003.

Blasco Herranz, Inmaculada, *Armas Femeninas para la Contrarrevolución*, Malaga: Universidad de Málaga, 1999.

Richmond, Kathleen J. L., *Women and Spanish Fascism – The Women's Section of the Falange 1934-1959*, New York: Routledge, 2003.

Cenarro, Ángela L., *La sonrisa de Falange. Auxilio Social en la guerra civil y la posguerra*, Barcelona: Critica, 2006.

Ofer, Inbal, *Señoritas in Blue: The Making of a Female Political Elite in Franco's Spain: The National Leadership of the SF de la Falange (1936-1977)*, Sussex: Sussex Academic Press, 2009.

Orduña Prada, Mónica, *El Auxilio Social (1936-1950)*, Madrid: Siglo XXI, 1996.

GLOSSARY

Absolutism Form of government in which there is no elected body to constrain the power of the monarch.

Accidentalism Political position which says that the form of a government, whether republican or monarchical, is less important than the content of the laws passed.

Afrancesado Spaniard who supported the French regime headed by King José Bonaparte between 1808 and 1814.

Africanistas Name applied to military officers who made their careers in the colonial war in Morocco after 1909. Francisco Franco was the most famous.

Anticlericalism Resentment or hatred of the Catholic clergy for its supposed alliance with the ruling elites and assistance in repressing the lower classes. It was expressed both verbally and, especially during the Spanish Civil War, in acts of violence against religious buildings and members of the clergy.

Autarky An economic policy aimed at achieving national self-sufficiency.

Autonomous Comunidades *(Autonomias)* The seventeen regions, roughly analogous to the devolved nations in the United Kingdom or the states in the United States, created by the Constitution of 1978.

Bienio Progresista Progressive Biennium. Two-year period following the Revolution of 1854 in which Progressives were in power.

Black Legend An interpretation of Spanish history which claims that, among European nations, Spain was uniquely prone to violence and religious fanaticism.

Cacique Originally a word for chief used by indigenous peoples in the Caribbean. In the nineteenth century it was applied to local bosses who acted as intermediaries between their communities and the central government.

Carlism The political movement which emerged in the 1830s supporting the claim to the throne of Don Carlos, the brother of Ferdinand VII who favored the return to the Old Regime.

Caudillo Spanish equivalent to Fuhrer or Duce.

Citizen movement Neighborhood and other locally based organizations which, during the Transition, called for more direct democracy, especially at the local level.

Civil Guard (Guardia Civil) Paramilitary national police force created in 1844, whose mission was to control rural areas and, at the beginning, the rooting out of banditry.

Clientelism A political system where local elites use their access to the resources of the state to do favors for their followers in order to retain their support. In Spain this system was known as *caciquismo*.

Concordat A treaty between a sovereign state and the Catholic Church.

Cortes Parliament or legislature.

Cortes constituyentes A convention, or special parliament, convened to draft a new constitution.

Demographic transition The process shared by most countries in Western Europe of moving from a demographic system marked by high birth and death rates and very slow population growth to one marked by declining death rates and spectacular population growth.

Disentailment Removal of restraints on the sale of land which were common under the Old Regime. It mainly affected the aristocracy, the Catholic Church, and municipalities.

ETA Acronym of *Euskadi Ta Askatasuna* (Basque Homeland and Liberty). A separatist organization which advocated armed struggle as the means of achieving an independent Basque state. Between 1959 and 2011 it had killed 829 people of whom 343 were civilians, as well as carrying out hundreds of kidnappings.

Ethnonationalism A type of nationalism that advocates a state for an ethnic group, which is usually defined by the possession of a shared language, a shared religion, and shared ethnic ancestry. Such movements are found within existing states and compete with state or civic nationalism.

Exaltados Radical liberals during the 1820s who later evolved into the Progressives and then the Democrats or Republicans.

Exiles A term that originally referred to people fleeing the French Revolution, but which has since been applied to any person fleeing political or social persecution. Such people are now called refugees.

Falange Española Small Fascist party founded by José Antonio Primo de Rivera in October 1933.

Falange Española Tradicionalista y de las JONS Official party of the Franco regime created in April 1937 by the fusion of the Falange and the Carlist Comunión Tradicionalista. Since the 1950s often referred to as the National Movement, it was dissolved in 1977.

Fueros Special laws applying to a region or social group in the Old Regime.

Generalitat Regional government of Catalonia. It comes from the name of the permanent committee of the Catalan Cortes that ruled the region while Cortes were not convened.

Generation of 1898 The group of Spanish intellectuals who wrote about the state of Spain following its defeat in the Spanish-American War of 1808.

Gross Domestic Product The total size of a national economy.

Guerrilla Literally small war. The name given to the irregular forces which fought against Napoleon's army between 1808 and 1814.

Indianos Spanish immigrants to the Americas who returned to Spain after making lots of money. Most came from northern Spain.

Indignados Literally the "indignant ones." The movement which began in May 2011 as response to government responses to the economic crisis of 2008. Predecessor to the Occupy movement.

Junta Council or committee, usually representative of the citizens of a town or region.

Krausism Philosophical movement founded by German philosopher Karl Christian Friedrich Krause which became influential among Spanish intellectuals in the second half of the nineteenth century. The highly influential school, the Institución Libre de Enseñanza, was created by Krausistas in 1876.

Liberal revolution Change from the social and political system of the Old Regime to a liberal, constitutional one which took place in the first four decades of the nineteenth century.

Mercantilism An economic theory predominant in Europe between the sixteenth and eighteenth centuries which believed that there was a fixed amount of wealth in the world and that a nation's prosperity depends on its ability to export more than it imported. In mercantilist systems, colonies existed to serve the economy of the European colonial power.

Liberal Triennium Period of constitutional government between 1820 and 1823.

Liberals Name given to the advocates of constitutional government in the Cortes of Cadiz. Their absolutist opponents were called "serviles" (Ser-viles, to be despicable).

Moderates More conservative strand of Spanish liberalism between 1830 and 1860.

Movida Youth countercultural movement of the 1980s and 1990s, most closely associated with Madrid.

National Catholicism A political culture that proclaims the consubstantiality of religion and the fatherland and recognizes the role of the Church in directing the cultural and moral life of society. It was a key part of the ideology of the Franco dictatorship.

National Militia Units of armed citizens created by liberal regimes to preserve public order and defend constitutional government. Particularly favored by the Progressives.

Old Regime Name given to the social and political system in Europe before the French Revolution.

Ominous Decade Name given to the period of reactionary government between the end of the Liberal Triennium in 1823 and the death of Ferdinand VII in October 1833.

Oposición Public examination by which public service jobs are allocated. Widely extended in the Spanish administration in the twentieth century, in order to fight favoritism.

Pistolerismo Use of hired gunmen by employers in Barcelona to fight against organized workers. Radical trade-unionists, particularly in 1919–22, responded by killing employers or politicians.

Popular Front Alliance of various Republican parties, the Socialist Party, and the Communist Party which fought and won the elections of February 1936. The term also refers to the strategy adopted by the Communist International in 1935 of promoting broad alliances of anti-fascist political parties.

Progressives More radical strain of Spanish liberalism between 1830 and 1860. On their left emerged the Democrat/Republican party.

Pronunciamiento A form of military revolt common in nineteenth-century Spain. Usually, a general, or senior officer, "pronounced" in front of his troops his political opposition to the government. It could lead to a bloody confrontation, but not always.

Reconcentration Counterinsurgency strategy developed by General Valeriano Weyler in the Philippines and refined during the Cuban War of 1895–98. It consisted of separating civilians from the rebel troops by moving them from rural areas into "reconcentration camps" (similar to General Westmoreland's "strategic hamlets" in Vietnam in the 1970s).

Regency A period in which the monarch is too young to rule in his or her own right and is represented by an adult. There were two regencies during the reign of Isabel II: her mother María Cristina (1833–40) and General Baldomero Espartero (1840–43) and one during the reign of Alfonso XIII, his mother María Cristina de Austria (1885–1902). There was also the provisional regency of General Francisco Serrano between the proclamation of the Constitution of 1869 and the coronation of King Amadeo I in 1871.

Regeneracionistas Intellectuals who, following Spain's defeat in the Spanish-American War, wrote books and articles diagnosing the ills (the "degeneration") of the fatherland and proposing remedies for its cure or regeneration.

Renaixença Revival of Catalan-language culture which took place in the nineteenth century. It preceded the emergence of politically oriented nationalism.

Restoration The political regime which lasted from 1875 to 1931, encompassing the reigns of Alfonso XII and Alfonso XIII. It began following the end of the First Republic and concluded with the proclamation of the Second Republic.

Sección Femenina Women's section of the Falange, headed by Pilar Primo de Rivera.

Separate spheres Ideology regarding the relations between genders which emerged in the nineteenth century and was particularly powerful after 1850. It posited a strict separation between the roles of men, who would act in the public sphere of business and politics, and women, who would be limited to the domestic sphere of raising children and taking care of the house.

Sexenio Democrático or *Revolucionario* The period between the Revolution of September 1868 which threw Isabel II from the throne and the military coup of December 1874 which ended the First Republic.

Silver Age Term applied to the Spanish culture of the first third of the twentieth century to emphasize its outstanding quality, considered second only to the Golden Age of the sixteenth and seventeenth centuries.

Substate nationalism A nationalist movement within a part of an existing state.

Ten Years' War War fought in Cuba between 1868 and 1878 in which sugar planters rebelled against Spanish rule and demanded independence.

Tobacco Monopoly Profitable government monopoly on marketing of tobacco in the colonies where it was produced. It was abolished in Cuba in 1817 but remained in place in the Philippines until 1880.

Total war A type of war in which all society and the economy are mobilized for the war effort and in which the separation between the front lines and the rearguard no longer exists.

Tragic Week Revolutionary general strike that ended in an outbreak of church burning in Barcelona between July 25 and August 2, 1909.

Transition Process of moving from Franco dictatorship to a democratic political system between 1975 and 1978 (or 1982).

Turno pacífico The prearranged rotation in power of the Conservative and Liberal parties that characterized the Restoration.

Unicameral A representative political system with only one chamber. The United States—House of Representatives and Senate—and the United Kingdom—House of Commons and House of Lords—both have two chambers, and are bicameral.

Urbanization Process in which an increasing percentage of a country's population lives in cities and predominantly rural cultures are replaced by predominantly ones.

Voluntary (or economic) migrants. People whose movement is triggered by lack of economic opportunities in their place of birth.

War of Africa War against Morocco fought between 1859 and 1860 which provoked an upsurge in Spanish nationalism, especially in Catalonia. It was part of a policy of imperial activities undertaken by General Leopoldo O'Donnell's Liberal Union government.

INDEX

Index

Index